System and Structure

Second edition

System and Structure

Essays in Communication and Exchange
Second edition

ANTHONY WILDEN

TAVISTOCK PUBLICATIONS

First published in 1972 by
Tavistock Publications Ltd
11 New Fetter Lane, London EC4P 4EE
First published in paperback in 1977
Second edition 1980
Reprinted 1984

Published in the USA by
Tavistock Publications
in association with Methuen, Inc.
733 Third Avenue, New York, NY 10017

© *1972 and 1980 Anthony Wilden*

Printed in Great Britain by
Richard Clay (The Chaucer Press) Ltd
Bungay, Suffolk

British Library Cataloguing in Publication Data
Wilden, Anthony
   System and structure.—2nd ed.
   1. Communication
   I. Title
   001.5   p. 90
ISBN 0-422-76700-X
ISBN 0-422-76710-7 (pbk.)

Library of Congress Cataloging in Publication Data
Wilden, Anthony.
   System and structure.

   (Social science paperbacks; 200)
   Reprint. Originally published: 2nd ed. London:
Tavistock, 1980.
   Bibliography: p.
   Includes indexes.
   1. Communication.   I. Title.   II. Series.
[P90.W475 1984]   001.5   83-22156

There is no more neutrality in
the world. You're either
part of the solution or
part of the problem.
There ain't no middle ground.

ELDRIDGE CLEAVER
Speech at the University of California at San Diego (1968)

You're either part of the
solution or part of the
problem.

RICHARD NIXON
Campaign speech (1972)

To René Girard and
Gregory Bateson

Contents

Preface to the First Edition

Some of the essays which follow, and parts of others, have been previously published. All have been extensively revised. In my revisions I have tried as far as possible to avoid repetitions, but often the logic of the argument in a particular text makes some repetition unavoidable. In fact, given the network of interconnected ideas with which these essays deal, a form of development which requires the constant return to certain central themes becomes a necessary principle of composition. The impossibility of a purely linear development of the theory of communication and exchange outlined in this book lies partly in the subject and partly in the evolutionary process I went through in writing it. Thus the reader may find that a concept or critique sketched out in an early chapter depends directly on a development of the same or a related position in a later chapter. In the hope of reducing the difficulties this may put in the way of the reader, I have added cross-references wherever it seemed useful to do so and tried to provide a comprehensive index.

The subject-matter of these essays can be summarized as follows:

Chapter I is a general statement about the interpretation of Freud by Jacques Lacan, the subject of an earlier book (Wilden, 1968a).[1] Certain aspects of the Lacanian theory are analyzed and criticized in Chapters V, IX, X, XVI, and XVII. Chapter II attempts to establish by means of two concrete analyses – a 'neurotic symptom' taken from Freud and a 'schizophrenic communication' taken from the work of Gregory Bateson – the value of Roman Jakobson's linguistic analysis of metaphor and metonymy to systems and communication theory. Through a study of Svevo's psychoanalytical novel, Chapter III deals with the Hegelian conception of

---

[1] References in parentheses refer to the bibliography at the end of the volume.
    Wherever possible, the date of the reference is that of first publication. Where this differs from that of the edition used, the bibliography so indicates. Translations from foreign sources are in general either my own or have been checked with the original and modified if necessary.

desire in the master–slave dialectic in order to establish it as a metaphor for goalseeking in the open system, and analyzes repetition in the terms of Bateson's theory of alcoholism. Chapter IV uses the double-bind theory of schizophrenia and the associated notion of metacommunication as a way of establishing a theory of interpretation based on the relationship between metalanguage (commentary) and referent language (text). Chapter V is a statement of the double-bind theory in relation to the problem of punctuating the context, which naturally leads to a consideration of Gödel's proof and of the theory of logical types. Chapter VI uses a systems model to get at the thermodynamic and mechanical models, derived from nineteenth-century physics, which underlie Freud's bioenergetics of the mind. Here I try to bring out the negatively entropic semiotic or communicational model in Freud which is obscured by his somewhat confused commitment to positively entropic principles.

Chapter VII tries to define the relationship between analog and digital communication, a distinction which is essential to all the other essays. By reference to Frege's logical foundation for the integers, to ecological anthropology, to information-processing in the nervous system, and to the elementary concepts of set theory, this essay seeks to establish what I call the paradox of digitalization, the paradox of the boundary, in relation to the differences between absence, zero, refusal, and negation. Appendix II to this essay reproduces an iconic communication from an undergraduate student, Vincent Hollier, about the analog and the digital. Chapter VIII seeks to establish the necessity of an ecosystemic or ecological approach to communication and exchange in open systems of all types, and introduces my version of Gregory Bateson's conception of the unit of mind and the unit of survival. Chapter IX applies the methodological distinction between analog and digital communication to anthropology, zoology, psychoanalysis, and Marxian exchange theory. It is concerned with the difference between the exchange of the 'symbolic object' in the unit of mind – which is not a mind or a brain – and the accumulative, exploitative exchange of Imaginary objects in our society. The appendix to this chapter is the work of another undergraduate student, Gerald Hall. Chapter X takes up the critique of phallocentrism in psychoanalysis and western culture, especially as it is used to justify the oppression of women, and applies this critique to a brief analysis of the memoirs of the most famous of all 'psychotics': Dr Daniel Paul Schreber. Chapter XI applies the previous analyses to a critique of equilibrium theory, game theory, 'structural causality', and the scientific ideology of law and order, in particular reference to Jean Piaget's 'genetic structuralism'. Chapter XII seeks to establish semiotic and systemic models for the processes of organic development, steady state, change of structure, natural evolution, and history. Chapter XIII employs Jacques Derrida's concept of writing and the conception of DNA as a text to further sketch the relationship between self-differentiation, the memory trace, the cultural memory (or 'instructions'), noise in the ecosystem, and the Event in history. Chapter XIV uses Ellul's definition of propaganda to provide a contextual critique of the use of the category of the so-called binary opposition in linguistics, semiotics, philosophy, anthropology, and psychoanalysis. This chapter concludes with a brief critique of the 'genetics of intelligence' (Arthur Jensen and Ernst Mayr).

Chapter XV analyzes the confusion between language, communication, and bioenergetic explanation, especially as this is represented in anthropology and in psychoanalysis. Chapter XVI summarizes the previous critiques and provides a detailed interpretation of Freud's primary and secondary process. By analyzing two of Lacan's slogans – "The unconscious is structured like a language" and "The signifier is what represents the subject for another signifier" – I introduce Derrida's attack on the logocentrism of French semiotics. Chapter XVII outlines Lacan's important contribution to communicational and exchange theory: the notion of the mirror-stage. This concept is analyzed in the terms of its source in existentialism and phenomenology and in terms of its ideological effects. Using the work of René Girard and Frantz Fanon, this chapter seeks to demonstrate the thesis about the logical typing of opposition first mentioned in the Introduction. It also seeks to demonstrate the Imaginary epistemology upon which Lacanian psychoanalysis and the theology of the scientific discourse are constructed.

Preface to the Second Edition

It is enough of a privilege to be trained to write books and then to be actually permitted to do so. It is even more of a privilege to be provided with the luxury of a revised edition in which one can attempt to remedy at least some of the more serious inadequacies of the first.

On reading this text over again, my first – and somewhat red-faced – response was to wish that more of it had been written in plain English. Following that, I found myself wincing at many of the sweeping declarations that the heady atmosphere of enthusiasm in which it was written gave rise to. It bears the stamp of its context in the 1960s.

That context of contestation has recently been replaced by another: the rising political consciousness of the people of the colony of Canada – accompanied by corporate concentration, resource exploitation, and governmental repression far more severe than in the country that took our colonization over from the British: the United States.

In retrospect, it appears to me that colonization in its many forms, but especially the contemporary colonization of consciousness, is the predominant theme of *System and Structure*, a theme it shares with many others in many fields.

The new Introduction to the present version seeks to outline and to clarify the various related themes that now seem to me particularly important. Other corrections and criticisms that could not be dealt with in the Introduction have been summarized in a series of Additional Notes placed in an appendix to the main text. The main text has been corrected for a number of significant errors of detail, as well as for specific ideological and epistemological faults. Details about this last type of error, as I can best understand it, will be found in the Additional Notes. I have also included an updated set of references and readings.

Note

I have taken the opportunity of a new printing to correct a number of minor errors. A French version of *System and Structure* (translated by Georges Khal), which permitted a thorough revision of the text and includes two new chapters, was published by Boréal Express in 1983 (5450 ch. de la Côte-des-Neiges, Montréal, Québec). In 1981 *The Language of the Self* (Lacan/Wilden) was reissued by The Johns Hopkins Press as *Speech and Language in Psychoanalysis*.

Acknowledgements

I should like to thank *Psychology Today* for permission to reprint parts of Chapter I; *Modern Language Notes*, for parts of Chapter III and IV; *Salmagundi*, for parts of Chapter VI; *Semiotica* for parts of Chapters VII and XI; and Gordon and Breach (New York), for most of Chapter VIII. A version of Chapter XII has appeared in *Communications* (CECMAS, Paris).

My thanks to Edgar Morin of the Centre de l'Étude des Communications de Masse, École Pratique des Hautes Études, for his support and assistance, and especially to Thomas A. Sebeok of the Research Center for the Language Sciences at Indiana University, without whose encouragement this book would not have been published. I owe a special debt of gratitude to Louis Marin of the École Normale Supérieure for a continuing critical dialogue around the themes of these essays, particularly on the subject of the violence of 'objectivity' or 'neutrality'.

I am most grateful to the Committee on Research at the University of California at San Diego for their continued support of my work over the past three years.

I am more than especially grateful to Judy Rosenthal, who has done such a magnificent job on the manuscript, and to Mathilde Vilas, both of whom have over the past two years relentlessly pointed out to me my male-chauvinist biases. I hope that at least some parts of this book may be a contribution towards the movement for the liberation of women for which they have been fighting so hard. Last, I should like to thank all my students at the University of California at San Diego – who taught me far more than they know. The errors which remain are, as usual, my own.

To thank by name the many people, not mentioned originally, whose aid, support, and criticism were such important contributions to this book, would take me far afield. But I must express my gratitude to Diana Burfield and John Harvard-Watts, whose refusal to be intimidated by obstacles placed in the path of this book made the original publication at Tavistock possible. And I must also thank Mrs Lilian Morrison, Patricia Wilden, Mark Wilden, and Paul Wilden for the kind of help that cannot be expressed in words.

Many other people have contributed to the development of this text since the first edition. There are others yet who cannot be thanked by name – and specifically those whose attitudes and conduct, especially towards people less privileged than themselves, have not let me forget the way oppression works in our society.

Introduction (1980)

The Scientific Discourse

KNOWLEDGE AS A COMMODITY

I

Theology is a science, but at the same time, how many sciences
there are! A man is a *suppositus*; but if one anatomizes him,
will he be the head, the heart, the stomach, the veins, each
vein, each section of a vein, the blood, or each humor of the
blood? A town or a countryside, seen from a distance, are a
town or a countryside. But as one draws closer, they are
houses, trees, tiles, leaves, grasses, plants, weeds, ants, legs of
ants, *ad infinitum.*   All this is enveloped in the name
'countryside'.
PASCAL: *Pensées* (1670: #29)

1. *The Prospective*

The essays in this book are an attempt at translation and integration. They
set out to translate between some of the many dialects of the discourse of
science in our culture; and, as a result, to bring together concepts and even
traditions which are generally associated with quite distinct fields of study
in the modern organization of knowledge.

The synthesis sought is necessarily both ongoing and open-ended. The
integration desired requires an active, critical, and transcending perspective.
This must be a perspective open to understanding the 'deep structures'
which actually unite the disciplines, both ideologically and epistemologically, as well as a perspective open to comprehending the communication
between the vested interests which are ultimately responsible for the seemingly psychotic splitting of the subject in academia today.

In the original sense of the term 'essay' – that for which Montaigne's
novel endeavors in the late sixteenth century provide us with the modern
model (or as he would say, the *patron*: the pattern; cf. pp. 88–109 below)
– the pages which follow seek to bring together as best they can concepts
derived most immediately from Anglo-American double-bind theory,
from French psychoanalysis, and from anthropology, both 'structural' and
'ecological', and concepts emerging from cybernetics and 'systems' theory,
from linguistics and semiotics, from ' information science' and communi-

cation theory, from metamathematics and ecological biology, and from Hegelian and Marxian dialectics.

A primary aim of these pages is to begin to set up a theoretical vocabulary and syntax which is not dependent on any particular science or discipline for its representative metaphors, nor on any specific jargon for its models of information and transformation, relationship and change. In contrast with both the disciplinary and the 'interdisciplinary' traditions, the following essays seek their basis in the transdisciplinary study of ongoing adaptive systems – symbolic, imaginary, and real. These are systems constrained by structures and bounded and regulated through their relationship to one or more environments – or levels of environment. Distinct from the general systems of physical theory, and unlike the mechanics of general systems, these adaptive systems are time-dependent, memory-bound, and reproductive. Thus they are open both to matter-energy and to the variety it bears, whether for the system-environment relationships in question that variety be coded variety (INFORMATION) or uncoded variety (NOISE).

As W. Ross Ashby said in his remarkable *Introduction to Cybernetics* – which deals with the (mechanistic) cybernetics of systems "closed to information and control" – "The truths of cybernetics are not conditioned on their being derived from some other branch of science" (1956: 1). There are nevertheless a number of traditional interpretative models related to what we used to call the cybernetic approach. One is the literary model of the novel as quest (Georg Lukács, René Girard), e.g., *Don Quixote*, Hegel's *Phenomenology*, Proust's *A la recherche du temps perdu*. Another is the Freudian model of the quest for the so-called 'lost object'; another the Heideggerian and Sartrean project of desire, the attempt to replenish what is designated as a primordial lack, an abandonment in the world corresponding to what one would now call a 'splitting of the ecosystem' in history (cf. pp. 217–27 below).

In a dialectical sense, these individual and collective quests are only versions of a more basic process: the goalseeking behavior of (organic and social) open systems in relation to their various environments. But the literary, psychological, or philosophical representations of this multidimensional process commonly take the open system out of its real biological and socioeconomic context, treating the relational realities we call 'individual', 'self', or 'mind' (for example) as if they were isolates. The goal of reconciliation that these representations propose (or reject) – reconciliation of an original splitting apart – is generally based on utopian or romantic forms of philosophical idealism. Liberation is spiritual rather than actual.

The modern quest for the 'spiritual' or 'psychological' liberation of the individual is surely a token, not of personal 'problems', on the one hand, nor of 'the human condition', on the other, as many would like to make it, but rather a statement about socioeconomic alienation in its modern forms. Consequently, unless we adequately integrate the contributions that literature, psychology, communication theory, semiotics, philosophy, anthropology, history, biology, ecology, and economics can make to the systemic understanding of wo/mankind as a collective being-in-process, then whatever one might have to say on the subject would be little more than a further contribution to the symptoms of the increasing decadence of western society. It would be a further contribution to the processes and structures through which our present socioeconomic system expresses and enforces the domination and exploitation of every resource it feeds on: nature, human beings, generations still unborn, the future.

At the basis of the ecosystemic approach introduced here there lie three particularly privileged models. The first is that which emphasizes the LINKING function of symbolic exchange across boundaries in the so-called 'primitive' society (ecological and structural anthropology). The second is that which seeks to understand the essential rationality of natural ecosystems (systems ecology). The third is that of the real and material teleonomic – but not teleological – processes of history. This is the model of 'civilized' history as the product of hierarchies of socioeconomic conflicts between goalseeking subsystems in socioecological organization: a version of the Marxian model.

With all its possible defects, the Marxian model has one scientific and epistemological quality which most other sociopolitical and socioeconomic theories lack. It rarely fails to be concerned with the CONTEXT in which change occurs. It is a systemic and structural model open to its environments, including the future. It seeks to establish a set of TRUTHS-IN-PROCESS which are derived from studying the deep-structure constraints and the systemic processes of the socioeconomic system itself, not by the aggregation, as it were, of information from 'other' disciplines. These 'truths', therefore, are not – or try not to be – derivations from any particular set of rationalizations seeking to justify the actual state of the system in question at any particular time. Of all the approaches brought together in these essays, the Marxian perspective is a truly scientific one in the sense that it is a critical, 'self-critical',[1] and transdisciplinary orientation, an

---

[1] The expression 'self' is a problematical one. The many English compounds in 'self-' began to become significantly popular in the revolutionary socioeconomic context of the seventeenth century (cf. p. 223n below). The problem is that whatever their Greek exemplars (for example) may have meant in the agrarian and mercantile context of antiquity, the novel emergence of these 'self-referring'

orientation which is also capable of explaining its own relationship to the context it is in.

Not that this capacity of the Marxian perspective is always recognized as such, or indeed employed in this way, by many of its modern exponents. On the contrary, the dead hand of nineteenth-century traditions – both epistemological and ideological – still lies heavy on many contemporary interpretations of the texts of Marx and Engels. But just as those texts themselves evolved in response to changing nineteenth-century socio-economic realities and in response to new understandings and discoveries, so too must their contemporary interpretations evolve. As with any text that time and place have turned into history, these texts must necessarily be re-read and re-incorporated into the critical discourse of each succeeding generation. The Marxian texts are not either 'outdated' or the 'truth'. On the contrary, they are both past and present to us, and can only be adequately understood, after the event, in terms of this double temporal relation, both synchronic and diachronic, which makes them part of the sociohistorical memory of our society – part of our contemporary context.

2. *Science and its Object*

> The brain is not an organ of thinking but an organ of survival,
> like claws and fangs. It is made in such a way as to make us
> accept as truth that which is only advantage. It is an
> exceptional, almost pathological constitution one has, if one
> follows thoughts logically through, regardless of consequences.
> Such people make martyrs, apostles, or scientists, and mostly
> end on the stake, or in a chair, electric or academic.
> ALBERT SZENT-GYORGI [2]

---

terms (Chapter V) in the century that invented solipsism makes them increasingly inappropriate metaphors to use in the context of an ecosystemic perspective. This difficulty is reinforced by the critique of the 'self' or 'ego' by Jacques Lacan, who terms it an Imaginary construct based on an either/or relationship of projection and identification with its correlate, or *alter ego*, the other (Lacan, 1956a, 1966; see the index to *The Language of the Self*). Indeed, many of the terms beginning with 'self' – such as the 'self-regulation' and 'self-differentiation' used so enthusiastically in 'cybernetic' viewpoints (including this one) – do tend to imply an ecological absurdity: the direct and unmediated reference of 'self' to 'self' in an Imaginary short-circuit of actual environmental relations (cf. pp. 316–18, 329 below; and Wilden, 1974). See also in particular Garry Wills' excellent commentary on the ideology of 'self-determination', 'self-control', and associated slogans (1969: 417–29, 462–9, 531–4, and elsewhere).

[2] Quoted in Zopf (1962: 340). Compare this with the example of another kind of 'hard-headedness' in the scientific discourse placed at the beginning of the next

Our contemporary socioecological reality has allowed us to recognize that the philosophy of science is no longer a discourse about knowledge of the 'object' of science – which is not of course an object – but rather a discourse about the knowledge of knowledge. In our twentieth-century context of crisis, the 'object' of science has necessarily become the DECONSTRUCTION of the scientific discourse itself.

This is not however just one more instance in recent history of a 'new paradigm' replacing an 'old' one, as in the idealist interpretations of the history of science persuasively offered by Thomas Kuhn. The overt discontinuities of the Kuhnian 'paradigms' all depend for their existence on an essentially continuous epistemological and ideological agreement about the nature and the goals of the scientific enterprise. In contrast, the deconstruction referred to here is an activity that puts science and its enterprise into question. Moreover, the source of this fundamental questioning does not lie in the scientific discourse itself, but in its environments. It lies in the deconstruction of our social reality by our society's own historical activities over time. This is a systemic transformation-in-process, originating not in consciousness but in the real; and for the first time in our experience it suggests that the future may be unimaginably different from what we have been led to expect.

Even a partial understanding of this systemic and structural transcendence (*Aufhebung*) of positivistic and normative science should lead automatically to a reconsideration of the function of the scientific discourse in our society. Unfortunately, in spite of Lévi-Strauss's analysis of the relationship of similarity between the function of the discourse of myth in the so-called primitive or 'cold' society and that of the discourse of science in the so-called civilized or 'hot' society (class society), with his attendant, if half-hearted and inadequate, critique of 'the idea of the primitive' (e.g., 'La science du concret', 1962a: 3–47) – and in spite of the ecologically-based demonstration, by Rappaport (1968) and others (cf. Vayda 1969), of the scientifically-based and context-sensitive ideology and reality of myth and ritual in some of these 'other' societies – we still find little by way of a creative understanding of such questions, much less a real recognition of what their 'to-whom-it-may-concern' messages actually have to tell us.

We have been brought up to believe that the scientific discourse should

---

section. An analysis of the mixture of science and ideology in Szent-Gyorgi's pithy remarks – the 'martyr complex' of the academician identified with Galileo, the projection of the individualist socioeconomic 'struggle to survive' onto nature, the elitism of the survival of the supposedly fittest in the university, the whiff of heresy used to help legitimize the local thought-police – would take a whole chapter, perhaps a whole book.

be, indeed is, the model for the dialects of all the sciences – i.e., of all the 'subjects' – in academia. It is held up as a model in the dual sense of 'a discourse to be imitated' (notably in its syntax) and as 'the discourse against which all the others measure themselves'. But, in reality and as we know, what has always constrained the expressed epistemology of the scientific (the academic) discourse is the dominant ideology of the social discourse, itself constrained by socioeconomic reality.   (One says 'expressed' because, our relation to reality being what it is, our ACTUAL epistemological relation to it must involve some type of survival value at some level.) Indeed, given that the function of ideology is to explain the past, present, and possible futures of a real live system, we would obviously expect that academia – whose goals are not significantly different – would be a repository of the dominant ideology in the abstract, as well as in the Real.

It might appear at first that the illusions about science and knowledge which the social discourse projects – the specular ideal of a discourse 'objectively' isolated from both the social discourse and reality itself, or the equally illusory image of science as a carefully constructed and repeatedly verified 'neutral' dialect within the overall communication of society (the occasional Mad Scientist excepted) – it might indeed be thought that this imaginary world of scientific rationality simply represents the vested interests of particularly powerful academics, and that the whole spectacular fiction of the scientific discourse is an expression of a relationship to society and to reality which scientists and other academics actively and consciously share between them.

This is not quite correct, however, in spite of the many privileges which academics share, including the privilege of commanding captive audiences. Ideologies, like reality, involve levels of relation; and they act not simply as the grounds of what will be called 'truth', but also and more significantly as the grounds of their own truth, which may or may not in different societies be adequately consonant with the Real. Ideologies metacommunicate at many levels, and in capitalist society one of their metacommunicative functions is to attempt to deny the ideological function of dominant discourses like the fiction of science, the academic discourse.

The fiction of science commonly appears in a positivist and objectivist form. In its mirror-image, the relativist and subjectivist form, the fiction of science abandons the 'One' for the 'All' by reducing all knowledge to the status of fictions like itself – while covertly maintaining that some of these fictions are more real than others. The point is that, as with the dominant ideology of our society, participation in the illusions of academia is neither generally voluntary, nor generally conscious. Thus, when it comes time for the oracle of the academic discourse to deliver its message, we find that the academic has not delivered the oracle – the oracle has delivered the academic.

3. Criteria

> The function of the University is to seek out and to transmit knowledge and to train students in the processes whereby truth is to be made known. To convert, or to make converts, is alien and hostile to this dispassionate duty. When it becomes necessary, in performing this function of a university, to consider political, social or sectarian movements, they are dissected and examined – not taught – and the conclusion left, with no tipping of the scales, to the logic of the facts.
> *Handbook for Faculty Members of the University of California* (c. 1968) [3]

The principal criterion of a critical and 'self-critical' viewpoint is simple to state, less easy to define. Any scientific theory or position that looks like a metaphor of the dominant ideology of our society, or which can be construed as contributing to the psychological, social, or material alienation of any class or group in world society, must come under immediate suspicion. It must then be subjected to a metascientific and contextual evaluation before being accepted as valid, or useful, or 'true'.

It requires also to be evaluated in terms of its probable contribution to the long-range adaptivity – the creation and the maintenance of systemic flexibility – which is necessary for human survival in the whole. Any scientific, technological, or political 'advance' – not to mention the still insanely escalating economics and technology of the relay race in armaments and other biocides – any 'advance' which evidently trades a short-term increase in pseudo-flexibility against a longer-range increase in systemic rigidity, must somehow be resisted – to say nothing of other developments which are less easily evaluated in terms of their negative contribution to the future. If this kind of condition is accepted (however difficult it may be to define positively or to put into practice), then it will also be recognized

---

[3] Quoted by Wills (1969: 318–19) in a singularly apt analysis of the unconscious ideology of the contemporary university. Compare Stephen Brush (1974) in *Science*: "I suggest that the teacher who wants to indoctrinate his students in the traditional role of the scientist as a neutral fact finder should not use historical materials of the kind now being prepared by historians of science: they will not serve his purpose. He may wish to follow the advice of philosopher J. C. C. Smart, who recently suggested (1972) that it is legitimate to use FICTIONALIZED, history of science to illustrate one's pronouncements on scientific method."

that neither statements about long-range survival, nor the proposed activities they refer to, are capable of ordinary proof, experimental or otherwise. They are however still subject to a conclusive testing of the most rigorous kind: the proof of the survival of the fittest ecosystem, where 'being falsified' means becoming effectively extinct.

In our thirty-year-old war against the toughest group of species on this planet, the insects, for example, we are still doing far greater damage to our food supplies, to farmworkers, to our children, and to ourselves, than we can possibly do the 'pests' which capitalist monoculture created in the first place.

(Cf. on this topic the ineptly ideological movie, *The Hellstrom Chronicle*, 1971, one of a latter-day series of zoological cautionary tales disguised as science, with its Kiplingesque representation of the so-called 'battle of the sexes' amongst the insects – and much more besides.)

To return to the question of evaluating the products of the academic discourse: obviously, any project of research, publication, or teaching that corresponds narrowly either to the conveniences of public or private funding or, equally narrowly, to the expediencies of academic competition, is particularly suspect. And when in the hands of an individual or research group the information being brought to public and private eyes betrays an ideological and technocratic subservience to a dominant caste or class or other social and economic grouping, then we should at the very least seek to discover who and what kind of people make up that dominant group in any particular case, or what system values are being served, to say nothing of asking why this information is being propagated at this time.

Nevertheless, if this metascientific evaluation is understood to mean, as it may well be, that we should simply be on our guard to recognize 'individual bias' or 'disciplinary imperialism' – each of which are perfectly real in the surface structure of the scientific discourse (where all biases are equal) – then we shall have failed to understand the task awaiting us. If this were all we meant to say, then we would have withered on the vine of our concrete bastions long ago.

Recognition of 'biases' as this term is ordinarily understood by academics is in effect a tried and true way of neutralizing any usefully radical critique of the vested interests represented in the discourse of science. The significant problems of evaluation and effect lie at the level of the DEEP STRUCTURES or CODES from which the messages of the scientific discourse are constructed, not in the particular messages as such which these codes permit individuals and individual bias to invent. These codings, which constrain the actual messages they permit, are commonly shared by the arts, by the sciences, by the humanities, and by society as a whole. It is here and at this level that we can begin properly to understand how what may appear to be adaptive or 'progressive' on the surface or in the short-range, may at deep levels or in the long-range turn out to become a COUNTERADAPTIVE relationship over time (Chapter VIII).

This imperative to look for the sources and the constraints common to whole sets of messages as such, rather than to limit ourselves to individual and particular messages, is of course implicitly the same as the imperative already expressed in both the 'mythic' and the 'scientific' discourses. It is the imperative expressed in the simple existence of these discourses – for, like all messages, they are at one and the same time report, command, and question. They tell us that before providing guidance or legitimization to any particular activity, the task of science and myth, in so far as they are useful to society-as-a-whole, is that of illuminating and teaching new generations about crucial PATTERNS OF RELATIONSHIP in the organic, the inorganic, and the social universes. No mythology does less, no science can do more.

4. *Aims*

> The law condemns the man or woman
> Who steals the goose from off the common
> But leaves the greater felon loose
> Who steals the common from the goose.
> *Eighteenth-century English Rhyme*

The ultimate goal of critical scientific inquiry must obviously be to contribute to the long-term well-being of humanity in its historical processes and global context. Amongst academics, only the more fanatical of the believers in 'pure' or 'objective' science would seriously disagree with this aim, along with other participants in the collective solipsism which this desire for purity entails. However, given the role of the university as an elitist aspect of the mass media in what many of its denizens fondly regard as the market-place of ideas, the 'long-term well-being of humanity' is too often confused by academics with the immediate well-being of the particular caste and class overwhelmingly represented in academia, and repeatedly replicated there.

It consequently becomes necessary to insist that, since all human commitments are also ideological and epistemological commitments, then no project of research or teaching that is unprepared or unable to investigate its ideological and epistemological foundations can ever do more than masquerade as science.[4]

---

[4] It is not always possible to distinguish easily between a dominant epistemology and a dominant ideology in human affairs. In general, the aspect of our world view

Nevertheless, on both the right and the left in western society, one still finds it assumed that (critical) science, social and physical, signifies a non-ideological or equivalently 'value-free' state of affairs. Given the awesome power of the dominant ideology and the dominant forms of communication in our society, the sources of this somewhat romantic belief are readily understandable. In a society dominated by commoditized relations and alienated values, the attempt to close science off from its relations with the values of its contexts makes a tortuous kind of sense. All the same, however, this undialectical and decontextualizing activity seems ultimately to betray an implicit allegiance to a now venerable religious, psychological, and philosophical tradition: THE QUEST FOR THE ABSOLUTE (as the early nineteenth century phrased it). Indeed, this particular characterization of the impotent in pursuit of the impossible may fittingly stand as an epitome of the Imaginary and even morbid quest of the academic discourse for what we might call the System of Systems – for the ultimate closed system where desires are facts and All is One. This is a quest that remains as common to logical positivism as it does to contemporary intellectuals for whom life has become explicable only as the pursuit of death (cf. Chapters III, VI, and XVII; pp. 364–7; and Atlan, 1972: 283–4, or Baudrillard, 1976, for example).

The foregoing passages outline in part and somewhat programmatically the general position from which, as far as is possible within both known and unknown limits, the essays in this book have been written.

It is also an underlying thesis of these pages that the human well-being just referred to cannot adequately be characterized or understood except by reference to the increasingly tragic plight of most of those who have so far managed to survive the twentieth century. This is to say that the long-range truths of the future require us to be capable of understanding and fighting the machinery of oppression and exploitation in the present, for without our informed enlistment in this struggle for life itself, the future we are all contributing to may well be the end of us. As apocalyptic as these phrases may sound, their source lies in a conviction, based on the best evidence I can muster, that long-term exploitation – as distinct from USE –

---

that we label epistemological has to do with the deeply-coded and often mainly SYNTACTICAL abstractions (in science, for example) which allow the more overtly valued or more obviously SEMANTIC-PRAGMATIC ideological world view to be communicated. Beyond the universals of all human experience, neither epistemology nor ideology are of course the immediate sources of predominant attitudes and values in a society, for these arise, after the event, in the socioeconomic organization of the real. Here they collude in the construction, not of a language, but of a dominant DISCOURSE – *pace* both Sapir and Whorf.

in any kind of ecosystem must eventually prove counteradaptive, and there-fore destructive, for the entire system over time.

Most recently, we have seen this happen within a decade to the ancient social systems of the Sahel in Africa. Where for many centuries the co-evolutionary relationship between these peoples' production systems and those of their natural environment ensured continuance down the ages, the imposition of 'context-free' (or 'context-buffered') colonial farming and herding on their original economic and ecological relationships has now ensured their collective and individual annihilation by the droughts they once knew how to survive.

In other words, we need a critical science of long-range survival with the courage to face up to the unprecedented dangers to which state and private capitalism have brought us. Here we must seek to understand pre-cisely what kinds of human creative potential are actually the targets of con-temporary alienation and exploitation. And if we can begin to understand what these targets are, then we can also begin to ask ourselves why it is apparently necessary, in society as we know it, for these human potentials to be subject to censure, to exploitation, or to other forms of oppression. In this way, we ought to be able, eventually, to begin understanding what it is in our socioeconomic system that makes exploitation profitable in the short term; what it is in our society that derives protection from the alienation of its citizens; and what it is in our present political economy that makes its multiple forms of oppression necessary.

II

5. *Context:* I

There are also differences in the degree of horizontal versus vertical communication within hierarchical levels. As one goes down the ranks in an organization, more communication flows are horizontal and fewer are vertical. Higher executives may communicate more exclusively in a vertical direction.

Generally, however, downward communication flows are more frequent than upward flows. Like water, communication in an organization tends to run downhill. A study of assembly-line workers found that 70 per cent initiated communication contact with a supervisor less often than once per month.
E. M. ROGERS and R. AGARWAL-ROGERS: "Organizational

Communication" in: G. J. Hanneman and W. J. McEwen,
eds. *Communication and Behavior* (1975)

Time flies like an arrow;
Fruit flies like a banana.
ANON

The reader will already have noted that, if there is one constantly recurring question for a critical and ecosystemic viewpoint, it is the real and material question of context. Obviously, the academic discourse, as well as the dissenting academic discourse, has signification only in terms of the real context in which it occurs. As has been pointed out, the systemic characteristics of this context, with its recognized and unrecognized codings of goals, are ultimately dependent on particular types of socioeconomic organization in history.

We recognize that there are no 'facts' in science, only an infinity of possible differences (and types of difference) among which to choose to make DISTINCTIONS, and that our choice to transform or translate a particular difference into a distinction cannot not be constrained by our 'hypotheses', both individual and collective. One hypothesis of these essays is that the assumption or goal of 'pure' knowledge is an outworn rationalization. ALL KNOWLEDGE IS INSTRUMENTAL. In the terms of modern communications theory, information (coded variety) is everywhere, but knowledge can occur only within the ecosystemic context of a goalseeking adaptive system peopled by goalseeking subsystems. If this is the case, then we are required to ask how the knowledge has been coded and filtered; and what it is being used for, and for whom.

Decisions about the varied instrumentalities of knowledge depend on recognizing the actual context and levels of variety within and amongst which INFORMATION will be distinguished from (what is defined or perceived as) NOISE, i.e., (as) uncoded variety. These selections can then be translated to the level of SIGNIFICATIONS (e.g., combinations of selections), at which level it will then be further possible to select and combine these distinctions into 'facts', and so on (cf. pp. 148–50, 168–70, and elsewhere below).

Knowledge – or the lack of it – which is used for the personal satisfaction and/or personal status of the knower in a context in which knowledge has a particular kind of exchange value, is of course the most common form of instrumentality. It is quite different from the understanding that knowledge without use, like 'pure' information, signifies nothing at all; and that it is the context in which it is used that gives it its semantic-pragmatic value. The relatively large amount of money spent on what is still strangely defined as 'research for its own sake', for example, would be perfectly justifiable in an ideal society; it is a peculiar priority in a society facing social, economic, and so-called 'environmental' crises that will almost certainly be beyond any kind of ordered resolution if allowed to escalate for too long. Thus one of the contexts of knowledge is the temporal context: past, present, and future. But the ideology of pure or objective knowledge to which the academic is expected to owe allegiance – besides protecting teachers and researchers from questions about the actual use value of their work – cannot deal adequately with time and place. It is an absolutist, non-contextual, non-temporal morality akin to that of a fundamentalist religion.

This is a fundamentalism that depends first on the misconstruction of closure and context; second on the correlative lack of understanding that contexts have levels; and third on its inability to deal with the real questions of logical typing in biological and social systems. The quotation from Pascal at the head of this Introduction puts this problem – which is that of the levels and extent of the PUNCTUATION of points of view – far better than I can.

This fundamentalism of day-to-day science and academia, along with its attendant censorships, is subject to a particular form of the Word of God; it is articulated on the image of the expert, the spectre of the 'subject-who-is-supposed-to-know' (Jacques Lacan).

It appears much more obvious now than it did a few years ago that the methodological requirements of closure in scientific analysis and synthesis are all too often the conscious and unconscious servants of unexplained or unrecognized ideological, psychological, and socioeconomic relationships. For example, the necessary abstraction of a system from its context in order that it may be studied – which should of course be accompanied by an overt attempt to avoid decontextualization by understanding the potentially paradoxical effects of such an abstraction – is quite commonly used, implicitly, to justify the pretended and actual abstraction or isolation of researchers from THEIR many contexts: from their socioeconomic status in a heterarchy of academic privilege, for example; from their actual functions in a system of liberal indoctrination; and from their spoken and unspoken commitments to ideological and political views – all of which the student may expect to find in one transformation or another in their work and in their teaching.

Indeed, it appears that without this repeatedly renewed personification and incorporation of the closures and the dead ends of the institutional structure itself, the academic phantasmagoria might actually have to begin to pay attention to what it is actually doing.

If knowledge is instrumental, then it is necessarily also political, for even the refusal of 'politics' is a political act. We used to be warned by people who called themselves the 'Old Left' in the 1960s not to 'politicize' the university – a warning that made little sense to those of us newly arrived in the academic propaganda machine. In retrospect, one realizes that by 'politicize' they meant that their experiences with past forms of censorship had led them to fear the imposition of new ones, if academics became seriously concerned about any contentious aspects of social reality – other than the business corporations and the government agencies which 'practical' academics have traditionally served in this century. The Cassandras were right, of course, as they had to be, since so many of them – along with some who called themselves 'New Left' – ended up collaborating with or acquiescing in the political purges, mostly of the younger faculty-members, that accompanied the economic retrenchment which followed the boom-years ending in 1968 and 1969.

So much for that. In those grand and tragic years of turmoil, we learned more than we believed possible about contexts, and not from books.

6. *Context:* II

> Ignorance, like knowledge, is purposefully directed.
> GUNNAR MYRDAL: *Objectivity in Social Research* (1969)

As has been pointed out in part, context, whether in theory or praxis, is a question of punctuation or closure – both AT a given level of relationship and, more importantly, BETWEEN levels of relationship (cf. pp. 55, 93–4, 110–17, 413–14, 420–4, and elsewhere).

Among the numerous but rarely touched on issues raised by attention to the contextual relation is that of the status of the HIERARCHIES of BOUNDARIES between systems and their temporal states, and between systems and their environments (cf. pp. 186–8, 276–7, 376). Indeed, and not the least because it enables us to distinguish between boundaries and BARRIERS (cf. pp. 315–16, 327–8), the simple methodological and epistemological distinction between CLOSED SYSTEMS and OPEN SYSTEMS provides us with the first chapter of a guidebook with which to question the ideological function of closure in the discourse of science. Simply stated, a closed system is one for which its context is effectively irrelevant or defined as such (e.g., the solar system, the cosmos as a whole); an open system, in contrast, is one that depends on its environment for its continuing existence and survival (e.g., an organism, a population, a society).[5]

---

[5] The usual thermodynamic classification of systems distinguishes between two types: those that are open to energy input (matter-energy) and those that are isolated or insulated from it. However, because of the (organic and inorganic)

This long-obscured distinction may now appear rather obvious to us. It must certainly have been behaviorally obvious to the inhabitants of the coevolved and coevolving societies that preceded us, as indeed it was to the Renaissance mystics and magicians who knew that the closure of the cosmos began and ended only with God (cf. Wilden, 1976a). But if we are now in the process of relearning much of what modern science and society induced our culture to forget, this ecological renaissance is not the result of some purported new 'advance of science'. Rather it is the result of the circumstance that our socioeconomic system has just discovered to its amazement that for some three centuries it has been an open system trying to behave like a closed one.

As we should expect, the very same behavior infects the scientific discourse, which for a similar period of time, and wearing similar blinkers, has been embarked on a similarly suicidal voyage. (This last is apparently the discovery now being celebrated in France by the recent outbreaks of new forms of intellectual nihilism and death-instinct metaphysics in that country.) Derived from its socioeconomic construction of reality, this kind of closure, this ideological artifice, is still one of the predominant characteristics of the scientific discourse. While not exactly closed to new information, as Ashby's cybernetic systems are, the discourse of science is nevertheless still relatively closed to new STRUCTURES of information, i.e., to the patterns of variety which it continues to dismiss as noise in its networks.

This insular characteristic, amongst others these essays will associate

---

systems with which they deal, where specific material inputs are significant, many systems ecologists prefer a tripartite classification (e.g., W. E. Cooper and H. E. Koenig). ISOLATED systems are closed both to the input of energy and to the input of material. CLOSED systems (e.g., the biosphere) are open to energy input (e.g., the sun), but do not depend on the input of new material. The OPEN systems that arise within the context of the isolated systems of physics (e.g., the cosmos as a whole) and within that of the closed systems of ecology, are dependent on the input of both matter and energy

In this text, 'closed' and 'isolated' are more or less synonymous. The open systems discussed here are generally organic and/or social systems (and include their representations or simulations). These (ecological) open systems are both open to matter-energy input and SENSITIVE to the variety (information/noise) which matter-energy bears. It is assumed moreover that the cosmos is the closed- or isolated-system context for all the open systems – e.g., life – which may arise within it.

One further point of clarification: some systems called open systems in physics are neither organic nor social. A flame, for example, whose entropy cannot be measured because it is dependent on the environment that supports combustion, is an open system. Similarly with the systems of meteorology (whose inputs include those of solar radiation, gravity, and the rotation of the earth). In the atmosphere, for example, a cloud is an open system.

with it, still remains a salient one, whether the particular aspect of the scientific discourse we choose to examine is traditional biology and genetics; or literary criticism and the 'sociology of knowledge'; or the recent resurgence of the century-old fascination with cosmic entropy;[6] or the bioenergetics of the social and cognitive sciences; or the phallocentric atomism of psychoanalysis and logical positivism; or the psychological foundations of modern economics, notably the 'subjective value theory' which reappears in Freud as the 'pleasure principle'.

Moreover, besides its historically peculiar attempts at closure from its real context and indeed from and between many of its own parts, the scientific discourse appears to have been composed by the inhabitants of Flatland (Abbott, 1884). We know that the discourse displays a dogged incapacity to deal adequately with system–environment relations (both practical and theoretical), even when they are considered on a single plane. But this incapacity becomes almost insignificant when understood within the context of the extraordinary ingenuity with which the scientific discourse persistently fails to recognize the realities of LEVELS OF RELATION and of RELATIONS BETWEEN LEVELS in open systems, in their environments, and, above all, between system and environment.

It is generally the case, for example, that the environment of a given open system is of a different and more inclusive level of relation (or LOGICAL TYPE) than the system it supports. However, in so far as the scientific discourse discusses such real and necessary hierarchies of BOTH-AND relations (distinct from the contingent HETERARCHIES[7] of class, race, and sex in modern society), it generally does so by putting 'system' and 'environment' into a bilateral and one-dimensional EITHER/OR OPPOSITION with each other.[8]

A case in point is the traditional (binary) 'opposition' between 'nature' and 'culture', or that between 'nature' and 'society'. The simple test for

---

[6] On the relationship between the second axiom of thermodynamics and the strange pseudobiological conceptions that led Freud to invent the notion of a bioenergetic 'death instinct' (*Todestrieb*), see Chapter VI. On death, see pp. 82–7, 405, 469–72, and elsewhere.

[7] Heterarchies are subset forms of hierarchy in which the dominant node or nodes may change place and function over time. The ecological necessities of hierarchical relationship, as well as the necessity of hierarchical information processing, should not of course be confused with the socioeconomic relationships of our present economic system.

[8] As it is becoming necessary to insist, Imaginary and either/or relationships remain dominant in our society, and in such a way that in general our system's both-and (cooperative) relations are derived from the either/or socioeconomic reality, rather than from the socioecological imperative of 'both system (at one level) and environment (at another)' to which the either/or must ultimately be subordinate if the system is to survive.

this kind of hierarchy is to ask oneself which of the two realities will survive if the other is removed or destroyed. Obviously – *pace* philosophical idealism – 'nature' survives no matter what happens to 'culture'. (So much for the slogan 'saving the environment'.) And yet so profoundly is this particular system–environment relationship misconstrued by the scientific discourse that the discourse will in some contexts actually invert the logical typing of the relation, with the result that science in its 'objectivity' carries forward the three-centuries-old Imaginary and ideological myth of 'man's mastery over nature' (cf. pp. 11–14, 117–21, 170–2, 219–23, and elsewhere). In considering social and economic relations, moreover, the scientific discourse generally maintains its deep-structure identity with the dominant ideology by indulging in the same syntactic juggling tricks. This it achieves by similarly SYMMETRIZING and/or INVERTING various contemporary hierarchies of relationship which involve levels of power and responsibility – e.g., the relationship between white and non-white, between 'man' and 'woman', between capital and labor.

This double process of symmetrization and inversion, by means of which extremely significant aspects of actual relationships are (temporarily) neutralized, can be illustrated by a simple example. The three relationships whose step-by-step COMMODITIZATION in history defines the novelty of the capitalist revolution – capital, land, and labor potential (or creative capacity: *Arbeitsvermögen*) – are hierarchically ordered. Under state and 'private' capitalism, capital dominates labor potential, and labor potential is consequently used to exploit land. But 'land' (photosynthesis) stands for our life-support system, the biosphere, and capital can be produced only by the creative capacity of human beings. Thus, since land is the source or 'ground' of labor potential, and labor potential the ground of capital, then the Imaginary and commoditized hierarchy invented and imposed by capitalism is precisely the inverse of the real one. These two hierarchies of relationship notwithstanding, however, most of modern economics prefers simply to symmetrize the three levels by reducing all three terms to a single plane of reality, each being defined as one of the three 'factors of production': 'land, labor, and capital' (cf. Chapter VIII).[9]

This hierarchical relationship and its inversion, as well as its 'one-

---

[9] Compare this to Abraham Lincoln, in his first annual message to Congress (1861): 'Labor is prior to, and independent of, capital. Capital is only the fruit of labor, and could never have existed if labor had not first existed. Labor is the superior of capital, and deserves much the higher consideration.' One notes that this judgement was made at a time when industrializing capital was about successfully to ensure that the commoditized market of 'free' laborers would become the dominant socioeconomic relationship in the United States, as it had rather less violently become in Britain a half-century previously.

dimensionalization' or symmetrization, can perhaps be more immediately visualized (i.e., less mediated by the particular medium of print) by means of the iconic representation of a diagram, as in *Figure 1*.

FIGURE 1
Inversion and Symmetrization

(a) The actual and long-term hierarchy of constraints between land, labor, and capital (distinctions):

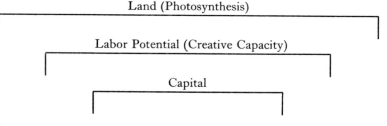

Land (Photosynthesis)

Labor Potential (Creative Capacity)

Capital

(b) The inverted hierarchy of commoditized power and control between the three components (contradictions):

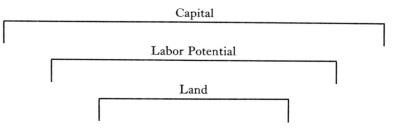

Capital

Labor Potential

Land

(c) The ideological symmetrization of both hierarchies into potential 'identities of opposites' (the 'three factors of production') (oppositions):

Land ----------------- Labor ----------------- Capital

To those readers familiar with the text of Marx, it will be evident that the relationships of *Figure 1* are among those which Marx was attempting to redefine, against traditional economics, in his systemic analysis of capitalism.[10]

7. Syntax

I am come in very truth leading Nature to you, with all her children, to bind her to your service and to make her your

---

[10] On the topic of systemic hierarchies and the related concepts of opposition and contradiction, see Notes 24 and 29 in the Appendix.

slave . . . So may I succeed in my only earthly wish, namely to
stretch the deplorably narrow limits of man's dominion over
the universe to their promised bounds. . . .
SIR FRANCIS BACON: *The Masculine Birth of Time, Or the Great
Instauration of the Dominion of Man over the Universe* (1603)

Questioning the function of (atomistic) closure in the discourse of science
tends to set off the rather stereotyped responses amongst positivists and
their kin to which I referred summarily in the first version of these pages.
I am chastened to discover how little these problems have changed in the
intervening decade, and in spite of the extraordinary succession of apparent
changes and real crises which those years have seen. These responses are
almost always based on the same unrecognized SYNTACTIC patterns or
structures in the scientific discourse – not to mention the socioeconomic
discourse – as those just remarked on: (1) the 'flattening out' and symmetrization of non-symmetrical relations (reduction of logical typing) – as in the
loaded phrase: 'My wife and I are equals'; and/or (2) the coincidental
activity of turning a real hierarchy upside down – as in the once traditional
American fiction of the supposed economic 'matriarchy' of wealthy widows
dominating the stock market (a self-serving story that could still be heard
on right and left in France in the 1970s); as well as (3) a correlative persis-
tence in viewing both 'horizontal' relations at a given level, and 'vertical'
relations between levels, as single-level relations of (binary) opposition
(EITHER 'either/or' OR 'both-and').

Such mispunctuations of social reality are of course greatly facilitated by
the equally syntactical activity of reducing the general and the systemic to
the individual, the personal, and the particular, as in 'some of my best
friends are . . .'.

What comes out quite specifically in the responses referred to is the
unrecognized absolutism of the dominant discourse. For example, one
stereotyped response to an explanation of the contextual relations of open
systems is still the query: 'Does this mean that everything is relative?' If
we 'decondense' this remark so as to bring out the unstated significations
communicated by the lacunae within it,[11] we find that it translates approxi-
matively as follows: 'Does this mean that [either] every-thing is [absolutely]
relative [or it is not]?'[12]

[11] Compare the decondensation (Freud's term) of the 'schizophrenic symptom':
'I'm an end-table made of manzanita wood' on pp. 56–60 below.

[12] Part of the answer, level by level, to this question is: 'All human RELATIONS are
relative to the long-range survival of the (social) system one is in; and this at
another level is relative to the constraints of the organic environment (which
includes humans-as-organisms). This at another level is relative to the constraints

As in the case of the 'cultural relativism', newly popular since the 'sixties – the self-referring relativism which translates the ideology of the 'free and equal' individual of nineteenth-century liberal capitalism into the newer form of 'all cultures are equal' – the questioner does not always recognize the hidden equation involved. What is not recognized is that (absolute) relativism ('all contexts are equal') is simply the Imaginary mirror image of (absolute) atomism ('all contexts are one'). Indeed, aside from the echoes of this confusion in Buddhistic solipsism, we are reminded that this Imaginary identity was one of the messages unconsciously borne by Leibniz's imaginary 'deep structures', the 'monads', in so far as each was both 'one' and 'all', in the eighteenth-century equivalent of science fiction. (Cf. p. 216 below; and pp. 86, 89, and 92 on 'Do your own thing'. Consider also the worldwide commercial success of Jacopetti's *Mondo Cane*, 1961 – translatable as 'We Are No Better Than The Savages' – which happens to include a grotesque misrepresentation of a New Guinea pig festival.)

I think there is little need to labor this point with the numerous other examples that must be familiar to the reader, except to remark that, even apart from the latest updating of the arms race (try *The Aviation Yearbook* for 1978, Denver: Jeppesen-Sanderson), in old-line neocolonial dependencies like Canada – where 'redbaiting' and other such ploys are still very much the political rule – the dominance of the either/or logic will manifest itself in classic style. This is the style which allows people to assume that if you make a critical comment about 'capitalism', you are *ipso facto* being nice to the Russians – and hence approving of their subordinate version of our now global economic arrangements.

8. *Systems*

> The cell membrane is not a wall or a skin or a sieve. It is an
> active and responsive part of the cell; it decides what is inside
> and what is outside and what the outside does to the inside.
> Cell membranes have 'faces' that enable cells to recognize
> and influence one another. The membranes are also

---

of the inorganic environment; which in turn is relative to the constraints of local or planetary (positive) entropy . . .'; and so on. Each time we approach a boundary in this hierarchy of relations – e.g., the boundary between 'life' and 'non-life' defined by the DNA-RNA communication system, or that between 'nature' and 'society' defined by the historical emergence of kinship-constrained production and reproduction (including the reproduction of society itself) – we are at the same time approaching the locus of what a given relationship will be relative TO. On the topic of kinship and production, see in particular Maurice Godelier's recent and pioneering work (1973, 1975).

communications systems. Things outside a cell do not necessarily act on the cell interior by passing through the membrane; they may simply change the membrane in some way that causes the membrane, in turn, to make changes in the cell interior.

DANIEL MAZIA: 'The Cell Cycle' (1974)

Before leaving the topic of the confusion of 'closure' with 'closed system', but without going into any details about the recent rise of 'systems theory', some aspects of which I have considered elsewhere (e.g., 1974, 1976a, 1976b, 1977), a word or two at the start on some of the current uses of the term 'system' seem necessary.

Leaving aside the Light Airborne Multi-Purpose System and the Utility Tactical Transport Aircraft System (both of which are helicopters), it should be noted that the evocation of a 'systems perspective', which is now becoming a fashionable ploy at the contemporary equivalent of cocktail parties, is no guarantee whatsoever against the mispunctuations of the discourse of science. Indeed, readers unfamiliar with what now passes for systems theory (general or otherwise) and for the theory of communication systems – especially in North America, where a new technocracy of mind managers, word processors, information movers, and people pacifiers is arising like Dracula out of the coffins of Management Science – readers unfamiliar with these developments would be well-advised to beware of the word 'system' and its associated jargon.

For many who refer to themselves as 'systems theorists' today, systems are as mechanical as they were for Adam Smith or for Isaac Newton's followers. For others, the terms 'system' and 'environment' reveal by their use that they are simply the familiar 'subject' and 'object' of the traditional Cartesianism of psychology and 'social' science, but now in a new disguise. In other versions, the system itself is viewed as an object, and moreover as an object to be viewed or even 'controlled' from an imaginary 'outside'. In other inappropriate punctuations, the concept 'system', with or without significant reference to an environment (usually without), will be found standing in for a number of equally invalid analogies in the human sciences, e.g., that which makes society a superorganism or some such biological and bioenergetic entity; or that which makes society a mechanical equilibrium system or a network of 'fields of force'. Two such 'systems analogies' are particularly revealing: that which abstracts society from its material basis, and, by calling it 'culture' or the like, makes it into one gigantic 'mind' (e.g., the perspectives of Bateson and Lévi-Strauss); and that which, as if by equal and opposite reaction, takes the organismic analogy to the point of making society the equivalent of the 'body' which was missing from the 'mind' of the other analogy (e.g., major aspects of functionalism, for which 'structure' commonly signifies 'institution').

For others associated with systems and structures, even open systems are strangely viewed as entities or objects in 'neutral' space, like atoms in the void, or galaxies in the cosmos. These include what I have come to call the 'social-contract' systems theorists, who use a systems model not significantly different in its syntax from the model of society invented in the seventeenth century by members of the rising class represented so faithfully by John Locke (cf. Wilden, 1974).

The basic model used by the social-contract systemists is, however, obscured by their reaction to the Newtonian atomism of 'The whole is the sum of its parts' by the less overt atomism of what is sometimes mistaken for holism, the dictum that 'The whole is MORE than the SUM of its parts'. As A. Angyal pointed out many years ago (1941), this revised formulation is still additive. Moreover, it still confers on the parts an ontological primacy over their relations. In other words, it may signify no more than that one calculates the sum of the (autonomous) 'parts', and then adds to this sum the sum of the 'relations' between them. It tells us nothing of value, for example, about those wholes, such as socioeconomic systems in their environments, whose relations are responsible for creating the historically-constrained characteristics of their parts, e.g., social and economic individuals (as distinct from the biological individuality which also sustains them). The revised dictum is thus a form of PSEUDOHOLISM.

If one looks at the basic characteristics of such 'systems' approaches, one commonly finds in them a constitutive kind of ideological projection which is not in the end difficult to identify. In the study of society and social relations, the basic characteristics of an approach can be expected to appear with considerable fidelity in the representative metaphors used to describe or evoke such nodal relationships as: the relationship between the individual and the whole; the relationships between different groups of individuals; the relationship to past, present, and future; the relation between 'mind' and 'body' (if and where such terms exist); the relation between work and play; the relationship to the natural environment; and so on. Thus, apart from considering the boundary relationship represented as existing between system and environment as such, one key characteristic we should look at is the representation of the boundaries – and KINDS of boundary – said to exist between the various subsystems within the whole.

Not long ago, for example, I had occasion to ask of a man who was implicitly defending the solipsistic subjectivity of 'Do your own thing', where in his view the boundary between us – between our 'selves' –

actually lay. His response was to draw an imaginary line in the air around himself, corresponding, he said, to the one I might draw around 'me'. When further asked what lay between these two supposed boundaries, he replied: 'Nothing'.

This response recalled significant features of Piaget's theory of systems (cf. in particular pp. 324–30 below), where the 'prototype structure' is said to be the 'organism'. It also recalled Sartre's analysis of the 'ego' in his *Réflexions sur la question juive* (1946). Just as Sartre identified in the anti-Semite a kind of frontier mentality around the borders of the 'self', so Piaget also seemed to identify a similar frontal barrier around the territory of his 'autonomous structures'.

By the early 'seventies, a number of people had already suspected that certain 'systems theorists' were in reality only performing a 'rectification of names', and moreover one which in the end led them right back to the same old categories they had started with. The radical import of the communicational and ecosystemic approach, as much for the understanding of present society as for understanding the one truly social and the one truly economic analysis it has received – I mean the work of Marx and Engels – was in this way being thoroughly neutralized. However, it was not easy at first adequately to characterize the pseudo-systemic approaches. These approaches were atomistic and flat – though lipservice was regularly paid to heterarchical and constantly-changing relations of dominance – and still seemed to owe a great deal to Newtonianism and Cartesianism, as well as to the bioenergetics of nineteenth-century 'field theory'.

But science does not produce society; societies produce science. Thus, the epistemological critique of these perspectives, while nevertheless illuminating for many of us, was inadequately understood in relation to the socioeconomic functions of these viewpoints. It was not until recently that it began to become clear that some of the commonest systems models shared a definite kinship, and sometimes even a lineage, with the Lockean version of the 'social contract', with its specifically bourgeois origins and its distinctively capitalist underpinnings. In the view of Locke, private property is anchored and imbedded in the individual 'self', and this 'innate' characteristic, like a metaphor of Newtonian inertia, enters into all social relations essentially unchanged – as do the Imaginary individuals who carry it around (cf. p. 222n).

Thus it is that the Lockean view of society is not based on the characteristics of social organization at all; it is based, like practically the entire domain of 'social' science today, on the psychology and/or the biology of the supposed 'human individual' or on that of the 'species' (cf. Piaget on the "psychobiological environment", p. 310 below). This is of course a confusion of the logical typing of distinct levels of organization. Characteristics stemming from the actual organization of the system are projected into the supposed 'instincts' or 'innate ideas' of an imaginary 'individual'.

One of the truly representative characteristics of the Lockean individual, as of the Cartesian one, is that it replicates in its own organization that SPLITTING OF THE ECOSYSTEM, scorned by traditionalists like John Donne, with which the Age of Discovery opened the world to colonialism and to the specifically modern domination of nature (cf. Leiss, 1972). This individual is, in other words, a peculiar dyad, split into 'body' and 'mind' – consider in this context the Lévi-Straussian categories of 'nature' and 'culture' – and this split is historically novel. It is a splitting of the subject in this world in which the supposedly dominant part – mind – not only 'controls' the rest (it is believed) – i.e., the body – but mind actually OWNS the body. And what can you do if you own something under capitalism? You can sell it. And not just sell it, in reality, but ALIENATE it, make it OTHER.

The mind-body relation in our society is a great deal more muddled and complicated than this – 'mind' or 'self', for example, often turn out to be modeled on the image of the body – but the crucial relation, the STRUCTURAL contradiction between 'capital' and 'labor' that makes capitalism capitalist, is represented here. And when we sell control over our creative capacity in the market (cf. Nicolaus, 1972: 318–19), our minds and our bodies and our hearts and our souls go with it.

Consider, if you will, the following extraordinary pursuit of the Lockean position on the individual to its ultimate conclusions – and just at a time when the commoditization of labor potential was becoming dominant under industrialization – penned by the man who invented the term 'ideology', Destutt de Tracy. In *The German Ideology* (1845–6: 245–6), Marx and Engels single out the following sentences from Destutt's *Traité de la volonté et de ses effets* (1826 edition):

'. . . Nature has endowed man with an inevitable and inalienable property, property in the form of his own individuality' (p. 17). [The individual] 'clearly sees that this *Ego* is the exclusive owner of the body which it animates, the organs which it sets in motion, all their capacities, all their forces, all the effects they produce, all their passions and actions; for all this ends and begins with this Ego, exists only through it, is set in motion through its action; and no other person can make use of these same instruments or be affected in the same way by them' (p. 16).

The quotation itself calls for more attention than we can give it here, especially since similar sentiments become a nineteenth-century commonplace in economics (e.g., W. S. Jevons' view of the worker's "monopoly of labor"). But to restrict the commentary to the major point being made, it is surely significant that this bizarre PSYCHOLOGIZATION and BIOLOGIZA-TION of a socioeconomic relationship invented in its ultimate dominance by the capitalist revolution alone – the commoditization of human energy and information as 'labor' in the market – should manifest such a structural or syntactic identity with the concept of 'system' blithely being used by so many people today. For the Lockean 'ego' – associated with what Locke called the 'little closet shut from light, with only some little openings left' (one of his metaphors for 'understanding' or 'mind': pp. 212–17 below) – the Lockean ego is as autonomous in its essence as a closed system would be; and the image of a barbed-wire fence around the 'territory' of the self, with gates here and there which can be opened or closed, is not in the least inappropriate to the Imaginary projections involved in this ideological construction.

What I am arguing, then, is that from two directions, as it were – from the projection of the Imaginary status of the 'self' into everyday life; and from the projection of the private-property relations of the dominant mode of production under capitalism (private property being quite distinct from the PERSONAL property with which it is often ideologically confused), from the projection of these novel relations of possession and production into the domain of biology and psychology – there arises in the scientific discourse a complex network of confused relations which by successive abstraction from the Real comes to masquerade in academia and in business as 'systems theory', as the theory of 'interpersonal communication', as 'environmental (i.e., human) engineering', as 'organization' (i.e., corporation) theory', as 'administrative communications theory' (or management by outright manipulation), or indeed as any number of other profitable or even patho-logical modes of translating an original alienation of the person into the production and reproduction of the 'self' as a commodity.

What we seem regularly to find in these pseudo-systemic approaches – i.e., neither communicational nor ecosystemic – is in other words a projec-tion, distinctively mediated and constrained by the codes of the present structure of our socioeconomic system, a projection of the experienced structures of ECONOMIC INDIVIDUALISM – which are not the same as the structures of sociohuman individuality – into the structure of society, into the structure of the person, and into the structure of the ongoing relationships between them. The 'system' thus constructed is, in sum, a mere aggregate or heap of (supposed) SELF-SUFFICIENCIES. It is an atomistic collection of so many Imaginary replicas of '(individual) human natures', as it were, an aggregate of a number of so-called 'humans-in-the-state-of-nature' (male organisms, of course), who apparently ran into each other while out for a constitutional in the woods one day; and then, for various reasons – depending on the author of the fairytale – sat down and invented society by means of a 'contract'.

Thus it was, so the story goes, that the originally 'free' and 'unconstrained' individuals – who keep popping up again and again in one of capitalism's ideological mirror-images, individualistic anarchism – came to invent the social system we live in, a social system which is represented at one and the same time as the only locus of constraint in their individually-motivated actions, and also as completely separate from them – as completely separate from them as they are from each other.

With due allowance for different emphases, this is the basic model. What we so often find hanging about under the rubric of systems theory today is only a more abstract – and decontextualized – representation of this fundamentally Imaginary system.

The foregoing seems at present to be the only adequately contextual explanation, which – besides being an explanation in which the concept of 'system' and the concept of 'society' mutually support and sustain each other – is also a direct way of answering to certain highly significant features of these 'systems approaches' – and notably to the implicit or explicit 'zone of neutrality', the 'no-person's-land', or perhaps even the 'demilitarized zone' which in all these views effectively bars each (supposedly closed) subsystem both from each other and from the whole.

To put it another way, the ghosts in these machines must spend most of their time running from one border post to another, the better to censor what gets in and out.

That the boundary between you and me might actually be distinct from both of us together, and not the double edge of the private property of our selves, for example; or that this boundary we share with others might also be the actual locus of all communication and exchange between us – such compendency in the Real seems not even to be dreamed of in most of modern systems philosophy.

Boundaries, far from being barriers, are the locus of relations for open systems in reality; and it is our relation to these boundaries, including our discovery of them and their discovery of us, which surely makes us what we become.

What is more, if the relations briefly outlined here do indeed qualify as basic sources of the (psychosocial or sociobiological) 'systems perpective' – cf. pp. 326–9, and the Index entry 'boundary' – then we might want to ask the social-contract systems theorists (leaving aside the obvious mechanists) why, if they are bringing us some newly useful theory, they seem nevertheless to have forgotten what we all must surely once have known as children: that the (communicational) 'space' between the open systems we call people is not only not some valueless void between the 'social atoms' of some contemporary version of an eighteenth-century 'social physics', but also happens to be inhabited by the rest of us.

III

9. *Values*

> The masters' right of giving names goes so far that it is
> permissible to look upon language itself as the expression of
> the power of the masters: they say: "this IS that, and that,"
> they seal finally every object and every event with a sound, and
> thereby at the same time take possession of it.
> FRIEDRICH NIETZSCHE: *The Genealogy of Morals* (1887)

> Profit is today a fighting word. Profits are the lifeblood of the
> economic system, the magic elixir upon which progress and all
> good things ultimately depend. But one man's lifeblood is
> another man's cancer.
> PAUL SAMUELSON: *Speech at Harvard University* (1976)

However corrupted by the constraints of capitalism the circulation of knowledge in the university may be, the production, reproduction, and exchange of knowledge in this academic subsystem nevertheless seems at first to correspond to the requirements of what in this book is called 'symbolic exchange' (cf. pp. 15–17, 248–61, and elsewhere). The structures and the processes of symbolic exchange in the so-called 'primitive' social systems correspond to the SOCIOECOLOGICAL requirements of goalseeking systems whose reality of values has been oriented by consonance and co-evolution towards long-range survival.

The essential requirement of such forms of communication within and between social systems and the real is that the processes of production, reproduction, and exchange which they employ shall maintain the socio-economic system's overall 'steady-state' relationship to its various environments, staying well within the carrying capacity of their territory, and thus ensure the long-range survival of the whole – both 'system', at one level, and 'environment', at another.

Without here going into details of relationships which are progressively developed throughout this text, and which have lent themselves to further refinement and extension since, it can be said that where the living and socioeconomic relationship to the Real is such that Symbolic structures and processes PREDOMINATE over co-existing Imaginary structures and processes in production and exchange – as seems to be the case in many of the 'other' societies – then long-range cooperative relations of survival-in-use will tend to be maintained.

Conversely, in societies like our own, where this hierarchical relationship is inverted so that Imaginary structures predominate in the reality of the socioeconomic system and its relation to its environments, then the (temporarily) dominant relationships will be those of short-range survival: 'either/or' exploitation and competition.

Moreover, since these Imaginary relationships are (temporarily) unconstrained by their relations with the Real, there can also predominate in our socioeconomic system other positive feedback processes with similarly destructive potentials in the long term (cf. *Figure 2* on p. 209, and the graph on p. 508). At one level in the system, the production of economic EXCHANGE VALUES undergoes repeated escalation, far beyond any real possibilities of rational use. At another level, that of the 'capital goods circuit', we find exponential and superexponential escalation of the production and reproduction of the means of production themselves, i.e., an escalation of the MEANS of producing exchange values (cf. pp. 390–4). This is the escalation of the production of 'productive capacity' in an economic system whose present stability continues to depend on the exportation of its instabilities into any and all available environments, and notably its own future. In other words, the present stability of capitalist economies depends on their future (quantitative) growth, as many economists now recognize; and this process is not the product of 'growth for the sake of growth' – a peculiarly 'self-reflexive' notion – but rather that of growth for the sake of (temporary) stability.

(On this topic, note the recently renewed concerns of economists for what their nineteenth-century predecessors, such as David Ricardo, believed should be avoided at all costs: the 'steady-state' economy, e.g., Daley, 1973. It is not clear that capitalism could sustain such a state without crisis, stagnation, or collapse – unless it also went through a restructuring in the process.)

Ideologically speaking, of course, it is this exponential and superexponential accumulation that has for at least two centuries now been called 'progress'.

The distinction between exchange value and use value depends on the context in which any particular relationship is used. (The distinction is obscured, and not by accident, by the 'subjective value theory' of (marginal) 'utility' in modern economics.) In order to define a relationship as one primarily of use or primarily of exchange, one has to decide which form of value is the DOMINANT characteristic in any given context. The point of difficulty for some people is, first, that they tend to assume that any 'object' (i.e., relation) must be EITHER one OR the other; and, second, that this common epistemological approach effectively precludes an understanding that exchange values have uses – one of which is of course that they are produced and exchanged – and that use values, in their turn, cannot find their expression except through production and exchange.

Exchange values are necessarily punctuated and mediated digitally (ascribed discrete boundaries), whereas use values are essentially analog. This text distinguishes between two major forms of (social and economic) exchange value, both of which are digital: Symbolic exchange value and Imaginary exchange value (cf. pp. 272–3 below).

Symbolic exchange values are constrained by socioecological use values; Imaginary exchange values, however – true to the myth of progress under capitalism – know no such limits. Imaginary structures are those we associate with symmetrized relations of either self or other in 'zero-sum games'. In the personal sense, the Imaginary WHEN DOMINANT is the domain of that loss of perspective and confusion of levels that we know as paranoia and/or psychosis. In the socioeconomic sense, the Imaginary when dominant is the domain in which (apparently) unconstrained competition is dominant over cooperation, and exchange values dominant over use values.

(On this topic, note in particular the discussion of what Marx calls 'commodity fetishism' – metaphorically defined by him on the model of the nineteenth-century illusionists' device, Philipstal's 'Phantasmagoria' (1802) – in the first volume of *Capital*; and his remarks on the exponential and superexponential expansion of accumulated capital in the third volume; also pp. 250–5, 390–4 below. On his derogatory use of the term 'fetish', see the remarks on 'myth' and 'civilization' in Note 26 in the Appendix.)

From the perspective being outlined here, a number of the production, reproduction, and exchange relationships of our society become easier to comprehend in terms of their actual interconnections. We can begin to see, for example, how the production, reproduction, and exchange of values in the university (including the qualitative values it labels 'neutrality' or 'objectivity' or 'quantification', and so on) have come to correspond in general to an ALIENATED and REIFIED form of Symbolic relationship – and hence to an Imaginary one.

The exchanges of academia are alienated in the sense that they are commonly treated as being quite separate from their real environments, and even from the persons that profess them. They are reified in the sense that knowledge in academia is generally treated as if it were a collection of objects – not as a many-leveled ensemble of messages-in-circulation – and moreover as objects of POSSESSION. As such, then, the academic disciplines and their inhabitants present us with an ideological model of private-property relationships under capitalism. In effect, each discipline and sub-discipline stands steadfast for so-called 'free' enterprise. Each discipline and subdiscipline seeks to retain unto itself the private ownership of the means of production and reproduction in which it specializes – the means of the production and reproduction of 'its' form of knowledge – and which it may then employ in competition with other disciplines, or with the many representatives of its own progressive fragmentation into more and more isolated parts.

A major aspect of the results of this 'possessive individualism' (C. B. Macpherson, 1962) of the disciplines is not so much a 'quest for truth', but rather a quest for the (illusory) stability of what many academics, especially in the social sciences and the various forms of positivism, still painfully call 'the facts' or the 'logic of the facts'. Other academics, moreover, while approaching such questions with rather more subtlety and suspicion (notably in the 'humanities'), will nevertheless fall into the Imaginary trap implicitly laid for them by the positivistic position: they fall into a negative identity with it, countering absolutism with relativism, and even indulging themselves in the privilege of viewing life, science, and reality as just so many games to be played.

Indeed, many of the latter will actually call upon Einsteinian relativity or upon Heisenberg's principle of indeterminacy to support their position. Apparently they do not realize that, in both of these relationships, the observer doing the observing is a constructed abstraction necessary in physics, an IDEAL observer deliberately abstracted from the reality of society-in-nature-in-history. As a result, the relativists fail to recognize that the physicists' relativity and indeterminacy are significant and useful ONLY in contexts where the sociohistorical context is not.

(A useful test for this kind of abstraction in physics is to ask whether in principle it could be replaced by a suitably designed and programmed machine. In the cases cited, it could – in principle, and whether or not such a machine could actually be constructed. In contrast, only a fanatical believer in the future of 'artificial intelligence' would suggest that a machine could replace participant-observers-in-history.)

The further result is that humanists and social scientists who confuse the physical order of relationships with the socioeconomic order commonly end up by doing physicists the disservice of translating physics directly (if unconsciously) into ideology. For, where Relativity tells us that all physical standpoints for observation are ultimately equivalent (equally valued), and where Indeterminacy tells us that at a certain level all such observations become equivalent (equally indeterminate) – both of which are clearly true – the liberal aspects of the dominant ideology, in one of its classic contradictions, tell us that all ideas (and therefore all punctuations) are equal in value – which is manifestly false.

(The conservative aspects of the ideology commonly restrict this pseudo-equality to the ruminations and representations of a specific caste, race, and class; and – like others – to a specific sex.)

What neither the diehard positivists nor the well-meaning relativists living in this opposition seem to recognize is that what is ultimately real for human beings in social and natural reality is not the result of its punctuation by 'truth', by physics, by God, or by the individual (solipsistic or otherwise). Nor is it ultimately the result of the punctuation of reality by the linguistic and non-linguistic dialects of the dominant classes. Not at all. What is real for us in reality are the products of the punctuation and the organization of reality by the activities of society in history. And whereas it is utterly insignificant in the end how the (positivistic) individual or the (individual-istic) relativist may choose to punctuate their relationship to their environments, this has never been the case for society. In the relationship between society and nature, inadequate, inept, or imaginary punctuations may lead to extinction.

Parenthetically, what are also commonly missing from such confusions between different orders of reality are the relatively distinct categories of time which are relevant at distinct levels in the overall social ecosystem. At the physical level, as in symbolic logic, time – past, present, and future – is a mere abstract BACKDROP for the operations taking place. At the qualitatively distinct biological or ecological level, a new punctuation of time appears against the backdrop; time past punctuated by the environment and the genetic memory of EVOLUTION, and time to come punctuated by the processes of biological reproduction. Again, at the qualitatively distinct socioeconomic level, there join the other categories of time, the time past of HISTORY and the future time of socioeconomic reproduction. For us as individuals, we live not only all these kinds of time, but also the past time of MEMORY and the future time of HOPE (cf. pp. 63–5, 74–5, 99–100, 104, 179n, 359–60, and elsewhere).

But the longstanding confusion about the natures of time in modern analytic logic – which, like information theory and popular forms of linguistics, is little more than a synchronic theory of syntax in a consciously and unconsciously closed system – is nevertheless readily understandable. The problem is that when you live in a society of time machines, it is not difficult to fall into the habit of thinking of time as mechanical and repetitious (cf. Zeno in Chapter III), like a production line, no doubt – or to become addicted to confusing the work of time with the works of clocks.

10. *Exchange*

> . . . Cultural relativism would be merely puerile if – in order
> to concede the richness of civilizations different from our own,
> and also to concede the impossibility of attaining a moral or
> philosophical criterion to judge the respective value of the
> choices which led each one of them to retain certain forms of
> life and thought by renouncing others – if this relativism felt
> obliged to treat with condescension or even disdain, the
> scientific knowledge which – whatever may have been the evils
> its applications have brought about, and whatever may be the
> even more destructive and overwhelming evils now on the
> horizon – does not any the less constitute a mode of knowing
> whose absolute superiority cannot possibly be contested.
> CLAUDE LÉVI-STRAUSS: *L'Homme nu* (1971)

> Interior Minister of Lilliput: 'But you're a Giant! A monster
> sent by our enemies to destroy us!'
> Gulliver: 'I'm not your enemy; I'm just different. . . .'
> Minister: 'Different! That makes you an enemy!'
> Gulliver: 'No, I'm different from you and you are different
> from me. So you see, we're both the same. That makes us
> equal. . . .'
> *The Three Worlds of Gulliver* (1960)

If the general contentions of this brief outline and analysis are accepted,
then, since there is no demonstrable long-range survival value in the 'pure'
knowledge, in the so-called 'advance of science', or in the so-called 'civilized
thought' of the academic discourse, we might well ask ourselves what the
function of the 'unit of knowledge' in the particular kind of bourgeois kinship system represented by the university can possibly be.

The answer is not far to seek. The function of the circulation of the 'unit'
of knowledge in the academic discourse seems to be primarily that of maintaining the homeostasis of the relationships of the academic establishment. As anybody who has attended more than one academic symposium
or read more than one or two scholarly journals must surely recognize, the
supreme value of remaining silent when you have nothing relevant to say
is not a recognized academic virtue. Somebody suggested a few years ago
that the first requirement for the receipt of the Ph.D. should be a promise
not to publish anything for at least ten years. But NOT to publish or perish
is unthinkable in an industry whose product is 'knowledge'. All the corporate necessities of production for the sake of accumulation under the con-

straints of competition would have to be rejected. Without such growth and accumulation, it is unlikely that the corporation would continue profitably to survive.

In retrospect, it seems clear that the so-called 'knowledge explosion' of the past thirty years or so has little to do with knowledge as such. It has primarily to do with knowledge as a commodity produced by the 'knowledge industry' (Clark Kerr). And like every other form of industrial production in North America today, its most significant side-effect is pollution: the pollution of minds. This explosion is an 'information explosion' only in the sense that the contemporary organization of the academic establishment depends upon everyone finding SOME-THING to exchange and communicate in order to obtain funds and to maintain and reproduce the system.

This communication of units of information would be perfectly rational if the university really were the 'primitive society with ownership in common' that its fantasies describe it to be. In reality, however, the communication processes of contemporary academia seem to serve explicitly or implicitly to deny or disavow the progressive alienation of the faculty member – and of most of the students – from any relation significantly resembling the real life of the rest of humanity, who are less privileged in terms of leisure, status, caste, and class.

Where once one might have tried to say that the work of the 'intellectual' or the 'artist' is essentially creative and unalienated, the logistics of the university's lines of production have demonstrated that its workers are alienated laborers also (if more in the spiritual than in the material sense). Whereas workers are alienated in the classic sense because they do not fully share in the fruits of their labor, academicians are alienated because their labor is, so often, quite fruitless. Academic products – books, papers, 'communications', footnotes, courses – thus become the objects of Imaginary production and exchange.

The alienation of the relationships between people which this process implies is indeed a mirror, as it were, of the impotence of the academic compared with the ruthless inefficiency of the university machinery. In this context, the question of whether the units of knowledge have demonstrable use value in their exchanges becomes less and less significant. These units nevertheless express a predominant exchange value; and in this sense they are indeed useful – as currency. Unfortunately this currency was devalued by the inflation of knowledge long ago.

The system of the academic exchange of knowledge does of course have a practical function: like the 'primitive' system, it is highly redundant and resistant to noise. But the collective injunction of reciprocal exchange in a 'primitive' and non-commoditized society – for which the environment is the world of nature and other similarly organized groups, and in which there is 'room to move' both spatially and temporally – performs a symbiotic and rational function. In contrast, the existence of such an anomaly in industrialized capitalist civilization (state or private) simply contributes to the long-range instability of the system it continues to serve.

In more recent years, however, academia has been constrained, mostly by economic realities, to recognize some aspects of its anomalous situation. Research must be more 'applied', we hear, teaching more oriented to the 'community', textbooks more 'relevant' to 'public service'. In form and in apparent goals such reforms sound most welcome. It is only when one examines the content of what actually happens as a result – the expansion of pseudoliberating and social control programs, such as 'organization theory', courses in 'How to Communicate', and criminology, for example – that one realizes that academia has once again been enlisted, along with other parts of the media – those that have been advertising a Depression for the last few years, for instance, judging by the quantity and indeed the quality of their mass-produced and computerized fantasies – academia has been enlisted in the latest of our social counter-insurgency programs: Attitude Change by Behavior Manipulation.

11. *Opposition*

All successful men have agreed on one thing – they were
CAUSATIONISTS . . . The biggest thing in the world is the law
of action and reaction, namely that for every action there is an
equal and opposite reaction.
RALPH WALDO EMERSON: *What is Success?* (1870)

Up to now, car stereo has been something of an either/or
situation. Either you got plenty of power . . . Or sensitive
controls . . . But the time has come for something
revolutionary in car stereo. The AND. 20 watts of power per
channel and separate bass and treble controls and dual-gate
MOS/FET and a phased-locked-loop multiplex demodulator
and automatic fine tuning and dual ceramic filters . . . and even
more, all in one. If you're tired of hearing either this or that,
drive over to your Audiovox dealer for a test-listen. You'll
find the sum of the parts sounds a lot better than just some of
the parts.
© 1977 AUDIOVOX CORPORATION: *Announcing the End of the
Either/Or Era in Car Stereo*

In looking at our situation as faculty members in the academic establishment, one comes to see little else besides a façade of (real enough) economic comfort which scarcely conceals a crumbling structure of garrulous desperation and hidden contradictions in values. As a group of (mostly) men, many of whom once had high ideals about 'objective' knowledge and about 'education' in the traditional elitist sense, we have progressively painted ourselves into a corner where what we say we are doing and what we actually do have less and less relation to each other. We have become imprisoned by the necessity of trying to explain what we are doing when, in reality, few of us can afford the risk of believing in it. Leaving aside the cynics, the Stalinists, the professional manipulators, and those whom one can only describe as academic racketeers, we could perhaps demand sympathy for our plight if it were not for the disastrous effects which our own alienation by the university machine has on most of the students committed to our charge. We have become lower-echelon – and not very efficient – managers in a corporation over whose balance sheets we have no control, and the metaphor of 'commitment' in the previous sentence begins to sound ominously like something applicable to a 'schizophrenic ward'.

The anomaly represented by the fantasy of the university – the 'free university in a free society' – does not lie in the fact that it is manifestly untrue. The anomaly is that such an 'open' university could only exist in a quite different kind of society, one not founded on exploitation. This fantasy of the academic community is in effect a fantasy of primitivism or utopian socialism. In other words, and to reaffirm what has already been said, the picture most members of the university have of the institution – a picture that is greatly strengthened when anything happens that might be construed as biting the governmental hand that feeds it – is one of a closed system, separate from the socioeconomic and political organization of the 'environment' which actually constrains it (at all its inputs), on the one hand, and which the university helps to maintain (by its output), on the other.

Within what has so inexorably become a managerial and administrative dictatorship, the artificial and ideological attempt to maintain closure engenders a contradictor: the 'negative academic'. This phrase – whether referring to student or faculty member – describes the situation of whomever is identified by an OPPOSITION to the academic establishment (cf. also pp. 74–9 below). For those of us who may find ourselves in such a relationship of (Imaginary) opposition, in spite of our best efforts to transcend it, two rather unhappy possibilities may impose themselves on us.

The first is that in criticizing the university we serve the ends of its higher management. By our very existence, we who dissent 'prove' that the system works, that there really is 'academic freedom'. Apart from the circumstance that academic freedom is an illogical socioeconomic privilege in a 'democracy' supposedly founded on freedom of speech (no wonder the average taxpayer finds the term so offensive), this freedom is of course as illusory as that of the 'free laborer' or that of the 'individual consumer'. One is 'free' to communicate what one wants, but only from and within limits which tend to ensure that it doesn't have any undesired effects. Most students and faculty members have never been offered the wherewithal to appreciate the thought control implicit in the illusion of freedom (to compete) in our society, much less act on it. In such a climate of willing and unwilling ignorance, dissenters may easily contribute to the short-range maintenance of the systems they wish to change.

The second possibility corresponds to the reality that so much of recent and current dissent is founded on psychological alienation, rather than on the political and systemic understanding of bread-and-butter issues of exploitation and oppression; that whenever the system makes even the most minimal reforms, a large number of the pseudo-political dissenters vanish in the equivalent of a puff of smoke. For if one's existence is crudely based on opposition TO something, then the disappearance of that something necessarily entails the disappearance of oneself.[13] This is the situation of the anti-Semite so imaginatively analyzed in Sartre's *Anti-Semite and Jew* (1946). Sartre's critique is not specifically directed against the anti-Semite as such, however, but rather against all those, right or left, conservative or radical, Jews and non-Jews, white and nonwhite, who substitute an either/or Manicheism, organized around themselves as a thing-like and closed ENTITY, for a personal and open relationship to the world.

12. *Identity*

> The Jews have a friend, nevertheless: the social democrat. But
> he is a feeble defender. True, he proclaims that all men are
> equal in rights . . . But his very declarations demonstrate the
> weakness of his position. In the 18th century, he chose, once
> and for all, the analytical spirit. He has no eyes for the concrete
> syntheses which history offers him. He does not recognize the

---

[13] Originally written in 1971. It has not been particularly pleasant to see how this judgement became true, e.g., the fate of two of the founders of the Students for a Democratic Society; the realization by Yippie leaders in the decade following 1968 that they were operating on the psychological assumption that the group called 'youth' was itself the equivalent of a socioeconomic class. Class is not a relationship you recover from just because you have grown older.

Jew, nor the Arab, nor the negro, nor the bourgeois, nor the worker; he recognizes only 'man', man in every time and every place equal to himself. He dissolves every collectivity into individual elements. A physical body is for him a sum of molecules; a social body, a sum of individuals. And by 'individual,' he understands a singular incarnation of the universal traits making up human nature . . . The result is that his defense of the Jew saves the Jew as 'man', and annihilates him as a Jew. Unlike the anti-Semite, the social democrat is not afraid of himself. What he fears are the huge collective configurations into which he runs the risk of becoming dissolved.

JEAN-PAUL SARTRE: *Réflexions sur la question juive* (1946)

In spite of its existentialist and psychological basis, Sartre's critique is so penetrating that it gives small comfort to anyone. If it attacks anyone at all, it attacks the liberal and the individualist. The critique is in fact directed against all those, Jews or non-Jews, who respond to one possible form of alienation – the reification of the self in a rock-like position – by another. In particular Sartre attacks those who, rather than be caught on 'one side' or the 'other side' of a set of oppositions which are vulnerable to criticism, respond not by making their ego and their position coterminous (as does the 'anti-Semite'), but by attempting to abdicate their responsibility to decide. Their situation cannot properly be called their fault, but the responsibility of their responsibility for it is theirs alone. Responsibility is not, however, absolute. Since responsibility is a function of the relative POWER to be responsible, and since power is presently distributed on the hierarchical basis of sex, race, and class, then not all responsibilities are equal.

Liberalism has had a most important historical function in freeing the now privileged classes from some forms of oppression, and some of this freedom has filtered down in bits and pieces to the less privileged. But in the present context of human crisis, those who choose to take refuge from their consciences, by coming out strongly and exclusively for respectable causes like whales, orphans, 'cleaning up the environment', and other forms of motherhood, are effectively resigning the most significant aspects of their responsibility to themselves within the collectivity. Once responsibility becomes neutralized by its tokens, its vehicles become what are known in the contemporary jargon as Uncle Toms, Red Apples, Tío Tacos, or Top Bananas. This is a position of cowardice and opportunism which has never had anything specifically to do with race; it corresponds to Sartre's description of the 'inauthenticity' of the 'social democrat'.

As has been pointed out, one of the recurrent themes in the essays of *System and Structure* concerns the difference between Imaginary communication and exchange and Symbolic communication and exchange (with their associated relationships to production and reproduction). The concept of the Imaginary order, an interpretation of the work of Jacques Lacan (cf. pp. 14–30, 147–51, 280–90, 460–86, and elsewhere below), can in retrospect be as readily derived from Sartre's conception of the ego (the 'thing-in-itself': cf. pp. 66–7 below) as it can from Marx's theory of fetishism. When dominant, the Imaginary centers on the function of mirror-like, one-dimensional oppositions as correlatives of identity in human relationships. Positive or negative identification with or against the Other as the oppressor (or whatever) is politically and psychologically dangerous, for it entails an implicit 'self-definition' in relation to the code of values defined by that Other. In other words, it implies a simple inversion of the relationship between master and slave, or between executioner and victim. The identities may change, but the (Imaginary) rationalization of the real relationship remains the same.[14]

IV

13. *Violence*

> To men a man is but a mind. Who cares
> What face he carries or what form he wears?
> But a woman's body *is* the woman . . .
> AMBROSE BIERCE: *The Devil's Dictionary* (1906)

> Woman's only weapon is man's imagination.
> JANE: In: *Tarzan and his Mate* (1934)

While fundamental socioeconomic change in Canada and in the world will no doubt be accompanied by a violence running counter to the many forms of violence making up the established system, any possible change will be no change at all unless the pitfall of the Imaginary IDENTITY OF OPPOSITES can be overcome. The double-binding, either/or oscillations[15] which the

[14] For an analysis of the role of Imaginary relations in colonization, as well as in racism, classism, and sexism, see the more recent work which emerged out of this revision: *The Imaginary Canadian* (Vancouver: Pulp Press, 1979).

[15] Amongst its other aspects, one aspect of the double-binding oscillation referred to in the text here – an oscillation which, in spite of the impression conveyed by my use of the term, is not necessarily pathogenic – needs further investigation and analysis. Some such oscillations are primarily digital and seem not to involve levels, e.g., positive/negative/positive/negative . . . An example here would be the paradoxical injunction involved in 'I am lying' (if I am, I'm not, if I'm not, I

Imaginary relations of projection and identification permit in class society must eventually be transcended in the real and material relationships of wo/mankind by the mediation of the Symbolic in its symbiotic relation with the Real. This is the locus, not of the 'identity of opposites', nor indeed of the 'unity of (so-called) opposites', but rather the locus of the unity of differences, distinctions, and contradictions – the real locus of the dialectical unity of BOTH 'both-and' AND 'either/or'. For here the both-and, long-term survival values of the actual system-environment relations which make us what we can be, come to transcend that pseudoholistic and idealistic 'both-and' which is simply a symmetrical REVERSAL of the already-given and one-dimensional either/or.

This is hardly an easy task. In our present society, the dominance of the Imaginary and all its energetic mechanics has the effect of what might be called a *reductio ad nauseam*. Consider, for example, how the Imaginary when dominant reduces the mediate to the apparently immediate, the manifold to the singular, the relational to the objectified, the analog to the digital, the multilevel to the bilateral, the asymmetrical to the symmetrical, the non-commutative to the commutative, the topological to the arithmetical, the transitive to the intransitive, the code to the message, and the message to the thing.

It is in this repeatedly renewed and reproduced subjugation of the Symbolic that the dominance of the Imaginary in our society alienates from each and every one of us the creativity that not simply makes us human, but EQUALLY human. For by 'creativity' is signified not the productions of the performance principle in our daily lives, but rather those human relations, such as the loving of a child, that in the dominance of the Imaginary do not count because they cannot be counted.

---

am, and so on *ad infinitum*). Other such oscillations seem to be more appropriately understood as analog (i.e., as not discontinuous), and they seem also to involve both levels and thresholds, e.g., x⟍ ⟋x⟍ ⟋x . . . The example here could be the surface-structure 'business cycle' under capitalism, or the ritual cycle of pig festivals and 'war' amongst the Tsembaga (pp. 117–24, 159–60, 174–8 below; see also the Index entry 'oscillation'). Although Tim Wilson and I were able to understand that it is the context in which it is used, and not the double bind itself, which may or may not be pathological or pathogenic; and although with the valued help of Jean Petitot, we were able to glimpse the deep-structure relationships between oscillations resulting from double binds and the 'stability oscillations' iconically represented by René Thom's simpler topological 'catastrophes' (Wilden and Wilson, 1976), we did not at that time realize that we were discussing analog and digital oscillations together, nor that Thom's simpler models provide representations of analog oscillation and analog-digital oscillation (for a useful account, see Zeeman, 1976).

The result of the dominance of the Imaginary relation in our present world is that, not just for philosophical idealists and for mechanical materialists, but also for every one of us constrained by the structure of capitalism to offer control over the expression of our creativity as a commodity in the market-place, the Imaginary becomes the Real.

This is quite a problem, to say the least, for, as Mark Twain once put it, we can hardly expect to see straight when our imagination is out of focus.

To put it another way, in a system such as ours, where competition is of a higher logical type in our relations than cooperation, then existing cooperative relations – e.g., cartels and oligopolies at the level of capital, unions in response at the level of labor – will tend generally to be mere reactions to mediation by competition. In our society, at the level of the Other – the locus of the mediating code – the metarule of competition constrains all other rules. In a rational and human system, in contrast, all competitive relations would be such as to remain the instruments of an overriding rule of mediation by cooperation, and this appears to be how we now have to learn to read the dominant relations in many of the other societies. Or, in Lenin's words, in a truly human society, contradictions would still exist, but antagonistic contradictions would not.

As intensely conscious as one may be of the reality that ideas alone can change nothing, one has nevertheless to begin somewhere. There is only one kind of escape from the oscillations between opposition and identity in our society, and it makes no difference whether one is talking or behaving in epistemological, ideological, or political terms. If dissent is to escape its own alienation, if it is to escape the automatic response of liberalism in its hostility to combinations and connections of ideas in realities (Wills, 1969), the response that a new theory is simply 'an interesting (personal) point of view', then dissent must transcend the status of negative identification. In short, ALL DISSENT MUST BE OF A HIGHER LOGICAL TYPE THAN THAT WITH WHICH IT IS IN CONFLICT. It will thus not make the Hegelian error of trying to reduce real and material differences to identity, for this is to be caught in an endless mirror-game from which there is simply no escape.

Hence the response to academic intellectualism cannot simply be an anti-intellectualism; the response to academic cynicism cannot simply be nihilism; the response to the crushing weight of institutionalized organization cannot simply be anarchism; the response to the *Realpolitik* of the system cannot simply be romanticism; the response to the indifference of the system cannot simply be a strident dogmatism.

The definition of effective dissent as necessarily being of a higher logical type should not be confused with contemporary moralizing about transcending (physical) violence by non-violence – a shopworn formula which it would be impossible to sustain if its supporters gave even a minimal consideration to the nature and the extent of institutionalized violence in the family, in society, and in the university itself. The position taken on violence by most academics is in effect an essentially rhetorical one. It is a position that fits well with the general refusal to recognize the actual violence of the 'rational' which, when you have power on your side, is simply devastating for its targets in the real. The most immediately obvious examples of such violence are collective and institutionalized racism, sexism, and – why is there no similar epithet for oppression by class? These and other exploitative '-isms' are neither accidental nor psychological in their origins; and the academic discourse, sounding brass and tinkling cymbal, continues to reproduce them.

Every course in the university is fraught with a potential violence against the student. Every faculty member is a potential executioner, not simply because of his or her personal characteristics, although these are certainly involved, but because of the traditions of the institution and the way it is actually organized. The controlling power of the predominantly digitalized discourse over attitudes is awesome. Too often one sees students simply stopped dead in their tracks by the facile manipulation of a few well-worn labels by the appropriate guardian. I suggest therefore that the first line of defense against the violence of the rhetoric of the establishment is to learn something about rhetoric. And that means to learn something about communication. But a line of defense is not enough; the victims must take the offensive. What is required – at this admittedly minimal level – is a GUERILLA RHETORIC. And, for a guerilla rhetoric, you must know what your enemy knows, why and how he knows it, and how to contest him on any ground.

14. *Dialectic*

Every sign, as we know, is a construct between socially organized persons in the process of their interaction.
Therefore, the forms of signs are conditioned above all by the social organization of the participants involved and also by the immediate conditions of their interaction. When these forms change, so does sign. And it should be one of the tasks of the study of ideologies to trace this social life of the verbal sign . . .
To accomplish this task certain basic, methodological prerequisites must be respected:
1. Ideology may not be divorced from the material reality of sign (i.e. by locating it in the 'consciousness' or other vague and elusive regions);

2. The sign may not be divorced from the concrete forms of social intercourse (seeing that the sign is part of organized social intercourse and cannot exist, as such, outside it, reverting to a mere physical artefact);
3. Communication and the forms of communication may not be divorced from the material basis.

V. N. VOLOSHINOV: *Marxism and the Philosophy of Language* (1929)

The question of developing and teaching an academic discourse of a higher logical type than that to which we are all presently subjected returns us to the point at which we began: the question of context. In an ecosystemic perspective, the position of higher logical type is simply that which is most capable of dealing with the most context and levels of context, and that which is most capable of understanding how methodological closures – like that of logical typing itself – inevitably generate paradox. It is also that position which can explain its own relationship to the context it is in. In addition, therefore, to the traditional and relatively static logical position dependent on principles of non-contradiction and identity (the analytic epistemology) which will work INSIDE a given dimension of the system one has isolated, there is a purely epistemological requirement for a logic of a higher type, a dynamic logic SUBSUMING the first, and one which will work WHEN ONE TRIES TO CROSS THE SPATIAL, COMMUNICATIONAL, ORGANIZATIONAL, OR TEMPORAL BOUNDARIES SET UP BY CLOSURE. Such a logic will subsume the Gödelian paradoxes of analytical logic by a process of metacommunication: it is the dialectical logic, not of Hegel, but of Marx.

But this is nonsense, somebody will object, because there is no such logic as a Marxian dialectical logic. That may seem true. But since logic and mathematics are communications systems, on the one hand, and models of relationships or process, on the other, all I mean to say is that we need a dialectical model of the Symbolic, Imaginary, and Real relationships between people in socioeconomic systems – the model that Marx set out to discover.

I hope to begin to show how a critical semiotic approach to such transdisciplinary theories as a non-mechanistic cybernetics theory, social systems theory, and deep-structure economics can contribute to the foundations of that understanding, as well as rescue it from the mechanistic (or bioenergetic) materialism represented by some of the more well-known writings of Lenin (e.g., the 'copy theory' of perception, which could have been derived directly from the philosophical spokesman for the 'Glorious Revolution' of 1688, John Locke). Looking at those writings now, one recognizes that they are very much beholden to the epistemology of the nineteenth-century scientific discourse (e.g., Lenin's flat-earth theory of contradiction). As a result, not only do these writings often take 'dialectical' positions which it is all too easy for the analytical thinker to refute, but they also carry with them the repressed metaphors of the dominant ideology of capitalism's bourgeois revolution.

As Marx so succinctly put it, the question of truth for humankind is not a theoretical question, but a practical question. The pragmatics of life, relationships, and meaning necessarily and invariably subsume the theoretics of knowledge, existence, and signification. Not only do the former CONSTRAIN the latter; they are also the environment without which the system represented by the scientific discourse could not survive. This relationship is similar to that between dialectics and analytics. BOTH the 'both-and' of dialectics AND the 'either/or' of analytics are necessary to any critical perspective: the relationship between the two logics is not oppositional, but hierarchical.

I expect to address myself again and more directly to some of the problems of what passes for 'dialectical materialism today' in a later book.

15. *Adaptation*

> The fundamental difference is that the slaves owe their
> origin to violence; the poor, to cunning.
> SCHOPENHAUER

> Technology is a continuing response to the needs of life.
> UNITED TECHNOLOGIES: *Television commercial* (1978)

If the reader finds the overt ideological commitment of these essays to represent a form of SYMBOLIC violence, the reader will be correct – in the sense that they are an attempt to formulate an adequately contextualized, a non-exploitative, and a metacommunicative response to the violence of the university and the academic discourse in a violent society. Obviously, no form of systemic violence – against persons or against nature – can ever be adaptive in the terms of long-range survival. Thus, in a system such as ours, where violence is rationalized and explained away by reference to short-range survival – as in the militarists' satisfaction at the huge number of lives saved by Hiroshima, Dresden, and Dieppe, for example – it now appears that various forms of subverting violence against the capitalist system and its works are not simply necessary, but also inevitable.

We may nevertheless be saved from having to survive this particular kind of unpleasantness by the activities of the system itself. As has been pointed out elsewhere (Wilden and Wilson, 1976), state and private capitalism appears now to be trapped in at least one systemic and material double bind – in the real paradox of an opposition between (quantitative) growth, on the one hand, and 'no growth', on the other (cf. Notes 4, 23, and 29). As best we understand it at present, it seems evident that if society is to survive the industrialization of capitalism, then this paradox must be transcended by a restructuring of the economic system. Now, since the logic of capitalism requires it to expand in every possible way in order to maintain its (temporary) stability, it appears equally evident that, provided our species does not become extinct, the socioeconomic system which eventually survives in the limited planetary environment will not be a capitalist one.

Capitalism is certainly a 'self-correcting' adaptive system – as Mobil Oil felt constrained to advise us (against what it thinks is 'Marxism') on the Op-Ed pages of many US newspapers in 1974 (now see Silk, 1974). But this adaptiveness does not preclude the possibility that, as with other systems, capitalism may end up adapting itself out of existence. Capitalism's final adaptation may well be a manifestation of the 'self-destructing prophecy' in tune with which one historically and environmentally constrained socio-economic system undergoes the morphogenesis of a deep-structure revolution that turns it into another one. After all, this was how capitalism came to be in the first place; and it is just possible that nothing will quite so become it as its manner of leaving us.

However, if this revolutionary restructuring is indeed on our horizons now, it is not, unfortunately, a future relationship to be overly sanguine about. For it has not been demonstrated or even argued, as far as I know, that what we now know as capitalism could not survive for some considerable time as a new and more subtle form of National Socialism.

Indeed, the works on 'popular ecology' in the 1970s by a number of well-known people on both sides of the Atlantic would seem to invite some such similar 'solution', whether intentionally or not. In 1972, with some justice, the Parisian journal *La Gueule Ouverte* was attacking the positions taken by certain popular ecologists as 'ecofascism' (cf. on this topic H. T. Odum's *Power, Environment, and Society*, 1971: 218–46; or Barry Commoner's counter-attack on Garrett Hardin's pseudo-anthropological 'tragedy of the commons': 1971: 295–8).

16. *The Other*

> For the colonized person, objectivity is always directed against him.
> FRANTZ FANON

> Relativism is the bad faith of the conqueror who has become
> secure enough to become a tourist.
> STANLEY DIAMOND : *In Search of the Primitive* (1974)

Whoever might wish to reinforce the now traditional psychologization of
society by placing an 'oedipal' interpretation on the obvious orientation of
these essays – or on what was called the 'violence of youth' or the 'violence
of the minorities' in the 1960s, or on the contemporary counterviolence of
militants amongst the feminine majority – will have inadvertently punctuated this system correctly. For, by reference to a myth which describes
the creation of a SCAPEGOAT who shall bear away in his own person the collective violence disavowed by its perpetrators in the City (René Girard),
the pyschological interpretation of contestation offered by defenders of the
status quo, such as Bruno Bettelheim and Jacques Lacan, will have correctly,
if unintentionally, assigned the responsibility for the violence to those who
have the power to be responsible for it.[16]

Oedipus' murderous feelings towards his father do not come from nowhere. Apart from one significant variant of the myth which tells how
Laius gave the riddle to the Sphinx in order to use the monster to kill off
aspirants to his throne, the commonly accepted version states quite plainly
that it was Laius, King of Thebes, not Oedipus, who introduced violence
into the City, for it was not Oedipus, but Laius, who chose to try to maintain his power by sacrificing his son. And in the Judeo-Christian mythology,
the perpetrator of the near-sacrifice of Isaac and the actual sacrifice of
Christ – as the scapegoat – was not 'man' as 'Man', but God HIMSELF.
We must inevitably conclude therefore that so long as the Other remains the
real and original locus of every form of exploitative violence in the system
of communication and exchange we call 'civilized' society, no human form
of society will ever be possible.

[16] For a classically conservative statement of this position, see Stewart Alsop's
strangely titled "The Oedipal Revolt and the Laius Reaction" (*Newsweek*, 23 June
1969). Alsop's concern for what he calls the "unfortunate King Laius" is altogether characteristic of the way contemporary ideology, whether labeled liberal
or conservative, confuses the logical typing of violence – besides the fact that Laius
is dead. As with the 'Electra complex', 'black racism' in North America, 'female
sexism', 'the Jewish question', or the theory of 'penis envy' (a male concern) –
and even the expression 'saving the environment' – the dominant ideology projects violence away from its source into its 'object'. Thus it makes the exploited
responsible for their own exploitation, the oppressed responsible for their own
oppression.

　　Also on this topic, R. F. Hammer has drawn my attention to Shulamith Firestone's illuminating political reading of the 'oedipal relation' in terms of socioeconomic power (1970: 47–55).

Nevertheless, as Svevo's Zeno reminds us, just because the world goes round is no reason for getting seasick.

La Jolla, California – Paris, France, 1971–2
Vancouver, British Columbia, 1978–9

Since the Young Hegelians consider conceptions, thoughts, ideas, in fact all the products of consciousness, to which they attribute an independent existence, as the real chains of men (just as the Old Hegelians declared them to be the true bonds of human society), it is evident that they have to fight only against these illusions of consciousness . . . This demand to change consciousness amounts to a demand to interpret reality in another way, i.e. to accept it by means of another interpretation. The Young Hegelian ideologists . . . are the staunchest of conservatives.

KARL MARX and FREDERICK ENGELS: *The German Ideology* (1845–6)

ALL of the many current threats to man's survival are traceable to three root causes: (a) technological progress; (b) population increase; (c) certain errors in the thinking and attitudes of Occidental culture.

GREGORY BATESON: *Steps to an Ecology of Mind* (1972)

[The Critical School] has at least learned from Hegel's *Phenomenology* the art of transforming REAL, OBJECTIVE chains existing OUTSIDE ME into solely IDEAL, solely SUBJECTIVE chains existing solely WITHIN ME – and hence the art of transforming all EXTERNAL struggles, material and physical [*sinnlichen*], into pure struggles of thought.

KARL MARX and FREDERICK ENGELS: *The Holy Family* (1845)

Chapter I

The Symbolic, the Imaginary, and the Real

LACAN, LÉVI-STRAUSS, AND FREUD[1]

All behavior is communication.
BATESON

Unlike the experience of psychoanalysis in the United States, Freud came very late to France, and he was more or less refuted by Sartre in *Being and Nothingness* before he had even properly 'arrived'. Curiously enough, however, it was during the very heyday of existentialism and existential psychoanalysis in the fifties and early sixties, that an unknown French analyst of Sartre's generation had begun a radical re-reading of the Freudian texts. His work was to have such influence by the seventies as to entirely rescue Freud from the positivistic medical orientation of the Paris psychoanalytical society, and to re-integrate the work of Freud into what the French still call *les sciences de l'homme*.

The man in question was Jacques Lacan, Director of the École freudienne de Paris – a hermetic and obscure stylist, a mesmerizing lecturer, an uncompromising and intransigent thinker intensely preoccupied with and jealous of his own writings and prerogatives – who was outlawed from the International Association when he and his colleagues broke away from the Paris society in 1953, mainly because of internal rivalries. There are undoubtedly a greater number of scurrilous and probably slanderous anecdotes circulating about Lacan in the incestuous intellectual climate of Paris than about any other influential thinker. But if Lacan's work means anything at all, we must separate Lacan's well-known personal idiosyncra-

[1] A version of this chapter has appeared in *Contemporary Psychoanalysis*.

sies from the unique contribution he has made to our understanding of Freud.

Although Lacan began his original work in the late thirties, under the influence of Husserlian phenomenology and Heideggerean existentialism, it was not until the sixties that he began to be really listened to in France, and his writings have only recently begun to reach England and the United States. Attacking French 'intellectualism' and the cult of the 'expert', British 'empiricism' and 'biologizing', and American 'adaptation' and 'behaviorism' in a series of blistering polemics, his work alone has made it impossible for any self-respecting French thinker to continue to ignore the texts of Freud. The integration of that text into the culture of the Cartesian *cogito* has already had startling and fertile results. It remains to be seen how much of Lacan will filter across to the United States – where the very enthusiasm of the original American acceptance of Freud has tended to reduce his ideas to triviality and his theories to the status of games people play.

We now discover, for instance, that we have another return to the Breuer–Freud theory of therapeutic catharsis – once popular as the psychodrama – in a new form of 'repressive desublimation': "primal-scream" therapy. But the heroes of the late-night talk-shows come and go with monotonous regularity, and, when all is said and done, we are always left with the great works of genius to ponder over: Hegel, Marx, Freud, Dostoevsky, Rousseau, Balzac, to mention only some of our more recent antecedents. And what we discover is that we must LEARN TO READ before we speak, that we must learn to read them from a critical social perspective, as free of ethnocentric, socioeconomic, and cultural prejudice as possible. In a word, we have to learn to read from a non-academic perspective, from the perspective of a life-experience in which these authors and their personal quests form part of our individual and collective quest. I would much rather read the *Interpretation of Dreams* as a novel, for instance, or the celebrated case of the 'psychotic' Doctor Schreber as philosophy, or the *Brothers Karamazov* as a metapsychological study, than the other way around. Lacan has helped to make this kind of reading possible.

Much of what Lacan sought to accomplish with his students in the fifties is of little interest now, because it was an attack on the therapeutic technique of a most untalented group of objectifying, culture-bound French psychoanalysts. But his attack on the 'ego psychology' of practitioners like Hartmann, Kris, and Löwenstein, or the 'behaviorism' of Massermann, still holds good (Lacan, 1956a; Wilden, 1968a: 1–87). And those who so vehemently opposed him in France now find that they cannot reject his critical analyses of the Freudian texts and still call themselves Freudians. But if Lacan has inspired a French school of analysis which claims to be

anti-institutional, anti-psychiatric, and profoundly critical both of the
'adjustment' of the individual and of those Marcuse called the neo-
Freudian revisionists, he has probably done no more for analytical practice
than what has been accomplished by therapists like Laing, Esterson, and
Cooper, in the United Kingdom, or by people like Ruesch, Bateson, Haley,
Weakland, and Jackson in the United States.

Moreover, psychoanalysis is a socioeconomic privilege restricted to
people with the money and the leisure to indulge themselves. The question
of the 'cure' is in any case entirely debatable, and we well know that
psychology, psychiatry, and psychotherapy in general have always been
vehicles of the values of the *status quo* (with the extraordinary exception
of Wilhelm Reich, whose theories unfortunately never matched the high
level of his social commitment). And since most of us can learn to live
with our hang-ups, whereas it is highly unlikely we can ever learn to live
with the alienating effects of our one-dimensional, technological society,
why bother with psychoanalysis at all? No one seeking a truly critical
perspective would attempt to build a theory of man-and-womankind
primarily on human psychology in any case, because the 'scientific discourse' of psychology is designed to deny or to omit the collective socioeconomic content in which psychological factors come to play their part.

I shall try to show later that the axiomatic closure of most psychoanalysis from that context in all its plenitude – and, I believe, in its primacy
– generates purely LOGICAL problems in the theory, problems that it is not
logically equipped to overcome. Thus, what appears in Bateson's logico-
mathematical theory of the 'double bind' (Chapter V) as an OSCILLATION,
necessarily appears in psychoanalysis under one form or another of a theory
of REPETITION. Lacan, for instance, has appealed to Kierkegaard (*Repetition*,
1843) to buttress his interpretation of Freud, and yet if one looks closely
at Kierkegaard's writings, especially his *Either/Or*, also published in
1843, one discovers that the whole theory depends upon Kierkegaard's
inability to transcend, either logically or existentially, the paradoxical
injunctions (double binds) he receives from his familial and social environment. Consequently he is condemned to oscillate interminably between an
'either' and an 'or'. What appears in Bateson's theory as a necessary response to injunctions emanating from relationships of POWER and DOMINA-
TION in the social order, usually appears in psychoanalysis, and specifically in
Lacan, as the 'compulsion to repeat'.[2] In this way, either the responsibility

---

[2] Thus a recent book by Gilles Deleuze, with the tantalizing title *Différence et
répétition* (1968), turns out to be founded on Kierkegaard's theory. Deleuze's
position is invalidated by even the most rudimentary knowledge of 'cybernetic'
oscillation in self-regulating open systems like the cell.

is thrown back onto the individual (via the 'instincts' or some other metaphor for these biomechanistic constructs), or else, as in Lacan, it is subtly transformed into a form of the 'natural order of things', via the paradoxes that language creates in the human condition.

Unlike the double-bind theory, both views assume a homogeneity in society which simply isn't there, and both serve as rationalizations of domination.[3] By refusing to deal with the relationship between power, knowledge, and oppression, they fail to see the difference, in society, between what Marcuse termed 'repression' and 'surplus-repression'. For all of Marcuse's lack of understanding of the 'clinical' Freud – and in spite of his reliance on the bioenergetic theory of the instincts – the distinction is important. Few American theorists, for example, would seriously consider the travail of the American minorities in their struggle for elementary socioeconomic rights, simply in the terms of a 'compulsion to repeat' a revolt against the father (or the mother).

I find it impossible to talk about either Freud or Lacan without using the contributions Bateson and Marcuse – in different and even mutually opposing ways – have made to our understanding of human relationships. We have on the one hand to deal with the reputation of psychoanalysis and psychology as rationalizations of the values of our culture (the oppression of women, in particular), and, on the other, to show how they may contribute to a devalorization of those values. Bateson's analysis of power relations through the double bind is, I believe, essential to social and psychological theory,[4] and I do not know how to explain Lacan's theory of the Imaginary without it. In any case, Freud does describe the relation between ego and ego ideal in terms similar to a double bind (in *The Ego and the Id, Standard Edition*, XIX, 34): "You OUGHT TO BE like this (like your father), but you MAY NOT BE like this (like your father)."

In the contemporary world of contestation, there would be no answer to the way psychoanalysis is regularly – and necessarily – put in question, if the Freud we are talking about is the hydraulic, instinctual, electromagnetic, and entropic determinist we all thought we knew. There is an

---

[3] See, for example, O. Mannoni's 1950 work, *Prospero and Caliban: The Psychology of Colonization*, refuted with remarkable restraint by Frantz Fanon (1952). Mannoni speaks of the "civilizing influence" of the French subjugation of Madagascar, and of the "dependency complex" of the Malagasy people (see Chapter XVII).

[4] See, for example, his subtle and remarkable analysis of alcoholic 'repetition' in "The Cybernetics of 'Self'" (1971a). Bateson locates the 'repetition' – an oscillation between mutually exclusive logical propositions – not 'in' the alcoholic, but in his relations with the social order. What Bateson calls "alcoholic pride in performance" is a version of Marcuse's "performance principle" (cf. Chapter III).

answer, however, if we discover the communicational and linguistic perspective behind Freud's explicit or implicit acceptance of the mechanistic tenets of nineteenth-century physical and economic science. After all, psychoanalysis is indeed the 'talking cure', as Lacan has never failed to insist, and pages upon pages of Freud's writings are concerned above all with language. Far more interesting than the entity-bound theory of ego, id, and superego, for instance, is Freud's view of the unconscious and the dream as scenes (*Darstellungen*) of distortions (*Entstellungen*) and (re)-presentations (*Vorstellungen*). More in keeping with contemporary concern for systems and structures than the later Freud's 'ego psychology', is his early model of primary and secondary processes. More significant than his determinism is his theory of the 'overdetermination' of the symptom or the dream, which is a concept akin to redundancy in information theory and to equifinality in gestaltism and biology. If we have to reject the mechanistic tenets of the pleasure principle, we can still discover the semiotic model of levels of communication in the early work of Freud. More useful than the 'second' theory of symbolism (derived from Stekel), which equates icons or images (analogs) with sexual symbols (Jones, Ferenczi, *et al.*), is the 'first' or 'dialectical' theory, dependent on the condensation and displacement of SIGNS (*Zeichen*). The dream must be TRANSLATED from image to text before it can be interpreted (by the dreamer), and repression is, as Freud put it in 1896, "a failure of translation". Moreover, no current theory of memory is essentially different from Freud's original metaphor of the 'grooving' of pathways by the memory traces in the brain.

I shall return to a more specific description of Freud's semiotic and linguistic orientation in a moment. The point is that, without the work of Lacan, I doubt whether we would have discovered this Freud at all – although Karl Pribram's analysis of the neuropsychological *Project for a Scientific Psychology* (1895) goes a long way in the direction of re-reading Freud at least in the terms of information theory and feedback (Pribram, 1962).

The problem with Lacan is that at first glance his writings are almost impossible to understand. His *Écrits* (1966) – and only Lacan could have the hubris to entitle his work simply *Writings* – read more like a 'schizophrenic discourse' – or like poetry, or nonsense, depending on your prejudice and your tendencies towards positive or negative transference – than anything else.[5] Lacan's hermeticism cannot be excused on any

---

[5] Harley Shands, in a review of the text, *The Language of the Self* (1968a) in *Semiotica*, 4 (1971), projects his justifiable annoyance at the hermeticism of Lacan onto me, constructing an image of me as the "disciple" of Lacan, "chosen" by the master to introduce his work to the English-speaking world. To set the

grounds – any more than his attitude to the reader, which might be expressed as: 'like it or lump it'. But although Lacan's personal destruction of French syntax makes him arduous enough even for the French reader, there is at least a fairly homogeneous intellectual tradition in Paris which makes Lacan less alien there than in Britain or in the United States. The phenomenological, existentialist, and Hegelian–Marxist tradition in France makes it less necessary there to explain what you mean when you mention Hegel, or Husserl, or Heidegger, or Kojève, or Sartre. And most people will recognize an idea anyway, even when you don't mention the source, or when you quote or paraphrase without references, for this kind of 'plagiarism' is generally acceptable in France.[6]

Significantly enough, though, Lacan could not have accomplished his analysis of Freud without the influence of the American–Russian–Swiss school of linguistics represented by Roman Jakobson, who has long exemplified the influence of Russian formalism and of Saussure's structural linguistics in the United States. But even that influence came to Lacan indirectly. The most important single influence on Lacan has been the French structural anthropologist Claude Lévi-Strauss, who met and worked with Jakobson while at the New School for Social Research in New York, in 1942–5.

---

record straight, I have to point out that I have never been such a disciple, and that I chose to put the book together simply because I thought Lacan's work interesting and important. With only the published texts of Lacan to go by, some of the problems of interpretation necessarily remained unresolved.

[6] One of the first tasks in understanding Lacan is to track down the sources of his text and to provide it with a CONTEXT. Since 1968, I have continued to come across new signposts. For example, in his theory of psychosis, which speaks of the "coming unanchored" of the Symbolic order (governed by language), Lacan describes language as being anchored to Symbolic meaning by *points de capiton* ('buttons' like those on the surface of a mattress). Like many of Lacan's images, this is probably more mysterious than it is worth. But in the context of Lacan's predisposition to invent complicated and ill-explained graphic diagrams and equally incomplete 'transformational' formulae, this image is illuminated somewhat by the 'buttons' in W. Ross Ashby's kinematic graphs, in his theory of transducers (1956).

The Lacanian school unfortunately chooses to operate like a Masonic lodge. Important texts, including résumés of Lacan's seminars by third parties, are deliberately withheld from publication, and circulated only among certain initiates. The 'sibling rivalry' this creates among his followers would be ludicrous if it were not so pernicious. The École freudienne has been riven by excommunication after excommunication – which has even gone so far as to include the 'old Soviet Encyclopedia trick' of excising names from articles being republished. Moreover, the withholding of texts from publication might well lead the uncharitable to suspect that Lacan is seeking for himself a posthumous reputation à la Husserl or à la Freud.

Lévi-Strauss tends to be rather vehemently disliked by American and British anthropologists beholden to the analytical and so-called empiricist tradition, which says a lot for him. He has been the originator of a new methodology and accompanying epistemology in the human sciences in France, which is usually called 'structuralism'. (By now, however, the term simply designates a fad, in the same way that existentialism came to do.) Structuralism, in the sense of a non-empiricist, non-atomist, non-positivist methodology of the LAWS OF RELATION, is complemented elsewhere by advances in general systems theory, in non-mechanistic cybernetics, in communication theory, and in ecological studies. Both the new structural and the new systemic–cybernetic approach seem in fact to bespeak a veritable epistemological revolution in the life and social sciences, about which we shall be hearing a lot more in the next decade (if we survive it, that is).

Lévi-Strauss sought to use the work of structural phonologists on the 'binary opposition' of phonemes as a model for the analysis of myth and of the exchange relationships of so-called 'primitive' societies – whose supposed 'primitivism' he proceeded to put in question. Noting that a relatively small number of 'oppositions' between 'distinctive features' (grave/acute, voiced/voiceless, etc.) are sufficient to form the acoustic infrastructure of any known language, Lévi-Strauss attempted to discover analogous sets of oppositions in kinship systems and in myth. His most recent work has concentrated on myth as music. With all that is dubious in his approach, Lévi-Strauss has nevertheless introduced a type of signification into the study of myth – previously concerned almost exclusively with content rather than with form – where none existed before. As with the work of Lacan – or that of Freud – the main problem of Lévi-Straussian structuralism lies not in the methodology, but in its application, that is to say, in the universal claims made on its behalf.

I shall take up the more detailed critique of 'structuralism' in later chapters. For the moment it will suffice to give a brief and purely illustrative example of Lévi-Strauss's use of the concept of 'binary opposition' in the study of myth (Lévi-Strauss, 1958: Ch. 11).

For him, the myth is a diachronic representation (succession through time) of a set of synchronic (timeless) 'oppositions'. He believes that the discovery of these synchronic oppositions is a statement about the "fundamental structure of the human mind". In later chapters, I shall analyze and criticize the term 'opposition' – which conceals the categories of 'difference', 'distinction', 'opposition', 'contradiction', and 'paradox'. I shall also criticize the concept of 'binary' relations – which conceals a whole set of misunderstandings about analog and digital communication in general, and specifically about 'not', 'negation', 'exclusion', 'zero', and 'minus-one', as well as about the relation between 'A' and 'non-A'. I shall also try to demonstrate the misconception involved in Lévi-Strauss's confusion between 'mind', 'brain', and 'individual'. This is closely allied to Piaget's conception of the organism as the "paradigm structure", and with the failure, in most current work in the life and social sciences, to understand the logico-mathematical and existential problem of BOUNDARIES and LEVELS in open systems of communication and exchange (systems involving or simulating life or 'mind', living and social systems).

Lévi-Strauss's method of reading myths is entirely novel, simple to understand, aesthetically satisfying, and all-encompassing. He suggests that we look at the myth the way we would look at an orchestra score in which the notes and bars to be played in simultaneous harmony by different instruments have become mixed up into the cacophony of a linear succession. Thus, if we represent this succession by the numbers 1, 2, 4, 7, 8, 2, 3, 4, 6, 8, 1, 4, 5, 7, we can re-establish the original score by putting all like numbers together in vertical columns:

1	2		4			7	8
	2	3	4		6		8
1			4	5		7	

This matrix is exactly what one might construct in the phonological analysis of a sentence, where a linear sequence of words can be shown to be constructed on a succession of binary oppositions between distinctive acoustic features.

Unfortunately for what Lévi-Strauss views as the keystone of his method, the analogy he draws between structural phonology and myth is false, whereas his methodology is extremely fertile. This problem points to the central difficulty involved in using the work of both Lévi-Strauss and Lacan. One has to show that the supposed sources of their new contributions to social science are not what they think they are; one has to demonstrate where and how their views serve a repressive ideological function; and one has to show the inadequacy both of many of the axioms of the method and of many of the applications claimed for it.

Without developing a detailed critique at this point, it can be said at once that it is an error to treat a context-free system of oppositions between the acoustic characteristics of 'bits' of information (distinctive features) as if it were isomorphic with myth, which is a system with a context. Myth is necessarily contextual because it manipulates information in order to organize and control some aspect of a social system, and it cannot therefore be considered as isolated from that totality. Unlike Lévi-Strauss's 'mythemes' (the "gross constitutive elements" of myth, by analogy with 'phon-eme'), phonemes are bits of meaningless and non-significant information. Phonemes and phonemic oppositions are the tools of analysis and articulation (whose basic characteristic is difference) in a system in which both signification and meaning are outside the phonemic structure. 'Mythemes' and 'oppositions' between mythemes, on the contrary, involve both signification and meaning: they have 'content'.

Lévi-Strauss is treating myth as if it were a language representable by a context-free grammar, or treating mythemes as 'information' in the technical sense of the quantitative and closed systems of information transmission studied by Shannon and Weaver. Information science concerns the statistical study of stochastic processes and Markov chains (Chapter IX) – and Chomsky has demonstrated that no known language can be properly generated out of a grammar modeled on such processes. It has further been shown that language is a system of a higher logical type than that which can be generated by context-free algorithms (grammars).

Although Lévi-Strauss speaks of the mytheme as of a 'higher' type than any similar element in language, the model of the binary phonemic opposition remains what he regards as the scientific basis of his method. Thus the mytheme becomes the equivalent of a tool of articulation (a distinctive feature) employed by a system of signification and meaning of another logical type (language). When we seek to discover what this other system is in Lévi-Strauss, we find the category of "mythic thought". But mythic thought is already defined on the basis of the mythemes themselves. It is a system of the articulation of oppositions by "a machine for the suppression of time" (the myth). What is missing from this circle is the real and material context in which the myth arises and to which it refers.

However, Lévi-Strauss will insist that his methodology, unlike pure formalism, is indeed 'contextual' (Lévi-Strauss, 1960a). He consistently refers to kinship categories, to the zoological and botanical context of the myth, and to the characteristics of material entities ('raw', 'cooked', 'rotten', and so on). In actual fact, however, all the 'material entities' and 'material relations' he employs come to the analysis already defined, tautologously, as categories of mythic thought. Consequently, the 'context' Lévi-Strauss evokes is invariably the context of 'ideas' or 'mind', which, like Kant, he conceives of as being antecedent to social organization, both epistemologically and ontologically. Within this idealist framework, he then makes a quick-step into the material categories of physics and chemistry, which he regularly evokes as the ultimate ground of his ideal categories.

But in between the context of ideas and the context of atoms and molecules (or even that of the genetic code) there is a single, but enormous, level of organization which is missing: the socioeconomic context of human reality. And this level of organization contains a parameter which cannot be found in physics, in biology, in information science, in language, in ideas, or in myths viewed as synchronic systems of oppositions: the punctuation of the system by the power of some of its parts to exploit the other parts (including 'nature' itself). All ideas, electrons, and 'bits' of information are indeed equal, none of them are more equal than the others, and no group of them exploits the others. And whereas in systems not involving social exploitation, myths can properly be regarded as performing a 'pure' or 'neutral' organizing function, in all other systems myths become the property of a class, caste, or sex. 'A myth which is the property of a class' is in effect a definition of ideology. The myth then ceases to serve the neutral function of organization pure and simple; it serves as the RATIONALIZATION of a given form of social organization.

The structural study of myth is, as Lévi-Strauss has often said, another variant of the myths it analyzes. Like them, it is a system of binary oppositions. But it is not a machinery for the suppression of time, however, it is a machinery for the suppression of history. And since 'structuralism' is indeed the property of a class, then we may correctly identify it as a system of ideological rationalization – which is not the same, however, as saying that it has no value.

Lévi-Strauss's mistaken analogy between a context-free system and a context-bound system – and all the subsequent edifice erected on it by the structuralists – is derived from a confusion between language and communication. On the one hand, such a confusion is only possible in theories punctuated so as to exclude the objective social category of exploitation. On the other, it depends upon a single real isomorphy, which is then used to reduce different levels of organization to each other: the fact that language, kinship systems, the structural study of myth, and the science of phonology are DIGITAL (discontinuous) communications about ANALOG (continuous) relations. A single characteristic of digital communication – that it is a system of communication involving boundaries and gaps – is reified by the structuralist argument so that it can be indiscriminately applied, as an implicit ontological category, at every level of complexity at which 'boundaries and gaps' occur. Such digital forms do necessarily occur, as the instrument of communication, at every level of biological and social complexity. Consequently, the reductionist argument of the structuralists is greatly facilitated. Moreover, the fact that binary opposition is also a significant category in classical physics (e.g., electromagnetism) allows structuralists to make the further epistemological error of confusing matter–energy with information.

The excluded term in the system of reductions involved in structuralism is, as I have said, the real context in which the 'system of elements involving boundaries and gaps' is used. Since information without context is NOISE, this exclusion provides a neat closure to the theory, an imperviousness to information generated at levels of context and organization of a different logical type from the logical typing of the theory itself. The uneasy feeling of simplistic reduction one often has in reading both Lévi-Strauss and Lacan has its real source in the actual logical 'flatness' of the theory. As much as it refers to levels, structuralism includes no theory of levels of communication. Consequently, it is impervious to the paradoxes it generates: all such paradoxes – which ought to require an evolution and an enlargement of the theory – are manipulated, by means of a flattening of logical types, into 'oppositions'.

As a new metaphor of the discourse of science in our culture, structuralism confuses meaning – which concerns survival – with signification – the instrument of meaning (Chapter VII). It is altogether characteristic, in consequence, that Lévi-Strauss should respond to criticism by drawing in his horns, disavowing his metaphysical pretensions, and explicitly limiting structuralism to what it always was: a methodology applicable to (some aspects of) "mathematical entities, natural languages, musical compositions, and myths" (Lévi-Strauss, 1971: 578).

In spite of the important contributions it has made – principally by changing the kind of questions to be asked – structuralism fails in the life and social sciences in exactly the same way and for exactly the same reasons that both structural linguistics and information science fail in those areas. They are all anti-semantic in that they substitute the supposed characteristics of a theoretically neutral INSTRUMENT OF ANALYSIS (the 'bit') for the USE to which it is put, as an INSTRUMENT OF COMMUNICATION, at given levels in a given goalseeking system, where no information is ever neutral. Meaning – the goal – becomes bounded not by the structure of the context in which it occurs, but by the structure of 'science'. As a result the methodology implicitly becomes an ontology.

Leaving aside the related problematic of constructing the structure of the myth to be interpreted – its PUNCTUATION (Chapter V) – we can immediately recognize in the two terms 'binary' and 'opposition', the more significant of the implicit semantic inputs into the 'neutral' structure from the non-neutral social context in which structuralism arose. Apart from whatever signification they have in the context into which Lévi-Strauss introduces them, both terms play an ideological function in the social discourse and in the discourse of science (Chapter XIV). Consequently, any structuralism based on these categories will necessarily serve to generate a set of propositions, not simply about the structure of myth, and not simply about the supposed structure of 'mind', but also – and most significantly – about the structure of contemporary ideology.

This said, we can employ a version of Lévi-Strauss's analysis of the Oedipus myth to illustrate what he means by a binary opposition, without prejudice to the subtlety and length of his other structural analyses. In the table on page 13, the story – highly condensed for the purposes of the example – reads from left to right in succession; the analysis concerns the 'oppositions' between factors common to the 'elements' or 'mythemes' in each column.

The 'opposition' between two common factors, "overvalued and under-valued blood relations", in A and B is clear from the myth itself.[7] The 'opposition' between C and D involves a further interpretation. The factor common to both is that they are statements about the autochthonous origin of mankind. In D, monsters 'born of the earth' who threaten human survival are killed. The act of killing is taken by Lévi-Strauss to be a denial of the power of 'born of the earth', which is a recurrent theme in many mythologies, including that of the Greeks. But in C, the theme of lameness affirms 'born of the earth', because in many myths, men so born are lame or they stumble (e.g., the Pueblo Muyingwu, "bleeding-foot", and Shumaikoli, "sore-foot").

The myth may thus be seen as representing two sets of UNRESOLVED, synchronic 'oppositions' (contradictions) in Greek ideology by means of a diachronic sequence of events, and the two sets of 'oppositions' are themselves in 'opposition'. These 'oppositions' may be interpreted in various ways: blood ties versus social ties; 'born of the earth' versus 'born of man and woman'; 'born of one' (the earth, the mother, 'mamma') versus 'born of two'; born of one 'family' versus born of two 'families'; the primary tie to the mother versus the power of the father; biological reality (bisexual reproduction) versus cosmological belief (the origin of the 'many' in the 'one').

[7] Note, however, that in order to follow Lévi-Strauss's analysis, the fact that A and B involve the digitalization of an analog continuum ('more' or 'less'), whereas C and D represent digital propositions related by 'not', has to be ignored. Moreover, the 'not' does not occur anywhere in the myth itself. Whereas A and B describe formal categories which can be extracted from the myth with the minimum of interpretation, C and D depend on an antecedent analysis of CONTENT. Thus if A and B are of the same logical type as the myth itself, C and D are not. The point is that 'oppositions' in the phonemic structure of language are of the same logical type or class, and that a binary opposition must oppose elements of the same logical type. This requirement, however, necessarily makes the analysis subject to the paradoxes inherent in logical typing itself (Chapter VII).

TABLE 1

The Oedipus Myth

A	B	C	D
			Cadmus, founder of Thebes, slays a dragon. Its teeth, sown in the earth, turn into warriors
	who kill each other.		
		The name of the next king, Labadacus, may mean 'lame'. The name of his son, Laius, may mean 'left-sided'.	
	Because of a prophecy, Laius tries to kill his infant son,		
		Oedipus (= 'swollen-foot'), by leaving him to die with pins driven through his ankles.	
	Oedipus kills his father,		
			slays the Sphinx by solving its riddle,
and becomes king of Thebes by marrying his mother.		Discovering his 'crime', Oedipus blinds himself and is exiled. He cannot walk without a guide.	
	The twin sons of Oedipus battle for Thebes and kill each other.		
Antigone, Oedipus' daughter, disobeys her uncle, the new king, by burying one of her brothers			
	and dies as a result.		

TABLE 2
Binary Oppositions

A *Affirmation*	B *Denial*	C *Affirmation*	D *Denial*
Ties of blood are MORE important than social relations	Ties of blood are LESS important than social relations	Man is born of the earth (born from one)	Man is NOT born of the earth (not born from one)

Relation: A is to B as C is to D

The validity of the interpretation is to be tested by including all known variants of the myth in the matrix. We can easily include the Freudian variant – the 'oedipus complex'. Amongst other matters, the oedipal theory concerns the child's unshaken unconscious belief in 'born from one' (in every sense of 'one'), and the relation between love for the mother (representing 'nature' and the 'home') and fear of the father (representing 'culture' and 'society'). We could in fact add to columns C and D the following remarks from Chapter VII of the *Outline of Psychoanalysis*, which immediately follow Freud's evocation of *Oedipus Rex*: "We are faced here by the great enigma of the biological fact of the duality of the sexes: it is an ultimate fact for our knowledge, it defies every attempt to trace it back to something else. . . . In mental life we only find reflections of this great antithesis . . .", which, continues Freud, is greatly complicated by the bisexuality of human beings. Thus, both the Greek mythmakers and Freud STATE the oppositions, but neither explain their social resolution.[8]

Lacan has attempted to show how a similar methodology – similarly claimed to be 'linguistic' – might be applied to the 'representations' of 'oppositions' in the psychic infrastructure: unconscious phantasies. Unfortunately, both Lacan's methodology and his exposition of his views entirely lack the kind of unified approach one finds in Lévi-Strauss. Lacan takes bits and pieces from everywhere and anywhere and jumbles them up

[8] Whereas Lévi-Strauss apparently thinks of the HISTORY represented in the myth as a REPETITION (or cycle) of oppositions, the story actually represents a diachronic development from questions about cosmological relations to the question of the relation between nature and culture (joined and separated by the digital boundary and boundaries introduced by the prohibition of incest), and from this 'societal' question to the POLITICAL question raised by Antigone. The problem of the synchronic and diachronic relationships between cosmological, social, and political categories is even further complicated if we introduce into the list of the variants of the myth that in which the Sphinx learned the riddle from Laius and was used by him to kill off 'illegitimate' aspirants to his throne (Thomson, 1940: 178–9).

– like the text of a dream – playing on ambiguities, etymologies, puns, analogies, poetic metaphors – again like the text of a dream – as well as on the reader's benevolent desire to understand. Lacan's argument is presumably that he is representing his theory in the very 'language' the theory is designed to analyze: if you understand the theory, you will then understand his exposition, and vice versa. Within all this, there appear strikingly important concepts, such as the theory of the Imaginary. Such an attitude nevertheless defies the simplest criterion of all 'science': that any theory must be demonstrably less complex than what it is intended to explain. Moreover, it is entirely in keeping with the implicit agreement between 'analyst' and 'patient', as members of a particular social class, that there is enough time and money available for analyses lasting twenty years or so, if need be (cf. Laing, 1961: 28). The underlying assumption – equally well represented by Lévi-Strauss – is that present biosocial arrangements have an unlimited future. The same value appears in the contemporary discourse of science as the 'unending pursuit of pure truth for its own sake (by successive approximations), limited only by time and money' (research grants). Minority groups, other exploited groups, and ecologists, however, tend to disagree with this conception of scientific leisure, with all that it says about socioeconomic privilege, ethnocentric comfort, freedom from the worst aspects of the production line, and a gracious lack of concern for the future of the human race.

Lacan consistently uses linguistic terms like 'signifier' in ways which gratuitously conceal the level of language he is discussing (Wilden, 1968: 225–6, 235–6). Moreover, his 'linguistic' model of the unconscious is derived directly from Lévi-Strauss's phonological analogy. Lévi-Strauss says that he was influenced most by Freud and Marx – and geology – and it was his reformulation of the concept of the unconscious as a locus, not of instincts, not of phantasies, not of energy or entities, but as a locus of a SYMBOLIC FUNCTION – a set of rules governing the possible messages in the system, a sort of syntax or code (Lévi-Strauss, 1950) – which allowed Lacan to declare in 1953: "The Freudian unconscious is the discourse of the other" (later "the Other"), and shortly afterwards: "The unconscious is structured like a language."

For Lévi-Strauss the unconscious consists of the rules which govern the possibilities of a "discourse" for which the "vocabulary" comes from the (preconscious) lived experience of the subject. Apart from his methodology, which is far from being purely linguistic or structural, his most significant other contributions may be his analysis of the gift as a 'symbolic object' of exchange (following Marcel Mauss) and his methodological distinction between nature and culture. The distinction between 'nature' and 'culture' in Lévi-Strauss marks the emergence of the symbolic function. This emergence provides for symbolic exchange, in which the COMBINA-TORIAL possibilities of the 'discrete element' (as with the integers, the alphabet, or with phonemes) allow a logically complex, but semantically weak, DISCONTINUOUS system of communication and exchange to emerge from the rich continuum of natural exchange processes. (In the terminology of communications theory, he is describing the emergence of the digital from the analog in interorganismic communication: Chapter VII; in the terms of Marxian exchange theory, he is describing the emergence of exchange value from use value: Chapter IX.) A kinship name, for example, turns a biological organism into something akin to a bit of information at a new level of communication. It defines, labels, or names – in other words, it makes a boundary distinction at the same time as it defines a locus in the system.

What separates nature from culture and in fact initiates symbolic exchange, is the mysterious but universal law of incest. (So universal, in fact, that it does not appear in the Ten Commandments, for which it is the necessary condition.) Not the law which says "Do not", however, but rather the positive aspect of the prohibition, which says in effect: "Give one member of your 'family' to another 'family' and you will receive another member of another 'family' in return." Unlike monetary exchange and contemporary systems of commodity exchange, in such a system of symbolic exchange, the 'objects' of exchange are insignificant compared with the function of the ACT OF EXCHANGE. (There is no particular reason, and certainly no reason known to the 'primitive' society, why members of the same 'family' should not reproduce the 'family'.) Like Malinowski's "phatic communion", the exchange of 'sister' or 'brother' is not so much the exchange of a biological ENTITY (matter–energy) as an exchange of SIGNS (information), and it is this exchange of signs which both organizes the system and holds it together. Thus, says Lévi-Strauss, a kinship system might be called a "matrimonial dialogue" in which marriage partners are exchanged "like spoken words". Methodologically speaking, then, language, society, and the law of incest must all be considered to have emerged "in one fell swoop" (Lévi-Strauss, 1950).

Obviously most reciprocal conversation serves a similar binding or linking function, and the analogy is persuasive. I shall criticize Lévi-Strauss's patrocentric position on the 'exchange of women' elsewhere. What is important for our purposes here is that Lacan interprets the phallus – not, please note, the penis – as the object of symbolic exchange within and between generations in the western family. Only from this or a similar perspective can one in fact make sense of the common psychoanalytical associations: breast–thumb–faeces–phallus–child. Although neither Lacan nor Lévi-Strauss would use this terminology, one can say that the 'part-object', the breast, is both an entity (matter–energy) and a sign (information) for the child. It is only because these 'objects' are what von Neumann called MARKERS – matter–energy bearing information just as the metal of a key bears the notches which say 'Open sesame' only to certain locks – that associations, displacements, and substitutions between them are possible. D. W. Winnicott's "transitional objects" (1953) are similarly bits of 'non-signifying' or meaningless information which take on their signification in the 'meaning-full' exchange of communication between mother and child, between the child as 'system' and the mother as 'environment' – and vice versa.

In order to fully appreciate the value of this viewpoint in psychoanalysis (to say nothing of biology, economics, and other realms of communication and exchange), we have to integrate Lacan's theory of the phallus and the phantasy as SIGNIFIERS [9] – Saussure's term for a linguistic sign – said to be controlled by laws similar to those found in language, with Bateson's seminal theory of play and fantasy (1955, republished 1972). Bateson asked himself why play and fighting among animals are so similar and yet so different. On the thesis that all behavior is communication, what is communicated in fighting as a bite becomes a 'playful nip' in animal play. He concluded that play involves the emergence of another level of communication, a new level that must in some sense be considered the logical prerequisite of both fantasy and language. In order that the 'nip' not be communicated as a bite, it is necessary that a message ABOUT the relationship be communicated. This message, the equivalent of 'This is play', would have to be of a higher logical type than the communication itself:

[9] Thus the phallus is said to be "the signifier of signifiers", the "signifier of desire". Phantasies are similarly described as signifiers. The accepted position of Lacan is that if the sound system of language is constructed on a rather small number of 'oppositions' between 'distinctive features', then psychoanalysis reveals that our concrete discourse is constructed on a relatively small number of 'oppositions' between phantasies ('inner/outer', for example) (cf. Laplanche and Pontalis, 1964). These will also be revealed in the discourse of the 'schizophrenic' who is said to speak the 'language of the unconscious' directly and to oscillate between oppositions (Laplanche and Leclaire, 1961). Consequently, Lacan has made much of the 'opposition' between the sounds 'o-o-o' and 'aah', REPRESENTING a relationship between presence and absence, in the well-known *Fort! Da!* ('Gone!' 'There!') of *Beyond the Pleasure Principle*, which founds Freud's discussion of repetition and the 'death instinct'. Most of the relevant texts of Lacan on this aspect of his theory can be found in the notes to my translation of his manifesto of 1953 (Lacan, 1956a). Laing (1961: 3–28) correctly locates the psychoanalytical category of opposition in ideology, rather than 'in' the unconscious.

it would be a METACOMMUNICATION. The emergence of metacommunication thus involves the possibility of 'talking about' relations, which is not possible in the same way at lower levels of communication within and between organisms. It also involves a form of something specific to language alone: the possibility of saying 'not'. (Animals refuse, they cannot negate.) Thus the 'nip' evolves as the sign of the bite: it is a bite which is not a bite.

Both Freud and Lacan consistently confuse linguistic negation ('not') with communicational refusal (e.g., ejection, rejection, disavowal) – while at the same time distinguishing 'neurosis' on the basis of negation (*Verneinung*), and 'psychosis' on the basis of rejection or disavowal (*Verwerfung, Verleugnung*). But the paradoxical situation of a message, the nip, which says: "This sign does not denote what the message for which it stands denotes' has everything to do with Freud's discussion of 'denial' and the emergence of the 'symbol of negation' in his 1923 article "Negation (*Die Verneinung*)". Freud says, in particular, that a denial in the analytical relationship is a "lifting-and-conserving" (*Aufhebung*) of a repression – an equally paradoxical metacommunication.

In the terms of communications theory, the distinction between bite and 'nip' points to the distinction between energy explanation and informational explanation, a distinction essential to the new paradigm which is emerging in the contemporary life and social sciences. Whereas in the bite, energy and information are one – as for example, when we step on the brake in a car: the movement both says 'stop' and does the stopping – in the nip, the energy involved becomes largely irrelevant; only the information counts. The primary characteristic of information is the triggering, the control, or the ORGANIZATION of matter–energy. Thus, when we step on the gas pedal instead of the brake, the energy of this movement, which says 'go faster', is almost entirely information. Moreover, it is not the same as the energy it TRIGGERS to make the vehicle accelerate. In psychoanalytical terms, one has only to say that the thumb is not the breast, that it is a sign of the breast, and that it involves an emergent metacommunication about the organization of the relationship between the mother and the child – based originally more on energy requirements than on informational ones (although the two cannot in fact be so easily separated, since mother and child are in a communicational relation from the moment of conception) – in order to point out that there are analogous emergences of levels of communication between child and environment. Bateson's theory is more subtle than I can indicate in this introductory chapter. Its full interpretation requires a theory of analog and digital communication (communication by means of continuous and discontinuous codes), the theory of logical types, and a theory of boundaries and levels in communication. But these few remarks should make it clear how seriously mistaken the whole Cartesian vocabulary of the 'object relation' is in psychoanalysis.[10]

Lacan does not use the terminology of communications theory, however, and, in spite of the communicational content of his own work, he knows practically nothing about the recent development of a non-mechanistic systems–cybernetic perspective in the life and social sciences in the United States and the United Kingdom. For reasons of historical influence and intellectual context – notably the mistaken tendency in France to subordinate semiotics or semiology to the terminology of linguistics – Lacan has persisted in a linguistic approach to Freud. It is this lack of understanding of the difference between language and communication – very evident in O. Mannoni's *Freud* (1971), for example, especially in the 'Afterword' to the American edition – which accounts for the present impasses in the theory, as well as for the problems of interpretation which I found impossible to solve in the first edition of my own work on Lacan. More recently, Lacan has said "the hell with linguistics", and has been working to develop what he calls a "logic of the signifier". He has been particularly chagrined by my own use of his work in a communicational perspective. But I have been unable to detect any significant evolution from what I would call an originally rationalistic and digital bias in the theory. I would say that Lacan's stated position is more mistaken than what he actually does.

Significantly enough, one can say the same of Lévi-Strauss, without whom Lacan would possibly still be a phenomenologist. Lévi-Strauss explicitly conceives of models in social science either as mechanistic (explanation of 'organized simplicity') or as statistical (explanation of 'unorganized complexity'). This position maintains him in the bioenergetic lineage of Freud – whose pleasure principle is a theory of mechanical equilibrium derived directly from nineteenth-century physics (G. T. Fechner), and whose 'death instinct' is a form of thermodynamic inertia or entropy, modeled on the second law of thermodynamics. (Thermodynamics concerns statistical relations of 'order' and 'disorder' in the energy relations of homogeneous 'entities'.) But Lévi-Strauss's theory of structure, in spite of similarities with Talcott Parsons's theories of 'social equilibrium', is a contribution to a universe of explanation quite different from that of the closed systems of classical physics: a contribution to the theory of ORGANIZED COMPLEXITY in the OPEN systems of feedback

[10] Cf. the critique in Chapter XI of Piaget's bioenergetic and physicist epistemology, grounded in phenomenology, which I use as a representative metaphor of the structuralist movement in France.

relationships between HETEROGENEOUS elements in the system–environment ensembles studied by the life and social sciences.

Lacan's work is by no means entirely free of the biomechanistic or bioenergetic perspective which still vitiates the epistemology of the human and social sciences. Moreover, the theory of castration is central to his theory, as it is in Freud (the woman is a 'lack' or the sign of a 'lack'). But although I object on theoretical and ideological grounds to Lacan's phallocentrism, I don't think it is any more essential to his theory than so-called penis-envy is to Freud's. (Penis-envy is in any case a purely MALE characteristic in any culture. The woman who supposedly manifests it can therefore only be a male chauvinist, a victim identifying with the executioner.)

As in the Kula trade described by Malinowski in his *Argonauts of the Western Pacific* (1922), the most interesting characteristic of symbolic exchange is that the symbolic object cannot actually be expropriated or possessed. Since the function of such exchange is not accumulation, but the maintenance – at all costs – of the relation between the exchangers, the possession of the object would break the circuit and the exchange would cease. (As, for example, in the children's game of passing an object behind their backs in a circle. When the one who is 'it' discovers who 'has' the object, the exchange stops. There is a sense, of course, in which the contemporary rituals of smoking pot seek to re-establish this symbolic relation between people.) Thus, if we assume that the phallus may, under the conditions of male domination, come to represent an object of symbolic exchange, any question about relationship which can be translated into the question of who HAS the phallus (and for whom) or who IS the phallus (and for whom) bespeaks a pathology (cf. Chapter X).

The phallus is exchanged in what Lacan calls the 'Symbolic order', governed by language and by the Other (with a capital O). There are two other 'orders' in the relationship between human beings: the Real and the Imaginary. The Real is simply what is Real for human subjects and does not require discussion here. The Imaginary is something else. In the first place it is not in the least 'imaginary'; it is the realm of images, doubles, mirrors, and SPECULAR identification. There is no Other in the Imaginary, only 'others'. This notion, which is probably Lacan's most important contribution to social and psychological theory, is derived from a phase of childhood that Lacan calls the "mirror-stage" (1949; cf. Winnicott, 1971: 111–18; Laing, 1969: 122). Briefly put, this is a period when the child comes to discover his 'Self' by a mirror-like identification with the image of another. This self is the ego, and there is some support in the earlier Freud, especially in the theory of narcissism, for such a view of the

ALIENATION of the subject (he who says 'I' and means 'I') from himself. The ego, on the other hand, may well say 'I', but that 'I' will designate 'the other'. (Cf. Freud on the 'body ego', 1953: XIX: 25-7.)

For Lacan the ego is an essentially paranoid construct founded on the OPPOSITION and IDENTITY between self and other. The ego involves the purely dual, either/or, relationship of master and slave. In a genetic sense, then, the child is born as an undifferentiated 'a-subjective' being. According to Lacan, the child's first discovery is that of DIFFERENCE: the difference between self and world. Through the Imaginary relationship to others, this difference will become an opposition. The child cannot become a subject until he or she can say 'I', but in learning to say 'I', the child will always begin by meaning 'he' or 'she'. So long as the child lives in the dual Imaginary relationship with the mother (whom Lacan calls the real Other, as opposed to the father, who represents, but who is not, the symbolic Other), the child is trapped in a short-circuit. It is through the oedipus complex, in which each apex of the family triangle comes to mediate the dual relationship between the other two, that the child passes into the 'normality' (one uses the word with reservations) of a three-way, Symbolic relationship, in which opposition is mediated by difference. In the Symbolic, the subject can say 'I': he or she has passed from the subject–object, object–object relationships of the Imaginary into what the phenomenologists would call the INTERSUBJECTIVITY of the Symbolic.

Thus Lacan's definition of the process of an analysis is that of a passage from the 'empty words' of an Imaginary discourse to the 'full words' of a Symbolic discourse, in which the analyst himself is equally and entirely involved. (The distinction is similar to Heidegger's distinction between "discourse proper" and "idle talk" – between *Rede* and *Gerede*.) Any other approach to psychoanalysis, says Lacan, sets the analyst up as "the subject-who-is-supposed-to-know" (he doesn't, of course) and thus defines the 'cure' as the identification of the subject's alienated ego with the equally alienated ego of the therapist. Ego psychology, says Lacan – in a typical image – is a Trojan horse. (For the ego psychologist, on the other hand, I suspect that Lacan is a Cheshire cat.)

"The subject begins the analysis by talking about himself without talking to you, or by talking to you without talking about himself. When he can talk to you about himself, the analysis will be over" (Lacan, 1966: 373). That this is an asymptotic notion is self-evident: it is impossible in language for the 'I' of any sentence to properly and entirely talk about the 'I' who emits the sentence. In linguistics, words like 'I' are called 'shifters': they designate a locus in the discourse, rather than a person. This linguistic fact is the basis of Lacan's version of the (irremediable) 'splitting of the subject' in the later Freud (*Ichspaltung*). In another terminology, this is to say that the subject of digital knowledge can never fully represent the subject of analog knowledge, as poets and artists have always known. Analysis ends when the patient realizes it could go on forever, said Hanns Sachs – but the splitting of the subject in Lacan's sense is an irremediable fount of anxiety only in cultures which believe that the digital is superior to the analog, rather than in a reciprocal relationship of difference to it. In other words, only in an individualistic and phallocentric culture of primarily digital communication and accumulation does the Lacanian analysis fully apply.[11] In this context, his analysis is indispensable – provided one knows how to go beyond it.

Behind the Symbolic lies the notion of mediated (unconscious) desire. The word translated 'instinct' in Freud clearly never meant instinct for him, and may very well be translated 'desire'. Moreover, Freud points out that there are no 'instinctual impulses' (*Triebregungen*) 'in' the unconscious, only "representatives of desire" (*Triebrepräsentanz*). Other Freudian concepts, such as wish-fulfillment and the *Lust* of the pleasure principle, also lend themselves to translation into a concept like 'desire'. Readers who know of Newcomb's 'A-B-X theorem' (Buckley, 1967: 113–16) will be familiar with the concept of mediated desire, which is of course Hegelian (and not restricted to desire for objects). "Man's desire", says Lacan, "is the desire of the Other."

The Other is not a person, but a principle: the locus of the "law of desire", the locus of the incest-prohibition and the phallus. According to Lacan, the Other – mythically represented in Freud by the Symbolic father of *Totem and Taboo*[12] – is the only place from which it is possible to say "I am who I am". The paradox of identity and autonomy which this involves – identical to or identified with what? – puts us in the position of desiring what the Other desires: we desire what the Other desires we desire. (Consider the situation of the ethnic minorities in England, France, or the United States, for whom all desires are coded white.) We therefore

11 For 'digital', one may read: language, 'objectivity', reason, mind, white, 'civilized', man, as the case may be. Similarly, for 'analog', one may read: nonverbal communication, 'subjectivity', emotion, body, people of color, 'primitive', woman. These represent some of the more significant of the pathological oppositions in our Imaginary culture. As Watzlawick, Beavin, and Jackson have remarked (1967), the distinction between the form and function of analog communication and the form and function of digital communication rather precisely maps that between the primary and the secondary processes in Freud. See Chapters VII, VIII, and IX.

12 In the case of 'little Hans' – conducted by Freud through the boy's father – the Freud 'standing behind' the real father came to represent the Symbolic father for the child, who knew Freud as 'the Professor'.

desire to TAKE THE PLACE of the Other in desire. When all is said and done, then, we do not desire objects, we desire desire itself (cf. Kojève, 1947: 1–30). Desire is represented by the phallus, which is not an object, but a "signifier".

The impossibility of satisfying such a desire – which is like trying to find a hole to fill up a hole – leads Lacan to make a most important distinction (partly to be found in the text of Kojève) between NEED, DEMAND, and DESIRE. Need represents the level of 'instinct' or 'drive'; desire is unconscious and ineffable; demand is the metaphoric expression of the relationship between need (which can be satisfied) and desire (which cannot). The emergence of desire is directly related to language, both ontogenetically and phylogenetically. The human *infans* cannot avoid learning to translate his needs into demands, through the acquisition of language. But language is controlled by and learned from the Other, not by and from any particular other. The Symbolic order of language awaits the child at birth: he or she has to discover where one fits into it. (Consider, for example, the length of time required for the child to master personal pronouns – and their early loss in some forms of schizophrenia and aphasia.) Not only may the child be already identified as an object of exchange in his parents' phantasies, he also has to find out where 'I' fits into the social universe of communication and exchange he discovers. This is the fundamental 'desire to know', and Lacan translates the "Who am I?" of Oedipus into "What am I there?" (in the discourse). Desire comes into the world because of the necessary relation with others that makes humans human; the child's helplessness to attend to his own needs results in the detour of need, through language, into demand, and it is this detour which generates unconscious desire as a fundamental and unfillable 'lack'.

We can interpret Lacan's reasoning as follows. A central problem in the text of Freud – a problem seriously obscured in its translations – is that of 'presentation', 'representation' (*Vorstellung*, usually translated as 'idea', 'concept', or 'image'), and 'representative' (*Repräsentanz, Repräsentant*), sometimes all combined in the somewhat mysterious term *Vorstellungs-repräsentanz* (see the invaluable *Vocabulaire* of Laplanche and Pontalis). The dream, for example, is a distortion or 'different placing' (*Entstellung*) of a set of RE-presentations in what Freud and Fechner called "another scene". The 'primal scene' similarly involves the problem of representation. Thus we can call demand 'metaphorical' because it re-presents a need. The child's original helplessness – which Freud regards as at the origin of all "moral principles" – requires that he appeal to an other to satisfy them. But whereas the need involved (e.g., hunger) can be satisfied, the original appeal (crying) cannot. And whereas it would seem that the acquisition of language – which the child sees as in the power of the Other and as giving others power over him – should make matters easier, in fact it does not. Although language, compared with crying, would seem to offer a huge gamut of possibilities of 'explaining what you mean', it is semantically and structurally much more limited than crying as a form of communication.

Language takes time, but for the child, crying says EVERYTHING AND ALL AT ONCE. What after all, is the message that crying represents? Although we all 'know' perfectly well what it is, IT IS IMPOSSIBLE TO SAY. As Lacan points out through his theory of the splitting of the subject, and as communications theory shows, language – in so far as it is a primarily digital instrument syntactically complex enough to transmit certain kinds of information with considerable precision – is incapable of properly representing the rich and ambiguous semantics of analog communication (relations).

This distinction between two modes of communication was originally based on the difference between the digital and the analog computer. The digital computer (e.g., an adding machine) computes by discrete steps, whereas the analog computer (e.g., a slide rule, a clock) employs continuous functions, which are then digitalized by the observer. In the on/off processes of the digital computer, 'no', 'not', 'zero', and 'minus' are all possible, whereas in the analog computer, one cannot say 'not'. The digital computer operates by means of 'either/or' identities, which, along with a way of saying 'not', are the sole prerequisites of any kind of analytic logic. But the analog computer communicates on the basis of 'more or less'. Consequently, identity is an impossible operation in analog communication (Chapter VII).

Freud's theory of desire (*Wunsch*) is based on the problem of identity. A wish is an attempt to establish an 'identity of thought' or an 'identity of perception' between a present situation of non-satisfaction and a past situation remembered as satisfaction. The anomaly involved is that identity is digital, whereas perception is analog: therefore any 'identity of perception' necessarily involves some process of TRANSLATION from the analog to the digital. Such translations always involve a gain in signification (the child says: "I want a . . ."), but a loss in meaning (the child cries).

Of course, only in cultures that supervalorize language is this necessity of translation any kind of problem. But by its demand that all communication be 'rational', by its insistent digitalization of analog relationships, our own culture is precisely one of those that becomes trapped in the contradictions between its ideology (which valorizes the digital) and its socioeconomic reality (which is both digital and analog). With the help of Lacan, however, it can easily be demonstrated that the Imaginary discourse of language in western culture – its reification in paradoxical concepts like 'individualism', 'identity', the 'autonomous ego', and 'doing your own thing (!)' – is not only no accident, but has a precise morphology in our socio-economic system.

We do have a word for what crying is about, of course: we call it 'love'. Lacan will say therefore that all demands are essentially demands for love. Thus, speech can be described as consisting of chain upon chain of words, all seeking to fill up the holes in communication, holes that cannot be filled. In communications terminology, these holes are in effect the 'gaps' which digital communication and signification necessarily introduce into the analog continuum of 'life', 'relation', and 'meaning'. Without these gaps – such as those between the integers, between the letters in an alphabet, or between the 'on' and the 'off' of the relays in a digital computer, or in the genetic code – language, as a particular system of the substitution and combination of discrete elements called signs or signifiers, would not be possible. Unconscious desire, then, in Lacan's sense, is the result of our being "creatures at the mercy of language". It corresponds to a kind of hole or "lack in being" introduced into being BY LANGUAGE ITSELF. (Note, however, that all goalseeking systems depend on 'lacks', and that all involve both analog and digital communication.)

In so far as the predominance of the Imaginary in our culture results in a reification of the natural and ecosystemic relations between human beings – in my own terminology, the conversion of interdependent similarities and differences (between 'man' and 'woman', for example) into pathological identities and oppositions (as between the IMAGES of man and woman in our culture) – the Imaginary order does not fulfill its function as an instrument of the Symbolic, it subverts and subjugates it. The analytic tendencies of western epistemology since Plato have invariably conceived of knowledge in the terms of perceptual images of identity and non-identity. The Greek for 'I know', from which the word 'idea' is derived, means literally: 'I have seen'. (I hope you can see what I mean.) But there are no identities in perception, as Hume took considerable pains to point out. Identities require boundaries and discreteness, but perception is by analogs, which have no intrinsic boundaries. Since gestalt theory, at least, we have known that boundary distinctions are introduced into open systems by the neurophysiological, linguistic, ideological, economic, or biological DECISIONS of parts of the system. And in our present culture, most of us have agreed to let language and economic relations make those decisions for us.

Consequently, in a pathological family – which we assume to be both the product and the 'socializing device' of a pathological culture – the child will remain trapped in the duality of an Imaginary relationship. He becomes trapped in an Imaginary discourse. All Symbolic exchange is impossible: the symbolic object has been expropriated. Thus it becomes crucial for him to solve the (insoluble) 'either/or' question of who has and who is the phallus, and for whom. The symbolic dialectic of the real differences between parent and child, or between male and female, become short-circuited by the oscillating double binds of identity and opposition. Instead of what Lacan calls a symbolic identification with a loved and loving model (the ideal of the ego), the child is captured in a paranoid relationship of specular identification with 'the other' (the ideal ego). His ego is an *alter ego*. As a sign or an icon exchanged in his parent's phantasies, the child becomes the equivalent of a WORD in somebody else's conversation. Survival becomes an impossible question of EITHER me OR them. The child – like contemporary youth, like the minorities, like the Third World – IS SPOKEN rather than allowed to speak.

There is a great deal more to the Lacanian viewpoint than I can discuss in detail here, notably his theory of the Symbolic father. Lacan suggests that 'psychosis' depends on the "cutting-out" of the "name-of-the-father" – the representation of the Symbolic Other – from the subject's discourse. This results in the 'repudiation' or 'foreclusion' (*Verwerfung* in Freud) of the Symbolic order, with resultant linguistic confusion between the literal and the metaphorical. For the 'psychotic', says Lacan, the Symbolic is the Real. According to Lacan, it is the Symbolic Other that 'supports' language, and when the relationship to the Other is cut off, the subject's discourse becomes 'unanchored' in the Symbolic reality which language represents for human beings:

> The Other as the locus of speech and guarantor of truth is compensated for in psychosis by the other. It is the suppression of the duality between the symbolic 'Other' and the 'other' as an Imaginary partner that causes the psychotic such difficulty in maintaining himself in the human Real, that is to say, in a Real which is symbolic (Wilden, 1968a: 130).

This aspect of Lacan's theory is one of the most debatable and the most culture-bound, since it depends on a patriarchal ideology (which is, in fact, Imaginary in Lacan's own terms). I shall not therefore elaborate on it at this point.

Apart from his theory of the Imaginary, perhaps Lacan's most significant contribution to the understanding of man-and-womankind has been that he has taught us how to read – specifically how to read Freud. He has taught us that any scientific theory is a set of metaphors, and that sometimes an analysis of those metaphors as metaphors, or their replacement by others, is the only way to get to the heart of a text. The DISCOURSE of all science is there to be analyzed – like a dream. But this is true only if we understand that dream analysis is communicational and linguistic analysis, and that it follows Freud's first theory of symbolism (his own great discovery in fact): the theory represented in the first edition of the *Interpretation of Dreams*, in the *Psychopathology of Everyday Life*, and in the book on jokes. And, if we try to understand, in the total social context, why Lévi-Strauss has insisted that the so-called primitive myth serves the same kind of function in that culture as the scientific discourse does in our own, we can understand very well why Freud compared the construction of the analyst and of the scientist to the delusions of the so-called schizophrenic.

The two most important processes in the dream-work, by which the 'word-presentations' of the dream thoughts regress 'through the unconscious' to perception, where they are represented as 'thing-presentations' or 'images', are, of course, condensation and displacement. The interpretation of the dream involves a decondensation and a re-establishment of the displaced elements by analysis of the words the dreamer uses to recount the dream. Thus Alexander the Great's dream of a 'satyr' shortly before his attack on the city of Tyre – the only correct interpretation of a dream in the old 'analogic' dream books, says Freud – is accurately decondensed into a Greek sentence representing the wish-fulfillment: "*sa Tyros*: Tyre is thine." (No doubt the image of the satyr had other associations also, for the overdetermination of dreams in such that they can never be fully interpreted.) In a dream analysis recounted by two former disciples of Lacan (Laplanche and Leclaire, 1961), a French patient's dream of a unicorn turns out to be a statement about a girl called 'Lili' and the patient's 'corne du pied' (sole of the foot), for the unicorn is *la licorne* in French.

Freud distinguishes the unconscious as involving only 'thing-presentations', whereas the preconscious and consciousness involve both 'images' and words. In dream there is a topographical regression from words to images; in 'schizophrenic speech', however, the patient speaks the 'language' of the unconscious directly: he 'treats words as if they were concrete', he treats 'word-presentations' like 'thing-presentations'. (This is essential to Freud's distinction between neurosis – involving repression and negation – and psychosis – involving projection and foreclusion or disavowal.) And, says Freud in the 1914 article on the unconscious, we cannot properly speak of the repression of drive or of a desire: only the idea or the presentation (*Vorstellung*) is repressed. Lacan translates: "It is the signifier which is repressed." Later we find Freud distinguishing between the fate of the 'information' (the presentation) in repression and the 'energy' (the quota of affect) which it does or does not trigger, in terms very similar to modern systems theory.

Another of Lacan's significant insights into the metaphoric dimensions of Freud's explicit energy model of the psyche is to suggest that what Freud describes as the "free flow of (free) energy" in the primary process can be read as a "free flow of meaning". Meaning arises in the relationship of the primary and the secondary processes, i.e., in the situation in which each is the CONTEXT of the other. The 'free meaning' of the primary process is without signification until it is 'bound' (digitalized) by the secondary process. The "bound energy" of Freud's secondary process thus becomes equivalent (as Freud himself seems to suggest) to *Bedeutung* (signification) in language. This 'binding of energy' can be described as the digitalization of an analog process of communication (as when we 'name' the images in a dream). It is in any case clearly related to the notion of cathexis (*Besetzung*), which in turn is related to the phenomenological concept of intentionality (Brentano, Husserl) and to the process of establishing the boundary between 'figure' and 'ground'.

If all symptoms, dreams, lapses, and forgettings are governed by the rules of condensation and displacement, and if the signification of the dream can be discovered only when its images are bound (i.e., defined or digitalized) by their intentionalization by language in the secondary process (the dream-text), then it does indeed appear that the crossing of the boundary between primary and secondary process may involve the 'domain of rules' described by Lévi-Strauss. (Systemic–cybernetic theory shows that digitalization is always necessary when communication crosses the boundary between different states or different systems – and that it creates the boundary in doing so.)

These rules, avers Lacan, are those of METAPHOR and METONYMY (synecdoche), more or less exactly as we find them in ordinary language. In Lacan's theory, metaphor represents condensation and the symptom, and metonymy represents displacement and desire (wish-fulfillment). This interpretation of Freud's theory of the dream-work and the processes of language comes directly from the structural linguist Roman Jakobson (1956). In his article on aphasia, Jakobson first explains that all linguistic processes involve a combination of two 'poles': selection and substitution (from the linguistic code), and combination and contexture (in the specific message). Thus, in speaking a sentence we select words from the code which we combine with other selections into the message. Each selection and combination places constraints on future selections and combinations. Since metaphors involve similarities and metonymies involve contiguities (whether in the thing described or in the words themselves), Jakobson speaks of language as consisting of a metaphoric and a metonymic pole.[13]

As it happens, these processes obtain in any system of communication whatsoever. But I shall not engage in the controversy over language and communication, or semiotics and linguistics, at this point. The mere correlation of these structural laws in language with the processes involved in the relation between consciousness and the unconscious is enough to engender considerable critical interest in Lacan's slogan: "The unconscious is structured like a language." It is enough to make us wonder whether the Freud we once learned about ever really had anything to do with the Freud represented in the twenty-three volumes of the *Standard Edition*. And that is surely enough. If Lacan has sent a whole new generation of French therapists, linguists, philosophers, literary critics, historians of ideas, and even Marxists back to a serious critical reading of the text of Freud, he has accomplished something extraordinary. And in spite of the denseness and obscurity of his own writing, he illuminates that text, even when he is wrong.

It can easily be demonstrated, for instance, that the 'specificity' or 'uniqueness' of psychoanalysis, as claimed by the Lacanian school – i.e., the implicit claim that psychoanalysis is somehow the privileged 'ground' or 'foundation' of all other theories in social science – is logically indefensible. Nevertheless, Lacan's analysis has opened up the text of Marx to new readings. We discover in retrospect that the Marxian theory of exchange value is a theory based on the Imaginary relations which Lacan has uncovered. Marx is concerned to demonstrate how commodities come to be valorized by the creation of a "general equivalent of exchange" (one commodity which comes to valorize all the rest, e.g., gold). He goes on to describe the valorization of the exchange-identities of commodities as a process by which "the body of commodity B acts as a mirror to the value of commodity A" (Marx, 1887: I, 52). In a 'psychological' footnote, Marx

---

[13] Thus, since in Jakobson's theory, the 'metonymic pole' of language represents its syntagmatic, connectional, or 'concatenated' aspect, Lacan states that metonymy IS desire. Using the Sartrean terminology derived from Kojève, he says that "metaphor is related to being as metonymy is related to lack of being". (Lacan, 1956b; Wilden, 1968a: 131). The phallus "signifies the lack of object" in the relation between mother and child; it is the "signifier of castration", a *manque à être*: 'a lack which has to be', 'a lack which is brought into being'. It is this representation of a lack or absence which circulates between human beings in the Symbolic order; what are exchanged in the Imaginary are things or representations of things. Consequently, possibly the most fundamental question in the analytic relationship is that both 'analyst' and 'patient' must recognize is that one cannot BE the phallus, for that is to be the desire of the Other.

compares this process of identification and valorization with the mirror-relationship through which a child comes to see himself as a human being by seeing himself "reflected" in others. (The common denominator in both Lacan and Marx here is, of course, the "desire for recognition" in Hegel's analysis of the relation between master and slave.) This correlation is quite surprising enough, I think, but it becomes even more significant when we reflect on Marx's thesis that under capitalism (symbolic) relationships between people are reduced to the status of (imaginary) relations between commodities or things. In this way, with the help of the concepts of analog and digital communication and exchange in living and social systems, Lacan's theory of the Imaginary is given a socioeconomic foundation.

Reading Lacan – especially his later work – is so tortuous and difficult that one hesitates to recommend him to the reader. But, as I have said elsewhere, there is a method in his madness. As one who 'knows', Lacan is above all devoted to the destruction of the status of the "subject-who-is-supposed-to-know". But we cannot destroy the master by simply taking his place; we have to make him IRRELEVANT – and that means to reduce his mastery to insignificance by transcending the oppositional relationship in which we find ourselves in a negative identification with him. To destroy exploitative mastery, we must do more than become the negative complement of the master, his mirror-image; we must know what he knows, which, in essence, is nothing we don't already know.

To read Lacan, Lacan demands that the reader "put himself into the text". Whether anybody reads Lacan or not, this I translate as an injunction to transcend the individualistic identities and oppositions of the Imaginary by an entry into the collective differences of the Symbolic. It is an injunction which is necessarily paradoxical, in Bateson's sense of a command that can be neither obeyed nor disobeyed. Nor do I believe that any such transcendence is possible in a socioeconomic system like our own, in which all Symbolic values are reduced to Imaginary profits.

Chapter II

Metaphor and Metonymy

FREUD'S SEMIOTIC MODEL OF CONDENSATION AND DISPLACEMENT

1. *The Two Theories of Symbolism in Psychoanalysis*

Traditional psychoanalysis has not been concerned with the problems of linguistics or semiotics. Psychoanalysis is indeed the 'talking cure', but in spite of all of Freud's discussions of language, and in spite of the semiotic and graphic metaphors which run through his work, the symbolism of the dream and the symptom has not generally been considered as a question of COMMUNICATION. This is in part the result of the theory of intrapsychic conflict, in part the result of Freud's own contradictions on the subject, and in part the result of simple ignorance of the texts. Freud both denies and affirms that the dream is a communication, for instance.

Symbols in the traditional textbook sense are not discursive phenomena. The orthodox analyst has always tended to suppose a natural connection between word and thing (e.g., spider) and a further natural connection between the symbol and the thing symbolized (spider = mother). This atomistic, non-contextual view of the symbol is in keeping with Freud's second theory of symbolism, which can be referred to as *die Symbolik* (Symbolism); it is opposed to his first theory – that upon which psycho-analysis was founded – which Lacan calls *le symbolique* (the Symbolic).

The atomistic view which severs the 'symbol' from language by a form of analogical interpretation is only a step past the oriental dream books against which Freud was writing in the first edition of *The Interpretation of Dreams*. And in fact, in later adding the second theory of a more or less 'fixed' symbolism, derived from Stekel, Freud warned that Stekel had probably damaged psychoanalysis as much as he had benefited it. This is not to deny the possible validity of a 'universal' cultural symbolism – how-ever monotonously unilluminating such theories may be. But Lacan's attack on simplistic, non-dialectical analogical interpretation (1956a, 1956b) has had the effect of making us reconsider Freud's semiotic and linguistic perspective.

The concept of the 'symbol' as a communication and of the Symbolic as a system of communication finds its support in anthropology and in the history of religion. Besides its legal sense of 'pact' or 'contract', the word *sumbolon* is probably equivalent to the Latin *tessera* – the two halves of a broken potsherd whose fitting together served as a token of recognition or password in the early mystery religions. Like the verb *sumballo*, the etymological source of the word symbol is that which implies a LINK (cf. Wilden, 1968a: 35, 101, 118–22, 209–49). Charles Sanders Peirce pointed to these correlations in 1897 in his "Logic as Semiotic: The Theory of Signs" (Peirce, 1955: 112–15).

In the complex systems of exchange examined by Mauss in the *Essai sur le don*, or by Malinowski in his *Argonauts of the Western Pacific*, the gifts exchanged can be called symbols. But they do not stand for what they 'represent' in some fixed relationship to an unconscious 'meaning'. They are the symbols of the act of exchange itself, which is what ties the society and its neighbors together. Thus they cease to be symbols in any important sense; it is the ACT of exchange, with its attendant *mana* or *hau*, which symbolizes the unconscious requirement of exchange through displaced reciprocity (I give you this, he gives me that) as a means of establishing and maintaining relationships between the members of that society or between one society and another. In Lévi-Strauss's terminology, these objects of exchange are often referred to as 'signs', which are exchanged like words in a discourse. The 'object' exchanged is part of a symbolic 'discourse' responding to a requirement of communication. It is thus part of a symbolic function, but it symbolizes nothing in itself. Even the appellation 'sign' turns out to be a dubious one in certain instances, since if we employ Peirce's definition of the sign as "something which replaces something for someone", Lévi-Strauss will ask how we can call an object with a specific function of its own, like a stone ax, a sign, since we cannot answer the question of what it replaces, or for whom.

It seems then that the word symbol may be better restricted to those kinds of 'analog' signs or icons which are not arbitrary representations. Saussure's distinction between the arbitrary sign (or signifier) and the symbol was that there is a "rudimentary natural link" or "rational relation-ship" between the symbol and the thing symbolized (1916a: 101, 106). Thus the symbol in the traditional psychoanalytical sense is an icon, where-as the symbolic exchange of the 'cool' society involves signs – and many a psychoanalytical 'symbol' may turn out to be a SIGNIFIER in the Saussurean sense and in the sense of Freud's original theory, as, for example, in the unicorn dream mentioned in Chapter I (Laplanche and Leclaire, 1961).

In traditional psychoanalysis, Fliess, Ferenczi, Jones, and others have insisted that the 'psychoanalytical symbol' is to be defined as the "use of a 'non-sexual' element to stand for a repressed 'sexual' one". For Jones in particular, this is a one-way process: the theory is reductionist, insisting in effect that the symbolized 'sexual' element is the 'efficient cause' of the symbol used for it. (For the inappropriateness of causal thinking in communication and the discourse, and for goalseeking or 'final causes' in cybernetics, see Chapters VI, VIII, and XII). Jung correctly criticized this misinterpretation of Freud by pointing out that it uses the term 'symbol' as an equivalent for 'sign' in the sense of an 'indicator' or 'symptom', as in medicine. From another point of view, Binswanger – drawing on the Heideggerean emphasis on the *logos* – sought in his existential *Daseinanalyse* to correct the tendency of orthodox psychoanalysis thus to reduce overdetermination to determinism, without falling into the idealization or romanticization of human behavior represented by Silberer's anagogic theory of symbolism, which has always been understandably popular with students of literature (cf. Binswanger, 1963: 59–83).

As Needleman points out (Binswanger, 1963), Jones defines the 'true' symbol as: (1) being a representation of unconscious material, (2) having a constant meaning, (3) being independent of individual conditioning factors, (4) having an evolutionary basis, (5) having linguistic connections, and (6) involving phylogenetic parallels (Jones, 1913: 87–142). Such a definition may be adequate for the theory of symbolism; indeed it would be surprising not to discover cultural and existential universals in human experience. We have only to restrict the implicit Lamarckianism of Jones's definitions to that aspect of our experience which is clearly Lamarckian: the transmission of 'technological' acquired characteristics through culture. But, as I shall find myself insisting again and again, the problem is not that of the interpretation itself, but rather of the LEVEL at which it is applied. To assent to the primacy which Jones ascribes to what he defines as the 'true' symbol is not simply to lay an inappropriate emphasis on the ELEMENT, rather than on the structural and systemic LAWS OF THE RELATIONS between elements. It is also to maintain an essentially reactionary and static theory of human 'nature' for which there is precious little properly scientific evidence. One has only to suggest that the 'collective symbols' as such are less important than the symbolizing PROCESSES of the social organization in which they occur, for instance, or to suggest that the USE of these symbols may depend on that social context, to realize that the question of primacy is still an open one. Among other things,

Lacan's critique of Freud has reopened this question. Jones does not properly understand that his 'symbols' are messages; he does not question the status or the function of the code or repertoire from which they are drawn; nor does he concern himself with the constraints of the context in which they appear. In other words, the orthodox interpretation of symbolism knows nothing of levels or of relative semiotic freedom in communications systems, and, by disavowing the context, it mimics the closed-system thinking of classical physics.

A symbol in the traditional sense is not distinguished solely by its differentiation and distinction from other symbols, as are Saussure's 'diacritic' semantics of the signifier (Wilden, 1968a: 212–18), nor can it generally be replaced by other symbols, and it certainly cannot be negated or defined by them. Symbolism in this sense is an analog-iconic communication system.

Kenneth Burke surely recognized the proper nature of the symbol in his "Freud – and the Analysis of Poetry" (1941: 221–50). In this article, Burke outlined his conception of how Freud's discoveries should be applied to "the structure of interrelationships" which make up the "motive" of a literary text – with an aside to the effect that the use of communication as a basic motivational category might resolve the paradoxes of reductionism lying in wait for critics who apply an "essentializing" strategy as opposed to a "proportional" one (pp. 224–5). Since Burke described what he was doing as "dialectical criticism", it is perhaps not surprising that he should have warned of the "lure of efficiency" offered by the 'short cuts' provided in all non-dialectical interpretations of symbols. He called for a contextual analysis of symbols and symbolic actions by means of variants on the Freudian method of free association. Burke rightly saw how the essentializing short cut affected the interpretation of the psychoanalytical models themselves by short-circuiting overdetermination (equifinality and multifinality):

> The trouble with short cuts is that they deny us a chance to take longer routes. With them, the essentializing strategy takes a momentous step forward. You have next but to essentialize your short cuts in turn (a short cut atop a short cut) and you get the sexual emphasis of Freud, the all-embracing ego compensation of Adler, or Rank's master-emphasis upon the birth trauma, etc. (p. 228).

2. Overdetermination and Equifinality: Relations between Relations

The dream, the lapsus, the forgotten name, and the symptom are all described by Freud as 'overdetermined'. None of these manifestations of an unconscious message are simple indicators of something, as the word symptom implies in medicine. Overdetermination may be read to mean 'determined' in some classically causal fashion, but in fact the notion is quite different from causal explanation. All it says is that, because of the semiotic freedom of the system of communication in which the symptom occurs, 'there is more than one way of getting there'. In other words, although the system is indeed determined in some sense by the repertoire or the code from which the possible elements of the message are drawn, and by the syntactic laws of combination in the message itself, this determination is similar to that in language itself. In language, there is a very large number of ways of saying the same thing, and an infinite number of possible messages. Determined as it is by its code and by its syntax, language is perhaps the most semiotically free of all representational and communicational systems – and it is not ruled by causality, but by possibility, constraints, and by its pragmatic–semantic function, that of the transmission and reproduction of variety in the system.

Although Lacan believes that overdetermination makes sense only in a linguistic context (Wilden, 1968a: 55, 116, 176), his assertion is not borne out by biology, by semiotic theory, or by the text of Freud. Since the concept of overdetermination is important for the understanding of all non-linear systems, it is essential not to confuse it with a purely linguistic model. Breuer implies that the idea of multiple determination (*Über-determinierung, Überbestimmung*) is original with Freud. Breuer employs it as if it were simply a non-deterministic theory of multiple causation (Freud, 1953–: *Standard Edition*, II, 212), and there is some justification for attributing a similar notion to Freud himself (*Standard Edition*, II, 263; XVI, 435–6). Freud does indeed speak of Wundt's 'principle of the complication of causes' (1900) in *The Psychopathology of Everyday Life* (*Standard Edition*, VI, 60–1), and he may have been influenced by John Stuart Mill's doctrine of the plurality of causes.

But Freud's conception of overdetermination is actually more subtle. He first uses the term in *On Aphasia* (1891: 74), where it is clearly equivalent to the concept of REDUNDANCY in information theory: "The safeguards of our speech against breakdown thus appear over-determined, and it can easily stand the loss of one or the other element." It is probably true that no system exhibiting redundancy can also be causally deterministic in the traditional sense; consequently, Freud's committment to 'causal therapy' (*Standard Edition*, XVI, 435–6) is already in question, well before the discovery of psychoanalysis proper. Bateson's early critique of causal thinking in psychiatry is particularly apt here (Ruesch and Bateson, 1951: 57, 74–7), for it provides a retrospective analysis of Freud's theory of the association of ideas:

In the extreme mechanistic emphasis of the eighteenth and nineteenth centuries, the causal chains for which scientists searched were, almost without exception, lineal, branching, or converging. The question 'why', the belief in single causation, and the stress upon the problems of etiology and assessment of disease overdetermined the answers. A chain of events spaced in time or a set of conditions patterned in space were linked together to build a theory of causality. . . . In such systems it appeared illegitimate to evoke final causes as a part of explanation. . . .

Bateson goes on to describe the changed twentieth-century emphasis, away from the Aristotelian 'class-theoretical' approach – which deals with types or categories and presupposes a certain atomistic autonomy of the various classes – towards 'field-theoretical' explanation, which deals with the processes and interactions in the circular and reticulate systems of human relationships (cf. also Bateson, 1967).

Cybernetic or communicationally oriented explanation is concerned with wholes, (open) systems, feedback, and relationships, rather than with parts, aggregates, entities, and forces; with circular, self-regulating, or structure-elaborating systems rather than with lineal chains; with homeostasis and morphogenesis rather than with equilibrium; with constraints, noise, probabilities, teleonomy, and goals rather than with efficient causes; with the information in circuit (which triggers and controls) rather than with energy. All systems involving or simulating life or mind are open systems, because they are necessarily in communication with another 'system' or 'environment'. Thus they are constitutively multifinal or equifinal – or, to use Freud's term, overdetermined. (On this point, see also Chapter XI, Section 4.)

In "The Psychotherapy of Hysteria", published in 1895 (*Standard Edition*, II, 288–92), Freud describes resistance (*Widerstand*) as "a structure in several dimensions which is stratified in at least three different ways". There is "a nucleus of memories or trains of thought in which the traumatic factor has culminated or the pathogenic idea [*Idee*] found its purest manifestation".

The three types of arrangement of the material leading to this nucleus are:

1 A linear chronological order of memories which is always accurately recalled, but in reverse order of occurrence. Freud describes these linear (and lineal) sequences (like a file of documents, a packet) as also having a thematic structure (*als Bildung eines Themas bezeichnet*).

2 Each 'theme' is "stratified concentrically round the pathogenic nucleus". "The contents of each particular stratum are characterized

by an equal degree of resistance, and that degree increases in proportion as the strata are nearer the nucleus."

3 The third type of arrangement is the most important, but is less easily defined. It is "an arrangement according to thought-content, the linkage made by a logical thread which reaches as far as the nucleus and tends to take an irregular and twisting path. . . ."

The first two are morphological, the third dynamic. Thus, whereas the first two "would be represented in a spatial diagram by a continuous line, curved or straight, the course of the logical chain would have to be indicated by a broken line which would pass along the most roundabout paths from the surface to the deepest layers and back . . ." (like the knight's course in chess). Freud concludes this description of the third 'logical chain' of associations as follows:

> The logical chain corresponds not only to a zig-zag, twisted line, but rather to a ramifying system of lines and more particularly to a converging one. It contains nodal points [*Knotenpunkte*] at which two or more threads meet and thereafter proceed as one; and as a rule several threads which run independently, or which are connected at various points by side-paths, debouch into the nucleus. To put this in other words, it is very remarkable how often a symptom is DETERMINED IN SEVERAL WAYS, is 'OVERDETERMINED' (II, 290, my emphasis).

In relation to the theory of information-processing networks, Freud's description again matches the concept of redundancy. It is clear that no psychological symptom whatever could possibly appear in any system which did not allow for a high degree of redundancy. Not only is the channel full of 'noise' in the purely technical sense, but part of the psychic system is actively opposing the transmission of the message in the first place.

However, Freud's description also matches in many respects the mechanistic and deterministic notion of a branching and/or converging lineal chain of causation. His general description does in fact match Locke's causalist explanation of the association of ideas: association by contiguity in space or time (Freud's linear chronological sequence); by similarity (Freud's 'themes'); and by cause and effect, which is really only another form of contiguity, just as Freud's third (spatio-logical) arrangement is a special case of the first.

As in so many other instances, we must go to the *Project* of 1895 (*Standard Edition*, I) in order to separate Freud's bioenergetic causal explanations from his semiotic understanding of communications processes. Karl H. Pribram (1962) brings out the importance of overdetermination, without actually dealing with it, in analyzing the theory of memory in the *Project*. The singularity of Freud's theory of the grooving (*Bahnung*, facilitation, *frayage*) of the neuronal pathways, is that there are always several pathways (that is to say that the *Bahnen* are overdetermined), which are independent of each other (that is to say, that the process by which the neuronal messages are transmitted is equifinal). Otherwise the transmissions in the network of neurons would be random (without pattern). For Freud, each cell in the nuclear system is in multiple contact with its neighbors. If the resistance to transmission were equally or simultaneously overcome at all these points of contact, the transmissions would in fact be random. They do begin in a non-structured and random way; they progressively become structured and organized (after the event) by a process of selection. What 'motivates' the overcoming of resistance and thus governs the selection of the overdetermined pathways is, in the final analysis, the Other, as 'environment', as the gratifier of the needs of the child, who cannot attend to his own needs. Pribram's analysis brings out the intuitive sense of 'open systems in communication' which, in contradiction with the more well-known bioenergetic views elsewhere, informs the work of Freud from the very beginning. For, as Wiener remarks in his *Cybernetics* (1948: 20), the concept of 'facilitation' is multiplicative, rather than additive, that is to say, it belongs to cybernetic explanation rather than to bioenergetic, causal explanation. (Information is multiplicative because each 'bit' affirms some 'thing' at the same time as it does not affirm some – undefined – other 'thing'. Thus 'Twenty Questions' may suffice to define 2^{20} 'objects'.)

The connection between overdetermination and equifinality – derived originally from gestalt theory, and unknown to 'behaviorism' – is thus very clear. Equifinality can be defined as the process by which the same final state may be reached from different initial conditions and/or by different paths (a simple example: once an animal has learned a task, it will continue to complete it by whatever means available to it). Von Bertalanffy's definition of the open system explains why: "In contrast to equilibrium states in closed systems which are determined by initial conditions, the [goal-seeking] open system may attain a time independent state independent of initial conditions and determined only by the system's parameters" (1962: 18). So long as the parameters of the system exhibit redundancy, there will be equifinality or multifinality, and this rule applies, not only to language, but to any information-processing system whatsoever. In Freud's words:

Since in fact our *I* always entertains goalseeking cathexes [*Zielbesetzungen*] – often a number of them at the same time – we can now understand both the difficulty of purely cognitive thought and also the possibility, in the case of practical thought, of the most various [neural] pathways [*Wege*] being reached or sufficing at various times under various conditions for various persons (*Standard Edition*, I, 377, translation modified.)

I introduce a more adequate distinction between equifinality and multifinality in Chapter XI, Section 4, and, of course, the problem of understanding the open (eco)system is one to which these essays constantly return. Having evoked the term 'determined', however, we are still faced with the specter of 'efficient causality' in the open system. Since the entire Freudian corpus is so impregnated with a causal terminology and epistemology, it becomes necessary to say something further about the problematic of causal explanation.

As Emery and Trist (1965: 242) and others have pointed out, von Bertalanffy's conception of the 'open system', which has been so important for the development of a systemic perspective, is in fact relatively closed. In von Bertalanffy's conception, the 'environment' is in essence a kind of passive 'ground' in which the 'organism' (the figure) moves. But in trying to correct this, Emery and Trist simply replace the inadequacy of von Bertalanffy's notion by another inadequacy: the concept of the "causal texture of the environment". (This term derives from an article of 1934 by S. C. Pepper.) What they obviously intend by it is of course the 'reciprocally interacting communication and control through the CONSTRAINTS in the CONTEXTURE of the ECOSYSTEM'.

The terms 'causal' and 'texture' represent a simple displacement – and not a transcendence – of the ideological and epistemological opposition between 'organism–organization' and 'environment' (cf. Chapter VIII). Moreover, especially and most clearly when the kind of reciprocal interaction in an ecosystem is partially controlled by the inadequate 'map' or 'image' one subsystem has of its 'environment', it is misleading to speak of causality as such. Certainly there are 'results' and 'consequences' in open systems (and it seems that we cannot do without a terminology of 'because') – but the lineal, closed-system constructs lying behind the term 'causality' are completely inadequate to deal with the fact that in the feedback relations of open systems, CAUSES CAUSE CAUSES TO CAUSE CAUSES.

In other words, as in the example quoted by Emery and Trist, of a company whose conservative management and inadequate map of its 'territory' brought it close to self-destruction, we cannot legitimately locate the 'cause' of this inadequate map anywhere. In the first place, according to our deeply imbedded conceptions of classical causality, changes in the environment ought to have caused changes in the subsystem's map (they did not). In the second place, the particular extent of the changes in the company's environment could not have taken place if the map had been adequate. It was precisely this inadequate map and the consequent rigidity of the company in question which, in combination with other factors (e.g., changes in consumer demand correlative with changes in the possibilities of supply), relieved certain constraints on other, much smaller companies competing in the same 'territory' or in interrelated 'territories' according to a different system of navigation. This then allowed for environmental changes to which the first company could not easily adapt (cf. Chapter VIII on positive feedback, counter-adaptivity, and rigidity).

In truth, neither the company, nor its competitors, nor the consumers 'caused' anything to happen. What happened was that the RELATIONSHIPS (and not the 'entities') changed. The socioeconomic ecosystem moved to another level of logical typing or organization while (and because) the company in question persisted in viewing the system as still at its previous level of relationship.

I know of no way in which classical or semi-classical conceptions of lineal causality ('strong' or 'weak') can be applied to relations – whereas they apply perfectly well to 'entities' (or to what are defined as entities). In this context, it will be noted that in the statement 'causes cause causes to cause causes', each con-sequential use of the term 'cause' is of a different logical type from that of the antecedent term. These 'causes' cannot add: they divide and multiply (cf. Marx's *Grundrisse* [1857–8]: McLellan, 1971: 106–18, especially p. 107).

RELATIONS BETWEEN RELATIONS CANNOT BE TALKED ABOUT in the analytic logic of lineal causality and unidimensional sequence. It is even possible that they cannot be talked about (digitalized) at all, whereas they can certainly be (and in fact always are) COMMUNICATED.

3. *The Freudian Points of View*

Freud uses several different points of view to represent the psychic system:

1 The functional: This term is usually applied to Freud's early attempts at systemization, concerned with the difference between memory and perception (e.g., *Standard Edition*, V, 571).

2 The descriptive: This viewpoint draws the line between consciousness and the unconscious as follows: *Cs./Pcs. Ucs.*

3 The topographical (or structural, or grammatic): *Cs. Pcs./Ucs.* This involves the concept of the double inscription (*Niederschrift*), which is examined in further detail below.

4 The dynamic: Here the unconscious is equated with the repressed. This view involves a further distinction between 'primary' repression and 'after'-repression or 'repression proper' (Chapter XVI).

5 The systematic: This is equivalent to the topographical view (levels of inscription) plus the dynamic view. The division is expressed as that between the secondary system or process and the primary system or process. This is the viewpoint of the *Project* of 1895.

6 The economic (essentially functional): This is the classically bio-energetic viewpoint, influenced by G. T. Fechner and the first and second laws of thermodynamics, which runs throughout Freud's work, from his early neurophysiology to the introduction of the so-called death instinct in 1920. It sets up an opposition between *Lust* or pleasure (release from tension) and unpleasure (tension) through which the system as a whole seeks to re-establish an original state. The 'free' energy of the primary process is said to be controlled by a 'principle of inertia'. The 'bound' energy of the secondary process seeks, through the 'principle of constancy', to maintain a level of energy sufficient to deal with the 'exigencies of life' (*Not des Lebens*).

7 The 'new topography' (1923): the ego, the id, and the superego (cf. *Standard Edition*, XXII, 78).

8 The 'semiotic' view (1914): The full significance of this Freudian viewpoint has been brought out only by Lacan. It involves a distinction between the primary process as consisting only of thing-presentations, whereas the secondary process involves both thing-presentations and word-presentations (signifiers).

4. *Cathexis and Intentionality*

Freud followed Brentano's course on Aristotle when he was a medical student. It is not really necessary to establish a historical influence, however, for the relationship between cathexis (*Besetzung*: investment, occupation) and phenomenological intentionality is very clear. Both the 'theory of deferred action' (*Nachträglichkeit*: the quality of being 'after the event') and cathexis reveal a relationship with the existential 'project' derived from the concept of intentionality. Brentano (1874: Book II, Chapter 1, No. 5) describes this process as follows:

Every psychical phenomenon is characterized by what the Scholastics . . . called the intentional (or sometimes the mental) inexistence of an object, and what we should like to call, although not quite unambiguously, the reference [*Beziehung*] to a content, the directedness [*Richtung*] toward an object (which in this context is not to be understood as something real) or the 'immanent-objectness' [*immanente Gegenständlichkeit*]. Each [phenomenon] contains something as its object, though not each in the same manner. In the presentation [*Vorstellung*] something is represented, in the judgment something is acknowledged or rejected, in desiring it is desired, etc. This intentional inexistence is peculiar alone to psychical phenomena. . . . And thus we can define psychical phenomena by saying that they are such phenomena as contain objects in themselves by way of intention [*intentional*].

The scholastic theory of the *intentio* (*sensibilis, intelligibilis, intellecta*) is linked with what is called the species theory of knowledge, which goes back to Aristotle's theory of the perception of the form (information) of an object without its matter(–energy). The scholastic theory does not, however, depend upon the necessity of the 'object', as Brentano's version does, or as Sartre intended when he spoke of the 'explosion of consciousness towards the world' (all consciousness being consciousness of . . .) in his early article on Husserl (1939). The fact that these versions of the theory speak of purely mental phenomena or of consciousness is, of course, irrelevant to the significance of the principles of the selection of information and the goalseeking behavior of communications systems which they describe. We have seen that Freud thinks of cathexis as an intention towards a goal (*Zielbesetzung*). For many of the later phenomenologists, intentionality becomes a principle of signification, just as cathexis is related to signification (*Bedeutung*) by Freud (*Standard Edition*, XIX, 187; Wilden, 1968a: 282–4). In the terms of the distinction between analog and digital communication developed in detail in Chapter VII, the relation between cathexis, intentionality, and signification is reinforced by Freud's conception of the binding (*Bindung*) of the primary process by the secondary process.

5. *The Semiotic–Grammatic Metaphor*

> The 'thing itself' – that of course would be pure,
> dead-end truth – is wholly incomprehensible even
> to the creator of language and in no sense worth
> striving for. He merely describes the relation of
> things to man and resorts for their expression
> to the boldest metaphors. A nerve stimulus
> first translated into an image! First metaphor.
> NIETZSCHE: *Truth and Lie in an Extra-Moral*
> *Sense* (1873)

The 'points of view' that are of most interest for this essay are the economic view, involving 'binding', the semiotic view, involving the conception of 'presentation', and the writing or grammatic (rather than phonetic) metaphor of the inscription or the trace (see also Chapter XIII).

Freud's earliest representation of the neural system is dependent entirely on semiotic metaphors (*Standard Edition*, I, 233–8, Letter 52, 1896):

> As you know, I am working on the assumption that our psychical mechanism has come about by a process of stratification: the material present-at-hand as memory traces [*Erinnerungsspuren*] is from time to time subjected to a restructuring [*Umordnung*] in accordance with fresh circumstances – it undergoes, as it were, a re-transcription.[1] Thus what is essentially new in my theory is the thesis that memory is present-at-hand not once, but several times over, that it is registered or deposited [*niedergelegt*] in various species of signs [*Zeichen*]. (I postulated a similar re-ordering some time ago, in my study of aphasia [1891], for the paths [*Bahnen*] leading from the periphery.) . . . I have illustrated this in the following schematic picture . . ., which assumes that the different inscriptions [*Niederschriften*] are also separated (though not necessarily topographically [*topisch*]) in respect to the neurones which are their vehicles. . . .

FIGURE 1

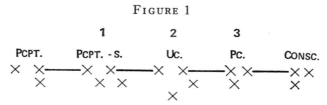

---

[1] *Umschrift*: a repeated inscription, another kind of inscription, a paraphrase. Another term which occurs in this letter, translated 'record', is *Fixierung* (fixation).

Pcpt. [perceptions] are neurones in which perceptions originate and to which consciousness is attached but which in themselves retain no trace of what has happened. FOR CONSCIOUSNESS AND MEMORY ARE MUTUALLY EXCLUSIVE.

Pcpt.-s [perceptual signs] is the first inscription or registration of the perceptions; it is quite incapable of being conscious and is arranged according to associations of simultaneity.

Uc. [unconsciousness, unconscious signs] is the second inscription arranged according to other associations – perhaps according to causal relations. *Uc.* traces may correspond to conceptual memories [*Begriffserinnerungen*]; they too are inaccessible to consciousness.

Pc. [preconsciousness] is the third transcription [*Umschrift*] attached to word-presentations [*Wortvorstellungen*] and corresponding to our official *I*. The cathexes proceeding from this *Pc.* become conscious in accordance with certain rules. This secondary 'thought-consciousness' is after the event [*nachträgliches*] and probably connected with the hallucinatory activation of word-presentations; so that the neurones of consciousness would once again be perceptual neurones and in themselves devoid of memory.

The successive transcripts represent a genetic process of development through which from stage to stage in the life of man there is a translation (*Übersetzung*) of the 'psychical material'. "A failure[2] of translation is what we know clinically as 'repression'." Thus repression, in the usual psychopathological sense of an 'after-repression' (*Nachverdrängung*) or 'repression proper', leading to illness (and not apparently considered to include the later concept of the 'primal repression'), is a frustration, a GAIN-SAYING (*ver-sagen*) OF TRANSLATION. In this way the neurological model, designed to be an analog of the brain, turns out to be a model of the processes of writing (the trace) and the process of metaphor in communication and in language, for a metaphor, a symptom, a substitute, is a transmuted sign or series of signs, a PARAPHRASE (*Umschrift*).

I shall say that each 'layer' of signs is related to the other layers as metalanguage to 'object' language, as COMMENTARY to TEXT. This conception requires an assumption of DISCONTINUITY between the layers, for which any notion of 'reflection' or 'homology', or 'attraction' or causality,

---

2 *Versagung*: 'gainsaying'. This is the word most commonly used by Freud for what is rendered in English as 'frustration'.

would be a totally inadequate metaphor – and this is in fact the only satisfactory way I can see of explaining the lines (continuities) and the gaps (discontinuities) in Freud's own diagram (*Figure 1*).

As Derrida (1967) has pointed out, Freud never gave up the inscriptive or "grammatic" model of the trace, for it reappears in 1925 in the model of the mind based on the 'mystic writing pad' (*Standard Edition*, XIX, 227–32): the endlessly erasable wax tablet made as a toy for children. This model is obviously connected with the metaphor of the dream as a palimpsest (James Sully, quoted in *Standard Edition*, IV, 135, note 2), and as a hieroglyph or pictograph (*Bilderschrift*).

In 1914 Freud sought to replace the inscription theory with a semiotic model based on the difference between iconic signs (thing-presentations) and word-presentations. It is typical of the many actual and apparent contradictions of Freud that this new model in no way contradicts the first, as he seems to assume, and that he introduced this 'new' viewpoint in the same year that he added the note about the erasure of writing on parchment (the palimpsest) to *The Interpretation of Dreams*.

Freud put the new problem of the relationship of presentation between the conscious and the unconscious in these terms:

What we have permissibly called the conscious presentation [*Vorstellung*] of the object can now be split up into the presentation of the WORD and the presentation of the THING. . . . We now seem to know all at once what the difference is between a conscious and an unconscious presentation. The two are not, as we supposed, different registrations of the same content in different physical localities, nor yet different functional states of cathexis in the same locality; but the conscious presentation comprises the presentation of the thing plus the presentation of the word belonging to it, while the unconscious presentation is the presentation of the thing alone. . . . Now, too, we are in a position to state precisely what it is that repression denies to the rejected presentation in the transference neuroses: What it denies to the presentation is translation into words which shall remain attached to the object. A presentation which is not put into words, or a psychical act which is not hypercathected [attended to], remains thereafter in the *Ucs.* in a state of repression (*Standard Edition*, XIV, 201–2).

Freud had previously said, and the distinction is again a crucial one:

Even in the unconscious, a desire [*Trieb*], cannot be represented otherwise than by a *Vorstellung*. If the desire did not attach itself to a presentation or manifest itself as an affective state, we could know nothing about it (XIV, 177).

In reference to unconscious "instinctual impulses" or desires (*Triebregungen*), he goes on: "Yet its affect was never unconscious; all that had happened was that its PRESENTATION had undergone repression" (XIV, 178). Or, in Lacan's terminology, "c'est le signifiant qui est refoulé".

6. *Condensation and Displacement*

> The memories of childhood come
> to life again when we reach the
> middle of our lives – like the lines
> of a palimpsest manuscript which
> are made to reappear by
> chemical processes.
> GERARD DE NERVAL: *Angélique* (1853)

In the passages previously quoted from Letter 52 and from the "Psychotherapy of Hysteria", one detects the Lockean principles of association by similarity (simultaneity) and association by contiguity (causality). Just as there is an internal connection in Freud's models between *Vorstellung* (translated 'idea', 'image', 'concept', 'presentation'), *Darstellung* ('representation', 'scene of a performance'), and the theory of distortion (*Entstellung*) in dreams and symptoms, the two processes of similarity and contiguity are clearly related to those of condensation and displacement in the theory of dreams, jokes, and symptoms.

Freud first came to recognize the "mechanism" of condensation (*Verdichtung*) in the simple fact that the dream itself is much shorter and much more compressed than its verbal representation (the dream-text). Dreams are 'laconic', as is the dream-text itself in relation to its later interpretation. Condensation represents the 'nodal point' (*Knotenpunkt*) of the dream; it will be like a railroad switch in the dream-work, always allowing multiple interpretations (overdetermination).

After noting that it is impossible ever to know whether a dream has been fully interpreted, Freud goes on to the use of words in dreams: "The work of condensation in dreams is seen at its clearest when it handles words and names. It is true in general that words are frequently treated in dreams as though they were things, and for that reason they are apt to be combined in just the same way as thing-presentations" (*Standard Edition*, IV, 295–6).

He often employs the related concepts of 'password' and 'switchword' in his analyses of symptoms and dreams.

Displacement (*Verschiebung*) is less clearly defined. It is a form of distortion (transposition) or 'indirect representation' in dreams, in respect of both words and images. The censorship will displace the center of the dream onto objects or words of minor importance, and thus reveal its latent content. Displacement in dreams, for Freud, not only covers any kind of "diversion from a train of thought but every sort of indirect representation as well", including "substitution by a piece of symbolism, or an analogy, or something small" (*Standard Edition*, VIII, 171). In this context (the context of presentations), he also employs the term *Verschiebungsersatz*: 'displacement-substitute'. Connected with the concept of displacement in his early writings are a number of other terms, including 'dislodge' (*dislozieren*), 'transpose' (*transponieren*), and *Übertragung* itself ('transference', 'translation') in the usual nontechnical German sense, as well as concepts involving 'false connections' and 'conversion'. Displacement as a mode of symptom formation is one of Freud's earliest methodological terms, referring to the transfer of a 'quantity of affect' from one presentation to another, or from a presentation to the body itself (hysteria). This device is especially evident in obsessional neurosis.

7. *Metaphor and Metonymy*

Lacan has sought to correlate Roman Jakobson's analysis of the two poles of language with Freud's condensation (metaphor or symptom) and displacement (metonymy or desire). Much of Lacan's interpretation of Freud seems impossible to justify from a critical semiotic perspective, but I shall not attempt any critique at this point. I mention Lacan's name as my immediate source of the correlation between psychoanalysis and linguistics (Lacan, 1956b), but it was in fact Jakobson who first established it.

Any linguistic sign, says Jakobson (1956: 55–82), involves two methods of arrangement: combination and contexture, and selection and substitution. Thus there are always two possible interpretants (Peirce's term) of the sign, one referring to the code and the other to the context of the message. The interpretant referring to the code is linked to it by similarity (metaphor), and the interpretant referring to the message is linked to it by contiguity (metonymy). For example, the word 'hammer' is linked by metaphor to the code where hammer stands for a 'tool for driving nails' and linked by metonymy to the rest of the message ("Bring me the hammer", "This is a hammer", "Hammer!", "Hammer?").

Selection (the relation of similarity) and combination (the relation of contiguity – the metaphoric and the metonymic ways – are considered by Jakobson to be the two most fundamental linguistic operations, whether at the level of phonemes or at the level of semantemes or words. In psycho-pathology he discovers that aphasia can be divided into variants of two broad types: CONTIGUITY DISORDER (where contextual, connective, and auxiliary words are the first to disappear) and SIMILARITY DISORDER (where the same contextual words are those most likely to survive). In the first, the patient may employ a telegraphic style, or he may be able to understand and say 'Thanksgiving', for instance, but be totally unable to handle 'thanks' or 'giving'. In the second, he might be unwilling or unable to name objects pointed to, but will perhaps offer some associated remark about them instead of the name. In the final chapter of his remarks on aphasia, Jakobson deals with the metaphoric and metonymic poles in the wider context of normal speech and literature:

> In normal verbal behavior both processes are continually operative, but careful observation will reveal that under the influence of a cultural pattern, personality and verbal style, preference is given to one of the two processes over the other. . . .
>
> In manipulating these two kinds of connection (similarity and contiguity) in both their aspects (positional and semantic) – selecting, combining and ranking them – an individual exhibits his personal style, his verbal predilections and preferences (pp. 76–7).

In literature, he continues, poetry is of course predominantly metaphorical, but the 'realistic' trend in modern literature (for instance the rise of the 'realistic' novel) is predominantly metonymic. Jakobson goes on to consider the application of this polarity in Freud: "A competition between both devices . . . is manifest in any symbolic process, either intrapersonal or social. Thus in an inquiry into the structure of dreams, the decisive question is whether the symbols and the temporal sequences used are based on contiguity (Freud's metonymic 'displacement' and synecdochic 'condensation') or on similarity (Freud's 'identification and symbolism')" (p. 81). It will be seen that Lacan's use of the polarity between metaphor and metonymy – the two processes cannot, of course, be actually separated from each other – is slightly different from Jakobson's. Freud's usage in this respect is ambiguous, but the equation of the relationship between these terms with that between condensation and displacement is not incompatible with Freud, since the importance of metaphor and metonymy in communication is correlative to the importance Freud assigns to condensation and displacement in the formation of jokes, slips of the tongue or pen, dreams, and symptoms in general: ". . . One . . . of these logical relations is very highly favoured by the mechanism of dream-formation; namely, the relation of similarity, consonance or approximation – the relation of 'just as'. . . . The representation of the relation of similarity is assisted by the tendency of the dreamwork towards condensation" (*Standard Edition*, IV, 319–20). And, of course, Jakobson's theory is no more than a linguistic version of Locke's theory of the association of ideas, already mentioned, which has a venerable lineage, including Plato, Aristotle, Condillac, J. S. Mill, besides Freud himself.

One of Jakobson's examples of similarity disorder (the choice of the metonymic pole) is so striking that it must be quoted here. It is taken from the work of the novelist Gleb Ivanovich Uspenskij (1840–1902). His first name and his patronymic (usually combined in polite intercourse in Russian) for him split into two separate beings: Gleb was endowed with all his virtues, while Ivanovich, the name relating the son to the father, became endowed with all his vices. A literary portrait typical of the writer, in which the parts totally obscure the whole, runs as follows (p. 80):

> From under an ancient straw cap with a black spot on its shield, there peeked two braids resembling the tusks of a wild boar; a chin grown fat and pendulous definitively spread over the greasy collars of the calico dicky and in thick layer lay on the coarse collar of the canvas coat firmly buttoned at the neck. From below this coat to the eyes of the observer there protruded massive hands with a ring, which had eaten into the fat finger, a cane with a copper top, a significant bulge of the stomach and the presence of very broad pants, almost of muslin quality, in the broad ends of which hid the toes of the boots.

The metonymic process here is clearly a progressive displacement; the order of top to bottom is not simply the result of a principle of literary style as such. As I mention at the end of the analysis of Freud's forgetting of the name 'Signorelli' below, there may be some theoretical value in seeking an overall preference for metaphor[3] in neurosis and for metonymy in schizophrenia, and Jakobson's example would certainly support such a correlation.

[3] Note Ella Sharpe's definition of metaphor (Fliess, 1940: 277) as something "which like a symptom, is a compromise between the ego, superego, and id". Depending on a version of the Lockean *tabula rasa* and upon an emergent theory of language (Grindon: "No word is metaphysical without its having first been physical"), she describes metaphor (i.e., speech) as possible ontogenetically only when the bodily orifices become controlled. This control allows for 'outer-ance' (i.e., *outrance*, utterance). Unfortunately, for all its interest, the article depends upon an atomistic and reductionist epistemology which replaces communication by intrapsychic conflict and overdetermination by predetermination.

What interests us here is the relationship between the paradigmatic (metaphor) and the syntagmatic (metonymy) in communicational and linguistic processes. Within a discourse or communication, these terms describe the relationship between synchrony (Saussure's 'axis of simultaneities') and diachrony (Saussure's 'axis of successions'). Related to this double process, when we consider the question of substitution, is Saussure's conception of the 'exchange value' of a word as opposed to its 'use value' (signification). Thus a word may be exchanged for an idea or for another word (substitution) or it may have a signification by its diacritic relation to and distinction from other words (combination) (1916a: 160).

Saussure points out that when he says that values

> correspond to concepts, it is assumed to be understood that concepts are purely differential, defined not by their content, but by their relationships with the other terms of the system. Their most exact characteristic is to be what the others are not (p. 162).

"In language, there are only differences, without positive terms." The proof of this lies in the fact that

> the value of a term can be modified without our changing in any way either its sense or its sounds, but only by the fact that some neighboring term or other has undergone a modification (p. 166).

It will be clear that the significance of Freud's forgetting of the name 'Signorelli' analyzed below – which, since it is a proper name, has neither signification nor meaning but only a designating power – only comes out in the relationship between the forgetting and the paralogisms which were exchanged for it. The signification of the substitutes for the missing name appears only in the difference or the relation (which is nowhere) between 'Signorelli' and what supplemented its absence.

8. The Repression of the Signifier

In September 1898, Freud forgot the name 'Signorelli'. His subsequent analysis is the first fully developed psychoanalytical approach to the question of the symptom in 'neurosis' and 'hysteria'.

There are three accounts[4] of the forgetting, which differ in significant

---

4 Letter 96 (September 22, 1898) (Freud, 1954: 264–5); "The Psychical Mechanism of Forgetfulness" (1898), Standard Edition, III, 289–97; The Psychopathology of Everyday Life (1901), Standard Edition, VI, 2–8; 12, note 2; 13 and note; 24–5; 26; 55–6.

details and emphasis. They are inextricably bound up with a whole set of other references to Freud's 'self-analysis' (with Fliess as the interlocutor).[5] For the purposes of this exposition, I shall simplify the overdetermination of the details of the incident here.

The three accounts should be read in detail, but the essence of the incident is as follows. While on holiday in Bosnia-Herzegovina, during a carriage drive with a chance acquaintance, and before coming to the subject of Signorelli's fresco *The Last Judgment* at Orvieto, Freud had been discussing the characteristics of the Turkish inhabitants of the area. He had remarked in particular on what he had been told by a Dr Pick about the extraordinary confidence of Turkish patients in their doctors and their great resignation to fate. In response to a doctor's death sentence, they are wont to reply: "*Herr*, what is to be said? If he could be saved, I know you would have saved him." But their attitude to sexual disorders was, Freud knew, rather different, and the example he quotes as immediately running through his mind also began with the patient addressing the doctor as *Herr*: "*Herr*, you must know if THAT comes to an end then life is of no value." Freud was speaking German at the time, but had for some weeks been speaking Italian, "translating it in his head", as he puts it. At the same time as he thought to himself that there was probably some intimate connection between these two attitudes, Freud 'delicately' avoided telling his partner in conversation of the second feature of the relation between death and sexuality as revealed in the relationship of Turkish patients to their doctor.

Thus, Freud sought to divert his conscious attention from the theme of death and sexuality. Shortly afterwards, the conversation turned to the subject of Italian painting, and Freud, by a rather natural further association, asked his companion whether he had seen the fresco at Orvieto by. . . . Impressed as he had been the previous year by Signorelli's work (at Bolsena in particular), and in spite of his admiration for this particular painting, he could not name the painter. The four-part fresco in question is variously called the *Last Judgment* (*Weltgericht*) or the *Four Last Things* (Death, Judgment, Hell, Heaven). It was at Orvieto that Freud had seen an Etruscan tomb, complete with two skeletons, which he later associated, in his well-known 'dissection' dream, with 'Old Brücke' (Freud's "greatest authority", whose judgment on his students was notoriously harsh, for all his 'kindly' qualities). He also associated the tomb with his own self-analysis through which the oedipal theme had emerged (1897), with his anxiety in the dissection dream over his body in bits and pieces and over

---

[5] Letters 48, 50, 54, 64, 65, 70, 71, 77; *Standard Edition*, IV, 238–40, 247–8; V, 427–9, 452–5, etc.

the chasm (*Abgrund, béance*) which yawned before him in it, and with his own entry into the grave (V, 452–5).

However, along with the loss of the signifier 'Signorelli', there rose in his consciousness an "ultra-clear" representation of Signorelli's self-portrait in the fresco. But this face, the symptom of his anxiety, was completely without signification for him, because he could not put it into words. What is not brought out in the third account (in *The Psychopathology of Everyday Life*) is the fact that the paralogism lasted for several days, causing Freud an "inner torment". Freud anguished over the absent name until it was supplied to him by another stranger some days later. And when the signifier returned, the ultra-clear vision of the master-painter's features faded away.

In his attempt to recover the name, he thought of two others: 'Botticelli' and 'Boltraffio'.

The elements of the overdetermination of the paralogisms explicitly mentioned by Freud are:

1 *Herr* (*Signor*) – Turks ("Herr . . .") – death and sexuality;
2 *Trafoi* (-traffio) – where a former patient of his suffering from a "sexual disorder" had just committed suicide – death and sexuality;
3 *Herz* (heart) – *Pick* (spade), the name of his Bosnian informant about Turkish attitudes to death and sexuality (III, 296, note 1);
4 *Herz* (heart) – which, "as a sick bodily organ, played a part in the thoughts I have described as having been repressed" (death and sexuality) (III, 296, note 1).

From the internal evidence of Freud's own discourse, we can add a number of other elements. These bring out oedipal and castration themes, as well as those of identification with the mother and the dead father. They emphasize the theme of the Last Judgment of the (Symbolic) Father, with his diminutive, the son, the little master (Signorelli), at his right hand.

The locus of the father is variously occupied by a number of persons. First, and obviously, it is occupied by Jakob Freud, *der Alte* (*senior*), who had died in 1896. 'Old Brücke' is the figure who demands the dissection in the dream about self-analysis, which ends in a representation of the Etruscan tomb Freud had seen at Orvieto, but with the addition in the dream of two dead children to match the two adult skeletons he had actually seen. (The décor of the dream is taken from Rider Haggard's *She* and *The Heart of the World*). Theodor Meynert, the former mentor and male hysteric who so vehemently opposed Freud's theory of male hysteria, occurs in the related 'absurd' dream about a dead father (who, like the father in the dream referred to in Chapter III, is dead but does not know it). Freud was suffering from hysterical symptoms of the heart trouble which had characterized his father's death, throughout the Signorelli incident. These symptoms are related to a dream of sexual exhibitionism associated with the "prehistoric" old nurse who played such an important part in Freud's 'self-analysis' (Letter 64, May 31, 1897; *Standard Edition*, IV, 238–40, 247–8).

The Meynert dream is related to Fliess by the date 1851, for Fliess had predicted that Freud would die at 51. (Freud begins Letter 54 to Fliess, written at the age of 41, with the words "Give me ten more years", and end with his choice of epigraphs for the projected article on sexuality: "From heaven through the world to hell.") Freud's fainting fit in 1912 ("How sweet it must be to die"), which was directly connected with the quarrel and break with Fliess in 1900, finds its interpretation in Letter 52 (1896): "Attacks of giddiness and fits of weeping [in hysteria] – all these are aimed at the Other [*den Anderen*] – but most of all at that prehistoric, unforgettable Other who is never equalled by anyone later" (I, 239). The oedipal theme is explicit in Letter 70 (1897), which also deals with the Godfearing old nurse, representing his mother, with whom Freud found himself identified in his dreams (Letter 71). The same dream also deals with the railway journey leading to his later railway phobia and with the vision on the train of seeing *matrem nudam*, as he delicately puts it. The injury to his face on the same or a similar railway journey, alluded to in Letter 70, is made explicit in the article of 1899 on "Screen Memories" – which often involve ultraclear (*überdeutlich*) images (III, 310, 312f). The one-eyed doctor and the one-eyed teacher of his past are also mentioned in Letter 71.

The overdetermination of this incident is already startling. But there is more. Throughout the analysis runs the theme of Freud's expected promotion to the title of 'Herr Professor', which was denied him in September 1897 because of his race, by the Minister of Education, the Freiherr von Hartel. Fliess had joked about the title in a letter of June 6, 1897 (cf. Letter 65), and in early 1898 (Letter 83), Freud returns to the subject:

There is a rumour that we are to be invested with the title of professor at the Emperor's jubilee on December 2nd [1898]. I do not believe it, but I had a fascinating dream on the subject; unfortunately it is unpublishable, because its background, its deeper meaning, shuttles to and fro between my nurse (my mother) and my wife. . . .

Shortly before the Signorelli incident (on August 31, 1898) Freud had described the Czar to Fliess as an untrustworthy obsessional neurotic

(Letter 95), a statement for which he had already provided the (decontextualized) psychological interpretation in Draft N (May 1897):

Hostile impulses [*Impulse*] against parents (a wish that they should die) are also an integral part of neuroses. They come to light consciously in the form of obsessional presentations [*Zwangsvorstellungen*]. In paranoia the worst delusions of persecution (pathological distrust of rulers [*Herrscher*] and monarchs) correspond to these impulses. They are repressed at periods in which pity for one's parents is active – at times of their illness or death. On such occasions it is a manifestation [*Äusserung*] of mourning to reproach oneself for their death (what is known as melancholia) or to punish oneself in a hysterical fashion (through the mediation of the idea [*Idee*] of retribution) with the same states [*Zustanden*] [of illness] that they have had.... It seems as though this death-wish is directed in sons against their father and in daughters against their mother (I, 254–5).

He goes on to speak of incest, displacement, formation of symptoms by identification (*Symptombildung durch Identifizierung*), and the MULTILOCULAR nature of symptoms and defense.

It is also perhaps possible to relate to the general theme the forgetting of the painter's first name, Luca (light), which came back to Freud immediately upon his being told the last name. Although he does not explain why, Freud indicates that it was this fact that showed repression to be at work and not true forgetfulness (Letter 96). It happens that Freud's first reported paralogism was to forget the name Mosen, while remembering the first name of the writer in question (Julius).[6] He thought that the forgotten surname might end in -*au*. It was on the train journey to Leipzig in 1859 that Freud first saw gas lighting, as the train passed through BRESLAU, and he described the lights as like "souls burning in hell". It was at Breslau that Freud had met with Fliess for the 'Congress' of December 1897, where Fliess first proposed the theory of bisexuality to him (which he later appropriated as his own). The early letters of 1898 are full of references to the town. Moreover, in his rememoration, Freud confused the train journey of 1859 with that in the opposite direction in 1860, when he saw his mother naked. (The dream of dissection, journeying, fear for his legs, and the grave at Orvieto includes an image of himself in a taxi passing through a house – an image which Freud describes as over-determined in several unspecified ways – much like a train passing through

---

[6] This he reported to Fliess on August 26, 1898, a few weeks before the forgetting of 'Signorelli'. Julius was the name of the young brother who died when Freud was nineteen months old, of whom Freud was extremely jealous (Letter 70).

a station). If this set of associations with Luca Signorelli is rather more speculative, it is nevertheless of prime significance that the man in the carriage for whom Freud avoided the topic of sexuality was a certain Herr FreyhAU. What was avoided for another in a discourse WITH a particular other became a message to and from the Other,[7] to and from the locus of the Other.

Although one's decision to describe metaphor or metonymy as synchronic or diachronic depends upon how one has chosen to view the system in question, the 'return of the repressed' in the Signorelli incident can be represented in the general way (which is illustrative rather than exhaustive) represented in *Figure 2*.

FIGURE 2

*Diachronic axis of succession: desire, displacement, combination, syntagm, message, contiguity.

†Synchronic axis of simultaneity: symptom, condensation, substitution, paradigm, code, similarity.

N.B. The sets of relations given above are to be read in terms of each other, and not as sets of simple synonyms. The placement of 'Signorelli' 'in' the unconscious is purely a matter of convention, since the primary process requires to be considered as an analog process of communication which cannot represent words as such (see Chapter IX).

'Botticelli' can be decondensed as follows:

BO(TTIC) → *Bo*snia → *Her-z-*egovina → "*Herr* . . ."
(death and sexuality) → *Herz* (death) — ELLI

The bracketed 'ttic' would represent an instance of what Freud calls the meaningless "hieroglyphic determinative" in the dream text, an element "not intended to be interpreted (or read) as the case may be" but whose function is "to establish the meaning of some other element" (XIII, 177). The 'nodal point' of the symptom is *Herr-Herz*. By the 'secondary revision' (XIV, 229) of the dream-text (to 'make better sense', since 'Botticelli' was

---

[7] In this interpretation, all the connections come from Freud's own text. Rosolato offers a set of more speculative and generalized associations around the theme of the forgotten first name ('Sigmund', of course, provides the first three letters of 'Signor') in his "Du Père" (1969: 36–58).

a ridiculous choice for a man of Freud's education, and in any case retained the '-elli'), the second substitute is produced, by metonymy from the first: the name 'Boltraffio', a painter Freud knew almost nothing about.[8] The image of Signorelli remains as the 'hallucinated' thing-presentation of the dream-wish, completely meaningless and without signification until it is put into relation with 'Botticelli' and 'Boltraffio'. (It is also a screen memory and a visual condensation of the theme of the Last Judgment.) Freud's *Angst* over the absence of 'Signorelli' gapes like an abyss before him as it did in the dissection dream. (Sartre's description of *Angst* evokes the same lack.) The image of Signorelli represents the "topographical regression through the unconscious" to perception in the dream-work.

The second symptom representing the name-of-the-father (*Signor–senior-Herrscher-der Herr Gott*, etc.) brings Freud closer to the identification of his own death with the death of the father (*Signor–Sig–ismund*), for the '-elli' disappears to be replaced by '-traffio' – the locus of a suicide. If 'Botticelli' comes primarily from its metaphoric relation to the code, 'Boltraffio' comes from the context, from its metonymic relation to the message (of Freud's desire). In a later repetition of the repression during a cardgame (III, 296, note 1), where Freud forgets the name of his informant about the Bosnian Turks (Pick), the theme of sexuality is muffled by the overriding theme of death, and no substitute appears:

$$\frac{(\qquad\qquad\qquad)}{\text{'Pick' (spades)} \leftrightarrow \text{'Herz' (hearts)}}$$

The "Bosnian authority" had already provided the necessary message of identification with the father when he remarked to Freud: "I'm not called *Her-z*, but Pi(c)k". The Lord and master and the heart are thus related, through the word for 'spades', to 'grudge' (*Pick, Pik, pique, rancoeur*) and to death.

9. *Manzanita Wood*

The trouble with the analysis of the Signorelli incident is that both it and the incident itself are simply unbelievable. On the one hand, it is easy to accuse Freud or a later commentator of just playing around with the ambiguities in language. "Anything can be proved that way" might be an understandable response. But it is not true that anything can be proved that way, because we are not concerned with just anything. We are con-

---

[8] At another level, 'Boltraffio' provides a set of associations around the theme of place-names (Freud had seen Signorelli's work at Bolsena in 1897):

BO → L → *Bol*sena → *Signor*elli (etc.) → *Trafoi* → TRAFFIO

cerned with the FUNCTION of the message, with its GOAL in a real and material context of senders and receivers. The precise importance of whatever aspect of this overdetermined symptom is significative for Freud himself is of course irrelevant to what we seek to show here. The incident is nevertheless a commentary on the oedipal relations between father and son in a typical Viennese family of the nineteenth century. I would certainly make no claim to extend this form of the oedipal theme to a general interpretation of mankind (cf. Fanon, 1952: 152, 180; Ortigues, 1966). Quite the opposite in fact. But it seems clear that in any society of alienation similarly constituted on patrocentric and phallocentric lines, similar symptoms will be found in the communication between individuals.

What I have sought to show here is the applicability of Jakobson's analysis of the two poles of language – which are actually the two poles of communication in the semiotic sense – to psychoanalysis, so that a similar polarity can be developed in the context of the goalseeking adaptive system (Chapter XII). But in an attempt to demonstrate the controlling function of language in any culture, I have also sought to show that psychoanalytic theory really does involve PLAYING AROUND WITH WORDS. And if anyone should say that it is all a semantic game, I am sure that Freud would be most gratified to hear it.[9]

I have said that the Signorelli incident is unbelievable and that the interpretation is open to criticism. I must therefore introduce an even more unbelievable incident of playing with words. This example further confirms the necessity of a contextual theory of symbolism. In the following example, taken from Bateson, no outside interpretation is possible until the subject who produced the message provides us with the key.

The example will, I think, illustrate the applicability of the relational categories of metaphor and metonymy to what is called schizophrenia. For Freud, the difference between the work of the symptom and dream and that of the schizophrenic 'language of the unconscious' lies in the absence of repression and negation, replaced in it by rejection (*Verwerfung*) or disavowal (*Verleugnung*). Freud explains the difference in "The Unconscious" (1915):

---

[9] This incident provides an excellent example of the necessary tautology of the axioms of the scientific discourse. If you accept the analysis of the Signorelli incident, then you must also accept the psychoanalytic theory of language. But the psychoanalytic theory of language is founded – both historically and theoretically – on this incident. Similarly, if you accept Newtonian mechanics, you will agree that the physical universe is ordered. But the 'ordered universe' is precisely the hypothesis upon which Newtonian mechanics is founded. Thus the celebrated "I don't make hypotheses" is the *Verneinung* necessary to the foundation of the Newtonian discourse (cf. also Chapter VIII on 'gravity') – and Leibniz never did believe it.

In schizophrenia words are subject to the same process as that which makes the dream-images out of latent dream-thoughts – they undergo condensation, and by means of displacement transfer their cathexes to one another in their entirety. The process may go so far that a single word, if it is especially suitable on account of its numerous connections, takes over the representation of a whole train of thought (*Standard Edition*, XIV, 186).

and in the "Metapsychology of Dreams" (1915):

In schizophrenia, what becomes the subject of modification by the primary process are the words themselves in which the pre-conscious thought was expressed; in dreams, what are subject to this modification are not the words, but the thing-presentations to which the words have been taken back. In dreams there is a topographical regression [to perception]; in schizophrenia there is not.

He goes on to say that in the psychoanalytic work of dream interpretation, this difference is not so obvious, for, since the interpretation follows the paths from the latent thoughts to the elements of the dream, since it "reveals the way in which verbal ambiguities have been exploited, and points out the verbal bridges between different groups of material", we get the impression now of schizophrenia, now of a joke, "and are apt to forget that for a dream all operations with words are no more than a preparation for a regression to things" (XIV, 229).

Although both operations are indissolubly linked, and although the question begs for further examination, if we consider metaphor to involve primarily a change in the selections from the code and metonymy to involve primarily combinations in the message, it may be useful to say that schizophrenia is more metonymic than metaphoric (cf. Jakobson's example quoted above). In other words, if we change the level of the analysis, the polar relation we began with in order to distinguish the processes within a certain level, can be applied to distinguish levels. Metaphor and metonymy are not entities. They are categories of distinction, not bags to put things in. Neither describes an isolable thing; they describe a relation – which is nowhere. That is to say, this polar distinction itself has signification only in a context, and since everything has everything else as its context, it is up to the commentator to define the context he has decided to talk about. (See below, Chapter V.) A re-reading of Jakobson's article will surely demonstrate this: if we change perspective, all his metonymies turn out to be metaphors, and vice versa.

The reason for attributing a preference for metaphor in so-called neurosis and for metonymy in so-called schizophrenia is a methodological one. 'Neurosis' and 'schizophrenia' are not distinct categories in reality, but in terms of the relationship between repression (and negation) and disavowal, it is useful to distinguish the processes involved. According to Freud, the operation of repression in neurosis is such that the 'patient' may defend himself against the return of the repressed by a *Verneinung* or negation. But the relationship of disavowal in schizophrenia is such that repression is not the primary factor. Instead of repression, one finds condensation, refusal, and disavowal, all of which are possible (as in analog communication) without the use of 'not'. (Freud does not, of course, imply that 'not' does not occur in patients diagnosed as schizophrenic.) As in animal communication, the 'schizophrenic' discourse – which treats words like things (Freud), which treats the abstract as though it were concrete (Goldstein) – will be obliged TO SAY THE OPPOSITE OF WHAT IT MEANS IN ORDER TO MEAN THE OPPOSITE OF WHAT IT SAYS (Bateson). For an animal to say "I don't want to fight", for example, he must refuse to fight. But for the animal to say "I am not fighting", he must fight and then stop fighting.

Repression can be thought of as a paradigmatic 'crossing of the bar' between the secondary and the primary system, as in *Figure 2*. Disavowal, however, in the sense of entirely contradictory attitudes or theories coexisting in the 'patient' and in his discourse, is to be thought of as syntagmatic. The example that follows, which is of course a carefully selected one, will demonstrate this difference.

It occurs in Bateson's "The Message: 'This is Play' " (1956), which is one of Bateson's most important contributions to the theory of animal and human communication.[10] Bateson describes a "symbolic form of construction" used by one of his patients as a statement to him that the patient was willing to give up a certain form of concealment. The patient complained that he was an "end-table made of manzanita wood". (Manzanita, 'little apple', is a California shrub.) Obviously, this is a rather ordinary example of the patient referring to himself as an object. But he also makes himself something simply CONTIGUOUS to something more important (end-table). It is also an example of the somewhat poetic 'schizophrenic' who tests the therapist to see whether he is indeed human – which in institutions, as elsewhere, is highly improbable. Bateson passed the test. The

---

[10] Bateson views animal play as a primordial metacommunication (in the strict sense of a message about the mode of a message) about the analog communication involved in fighting. In my interpretation, we can say that the 'nip' is the METONYMIC SIGN of the bite (contiguous part for a whole), but not the bite itself, which is a signal. The nip thus becomes a METAPHOR in a new code of communication. Cf. Chapters VII and IX.

patient was refusing food at the time, and the institution wanted to force-feed him. Bateson sought to put him in a situation where eating food could be dissociated from the institution and succeeded in getting him to eat a meal in a restaurant. After the meal, the patient sat back in his chair and said: "Man's an eater. If the circumstances were resolved, he would."

This metonymic chain can be represented as a decondensation:

MANZANITA (if the circumstances were resolved, he) WOOD

(There was also an overdetermined reference to a woman called 'Anita' – Man's Anita – which was not resolved). Here the symptomatic absence occurs within the message itself, not as a metaphoric presence or absence at the level of the code. In 'manzanita wood', there is no failure of translation (*Versagung der Ubersetzung*), no misplacing (*Entstellung*), no regression through the *Ucs.* to perception, no 'secondary revision', no 'other scene', no *Darstellung*, but only simple homophony in which the 'literal' and the 'figurative' coalesce. 'Manzanita wood' is what Bateson calls a "metaphor which is meant", in which the Wine IS the Blood. Whereas both the translation of 'Signorelli' and the absence of 'Pick' in the two previous examples tend primarily towards selection and substitution (at the same time as they are dependent on contiguity and displacement at another level), 'manzanita wood' tends primarily towards combination and contexture (at the same time as it depends on similarity and condensation). In both examples, however, it is at the level of displacement in the message that the desire (*Wunsch*) is expressed. (Suicide, said one 'schizophrenic' patient, means 'jumping to a conclusion'.)

And if you have ever seen a manzanita shrub in the California desert, you will find this example even more delightful. As the shrub grows, a dead gray area splits the warm and silky red stem from itself: the tree itself is 'schizophrenic'.

10. *Postscript*

Cameron (1939: 54) deals briefly with the prevalence of the 'metonym' in 'schizophrenia'. However, since his so-called experimental method involves asking questions about causal relations, they would tend to force the patient into metonymic replies. In distinguishing schizophrenia from aphasia as such, Goldstein (1939: 27) makes the point about metonymy in a different way: "A word when used by a schizophrenic appears as PART OF an object or situation, not as a representative of it", as is the case for some patients with organic brain disease. In the same text, Von Domarus (1939: 108–13) gives examples of missing metonymic links. In discussing "paralogical thinking" in the terms of the "excluded middle" in the mode Barbara,

A: Certain Indians are swift
B: Stags are swift
C: Therefore certain Indians are stags

he points out that it is the intersection between A and B (the part common to both wholes) which allows for the confusion. Moreover, since everything which lies outside the intersection is irrelevant for the identity set up between each element of A and each element of B, the "law of contradiction is excluded from paralogical thinking" (cf. Chapter VII below, on boundaries and logical types). Thus a patient identified Jesus, cigar boxes, and sex, because, he said, Jesus is surrounded by a halo, the cigar box, by the box band, and the woman, by the 'sex glance' of men. (Compare Leach on the "tabooed overlap", 1964: 36.) Further on in this text, Angyal refers to 'schizophrenic' writing, which is often interspersed with drawings. These are not usually "illustrations" of the text, but a "continuous presentation" of the patient's ideas. (Such writing involves a switch from the digital to the analog in order to express the same set of 'thing-presentations'; cf. Chapter VII.) The pictures themselves often involve incongruous "system-connections" in the context of the "holistic organization" of the representation (pp. 115–23).

I cannot avoid remarking on the context in which these analyses are conducted. Benjamin (p. 74) refers to the" stupid" answers of the 'patients', thus annulling the context of a desire to please or displease on the part of the 'patient' in an institution full of men in white jackets who never get tired of asking silly questions and treating everybody like children (e.g., Kasanin, p. 131).[11] The implicit violence of the 'expert' who believes he is an 'expert' (cf. Lacan 1966: 280; Wilden, 1968a: 43, 151), is well

---

[11] In trying to distinguish between the categories of 'infantile', 'pathological', and 'primitive' thought – which are repeatedly reduced to one another by the one-dimensional thought of psychologists and anthropologists – Lévi-Strauss makes a similar point (1947: 111–13). He remarks on the fact that it is the constant (digital) questioning of the Navajo's (analog) learning processes by white anthropologists that convinces the Navajo that all whites are simple-minded or mentally retarded. In parallel fashion, one of Maruyama's 'in-culture anthropologists' wanted to research Navajo opinion on the first moon landing (1969: 234). As the Navajo pointed out, a Navajo had already been there, and the trip had taken him only one day, so why was it going to take the white man several days? But Lévi-Strauss manages to make what he says about the Navajo 'point of view' into an identity of opposition with the white 'point of view' (p. 111). Here he does not introduce the context through which the Navajo 'opinion' is not a simple opinion, but a critical metacommunication about white values.

demonstrated in the case of Cameron. He expresses surprise at one patient's insistence on writing down for him, what the patient had replied to "I get warm when I run because . . .":

> Quickness, blood, heart of deer, length,
> Driven power, motorized cylinder, strength.

Cameron comments (p. 53) that such an answer is not 'incoherent' or 'nonsense', but still, he adds, "it is very poor material for a conversation".

To conclude on a general note: in the progressive personal and material alienation of our times, one hears less and less about hysteria and neurosis, and more and more about schizophrenia. Whether or not one might legitimately conjecture a connection between this apparent change and the metonymic tendencies Jakobson notes in the nineteenth-century novel, I don't know, but the schizophrenic quality of the discourse of art and literature seems to have taken on collective characteristics in this century. If there is any truth to this speculation, it would bear investigating – with the double bind in mind – from the point of view of the increasing control of people through the communication of the mass media. One notes that Marcuse's analyses in *One-Dimensional Man* (1964) pick up many striking examples of metonymic disavowal – 'the clean bomb', SHAPE, NATO, STAGE – this last standing for 'Simulated Total Atomic Global Exchange', one of the games people play in the Pentagon.

Chapter III

Death, Desire, and Repetition

COMMENTARY ON SVEVO'S CONFESSIONS OF
ZENO

I

En pensant à présent à tous les fous que j'ai
connus chez le père Baryton, je ne peux
m'empêcher de mettre en doute qu'il existe
d'autres véritables réalisations de nos profonds
tempéraments que la guerre et la maladie, ces
deux infinis du cauchemar. . . . Cauchemar
d'avoir à présenter toujours comme un petit idéal
universel, surhomme du matin au soir, le
sous-homme claudicant qu'on nous a donné.
CÉLINE: *Voyage au bout de la nuit*

To speak of death and desire in Svevo's *Coscienza di Zeno* (1923) is to
speak of repetition and therefore of the kind of time in which repetition
operates. This is not the undifferentiated flow of an *a priori* time 'in itself',
nor is it the biological time of 'instinctual' repetition, but rather the time
of 'forward recollection' in a Kierkegaardian sense, where the subject
seeks in vain to correlate the future with the past according to a specific
model. Svevo's Stoic or Eleatic hero lives this kind of time and seeks
escape from it. While one part of him is involved in a (compulsive) repetition, the other seeks a paradoxical immobility:

Nothing helps one to concentrate so well as gazing for a long time at
running water. One remains perfectly still oneself and all the necessary
diversion is provided by the water, which is never the same for a single
instant. . . .[1]

[1] *The Confessions of Zeno* (Svevo, 1923: 381). The English title unfortunately
obscures the triple sense of the Italian: Zeno's conscience, knowledge, or consciousness. But *coscienza* of what?

Zeno's name, and this deliberate evocation of the Heraclitean flux, both clearly suggest the nature of Svevo's metaphysical preoccupation with time, inseparable as it is from movement; moreover, Svevo's dialectical psychology and his Hegelian view of human desire are intimately linked to an 'ek-static' conception of human time.

It is true that, outside the domain of science, very little has been added to what Saint Augustine had to say about human time, but obviously our consciousness and use of the category of time has greatly changed, especially since Hegel, and since the growth of the modern novel in which DURATION is not a simple décor, not an *a priori* outside the characters and outside their time, but more like a character in itself. Human time is that in which the future is primary; it is articulated on human desire. Using the Augustinian categories, one would say that the present of things future (hope) becomes the present of things present (perception) through reference to the present of things past (memory). The whole process is dependent upon that aspect of the human discourse which confers SIGNIFICATION upon hope, perception, or memory. Not only is the dialectic of human desire (desire of another desire, desire for recognition, desire of the Other) primary for Svevo's hero, but the intentionality of his discourse precisely fulfills the digital role of language in ordering time and in rendering his repetition meaningful. Kant had discovered that man needs both time and words to think in categories, and this notion was essential to Hegel's view of the dialectics of human existence in the *Phenomenology*, where he sought to chart a RATIONALIST path between the old antinomies of 'idealism' and 'realism'.[2] As Kojève remarks in his commentary on Hegel's view of time, language, and death (1947a: 370, 374):

> The real presence of Time in the world is . . . Man. . . . The real which disappears into the Past is maintained (as non-real) in the Present in the form of the Word-Concept. The Universe of the Discourse (the World of Ideas) is the permanent rainbow which forms over a waterfall; the waterfall is the temporal reality which is reduced to nothing or negated in the nothingness of the past.

This very image of the One and the Many in time and motion recalls Zeno himself on the river bank.

The Hegelian *Phenomenology* is a dialectic of opposition and identity

---

[2] "The concept [*Begriff*] without the intuition [*Anschauung*] is void; the intuition without the concept is blind." Hegel simply pushed this conception of the complementary relationship of digital and analog communication (or thought) to its limit. He denied the *a priori* category of time: "Time is the concept itself which is there in empirical existence and which presents itself to consciousness as an empty intuition" (Hegel, 1807a: 558).

which confuses the unity of oppositions (the symbolic differences of the 'unit of mind')[3] with the mirror-like identity of opposites (Lacan's Imaginary). But although Hegel's 'journey of consciousness' depends on the illusory reduction of difference to identity – the reduction of the difference between subject and object in the Absolute Spirit – the Hegelian conception of desire is what lies behind or explicates most modern conceptions of intentionality (Brentano, Husserl), of cathexis (Freud), of project (Heidegger, Sartre), and of goalseeking (non-mechanistic cybernetics). These concepts can also be related to the 'theory of deferred action' (*Nachträglichkeit*) in Freud, whereby the memory of past time depends on the present project of the subject: the intentionalization of the past changes with the intentionalization of the future. And, of course, as Lacan (1966) has pointed out, the words translated 'instinct' or 'drive' or 'instinctual impulse' in Freud (*Trieb*), as well as the concept of pleasure (*Lust*) and wish-fulfillment, can all be subsumed under the general category of desire, which is to be distinguished from instinctual need and from demand.

In his Heideggerian–Marxist reading of Hegel, on which most current views of Hegel depend, Kojève seeks to distinguish the digital and discontinuous realm of reason, discourse, logos, and concept from the analog continuum of exchange processes in nature. Although he shares the digital prejudices of most western thinkers, including Hegel, and tends to fall prey to a kind of existential utopianism, Kojève's commentary is essential to the concept of desire as goalseeking. At the end of the *Phenomenology*, Kojève points out, Hegel says that

> Nature is Space, whereas Time IS History. In other words: there is no natural, cosmic Time; there is Time only in so far as there is History, i.e., HUMAN existence, i.e., SPEAKING existence. Man who, in the course of History, reveals Being by his Discourse, is the "empirically-existing Concept" (*der daseiende Begriff*), and Time is nothing other than this Concept. Without Man, Nature would be Space, and only Space (1947a: 366).

In his commentary on the master–slave dialectic, Kojève defines desire as follows (1947a: 12, 14):

> For there to be Consciousness of self, it is therefore necessary that desire bear on a non-natural object, that is, on some thing that goes beyond given reality. This . . . is desire itself. For desire taken as desire – that is to say, before its satisfaction – is in effect only a revealed nothingness, only a non-real void. . . .

[3] See below, Chapter VIII. The unit of mind is the message-in-circuit in the ecosystem.

Man proves himself human by risking his life [in the struggle between the master and the slave] in order to satisfy his human desire, that is to say, his desire which bears on another desire. To desire a desire is to want to substitute oneself for the value desired by this desire. . . . To desire the desire of an other is thus, in the last analysis, to desire that the value that I am or that I 'represent' be the value desired by that other. . . . In other words, every human, anthropogenic, desire . . . is . . . a function of the desire of 'recognition'.

The relationship between desire and the 'existential' project – which is not simply existential, since all organisms are goalseeking systems – is further elaborated (1947a: 367, 368):

The movement engendered by the Future – this is the movement which is born of desire, that is, of specifically human desire, of desire which creates, . . . of desire which bears on an entity which does not exist in the real and natural World and which [as project] has not existed there. . . .[4]

The future is

. . . what is not (yet) and what has not (already) been. We know that desire can bear upon an absolutely NON-existent entity only on the condition of bearing upon another desire. . . . Desire is the presence of an ABSENCE: I am thirsty because there is an absence of water in me. Desire is thus clearly the presence of a future in the present: of the future act of drinking. . . .

If desire is the presence of an ABSENCE, it is not . . . an empirical entity. . . . It is, on the contrary, like a lacuna or a 'hole' in Space – a void, a nothingness. . . . Desire is thus necessarily the desire to negate [nier] the real or present given. . . . The NEGATED real – this is the real which has ceased to be: it is the PAST real, or the REAL Past.

In the Sartrean terminology, which is derived from Kojève, it is 'lack of being' (manque d'être), as 'ontological absence', which provides the possibility of the pour-soi's desire (Sartre, 1943: 652):

The for-itself is described ontologically as lack of being, and the possible belongs to the for-itself as what is lacking to it. . . . Liberty is the concrete mode of being of the lack of being. . . . Man is fundamentally desire of being . . . [for] desire is a lack. . . . The being lacking to the for-itself is the in-itself.

[4] The 'animal desire' and the 'human desire' which Kojève is seeking to distinguish here (but not entirely coherently) are the direct antecedents of Lacan's distinction between need and desire.

The in-itself (*en-soi*) is variously the plenitude of nature (which is necessary, whereas man, the for-itself, is contingent), Being (as opposed to existence), and the ego (as one's own alienation or one's own past). These somewhat dated metaphors continue to appear in new forms. It is around the conception of the in-itself as 'Being', that Sartre interprets man's past as his essence and his future as his existence, following the Hegelian aphorism: "Wesen ist was gewesen ist": "Being (or essence) is what was". The 'I' is existence, the 'me' or 'ego' is the essence. The pathology of desire is to seek to 'fix' that essence: to desire to be some 'body', and thus to turn one's 'self' into a thing (Sartre: 1946).

The connection one makes between the existential project and the alienation of the subject in the fixity of his 'ego' described by Sartre, depends on the perspective from which one views existentialism, as Sartre has demonstrated in his self-critical autobiography, *Les Mots* (1964). The goal of desire in the *Phenomenology*, for example, the "promise [*Wort*] of reconciliation" (*Versöhnung*), seems to be equivalent to the role of death in Freud. The difference is that for Freud the Being-towards-death of the 'death drive' or the 'desire for death' (*Todestrieb*) is a bioenergetic explanation for the behavior of the goalseeking system he is studying (and inadequate so long as it reduces all goals to the biological level), whereas for Hegel, reconciliation is what he believes to be a fully realizable goal of non-difference, a spiritual utopia which has its material correspondents in utopian socialism from Cabet to the contemporary 'love generation' and the 'Jesus cults'. Hegel's error, and the error of the human systems studied by Freud, is to confuse the socially and epistemologically coded relationships of opposition in our culture with the real material differences from which these oppositions derive, and to confuse the PROCESS of goalseeking with the goal itself. This is the reification of the lived dialectic. As Proust discovered in writing *A la recherche du temps perdu* (1913–27), the work of writing the novel itself was his goal. The *temps retrouvé* of the final pages does not represent the recovery of the lost object, but rather the critical realization that he is now ready to write the novel. As with Montaigne and his own 'novel of self-experience', the *Essays*, however, death was already about to provide the final punctuation mark to this individual quest, and thus raise it to the level of the collectivity.

II

It rests by changing.

HERACLITUS

Svevo's *Zeno* is above all a psychoanalytical novel written AGAINST psycho-analysts: an attack on the concept of mastery, on the subject-who-is-supposed-to-know. It is furthermore a sustained critique of the Imaginary (specular) values of western culture:

> Health cannot analyze itself EVEN IF IT LOOKS AT ITSELF IN THE GLASS. It is only we invalids who can know anything about ourselves (p. 146, my emphasis).

One can discover in Svevo's works many of the more important of the converging currents of twentieth-century thought some twenty or thirty years before we became ready to comprehend them. Apart from Hegel and Kierkegaard, *Zeno* immediately calls to mind the early Heidegger, the later Freud, and the most current readings of the Freudian texts. It is in this sense that – quite apart from his Heideggerean reflections on the 'absolute Master', death – Svevo wrote a novel about the master–slave dialectic of analysis and the problem of countertransference long before these difficul-ties had become matters of general technical concern; moreover, he made his novel depend upon the repetition discovered by Freud in 1914 and later extended to the whole process of analysis, even to life itself.

Zeno wants to kill his father and sleep with his mother. Fine. But Zeno says: So what?, and he sets out upon a work of analytic sabotage, bent on demanding to know what "Sophocles' diagnosis" (*sic*) can possibly mean. Through the studied use of every kind of alibi, protestation, self-justifica-tion, and denegation (*Verneinung*), through a liberal sprinkling of phallic, fetishistic, and incorporative symbols, through carefully chosen images, 'hysterical' (psychosomatic) symptoms, and a series of identifications, Zeno reveals that the oedipal interpretation offered by Dr S. in the final chapter of the book is in fact the 'correct' and 'orthodox' construction to be placed on his (triangular) relationship with the Other. And, as Zeno knows, his very denials reinforce the doctor's interpretation. The task of the novel, however, is to offer another interpretation, but in a mode of sustained irony which offers pitfalls for the unwary: for the alienated intellectual, for the *belle âme*, for the 'orthodox' analyst.

Dr S., who is the supposed editor of Zeno's psychoanalytical memoirs, sets the ironic tone of the novel in his *Preface* by confessing his annoyance at his patient for breaking off the analysis. But Zeno's attack on Dr S. is

conducted with all the subtlety of a patient who knows that he is manifesting a negative transference – and who knows that his analyst doesn't know
he knows.

There is no need to go into Zeno's "mass of truths and falsehoods" in
detail, but before coming to the central incident in the novel – his father's
death – something must be said about the general situation which is set up
in it. From the analyst's point of view everything Zeno says or invents
either inside or outside his analysis goes to reinforce the basic oedipal
interpretation. His phantasies and inventions could in fact be used to
support Freud's contention that it is not necessarily important, and sometimes impossible, to distinguish the 'real' rememorated material from the
'false'. But all of Zeno's resistances, symptoms, and defenses really serve
to put the theoretically omniscient and healthy analyst, and therefore the
society he represents, into question. For all his psychosomatic pains, his
limping, and his obsessions, Zeno doesn't seem particularly 'sick' at all,
and especially not in relation to the decaying bourgeois society of pre-1914
Europe to which he is expected to conform.

Early in the novel, quoting something his father-in-law had told him, he
states his position, which is amply justified by the book itself: "One must
always explain the matter clearly to one's adversary, for only so can one be
sure of understanding it better than he" (p. 89). He has to do with many
doctors in his 'confessions', and his thesis seems fairly clear: "It is worth
recording that I detected symptoms of disease in what the specialist regarded as healthy, and that my diagnosis turned out to be right" (p. 14). In
speaking of his wife, Augusta, whom he regards as perfectly healthy, he
makes the point more subtly:

> I am trying to arrive at the source of her well-being, but I know I cannot
> succeed, for directly I start analyzing it, I seem to turn it into a disease.
> And now that I have begun writing about it [twenty years later], I begin
> to wonder whether health like hers did not perhaps need some treatment
> to correct it. But during all the years I lived with her such a doubt never
> crossed my mind (p. 142).

We know that the fundamental question for Zeno is the relation of death
and desire, both linked by their essential nature to time. He desires escape
from what he sees as the degradation of lived time, he desires the certainty
of essence, he fears death – but like any mother's son in the social organization which has formed him, he also desires supremacy over those around
him, that is to say, he desires the death of others. From the very first words,
the whole novel is articulated on the Hegelian dialectic of the master and
the slave. Lurking in the wings is one of Zeno's questions, the question of

the child who asks "Am I EITHER good OR bad?" (p. 300), and Zeno makes sure that the answer is 'neither', for nothing bad he ever does is without good reasons, nothing good without bad reasons. Thus he successfully disposes of any ego-bound theory that might seek the 'real' Zeno in his essential goodness or badness, or in his degree of 'adjustment' or conformity. Like Rameau's Nephew in his experience of masters and slaves, Zeno is always other than what he or the reader thinks he is.

Zeno's 'problem' is not in himself but in his relationship to the Other. He sets off dutifully to get a "clear picture" of himself in response to the doctor's request for his memoirs, but nothing is revealed in them except a relationship to the Other which is dependent upon the alienation of Zeno's desire by the Other. At the very beginning of the novel, Zeno recounts how he was encouraged in his central (symbolic) vice, cigarette-smoking, by a friend who treated him and his brother to gifts of cigarettes. "But", says Zeno, "I am positive that he gave my brother more than me, and that therefore I was obliged to try and get hold of some for myself" (p. 6). In this seemingly trivial instance, Zeno carefully reveals, as authors like Proust and Stendhal had done before him,[5] that it is the social and socializing function of human desire to structure our desires on what the Other desires (or desires us to desire), the desired 'object' serving as a simple mediator between desiring subjects, or disappearing altogether in the mutual desire for recognition – the desire of a desire – which articulates the clash between the master and the slave. It is only a short step from here to that model of mediated human relationships in bourgeois society, the oedipal triangle itself, and this is in fact the step which Zeno takes.

Zeno steals money from his father to buy cigarettes, and later he steals his half-smoked cigars. There is presumably no need to dwell on this act of substitution for (and aggression against) his father. Later, again in relation to these thefts, he is the silent auditor in a simple scene between his mother and his father, which ends with the deliberately significant remark, picked up again later in the novel: "Her smile made such a deep impression on me that I immediately recognized it when I saw it one day long afterwards on my wife's lips" (p. 7). For Zeno, smoking and stolen cigars are the instruments in his struggle towards mastery over his peers and equality or better

[5] See René Girard, *Mensonge romantique et vérité romanesque*, translated by Yvonne Freccero as: *Deceit, Desire, and the Novel* (1965b). In spite of its idealistic and religious context, Girard's conception of triangular desire and his attack on the notion of autonomous desire are essential. All desire is mediated by an external or internal model, who, in the case of 'romantic' desire is inevitably a rival. *Le désir romanesque*, on the other hand, involves a self-critical transcendence of the dualistic and oppositional symmetries of the noble soul or the romantic or existential hero.

with the central master-figure, his father. Naturally, later on he character-istically denies this aggressive competition with his father (p. 375). The symbolic importance of smoking for this Napoleonic hero is reflected in his internal division into two personalities, as he puts it, the one seeking to continue smoking, the other to give it up. Smoking is the mediator in this conflict, which in itself supports his belief in his "latent greatness", for, he says, if he could only give up smoking, he could concentrate on "perfect-ing" himself. But in the conflict between his desire to smoke and his demands to give it up, he realizes something profound about the nature of his continually broken resolutions, something intimately linked to the transposed repetition of the oedipal situation throughout the rest of the novel. In making resolutions, he says, "you strike a noble attitude and say 'Never again!' But what becomes of the attitude if you keep your word? You can only preserve it if you keep on renewing your resolution. And then Time, for me, is not that unimaginable thing that never stops. For me, but only for me, it comes again" (p. 11).

This passage is central to the novel. It precisely describes what Bateson calls the "pride-in-risk" of the alcoholic (1971a). Bateson traces alcoholism to its source in the counter-adaptive, dualistic, epistemology of western society. Zeno has already discovered that his addiction to cigarettes in-volves a schizoid battle between a 'self' and an 'other'. This 'splitting of the subject' is symptomatic of the mind–body split endemic to our form of socioeconomic organization. It is this pre-programmed splitting which allows the alcoholic to personalize his battle with the bottle by depersonal-izing himself. He becomes the mind ('I'), and the bottle becomes the body ('it'): "*I* can resist IT". What he has done, of course, is to consciously make himself the equivalent of an 'it'.

In keeping with the schizoid values which necessarily result from the ideology of atomistic individualism (Chapter VIII), the bottle represents the 'body' that the 'mind' (the alcoholic) is supposed to be able to 'control'. However, once the alcoholic has made the bottle into the 'other', he has also projected his 'drinking problem' outside of his 'self'. He has – i.e., pos-sesses – a problem, and his problem is the bottle. Because the alcoholic naturally projects the anti-relational values of our social organization onto his own situation, he cannot understand that his problem is a relation, and not a thing. His objectification of the problem outside of the entity he has been taught to call his 'self', is consequently achieved at the price of making his atomistic 'identity' into a thing. Having made something of himself, the alcoholic is now in an ontological competition with another thing, the bottle – which represents his 'other' self. As Bateson remarks, the re-lation between the alcoholic and the bottle, after the event, is a highly personalized one. The classic rationalization for taking the one drink that will set him off on another binge is a conversation with this *alter ego*, the bottle, beginning: "Okay, baby. Let's you and me kiss and make up."

As an embodiment – at its 'highest stage' – of the competitive either/or values of our society, the alcoholic will necessarily and inevitably OSCILLATE between being on the bottle and being on the wagon. This oscillation is the result of what Bateson calls the alcoholic's deeply programmed sense of "pride". This is in fact a metaphor of what Marcuse has so aptly called the "performance principle" (1955). The alcoholic's 'pride' is not derived from something 'in' him. In order to 'survive' and 'succeed' in our society, one must 'perform'. The objectifying effects of 'performance' – making it, being some-body or other – are in effect derived from the primary processes of the SOCIOECONOMIC system, and not from the primary process of the alcoholic.

The alcoholic's pride in his performance – especially while he is still convinced that he can stop drinking whenever he chooses – cannot be reduced or eliminated by 'reason'. This is not simply because his 'pride' is so deeply programmed. Rather it is because the very values placed on 'rationality' in our society are the immediate sources of the irrational binary opposition between things in which the alcoholic now finds himself.

As Bateson emphasizes, quite apart from the specific difficulties which may encourage a person to take refuge in alcohol, social drinking in our society is almost entirely regulated by symmetrical relationships of competition. One either takes pride in being (or in having been) more drunk than anyone else, or else one takes pride in 'holding' one's liquor. In Zeno's language, whatever you do, you "strike an attitude". The incipient or actual alcoholic soon discovers that the bottle always represents a 'challenge' for him. And he never fails to try to meet the challenge of whether or not he can control his drinking. It is precisely because his personal and psychological survival depends, he thinks, on demonstrating the strength with which he can meet that challenge, that the bottle will always defeat him. This defeat is the result of the rules of feedback and goalseeking in Imaginary systems of opposition and identification (Chapter IX). It can also be explained in terms of desire. The confusion of process and goal engenders the OBSTACLE. As a result, desire is neither aimed at the process of seeking the goal, nor aimed at the goal itself. Desire becomes a desire for the obstacle, period. Since by definition – by the definitions of the desiring subject – an obstacle TO desire cannot be the effective goal OF desire, what happens if the obstacle is removed? As Zeno knows only too well, the subject is then faced with what seems to amount to an ABOLITION OF DESIRE ITSELF. It consequently becomes necessary to invent a new obstacle.

All self-destructive addiction is in essence an addiction to the obstacle.

What happens in the case of the alcoholic is the following. Besides its dangerous and frightening physical effects, the humiliating psychosocial effects of addiction to alcohol destroy the alcoholic's pride in his 'performance' and in his 'self-control'. Consequently, he takes up the challenge to his ability to perform as it is expressed by the demands of the others around him. He stops drinking. But his sobriety necessarily and inevitably destroys the very challenge which generated his state of sobriety in the first place. He has no way of continuing to prove himself against the challenge, for the challenge to stop drinking is gone. As Bateson puts it: "the CONTEXTUAL STRUCTURE of sobriety changes with its achievement" (my emphasis). Pride in performing AGAINST the 'other self' represented by the bottle can now be achieved ONLY by taking 'one little drink', for "symmetrical effort requires continual opposition from the opponent".

We can put this another way. When the bottle is the 'master', the alcoholic is in a complementary (one-down) relation to it. If this relation continues, it will destroy him. When he is on the wagon, on the other hand, he can never achieve 'mastery' over the bottle. Like Rabelais' *dive bouteille*, it simply sits there saying 'Drink'. The alcoholic is now in a symmetrical relationship of opposition and RIVALRY with the bottle. The only way, then, that he can 'prove' his 'mastery' over the bottle is to put himself in the one-down position again. He has to do what the bottle tells him to do: 'Drink'.

As Bateson concludes, unless the alcoholic can undergo the kind of spiritual (epistemological) conversion offered by the subtle and effective therapeutic techniques of Alcoholics Anonymous, he is lost. In the terminology of Chapters IV and V, the alcoholic is in a situation which he has MADE into a double bind (see note 9). Whether he drinks or does not drink, he never escapes his oscillation between these two impossible poles. If he has really 'hit bottom', however, then Alcoholics Anonymous can help him put himself into a 'therapeutic double bind' whose transcendence will restructure the programming rules, the values, and the perceptions which allowed him to create the alcoholic double bind in the first place.

Like 'schizophrenia', alcoholism projects epistemological errors about relationships into the domain of ontology. To drink or not to drink is an individual question. But alcoholism – like 'schizophrenia' – derives not from the individual, but from the organized destruction of analog or Symbolic relationships by the performance principle. If 'schizophrenia' tends to arise in the pathological communication of the family, alcoholism is its complement at the societal level. Here the pressure to conform to the desire of the Other by PROVING oneself – by proving one's self in relation to the apparently 'model performances' of others – drives us into a relationship of rivalry with those others. Both 'schizophrenia' and alcoholism are the products of the pathological organization of communication in the society at large. To perform means to be alienated by the desire of the Other; not to perform is already – by definition – either 'schizophrenic' or alcoholic.

This Other is not 'Otherness', in the sense of a necessary principle of relation to a collectivity. This Other is simply the personification of the underlying principles of our particular socioeconomic system. Like money, this Other is the general equivalent of all exchanges in the system; like money, this Other is Imaginary. Consequently anybody in a position of power or authority can come to represent the Other. For Zeno, this Other is his father, and Zeno's repetitions are an attempt to reconstitute his former position of slavery so as to maintain his psychosocial status as an entity defined by his opposition to others.

In this sense, Zeno is a representative of that class of people whose alienation by our alcoholic societal values is so far advanced that a dependency relationship of being a negative Other, or even a willing slave, is necessarily preferable to having, perhaps for the first time, to think about what they are actually going to do. The prospect of freedom from certain forms of competition and self-alienation, the prospect of freedom from the desire of the Other (as distinct from Otherness), is a frightening one indeed: in our epistemology – as in Zeno's – it is a definition of death.

Kierkegaard had already made Svevo's point about the synchronic value of repetition, in 1843: "The difficulty facing an existing individual is how to give his existence the continuity without which everything simply vanishes"; and he had answered the question by: "The goal of movement for an existing individual is to arrive at a decision, and to renew it" (quoted in Blackham, 1961: 9). For Zeno, existence is a similar double-binding tension between oscillating opposites, each repeated resolution being progressively subjected to an *Aufhebung* which maintains the process, and at the same time denies or disavows the problem. Faced with a doctor's order to give up smoking entirely, he sees "a great void and no means of resisting the fearful oppression which emptiness always produces". Naturally his father has only to encourage him to obey the doctor for him to smoke more vehemently than ever.

But the resolutions have another importance: they are put into WORDS: "It is curious how much easier it is to remember what one has put into words than feelings that never vibrated on the air" (p. 11). Moreover, they are DATED.[6] If they were not, they could not so easily be (symbolically)

---

[6] Cf. Heidegger (1927: II, 6: 81): ". . . The future as ecstatically understood – the datable and significant 'then' – does not coincide with the ordinary conception of the 'future' in the sense of a pure 'now' which has not yet come along but is coming along."

repeated, that is to say, integrated into a continuing *projet* or expectation on the basis of past repetitions. The resolutions should be linked, if possible, to 'objective' time, he says (e.g., the end of smoking linked to the end of the month), and Zeno even wishes that the dates themselves would repeat (p. 381).

Words imply the digitalization of time and impose order. Zeno unfortunately believes that in the human world it is the discourse of the subject (his self-organization), rather than the supposed 'non-order' of his analog 'feelings', which constitutes him in his humanity. "Time [in itself, as distinct from Time for me] is really very ill-ordered" (p. 381). The digital aspects of language and subjective time come to the subject from the Other and provide the means for his advent to subjectivity; language, the (usually) digital instrument of the analog goals of relationship (desire) can pervert those goals in cultures which overvalue the digital in communication and exchange (Chapters VII, IX).

Because of the overvaluation of the digital in modern industrial society – a valuation which is intimately connected with individualism, atomism, competition, and the historical development of capitalism and technology (Chapter VIII) – modern man is constitutionally divided from himself. And if Zeno talks constantly about his neurosis, his splitting from himself is more accurately to be described as schizoid or schizophrenic. Neurosis is in any case out of fashion these days (and not by accident). Such a splitting is only possible in societies whose socioeconomic organization inverts the logical typing of the analog and the digital. Zeno seems never to really escape the oppositions which are induced by the resultant alcoholic ideology. That all of the women in the novel (as elsewhere in Svevo's work) have names beginning with A is not fortuitous. The question of the absolute first and last is as central to Zeno's oscillations between impossible contraries, as is the question of the relationship between master and slave. The divisions around which Zeno's existence is articulated always and inevitably involve an oscillation between analog desire (goals) and digital control (reason).[7]

Zeno's considered diagnosis of his symbolic illness is that he suffers more from his resolutions than from his cigarettes, that his "personality . . . had become divided in two, one of which gave orders while the other was only a slave which, directly the supervision was relaxed, disobeyed its master's orders out of sheer love of liberty" (p. 16). Thus is the tension of the

[7] Cf. Kojève (1947a: 375, note 1): "For Man the adequation of Being and Concept is a process (*Bewegung*), and truth (*Wahrheit*) is a RESULT. It is only this 'result of the process' which merits the name of (discursive) 'truth', for only this process is Logos or Discourse."

obstacle maintained. In attempting to circumvent the resolutions against smoking with which he tries to order and control his life, Zeno becomes involved in another disagreeable enslavement. His 'pride-in-risk' makes him bet his business manager that he can stop smoking: "That bet proved excessively damaging to me. I was no longer alternately master and slave, but only a slave, and to Olivi, whom I hated. I immediately began to smoke" (p. 16).

Zeno's experience with Olivi (who, by his father's will, is the master of his money) is of course a repetition of the relationship with his father, and the necessity of his return to his resolutions is related to his profound desire for regularity and fixity in the flow of time. After his marriage, he is delighted by the fixed times for meals and so on: "All these hours had a genuine existence and were in their right place" (p. 142) – their right place, for this is symbolic of how Zeno, like the novelist, seeks to mark time. Only the present of things present has genuine existence, and that is nowhere. Thus it is that Zeno, embroiled in a diachronic process of transposed repetition, has the highest regard for any evidence of synchronic repetition – which conceals the flow of time: "Then Sunday came. . . . Though I work so little, I have always felt a great respect for this holiday, which divides life into short periods that make it endurable" (p. 96). "Things often repeat themselves with me: it was not at all impossible that I might pass that way again" (p. 26).

The assertion that, for Zeno, time "comes again" (but not 'in itself') returns us to another passage from Kierkegaard:

> [Repetition] explains the relation between the Eleatic School and Heraclitus, and that properly it is repetition which by mistake has been called mediation. . . . In this respect the Greek reflection upon the concept of κινήσις, which corresponds to the modern category of transition, deserves the utmost attention. The dialectic of repetition is easy; for what is repeated has been, otherwise it could not be repeated, but precisely the fact that it has been gives to repetition the character of novelty (1843: 52).[8]

Time is 'counted movement', said Aristotle, and it was precisely the impossibility of counting the repeated instants of movement in time which led Zeno of Elea to pose the famous paradoxes. Indeed the relationship of

---

[8] Note that both from the point of view of Constantine Constantius and from that of Kierkegaard himself, what is being analyzed in S.K.'s essay is the DESIRE for repetition. Kierkegaard is himself trapped in a series of Imaginary either/or oppositions, which accounts for his attempt to reduce Hegelian mediation to repetition.

the Heraclitean flux to the Parmenidean One is precisely that of a diachronic process to its synchronic states – the contemporary disguise of the
problem of change – where once again the mediator is homeostatic repetition in time. Zeno's paradoxes, answered by the anomaly that the sum of
a converging infinite series is finite, could very well be the models for the
problems of time and history with which his latter-day namesake is concerned. What, after all, is the central instance of repetition in the novel? It
is Zeno's relationship to his father, and, as will be clear presently, a special
instance of the discovery of finitude through the LOSS of that relationship.
The Eleatic's impossibly immobile arrow is in fact an open appeal to
essences, to fixity, perhaps even to immortality. Some people are attracted
by the permanence of stone, and this seems to be part of what Valéry is
saying in the well-known verses from the *Cimetière marin*:

> Zénon! Cruel Zénon! Zénon d'Elée!
> M'as-tu percé de cette flèche ailée
> Qui vibre, vole, et qui ne vole pas

Yet naturally, true repetition is impossible; outside the momentary and
ineffable flash of involuntary memory, nothing repeated is ever the same,
for if it were, the desire for repetition, for the obstacle, would be satisfied
and consequently . . . vanish.

III

> What we cannot reach flying, we must reach limping.
>
> .   .   .   .
>
> The Book tells us it is no sin to limp.
> (The last words of *Beyond the Pleasure Principle*)

In the second chapter of the book, Zeno watches his father die. But,
whereas he had found it comparatively easy to get over the earlier loss of
his mother, the death of his father cast a pall over the rest of his life:

> My mother's death and the healthy emotion it caused made me feel that
> everything was going to get better.
> My father's death, on the contrary, was an unmitigated catastrophe.
> Paradise had ceased to exist for me, and at thirty I was played out. . . . I
> realized for the first time that the most important, the really decisive
> part of my life lay behind me and would never return. . . . His death
> destroyed the future that alone gave point to my resolutions (p. 28).

The overture has been played. Having been trapped in the Imaginary world
of being a 'negative father', now Zeno tackles the central theme in earnest:

the death of his father and the transformation it effects on his own view of life. Naturally, he begins by expressing his guilt: "If only I had been nicer to him and mourned for him less, I should not have been so ill" (p. 28). His relationship to his father is a classic instance of the son who must admire, respect, and imitate his father, who must consequently hate him as the rival who possesses what the son desires, and who must seek by every means to proclaim his (illusory) liberty by surpassing him.[9] But it is a liberty, as we shall see, which Zeno must refuse. Compared with the old man and his stolid bourgeois moral and religious stability, his vacillating son is the weaker. Nevertheless, Zeno feels that he is the stronger of the two, because in contrast to his father's self-satisfaction, he has "a strong impulse to become better", but, he adds, in an immediate *Verneinung* which is a recurrent feature of especial significance in the novel, "this is perhaps my greatest misfortune" (p. 29). A few pages later, he reveals the unimportance of the question of who is "really" the stronger: all that is important is that the two subjects be RELATED BY OPPOSITION:

> Compared with him I felt myself strong, and I sometimes think that the loss of this weaker person with whom I could compare myself to my own advantage made me feel that my value had definitely diminished (p. 31).

As it happens, he recovers his 'value' later on, again through his dependence on the Other, by an extended repetition of his relationship to his father in his relationship to his brother-in-law, Guido: "Supporting himself comfortably on the unresisting balance-sheet, [Guido] played to perfection the part of lord and master" (p. 297). "Although he made a show of being strong, he seemed to me a weak creature who was in need of the protection I was so anxious to give" (p. 246). The net result of this protection is Guido's suicide.

Zeno's relationship to his father is, of course, a two-way street. Zeno

---

[9] This relationship of opposition and identification is of course another classic instance of the 'double bind' or the 'paradoxical injunction' (Bateson, Jackson, Haley, and Weakland, 1956). (See below, Chapter V.) Freud provided us with the 'categorical imperative' of the primary paradoxical injunction in the bourgeois family, in *The Ego and the Id* (1923). The relation of the superego (here equivalent to the ego ideal) to the ego "is not exhausted by the precept: 'You OUGHT TO BE like this (like your father)'. It also comprises the prohibition: 'You MAY NOT BE like this (like your father)'. . . ." This Freud describes as the "double aspect of the ego ideal" (*Standard Edition*, XIX, 34). I would describe it as a question of the difference between Imaginary opposition and Symbolic difference. The Christian mystery of the Trinity had already posed the problem. Over the question of whether the Son was ὅμοιος (like) or ὁμός (identical) to the Father, the Council of Nicaea (A.D. 325) decided in favor of the latter, and all hell broke loose.

detects his father's disappointment in him, his "old desire to punish me" (p. 32), and the old man's intention to continue to control his son after his death through the financial provisions of his will. Zeno is especially submissive at this point: "I was so docile and accommodating [over the will] that when I am tortured by the thoughts that I did not love him enough before he died, I always try to call up that scene" (p. 32). But even this submission is only a normal act of combined love and guile: "So long as my father was alive (no longer) I always felt contrary . . .' (p. 35). In the mutual struggle for recognition between himself and his father, Zeno knows that one of the protagonists must submit or die – and perhaps he also knows to what extent his desire for mastery over his living father will enslave him to the dead one.

The description of his father's death is designedly revealing:

I wept because I was losing my father for whom I had always lived. . . . Had not all my efforts to become better been made in order to give satisfaction to him? It is true that the success I strove for would have been a personal triumph for me as against him who had always doubted me, but it would have been a consolation to him as well. And now he was going away convinced of my incurable incapacity (p. 41).

Zeno's father falls into a coma and is clearly on the point of death. "What could I do", Zeno asks himself, "to make him feel how much I loved him?" and his answer is to pray that his father will die without recovering full consciousness. Zeno is beside himself with rage at the doctor who attempts to bring his father round as a purely medical exercise, since the old man is doomed anyway:

But I don't really know whether my childish fury was directed against the doctor or against myself. Myself perhaps first, because I had desired my father's death, but had not dared to say so. It was true that I had desired it solely out of filial affection, but the fact that I had remained silent about it made it a crime which weighed heavily on my mind (p. 46).

He goes on to reveal his ambivalence about his 'crime' by means of a dream in which he and the doctor reverse their roles in relation to the patient: "Distant shades!" he concludes. "It seems one can only recapture you by an optical illusion which turns you upside down" (p. 47).

But Zeno's father does recover full consciousness momentarily, in "that terrible, unforgettable scene which threw its shadow far into the future, and deprived me of all my courage and of all my joy in life" (p. 52). All the old man can do is to shout "I am dying!" and to strike his son in the face at the very moment of death. Zeno's resentment (p. 48) against his father's lengthy illness is replaced by the shocked realization that his father sought to punish him for the crime of having desired his death: "He was dead and it was impossible for me to prove my innocence" (p. 53). "I persuaded myself that the blow he had given me could not have been intentional. I became gentle and kind, and the memory of my father was always with me and grew ever dearer to me. It was like a delightful dream; now that we were in perfect agreement, I was the weak one and he the strong" (p. 53–4).

This final passage brings us to the central element in the novel, that upon which its successive moments depend. The account of the death of Zeno's father seems clearly to be related to a dream reported by Freud and added in 1911 to *The Interpretation of Dreams* (Svevo had in fact been involved in a project to translate the *Traumdeutung*):

> For instance, a man who had nursed his father during his last illness and had been deeply grieved by his death, had the following senseless dream some time afterward. His father was alive once more and was talking to him in the usual way, but (the remarkable thing was that) he had really died, only he did not know it. This dream only becomes intelligible if, after the words 'but he had really died' we insert 'in consequence of the dreamer's wish' and if we explain that what 'he did not know' was that the dreamer had had this wish. While he was nursing his father, he had repeatedly wished his father were dead, that is to say, he had had what was actually a merciful thought that death might put an end to his sufferings (*Standard Edition*, V, 430).

Zeno's father, of course, is dying but he does not know it, and Zeno's attempts to prevent his return to consciousness are thwarted by the old man's mute accusation of murder. In other words, in contrast to the situation of the dreamer in Freud's text, the signification of Zeno's real situation – which he later attempts to reverse by replacing it with a dream of "full agreement" and reciprocity, or in other words, by disavowing the death of his father – is immediately interpreted for him by a mute word from the discourse of the Other (the unconscious), symbolically represented by Zeno's Other, his father. Intentional or unintentional, whatever it was, the blow reveals Zeno's own unconscious desire to him. The same situation is later repeated with his rival in love, Guido, whom Zeno has seriously contemplated murdering. Guido's 'accidental' suicide by poisoning as a result of Zeno's advice produces another situation in which a man is dying but does not know it, since Guido expects to awaken from the effects of the drug, and the blow is now replaced by the look of reproach on Guido's dead face. The subjective necessity of reading his dead friend's face, as opposed to the objective fact of being struck, is correlative to Zeno's conscious wish to dispose of Guido as opposed to his unconscious desire to kill his father. And, of course, Zeno is full of poison, too (p. 375).

Zeno provides us with an explicit interpretation of this repetition in another instance, this time in relation to his father-in-law, Giovanni, whom he refers to as his "second father". Giovanni becomes terribly short of breath one evening, and a friend sees this as a dangerous symptom: "There's a real invalid for you!' said Copler. . . . 'He is dying and he doesn't even know he is ill'" (p. 157). When Copler himself dies, however, also breathing heavily, as all of Svevo's moribunds do, Zeno refuses to enter his room: "I had been looked at reproachfully by too many dying people already" (p. 198).

The rest of the novel could readily be conceived in certain respects as a commentary on the dream reported by Freud, and especially on Freud's closing remarks, added in 1919: "But I will willingly confess to a feeling that dream interpretation is far from having revealed all the secrets of ['absurd'] dreams of this character."

What is significant about this repeated situation in the novel, is that it only occurs in relation to people with whom Zeno has identified himself or with whom he is in a transference relation. It is as if Svevo had read the following passage from Freud's "Remembering, Repeating and Working-Through", first published in 1914:

> . . . The patient does not remember anything of what he has forgotten and repressed, but ACTS it out. He reproduces it not as a memory, but as an action; he REPEATS it, without, of course, knowing that he is repeating it. . . . What interests us most of all is naturally the relation of this compulsion to repeat to the transference and to resistance. We soon perceive that the transference is itself only a piece of repetition, and that the repetition is a transference of the forgotten past not only on to the doctor but also on to all the other aspects of the current situation (*Standard Edition*, XII, 151).[10]

Human desire is dependent upon non-realization. The death of Zeno's father leaves him facing a void, because his desire has come to fruition. Suddenly he doesn't know what to do with himself: "I was probing the future, and trying to discover in it some motive for continuing my efforts at self-improvement" (p. 51). Self-improvement means nothing to Zeno if there is no Other to improve against; for Zeno, it is a function of the desire

[10] This is the first mention of the *Wiederholungszwang*, central to *Beyond the Pleasure Principle* (1920), where it is related to the death-drive. Cf. Zeno on his compulsion to work with Guido, p. 295.

for the obstacle in which he has been implicated from the moment of his creation. What all the doctors in the book (including himself) seek to cure him of, he fears, is desire itself. In classic style, he refuses the proffered cure: "One day [the analyst] told me I was like someone recovering from an illness who has not yet got accustomed to doing without fever" (p. 373). But this fever is life itself: "Unlike other diseases, life is always mortal. It admits of no cure. . . . Every effort to procure health is in vain" (p. 397). For Zeno, health seems to suggest the abolition of desire and the end of the illusions of immortality upon which Eros depends: "I had never known life without desire, and illusions sprang up afresh for me after every shipwreck of my hopes, for I was always dreaming of limbs, of gestures, of a voice more perfect still" (p. 382). "Health . . . is really only a suspension of movement" (p. 287).

But Zeno felt none of this before his father's death. The key to the change lies in a simple projection of his own thoughts upon his almost speechless father during the illness. Zeno finds him staring at the stars and fears once more that his father will realize that he is dying: "I thought with horror: Now he is considering the problem he has always avoided" (p. 50), but it is of course Zeno who is considering it. Zeno's illness is "the fear of death" (p. 145), and it is only contracted after the death of the Other.[11] It is significant that the first involuntary memory he resurrects from the past is a symbol of his father's laboured breathing, a symbol of the fact that "his whole being was concentrated on the effort to get his breath" (p. 49). Existence for Zeno, until now, has been no more than a definition of himself for and against the desire of the Other, in the undifferentiated flux of time which he tries to order by his resolutions. At the old man's bedside, however, he shares his suffering and he is obliged to face the void his father's death will open up. He begs the doctor to let the old man die in peace – but in the midst of doing so, it is himself he prays for: "In an absolute fury, but still crying piteously all the time, as if imploring for mercy, I declared that it seemed an unheard-of cruelty not to let a condemned man die in peace" (p. 44).

But it is Zeno who is in fact the condemned man now. His introduction to death is his introduction to existence and to his own sense of finitude: "Pain and love – the whole of life, in short – cannot be looked on as a disease just because they make us suffer" (p. 396).

[11] Cf. the following passage from Svevo's *Senilità* (1898): "The image of death is great enough to fill the whole of one's mind. Gigantic forces are fighting together to draw death near and to expel it; every fibre of our being records its presence after having been near to it. . . . The thought of death is like an attribute of the body, a physical malady."

IV

> The after-life will be a repetition of terrestrial
> life, except that everyone will remain young,
> disease and death will be unknown, and no-one
> will marry or be given in marriage. (Andaman
> myth quoted by Lévi-Strauss)

In this implicit interpretation of the relationship between father and son,
Svevo introduces the existential anguish of Being-towards-death, later to
become so popular amongst intellectuals with the affluence and the leisure –
like Zeno's – to indulge themselves in it. What is so striking about this
novel of bourgeois anguish, is that its suggested reading of Freud is very
similar to the contemporary interpretation of Freud by Lacan. Lacan has
given his own interpretation of the dream-text represented by: "He was
dead (according to my wish), but he didn't know (that I had desired his
death)" in a seminar of 1958–9 (Lacan, 1960):

> We could use the words ACCORDING TO HIS WISH in several ways. We
> could say that it designates what the subject expressly willed while he was
> taking care of his father. Or we could call it the infantile desire for the
> death of the father (the infantile desire which Freud describes as the
> CAPITALIST of the dream and which finds its *entrepreneur* in the present
> desire). . . .

However, continues Lacan, at this oedipal level,

> the interdiction carried by the father furnishes the subject with a
> support, an alibi, a sort of mortal pretext not to affirm his desire. And for
> an analyst to interpret the dream at this level would simply permit the
> subject to identify himself with the aggressor, which would only be another
> form of defense.

This is of course the interpretation proffered by the omniscient Dr S.,
and Zeno does in fact seize upon it to use as a defense throughout the last
chapter of the book. The aggressor is the analyst and his counter-transfer-
ence; Zeno consequently reacts in a classic fashion, the point being that to
tell him what he already knows, with "an air of Christopher Columbus
discovering America" (p. 376), is of no help: "I . . . can only suppose that
he abstained [from seeking objective confirmation about my past] from fear
that this whole edifice of false charges and suspicions would crumble, when
confronted with the facts. I wonder why he took such a violent dislike to me.
He is probably also a hysteric, who avenges himself for having lusted after

his mother, by tormenting innocent people" (p. 377). Zeno later claims to have cured himself (by "self-persuasion") in opposition to the doctor, but precisely of what we are never able to determine. He returns to his "former good resolutions", he says, and gives up smoking – but implies that he will begin again, as he has always done. It is only in the very last few pages that we are given an explicit hint of what he really objected to in the doctor's oedipal interpretation: "I feel much better already, since renouncing the LIBERTY which that fool of a doctor forced on me" (p. 381).

Zeno is the man who knows too much and who must therefore seek refuge in irony. He is a Dostoevskian hyperconscious man in a minor key; like the underground man he knows the relationship between consciousness and suffering. In this sense, the movement of the novel is both to reveal and to reduce that consciousness, for the illusion of freedom offered by the 'psychical adventure' of psychoanalysis is insupportable. As the subject of desire, Zeno needs the lack his self-improvement seeks to fill; he needs his enslavement to the desire of the Other – an enslavement from which he knows his victory over any particular other will not free him – provided that he can knowingly seek to conceal it from himself. Full consciousness without illusions means paralysis, the "disease of the fifty-four move-ments" (p. 95):[12] "At whatsoever particular spot of the universe one settles down, one ends by becoming poisoned; it is essential to keep moving" (p. 287). And as he says of the willing sacrifice of his freedom to Guido: "It was either a real manifestation of disease or of great benevolence, both of which qualities are closely related to each other" (p. 248). Zeno is dimly aware that there can be no liberty purchased at the expense of other people's enslavement, and that somehow or other his illness corresponds to a social sickness. But what to do about it, he can never decide.

Lacan continues by saying that in watching his father die, the dreamer became fully aware of suffering as "the pain of existence when nothing more inhabits it except existence itself" and after excessive suffering had abolished the "desire to live".

> The subject knew of his father's suffering, but what he does not know is that he is in the process of taking that suffering onto himself. . . .

This explains the repudiation of the dream as 'absurd', for

[12] In a kind of image recurrent in the fiction of the modern alienated hero, Zeno discovers that to take one step requires fifty-four muscle movements. He begins to limp the moment he thinks about it: "Even today, if anyone watches me walking, the fifty-four movements get tied up in a knot, and I feel as if I shall fall down" (p. 95). The narcissism projected from self to other in the necessity of being watched nicely matches the Imaginary construction of 'self' by 'others'.

the subject can see that his father did not know that he (the son) wished him to die. . . . He can or he cannot see (depending on the point of view of the analysis) that he has always wished that his father, as his rival, would die.

But he doesn't see that in taking on his father's suffering, "he intends to maintain before himself an unawareness he needs: that there is nothing at the final limit of existence except the pain of existing". He rejects that unawareness onto the other. Thus,

the desire for death here is the desire NOT to awaken to the message: that, by his father's death, he is henceforth faced with his own death – with the death from which his father's presence had protected him until that very moment.

At the moment of the death of the father, says Lacan, the "wish to castrate the father falls back on the son".[13] Thus the "subject consents to suffer in the place of the other", but this involves an oppositional trap: "the lure of the murder of the father as an Imaginary fixation".

Language allows the dead father, now in the position of Lacan's Other, the symbolic father, to continue to exist in the WORDS "he is dead". What is really in question, says Lacan, is not the father's unawareness that he is dead, but the dreamer's unawareness of the signification of the dream and of the nature of the suffering he is participating in, which is: "the pain of existence as such when all desire is effaced from it". Thus the subject seeks to interpose between himself and the void or "abyss" which opens up before him when he is confronted by death

an image which serves to support his desire: his rivalry with his father. In bringing this image to life again, he finds a narrow footbridge which saves him from being directly swallowed up.

His triumph, then, is to know, whereas the Other does not know. But "in actual fact, the death of the father is felt as the disappearance of a shield between him and the absolute master: death" (Hegel's *absolut Herr*).

Or in other words, when one has spent one's life in rivalry and

---

[13] For the question of the asymptotic nature of the cure, for castration, and for the master–slave dialectic of analysis, see the 1937 article on finite and infinite analysis, *Standard Edition*, XXIII, 216. In relation to Zeno's confessions and his objections to psychoanalysis, the following passage gives Freud's interpretation of the problem: "The rebellious over-compensation of the male produces one of the strongest transference-resistances. He refuses to subject himself to a father-substitute, or to feel indebted to him for anything and consequently he refuses to accept his recovery from the doctor" (p. 252). For Freud the treatment has reached the bedrock beyond which it cannot go: the castration complex.

opposition, the disappearance of the other term leaves little alternative but a quick exit in the first convenient puff of smoke.

The alienated Zeno is thus introduced to Being-towards-death, which, in the philosophical consciousness of a century of increasing alienation, exploitation, and control, becomes the paranoid projection of material and social anguish into the realm of the individual and the idea. 'Authenticity' in the sense of a personal, spiritual liberation, becomes the Imaginary value of life in a society in which the real relationships of class, race, economics, power, and responsibility are consistently disavowed, to be replaced by idealistic and essentially SCHIZOID values of equality and personal responsibility. Whether in existentialism, in the 'hippie' movement, in the Jesus-movement, or in group therapy, the contemporary categorical imperative is "Do your own thing". But as Montaigne and the existentialists reminded us, the only thing we can do as our own is TO DIE. "Do your own thing" becomes another existential metaphor for Being-towards-Death.

For Heidegger death is related to authenticity – a curious word in the discourse of an active National Socialist: "The inauthentic temporality of everyday Dasein [which is 'fleeing in the face of death'] . . . must, as such a looking-away from finitude, fail to recognize authentic futurity and therewith temporality in general" (1927, II, 6: 81). Kojève falls into the same Imaginary trap of absolute liberty as did the early Sartre: "Man is the *Dasein* of the Concept in the World. He is therefore the *Dasein* in the world of a Future which will never become Present. This future is for Man his DEATH" (p. 379). ". . . In arriving at Wisdom, Man comprehends that it is only his finitude or his death which assures him of his absolute liberty" (p. 380).

In order to maintain a barrier between himself and his consciousness of his own death-to-come, Zeno needs his crime and his punishment as much as he needs the Other.[14] Caught in an Imaginary value system of opposition and identity, Zeno cannot transcend the double binds it engenders. He cannot liberate himself in the material world; therefore, he must seek an illusory liberation of the spirit. Like many of the 'love generation' and many so-called political radicals, he thus becomes a NEGATIVE BOURGEOIS: a victim who cannot transcend the values of the executioner in order to try to embark upon the real and material liberation of himself through the liberation of others. Unlike Mastroianni's role as the neurotic aristocrat in a

---

[14] Proust's Swann faces and rejects an identical 'cure' of his enslavement to Odette – the liberty of indifference to her: "But, to tell the truth, at the heart of his morbid state, he feared such a cure like something akin to death itself, a cure which would in fact have been the death of everything he was at that time" (1913–27, I: 300).

London ghetto in the film *Leo the Last*, Zeno remains forever a bourgeois voyeur, unable to transcend his essential decadence and parasitism.

But Zeno is not unaware of his own role as voyeur. In his attack on the subject-who-is-supposed-to-know – the analyst representing the established values of his culture – he transcends the simple question of his own sickness or health by placing the overall responsibility for his condition elsewhere. This 'psychoanalytical' novel does not end on a personal plane; it ends with a world war and a society facing destruction. The apocalyptic final pages of the novel, with their evocation of a Wellsian bomb, are an integral part of the book. Death will come as a surprise to some of those caught in the war (p. 392): they are members of a SOCIETY which is dying and which does not know it.

Whether Zeno is 'cured' or not ("I really am well, absolutely well' – p. 396) – and there is a Hegelian finality about the punditry of the final pages – whether he really becomes "a privileged person amongst so many martyrs", nevertheless it is western European society which is discovering its own historicity and finitude in the convulsions of the war to end all wars. Zeno's apocalyptic death-wish for *homo faber* is his last great act of repetition.

Svevo's novelistic interpretation of the problematics of health and existence in a sick society naturally involves the problem of freedom, freedom from the desire of the Other. But the repetition of Zeno's deadly relationship to the Other raises the spectre of determinism, and, determined or not, or to whatever extent, the most one can be sure of is that his protective repetition is desired. It is desired as the only possible kind of communication in a context of pathological communication. Nineteen-fourteen and after had no doubt engendered in Svevo a particularly acute existential sense of man's 'abandonment in the world', a sense of the loss of the 'transcendental essence', a sense of something lacking which one finds throughout the modern period, beginning (at least) with the *Deus absconditus* of the seventeenth-century Jansenists and present today in the Nietzschean God who is also dead but doesn't know it. *Coscienza* of death or of a collective death-wish, the Zeno who had said at the beginning of the book: "I stuck to my idea and asserted that death was really the great organizing force of life" (p. 71), now, at the end, joins Valéry in crying: "Nous autres civilisations, nous savons maintenant que nous sommes mortelles" (1919).

Chapter IV

Montaigne on the Paradoxes of Individualism

A COMMUNICATION ABOUT COMMUNICATION

An analysis terminates when the
patient realizes it could go on
for ever.

HANNS SACHS

1. *The Ideology of the Self*

Montaigne, or rather the subject who says 'I' in Montaigne's *Essays*, stands at the historical frontier of the ideology of bourgeois individualism like one of the multilingual signs in occupied Berlin: economically, sociologically, and psychologically, you are entering another sector. Whatever else they are – philosophy, hobby, literature, personal therapy – the *Essays* are both a commentary on and an expression of Montaigne's times and Montaigne's relationship to those times. As he says near the beginning of the essay "On Vanity", which is the one essay I shall particularly concentrate on here: "Scribbling seems to be a sort of SYMPTOM of an unruly age [*un siècle désbordé*]. When did we write so much as since our dissensions began?" (III, 9, 722–3b [923]).[1]

---

[1] "... depuis que nous sommes en trouble." Book III, Chapter 9, page 721, layer b, in Montaigne, 1595b. The number in square brackets gives the pagination of the French edition used: Montaigne, 1595a. The dates of the various 'strata' are: (*a*) before 1588, (*b*) 1588, (*c*) after 1588. Montaigne retired from public office and began the *Essays* in 1572, after the death of his father (1568) and that of his colleague and friend, Etienne de La Boétie (1563). The first edition (Books I and II) appeared in 1580, after which Montaigne travelled and was elected Mayor of Bordeaux (1581–5). An enlarged edition of Books I and II

Thus the *Essays* represent an ideology which is open to analysis at a number of different levels. Montaigne's ideology of the self – his view of the *moi* as a substantial, Cartesian-like rock of stability – is an expression of the central contradiction between desire (for certitude and solidity) and experience (of doubt and fluidity) out of which the *Essays* were generated. There is in every man a *forme maistresse*, he says, a master-pattern (*patron*). In himself, he repeats, there is an innate, unchanging *jugement* or *raison*, an essence, a soul which must always "retain its footing", an entity which refuses the "natural" "relationship to others", refuses *l'estranger faict*, public opinion, public vanity.[2] All these statements of belief in the atomistic individualism which Descartes was to formalize into the basis of a philosophy some fifty years later, are repeatedly related to the Delphic precept "Know thyself", especially in the later editions of the *Essays*, where the references to self-knowledge take on an increasingly justificatory tone.[3] Moreover, Montaigne also sees the self, in Sartrean terms, as an object of consciousness, a transcendental ego, which he can "distinguish and consider at a distance, like a neighbor, like a tree" (III, 8, 720c [921]). This self-image can only be a false one if it is considered as something attainable in isolation, and it is the merit of the *Essays* as a literary document to demonstrate the falsity of this notion of the self at the same time as their author believes in it.

But this is the fate of any ideology: to reveal the source of its contradictions at a theoretical and practical level. It is not necessary to attempt the impossible task of deciding precisely what Montaigne or anybody else means by 'self' in order to comprehend the real function of this mental construct, that of an image or phantasy, or to recognize the consequence, which Marx emphasized so clearly, that intellectual antinomies are not contradictions in 'reality' but rather an expression of a paradoxical

---

and a third book were published in 1588. Montaigne continued to re-read and annotate a copy of this edition until his death in 1592. The Bordeaux edition dates from 1595.

[2] See, for example (in the French edition): pp. 789, 785, 1052, 641, 790, 793, 359, 877–8, 932, 18, 979–80. Montaigne takes up the Thelemic injunction of Rabelais: "Fay ce que voudras" by his own version of "Do your own thing": "Fay ton faict et te cognoy." Paradoxical injunctions like these often appear in times of trouble amongst the members of a literate class which is being split from itself.

In *Les Paysans* (1844), Balzac calls Rigou, the usurer, a 'Thelemite'. As a member of the rising middle class at the beginnings of industrial capitalism in France, Rigou allies himself with the peasants against the landed aristocracy and wins out over both. The peasants discover – too late – that doing their own thing means doing the Other's thing for him. Cf. Lukács, 1938: 21–46.

[3] For example (in the French edition): pp. 360, 378, 18, 979, all added after 1588.

relationship between the subjective (ideological) and the objective (actual) 'life-situation' of an individual or a society. Viewed from the point of view of the transcendental observer implicit in Marx's social psychology, there is no 'real' conflict between the subjective and the objective in the total social context, only a series of relationships. There is no 'pure consciousness', only the "practical consciousness" of language, which arises from the necessity of relationships and communication with other men (Marx and Engels, 1845–6: 41–2; Marx, 1844: 162).

If Montaigne's subjective 'ideology of the self' is in conflict with the actual 'phenomenology of the self' represented by the *Essays*, the conflict is between what Montaigne believes and what he knows, between what he desires and what he attains, between a normally phantasized past and a phantasized future. As a concrete individual, Montaigne sought to establish the isolated essence of his 'self'. As the locus of a subject in an ongoing system of communication, the subject-who-says-I-in-the-*Essays* felt that he had lost himself, that he was being stolen from himself, that the vanity of the world was smothering his authentic self in its inauthenticity ("On Vanity", p. 766 [979–80]). He writes 'for himself' – but then he publishes his writings for others. 'Isolation' and 'society' are but two more polar terms in his ideological conflict – like 'self' and 'other', 'stability' and 'fluidity', 'being' and 'becoming', they invite TRANSLATION into the terms of relationship which is the aim of this paper. These antitheses are every bit as metaphorical as are the images of ebb and flow which are repeated in the *Essays*. Montaigne regularly opposes "living the stream of life" to battling "upstream" against it towards a source of stability, towards a fixable point of origin, towards a spatial transcendence of becoming, a ME "like a neighbor, like a tree". But the *Essays* as a whole reveal the non-satisfaction of Montaigne's desire for this transcendental home, the desire without which they could not have been written in the first place. At the same time, because they are a communication in a context of communication, they reveal rather clearly the network of conditions under which human communication takes place.

Like any ideology, Montaigne's ideological conflict (as he says himself) is symptomatically related to other levels of existence. A symptom (or metaphor) in this sense is not so much a 'sign' pointing to some sort of 'more real' cause, as it is an overdetermined statement in a metalanguage about some relationship in an object language.[4] Thus the symptomatic

---

[4] See below, Chapter XII, where the term 'object language' is replaced by the more suitable term ' referent language'. In this essay, 'metalanguage' and 'object language' include the sense of 'metacommunication' and 'communication'.

statement of an antithesis is completely valid at its own level of language and irreducible in fact to any other level. The fact that it is a rationalization about behavioral statements at other levels does not *per se* make any one level more 'true' or more 'real' than any other, for objective theoretical reasons which I shall consider in more detail presently.

The economic changes of the sixteenth and seventeenth centuries are necessarily represented symptomatically in the scientific and theological discourse. If the ideology of the medieval *communitas* is represented – at the moment of its rupture – by an Aristotelian teleological continuity between the city of man and the city of God, the most striking symptom of the real manifestation of that break (after the event) is surely the barrier drawn between man and God by the *Deus absconditus* of the Jansenists or by Pascal's "eternal silence of infinite space" (Goldmann, 1955). The Renaissance was still seeking to read the signs of the sacred text in the great book of nature, the writing that necessarily precedes speech, but the economic relationships of the period were such as to require man to become no longer the reader, but the exploiter, of that text. Western society begins in the sixteenth century to mark nature herself with an indelible imprint: the individual entrepreneur takes over the task of scribe from God.

The atomization of social relationships which was the necessary corollary of the atomization of economic relationships produces that impossible and Imaginary entity: the bourgeois individual. The movement of the physical sciences away from an 'organic' (Aristotelian) viewpoint towards a 'geometric' and 'technological' (Archimedean) viewpoint, or towards a 'mechanistic' (Cartesian and Newtonian) viewpoint, was a necessary product of the introduction of more and more highly developed TECHNIQUES of organization at every level of production, including the level of ideas. The kind of social organization required by a technological society in the modern sense is one in which the EFFICIENCY of the interchangeable machine part – the digital component which can be combined in many different ways – becomes a principle of social relationships. If the unit of communication in relatively less technological or 'cool' societies is the (analog) 'person', that of an industrialized and technological 'hot' society is the (digital) 'role'. It is only a short step from Montaigne's 'I' to Descartes' *cogito*, and thus to the "clear and distinct". The "clear and distinct" is the representative metaphor of an ideology of the entity, which was necessarily the product of the sixteenth-century advance in physics engendered by technology, an ideology which sought to justify a program which would not concern itself with the "government of men" (theology) but with the "administration of things" (natural science). The "administration of things" turned out to be a new form of the justification of objectification: the rationalization of the reduction of the 'person' to the status of a cog in the social machinery. For if you must have social and material alienation, and if you must justify the economic exploitation of men and women, then you must also engender a value system of personal and individual freedom and responsibility which will assist the slaves in identifying with their masters. "Do your own thing" is a useful metaphor to play with when the things are doing you.

The birth of modern individualism is the story of the birth of the myth of autonomous desire. The question of the desire of the Other – Don Quixote's Imaginary identification with the fictional Amadis of Gaul, for example (Girard, 1965b) – cannot become a SOCIAL question until the Other ceases to be God. And such a question, which concerns the real punctuation of relationships of power and responsibility between masters and slaves, must be repressed or disavowed if one is to adjust properly to the social machine, to the harmonious Newtonian equilibrium of 'attraction' and 'repulsion' for which all change is the work of 'external forces'. For Montaigne, however, who hates 'novelties' so much, the disruptive force is the coming Newtonian social universe itself.

The autonomy of desire is a paradox, because all desire – for 'objects' or for 'subjects' – is a desire for relationship. All desire is fundamentally an expression of the analog relationships between human beings; it is therefore mediated by those relationships. But the Imaginary desire for things in a social context in which everyone ELSE is a thing, is a perversion of those relations. Stemming from the relations of production as a result of which all social relationships are manipulated and explained as the administration of things, Imaginary desire justifies the digitalization of relationships which splits man from man, man from nature, man from woman, 'civilized' from 'savage'. In such a world of social atomism, the thing-like values of competition and accumulation become the dominant rules of relation. The internalization of the digital – the efficient, the 'rational', the 'technical' – as the agent of exploitation (rather than as the instrument of relationship), engenders a SPLITTING OF THE SUBJECT into mind and body, reason and emotion, self and other, male and female. The schizophrenia of modern society can be explained only in these terms: in the terms of the supervaluation of opposition and identity at the expense of the real and material differences upon which all communication depends. And once a society is founded on oppositional relationships, the contradiction between Symbolic and Imaginary desire becomes irresolvable without a change in the MATERIAL conditions which engendered those magnetic polarities in the first place (cf. Chapters VII and IX).

This is Montaigne's concern. How he tried to deal with it depends on an understanding of the relationship between communication and meta-communication, based on the premise that all desire is a desire for MEANING, which is possible only within real relationships. Signification, on the other hand, demands only a context, the context of the desire for meaning; it may thus be a repression or a disavowal of the context in which it occurs.

2. Levels and Mirrors

Psychoanalysis is the work of Oedipus.
GIRARD

In trying to establish theoretically the levels of communication and meta-communication, we must beware of thinking that the 'object' language (the text) or the metastatement (the commentary) is in itself the 'real' significa-tion of the metastatement (or vice versa). Such judgments depend on punctuation, and punctuation involves history, responsibility, and power. Punctuation is a semantic question only in the sense that all semantics is based on pragmatics. It is the notion of a theoretically detectable and somehow absolute level of 'real meaning' in what has been traditionally viewed as a relationship of REFLECTION (*Widerspiegelung*) which has misled so many commentators into the fallacies of reductionism. Obviously any commentary necessitates reduction – and in fact without the powerful systems of reduction revealed in human perception (gestalts) and in human communication (signs and signifiers), digital knowledge would be im-possible – but the reductionist fallacy differs in that it confers a privilege on a certain level. The notion of a reflective relationship always implies a more or less absolute noumenal level to which the phenomena are to be related. This concept of reflection is a particular kind of abstraction which leaves us without any understanding of the intentionalization of the various levels or analogs or mirrors as signification, because it is essentially one-dimensional.

The Imaginary mode, although part of the human communicative pro-cess, is what makes it possible to attempt to SHORT-CIRCUIT communica-tion by making it unnecessary. As the psychological area where identifica-tion and projection operate, the Imaginary seeks to deny difference by seeking actual identity (it is constitutively reductionist), and thus to replace the essential asymmetry of communication by a symmetry of silence. To put it another way, mirroring oneself in another or mirroring the other in oneself is a sort of quantum jump over the necessity of communication between self and other in order to be immediately at the point towards which alienated human communication tends and which it cannot reach: in a state of total and absolute equilibrium. Although one may often speak of the relationship of identity $(x = y)$, we are all aware that in psychological and philosophical terms there is no way for x to equal y without ceasing to be x. Unlike similarity, total identity (or total equilibrium) is not in essence a relationship at all – for Freud, it was death. Total communication is in effect perpetual motion (Shands, 1970: 385–6).

If we apply this psychological analysis of the Imaginary to the relationship between noumena and phenomena, it seems clear that the whole notion of reflection as an interpretative tool (whether explicit or implicit) is deficient in that it seeks to make identical what is not identical. At the same time, because there is no metalevel within the Imaginary (which is analog in form, and thus cannot comment on itself, as language and digital communication can), the notion of reflection has the curious result of implicitly denying that there is any relationship between what reflects and what is reflected – as any freshman student of Plato's metaphysics could tell us. The reflection of the object is neither the object nor a statement about the object.

It is proposed therefore that we substitute for the venerable notion of a 'real' (noumenal) level and a phenomenal level, the far more fruitful and objectively valid notion of the relationship between levels, and use as our interpretative schema the objectively verifiable existence of levels and metalevels in language and in communicative processes. It might be argued that this viewpoint supposes a theoretically attainable totality of 'vertical' and 'horizontal' relationships within and between levels viewed from the position of an impartial or transcendental observer – who, it will be added, seems to have replaced the absolute noumenal level or absolute object language we are trying to rid ourselves of. In reality, however, since the observer is also part of the system of relationships – my main point when I return to the analysis of a portion of Montaigne's text – this notion of totality and impartiality has only a methodological value. We are, in fact, in a Gödelian situation. There is no ultimate metalanguage which can comment on the system of relationships, because the means of analysis – metalanguage – like the observer, is also part of the system being analyzed. In a word, we must always and inevitably face paradoxes and contradictions – both existential and logical – which cannot in any circumstances be resolved.

3. The Communicational Model

No pleasure has any savor for me without communication.
MONTAIGNE: "On Vanity"

In an earlier paper on Montaigne I tried to deal with Montaigne's relationship to the Other on the model of his relationship with La Boétie, the friend whose early death, as Montaigne reveals, had a great deal to do with the genesis and the form of the *Essays* (Wilden, 1968b).[5] The idealized image of La Boétie is at a profound personal level the object of Montaigne's desire. His desire for plenitude, which is his reaction to the experience of emptiness and void, is a metastatement about that desire.[6] But we must avoid any suggestion that the one is reducible to the other, or that Montaigne's view of "La Boétie" as a "full soul", as a "pattern" modeled on the great men of antiquity, is more 'real' or more significant that the conflict between the desire for being and the discovery of becoming which informs the *Essays*. My point is that they are only understandable in terms of each other; each has its own language and its own validity. Neither is fully comprehensible without the other, and of course a great number of other relationships (theoretically an infinitely large number) are also involved. But more important yet is the fact that since we are dealing with a communicational context, there are certain unavoidable limitations to the analysis. It is to these limitations we must now turn.

Unlike the atomistic view of the individual and its correlative, the notion of linear, chronological development, evolution, or change, both the diachronic and the synchronic communications systems in which human beings are actually involved require some version of the notion of dialectic, which in communications theory would be called feedback. Feedback is a technical notion drawn from cybernetics, and in particular from the theory of goalseeking adaptive systems (e.g., the thermostat and, unfortunately, the radar gunsight). Translated into the terms of human communication, it not only precisely describes the formal conditions allowing messages to pass between senders and receivers, but also delineates the existential action and reaction between subjects in such contexts. In the psychoanalytical situation, one level of the feedback between analyst and patient is known as transference and countertransference, both being examples of a

[5] I am intrigued to discover that the title of this earlier essay, which is that of Chapter I of Montaigne's *Essays*, "Par divers moyens on arrive à pareille fin", is a metaphor of goalseeking, overdetermination, redundancy, and equifinality.

[6] In another terminology, the relationship between the plenitude of relation and the emptiness of reason in Montaigne represents the split, in the modern world, between the subject of analog knowledge and the subject of digital knowledge.

dialectical opposition, which the therapy must bring under the control of the mediation of difference if it is to be successful. A system with this type of feedback is an 'open' system; it cannot be interpreted from the point of view of a unilinear sequence of causes and effects, nor yet from that of simple linearity in time. In a macroscopic 'closed' system, on the other hand, such as a falling body or a sealed chemical reaction, there is no feedback.[7] There is a unilinear and chronological sequence of changes which can theoretically be reduced to the knowledge of the properties of the individual elements or forces from which it began. The sequence can also be reversed, at least in theory. In other words, in a closed system, both scientific prediction and scientific history are possible – and it happens that the closed system has long been the model *par excellence* of evolution and analysis in all fields of inquiry. What Susanne Langer (1962) calls the "genetic fallacy" of the British empiricists is one excellent example of this tendency: their "plain historical method" was more nearly a "plain logical method" derived from an artificial model of how things had to be (the complex derived from the association of the simple, for instance; language derived from denominating 'grunt-nouns'). This linear model of relationships between indivisible atoms has always been a totally inadequate grid to apply to the human communicational situation, where two types of open feedback will be found, both making the evolution of the system unpredictable and irreversible.[8]

In order to deal with the feedback model, the sender and receiver can be profitably viewed as two 'black boxes' (called subjects), both of which are fitted with facilities for input and output. Feedback compares the output of the black box with its input and adjusts the output accordingly. Negative feedback aims at homeostasis (input equal to output); positive feedback aims at change. Hegel's 'dialectical negation' (*Aufhebung*), for instance, could be viewed as positive feedback coming under the control of second-order negative feedback (Chapters VIII and XII). Since both black boxes have their own characteristics and since there are many levels of possible

---

[7] Some scientists and mathematicians would regard this assertion as an overstatement, since theoretically, any process whatsoever involves feedback in some form or other (for example, the relationship between momentum and gravity which prescribes the parabola of a projectile). To answer this objection it would be necessary to talk about 'weak' as opposed to 'strong' feedback in much the same way as it is possible to speak of 'weak' and 'strong' causality in physics. (After writing this, I discovered in the cybernetic literature the accepted term for what I called 'weak feedback': pseudo-feedback.)

[8] In what follows, as in much of the preceding, I am indebted to the lucid summary of communicationally oriented psychotherapeutic theory in Watzlawick, Beavin, and Jackson, 1967.

input and output, the relationships between these two *loci* in a human context are extraordinarily complicated. However, in theoretical terms, the dependence of one black box upon the other for its own level of output is clear, since its output is viewed in relation to the other's output, and adjusted accordingly. But the internal organization of each black box also includes other black boxes: ego, id, superego; consciousness and the unconscious; preconscious memory; repressed memory; phantasies. These other schemata have been gradually written into the network as a result of anterior relationships while the 'individual' developed. Since communication occurs in the here and now, these elements of the larger system are not empirically observable; memory, for instance, is simply what is empirically absent for the observer from the present system of communication, and its effects must be inferred (Ashby). For the individual, however, the output of the black box labelled 'memory' – which is a memory only of relationships with Otherness – that is, its intentionalization in the present by the secondary system (*Cs. Pcs.*), will inevitably be compared with the present input of the system. Thus there operates what Sartre called the *projet* and what Freud described as *Nachträglichkeit*: the programming of a future output on the basis of a open feedback loop between the present situation of the subject (*pour-soi*) and the present memory of a past relationship (*en-soi*).

Consequently, although communication cannot escape the here and now, and although the extreme difficulty of tracing back the evolution of an open system tends to turn the modern theorist or therapist away from any sort of archeology of the subject (a past he believes he cannot change) and towards the future communication of the subject (which he believes he can modify more easily), there is always in any given communicational context both a diachronic system of communication (operating synchronically on the basis of the present intentionalization of memories or phantasies) and a synchronic one (operating diachronically because it is constantly replaced in a system which is 'ongoing' in time). The Other in the system will always be both this other here and now (real and phantasied) and that other then.

A purely synchronic system of communication (a timeless slice through the here and now) would, however, be simply circular (if the spatial metaphor be permitted); the diachronic system, on the other hand, can best be described as a helix. Both Hegel's *Phenomenology* and Proust's *A la recherche du temps perdu* (sometimes called circular) can be usefully viewed on this model (cf. Dance, 1967: 296). Since the faculty of memory somehow allows the 'stratified' loops of the spiral to communicate directly (the constant communication within the large black box between present systems and past-but-now-present systems), and since the cycle of 'action' and 'reaction' between subjects in a communicational context is also spiral, we have to face the crucial problem of punctuation. The punctuation of an ongoing system either by the subjects involved or by the observer may be tendentious or arbitrary. It may often be the equivalent of a short circuit, or the system may defeat the punctuation by means of its own short circuits. ("You started it", says the wife. "I wasn't in a bad mood until you came in", replies the husband.) It is only by means of an analysis of the synchronic and diachronic CONTEXTS of the interaction that any ongoing interaction which is not simply a *folie à deux* can be properly punctuated. And that punctuation will inevitably depend, in the last resort, on an ETHICAL decision (in the pragmatic sense), for there are no judgments which are not essentially judgments of value.

These considerations return us to the question of the primacy or the priority to be assigned to the language of being and becoming in Montaigne as opposed in this instance to the language of the lost self (the desire mediated by the IMAGE of Montaigne's relationship with La Boétie). The Freudian psychoanalyst, for instance, might wish to punctuate the system by introducing the 'real' level of sublimated homosexuality[9] in the relationship between Montaigne and La Boétie, or he might speak of the 'instinctual' level of Montaigne's desire for union with the Other (the non-difference of Eros). But it would be equally convincing to interpret that 'real' level as derived from the 'more real' level of "ontological insecurity" as an existentially oriented analyst like Laing might do, viewing the desire for union as the result, not the cause, of a disturbance in Montaigne's being-in-the-world. These two possibilities, as well as all the others one could examine, will, I hope, reinforce the point that we are dealing with an overdetermined and multifinal open system of communication and relationship. The various levels of interpretation have their own validity, and they are not as such reducible to each other. But in a given social context, and from as critical a perspective as it is possible for a (self-critical)

---

[9] As a matter of fact, it is only the word 'sublimated' which prevents this from being an erroneous punctuation. The notion of sublimation allows the psycho-analyst to get around the paradox that the 'symptoms' of homosexuality in Montaigne's text do not denote what they seem to denote. As a map, these symptoms do not denote the real territory of homosexuality, but only another map for which the term homosexuality is still no more than an appropriate symbol and not a reality. The 'reductionist' interpreter thus commits two errors: he confuses the map with the territory, and he fails to recognize that there is more than one map and more than one territory to which any symptom refers. In the terminology of Gregory Bateson, Montaigne's 'homosexuality' is a metaphor which is not meant (Bateson, 1955).

observer within the system to attain, it will be very clear what priorities are to be assigned to what. The priorities of the therapist's office – I refer to an ideal therapist not concerned to reinforce the values of the *status quo* – are not the same as those which obtain when we consider not an individual, but a class of 'individuals', in a given society. It is in the sense that a particular individual, called Montaigne – who undoubtedly had all sorts of 'personal problems' – IS SPOKEN BY the socioeconomic discourse of his time, and by the discourse of the class with which he identifies himself (the landed aristocracy), that we choose to view his relationship with La Boétie as a metaphor of the disintegration of a society, rather than simply as a symptom of some psychological problem or other. And we choose to view Montaigne's metacommunication about that relationship as a metacommunication about the Other who is speaking him, rather than simply as a personal 'analysis'.

The theoretical requirements of the communications model outlined above add further to our understanding of a text and our own relationship to it. Since in an open system involving feedback loops which are not closed – talking, thinking, acting, writing a novel, for instance – neither scientific history nor scientific prediction is possible without our deciding on a punctuation of the system, we have a new insight into the function of beginnings and endings. Unlike what is involved in the actual mosaic and analog structure of a picture or statue, language and writing make chronology; they make beginnings and endings. Even if a novelist were to write his novel backwards or from the middle outwards, we would still punctuate it in the arbitrary way he has asked us to (given the fact that the author is only partially conscious of this arbitrariness and only partially in control of it): from 'beginning' to 'end'. Montaigne's 'novel of self-experience', the *Essays*, has a printed beginning and a printed end, for example, but where it 'really' begins or ends can never be determined. Because of the nature of human time, this would be true even if we did not know that Montaigne wrote the *Essays* in all directions at once over a number of years, with death as the final punctuation mark. Furthermore, the function of *projet*, *Nachträglichkeit*, and feedback in open systems requires a new view of the function and nature of time in novels of self-experience like the *Essays*. In the closed literary system, time is pure sequence or pure background; correlatively, the narrator is omniscient, timeless, like St Augustine's God. On the stage of the open system, however, time is also one of the players – as Georg Lukács (1920) said of Flaubert's *Éducation sentimentale* – and the narrator is *imbriqué* (cf. Margenau, 1964: 445). The time of this type of novel is not simply unilinear or sequential: it may be synchronic, diachronic, mythical, repetitive, ostensibly circular, actually spiral, or structured (but not read) like a mosaic. Time – and therefore the reader – is one of the *dramatis personae* in Montaigne's personal quest. The past is always remembered, re-presented, just as the Other is remembered, represented, Time is lost and regained; it is subject, object, and relationship in itself. Montaigne speaks to his past, and the past replies with advice about the future, for human time is not chronological, but dialectic.

4. Bildung *and* Entäusserung

> To understand himself man
> needs to be understood by
> another. To be understood by
> another he needs to understand
> the other.
> THOMAS HORA

Given these considerations, it is possible to analyze a specific example of the communications system represented by the reader (Montaigne's Other, in one respect) and the text (the reader's Other, in another respect). Certain of the determinants of this system are delineated in the *Essays* through Montaigne's own relationship to particular others; the rest occur in passages where Montaigne addresses the reader, obliquely or directly, or where he reacts to what the Other has told him (reacts to the ideology of the totality represented by his historical context). Thus he gets into arguments with possible (or actual) critics of the novelty and egocentrality of his project; he talks at length with the great writers of antiquity; he attacks scholastics, barbarians, innovators; he criticizes the failings of the particular time of troubles in which he lived; and so on. His announced project to follow the Delphic precept "Know thyself" (I, 3, 8–9c [18]) is mediated by the past 'self' he discovered he had lost – his re-intentionalization (after the event) of his specular identification with La Boétie – as well as by the type of future 'self' he intended to find, and by his desire that the Other recognize his self, his loss, and his quest. "Whatever I may be, I want to be it elsewhere than on paper" (II, 37, 596a [764]). His relationship to his book is such that the book itself, as organization and as Other, contributes its 'in-formation' to his *formation*: "I have no more made my book than my book has made me. . . ." (II, 18, 504c [648].)

The connection between necessary 'alienation' (equivalent in some sense to Laing's "depersonalization") and 'formation' is rather well brought out by Hyppolite in his commentary on the Hegelian *Phenomenology* (1946: II, 372):

... The two terms 'formation' [*culture*: *Bildung*] and 'alienation' [*Entäusserung*] have a very similar meaning [for Hegel]. It is by the alienation of his natural being that a determinate individual cultivates and forms himself for essentiality. One might put it more precisely by saying that for Hegel self-formation is only conceivable through the mediation of alienation or estrangement [*Entfremdung*]. Self-formation is not to develop harmoniously as if by organic growth, but rather to become opposed to oneself and to rediscover oneself through a splitting [*déchirement*] and a separation.

Hyppolite thus implicitly opposes a homeostatic 'organic' system to a self-differentiating system in essential relation to an environment (Chapter VIII).

The context of Montaigne's last remark is of particular importance to the desire for recognition which pervades the *Essays*, since it is a reply to Montaigne's rhetorical question of what good the *Essays* would possibly be if no one actually read them. In view of his re-membering of the reciprocity, unity, and feeling of plenitude he felt he had experienced in his relationship with La Boétie, and in view of his several direct requests for a reader (who should be like La Boétie), one can see in this affirmation of the autonomy of his own intrapsychic system, a defense against the possibility of non-recognition by the Other. By telling the reader in advance that he doesn't need him, Montaigne reveals how much he depends on him. Montaigne never experienced again the reciprocal recognition – the confirmation of the implicit statement: "This is how I see myself (in my present relationship to you)" – that he felt he had experienced in the "indivisibility' of his friendship with La Boétie. For Montaigne, there remained only the present signifier in his present discourse: the word 'La Boétie'. And whereas Montaigne constantly writes in the light of the possible 'rejection' of his demand for recognition by the Other, what he really fears, as do we all, is what has been labelled 'disconfirmation' – that message from the Other which says: "I do not see you at all; for me you do not exist." Montaigne had discovered the reality of this possibility in his original project to isolate and examine himself in solitude, his project in fact to escape the Other in the hope of finding himself. But in this attempt to establish himself in a state of intransitiveness, he tells us that he fell prey to "monstrous phantasies". He could not escape the human necessity of transitiveness; consequently he began to write (I, 8, 21a [34]). By retiring from the world, he had discovered that the desire to lose being-for-others amounts to losing being-for-oneself (Laing, 1960). Thus, the affirmations of autonomy which are repeated in the text can be seen as symptomatic metastatements about the impossibility of autonomy (escape from Otherness).

But there is also another level of metastatement about this same realization on Montaigne's part – and this is directed at ALL his readers (as distinct from remarks directed at an ideal reader). One could choose a large number of passages to make the following point: that Montaigne's demand for recognition of Montaigne's 'self' by the reader is coupled with the demand that the latter recognize Montaigne as 'one up' (the master) in the dialectic of recognition by virtue of the fact that Montaigne recognizes both the vanity of his self-image and the vanity of the reader's self-image. But before picking out of a number of possible examples the one key sentence which gave me the idea for this essay, let me introduce it by two passages, which typically contradict Montaigne's own explicit ideology of the self. The first occurs very near the 'end' of the *Essays*:

I, who boast of embracing the pleasures of life so assiduously and so particularly, find in them, when I look at them thus minutely, virtually nothing but wind. But what of it? WE ARE ALL WIND. And even the wind, more wisely than we, loves to make a noise and move about, and is content with its own functions [*offices*], without desiring stability and solidity, qualities that do not belong to it (III, 13, 849c [1087], my emphasis).

The passage implies very clearly that Montaigne has never reached the state of equilibrium or homeostasis he desires (he had attained it – after the event – with La Boétie, where input matched output in what he describes as a "fusion" of their respective selves), and it demands that the reader recognize his own stake in reading Montaigne, in following Montaigne on the quest of self-knowledge. What I particularly like about the metaphor Montaigne employs here is that with the help of a little meteorological information unavailable to Montaigne, one could analyze it as his own description of a communications system – for the wind is the expression of a relationship between centers of high and low pressure, and the weather itself can be regarded as an open system regulated by feedback. But it is not necessary to press the point so hard, except in so far as this passage is in any event a metastatement about what Montaigne might have called the 'autonomous ego', if he had been familiar with one of the more curious branches of psychoanalysis. Our mental life, like Montaigne's 'wind', is the expression of relationships; we ARE what we communicate. "We are all wind" is not so much one of Montaigne's replies to his central question "What do I know?", as a comment on the reason the question was posed in the first place.

The second passage will, I think, be self-explanatory, in view of what has already been said. Speaking of himself, he says:

(a) It is no less peculiar to the kind of temperament I am speaking of that it wants to be stimulated . . . to be roused and warmed up by external, present, and accidental stimuli [*par les occasions estrangères, présentes et fortuites*]. If it goes along by itself, it does nothing but drag and languish. Agitation is its very life and grace. (b) I have very little control over myself and my moods. . . . The occasion, the company, the very sound of my voice, draw more from my mind than when I probe it and use it by myself. . . . (c) This also happens to me: that I do not find myself where I seek myself [*je ne me trouve pas où je me cherche*]; and I find myself more by chance encounter [*par rencontre*] than by searching my judgment (I, 10, 26–7 [41–2]).

This chance encounter is both in the world and in his re-reading of his own book.

5. *The Paradoxes of Existence*

If the first passage quoted establishes a particular relationship to the reader, it does so more by direct attack combined with a sidelong appeal for sympathy than by the much more profound and subtle device Montaigne employs elsewhere. This is his intuitive recourse to the paradoxical injunction or the double bind. What I shall call the 'existential paradoxes' in Montaigne's *Essays* all have the form of paradoxical injunctions. Montaigne receives these injunctions from the Other – his particular genius lies in how he turns them round until they are directed at the reader.

We can define the paradox in general by saying that it is a logical contradiction arrived at through valid deductions from apparently non-contradictory premisses. The existential paradox is the conscious or unconscious intentionalization by a subject of something about life which denies the usually accepted categories of truth and falsity about 'reality' – something 'inexplicable'. The existential paradox differs from the purely logical paradox in that it involves subjects and is primarily dependent on communication. Moreover, it is part of an open system involving feedback and human time.

Montaigne was more than simply interested in the logical paradox, as is demonstrated by the lengthy attack on reason in the *Apologie de Raimond Sebond* (II, 12). Various logical and existential paradoxes occur in this essay. The 'I am lying' paradox, for instance, occurs on p. 393 (508), where it is immediately followed by a remark about the need for a "new language" to deal with this sort of difficulty (just as Carnap's theory of metalanguage and Russell's theory of logical types eventually did, in part), and then by Montaigne's celebrated appeal: *Que sçay-je?* The juxtaposition of these three ideas is significant, since in one respect the *Essays* as a whole represent a new type of language applied to the existential paradoxes of human existence, and the attack on reason itself seems clearly to be a report about experience which Montaigne would much rather not have been driven to make. The attack on reason amounts to a denial of the rationality of Montaigne himself, and the entire *dialogos* of the *Essays* can surely be read as an OSCILLATION between Montaigne's reiterated belief in the value of the rational discourse and his discovery of the irrationality of that discourse.

In an existential context, however, "I am lying" is not a paradox at all. Existentially, it can only occur in an interactional context (whereas the logician's "I am lying" is not spoken by a subject, but rather by the Other as an ideal speaker, and even if it were, that subject is implicitly a monad). It might be the reply to "Are you telling the truth?" In other words, because the syntagmatic mode of communication involves both a human context and human temporality (as opposed to the pure sequences of logic, which is concerned, as in symbolic logic, primarily with the timelessness of paradigms), as well as a receiver, it supposes a sender–receiver relationship in which the 'subjective' meaning in a context of 'action' and 're-action' is more important than the 'objective' meaning. "I am lying" is simply a metacommunication, about another, temporally anterior, statement. In the metacommunication, the subject is talking about his time, not the time of grammar books. It is our automatic metacommunicative response to the statement which makes "I am lying" existentially valid and not in the least paradoxical.

The existential paradox is of a different order. Basically it represents a command that can be neither obeyed nor disobeyed. In Bateson's theory of schizophrenia, paradoxical injunctions are actual commands of this type. They are directed by the Other in a familial system of pathological communication at the 'schizophrenic' member of the system, eventually forcing him into the typical schizophrenic double bind of trying not to communicate at all (which is, of course, impossible, since even silence is communication). Paradoxical injunctions or double binds are common enough. A classic example of the absolute paradoxical injunction is a sign bearing the words "Disregard this sign". At its own level of language, the injunction can be neither obeyed nor disobeyed. It can be dealt with only by metacommunication: by the realization and the expression of the realization that the sign is self-reflexive (like the logical paradox: "I am lying"), and therefore logically meaningless, because the 'this', in logic, can only refer to another sign about which the first sign is communicating. Since the 'this' of the sign is both referent language and metalanguage, "Disregard this sign" is not a valid statement. But in the pathological milieu of the schizophrenic family, the system automatically adjusts to the responses of the schizophrenic member so as to prevent or disallow his attempts to metacommunicate. (The system is punctuated arbitrarily[10] at the schizophrenic; but it is surely the others who are insane). The function of the therapist, for as long as he does not himself become double-bound by the system, is to provide an avenue for this metacommunication (the 'cure'). Without this avenue, "the paradoxical injunction . . . bankrupts choice itself, nothing is possible, and a self-perpetuating oscillating series is set in motion" (Watzlawick, Beavin, and Jackson, 1967: 217).

6. *Know Thyself*

> Our world divides into facts because we so divide it.
> SUSANNE LANGER

Like all of us, Montaigne experiences his share of double binds. He seeks to metacommunicate about certain of them to the reader, but he uses them on the reader too. The particular double bind towards which I have been directing the argument of this chapter occurs in the first sentence of *De la vanité*: "There is perhaps no more obvious vanity than to write of vanity so vainly" (II, 9, 721b [922]). It might be objected that this statement is not strictly speaking an injunction: the point is that it RE-presents one. It represents injunctions about vanity which Montaigne has received from the Other, and it is at the same time Montaigne's feedback to those injunctions. Thus it becomes an implicit injunction directed at the Other represented by the reader. But is it a true paradox? Not at first sight, since all it says in effect is "Disregard this sign" and the 'this' refers to the title: "Of Vanity". At this level, the first sentence is simply a logical contradiction: "Read this essay on vanity in order to find out about vanity but do not expect to learn about vanity from a man whose writings are simply vanity." Choice is possible; there is no double bind. But then Montaigne goes on to state explicitly that the essay on vanity is only the result of his own vanity: "Who does not see that I have taken a road along which I shall go, without stopping and without effort [*travail*], as long as there is ink and paper in the world?" (ibid.)

---

[10] That is to say that it is necessarily punctuated there by the social context in which the 'psychological problem' – the 'mad or bad' victim – occurs.

It is now immediately obvious that the implicit injunction about vanity is in fact a double bind for Montaigne ("I cannot obey or disobey what the Other tells me about vanity, and I can't help it"). The Other is telling him: "Be vainly authentic" or "Be authentically vain." Whereas the reader is still free to obey or disobey Montaigne's "Disregard this sign", Montaigne has never been free to do either one or the other.

With this realization, however, the reader who has decided to ignore Montaigne's self-contradiction and to go on reading anyway suddenly discovers that he is now sharing Montaigne's double bind. Montaigne has enjoined him to judge the authenticity of Montaigne's vanity and the vanity of Montaigne's authenticity – either of which means that if the reader understands Montaigne's predicament, he is automatically part of it. Montaigne has taken over from 'his' Other the function which makes him the reader's Other, and the reader is now precisely where Montaigne was when he wrote these lines. "Judge not," says Montaigne, "that ye be not judged", and then both he and the reader continue their quest together.

"Recognize my vanity", says Montaigne, "but you will not succeed in 'seeing me as I want you to see me' unless you can see yourself." Montaigne's statement surely has everything to do with truth, but no one would pretend that this truth is the 'objective' truth of logic. As an isolated logical statement, the first sentence of *De la vanité* is meaningless, because it is self-reflexive; it judges its own validity. As an existential paradox, however, it has several levels of meaning or truth. It expresses Montaigne's double bind, and it involves the reader in it. Equally important, perhaps, it expresses the reiterated message of the *Essays*: Montaigne's demand for recognition of himself, of his self, of his view of the self. Obviously, its truth-function is not a logical truth-function. Although it is necessarily expressed in the digital form of language and speaks the binary language of analytic logic (true/false), the statement is in effect an injunction about a relationship. Its form is digital, but its function is analog. Analog communication[11] is inherently ambiguous, it is continuous, and it involves a significant ambivalence about 'negation'. If disconfirmation were negation, for instance, then the disconfirmed would presumably cease to exist – or at least his demand for recognition would be stilled. But the relationship

---

[11] On the model of the analog computer: "Human beings communicate both digitally and analogically. Digital language has a highly complex and powerful logical syntax but lacks adequate semantics in the field of relationship, while analogic language possesses the semantics but has no adequate syntax for the unambiguous definition of the nature of relationships" (Watzlawick, Beavin, and Jackson, 1967: 66–7).

cannot be negated; if he seeks to treat himself as a non-person, an object, he is nevertheless conforming to the desire of the Other. Thus, the function of Montaigne's double bind is not to establish truth or falsehood but to establish the sender in a particular metacommunicative relationship of recognition with the receiver through analog statements pregnant with meaning because of their ambiguities.

Another level of meaning in Montaigne's double-binding injunction on vanity is only brought out in the closing words of this lengthy essay. In fact it is only the double bind at the beginning which adequately explains the curious change of tone in the last two paragraphs, where Montaigne makes his strongest attack on the desire of the Other and on the Delphic injunction:

> If others examined themselves attentively, as I do, they would find themselves, as I do, full of inanity and nonsense. Get rid of it I cannot without getting rid of myself.
>
> . . . In order not to dishearten us, Nature has very appropriately thrown the action of our vision outward. We go forward with the current, but to turn our course back toward ourselves is a painful movement. . . .

We are forced always to "look high or low, or to one side, or in front, or behind us" – in other words, we cannot avoid communicating.

> It was a PARADOXICAL COMMAND that was given us of old by that god at Delphi: 'Look into yourself, know yourself, keep to yourself; bring back your mind and your will, which are spending themselves elsewhere, into themselves; you are running out, you are scattering yourself; concentrate yourself, resist yourself; you are being betrayed, dispersed, and stolen away from yourself. Do you not see that this world [i.e., what Montaigne sees as a world of closed, autonomous systems] keeps its sight all concentrated inward and its eyes open to contemplate itself? It is always vanity for you, within and without; but it is less vanity when it is less extensive. . . . There is not a single thing as empty and needy as you [O man], who embraces the universe: you are the investigator without knowledge, the magistrate without jurisdiction, and all in all, *le badin de la farce* (III, 9, 766b [979–80], my emphasis).

7. Pathological Communication

It is here, surely, that we can recognize a fundamental double bind both for us and for Montaigne: 'Know thyself' means on the one hand seek to isolate and examine the alienated, mediated, and inauthentic construct we call our self; on the other, it means that we cannot know ourselves 'authentically' unless we are in the world, unless we know others, for our self has no meaning and no existence except in its relationship to Otherness. But in our mediation by the Imaginary Other, we lose ourselves in the objectifications of the socioeconomic discourse. Our cherished self turns out to be a thing, a piece of property, a commodity. 'Self' or 'other' become the two terms of a self-perpetuating oscillating series in a schizophrenic system of communication. The *Essays* are replete with sets of such impossible alternatives. But are we therefore to say that Montaigne was schizophrenic or schizoid and leave matters there? Not if we understand that schizophrenia in this sense is a social condition. Not if we understand that the double bind is one of the most powerful weapons used against the individual members of our society to prevent metacommunication about its Imaginary values. Not if we understand that only if we share in this epistemology of opposition and identity can we be trapped into the counter-adaptive antinomies of class, caste, race, and sex.

Montaigne's reply to the double binds he perceived was to make a remarkable attempt to metacommunicate about them. Unfortunately, his metacommunication is usually translated by his readers as a commentary, not about the disintegrating social organization in which Montaigne found himself, but only about the eternities of the HUMAN CONDITION. It is true that the *Essays* are ALSO about the Gödelian paradoxes of a creature who communicates digitally with his fellows, with his past, and with himself, for all digitalization is inherently paradoxical (Chapter VII). But since there is indeed a necessary connection between the form of the paradox which disjoins the subject of digital knowledge and the subject of analog knowledge in our society, and the particular socioeconomic organization of western culture, our particular version of the human condition is not in any demonstrable sense the fate allotted by the gods to all of man-and-womankind. And as far as that condition is concerned, it is about time we dropped in to see what condition our condition is in.

So long, however, as a dominant ideology requires us to repeatedly ask: "Who am I?" – the precise digital correlate of "What do I know?" – then the required level of metacommunication about our social double bind is beyond us as individuals. The therapist at this level can only be God himself. In the pathological system of communication represented by modern society, we cannot hope – as individuals – to transcend the paradoxical injunctions of our social existence. On the one hand, the specific form of these paradoxes is a product of the atomistic organization of the system itself. On the other, as we cast about for room to move, the system falls into step with us and adjusts its feedback to match our output. Like Montaigne or Zeno – as individuals – we are equally bound to go on oscillating back and forth between our own logical, communicational, psychological, and material antinomies. Given our status as discrete, combinatory units in the system, we are therefore required either to learn or not to learn to face what Montaigne ultimately learned to face: the realization that the INDIVIDUAL analysis is endless (*unendliche*).

But there is an avenue of metacommunication that neither Montaigne nor the therapist can be said ever to really consider.

The only avenue of metacommunication that can escape the oscillations of the individualistic ethic on which the paradoxical injunction depends in our present pathological context, is that of the collective praxis of human kind: the reduction of the digital to its natural function as an instrument of relationship, where now it is an exploitative device. For whereas there is no possibility – and no necessity – of overcoming our relation to Otherness, and no need for a metalanguage which will disprove Gödel, there will eventually have to be devised a way of overcoming our present enslavement to the Imaginary Other. This enslavement depends on a value-system based on the maintenance of exploitative oppositions and identities. If our species is to survive, humankind must find a way of reintroducing the mediating function of difference and similarity into the social ecosystem. As the young Marx put it (1844: 162):

It is only in a social context that subjectivism and objectivism, spiritualism and materialism, activity and passivity cease to be antinomies, and thus cease to exist as such antinomies. The resolution of the THEORETICAL contradictions is possible ONLY through practical means, only through the PRACTICAL energy of man.

Chapter V

The Double Bind

SCHIZOPHRENIA AND GÖDEL

> The primary form of
> mathematical communication is
> not description, but injunction.
> G. SPENCER BROWN: *Laws of
> Form*

1. *Closure and Context*

It is not for nothing that Freud often compared the constructions of the analyst and the philosopher to the delusions of the so-called schizophrenic. For the theory of the double bind in schizophrenia mediates the relationship between schizophrenia and science. It is a logico-mathematical construction through which we may discover the explanation of the delusions of the philosopher in the communicational processes of the schizophrenic relation.

The double-bind theory of schizophrenia evolved out of research into the schizophrenic relation in the family, rather than 'into' the so-called schizophrenic, and took as its starting-point the phenomenology of communication. A phenomenological approach to communication implicitly or explicitly assumes that all behavior is communication. As a result, the schizophrenic (relation) can no longer be described as the product of 'disease' or 'illness' or 'instinctual conflict' or 'intrapersonal conflict'; it can only be described as a product and a form of PATHOLOGICAL COMMUNICATION.

It may be objected that 'communication' is a linguistic concept, or that it refers to 'understanding', to 'speech', or to 'communion'. Although I use the word in a scientific, rather than in an everyday sense, it does not entirely lose its everyday usage. But it is a semiotic and not a linguistic concept: it refers to the transmission of signals, signs, signifiers, and symbols in any communications system whatsoever. This may include interorganismic or intraorganismic communication, communication in biological systems, communication between animals or between human beings, psychosocial or socioeconomic communication. As such the term has the Marxian sense of *Verkehr*. 'Communion' is the product and the goal of all exchange and all communication, and pathological communication in a society or in a family is as sacred a form of communion as any other. All that is necessary to avoid reductionism or to avoid the false analogies of 'organismic' approaches to societies or 'historical' approaches to organisms (for example) is a careful distinction of levels of communication, a distinction based on the relative semiotic freedom (flexibility, manipulability, freedom within constraints) of the various levels one can methodologically distinguish.

One of the most important contributions of the cybernetic and communicational theory I am outlining here, especially that aspect of it directly concerned with the double bind, involves the epistemological problem of context. Before dealing with the double bind as such, therefore, it is necessary to situate the theory itself in context.

If we use the term 'pathological communication', it is obviously of importance to indicate some set of values by which 'normal' communication can be measured. But since such values are always ideological and cultural, no such 'scientific' – or 'quantitative' or 'objective' – set of values exists as such, nor is it likely to exist. The communicational viewpoint necessarily destroys the 'objective' values of scientism, and even in physics, especially as a result of relativity on the one hand and of quantum mechanics on the other, it is almost universally accepted that the behavior of any system, open or closed, informational or energetic, organic or inorganic, is a function of the way the observer-participator PUNCTUATES it. The philosophy of science is the epistemology of our knowledge of 'science'. Moreover, to call any system open or closed, or to call it informational or energetic, or to call the observer a participator, are all acts of punctuation, if at a more abstract level than the punctuation which occurs in the 'observation' itself.

The relation of 'text' and 'context' is one of punctuation, for it involves the problem of boundaries, a question to which we shall return in considering Gödel's proof. Rather than being errors in SYNTAX, as the logical positivists would have it, all epistemological errors in science and philosophy are errors of punctuation. By error, I do not mean mistakes about facts, but rather the implicit or explicit application of hypotheses derived from a part of the field, whether derived 'ideologically' or 'scientifically', to the field as a whole. The implicit or explicit application of equilibrium or inertia theory, derived from mechanics or thermodynamics, to communications systems is an example of such an error. The reason for using the term punctuation rather than syntax, is that syntax is either a strictly linguistic term or else it refers to the modes and rules of articulation within a given system (language, for instance). Punctuation, however, may refer to the interference of another system with the given system. Thus gestures, facial expressions, intonation and so forth, punctuate a spoken discourse; the logistics of print and paging punctuate a written discourse; death punctuates life.

If we leave aside that level of communication at which the retina of the eye, for example, punctuates 'reality' in ways over which we have very little control and which we can only talk about, it is evident that most of the epistemological errors of punctuation which are not the result of accident (as when DNA becomes wrongly punctuated), can have their source only in the SEMANTICS – and therefore, in the final analysis, only in the PRAGMATICS – of human communication.

The semantics of communications systems (organisms, societies, etc.) concern the way in which information is given meaning in the circuit between sender and receiver (outside that circuit, all information is noise), in order to trigger or control energy in the interests of organization. The semantics of the organism or of the social system or of the family thus concern the use of information in the interests of the WORK to be done by the senders and receivers, which may or may not be consonant with the long-range or short-range goals of the system as a whole, or of certain subsystems within it. Semantics and pragmatics are consequently indissolubly linked, for all interests are vested interests. The syntax of the system is at one and the same time in the service of its goals and an unavoidable constraint on the system's possibilities. Syntax is thus directly related to semiotic freedom. The highest level of semiotic freedom is that which allows multiple levels of metacommunication, such as is possible in language.

To provide a specific instance of punctuation, let us take a simple example from Gregory Bateson (1971a: cf. also Buckley, 1967: 54–5), who is the man primarily responsible for the double-bind theory. In this example, the sender–receivers A and B exchange the following set of messages: *a-b-a'*. The isolation of this set is already an arbitrary punctuation of a circuit of communication, and, of course, in the venerable language of S–R theory, each message, *a* or *b* or *a'*, is simultaneously stimulus, response, and reinforcement. Let us assume that we are interested in questions of power, responsibility, and dominance–dependence in the relationship of A and B. According to most current theory and our own ingrained attitudes, if we substitute an innocuous set of messages in this (isolated) arc of the circuit between A and B, we should be able to discover who is the dominant partner:

A: Please give me a glass of water
B: (Hands the water to A)
A: Thank you

Obviously B is dominant, for A made a REQUEST, B decided to accede to it, and A reinforced the dominance of B by thanking him for his kindness. But what if we punctuate A's first message as a COMMAND? We discover immediately that A was dominant all along, for B obeyed the command, and by replying "thank you", A reinforced B's submission to him.

It is immediately obvious that the definition of the relation depends upon an arbitrary decision on the part of the observer and the participators, for both A and B may regard themselves as dominant or submissive (or both at once). The relationship may in fact be mutual (reciprocal) or pseudo-mutual, or any number of things. What is self-evident – as Dostoevsky could have told us – is that each communicator is dependent on the other at a higher level of logical typing (see below) than that of their dominant–submissive relation.

But thus to introduce the dependency relationship of the master on the slave, of the victim on the executioner, is only another way of mispunctuating the system. Not only did we originally isolate a triad from the total context of the messages between A and B. We have also isolated the obvious verbal and active part of the communication (its either/or digital aspect) from its non-verbal and possibly unconscious context (its both–and analog aspect). Quite apart from the HISTORY of the relationship, it makes a great deal of difference to know in what tone of voice A spoke, what expression there was on his face, what his bodily attitude was, and so on. But even this is not enough, of course. What about the PHYSICAL, CULTURAL, and POLITICAL context of A and B, whom we have isolated from that context in this example? It would make a difference, for instance, to discover that A and B are in a psychological testing laboratory as opposed to being in bed together.

And it would make the most significant difference of all to discover that B was on welfare, or that he was a Viet Cong, an Algerian, a black, a Jew, a chicano, a member of the working class, or a woman, whereas A was a male white Anglo-Saxon Protestant 'professional' or his equivalent.

In other words, NO COMMUNICATION CAN BE PROPERLY DEFINED OR EXAMINED AT THE LEVEL AT WHICH THE COMMUNICATION OCCURS. But this is almost never true of the way in which most communications are in fact explicitly or implicitly defined in our culture. The communication can only be properly examined by reference to the metacommunicative levels of punctuation and context. Interestingly enough, but hardly a matter for surprise, is the fact that the very psychotherapists and psychoanalysts who make constant explicit or implicit reference to and use of meta-communication, are also those most likely to be seriously deficient in fully understanding the question of context. This deficiency is as evident in the people who developed the theory of metacommunication, including Bateson himself, as it is in Freudian analysts, like Lacan, or in 'genetic structuralists' like Piaget. By reference to the family context, to the genesis of the epistemic subject, to the past history of the patient, to the analog components of the communication, or to the unconscious, and so on, all such therapists, analysts, and psychologists seem to be pursuing and utilizing a critical theory and practice concerned with metacommunication, punctuation, and context. But in fact they are not, for their concept of context is almost invariably restricted to the MANIFEST context of the 'here and now'.[1]

Given the omnipresent nature of contextual relations, it is obvious that all theories of relationship require a certain artificial closure. We are not particularly concerned about the physical effects of the moon – as opposed to its possible psychological and cultural values and effects – on A and B, for example. But the closure evident in the theories I am criticizing is not such a necessary METHODOLOGICAL closure. It is a closure stemming from cultural values, ideological values, or ignorance – and ignorance of the context happens to be one of our most highly developed cultural values.

There is little point in elaborating in detail the numerous examples of this ignorance which could be given. It is not so much the theory that is or may be in question as it is the ignorance of his OWN context on the part of the theoretician, for, although our critique may indeed involve an attack on the methodology, the epistemology, or the ideology of the theory itself,

---

[1] Cf. Watzlawick, Beavin, and Jackson (1967: 44):

> All this brings us back to the attribution of 'meaning', a notion that is essential for the subjective experience of communicating with others but which we have found to be objectively undecidable for the purposes of research in human communication.

See also Laing's implicit and objectionable assumption of the symmetry between 'Jack' and 'Jill' in his examples of pathological communication (*Knots*, 1970). With all that Laing has done to liberate the 'patient' from the violence of the 'therapist', he can still fall into the trap of excluding that part of the social context which makes Jills the slaves of Jacks – thus perpetrating the violence of male chauvinism in the most alienating way of all: not noticing it.

it is at the analog level of context, rather than at the digital level of text, that its most searching questions will be directed. In a word, the critique will focus on the inability to recognize or the refusal to recognize the LOGICAL CONSEQUENCES of the theory. This failure on the part of the practitioner of the theory has nothing to do with science, with intelligence, with 'truth', or with the 'objective facts'. It is a question of values, an ethical and political question, a question of praxis.

For when the therapist has reduced all problems to psychological problems, all motivation to the equivalent of a pile of shit; when the sociologist has reduced all social interaction to a variety of equilibrated attraction and repulsion; when the anthropologist has reduced human reality to structure and function; when the economist has reduced the violence of the economic system to a management problem to be corrected by 'adjusting' or 'tuning' the system – and then when each 'specialist' or 'expert' has uncritically extended his knowledge of part of the field to the whole of the field, each has done no more than to manifest a kind of disciplinary imperialism.

But it is the therapist with whom we are the most directly concerned here. He is the epitome of liberalism, for in psychotherapy all ideas are equal. But the ideological imperialism of psychotherapeutic and psycho-analytical theory is in essence only a justification of the privileged economic and cultural position of the therapist. We can understand entirely why his Hippocratean ethic requires him to treat the executioner as well as the victim. But we cannot agree that his oath requires him to extend his ethic to the biosocial context of all mankind. Because his ethic is a 'biological' one – concerned, that is, with psychobiological life and death – it is a confusion of levels of organization to extend it to the psychosocial sphere.

There is never any justification for unrecognized self-justification. There is no meaning – not even 'noise' – without context, and no theory can occur outside a context. Moreover, a theory is only another version of a com-munications system: it is goalseeking, adaptive, essentially dependent on its 'environment', and open to it. Like all such open systems, it exists in a context of selection: its goal is to survive. There is of course some value to theories of human behavior which are derived from, and thus entirely uncritical of, their socioeconomic context – they do at least serve as meta-phors of what they deny or repudiate.

With the word 'survive', we can approach a definition of the value system against which to measure the term pathological communication. Drawing on Bateson (1970) and on my own extension of his theory, we can say that the concept of long-range survival in nature does not concern the 'fittest' individual or the 'fittest' species. Since all organisms are open systems dependent on an environment to survive in, the concept of survival must be one which considers the unit of survival to be 'organism-plus-environment' (including other organisms). In other words, since the organism (or system) which destroys its environment necessarily destroys itself, what must survive is not EITHER the 'organism' OR the 'environment', but BOTH subsystem AND context. But the dominant ideology has long been one which places mankind in a relationship of opposition to nature. Such a relationship of opposition is pathological, not just because it is exploitative (which does after all provide a simple ethical justification for calling it pathological), but rather because it substitutes short-range survival value (competition) for long-range survival value (cooperation).

On examination, we find that the entity-oriented, bioenergetic values of our culture tend to turn all natural differences into similar artificial oppositions. By drawing an Imaginary epistemological line between 'organism' and 'environment', the ideology of our culture justifies all such lines. The message-in-circuit between man and woman, self and other, white and Third World, reason and emotion – all such totalities which are actually dependent on the survival of a relationship of non-exploitative difference between one part of the circuit and the other – are converted into exploitative relations of opposition. They are punctuated in this way by those who have the power to punctuate – and therefore the power to be responsible for the punctuation. And no matter what ecosystem we consider – natural, social, psychological, economic – the punctuators tend both individually and collectively to be white, male, industrialized, affluent, and usually Protestant. That is to say, they are either the actual physical embodiment of these terms, or, like the black bourgeoisie in America or West Africa, or the mandarins of South Vietnam, they are representatives of the values embodied in such terms. Their fundamental ethic is very simple: if you are on the 'right' side of the Imaginary line, you are justified in exploiting whatever is defined as being on the 'other' side. Having initiated or accepted a relation of violence and oppression through the abuse of power, you are then justified in developing a theory of self-defense: you may justifiably project your violence onto the 'other' and be afraid of him (her).

Thus we can define as pathological all communication which is exploitative – of self, of others, of nature, of the Third World – in the sense that it substitutes Imaginary survival values for the long-range survival values of the natural ecosystem. And we must assign the overall responsibility for pathological communication in our culture to those who have the (economic) power to change it. Individual responsibility remains unaffected by the doctrine of overall responsibility; it is simply a responsibility of a lower logical type (see below). The parent who makes the child a signifier in his own phantasies remains no less responsible for the effects of his communication, and no less responsible for discovering the source of the exploitative value system to which he subscribes. Since not all societies manifest the kind of exploitative alienation evident in our own, the primary source of that exploitative value system – no less dangerous to the parent but more immediately devastating for the child – must lie in the socioeconomic organization of relationships in the culture. In a word, there is not only a logical typing of communication in our culture, but also a logical typing of EXPLOITATION. In the social organization of opposition and aggressivity, human psychology may well provide the keyboard, but it is society which plays the tune.

The foregoing is necessarily an oversimplification of the problematic of punctuation, but it performs the function of indicating the context in which it is possible to talk relevantly about the double bind. For just as all behavior is communication, all communication, including logic and mathematics, is susceptible to double binds.

2. Logical Conditions for the Double Bind

> τῆς φύσεως γραμματεὺς ἦν, τον
> κάλαμον ἀποβρέξων εἰς νοῦν.[2]
> SUIDAS

In what follows, I am summarizing and elaborating on the original publication on the double-bind theory of schizophrenia (Bateson, Jackson, Haley, and Weakland, 1956). Page numbers indicate close paraphrases of the text.

The central thesis depends upon Russell's theory of logical types, according to which there is a discontinuity between a class and its members. The class cannot be a member of itself, nor can one of the members BE the class, because the term used for the class is of a different level of abstraction or logical type from the terms used for the members of the class (p. 251). In the psychology of 'real' communications, however, this discontinuity is continually and inevitably breached – it is in fact a condition of human creativity – and when this confusion occurs in certain power relationships, such as that between parent and child, it may lead to pathological communication which is at least formally equivalent to 'schizophrenic' communication.

---

[2] From the tenth-century Greek encyclopedia based on the lexicon of Hesychius: "He was the scribe of *physis*, nature, dipping his pen into mind."

The diversity of communicational modes amongst human beings allows the breaching of the boundaries between logical types both WITHIN the message in any given mode of communication and BETWEEN the message and its contexts. Thus logical typing may be breached within a digital message, or between the digital message and its analog context (and vice versa). As we shall see later, the locus of the breach is significant for the understanding of paradoxes, contradictions, and boundaries.

The main aspects of the original version of the theory are as follows:

1 The signals or signs which 'frame' or 'label' the message (or which metacommunicate about the communication in the message) are obviously of a higher logical type than the messages they classify. The complexity of this metacommunication is so elaborate that we have only a poorly developed vocabulary to deal with it as context (p. 252). This vocabulary is INHERENTLY restricted by the well-developed semantics but almost non-existent syntactics of analog communication, whose goal is to define relationships, as opposed to the weak semantics but powerful (logical) syntax of digital communication, whose goal is to transmit 'information' in the non-technical sense (concepts and ideas about objects, events, and relations).

2 Humor is the most obvious form of the CONDENSATION of logical types. The punch-line of a joke has the peculiar effect of requiring a re-evaluation of anterior logical typing. Thus a previous message in the joke, which appeared as a communication (as literal), may be re-evaluated by the punch-line so that it becomes a metacommunication (a metaphor), and it is the oscillation between message and meta-message which is amusing. In Freud's 'famillionairly' joke, for example, 'millionaire' types the person (digital) and 'familiarly' types his attitude (analog).

3 Metacommunicative messages between human beings may be falsified, consciously or unconsciously.

4 Communication and learning involve levels of logical typing. A message which is simply received represents a first or zero level of learning. Identifying the message as belonging to a set or context involves a second level of learning. The progressive re-programming of the message from the level of 'surprise' to that of 'habit', or from 'conscious attention' (hypercathexis) to 'hard programming' (cathexis), involves a third level: that of LEARNING TO LEARN. There is at least a fourth level of learning, and each is of a higher logical type than that which 'precedes' it.

5 'Schizophrenic' communication is characterized either by a refusal to

label metaphors and contexts, or by unconventional labeling. Schizo-phrenic communication is nevertheless a perfectly adequate communi-cational response, WITH SURVIVAL VALUE, to a context of paradoxical injunctions (double binds). Although the original and subsequent versions of the theory do not use this terminology, we can distinguish at least three levels of paradoxical injunction: those emanating from the 'other' in the family context, those emanating from the Other in the sense of the sociocultural context, and those emanating from Otherness in the sense of the constraints on both analog and digital thought, and on their presentation in language and logic (the human condition). The double binds used by the others in the family context may or may not call upon these two higher levels of paradox.

All double binds emanating from the others involve a deliberate but usually denied or repudiated confusion of logical types. When Bateson says that the 'schizophrenic' confuses the metaphor with what is meant, or when Freud says that he 'treats word(-presentations) like thing (-presentations)', or when Lacan says that for the psychotic 'the Symbolic is the Real', they are all talking about LEARNED confusions of logical typing in a pathological context.

6 In order to understand the sense of 'injunction', it must be realized that (*a*) in a communications system 'nothing never happens' (Bird-whistell), (*b*) every message in any system whatsoever is simultaneously a report on a situation and a command to do something (which may be 'nothing') about it (McCulloch), and (*c*) since one cannot NOT com-municate in the analog, silence itself is a communication.

3. Real Conditions

> In other words, I can't be anything but
> myself, and if people don't like me the way
> they am – ah, the way I am – then I appreciate
> when they – tell me or something, is what it
> amounts to.
> DAVE, a victim

Double binds create 'unresolvable' sequences of experience. This charac-teristic of unresolvability depends on the level of the double bind: it may only be perceived as one by the receiver, or he may be prevented from not perceiving it as one, for all double binds can be transcended. The condi-tions under which one member of the family may attempt to transcend the pathological communication of his milieu by attempting to cease communicating – i.e., by going 'mad' – are described as follows in the original publication. (Note that, in keeping with the well-known fact that 'going mad' is the beginning of the cure, it is also the only level at which the victim who is subjected to the conditions which follow can at first transcend the double bind.)

1 A 'victim' chosen by those who have the power to make such a choice.

2 Repeated experience of paradoxical injunctions on the part of the 'victim'.

3 A PRIMARY negative injunction defining learning as the avoidance of punishment. Punishment may involve the expression of hate or anger, physical abuse, withdrawal of reward, 'withdrawal' of love, or an attitude of helplessness on the part of the parent in relation to the child.

4 A SECONDARY injunction conflicting with the first at a more abstract level, usually communicated by analog means.

5 Most important, a TERTIARY injunction at a higher level yet, which prohibits the victim from escaping the pathological communication of the first two levels (e.g., the promise of love to come).

6 Once these conditions have been sufficiently programmed into the victim, the complete set of ingredients is no longer necessary. Almost any part of a double-bind sequence may precipitate panic or rage in the victim. The pattern of conflicting injunctions may even be taken over by hallucinatory voices (pp. 253–4).

The authors then go on to comment on the use of the double bind in Zen Buddhism. The master may hold a stick over the head of the pupil and say: "If you say this stick is real, I shall hit you. If you say it is not real, I shall hit you. If you don't say anything at all, I shall hit you." The significance of this example lies in the implicit representation of the tertiary injunction, condition (5). So long as the Zen master is defined as the subject-who-is-supposed-to-know by the pact between master and pupil, the pupil is in a double bind. That is, he can neither obey nor disobey the master. But if he perceives the real nature of the situation, he has only to metacommunicate about it in order to be released from the double bind. He can communicate with the master at a higher level of communication: he can grab the stick and take it away, or he can hit the master with it. All such paradoxical injunctions emanating from 'others' or from the culture involve a definition of a power relationship in which the subject-who-is-supposed-to-know is the locus of violence in the communication. This violence can only be met by metacommunication or by counterviolence. But the Zen Master's double bind is essentially benevolent. The authors go on to point out the implicit and explicit double binds benevolently used in the therapeutic relationship. Bateson has later said that all therapy depends on the proper use of the double bind. (Cf. also his analysis of alcoholism and the work of Alcoholics Anonymous.)

Since the original article was written, Bateson has pointed to some of the errors and inconsistencies in it (1969b), of which the most important is the lack of a distinction between CONTRADICTORY or CONFLICTING injunctions and paradoxical injunctions. It is too easy simply to define the double-bind relationship as one in which one terminal of the message circuit has the power – and uses it – to continually change or falsify the rules by which the other terminal has learned to communicate with him.[3]

FIGURE 1

The point is that the double bind goes beyond the level at which it is most commonly described: "You're damned if you do, and damned if you don't." The double bind is endemic in all human communication, especially in logic and mathematics, for it is founded not on contradiction, but on paradox.

[3] This is in fact how the so-called 'experimental neuroses' are induced in animals. There is obviously no way that an animal that has not been TRAINED to accept an artificial context of learning and of learning how to learn – the context of the experiment – can be driven 'crazy', for if he has not learned the arbitrary rules laid down by the experimenter, the experimenter cannot annul or falsify them. Note that this falsification occurs at the FOURTH or trito level of learning. It does not occur at the zero level (the reception of information), nor at the deutero level of the rules of learning how to learn it. All paradoxical double binds involve the fourth level, the higher level of METARULES, that of therapeutic efficacy.

Visual double binds, like visual illusions, also have their source in metarules, the rules of learned three-dimensional perspective applied to two-dimensional planes (*Figure 1*). Thus, in the work of Escher (1960), for example, the rules are posited at one level in the print and annulled at another level (e.g., prints #62–#76). Irresolvable oscillations are consequently set up. The oscillation between the two faces and the vase in the well-known gestalt illustration of the figure–ground relationship is a common example of another type.

As Teuber's excellent article on Escher now shows us (1974), many of Escher's 'metamorphic' prints use a matrix of 'ambiguous' figure-ground figures as an iconic mapping of the – ever-smooth and yet ever-distinct – BOUNDARY between figure and ground (cf. also p. 315). (Figure and ground involve a perceptual manipulation of levels.) These prints are VISUAL discussions of the paradox of the boundary.

4. The Paradox of Paradox

> The earth – our mother – and I are of one mind.
> INDIAN CHIEF: The 'frame' of his response
> to white demands for territory

An analog message may contradict a digital message, and the victim may well perceive this contradiction as an injunction which he can neither obey nor disobey. But properly speaking the paradigm of the paradoxical injunction is the Cretan paradox 'I am lying' or some such message as 'Do not read this'. For our purposes here, it is not important whether we use Russell's theory of logical types or Carnap's theory of metalanguage and object language to resolve a particular paradoxical injunction; nor whether we follow the distinctions between various types of paradox made by Watzlawick, Beavin, and Jackson (1967: 187–229).

The only points I wish to make here are (1) that the transcendence of any paradox or double bind, in logic or in life, involves some form of metacommunication, and (2) that the transcendence itself engenders paradox at the metacommunicative level – or at the level of the next higher logical type. In other words, Russell's theory of logical types, Carnap's levels of language, and the double-bind theory of schizophrenia are all paradoxical in themselves. It is easy to see why. On the one hand, all such theories correspond to the necessity of digitalizing analog continuums by introducing discrete boundaries into the non-discrete. On the other, in logic and in language they involve the use of 'not'. 'Not' itself is a metacommunicative boundary essential to the 'rule about identity' which is the sole sufficient and necessary condition of any digital logic. In other words, boundaries are the condition of distinguishing the 'elements' of a continuum from the continuum itself. 'Not' is such a boundary. It is the question of boundaries between logical types that generates the limiting paradox of the Russellian theory, which was designed to solve the antinomies involved in defining class membership, i.e., boundaries.

Gödel's proof is of course the one theory of a high enough logical type to explain the impossibility of ultimately transcending paradox in human communication. As Nagel and Newman put it (1956): "Arithmetic is ESSENTIALLY incomplete, for even if the true [meta-axiomatic] formula G were taken as an axiom and added to the original axioms, . . . we could still construct a true formula which would not be the case no matter how often we respected the process of adding axioms to the initial set." In a word, every consistent deductive system will generate Gödelian sentences which we know to be true but which cannot be demonstrated within the system.

And a system of meta-axioms will engender a meta-sentence, and so on *ad infinitum*.

This implies that all human communication, including mathematics and logic, is an open system which can be subject to closure only for methodological reasons. The problem of the punctuation of the analog by the digital is irresolvable for humankind: it is in fact that upon which Lacan founds his theory of the 'splitting' of the subject. But if the double bind generates irresolvable oscillations between 'yes' and 'no', it can do so only with a digitalized context of either/or: the context of analytical logic. Such oscillations do not present a problem for dialectical logic, which is of a higher logical type than analytical logic and (paradoxically) subsumes it. In other words, double binds are irresolvable only when metacommunication – in logic or in life – is prevented through the way in which allowable communication is framed or punctuated by those with the power to do so. Similarly, in evolution or in history, counter-adaptive oscillation is only irresolvable – i.e., self-destructive – when renormalization is cut off by the ways in which the boundaries of the system are defined.

It will be recalled that Zeno's arrow is said to be immobile in the famous paradox (pp. 76–7 above), because it cannot (logically) cross the infinite number of boundaries between each point in space (or time) and the next in any finite time (or space). The ontological base of Greek mathematics in the fifth century B.C. produced this particular version of the paradoxes involved in digitalizing the analog continuum because of its conception of boundaries. For Zeno of Elea and his contemporaries, the static, concretized, and purely structural definition of a boundary as a FIXED LIMIT between two regions prevented any process-oriented conception of a converging series such as we find several centuries later in the dynamic, anti-Platonic, and non-Atomist ontology of the Stoics. Stoic ontology speaks of a 'force-field' of *pneuma* and 'sympathy', and of the flux of an organic–holistic continuum in the process of becoming (e.g., Chrysippus, Posidonius) (Sambursky, in: Northrop and Livingston, eds., 1962: 237–53).

The conception of 'natural sympathy' reappears in the Renaissance (see Chapter XI), and the IDEOLOGICAL conception of the boundary as a BARRIER reappears at various levels in contemporary structuralism. Here we see a new form of the rationalization of the economic sources of the 'splitting of the ecosystem', a rationale based on the refusal to recognize what it means to say that the logical typing of any boundary is distinct from that of what it defines (Chapter VII). As we know, Zeno's paradox was not solved until the nineteenth-century invention of the mathematical limit replaced the concept of the infinitesimal which had allowed for the invention of the differential calculus in the seventeenth.

What is significant is that the great strides made in mathematics in the nineteenth century resulted in the grounding of logic and mathematics more firmly in paradox than ever before. Zeno's particular paradoxes may have been solved, but the paradox as such has moved from the status of a 'problem' in logic to that of the very source of mathematics itself. For example: Cantor's infinite sets of (countable and uncountable) transfinite cardinals; Russell's antinomy about class membership already mentioned; the persistent mismatch between geometrical intuition about continuity and the logical status of continuity (or, more recently, 'smoothness') in topology; Cantor's proof that there are more classes of things of a given kind (infinite or not) than there are things of that kind – i.e., that there is at least one class larger than the class of 'everything': the class of the SUB-CLASSES of everything; and so on.

Logicians distinguish the 'I am lying' paradox from other paradoxes in different ways, but, precisely because it includes the term 'I', it appears to be the ground of all possible paradoxes. Rather than relate it to questions of class membership, it is more usual to employ Carnap's and Tarski's theories of levels of language to 'I am lying'. In this way, it is pointed out that 'I am lying' is both a statement in an object language (about 'I') and a statement in a metalanguage (about 'I am lying'). Since it is consequently a SELF-REFERRING statement which judges its own validity, it has no significa-tion – in logic, at least. But it is in fact also a statement about classes and class membership – and pregnant with MEANING as a result. Russell's antinomy showed that in the foundations of mathematics and general set theory, no 'natural' or intuitively consistent schema enabling one to define the boundary (the membership rules) of sets is possible. Any rule about set membership that itself mentions membership or non-membership falls into the trap of self-reference, and sooner or later generates antinomies at higher levels in the theory. (As a result, in some current versions of set theory, the law of non-contradiction may be subtly violated.) Russell's statement that there is NO class that has as its members precisely the classes that are not members of themselves is itself such a rule (Quine, 1962, 1964).

The point about 'I am lying', then, is that the 'I' in the statement is a rule about membership IN the class of 'I' BY a member of the class of 'I'. It both makes a distinction in a universe of discourse and defines the locus of an INTERVENTION into that universe (cf. pp. 183, 186–7 below). We have to conclude that the paradox of paradox is the result of the self-referring characteristics of the human subject – as REPRESENTED in the (digital) dis-course by the linguistic shifter 'I' – the subject of both the proposition 'I am lying' and of the goalseeking, TIME-DEPENDENT subsystem that proposes it.

Chapter VI

Beyond the Entropy Principle in Freud

Life is a contradiction which is present in
things and processes themselves, and which
constantly originates and resolves itself; and as
soon as the contradiction ceases, life, too, comes
to an end, and death steps in.
ENGELS: *Anti-Dühring*

1. *Introduction: The Biomechanistic View*

For one of the possible Freuds in the text of Freud, a human being appears
to be a neurotic steam-engine fluctuating between quiescence and runaway
activity, with two conflicting *kybernetai*, Eros and Thanatos, at the controls,
each haggling with the other over what is to be done with the daily delivery
of coal. In so far as this machinery seems sometimes to be regulated by
some sort of governor seeking to maintain a constant level of available
energy in the system (the Freudian 'principle of constancy'), another Freud
presents us with the human being as a self-regulated homeostatic system.
For another Freud, the human being is a mechanical system striving for
equilibrium. For yet another, the human is a thermodynamic system
condemned to the entropy of the 'death instinct' (the Freudian 'principle
of inertia'), or else he or she is a biological system regulated by dubious
'biological' principles (the "desire inherent in organic life to restore an
earlier state of things": the inorganic state). The mind – brain or psyche –
appears here as an anatomy, there as a neural network, elsewhere as a
system of writing, and yet elsewhere as a nation containing individual
provinces or agencies (*Instanzen*), ruled by organismic Id or Ego – or by
that totally different *principe*, Superego (who is not an organism, but an
environment) – an Austro-Hungarian empire grooving with the Tsar.
Sometimes it is a question of topology or topography (*Topik*), sometimes

a question of primary and secondary systems, sometimes that of the dynamics of repression, sometimes that of thermodynamics and the ideology of psychic economics. Here, for instance, the libido is a vast hydraulic system; elsewhere, not unnaturally it is electrical; and sometimes it simply seems to be the negative of entropy (that is to say, a principle of organization opposed to Thanatos, the principle of disorganization). The neuronal energy of the early works becomes psychic energy, without any fundamental changes in the modular metaphors, and the neuronal network seems clearly to be a foreshadowing of contemporary models of the brain and human beings as information-processing systems. The mind is a camera, a telescope, a city under archeological excavation, a network of traces (*Spuren*), a "mystic writing pad", a system of layers of signs (*Zeichen*) – waiting to be trans-lated (*Um-setzung*: transformed, restructured, communicated at another level of communication) or simply read (inevitably *nachträglich*). Psychological resistance is described in the terms of a theory of warfare, and repression in the terms of a Department of Immigration– refusing entry to political, cultural, and pigmental undesirables. Repression produces a conscious discourse full of holes (*lückenhaft*), like a Russian newspaper at the hands of the Austrian censor. The superego is sometimes a kind of fearful political oppressor, sometimes a kindly commissar, and energy (labor) is invariably considered in the terms of price – a viewpoint not unconnected with 'working through' (*durcharbeiten*) at 20 marks an hour.

One could multiply these examples almost indefinitely, for Freud was surely one of the most metaphorical men that ever wrote. But there is more to the question than the simple metaphors of science, and quite apart from the fascinating problems of the way Freud used the models he inherited from the nineteenth century, the METAPHOR AS SUCH is Freud's profoundest paradigm. By metaphor in this sense I mean a category of the discourse exactly as the principle of explanation in cybernetics corresponds to what Bateson (1967) calls "rigorous metaphor". I do not therefore mean only 'figure of speech', nor am I necessarily referring to the particular illustrative figures and analogies employed by Freud, but rather to metaphor as a label for what goes into the construction of a figure of speech – or into a psychological symptom, a slip of the tongue or pen, a dream, an ideology – that is to say, metacommunication. The metaphor becomes a paradigm for the relationship between the 'phenomenon' (the symptom, the ideology) as a signifier in a discourse and what it signifies, because the metaphor involves a communication about a communication (a message about a message) or simply communication about communication, period. The metaphor has already been defined as an overdetermined statement in a metalanguage about some relationship or other in a referent language. If there is indeed one primary referent 'language', the question arises as to whether the primary level of communication is the erotic/aggressive relationship of self and other bound by the lost object as in Freud, or the "language of real life", the "material communication [*Verkehr*] of men" as in Marx. Since the primary function in both these discourses is goal-seeking exchange, and since both are overdetermined, they are not necessarily exclusive.

The communicational–semiotic dimension of Freud has been opened up by Lacan. Pribram in neuropsychology (1962), Burke in philosophy (1941), and Marcuse in 'culture criticism' (1955) have also contributed to our reading Freud in new lights. Nevertheless, in all these perspectives, the basic bioenergetic model of Freud remains untouched – in Marcuse, for instance, it is elevated to the level of a new principle (Wilden, 1970a).[1]

But the mechanical–biological model explicitly elaborated by Freud can no longer be viewed as founded in the phenomenology of the human mind, as Freud would have it. Nor can it properly be called a dialectical model, if by dialectics we mean a materialist theory of communication and exchange in relation to labor. The similarities between the Freudian and the Hegelian model, both in a practical and in a theoretical sense, have provided for a first-level liberation of the Freudian model from its 'instinctual' base (Hyppolite, 1957; Lacan, 1966: 215–26 [1951]). There are differences between the status of the 'Hegelian subject' and the 'Freudian subject' in their relationship to desire, to knowledge, and to the goal of 'reconciliation' (Lacan, 1966: 802–10; Wilden, 1968a: 307–8, 133–4). The similarities between Freud and Hegel are to be found in their representation of the genetic development of the individual, on the one hand, and in relation to the asymptotic progress of an analysis, on the other. In other words, if we use the terminology established in Chapter XII to distinguish three types of diachrony or change – homeorhesis (development), homeogenesis (repetition) and morphogenesis (evolution, revolution) – we can say that both the Freudian and the Hegelian models are basically homeorhetic at the material level (describing teleonomic 'developmental trajectories'), homeogenic at the level of the 'human condition' (repetition of homeomorphic structures), and morphogenic only at the IDEAL level of the 'evolution of consciousness', on the one hand, and at that of the 'cure', on

[1] The essays in this book are at one level an elaboration of the basic ideas which originally made up my criticism of Marcuse's 'instinct theory', and at another level, a critical reformulation of the relationships between organism and environment, between language and communication, between opposition and difference, and between the analog and the digital, as originally expressed in 1969, in the article on Marcuse and Freud.

the other. Although both involve a historical dimension of sorts, in Hegel this dimension is vitiated by its finalist teleology (as opposed to the teleonomy of the goalseeking system), and in Freud, it is vitiated by its developmental aspects. Thus, whereas we can describe the Hegelian *Phenomenology* as a great spiral of IDEAS, we find at the basis of the Freudian model a form of circular repetition within the physical universe – an astronomy of entities, attractions, repulsions, and steady states – overlaid on a genetic model of organic development and growth.

The Hegelian form of the spiral-like 'dialectics of opposition' is a necessary principle in any theory of the subject–object relations of the phenomenology of consciousness (or of the unconscious). In spite of Hegel's understanding of the mediation of opposition by difference, the theory is beholden to Imaginary identity. Marcuse summarizes the process as follows (1955: 102–3):

> When mere consciousness reaches the stage of self-consciousness [i.e., consciousness-of-self], it finds itself as EGO, and the ego is first DESIRE: it can become conscious of itself only through satisfying itself in and by an 'other'. But such satisfaction involves the 'negation' of the other, for the ego has to prove itself by truly 'being for itself' AGAINST all 'otherness'. This is the notion of the individual which [*sic*] must constantly assert and affirm himself in order to be real . . . so that he can exist only by incessantly winning and testing his existence against something or some-one which contests it.

This is in effect an epitome of the whole of western metaphysics: "the antagonism of subject and object" (p. 101). Missing from it is the real and material context of the 'oppositions'.

Freud's views are similarly dualistic and founded on fundamental antagonisms. The goal of all desire is 'object choice'. His 'mechanistic organicism' is similar to Hegel's. Moreover, the projection of what he saw as fundamental processes in the individual, into the plan of history, is similarly dependent on limiting the context to his own caste, class, and time. This lack of a context for his 'instinctual' model is the necessary result of the sources of the instinctual model: the scientific consciousness of the nineteenth century. His basic model is linear, bioenergetic, causal, and above all ENTROPIC. However, the model of entropic degradation which he took over from classical physics is overlaid and confused with a homeostatic model, derived from nineteenth-century physiology. This mixture of organicism and mechanics is well expressed in the pioneering work of Claude Bernard, for example, in the following quotation from his *Science expérimentale*:

The primary cause of life results in evolution or in the CREATION OF THE ORGANIZED MACHINE. But the machine, once created, functions by virtue of the properties of its constituent elements and under the influence of physico-chemical conditions which act on them (my emphasis).

A similar set of insights and confusions had already appeared in the work of Saint-Simon, *De la physiologie appliquée à l'amélioration des institutions sociales:*

> Society is not at all a simple agglomeration of living beings whose actions, independent of any finite goal, have no other cause than the arbitrary will of individuals and no other effects than chance events, ephemeral and unimportant accidents. On the contrary, society is, above all, a veritable organized machine, all of whose component parts contribute in a different way to the working of the whole (quoted in Jordan, 1967: 132).

The significant understanding that "society is the true reality and the individual the abstraction", which is common to Saint-Simon, Comte, and Marx (ibid.) is consequently obscured by the projection of models derived from technology – mediated by 'science' – into the social dimension. "Machine" in this text means 'machine', 'organism', and 'social physiology' at one and the same time.

There are many fundamental contradictions in the Freudian texts, and no attempt to employ what is valuable in the Freudian corpus can be anything but selective. What is of first interest here is the contradiction between Eros and Thanatos. Eros and Thanatos are usually placed in a relationship of binary opposition by Freud's determined dualism, and the Manichean struggle between them is what Marcuse (1955) chose to use in his attempt to liberate Freud from his political economy of 'struggle in the face of scarcity'. In other passages, however, Freud elevates either Eros or Thanatos above the other as a primary principle. In his later work, it is the 'death instinct' and repetition which enjoy the upper hand. Through a critique of the energetic base of the model of drives or instincts, it can be shown that these two principles, Eros and Thanatos, come from entirely different orders of reality, and are consequently fundamentally incomparable. As 'psychic' or 'human' principles, their opposition derives from a set of assumptions about science, and from a set of projections of the social discourse into the scientific discourse, not from the study of human beings-in-relation.

The battle between the determinists and the vitalists at the end of the nineteenth century had raised an epistemological problem which had not been solved by the defeat of the vitalists, who had recognized in a nebulous way, without being able to justify their position in scientific terms, that the linear causality of physics did not properly apply to living systems. It seems that this problem is now open to a solution. At least we can now say that the question of the *élan vital* or the 'vital force' is a false question, which is usually how such problems are resolved. But Freud knew nothing of the advances in linguistics, in statistical thermodynamics, in the fledgling theory of information, and he MANIFESTLY chose for the epistemological model of psychoanalysis the physical model of energy and entities in a Newtonian universe. Nevertheless, his clinical analyses and the 'self-analysis' he conducted with Fliess as the necessary interlocutor – and especially his neuropsychological model of the brain – contradict the manifest text at a different level from the simple contradictions IN the text. In order to understand this, we have to address ourselves to the unconscious level of the Freudian texts, to the invisible text, to their latent content.

This means at the same time to address ourselves to the latent text of nineteenth-century science. We could look, for instance, at the work of Clerk Maxwell, Freud's contemporary. A century ago, Maxwell sought to understand the behavior of the self-regulating system (the governor). Moreover his 'ideal' experiment, the 'Maxwell Demon',[2] which was posed in the energy terms of the second law of thermodynamics, revealed itself to be insoluble except in the terms of the statistical thermodynamics of order and disorder through which an equivalence could be established between negative entropy and information.[3]

[2] The Maxwell Demon is a mythical, microscopic, metaphysical thermodynamic being, who apparently disobeys the second law by decreasing the entropy of a thermodynamic system (in this case a gas). He sorts its molecules through a trap-door according to their level of energy, thus increasing the gradient. He does not in fact disobey the second law, as Maxwell supposed, because, as Szilard showed in 1929, any decrease in entropy is correlative to the information (the negentropy) which the Demon feeds into the system by his decisions about energy levels. Such local increases in negentropy are necessarily matched by increases in positive entropy elsewhere. Schrödinger has said that life consists in continually sucking information from the environment. The Maxwell Demon thus invites an analogy with repression as it is conceived by Freud. Since repression is TRANSSUBJECTIVE – coming from the Other – it can be said to involve a constant 'sorting' of information in order to maintain the gradient of the reality principle against the mortal entropy – in Freud's conception – of the pleasure principle.

[3] The continuing debate over this equivalence in the statistical world of thermodynamics and information science is undoubtedly of some significance at that level of explanation. But it is irrelevant to the way in which these terms are used here. It is irrelevant because nothing at all can be said about the domain of open systems if one is restricted by the mythical ideal of quantification, statistical analysis, and unambiguous mathematical formulation.

Claude Bernard was undoubtedly one of the earliest physiologists to understand the principles of organization and homeostasis in the organism. Unfortunately, for lack of a distinction between mechanistic–energetic explanation and informational explanation, the hastily constructed Darwinian–Spencerian organicist models of social systems (Hofstadter, 1947; Buckley, 1967: 7–40), on the one hand, and the reduction of organization to inadequately understood biomechanistic categories, on the other, resulted in the necessary repression of these fledgling systemic models – especially by logical positivism – until cybernetics came to revive them in the thirties, forties, and fifties. In the meantime, however, they had served valiantly on the socioeconomic frontier of the public consciousness, as propaganda for the 'bio-social-sexual' imperialism of monopoly capitalism.[4]

2. Cybernetic Explanation

In the cybernetic methodology, the symptom, the ideology, the super-structure, or any equivalent metastatement is a 'mapping' or a 'transform' of some other proposition or communication. As communication, behavior implies an information-processing network in which messages, borne by energy, pass along mediated channels disturbed by 'noise'.

Information, in this technical sense, can be distinguished from both signification and meaning; we can define it as a "mapping between sets of structured variety" (Buckley, 1967). This approach provides us with a LOGICAL model of behavior, although the kind of logic eventually necessary will undoubtedly be alien to most 'behaviorists' (cf. Chapters VII, XIV). Buckley (1967) deals at some length with the kind of methodological and theoretical restructuring which the new models provide, and I am indebted to his analysis for much of my own perspective. Bateson describes the change as follows (1967: 30):

> Outside of cybernetics, we look for explanation, but not for anything that would simulate logical proof . . . [which] is something new. We can say, however, with hindsight wisdom, that explanation by simulation

---

[4] It would seem a tedious business to quote the vicious and violent theories of William Graham Sumner, if it were not for the fact that apart from their function in the American myth of 'rugged individualism' à la Herbert Hoover, they still survive in attenuated forms as the contemporary values of our culture. Thus Sumner's version of Bacon's *Instauration* – mastery over nature – is a sexist rape-phantasy: "Nature is entirely neutral; she submits to him who most energetically and resolutely assails her. She grants her rewards to the fittest . . ." (quoted in Hofstadter, 1947: 224). Sumner forgets that with the evolution of humanity and the development of technology, 'nature as neutral' ceased to exist.

of logical or mathematical proof was expectable. After all, the subject matter of cybernetics is not events and objects, but the INFORMATION 'carried' by events and objects. We consider the objects or events only as proposing facts, propositions, messages, percepts and the like. The subject matter being propositional, it is expectable that explanation would simulate the logical.

As many biologists and others have always understood, no explanation of open or living systems can escape the necessity of supposing levels of behavior and organization. I have already pointed to the semiotic metaphor of 'levels of signs' in the early Freud (Chapter II, Section 5), and it is this metaphor which opens up the Freudian texts to analysis in the terms of language and metalanguage, communication and metacommunication, both structured around the notions of metaphor and metonymy. The level of reality we are concerned with here is not that level which can be analyzed by the closed-system models of classical physics, but that of 'organized complexity', which requires an open-system model: that of the goalseeking adaptive system. The principle of explanation involved thus requires a methodological distinction between energy and information, between closed and open system. Elsasser, for example (1966: 14, 45–6) – commenting on the "radical inhomogeneity" of the phenomena of life – points out that what is required is an "open theory" in which many questions will have no binary (yes/no) answers:

> There exist regularities in the realm of organisms whose existence cannot be logico-mathematically derived from the laws of physics, nor can logico-mathematical contradiction be construed between these regularities and the laws of physics.

In other words, there is a distinction in logical types involved. (See Chapter VII on many-valued analog or dialectical thought.) (Now see Note 9.)

3. *Critique of the Energy Model*

Let me begin with a quotation from Marcuse, which sums up the essence of Freud's bioenergetic model:

> Now the (more or less sublimated) transformation of destructive into socially useful aggressive (and thereby constructive) energy is, according to Freud (on whose instinct-theory I base my interpretation) a normal and indispensable process. It is part of the same dynamic by which libido, erotic energy, is sublimated and made socially useful; the two opposite impulses are forced together and, united in this twofold trans-

formation, they become the mental and organic vehicles of civilization. But no matter how close and effective the union, their respective quality remains unchanged and contrary: aggression activates destruction which 'aims' at death, while libido seeks the preservation, protection, and amelioration of life. Therefore it is only as long as destruction works in the service of Eros that it serves civilization and the individual; if aggression becomes stronger than its erotic counterpart, the trend is reversed. Moreover, in the Freudian conception, destructive energy cannot become stronger without reducing erotic energy: the balance between the two primary impulses is a quantitative one; the instinctual dynamic is mechanistic, distributing an available quantum of energy between the two antagonists (1968: 257–8).

In the last sentence of this quotation, Marcuse restates his acceptance of that aspect of Freud's quantitative energy model which involves the first law of thermodynamics, the conservation of energy. This model also involves a principle of constancy, a principle of inertia (the Nirvana principle), and a relationship between 'free' and 'bound' energy (related to the 'binding' force of Eros). It is also a homeostatic-equilibrium model which is both organismic and mechanical, and essentially closed. The sources of this model are especially significant in the sociological Freud, where Freud extrapolates on the 'instincts' discovered in the individual (system) so as to extend their effect to the aggregation of the instincts in the societal or species-specific system. Here – and notably in *Beyond the Pleasure Principle* (1920) – the apparently normative equilibrium of the fusion of Eros and Thanatos in the individual is converted into a degenerative model of the life of the species where the conservatism of the 'instincts' – principally the death instinct – the omniscience of the Nirvana principle, and "the compulsion to restore an earlier state of things", appears on the one hand as entropy (loss of gradient, of organization) and, contradictorily, on the other, as repetition (oscillation and/or steady state). Eros binds (organizes) and Thanatos destroys (disorganizes), both in TIME, but somehow in Freud's mind the retrogressive, temporal nature of actual return to a past (inorganic) state – the expression of a return to inertia or zero (mechanical or thermodynamic equilibrium) – is seen as synonymous with the attempted refusal of lived time, in other words, with the synchrony of repetition and oscillation (cf. Jones, 1956–8: II: 291–2).

I have already remarked on this process in Svevo's novel, and on its similarity to Kierkegaardian repetition (cf. Lacan, 1966: 46; Wilden, 1968a: 57, 141). *La Coscienza di Zeno* (1923) seems therefore to be strikingly faithful to the deepest levels of the Freudian model: it describes the relationship between the 'compulsion to repeat' and death at the same period as Freud was formalizing it in *Beyond the Pleasure Principle* (1920). The novel accurately represents the repetition discovered in analysis and in the play of children. However, as is clearly the case with Zeno's addiction to the 'challenge', or with Kierkegaard's psycho-ideological attempt to refute the 'philosophy of mediation' by making history match the self-perpetuating, oscillating series of his own double binds, the psychoanalytical theory of repetition seems to be no more than the tautologous product of the theory's CONSTITUTIVE lack of context. The tighter the theoretical closure, and the smaller the number of levels of logical typing the theory is prepared to entertain, the sooner the theory will discover that it is paradoxically double-bound by being, in effect, OUTSIDE itself. The 'universality' of repetition may consequently be no more than an ancillary proof of the applicability of Gödel's theorem to all theories which impose SELF-REFERRING forms of closure on themselves. Being innately paradoxical because of the inadequacy of its theoretical structure to account for the vast field to which it is applied, the theory will do well to identify all oscillations and repetitions as innate and universal characteristics of its 'object', rather than recognize them as its own products. In any event, no current psychoanalytical theory has at its disposal at present a theory of logic and communication and a sufficient contextual understanding which would enable it to deal either theoretically or practically with the question of the transcendence of INDIVIDUAL psychological double binds in the real and material domain of the collective. (Cf. the rationalization of this problem in Deleuze, 1968: 12–17.) As far as the child is concerned, repetition is in any case an essential part of his developmental trajectory through the Imaginary, and it may or may not be transcended, as the case may be. The question of time, like truth, is essential here, for only in an open system (with memory) can time be an essential – i.e., lived – category. We shall see that this requires a relationship to an environment: it cannot be an 'innate' category.

The notion of a restricted "available quantum of energy" for the drives is one of Freud's earliest methodological assumptions, taken more or less directly from G. T. Fechner's 'stability principle'.[5] Fechner was concerned,

---

[5] Fechner actually defined four states of stability: (1) absolute stability (particles in a state of inertia); (2) complete stability (movement between particles such that oscillations between perturbed states and the original configuration of the system repeat themselves at regular intervals); (3) approximate stability (a version of complete stability); (4) absolute instability (random distribution) (Penrose, 1931: 90). Penrose sees an analogy between Fechner's first three states and the three Freudian principles: the Nirvana principle, the pleasure principle,

amongst other things, to introduce the recently stated first law of thermo-dynamics (e.g., Helmholtz, in 1847) into the theory of organisms. Freud quotes from one of Fechner's works (1873) in *Beyond the Pleasure Principle* (*Standard Edition*, XVIII, 8), in which Fechner relates pleasure and un-pleasure to psychophysical stability and instability. Beyond a certain limit, pleasure is said to be proportional to the approximation of stability, and unpleasure, similarly, to deviation from stability. This is essentially a mechanical equilibrium model, with pleasure (stability) as the norm, equivalent to the stable equilibrium of a ball in a cup. From this Freud goes on to enunciate the combined principle of constancy and inertia originally stated in the *Project* of 1895: "The mental apparatus endeavours to keep the quantity of [free] excitation present in it as low as possible [inertia] or at least to keept it constant [constancy]" (p. 9). The pleasure principle is thus a purely physical model at this level (in spite of the important contradiction between inertia and constancy): unpleasure simply means tension and pleasure means release from tension.

In the neurological model of 1895, however, inertia and constancy are distinguished more clearly. Inertia is posited as the primary principle – the principle of keeping the neuronic network free from external stimulus through motor discharge. But endogenous stimuli, that is to say the later 'instincts' (here; "the major needs: hunger, respiration, sexuality"), cause a break in the principle of inertia. Motor discharge (for example, flight from external stimuli) cannot take place in response to internal needs, and a "specific action" is called for (e.g., eating) (*Standard Edition*, I, 296–7).

With the help of the articles on the three Freudian principles in La-planche and Pontalis' *Vocabulaire de la psychanalyse* (1967), we can see that in the *Project* of 1895 the principle of inertia regulates the free energy of the primary process, whose task it is through reflex or other action to keep itself free from external stimulus. The reactions of the primary process give rise to a secondary process ("imposed by the exigencies of life") which discovers certain other paths of discharge to be necessary. The primary process and its free energy thus corresponds to the pleasure principle, which is regulated by inertia, or reduction of tension to zero, whereas the secondary process, whose energy is 'bound' (*gebundene*),

---

and the reality principle. The fourth state could represent Thanatos, disorder. In keeping with the reductionism so common in psychoanalysis, some analysts in the thirties were seeking to prove that the psychic 'death instinct' was a principle of 'delayed' positive entropy in organisms (without dealing with its supposed manifestation in society). In this kind of speculation, the levels of 'organism', 'person', and 'social being' are all short-circuited or 'essentialized' (see Chapter XII, Section 7).

corresponds to the reality principle, which is regulated by constancy, or by the maintenance of enough tension (unpleasure) to deal with the exigencies of life.[6]

Freud's free and bound energy are exactly the opposite of the free and bound energy of thermodynamics. The bound energy of the *Ich* represents a higher level of organization (gradient) than the free energy of the primary process, whereas in thermodynamics, bound energy is equivalent to disorder, degradation, and disorganization; it is entropic energy from which no further work can be obtained. Freud's energy is not, however, the same kind of energy; it is rather the metaphor of *energeia* (process) on which the energy of physics was originally modelled. His organismic energy begins in the *Project* as a 'nervous' energy, metaphorically akin to electricity, and eventually becomes 'psychic' energy in the later works, where it can generally be equated with 'instinctual energy'. It is important to note that the energy of the *Project* seems to be equivalent to the much later so-called 'neutral' (*indifferent*) energy suggested by Freud, which can attach itself to either primary 'instinct' (*Standard Edition*, XIV, 78 and XIX, 44. See the editor's remarks on Q, *Standard Edition*, I, 395).

These notions all lie behind the theory of the death instinct in *Beyond the Pleasure Principle*. Freud was driven by the realization that there are many instances of pleasurable tension to modify his earlier correlation, derived from Fechner, between the principle of inertia/constancy and the pleasure principle. We have already seen that the pleasure principle of 1895 is closer to mechanistic inertia than to organismic constancy, so that it is not surprising to find it equated with the Nirvana principle in *Beyond the Pleasure Principle* and in the "Economic Problem of Masochism" (1924) – although he calls it there the principle of constancy – both principles being "in the service of the death instinct, whose aim is to conduct the restlessness of life into the stability [i.e., the 'inertia'] of the inorganic state". Freud then goes on in this article to characterize the pleasure principle as involving some sort of qualitative characteristics, which, he feels, may be related to "the rhythm, the temporal sequence of changes, rises and falls in the quantity of stimulus" – that is to say, in

---

[6] Although Freud views these 'exigencies' (*Not des Lebens*) as the INTERNAL demands of the organism (e.g., hunger), they necessarily involve its essential and open relationship to an environment. This is an openness not only to energy (food), but also to information (communication with others). For the child, it is his 'helplessness' to administer to his own needs which allows these 'exigencies' to subject him to the domination of the Other. They require an appeal to another person (a demand). Freud says in the *Project* that this relationship is the original source of 'moral motivations' (i.e., the later 'superego'). Cf. my remarks on Waddington's view of 'interorganismic authority' in Chapter IX, Section 11.

spite of the word "temporal", to something like repetition. Since repetition was the central empirical fact that led him to go 'beyond the pleasure principle', and since he goes on to say that the Nirvana principle is modified into the pleasure principle because it belongs to the death instinct, it becomes impossible for us to see any difference whatsoever between the two principles and the death instinct: all represent an inertial equilibrium model in mechanics or an entropic equilibrium model in thermodynamics. It is clear that there is nothing in fact beyond the pleasure principle – except the libido, Eros, which 'tames' the death instinct (*Standard Edition*, XIX, 159–60, 164). But Eros was defined by Freud as the "restlessness of life" – or in other words as gradient, tension – as a type of NEGATIVE ENTROPY which is impossible in the type of closed system he is building. Eros does not 'run down': as a principle of the 'binding' of matter–energy by intentionality (information), it must remain in process until the very end.

As Bateson has made clear (Bateson and Ruesch, 1951), the simplistic energy model is a disastrous one. The recognition of Freud's explicit commitment to the bioenergetic or inertial model has contributed to his fall from favor, at the same time as most social and psychological theory remains committed to the very same kind of principles, if now expressed more subtly.

One of Freud's difficulties, and one which contributed mightily to the whole problematic of the drives, was that there was no acceptable definition of teleonomy that Freud – as a 'scientist' – could use, whereas now cybernetics and systems theory have defined for us the general characteristics of the complex, adaptive, goalseeking system – controlled by information – to which the term teleonomy is entirely applicable. For Freud, the concepts of psychic energy, attraction and repulsion, and the 'drive', were the only available answers – and *Trieb* or *Lust* or *Wunscherfüllung*, the best available words – to make 'motivation' 'scientific'. I have already pointed out that these terms conceal a version of the existential *projet*, which is itself a rudimentary 'cybernetic' or 'systemic' principle.

But the basic Freudian conception of psychic energy as an indestructible SUBSTANCE, a substance necessarily transformed – not created or destroyed – and limited in quantity, cannot be maintained in the face of the communicational perspective. The bioenergetic metaphors will, however, tend necessarily to be retained in sublimated forms in any 'linguistic' or 'digital' perspective. In such a perspective, a concept like 'desire' will have to be employed to explain 'motive', and desire remains useful only so long as it is integrated into an ecosystemic view. Unlike energy, information is not a substance. Although memory retains 'LOCATABLE' information in patterns, the information cannot be 'LOCALIZED', because it involves a relationship between patterns. (Compare Freud's repeated attempts to localize the 'drives' and the 'libido'.) Negentropy, or order, or pattern, or improbability, or information, or redundancy (all these terms are operationally synonymous here) can be and is continually created and destroyed – either by purposive beings in the struggle, not for life, but for pattern or structure, or by 'random' intrusive events (noise). As Ashby's law of requisite variety puts it, only variety can destroy variety (1956: 207). But, for Freud, energy is independent in quantity and type from the purposes or state of mind of any organism – there is just so much available regardless of our desires or of our intake of information. Negentropy or information, on the other hand, if still a quantity, is nevertheless dependent upon the purposive being that emits or receives it. "Entropy is a statement of a relationship between a purposive entity and some set of objects or events" (Bateson and Ruesch, 1951: 248–50).[7]

It is not that we can do without some concept of energy in a theory of open systems, but that the energy is subordinate to the information it carries, as Buckley points out (1967: 47):

Though 'information' is dependent upon some physical base or energy flow, the energy component is entirely subordinate to the particular form or structure of variations that the physical base or flow may manifest. . . . This structured variation – the marks of writing, the sounds of speech, the molecular arrangement of the genetic code of DNA, etc. – is still only raw material or energy unless it 'corresponds' to, or matches in some important way, the structure of variations of other components [i.e., 'receivers'] to which it may thereby become dynamically related. A person speaking a language foreign to a companion is emitting only noise or vibrating energy as far as the latter is concerned, because there is no mapping of the structured variety of the vocal energy with the repertoire of meaningful sounds structured in the mind of the companion. . . .

Thus information is not a substance or concrete entity but rather a RELATIONSHIP between sets or ensembles of structured variety. . . .

4. Homeostasis and Repetition

Although Cannon's concept of homeostasis has been used by various writers in many different ways, it should be distinguished from equilibrium,

---

[7] Bateson is seeking an operational definition of information in relation to meaning, such as that offered by D. M. MacKay (1969) which is quoted at length in Chapter IX, Section 2. On entropy and communication, see also Shands (1970), especially pp. 20–3, 384–6.

which is better restricted to thermodynamics (entropy) and to mechanics (inertia). An equivalent but usually mechanistic term is 'steady state' (constancy).

The confusion between closed-system energy concepts like equilibrium and relatively open-system, energetic-informational concepts like homeostasis bedevils Freud's work, to say nothing of later psychoanalytical theory. Homeostasis has its material source in information, but its THEORETICAL source is bioenergetic, for it is the first cousin of mechanical equilibrium. It continues to be misinterpreted and misused (cf. Chapter XI on 'structure'). In general, however, it is now taken as a cybernetic concept, concerned with regulation and therefore with the processing of information, which organizes and controls energy ingested from the environment. By contrast, inertial and entropic equilibrium applies only when there is no source of change within the system itself and when no open exchange of energy and/or information with an environment takes place. A homeostatic system is neutrally entropic; it does not increase in order of complexity of organization, although it may reproduce itself or increase in extent.

If some aspects of homeostatic theory represent an advance in adequacy of explanation over the purely mechanistic equilibrium notions derived from physics, which are still being employed in biology, psychology, sociology, and elsewhere (e.g., Zipf's attempt to use the Maupertuis–Planck 'principle of least action'), homeostasis reveals itself to be too restricted in scope even for biology. Von Bertalanffy (1968: 89–119) has pointed out how the concept of homeostasis has been used in (bioenergetic) psychoanalysis as an equivalent of the primary principle of 'need gratification' or 'tension reduction' in response to outside stimuli (one version of the ubiquitous and utilitarian pleasure principle). Note that by REDUCING the informational aspect of homeostasis to energy ('need') in this way, the informational categories of variety, complexity, and organization are simply wiped out. In this sense of the concept, no place is allowed for the experimentally observed autonomous activity of the organism. And the reduction of information to energy produces a model which is not very different from the 'reactive automaton' supposed by stimulus–response theory.

As Waddington has pointed out (1968: 1–32), homeostasis is founded on the assumption of NON-TEMPORAL relations. It must therefore necessarily reduce the real temporality of the 'developmental pathway' to some form or other of repetition, for repetition is its first axiom. And it will necessarily be unable to deal with quantum jumps in organization (cf. note 5 on Fechner's 'complete stability'). Moreover, it is not clear to me that homeostasis as it is often used necessarily implies the two central characteristics of the open system: memory and reproducibility.

As Karl Deutsch has pointed out in his critique of the organic model, homeostasis is not a concept of a sufficiently high logical type to account for the complexity of learning, adaptation, and dynamic process in human and social systems. It is rather a special case in such systems, for it cannot adequately describe "either the INTERNAL RESTRUCTURING of learning systems or the combinatorial findings of the solutions". ". . . It is change rather than stability which we must account for" (quoted in Buckley, 1967: 15). Homeostasis in effect reduces all change to mechanical oscillation around a position of stability, and in mechanics oscillation and repetition are effectively identical. (Note that Ashby's homeostat, with its several thousand 'positions', is a linear machine with only one state of equilibrium and no memory; consequently it can choose between only two states: stability and instability [1960: 141, 153].)

Furthermore, the highly significant question as to whether by 'open', we mean open to energy, to information, or to both, finds no answer in the concept of homeostasis. Even more important is the question of the EXTENT and the ORDER of the PHASE-SPACE of VARIETY to which the system is open (its relative semiotic freedom or flexibility). Obviously, any theory – psychoanalytical or otherwise – which forces contextual closure on itself by choosing a term for 'motive' or 'control' which is overtly or covertly bioenergetic, will continue to reply to these questions about complexity – about organization, variety, interdependence, control, susceptibility to change, flexibility, creativity, relative closure, levels, logical typing, and so on – by essentially the same limited and heavy-handed reductions as those employed by Freud: entropy, innate 'drives', Benthamesque tension-reduction, repetition, and so forth.

Apart from its inadequacy to describe the programmed development of the organism in relation to an environment, the concept of homeostasis, as it is usually used, also excludes the self-differentiating or self-organizing open systems (such as minds, socioeconomic systems) which import energy from an environment to fuel the changing ORDERS of organization in the system. Such systems are negatively entropic: they tend to increase in order of level of organization. They have an essential feature which goes beyond the power of a homeostatic system: the power to elaborate new structures, which has been called 'morphogenesis' (Maruyama, 1963).

According to most current psychoanalytical theory, or any theory similarly dependent on closed-system parameters like the 'drive' – and including the theory of 'structural causality' in structuralism – Zeno's addiction to cigarettes and his succession of substitute father-relationships can be explained as a 'compulsion to repeat'. In Freudian theory, this 'repetition' is founded on the *Fort! Da!* example at the beginning of

Beyond the Pleasure Principle, where Freud's grandson would repeatedly throw away and pull back a toy on a string. According to Lacan, he is repeating the representation of an unconscious 'opposition' (supposedly analogous to a phonemic opposition) between presence and absence.

But in his unpublished seminar on the "Ethics of Pscyhoanalysis" (summarized by M. Safouan), Lacan talks about "overgratification" in the child's relation to the "primordial object" (*das Ding*), represented by the mother. This is the equivalent of an overload of information, and R. L. Marcus (1962) had already used the same idea for his analysis of the behavior of a light-seeking automaton in an attempt to clarify the concepts of 'instinct' and 'repetition'. The notion of 'overload' provides us with a way to begin to distinguish between closed-system or instinctual or programmed repetition and the OSCILLATION induced in goalseeking systems, not as a result of 'causes' emanating from their 'internal properties', but as a result of constraints imposed on them by an environment. As I have already suggested, what Kierkegaard called a 'repetition' implicitly inherent in individual human 'nature' is in fact an oscillation between logically paradoxical propositions imposed on an ensemble of messages by an ensemble of rules of a higher logical type than those governing the message transmissions themselves (Bateson, Jackson, Haley, and Weakland, 1956; Laing, 1970, 1971). In keeping with the static concepts of analytical logic, Kierkegaard believes that repetition explains the relationship between the Parmenidean 'One' and Zeno of Elea's paradoxes of motion (founded on the paradox involved in the digitalization of continuous processes), on the one hand, and the Heraclitean 'flux', on the other. He thus confuses his own double-bound situation, which generates oscillation, with the mechanical 'repetition' of, say, a revolving or rolling wheel. (Cf. Lacan in: Wilden, 1968a: 57, 141.) The distinction between repetition and oscillation, and between homeostasis and (organic) development is of considerable import for social and economic theory. Unlike the way these and allied concepts are usually used in the social sciences, it is clear that in biology at least, homeostasis and cyclic functions are SECONDARY functions in relation to ontogenesis and phylogenesis.

5. *Energy and Information*

By using Bateson's application of Carnap's categories of object language and metalanguage to human communication, it is possible to view the synchronic processes of the morphogenic goalseeking system as a combination of messages within norms (i.e., codes) according to primarily metonymic principles, and the diachronic emergence (*Aufhebung*) of the metasystem from the referent system as a metaphoric event, involving a code-switching quantum jump (selection from a set of metacodes). The regulated metonymic processes of the synchronic system are controlled by negative feedback (i.e., the contradictions are differences); the metaphoric event is brought about by the intensification of the contradictions, that is to say, by their conversion into irreconcilable oppositions related by positive feedback (Chapter XII). In view of the necessity of incorporating both a systemic and a structural view into the model, it may be possible to consider the metaphoric change of code as a transformation of the preponderance of structure into a preponderance of system, or vice versa, within a perspective which accounts for the general preponderance of structure as such at the lower levels of organization.

It is important to note that any such conception of levels of organization and metarelations seeks isomorphies between systems which differ concretely, but that it avoids the Imaginary error of seeking a relation of isomorphy, analogy, homology, identity, or reflection between metasystem and referent system, or between superstructure and base (as in the 'analogic Marxism' of Lucien Goldmann). The superstructure and the base, like consciousness and the unconscious, or the signifier and the signified, are of different logical types.

Buckley remarks, as W. Ross Ashby has done, that the relationship between energy and information involves a much more complex view of relationships in general, since the minute amount of energy required for a sender to communicate the message "Look out!" may be capable of 'triggering' a relatively enormous energy response in the receiver, just as the perception of an impending blow may do within the receiver's information processing system itself. The significance of this shift in emphasis is correlative to the understanding of the difference between lower-level and high-level behavioral systems. Higher-level systems have a vast potential of energy, internal or external, which may be triggered by information flow, without the necessity for the spatial or temporal proximity required in lower-level systems.

Lower-order open systems depend relatively more on proximity for communication than do those higher-order systems which can overcome space and time through the use of signs. Buckley concludes that 'information' does in every real sense 'represent' structure or organization, and thus can preserve it, transmit it over space and time, and change it. This representability is a function of the system's order of complexity:

The evolution of levels leading up to the socio-cultural system shows greater and greater dependence on independent, arbitrary, or symbolic communication linkage of components and less and less on substantive and energy linkages, until at the sociocultural level the system is linked almost entirely by conventionalized information exchange, with PROCESS overshadowing any rigid substantial structure such as is found at organismic levels (1967: 50).

And since the environment is essential to an open system (part of its 'essence', as the Other is for human beings), an 'intrusion' from the environment does not necessarily lead to dissolution, loss of organization, or simply to another level of equilibrium as it does for the typical closed system. It may lead rather to a restructuring or an elaboration of structure, at a higher level. The reason is that environmental interchange is not a RANDOM or UNSTRUCTURED event, or does not long remain so (remain as 'noise'), because of the mapping, or coding, or information-processing capabilities of the open system: its adaptiveness.

Buckley goes on to speak of the necessary TENSION in open systems ("the inherent instability of protoplasm" – of which Freud speaks – "tension or stress in animals, and psychic energy or motive power in men"). We are reminded of Freud's equation of *Trieb* with *Tendenz*, and of his definition of the pleasure/unpleasure principle in terms of release from tension. We can see at once that whatever the case may be for that lower-order relatively open system, the human organism, for the higher-order open system, SOCIOCULTURAL humanity, release from tension (i.e., Freud's pleasure) is a utopian myth. We know that it was pleasurable tension that caused Freud to seek to go beyond the pleasure principle: the tension of sexual desire, the tension of anticipation, of projecting towards the future and towards the Other.[8] We can now see why *Beyond the Pleasure Principle* is so full of internal contradictions. Equilibrium (constancy) and inertia, besides contradicting each other and besides being characteristic of closed or of bioenergetic homeostatic systems, correspond to the fundamental error of the Freudian model, derived from Fechner. This is that tension is DEVIANT or an environmental intrusion; whereas in fact tension is one of the products of organization itself.

Thus, in spite of the bioenergetic language, whereas Thanatos cannot be properly applied above the physical or biochemical level, the principle

[8] As a matter of historical interest, Husserl can be seen working towards some such definition of intentionality as the "intersubjective drive" (the sex drive) in an (undated) fragment, "Universal Teleology", recently published in *Telos* (Husserl, 1952). He struggles with the implicit masculinity of this drive (the libido is clearly a masculine 'force' in Freud): The fulfillment of the "intentionality of copulation" as "penetration into the other 'soul' " is not a "reciprocal feeling oneself in the other . . . and thus it is not at all related to the other, as an act of compenetration which is in the life of the world" (p. 179).

of Eros as 'project' or as 'goalseeking unity' still has some value. As the tension-producing principle of organization, as the gradient-retaining input from the 'environment' towards which Eros tends, as the "restlessness of life", the concept of Eros is an attempt to provide for a principle of information or negative entropy. Norman O. Brown (1959) has described the fundamental metaphor behind the instinctual language of Eros as a principle of "being one with the world". Since Thanatos can explain only the behavior of closed systems, whereas Eros tries to explain that of open systems, we can not only rid ourselves of the notion of instinct or drive at the human level, but we can also dispose of the fiction of the 'death-drive' altogether. There is no 'psychical inertia' in the higher-order system we call the mind – which is in any case a social category. We do not have to suppose a separate principle to explain tension, for Eros, as a goalseeking principle, will necessarily engender and depend on tension. Freud was essentially correct in wavering over the possibility that – as Marcuse (1955) has emphasized – there may be no drives other than the libidinal (negentropic) ones. Tension is as much a part of the human ecosystem as is 'Otherness'. The manipulation of this necessary gap between intention and goal so that it appears as interhuman aggressivity is a derivative of the particular state or kind of organization of the social order in which it occurs. Unlike the organism, which is adaptive only within a homeostatic plateau and changes only according to the programmed instructions of its homeorhetic 'developmental pathway', the social order can be restructured within very wide limits. Natural death is not therefore a part of the psychic system at all, and it is in no sense a principle of organization at the social level. Death is an 'environmental intrusion' from the lower-order INDIVIDUAL system, the organism, for which no further possibility of restructuring exists. (See Chapter XII, Section 7, on the concept of biological death as the result of the entropic accumulation of errors in cell reproduction and repair.)

The distinction between energy and information enables us to emphasize the undifferentiated (*indifferent*) energy available to the system, which can be 'bound' and 'triggered' by the secondary process in various ways. The problems in the Freudian texts over the *Triebrepräsentanz*, the 'representative of the drive', with its component *Vorstellung* and its component *Affektbetrag* (quota of affect), become more easily comprehensible if we view the *Vorstellung* in repression as the information born by the representative and the quota of affect as what may be 'triggered' in various ways by it.

Freud returned constantly to the problem of formalizing the relationship between the 'quota of affect' and the 'presentation'. The notion of the possibility of 'repressing' or 'suppressing' energy is obviously problematic in a viewpoint which depends on the first law of thermodynamics. On the one hand, it says that the 'repressed' or 'suppressed' energy must 'find a way out' somewhere (which agrees with the principle of conservation). On the other, it cannot fully explain the 'transformations' or the 'absences' of this 'indestructible substance'. The blocked 'aggressive energy' in the psychic system is variously said to be transformed into guilt or into anxiety: "When an instinctual trend undergoes repression, its libidinal elements are transformed into symptoms and its aggressive components into a sense of guilt" (*Standard Edition*, XXI, 139. Written in 1929). Thus both 'anxiety' and 'guilt' become other types of substances in the system. But in *Inhibitions, Symptoms, and Anxiety* (1926), Freud at least temporarily abandoned the notion of the possibility of a repressed affect. Here he speaks of the ego as sending SIGNALS (*Unlustsignals*) to control the energy available to the id. Thus he does himself partially formulate a distinction between energy and information which corresponds to the viewpoint expressed here.

This perspective of Freud's is in significant contradiction with his whole Cartesian and electromagnetic vocabulary of the 'object relation' (cf. Chapter XI). We can take as an example his explanation of the constitution of the 'part-object' in the posthumous *Outline of Psychoanalysis* (1940):

A child's first erotic object is the mother's breast that nourished it; love has its origin in attachment to the satisfied need for nourishment. There is no doubt that, to begin with, the child does not distinguish between the breast and its own body; when the breast has to be separated from the body and shifted to the 'OUTSIDE' because the child so often finds it absent, it carries with it as an 'OBJECT' a part of the original narcissistic libidinal cathexis. This first object is later completed into the person of the child's mother . . . (*Standard Edition*, XXIII: Chapter 7).

The operative terms are those referring to the part-object's 'carrying' away with it a 'portion' of the 'libidinal cathexis', as a piece of steel will carry with it the molecular rearrangement induced in it by contact with a magnet. What is in fact involved, however, is the child's discovery of his distinction from an environment by means of the INFORMATIONAL characteristics of the part-object. The breast is the bearer of a 'bit' (or 'bits') of information exchanged between mother and child; it represents both the skin-bound barrier and the channel of communication between them. (In the terminology of Chapter VII, the absence of the breast or its equivalent induces the digitalization of an analog relation.) At this point, the digital code which mediates the relation between mother and child has only two terms: presence and absence. The boundary between them is the result of a decision by the child, not a property of 'objective' reality.

6. Secondary Process and Signification

Laplanche and Pontalis (1967) summarize the relationship between 'free' and 'bound' energy in the *Project* as follows, under 'Principe de Constance':

In effect, what Freud makes the principle of inertia regulate is a type of process whose existence the very recent discovery of the unconscious had caused him to postulate: the primary process. This is described in the *Project* by a number of privileged examples, such as the dream and symptom-formation, in particular their occurrence in the hysteric. The primary process is essentially characterized by an unimpeded flow, an 'easy displacement'.'At the level of psychological analysis it was realized that one presentation could come to be completely substituted for another, could come to take from it all its properties and its effects: "But the hysteric who is reduced to tears by [the symbol] A is unaware that this is because of the association A–B, and B itself plays no part whatever in his mental life. In this case, the symbol has been completely substituted for the THING." The phenomenon of a total displacement of signification from one presentation to another and the clinical proof of the intensity and the efficacity presented by substitutive presentations, very naturally find their expression for Freud in the economic formulation of the principle of inertia. The free circulation of meaning and the total flow of psychic energy to the point of complete evacuation [inertia] are synonyms for Freud. In the final analysis the unconscious processes . . . suppose an indefinite flow or transposition of significance, or, in energy language, a totally free flow of the quantity of excitation. The secondary process, as it is defined in the conscious–preconscious system . . . supposes a binding of energy, this binding being regulated by a certain 'form' [i.e., gestalt] which tends to maintain and re-establish its boundaries and its energy level: the *Ich*.

Laplanche and Pontalis feel that the Freudian ego can only be clearly interpreted as a gestalt built upon the model of the organism, "or, if you wish, as a realized metaphor of the organism". The ego is of course precisely this type of open system for Freud, because the easy analogy with an organism allowed him to gloss over – by the vague notion of growth – those troublesome elements of his mechanistic views which, because they were derived from a closed system, could not handle 'life'. (On the question of binding, see also *Standard Edition* V, 598, 599.)

I shall not introduce in detail at this point the distinction between meaning and signification (Chapter VII), nor the correlation between the primary process and analog communication, and that between the secondary process and analog/digital communication (Chapter IX). These distinctions are intimately connected with the notions of emergence and meta-communication described in Bateson's theory of play and fantasy (1955) (Chapter IX). We can simply summarize the relationship established by Laplanche and Pontalis as follows: The bound energy of the secondary process – the preconscious and conscious *I* – can be described as a process of signification. The free energy of the primary process, on the other hand, implies a free flow of MEANING in an analog system which has not somehow been 'stabilized' or 'anchored' within the digital context which makes signification possible.

7. *The* Fort! Da! *of* Beyond the Pleasure Principle

Although the free flow of meaning in the hermeticism of the Lacanian texts makes their signification difficult to establish, it is clear that the original conception of the mirror-stage situated both Eros and Thanatos in the Imaginary (cf. Chapter XVII). Through the vision of his body as a harmonious totality at a time when it is experienced by him only as an uncoordinated aggregate, the child, says Lacan, is "precipitated" from an organic insufficiency into an anticipation of a future coming to realization as a whole. There is thus a primordial "disturbance" between the lived gestalt of the child and the visual gestalt of the mirror-stage. This alienation in an Imaginary identity is the source of the child's impossible desire to be one-with-the-world.[9] Eros is consequently a primordial double bind.[10]

[9] Cf. the early Hegel on love: "In love life finds itself, as a duplication of itself, and as its unity."

[10] Compare the Renaissance theory of sympathy and antipathy in Porta's *Magia naturalis*, summarized by Michel Foucault (1966: 39):

> Sympathy is an instance of the SAME so strong and pressing that it does not rest content with being one of the forms of the similar; it has the dangerous power of assimilation, of making things identical to each other, of making them disappear in their individuality – thus sympathy has the power of making them alien to what they were. Sympathy transforms. It alters, but in the direction of the identical, in such a way that if its power were not counterbalanced, the world would be reduced to a point, to a homogeneous mass, to the mournful figure of the Same. All its parts would hold together and communicate with each other without rupture or distance, exactly like chains of metal pieces suspended by sympathy through the attraction of a single magnet.

Sympathy is counterbalanced by antipathy, which is why the world remains what it is, related internally by similitude (resemblance), *convenientia*, and analogy.

The Imaginary is not of course the original constitution of a goal, for the child has been a goalseeking system passing from level to level of organization since the moment of conception. He has for months been stimulated at many levels by the ANALOG information in the circuit of the unit of mind constituted by his ecosystemic relationship to his mother. He has long known difference. What Lacan is describing as the erotic relationship of the Imaginary is the emergence of an ALIENATION of the analog goals of the child, the objectification of the goal by an image of opposition and identity (cf. Chapter VIII). The child begins in the Symbolic world of difference. By his birth, he discovers distinction. Through the mirror-stage, he discovers opposition. In the collective, his goal must be to transcend oppositions by the relations of higher logical typing offered by difference. He cannot follow Hegel into the individualistic identity of the Absolute Spirit without losing himself and the other. He must therefore become reconstituted in the Symbolic collectivity at another level, that of the exchange relations of the unit of mind (Chapter IX).

R. L. Marcus (1962: 145) has pointed out that whereas directedness and goal are an inherent aspect of the instinctual concept, a specific goal for any instinct is difficult to define.[11] He thus restates the problem Freud faced by dropping the untenable notion of the 'specific action' corresponding to an instinct (as this notion appears in the *Project*, for example) and substituting for it the concept of the 'mobility of the libido'. Marcus's point is to distinguish between "a process with a goal, a direction, or purpose" and a process "manifesting a need [i.e., desire] for a goal, directiveness, or purposefulness". Since goalseeking is characteristic of any kind of feedback system, it seems clear that it is not the manifestation of goals or purposes that is specific to higher-order systems such as human beings, but rather the desire for purposefulness itself.

This desire for purposefulness is surely no less than the desire of the Other. Desire would be termed a "goal-gap ratio" by operationally minded general systems theorists, and it is this goal-gap ratio which is described by G. G. Lamb as "the intensive factor or driving force in information energy" or the "amount of motivation felt by the goal-seeking animate systems". This is a bioenergetic statement of the notion of lack or absence to be found in Sartre or in Kojève.

Lacan has made a great deal of a supposed 'binary opposition' between 'presence' and 'absence' in the child's discovery of 'difference' (cf. Wilden, 1968a: 163–4, 191, 307, and elsewhere). I have pointed out that the child knows difference long before the point in development that Lacan calls

---

[11] The basis of this article in mechanistic cybernetics and closed-loop feedback systems does not vitiate Marcus's argument.

difference. In Chapter VII, I point out that presence and absence are a binary RELATION in the analog continuum, with no boundary between them equivalent (at this first level) to the digital distinctions of discrete elements (binary oppositions). Lacan almost says as much himself (1966: 594 and note), but goes on to further confound the whole issue by confusing 'zero' with the '0' of the digital computer, while still recognizing the "essential function of the PLACE in the structure of the signifier". Any supposed opposition between presence and absence is thus not only a confusion between the digital and the analog, but also (at this level) a confusion of logical types, for absence is the 'figure' on the 'ground' of presence, and the two involve levels of logical typing (cf. Chapter XIV). As Bateson has said, the difference between logical types cannot be stated, and it is here that the whole set of confusions between absence, negation, zero, refusal, and so on is repeatedly articulated. In Chapter XV (Section 1), I point out that lack or absence is not specific to human systems, as seems often to be believed. What is specific to such systems, however, is PARADOX (Chapter V).

This epistemological and communicational critique allows us to restate what is important in Lacan's commentary on *Beyond the Pleasure Principle*. What is of some significance is that from the moment one frees presence and absence from the ideology of opposition, the supposed universality of the 'compulsion to repeat' derived from this text is put in question, and its purely cultural characteristics are revealed. Through this reformulation, we can also examine the sources of an equivalent kind of error in Freud: the confusion between refusal and negation.

Freud begins *Beyond the Pleasure Principle* (*Standard Edition*, XVIII, 14ff.) with a description of the play of his grandson, who would alternately throw away and draw back a toy on a string, uttering an "o-o-o" and a "da" as he did so. Freud interpreted these phonemes as representing the German words *Fort!* ('gone') and *Da!* ('here'). He describes this apparently unpleasurable 'compulsion to repeat' as evidence of the child's learning to master his environment actively through speech, for the active repetition seemed clearly to replace the passivity of a situation where the child's mother was (inexplicably for him) alternately present and absent. The throwing away was eventually coupled with a "Go to the fwont" obviously addressed to his father, who was away fighting in World War I, and it is clear that the difference between presence and absence was the essential feature of the game, for by means of a mirror the child soon learned to make himself disappear in conjunction with the appropriate phoneme.

Much has been made of the discovery of the binary phonemic opposition in phonology – stemming in part from Ferdinand de Saussure's notion of the 'differential element' – since the work of Roman Jakobson and Troubetskoy in the thirties. But the phonemes uttered by Freud's grandson do not even involve a phonemic opposition in the proper phonological sense, for they are in fact 'holophrastic messages' (Chapter VII), not simple sounds. Nor can the 'o' be said to represent zero or 'no', as Lacan suggests. It is significant that Lacan uses a mathematical metaphor derived from Frege's theory of the integers to describe the supposed progression of the child from difference to opposition (Wilden, 1968a: 191). For what he is in fact describing is the emergence of DIGITALIZATION from an analog continuum (Chapter IX), and Frege's theory is of course a theory of the digits as distinct from the uncountable.

What the child discovers as he passes out of his 'objectless' and 'a-subjective' world – a world of pure difference, of *différance* in Derrida's sense of "postponement" (Chapter XIII), and analog patterns of relationship – is a distinction, equivalent to that between figure and ground. This distinction is then taken up at the level of phantasy and projected onto objects in the world. This is the primordial constitution of the Imaginary out of the Symbolic. It is a necessary step, and does not suppose any alienation by the image of the other (Chapter XVII). The appearance and disappearance of the toy – acceptance and rejection – are clearly a first step towards control over the comings and goings of the one who feeds him, as Freud points out. The holophrastic messages of the 'o' and the 'a' can be said to represent an appeal and a refusal – but not as yet anything like negation.

What appears here is the 'discrete element' (Chapter IX). The discrete element allows for the logical complexity of digital selections and combinations (signification) on the ground of the semantic richness of analog meaning (goals). It is of interest that Lacan does describe the *Fort! Da!* as a relation between the continuous and the discrete, by an allusion to the Chinese *kwa* (Lacan, 1966: 276; Wilden, 1968a: 39, 125): a continuous and a broken line (cf. Leach, 1962). The error involved, of course, is to confuse the *phonē* with the *graph* (Derrida, 1967a, 1967b; Chapter XIII), for the *kwa* is not a phonemic representation of the *logos* it is WRITING. Hegel (1952: 253–7) in fact uses it in discussing the difference between hieroglyphic writing (representation) and alphabetical writing (signs on signs). In this relationship, the first is analog or iconic, and the second is digital.

But we have still not approached the domain of language. The 'o' and the 'a' represent a step in the emergence of digital communication, which thus allows for all kinds of other representations and signs to be substituted for them. The 'o' and the 'a' in turn may represent the presence and absence of the breast, or of the child's own thumb and so on. The 'o' and the 'a' are not signifiers, however. The common description of the signifier as a presence made up of an absence, or as representing one, gratuitously confuses logical types. The 'o' and the 'a' are another level of the primary digitalization Bateson discovers in animal play (1955): the emergence of the sign 'nip' from the signal 'bite'. In the same way as the energy and the information of the bite are one, whereas in the nip there is a distinction between energy and information, the 'o' and the 'a', at a different level, represent the discovery of pure digital information, separate from the matter–energy (and information) of the toy and what it re-presents. The *Fort! Da!* is another form of the metacommunication 'This is play'. A new behavioral FRAME has been constructed.

Bateson describes the evolution of possibilities of communicating about the KIND of communication taking place as a significant and necessary stepping-stone in the emergence of language in evolution. Without confusing natural evolution with the development of the child (the second is teleonomic, the first is not), we can note the striking resemblance between the two processes. Play is usually assumed to involve a selective survival value in evolution – as practice, learning – just as dance and ritual undoubtedly perform some similar function. There is little doubt that, as 're-presentation', play has a parallel value in the child's learning processes. Bateson summarizes his point (1955: 40):[12]

> If we speculate about the evolution of communication, it is evident that a very important stage in this evolution occurs when the organism gradually ceases to respond quite 'automatically' to the moodsigns of another and becomes able to recognize the sign as a signal: that is, to recognize that the other individual's and its own signals are only signals, which can be trusted, distrusted, falsified, denied, amplified, corrected, and so forth. . . . Not only the characteristically human invention of language can then follow, but also all the complexities of empathy, identification, projection, and so on.

Threat, histrionics, and deceit are all observed in animals, he continues. Bluff, teasing play in response to threat, gambling, risk, spectatorship, self-pity, ritual, phantasy – in the world of human communication, these all involve metacommunication of the type of 'This is play' (p. 42). But what is not observed in animals, as Lacan has pointed out (1966: 525), is the pretence of deceit, which is essentially human, a communication of a different order from 'This is play' ('This is/is NOT play').

The 'nip' is paradoxical. It is not a 'presence made of absence', but

[12] In the following quotation, 'moodsign' refers to an iconic sign, and 'signal' to a form of digital sign.

something far more complicated and significant. Without any use of negation, it says: 'The sign which is now being communicated does not denote what would be denoted by the same act (the bite) which this act (the nip) denotes.' "The nip denotes the bite, but it does not denote what would be denoted by the bite" (p. 41). It is a message of a different logical type, a map for which there is no longer a simple, one-dimensional territory.

Bateson concludes by remarking that naming is a metalinguistic function:

> Denotative communication as it occurs at the human level [digital language] is only possible AFTER the evolution of a complex set of meta-linguistic (but not verbalized) rules which govern how words and sentences shall be related to objects and events (pp. 41–2).

Play thus involves what could be called a 'kind' of negation, if it were not that there is, strictly speaking, only one kind of negation: the word 'not' and its equivalents in language.

8. Verneinung *and* Verleugnung

In his article on "Negation" (*Standard Edition*, XIX, 235–9), Freud seeks to make a correlation between affirmation (*Bejahung*) and 'introjection into the primary *I*', on the one hand, and between *Verneinung* and 'expulsion out of the *I*', on the other hand. The connection between this relationship and the alternating throwing-away and pulling-back of the child's toy is an obvious one. Freud goes on to use the relationship between introjection and expulsion as a model of a primary form of judgment (of attribution, and of the existence or the reality of 'things'). This is mapped against the distinction between the 'subjective' and the 'objective', on the one hand, and against that between Eros and the death instinct, on the other: "Affirmation – as a substitute for uniting – belongs to Eros; negation – the successor to expulsion – belongs to the instinct of destruction."

But we know from Frege (Chapter VII) that negation is of a different logical type from affirmation: 'not' is a metacommunication about affirmation. The binary relation of exclusion between introjection and ejection cannot simply be mapped against the negation possible through the digital aspect of language. Freud confuses analog acceptance and refusal, which are distinguished by the logical typing of figure and ground, with digital affirmation and negation, which are related by metacommunication. Since the distinction between neurosis and psychosis in Freud involves a distinction between a process involving repression and denegation ('no-saying') and a process involving disavowal (*Verleugnung*), rejection (*Verwerfung*), or refusal, this confusion of the digital and the analog is somewhat surprising.

In his article "Le Fétichisme" (1969), Guy Rosolato points out with abundant evidence from Freud that disavowal always involves perception or presentation. Since the primary process seeks to establish, in Freud's terms, an identity of PERCEPTION, and the secondary process, an identity of THOUGHT, Rosolato goes on to suggest that "disavowal is to denegation as the primary process is to the secondary process". Freud's use of the term *Verneinungssymbol* (i.e., 'not') to describe 'neurotic' denegation, and that of the expression "SUCCESSOR to expulsion" to describe negation, suggests a certain uneasiness in his reduction of the analog and the digital. The text does indeed suggest the distinction between negation and disavowal, for negation is a "hallmark of repression" (not of disavowal). In other words, it is the hallmark of 'normal' and 'neurotic' language, both of which maintain the distinction between the (iconic) thing-presentations of the unconscious and the (digital) word-presentations of language. The same is not true for the language of 'schizophrenia', nor is it true of fetishism. Here there operates a refusal of an (iconic) identity of perception, whereas the denegation which negates an identity of thought (i.e., discourse) involves digital processes.

Freud's categorization of 'schizophrenic' speech as the language of the unconscious was obviously never meant to imply that the 'schizophrenic' or 'psychotic' cannot say 'No'. To thus assume that there is some real regression to an unconscious level in the psychoses is reductionist and positivistic. But the 'psychotic' who says 'No' may be primarily refusing, for digital elements can be used analogically. (We are all familiar with the anecdote about the patient who when asked to say "No", replied "No, I can't say it".) I have already remarked on the absence of the 'law of non-contradiction' in 'schizophrenia' (Chapter II, Section 10). Since this involves 'identities of thought', it is a digital relation. Thus, as a result of the complexity of what actually happens in 'psychotic' or 'schizophrenic' relationships, Rosolato defines disavowal as "an IMPLICIT denegation". It is not as if the subject says to himself 'I did not see what I saw', but rather that he simply doesn't perceive what he sees, except in the terms of projection, which is a form of refusal (cf. Wilden, 1968a: 275–84).

What seems to be in question in 'schizophrenic' relationships is that the RELATION between the analog and the digital is disturbed: the 'schizophrenic' uses 'words like things', confuses the literal with the figurative, the abstract with the concrete. This is what Freud expresses when he says that, unlike dreams, in 'schizophrenia' the communication between pre-conscious word-cathexes (intentionalizations) and unconscious thing-cathexes has been cut off (*Standard Edition*, XIV, 229). There is no longer a metaphoric relationship of metacommunication or 'distance' between them ('Botticelli'), but rather a word-to-word metonymic coalescence ('Manzanita wood').

Moreover, the whole conception of the splitting of the ego, where mutually contradictory propositions exist in coincidence with each other, does not involve a situation which can properly be characterized by saying that one proposition negates the other. They simply refuse each other, turn their backs on each other. It is equally significant that the schizophrenic double bind CANNOT be negated; it can only be communicated about at a higher level of communication.

There is a perhaps hidden genetic model discernible here. In 1905, Freud described repression as an intermediate stage between a 'defensive reflex' and a 'condemning judgment' (*Urteilsverwerfung*) – this last being an equivalent for disavowal (*Standard Edition*, VIII, 175). What he seems to seek to establish is a genetic sequence: (1) biological reflex; (2) the primary repression constituting the primary process (as analog) and the secondary process (as both analog and digital); (3) condemnation or analog refusal, IMPLICITLY involving 'something like' negation; and (4) the emergence of the digital 'symbol of negation' itself. Each emergence defines a system of a higher and higher order of complexity and dimensionality. At least this sequence explains to me the cryptic proposition in "Negation" (p. 236): "Through the MEDIATION of the symbol of negation, thought frees itself from the consequences of repression and enriches itself with a content necessary for its accomplishment" (my emphasis). This, Freud says, is an essential prerequisite to the function of judgment (*Urteil*). If 'not' frees thought from the 'compulsion' of the pleasure principle (the 'free flow of meaning'), then presumably it is that which provides for the 'binding' of significations by the reality principle (XIX, 239, 237).

The foregoing analysis has depended on the methodological distinction between analog communication and digital communication. It is now time to turn our attention to an analysis of this distinction.

Chapter VII

Analog and Digital Communication

ON NEGATION, SIGNIFICATION, AND MEANING[1]

To EXPLAIN, literally to lay out in a plane where particulars
can be readily seen. Thus to place or plan in flat land,
sacrificing other dimensions for the sake of appearance.
Thus to expound or put out at the cost of ignoring the
reality or richness of what is so put out. Thus to take a view
away from its prime reality or royalty, or to gain knowledge and
lose the kingdom.

G. SPENCER BROWN: *Laws of Form*

All natural systems of communication employ both analog and digital communication at some level in the system. It is useful to make a methodological distinction between these two modes of information transmission.
The distinction is modeled on the way information is transmitted and used
in certain manmade primitive 'organisms': cybernetic devices, control
mechanisms, computers. It is equally applicable to or derivable from the
way information is transmitted within the human organism, or in an ecosystem, or from the way it is transmitted between human organisms.

Let us first consider the FORM of the information transmission in
manmade analog and digital devices (which I shall call 'computers'
whether they actually compute in the strict sense or not).

1. *The Analog Computer*

An analog computer is defined as any device which 'computes' by means of
an analog between real, physical, CONTINUOUS quantities and some other

---

[1] A version of this paper was originally presented at the Meeting of the American
Anthropological Association, San Diego, November 19, 1970, in a symposium
on Lévi-Strauss organized by Ino Rossi.

set of variables. These real quantities may be the distance between points on a scale, the angular displacement, the velocity, or the acceleration of a rotating shaft, a quantity of some liquid, or the electrical current in a conductor. Examples of the analog computer thus include a number of common devices: the flyball governor (which first led Clerk Maxwell to found the theory of goalseeking or cybernetic devices[2]), the map, the clock (water or mechanical), the ruler, the thermometer, the volume control, the accelerator pedal, the sextant, the protractor. Specialized computing devices employing analog representation include the slide-rule, the planimeter, the harmonic analyzer and synthesizer (e.g., Kelvin's tide predictor), the mechanical or electrical differential analyzer. These machines differ from each other in that the ruler, the thermometer, and the volume control employ direct analogy, whereas the differential analyzer employs indirect analogy. That is to say, the differential analyzer is a direct analog of a mathematical formula which is an analog of a real situation, whereas no such mediator intervenes between, say, the distance on a ruler and the distance on the line being measured. The central feature of both types, however, is that they are 'continuous function computers'. In this sense the humoral system of the body, dependent upon the release of 'more or less' of something into the bloodstream, is an analog system.

2. *The Digital Computer*

The digital computer differs from the analog in that it involves DISCRETE elements and discontinuous scales. Apart from our ten fingers, the abacus was probably the first digital computer invented. Pascal's adding machine, the Jacquard punch-card loom, and Babbage's difference engine are further historical examples. Any device employing the on/off characteristic of electrical relays or their equivalents (such as teeth on a gear wheel) is a digital computer. Thus the thermostat, although it depends upon continuous analog quantities (the bending of its thermocouple in response to temperature) involves a digitalization at a second level, because the thermocouple is connected to a switch which either turns the furnace off or turns it on. Similarly, the central nervous system involves neurons which receive

---

[2] Gregory Bateson has often pointed out that A. R. Wallace – in the famous letter of 1858 to Darwin about his independently conceived notion of natural selection (conceived in the analog and somewhat psychedelic world of a malarial delirium) – compares the process of natural selection to the imperceptible movements of a flyball governor controlling a steam engine (Cooper, ed., 1968: 36–7). The point, of course, is that both a governor and natural selection are cybernetic devices. (The first cybernetic device invented is presumed to be Ktesibios' level regulator for water clocks in the third century B.C.)

quanta or packages of information via the axons and through the connecting synapses. Upon arrival at the synapses on the body of the neuron these quanta are said to be summated, the result of which is either the firing or the inhibition of the firing of the neuron. That is to say, at the moment of 'summation' (the process does not in fact seem to involve sums), the neuron either fires or does not fire. Thus the neurons may be said to operate digitally, but the synapse and axon which connect them appear to be complex analog devices (Dreyfus, 1965: 56).

3. *The Computer and the Brain: Boundaries and States*

Whereas in manmade information-processing devices the boundaries of the analog/digital distinction are fairly clear, the same is not true for other systems or for the intraorganismic communication of the human body (this is in fact the most significant aspect of the problem of artificial intelligence). And even the distinction in manmade machines requires careful definition, for the digital computer involves a code, and any code considered in its totality is an analog of something (a 'map' of some 'territory' or other). In the case of the digital computer, the machine processes are analogs of mathematical formulae which are digital representations of the behavior of some system or other. Moreover, given perhaps almost unlimited computing time and memory capability, it is possible in principle to represent the behavior of any analog system or computer in a digital computer, provided only that the problem can be stated in a finite number of unambiguous 'words' (McCulloch and Pitts). (See Appendix II.) But some of the most common human communicational acts are probably not definable in this way and almost certainly do not involve only digital processes. The most significant examples are the phenomena involved in fringe consciousness, in attention or 'zeroing in', in the distinction between the essential and the non-essential or between figure and ground, in pattern recognition, in the context-interdependence involved in language translation, and obviously, in the necessary human tolerance for ambiguity which allows us to define and redefine the rules for any given situation. At present these decisions or ways of dealing with them have still to be made by the human programmer, who perhaps provides the necessary analog component to complement the amazing brute-force problem-solving capabilities of the digital computer (Dreyfus, 1965).

Von Neumann deals in some detail with the question of the analog and the digital in the brain, in the Silliman Lectures interrupted by his death (1958: 39–82). He points out that what he calls the *prima facie* digital behavior of the neuron is a simplification. It is true that neurons either fire or do not fire, but this firing may be modified by the recovery time of the neuron. Similarly, a neuron may represent a simple, two-valued logical network: its firing after a combined and/or synchronized stimulation by two connecting synapses represents 'and', and its firing after stimulation from one or the other of two synapses represents 'or'. But most neurons embody synaptic connections with many other neurons. In some cases, several connecting axons or branches (ending in synapses) from one neuron form synapses on the body of another. Moreover, the axons themselves may stimulate or be stimulated by their neighborhood, the 'impulse' then travelling in both directions, towards the neuron and towards the synapse. Thus, quite apart from the estimated 10^{12} synaptic connections in the network, and without considering the dendrites or the phenomenon of direct axonal stimulation, the possible patterns of stimulation do not involve only the so-called 'impulse' (which is probably to be considered as much more like a PROPOSITION, in every sense of the term). These patterns probably also include the FREQUENCY of the series of impulses in a single axon, the SYNCHRONIZATION of impulses from different axons, the NUMBER of impulses, and the SPATIAL ARRANGEMENT of the synapses to which the impulses arrive, as well as the so-called summation time. (This, again, is quite apart from the interrelated physical, mechanical, chemical, and electrical processes in the axon which propagate the message: Section 10 below.) Some of these aspects, such as frequency, spatial arrangement, and the chemical processes, are analogs.

Von Neumann also points to the constant switching between the analog and the digital in the behavior of the message systems of the body at another level: a digital command releases a chemical compound which performs some analog function or other, this release or its result is in turn detected by an internal receptor neuron which sends a digital signal to command the process to stop or sets off some other process, and so on. Similarly, the genes are part of a digitally coded system, but depend for their effects upon the formation of the analogs (enzymes) specific to them (1958: 68–9). It has been suggested that we think of these processes not in terms of 'impulses', which imply a basically energetic model of what is obviously an information system (which 'triggers' energy in order for 'work' to be done), but rather in terms of logical types and classes. The neuron could be said to fire or not to fire if and only if the requisite analog and digital logical arrangements have been completed.

The logical complexity of such a system would hardly seem to be that of a two-valued, analytic logic, but rather that of a many-valued, dialectical one. This way of looking at the brain seems to confirm the notion that every representation in its totality is analog-iconic.

Another feature which emerges from the study of the nervous system seems to be that digitalization is always necessary when certain boundaries are to be crossed, boundaries between systems of different 'types' or of different 'states', although how these types or boundaries might be operationally defined is unclear. Descriptively speaking, Mandelbrot's analysis of the relationship between the continuous and the discrete at the phonological level of language appears to support this notion (see Section 6 below), as does the application of the analog/digital distinction to psychoanalysis, play, exchange theory, and anthropology (Chapter IX).

I shall return to the complex epistemological problem of 'boundaries' in Sections 9 and 10 below. For the moment it will suffice to point out that the question of 'different' systems or different 'types' of system is never an objective fact, but the result of a definition made by some subsystem in the wider ecosystem. For example, the behavior of animals in relation to the so-called territorial imperative, and especially the marking of trails and limits by chemical messages (Sebeok, 1967), is one way in which such a definition is arrived at. Certainly, in the macroscopic domain of communication, one system is distinct from others because some organism or group of organisms has 'decided' to make it so.

It seems likely that all such delimitations correspond in general, not so much to the survival of the individual organism, species, or group, but rather to the survival of the ecosystem without which no subsystem can survive (Chapter VIII). A 'territory' corresponds in no sense to 'property', but rather to the maintenance of the necessary ecological space to regulate such things as the genetic pool and the food supply (cf. Hardin, 1969).

The chemical trail or the territorial boundary thus seems to be equivalent in some rudimentary way to the differentiation of figure from ground in perception. As in the case of the spermatozoa or pin-prick which MARKS the pole for one of the infinite number of bipolar and radially symmetrical meridians of the frog's egg to become the locus of the bilateral symmetry of the frog, a 'bit' of information is used to select one difference from an infinite number of possible differences. This difference then becomes DISTINCT from all the others. If the chemical message, for instance, marks a line which is not to be crossed, or a line which is to be followed, then it clearly has a rudimentary 'on/off' or 'either/or' function: it turns a difference into a distinction (see below, Section 6). Since the 'bit' marks a boundary – indeed, since we can actually call it a 'bit' – it is a rudimentary digitalization of the analog; it introduces some form of discreteness into a continuum.

At a more complex level of communication, Rappaport has shown how the Tsembaga of New Guinea employ a digital device to regulate the analog relationships of the biosocial ecosystem in which they live (1968, 1970). The boundary between 'not enough pigs' (to propitiate the ancestors) and 'too many pigs' (for the local ecosystem to support) is indicated by the planting or the uprooting of a symbolic tree. The either/or status of the tree indicates 'to whom it may concern' that the relationship between system (the Tsembaga) and environment (nature, pigs, other local groups) is about to change. The system is complex, having to do with war and peace, ritual, and the amount of available protein (energy = pigs) in the system. At the termination of intergroup hostilities, there are never enough pigs to slaughter to properly propitiate the ancestors for future success in war. A symbolic debt is created. After a certain period of truce during which the pigs are allowed to multiply, however, the pig population becomes too great for the local ecosystem to support. When the complaints about the pigs' destruction of vegetable gardens reach a certain intensity (when there are 'more' rather than 'less' pigs), the tree is uprooted, the ritual preparations for war begin, and the mature pigs are slaughtered.

Thus, just as the on/off characteristics of the thermostat halt the positive feedback (escalating difference) of a continuously increasing or decreasing temperature by introducing negative feedback, so does the status of the symbolic tree indicate by digital means that a particular level of difference – 'too much' or 'too little' – has been reached. The result is the homeostatic control of the available energy in the system to maintain neutral entropy, and thus to preserve the RELATIONSHIP between the Tsembaga and every facet of their environment. The tree does not in this case indicate a physical or spatial boundary, but rather a boundary between acceptable and non-acceptable energy levels in the system. Digitalization is thus a TOOL employed to maintain an overall analog relation: the survival of the ecosystem as a whole.

We find exactly the same characteristic analog/digital relationship in cellular processes. Although Goodwin (1968: 134) does not differentiate between the ECOLOGICAL characteristics of the analog and the LOGICAL characteristics of the digital on any epistemological or ideological grounds, he makes the following significant point (p. 136):

A fundamental question in relation to control dynamics in cells is whether or not gene action has an all-or-none character, a gene being full on when its repressor level is lower than a particular threshold value and shut off when it is above this value. Such on–off characteristics would make the gene a two-state module and the cell an essentially digital-type mechanism at this level of control. However, the evidence available is fairly conclusive in demonstrating that those genes so far investigated (for alkaline phosphatase and β-galactosidase) can be continuously regulated over an order of magnitude by continuous variation of repressor level. This transforms the problem of gene regulation into one of control rather than strictly logic. . . .

To return to the analog and digital characteristics of the brain: it is as a result of the 'totalizing' complexity of the brain that it is suggested that "general electric potentials [analogs] play an important role". The system "responds to the solution of potential theoretical problems *in toto*, problems which are less immediate and elementary than what are normally described by the digital criteria, stimulation criteria", and so on (von Neumann, 1958: 59). This characteristic of the brain as a whole is presumably related to Lashley's theory of mass action, according to which "the activities of any part of the cortex in the acquisition, retention, and performance of more complex integrative functions are conditioned by the activities of all other parts" (Roy, 1967: 163).

The conception of a sort of totalized adaptive response – for the 'work' to be done is always concerned with an adaptive or counter-adaptive relationship to some environment or other – has presumably some relevance to the known effects of hallucinogenic drugs, which heighten analog thinking and perception, but apparently impair digital thought. Since the relationship of an organism to its environment is primarily an analog one, the conception outlined may also be relevant to the 'chicken and the egg' question of the relationship of brain (an entity) and mind (a relation) in so-called schizophrenia: is it the chemical or electrical changes in the brain which induce the 'disease'? Or is it the pathological communication of schizophrenic relationships which set off these changes?[3]

4. *Distinctions in Logical Form*

Since the analog computer employs continuous linear quantities to represent other quantities, there are no significant 'gaps' in the system. Equally important, there is no true zero (at 'zero' the machine is 'off'). All the quantities involved are positive; there are no minus quantities.[4] The

[3] I suspect that the answer lies in the way the observer defines the system under study. Like the present controversy over 'hyperkinetic children' with 'minimal brain dysfunction' (in the words of the companies selling the drugs to quiet the children), the definition of the disease seems to be logically equivalent to the dormitive virtue found in opium, because it substitutes the name of a thing (MBD) for an explanation of a relation to an environment.

[4] It is of some historical interest to remember that the Greeks thought of numbers as real and positive quantities. Both zero and minus numbers, which are more

quantities represented are relatively imprecise. The digital computer, on the other hand, depends upon the combination of discrete elements made possible by its on/off processes. Zero is essential to it, and since its combinatorial possibilities depend only upon the PLACING and the ORDERING of its discrete elements, rather than upon their nature or their location as such, the digital computer can represent negative quantities. Its representations are relatively precise.

The analog computer maps continuums precisely whereas the digital computer can only be precise about boundaries.[5] The units of communication or computation in the analog machine may in principle be repeatedly divided without necessarily losing their signification or use, whereas those in the digital computer cannot be divided below the level of the discrete unit on which it depends. (And the 'gaps' cannot be divided at all.) The direct analog computer is a concrete, ICONIC representation of the behavior it maps; the digital computer is an entirely abstract, ARBITRARY, and more nearly linguistic representation. (It employs an artificial language.)

These formal distinctions between two kinds of machines already sound similar to a number of other long-standing distinctions involved in communication in general. The most obvious involves the distinction between what Pascal called the *esprit de finesse* and the *esprit de géometrie*.

It is impossible to represent the truth functions of symbolic logic in an analog computer, because the analog computer cannot say 'not-A'. Negation in any language or simulated language depends upon SYNTAX, which is a special form of combination, and the analog computer has no syntax beyond the level of pure sequence (and that only in a positive direction). There is no 'either/or' for the analog computer because everything in it is only 'more or less', that is to say: everything in it is 'both-and' (see Note 10). The analog computer cannot represent nothing (no-thing) because it is directly or indirectly related to 'things', whereas the 'language' of the

---

clearly relations rather than 'entities', were invented much later. Note also that the introduction of zero into a scale applied to an analog computer involves digitalizing it, and that turning it off generates a false zero.

[5] Perception involves the transformation of analogs or icons into digital messages to the brain through both digital and analog processes. (Note that the retinal receptors are sensitive enough to be stimulated by the 'smallest possible energy difference', a single quantum of radiant energy, and that the result at every moment must be like the digital process of the half-tone print which an analog machine like a Xerox copier cannot properly reproduce.) Optical stabilization of the image on the retina, which defeats the purpose of saccadic eye movement, results in a fading of the image. But if that image contains large areas of non-difference, as in the image of a sheet of paper, only the areas of distinction, the BOUNDARIES, fade, for the visual system contributes to perception by extrapolating between boundaries (Gregory, 1966: 42–50, 78).

digital computer is essentially autonomous and arbitrary in relation to 'things' (except in so far as all information requires matter–energy in the form of markers for its transmission). The analog computer is an icon or an image of something 'real', whereas the digital computer's relationship to 'reality' is rudimentarily similar to language itself. In fact, we can say that in human communication all non-conventionalized 'gesture language', posture, facial expression, inflection, sequence, rhythm, cadence, and indeed the CONTEXT within which human communication takes place, is a type of analog or iconic communication in which the signal or sign has a necessary relation to what it 're-presents', whereas all denotative, linguistic communication is arbitrary and digital (Watzlawick, Beavin, and Jackson, 1967: 60–7).[6] Obviously, whatever the nature of the underlying processes, all non-linguistic communication through the senses, between person and person or person and world, with the single exception of conventionalized signals, involves analog and iconic communication.

The relationship between the absence of 'zero' and the absence of 'negation' in the analog machine does not appear to be an accidental one. I shall return to this point later.

The interest of the distinction between analog and digital machines is even more striking if we consider the relationship between semantics and syntax in these two forms of communication. The analog is pregnant with MEANING whereas the digital domain of SIGNIFICATION is, relatively speaking, somewhat barren. It is almost impossible to translate the rich semantics of the analog into any digital form for communication to another organism. This is true both of the most trivial sensations (biting your tongue, for example) and the most enviable situations (being in love). It is impossible to precisely describe such events except by recourse to unnameable common experience (a continuum). But this imprecision carries with it a fundamental and probably essential ambiguity: a clenched fist may communicate excitement, fear, anger, impending assault, frustration, 'Good morning', or revolutionary zeal. The digital, on the other hand, because it is concerned with boundaries and because it depends upon arbitrary combination, has all the syntax to be precise and may be entirely unambiguous. Thus what the analog gains in semantics it loses in syntactics, and what the digital gains in syntactics it loses in semantics. Thus it is that because the analog does not possess the syntax necessary to say 'No' or to say anything involving 'not', one can REFUSE or REJECT in the analog, but one cannot DENY or NEGATE.

[6] The mention of 'discrete analog quantities' in this text is totally misleading.

5. *Distinctions in Function*

If we leave the computers from which the distinction was originally drawn and look at communication between organisms, it seems that human beings are the only organisms to use the FUNCTIONS of both processes for communication with their peers. Moreover, humans seem to be the only animals capable of using one mode in place of the other, for natural language and human communication are both digital and analog in both form and function. Formally, the poet may employ devices such as alliteration or onomatopoeia or association to make the digital elements on the page or in his reading into analogs or in order to evoke analog sensations. Functionally, the politician may employ the analog context of his digital text to obscure or replace the text, as we saw in the television campaign for the 1970 US elections, for example. He may in other words be apparently conveying denotative information about issues and events when in fact he is actually talking about his relationship to his audience and their relationship to the image and images he projects. In such a context, the 'conceptual' value of the digital information is zero (cf. the Introduction).

This is in essence the prime distinction between the function of the digital and that of the analog. The digital mode of language is denotative: it may talk about anything and does so in the language of objects, facts, events, and the like. Its linguistic function is primarily the sharing of nameable information (in the non-technical sense); its overall function is the transmission or sharing or reproduction of pattern and structures (information in the technical sense). The analog on the other hand talks only about relationships. In human communication there are often serious problems of translation between the two.

Analog communication thus accurately describes all that we know about the function of macroscopic animal communication, for we know of little, if anything, approaching denotation in the animal world. Such rudimentary systems of food calls, danger calls, and so forth as do exist do not seem to involve anything beyond the level of the signal or the rudimentary sign, and it seems at first to be unnecessarily anthropomorphic to suggest that such and such a noise 'signifies' SOME-THING when it is clear that it only signals something about the relationship of the animal calling to his environment and thence about his relationship to the receivers of his message.

But in order to avoid confusion about the terms 'form' and 'function', a further clarification is necessary. Since a food call is a metacommunication about an analog relationship, it is not quite correct to say that it does not signify something. Since it sets up a boundary between one state of a system ('absence of food') and another state ('presence of food'), it is a FORM of digitalization. We need therefore to introduce at least two main levels of semiotic freedom in the form of the digital:

1 The level of the signal or sign, which is arbitrary in one sense and fixed in another (a noise has no essential connection with food but all gibbons make the same set of noises to indicate food). Like the firing of a neuron, such a first-level digital message has only to do with decisions about the difference between presence and absence (a continuum), and cannot be substituted for the overall analog function of the communication. At this level, it would appear that no metacommunication about the message is possible.

2 The level of the linguistic signifier, which is arbitrary in one sense and has a high degree of semiotic freedom in another sense (there are many ways to indicate the presence or absence of food in language). Unlike the on/off decisions of a neuron or of animal signals about food, danger, territorial boundaries, and so on, this second level in the form of the digital is capable of more than simply labeling a certain difference as distinct. This is the level of double articulation (duality of patterning) and negation. It is capable of taking over or replacing the analog in terms of both form and function. At this level, messages about messages (logical typing) are clearly possible.

As an example of the kind of 'primary digitalization' described by (1) above, Hockett and Altmann's analysis of gibbon calls is useful (1968: 70–1). They point out that the danger call and the food call are "holistically different" from each other and belong to a finite repertoire of calls from which the gibbon can choose. Yet the 'danger call' turns out to be "a continuous range of possible calls, varying within certain rough bounds as to intensity, duration, and number of repetitions". To some extent these variations are directly related to the relative seriousness of the perceived danger.

Thus, we must say that the SINGLE gibbon call . . . is in fact a continuous open repertoire of possibilities within which any actual utterance occupies a systematic position; in this respect the 'single' gibbon call is like the entire repertoire of bee dances. A human language is open, but discrete rather than continuous, so that the mechanism of openness (of free coinage of new messages) is necessarily quite different from that of bee dancing.

This paper moves away from considering 'design features' atomistically, by incorporating Bateson's conception of 'frames' and 'metacommunication'.

The conception of the analog as communication about relationship is equivalent to Malinowski's phatic communion: "a type of speech in which ties of union are created by a mere exchange" (quoted by Sebeok, 1962: 434). Jakobson has suggested that the phatic function of language is the only one other species share with human beings and that it is the first 'verbal function' acquired by infants (ibid.). In the terminology of this essay, one would say that the phatic function long antedates verbal communication in ontogeny, and is more accurately to be described as analog communication. Verbalization and symbolization involve the digitalization of the analog, for the infant knows how to communicate with his sphincters and other orifices (Lacan in: Wilden, 1968a: 24) long before he comes to emit anything more than analog sounds.[7]

No known animal communication is digital in function, and none is known to involve second-level digitalization, although the complexity of dolphin communication and the whale's song offer intriguing possibilities for research into an area where the methodological assumption of a discontinuity between animal and humankind is necessarily contradicted by the continuum of reality.[8] The example of the communication of the bees is

---

[7] I would also speak of analog thinking or knowing and digital thinking or knowing, as well as of analog and digital communication. The analog would cover the emotive, the phatic, the conative, and the poetic; the digital, the cognitive and the metalingual. Phatic communion describes the main aspects of the symbolic function in Lévi-Strauss and Lacan (Chapter IX).

Not all languages are equally digital in form or in function. If Granet is correct in his analysis of ancient Chinese language and epistemology (*La Civilisation chinoise* and *La Pensée chinoise*, reviewed by C. Wright Mills, 1963: 469–524), the OVERALL analog function of digital communication is much more evident in ancient Chinese culture. Of course Chinese written language is emblematic or relatively iconic in form. Ancient Chinese epistemology and education emphasize totality, homeostasis, natural and social context, response, consummation, interrelation, and wisdom rather than analysis, pure knowledge, so-called 'reason' or 'rationality', and the various separations and dichotomies which underlie all western epistemology.

Something of the flavor of the subtleties available in Chinese is brought out in Chao (1959: 7–8). He points out that, without counting intonation and voice qualifiers, there are 81 ways in Chinese of posing the either/or question "Will you eat rice or noodles?"

[8] The epistemological necessity of mapping discontinuity onto continuity must be emphasized. Epistemology is a matter of where you draw the line; every *logos* deals with boundaries. The same is true of any conceptual relation: metaphor and metonymy, closed and open system, energy and information – and, of course, the analog/digital line itself.

This is not to say that all knowledge is digital, although many philosophers seem to think so, or at least to behave as if it were. Most knowledge is analog. Only the divine power of abstraction (*Verstand*), to use Hegel's term, is digital. Most of our knowledge or understanding (in the usual sense) is communicated

instructive. (Even though the more it is studied, the less we seem to know about it: cf. Sebeok, 1963.) No bee constructs a message out of or about another message (there is no metacommunication about messages as is possible in digital communication); in other words, no bee can "dance about dancing" (Hockett). The 'gesture language' of bees involves perception (perceptual representations are analogs of what they represent). Moreover, no bee who has not flown the course to find the nectar can send the message 'about' where it is, no bee can tell where the nectar or the pollen WILL BE, no bee can say where the nectar ISN'T. It is significant that there are two sorts of dance and that the sense of smell, which is analog (Sebeok, 1967) is also involved. (There are auditory elements also.) The circular dance has the specific function of analog communication: it simply says something about the dancing bee's relationship to the food near the hive, but it cannot say there is no food there. The wagging dance uses a code of signals to point; it is a more complex analog message. In neither case does there seem to be a possibility of a methodological analysis of these forms into discrete elements with a duality of patterning similar to that of morphemes and phonemes, for the indications of distance in the wagging dance are frequencies and times, and relatively imprecise (cf. Sebeok, 1962: 435; Esch, 1967).

Only if we anthropomorphize the bee can we be deluded into thinking that the REPORT aspect of the dance (all messages being simultaneously reports on situations and commands to do something about them – McCulloch) is a statement, for the bees, of where the nectar is. The dance is a report about the dancing bee's relationship to the hive and to its needs, and a COMMAND to the other bees to put themselves into the same relationship. The bees obtain food, but nobody 'knows' where it is. Similarly, the cat who rubs against our leg when we open the refrigerator door is probably not saying anything like "I want some milk" or "Give me some milk," but something like a question or a PROPOSITION about a relation: "Will you put yourself into a mother relationship to me?"

---

analogically, by imitation, for example. In our universities, significantly enough, analog knowledge – and especially the (analog) context of (digital) knowledge – is generally denied, rejected, or ignored – except where its recognition can't do much harm, as in art and music departments, or where it simply has to be taken into account, as in medical schools (which are very interested in the problem of analog simulation), for no amount of digitalization can properly describe the touch of a surgeon's knife, which can have rather sudden either/or effects.

6. *Difference, Distinction, and Opposition*

It is important to distinguish the form and the function of the two types of communication, but they seem always to be found together in all communications systems, and at every level of communication. Digitalization at the first level is necessary for all systems controlled by negative feedback, and since cells are such 'oscillators', they must involve digital controls at some level. For the elementary light-seeking organism or for the frog's visual relationship to small moving blobs, the function of the communication is analog (relation to environment), but its form is digital: the receptors say whether there is or is not light of a sufficient intensity and the frog's tongue either is or is not directly energized by the retinal perception of the approaching winged insect (Gregory, 1966).

Obviously without the digital, we could not speak of the analog. As communication of information, both are to be distinguished from energy-transfer. The digital is assumed to involve higher levels of organization and therefore lower levels of logical typing. If natural language is both digital and analog, artificial languages are digital only. In human communication, where we can see a diachronic evolution or accession from the analog to the digital (from suckling, play, and noise-making to speech) and a synchronic coincidence between them, the primary functional difference bears on the distinction between relation and denotation. In human communication, translation from the analog to the digital often involves a gain in information (organization) but a loss in meaning. Translation from the digital to the analog (as in the psychosomatic symptom) usually involves a loss of information and a gain in meaning. Such translations may generate paradox and contradiction.

It is important to reiterate that the distinction does not say that the digital is restricted to human language. Digital is a necessary condition for natural language, but not a sufficient one, since the following remark is also a statement in a digital language: "1234", as is "#$%¢&". Moreover, DNA involves a digital code, which may be said to be doubly articulated or dually patterned, in some way, since the genetic information in the four-letter code of DNA has to be translated into the twenty-letter code of the amino-acids before it can be 'used'.[9] And from a wider perspective, in so far as any system of signifiers is a mapping or transform of a system of signifieds, the relationship of one system to the other in its totality is analog.

[9] But if DNA is to be viewed as a 'text', as Waddington suggests (personal communication), and messenger RNA as the 'reader' who tells the proteins what to do, it is not clear to me that this 'translation' is equivalent to the relationship between phonemes and morphemes in language.

There are thus two kinds of DIFFERENCE involved, and the distinction between them is essential. Analog differences are differences of magnitude, frequency, distribution, pattern, organization, and the like. Digital differences are those such as can be coded into DISTINCTIONS and OPPOSITIONS, and for this, there must be discrete elements with well-defined boundaries. In this sense, the sounds of speech are analog; phonology and the alphabet are digital. In the same way, the continuous spectrum of qualitative, analog differences ranging from black to white in the visible color spectrum may be digitalized by the boundaries of a color wheel or coded around the opposition of black and white (which, for another system of explanation, as the absence of color, are identical). Similarly, in order for the analog differences of presence and absence, raw and cooked, 'o' and 'a', life and death, or the analog and the digital themselves, to be distinguished or to be opposed, they must first be digitalized either by the sender or the receiver or both in a language of discrete elements. It is interesting in this context to note the use of the terms 'differential elements', 'distinctive features', and 'binary oppositions' in modern linguistics, terms which need to be more clearly differentiated from each other (cf. the critique of 'opposition' in Chapter XIV).

These generalizations seem to be borne out by Sebeok's intensive analysis of the distinction, although the terminology differs. In dealing with expressive or 'paralinguistic' phenomena, he cites Trager on the concept of the analog code:

> [The] voice qualities as described seem to involve paired attributes, but the pairs of terms are more properly descriptive of extremes between which there are continua or several intermittent degrees (Sebeok, 1962: 437).

There are indeed binary relations or differences in the analog, but they do not seem to be either functionally or formally equivalent at one and the same time to the binary oppositions of phonemes. And Haldane asserts that "animal signals grade into one another" (quoted in Sebeok, 1962: 439). Thus it seems that we might talk of binary differences in the analog (e.g., presence and absence), and of binary distinctions and oppositions in the digital, without violating the spirit of the usage of these terms by linguists.

Sebeok goes on to cite Mandelbrot's argument for the necessary relationship of the continuous and the discrete in linguistic change. The discrete character of the signifier follows from its continuous substratum: the signifier is 'carried' by continuous sounds, discreteness is thus never sufficiently established, and the system changes (p. 439). The notion of the discrete being borne by the continuous is an interesting one, for it can be read as corresponding to the relationship between energy and information: continuous energy processes bear both (analog) differences and (digital) distinctions. Energy interferences in the channel contribute noise, and noise, as Bateson has pointed out, is the only possible source of new patterns (1967). It is 'noise' in the genetic code which constitutes random variation in evolution. Information, by definition, is not random, and the 'noise' does not long remain as such, because of the adaptive characteristics of goalseeking open systems (language, minds, societies, organisms, ecosystems).

To sum up the logical, mathematical, and pragmatic signification of distinction, I quote without comment the first definition in G. Spencer Brown's *Laws of Form* (1969):

DISTINCTION IS PERFECT CONTINENCE.

That is to say, a distinction is drawn by arranging a boundary with separate sides so that a point on one side cannot reach the other side without crossing the boundary.

Once a distinction is drawn, the spaces, states, or contents on each side of the boundary can be indicated.

There can be no distinction without motive, and there can be no motive unless contents are seen to differ in value.

If a content is of value, a name can be taken to indicate this value.

Thus the calling of the name can be identified with the value of the content.

7. Logical Typing

Analog communication employs no subject function (no 'shifters' like 'I' or 'here'), and no message transmitted in an analog mode can be precisely repeated by another communicator, although it may on occasion be imitated. In other words, analog communication does not lend itself easily to the sort of relay from subject to subject which digital communication makes possible, and in fact requires. Natural language is the most highly organized form of digital communication, the form with the greatest semiotic freedom, the form which allows for the representation of the past and the future, the possible and the impossible, the form which is the least dependent upon PROXIMITY for communication (not withstanding the fact that audio and video transmission involves analog processes). The more highly organized a system is, the more distinct information is from the energy that bears it. (But see Sebeok, 1967, on chemical zoosemiotics.)

All behavior is communication. Language is behavior, but it is also language, and obviously involves properties specific to it as well as properties to be found in all other forms of communication. One specific property of language, as I have pointed out, is that it can talk about itself, it can metacommunicate. ("This sentence is in English.") This implies that language involves logical typing (the sentence about the sentence in English is of a different logical type from that of the sentence it refers to), and logical typing seems to be a property only of digital or mixed systems, because of the boundaries (classes) it requires. It is true that an analog message about a relationship (a look of dislike) may be a metacommunication about a digital one ("Pleased to see you"), or vice versa, but it is probably impossible to conceive of an analog commenting on itself. An artist might produce a painting apparently commenting on itself, but in fact the artist would be the commentator. It is probably correct to say therefore, that metacommunication requires some form of digitalization. (We are not concerned at this point about whether the metacommunication is 'conscious', but only about whether it can be 'recognized'.) In fact, any digital message MUST at some level be a metacommunication about an analog relation. The chemical sign-trails of animals and insects and the symbolic tree of the Tsembaga correspond to the necessity of 'drawing the line somewhere' in the interests of long-range survival, and survival is an analog function. In the widest sense, that line seems always to be related to the line between negative feedback (control, maintenance) and positive feedback (runaway, destruction). (Cf. Chapters VIII and XII on positive feedback in symmetrical and complementary relationships.)

The relationship between levels of logical typing and levels of organization is not easy to define (because the explanations are of different types). "This message is in English" can be called a metacommunication of a HIGHER LOGICAL TYPE than the message to which it refers. It is the class of all messages in English. But the message to which it refers is of a MORE COMPLEX LEVEL OF ORGANIZATION. There seems therefore to be an inverse hierarchical relationship between levels of organization and levels of logical type. (A rule or a code is of a higher logical type, but of a less complex level of organization, than the messages it gives rise to.)

For reasons which will be apparent in the following remarks about Bateson's theory of play, the simple statement of this inverse relationship is inadequate. Any message which 'frames' another message is, synchronically speaking, of a higher logical type than that which it frames. But in ontogeny and phylogeny, the negentropic emergence of more and more complex levels of organization requires that we decide whether a new level of organization (such as the child's learning to speak, the emergence of play in mammals, puberty in adolescents, and so on) 'frames' or 'is framed by' whatever diachronically preceded it. Either interpretation is valid, and depends only upon what one wants to do with the analysis, rather than upon some sort of 'objective' considerations. Logical typing applies strictly only to the overall synchronic analysis of a system (logical types do not 'evolve' the one into the other), whereas levels of organization can be applied to the synchronic analysis of the system, to its synchronic state, and to the diachronic processes involved (organization in open systems has 'evolved' to more complex levels over time). Logical typing thus properly applies to certain abstract characteristics of the system (for example, the relationship between codes and messages within it, or the relationship between various messages), and is not to be confused with the STATE of the system at any given time, to which the concrete description of organization more properly applies. And every diachronic emergence of a new level of organization must necessarily require the reorganization of the logical typing of the system.

8. *Play*

It is around the concept of metacommunication that Bateson constructs his theory of play (1955, 1956) already mentioned. He proposes that the communicational processes of animal play provide us with a methodological insight into the genesis of digital language, and a yardstick to distinguish animal communication from human language. That is to say, it seems useful to suppose a methodological discontinuity in the continuous process which produced language, and to use the amorphous domain of play to mediate the distinction. It is possible to see animal play as a primordial metacommunication – in the strict sense of a MESSAGE ABOUT A MESSAGE – of a different logical type, about the analog communication of fighting. In play, the nip is the METONYMIC SIGN of the bite (part for whole), but not the bite itself (which is a signal). Whereas the bite is what it is, the nip re-presents what it is not. The nip signifies the absence AND the presence of the bite just as the thumb signifies the presence/absence of the breast, or the holophrastic *Fort!* ("Gone!") of the child's play at the beginning of *Beyond the Pleasure Principle* signifies the presence/absence of the toy he has thrown away (or that of the mother, the father, the child himself, and so on as the 'game' progresses) (Chapter VI). The process involved in the child's game RE-presents, in a communication at a higher level of organization, the analog communication of his relationship to what is called in psychoanalysis the lack of object, and thus to the primordial discovery of the analog difference between presence and absence, which is then digitalized by the child in the terms of the Imaginary opposition between self and not-self (*Standard Edition*, XIX, 239; Lacan, 1966; Wilden, 1968a, 1971e).

By introducing at a more complex level the possibility of communicating about communication, play provides the potentiality of truth, falsity, denotation, negation, and deceit. (The nip says "This is play." The next step is to be able to say: "This is not play." And then: "This is/is not play." Only human beings pretend to pretend.) The introduction of the second-level sign into a world of first-level signs and signals detaches communication from existence as such and paves the way for the arbitrary combination of the discrete element in the syntagm. It is thus a discovery of difference at a higher level of communication or organization. The nip is originally a metonymy (formed by contiguity), but its integration into another level of communication makes it into a metaphor (a substitute) – both a statement in a 'language' and a statement in a 'metalanguage' about (overdetermined) relationships in a 'referent language' from which it emerged and with which it coexists. The bite was a message in a 'natural' code; the nip is both part of a new code and at the same time signifies the 'agreement' or the 'relation' which is the mediating function of a code.[10] Once the digital signal or sign (a distinction) has been constituted out of a world of analog differences, the way is open for the linguistic signifier (which must be digital in form). The amorphous domain of play provides a sort of bridge to conceptualize the digitalization of the analog which is the necessary condition for language. The way is then open to the binary opposition – and, unfortunately, open also to paranoia, for what is available to digitalization in interhuman communication is available to the either/or oppositions which characterize the Imaginary or specular order in Lacan's reading of Freud.

The conception of the nip emerging from the bite as a metonymy and then becoming part of the code (as a metaphor) once it has been integrated into a higher level of communication, seems to be borne out by a number of studies of animal and infant communication. Bronowski (1967: 385) points out that "the normal unit of animal communication, even among primates, is a whole message", and Bruner emphasizes McNeill's argument that the child's first semantic system is a holophrastic 'sentence dictionary' in which words correspond to complete sentences. The ultimate solution for the memory load that such a dictionary entails is of course a word dictionary, a dictionary in which the discrete units are 'subtracted' from the continuum of the various sentences (1967: 432–3).

Thus, if we avoid the tendency to make a positivistic interpretation

---

[10] A digital code is 'outside' the sender and receiver and mediates their relationship; an analog code IS the relationship which mediates them.

which demands to know what entity is to be compared with what other entity, I think it can be correctly said that the nip in relation to the bite suggests an isomorphy with the word in relation to the sentence. That is to say that the 'words' within the holophrastic sentence dictionary are the original units of communication representing whole messages, and are later replaced by words as such: the 'words' of the sentence dictionary are related to the sentences they express by metonymy; the invention of words as combinatorial units makes words into metaphors (units of the code). The original dictionary is a dictionary of messages; it is replaced by a dictionary of the code.

9. *Digitalization and Decision: The Nerve Axon*

The analog is the domain of difference; it cannot represent the either/or opposition because its 'more or less' is always of the ambiguous but naturally rational realm of the 'both–and' of the natural ecosystem (Chapter VIII). It is therefore the domain of similarity and resemblance. The digital world, on the other hand, is the domain of opposition and identity as well as difference; it allows for the analytic epistemology of either/or as well as for the dialectical epistemology of both–and.

The transmission of information between different systems or between different levels of organization depends upon the codification and combination of the difference between discrete elements, whether these digital 'bits' are coded into or out of the message by the sender or by the receiver or by both. A gestalt, for example, is formed by the decision to digitalize a specific difference, so as to form a DISTINCTION between figure and ground. There is in effect a decision – which may be neural, or conscious, or unconscious, or habitual, or learned, or novel – to introduce a particular boundary or frame into an analog continuum. The introduction of such a boundary into the perceptual field by the perceiving subject always involves at least one other frame or boundary: that which constitutes the perceiving subject himself. The subject introduces a desired closure into a continuum, which distinguishes a certain 'part', and by the same act he constitutes himself as distinct in some way from the environment he perceives. In order for a system to be open to an environment, in other words, the system must be capable of punctuating itself as distinct from that environment so as to select messages within it. (Cf. p. 124.)

A difference that makes a difference may introduce a distinction into the continuum of difference. This distinction depends on the relationship and the goals of the senders and receivers involved. The energy or quantity or spatial relationships of the analog computer, for example, may be digitalized by the application of a longitudinal or circular scale, or by that of a system of space or time coordinates (as in the system of longitude and latitude). The character of this digitalization depends on what it is desired the computer should do. Digitalization may not involve any visible scales. The continuous variations of the flyball governor or the wind vane, for instance, are differences which might be viewed as equivalent to the infinitesimal in the calculus (the smallest possible difference) or to the quanta of radiant energy borne by the waves of the electromagnetic spectrum. But, given that these devices are negative feedback control mechanisms, they are designed to decide between 'more' or 'less' difference, and thus to introduce a digital decision into a continuously variable fluctuation. The digital scale involved is inseparable from the physical design of the system (e.g., the way the rotating balls of the governor are mechanically linked to the throttle of the engine), and one cannot 'see' this digital aspect the way one can see the switch attached to the thermocouple in a thermostat. The 'on/off' digital control characteristics of both flyball governor and wind vane occur only at the moment when they change direction: from inward to outward or from clockwise to anticlockwise.

If we take the specific example of the propagation of a single 'signal' in the nervous system, we can see the same characteristic relationships – between difference and distinction, continuity and discontinuity, positive and negative feedback, and analog and digital processes – as we found in the Tsembaga example (Section 3 above). As in the Tsembaga example, it is the function of the boundary between states of the system, and between the open system and its environment, which draws our attention.

The axon of a nerve cell serves to transmit messages to the synaptic connection (which is in fact a gap) between one cell and another. The way the message is propagated in the axon depends on the selective properties of the membrane which separates the inside of the axon from its outside. The permeability of the axon membrane defines the inside as an open system in a selective relation to the outside. The propagation of the signal depends upon the way this permeability punctuates the relation between inside and outside, and on the way the punctuation changes.

The axon is not a conductor (like a wire), but an amplifier. It operates by copying, rather than by simply conducting, the input signal (Katz, 1961). In the resting state, when no message is being propagated, the selective permeability of the membrane to certain ions maintains an electrochemical gradient, called the 'resting potential', between the aqueous solution inside the axon and that outside it. When an input is applied to the axon, a change in the membrane's selectivity reverses the gradient to produce the 'spike', or 'action potential', which re-presents the original message or input. In its turn, the reversal of the gradient engenders a return to the resting potential at one point on the axon and a new representation of the message by another spike further down the axon. The spikes are of more or less constant amplitude, but vary in frequency: the system is thus frequency modulated. The distance between spikes depends on the characteristics of the input, on the one hand, and on the recovery time (the 'refractory period') of the axon, on the other. An oscilloscope will show the propagation of the message as a continuous variation between potential (millivolts) and charge (plus or minus), with the resting potential as the base of the series of spikes.

The aqueous solution outside the membrane is composed largely of positively charged sodium ions and negatively charged chloride ions. The solution inside is principally composed of positive potassium ions and other organic particles, which are negatively charged. The membrane operates like a Maxwell Demon: it sorts ions. In the resting state, it is much more permeable to potassium ions (+) and chloride ions (−) than it is to sodium ions (+) and the other organic ions (−). The resulting continuous outflow of positive potassium ions and inflow of negative chloride ions in the resting state gives rise to a gradient of between 60 and 90 millivolts across the membrane, with the inside negative in relation to the outside. This is combined with other (negentropic) processes which employ energy to maintain the electrochemical gradient (i.e., the 'sodium pump').

The relation between inside and outside is not a simple 'binary opposition' between positive and negative, however, because it is a relation between a continuously differentiated potential and a threshold. The message in the axon thus appears as a distinction engendered on the ground of difference. This distinction is in turn dependent on the punctuation of the distinction between inside and outside by the membrane.

Once a message induced in the axon passes a certain threshold – i.e., becomes 'more' rather than 'less' – the axon will 'decide' to transmit. This decision is accomplished by a change in the selective permeability of the membrane, which is a function of changes in the electrochemical gradient across it. In their turn, these changes in potential are controlled by the properties of the membrane. In other words, the permeability of the membrane depends on a threshold which regulates the voltage differential across it, and the voltage differential depends on a threshold which, in turn, regulates the permeability of the membrane. The result is a self-perpetuating regeneration of the original input (the distinction) down the whole length of the axon.

The input of a signal lowers the voltage differential across the membrane. This has the effect of making the membrane locally more permeable to the sodium ions outside it. The entry of positive sodium ions into the axon lowers the local voltage differential even further, which makes the membrane even more permeable to sodium ions. The accelerating entry of these positive ions eventually – within milliseconds – cancels out the excess negative charge within the axon. This is in effect a process of positive feedback which eventually reaches a threshold in a continuously variable set of differences. Passing the threshold reverses the original distinction between the positive and negative charge outside and inside the axon. The inside becomes locally positive. (Note that 'positive' in 'positive feedback' concerns the amplification of differences and has nothing to do with positive electricity. Similarly, negative feedback refers to the reduction of differences or to the reversal of positive feedback, not to electrical charge.)

From an originally negative resting potential of about 80 millivolts, the inrush of positive ions creates a positive action potential in the axon (the spike) of about 40 millivolts. This local change in potential has two linked effects. It makes the membrane immediately ahead of the spike more permeable to the same sodium ions, thus creating the conditions for a second copy of the input to be created by a reversal of the negative resting potential further down the axon. At the same time, the rising positive action potential of the spike is in the process of reversing the local selective permeability of the membrane at the point of the spike: the membrane ceases at this point to be permeable to positive sodium ions and becomes permeable to positive potassium ions again. The resulting outflow of positive potassium ions in the direction of the reversed electrochemical gradient (inside positive, outside negative) then restores the original negative charge in the interior of the axon (the resting potential).

In other words, the continuous escalation of difference (positive feedback) engenders a distinction in the axon (the message), and this distinction is both the condition for another copy of itself further down the axon (positive feedback), and the condition for its own cancellation at the point where it occured (negative feedback). An analog continuum of difference engenders a digital distinction (a decision) which is dependent on the properties of the boundary between the two parts of the system. The membrane is the boundary in an open system which enables a part of the system to be used to make other boundaries in order to propagate what is not perhaps to be called a signal, but rather a SIGN. The so-called nerve impulse is in effect a digital decision about relations between differences.

In its turn, the distinction propagated in the axon arrives at another boundary: the terminal between the nerve cell which is sending and its receiver. In the case of the nerve-muscle junction, we can see here a somewhat similar set of relations between difference and distinction, which are used to pass the sign of the distinction across the gap between the end of the axon and the receiver. Just as the reciprocal relation between potential and permeability at the membrane changes the RATE of a continuous process of ion flow, the arrival of the message at the nerve terminal alters the local membrane potential. This has the effect of enormously increasing the rate of secretion of packets of molecules of a transmitter substance (acetylcholine). This acceleration – again a digitalization – allows the message to pass from one system (the nerve) to another (the muscle). In each case the smallest possible differences in the system (ions, packets of acetylcholine) are manipulated by the digital function of a boundary in order to propagate digital distinctions (messages, decisions) which are capable of crossing the boundary between different systems. Particularly significant for the theme of these essays is the fact that what we decide to characterize as analog or as digital in any given ensemble of communication is dependent on how we have methodologically drawn a boundary around the system we are studying – and that this decision is an exact epistemological equivalent (if of a different order of complexity) of the way the nervous system depends on the selective function of boundaries to make its own decisions.

Thus, since both the analog and the digital depend on difference, the distinction between them depends upon the same methodological necessity as that which requires us to conceptualize the continuous processes of evolution as a series of quantum jumps (the emergence, through random variation and natural selection, of metasystems from referent systems – Chapter XII). There will always be a place – as in the paradoxical question of play – where the distinction will no longer hold, because there simply aren't any gaps or holes in the natural world (although there are isolates and species, which are presumed to have resulted from various natural boundaries within and between ecosystems). Like the question of distinguishing system and environment, the distinction between analog and digital depends very much upon the way the distinction is defined for any particular system of explanation or level of system or set of circumstances. In other words, as systems theory never fails to point out against positivism, scientism, and reductionism, we must not forget that we are talking about models constructed for the purpose of explanation, not about reality, which has no purpose in explanation, no purpose to explain.

10. *Zero and Not*

As I pointed out above, there seems to be a relation between the absence of zero and the absence of negation in the analog machine. Neither 'zero' nor 'not' is correlative to nothing, to a simple absence of something, or to a simple exclusion, although all these ideas are often confused with each other.[11]

Following Frege (1884), we can speak of 'zero' as the number belonging to an 'objective concept'.[12] Object (*Gegenstand*) for Frege is not related to space, to existence, or to 'reality', since "not every object has a place" (#61). (But, we must add, every object does have a locus.) The number 4, for example, can be called an 'objective object' belonging to the concept F (under which a number of objects may fall) so long as F is a "unit relative to a number" (a concept) which isolates the objects under it in a countable manner. Thus 'red' is not a concept relative to any finite number, but 'moon' is. "The number of Jupiter's moons is identical with the number four" is a statement meeting the criterion, which implies that a number is not an attribute or a predicate, but a "self-subsistent object". (By 'self-subsistent' Frege clearly means no more than 'bounded'.)

In his theory of the natural integers, Frege 'saves the truth' (which is of course the most important principle in metamathematics) by first defining zero, in distinction from all the 'other' integers, as "belonging to the concept under which no object falls' (#55).[13] This leads to the more adequate definition of zero as "the number which belongs to the concept 'not identical with itself'". Thus zero is implicitly defined as a META-INTEGER, and indeed its definition is what provides the RULE for the series of integers which follow it:

---

[11] Von Neumann (1958) unfortunately skips over the representation of 'not' in the brain, and mentions, without explanation, "ways of getting around it".

From a philosophical perspective, Kojève's theory of Language illuminates the question of negation, if not that of zero:

> . . . One obtains the concept 'Being' by SUBTRACTING being from Being: 'Being' minus being equals the concept 'Being' (and not nothing or 'zero'; for the negation of A is not nothing, but 'non-A', that is, 'something'). This subtraction . . . takes place literally 'at every instant'; it is called Time (1947a: 375, note 1)

Time, in Kojève's sense, is not equivalent to time as the 'background' of analog and digital communication in the way that 'time' in logic and arithmetic is such a background (and therefore not part of the system). Kojève's Time is Hegelian; it is part of the process, an actor in the drama, it is human, dialectical time (cf. Lukács [1920] on time in the nineteenth-century novel).

[12] The equator is an objective concept in this sense, i.e., it is not personal, not subjective, not imaginary, not an image, not a sense datum.

[13] The second definition in #55, brought in to avoid replacing zero by 'no' ("which means the same"), replaces 'no object' by 'does not fall'. Frege later abandoned his thesis that the foundations of arithmetic lie in logic when he ran afoul of Russell's antinomy.

... In order to arrive at the number 1, we have first of all to show that there is something which follows in the series of natural numbers directly after 0 (#77).

In keeping with Frege's claim that a statement of number contains an assertion about a concept, the following proof depends upon the logical consequences of the definition: "The number which belongs to the concept 'identical with 0' follows directly after 0" (#77). The proof itself need not concern us here, except to say that it depends upon the distinction between 0 as an object falling under a concept, and 0 as the number belonging to a concept. All that needs to be established is that zero is not simply a number as such, but a rule for a RELATION between integers. The number which belongs to the concept 'identical with 0' is also the interval or gap between the integers (the number one). Thus a^0 (but not 0^0, which equals 0) is arbitrarily defined as 1, because it is the BOUNDARY between a^1 and a^{-1}.

The logical definition of zero naturally has its correspondent in set theory (Warusfel, 1969).

In order to 'save the truth' that the complement of any subset A in set S is subset B ($S = A + B$; $A = S - B = \bar{B}$), it is necessary to define the complement of set S as the EMPTY SET ϕ ($S - S = \phi$). The empty set is a unique set which contains no elements. It is not only the complement of S but also a subset of S ($S + \phi = S$). Therefore the complement of the SUBSET ϕ is also S, for ϕ is symmetrical with ($S - \phi$). If S itself is the empty set, then it has one subset only, which is also its complement (ϕ). Like zero, the empty set had to be invented. And as with zero, for good reason, the 'subtraction' of set S from itself does not have nothing as its product, but rather a METASET (ϕ), just as the 'subtraction' of being from Being provides us with the concept of 'Being'. The empty set is a statement about the relation between a set and itself. As an object it falls under the concept 'identical with itself' (as does the number zero); as a 'number', however, it belongs to a concept under which no object can fall: that is, it has no elements ($1 - 1 = 0$).

In both cases the definition of the 'rule of relation' zero or ϕ depends upon distinguishing 'the number zero' or 'the empty set ϕ' (objects falling under concepts) from 'zero' and 'ϕ' (concepts). For Frege, such definitions appeal implicitly to his later formulation of the difference between *Sinn* ('sense') and *Bedeutung* ('reference').

This distinction allows us to turn to the question of negation from another angle. Interpreting Frege's presentation of number theory, one notes that the distinction between object and concept (which founds the integers in their own right – they are not proper names for or derived from things) can be mapped onto another distinction: that between energy and information. The distinction between energy and information is itself equivalent to Wittgenstein's warning not to confuse the signification (*Bedeutung*) of a name (the information) with the BEARER of a name (its 'marker') (1945-9: #40). Since we have defined the digital as the set of elements which DENOTE, this distinction, as a relation (and not as a mapping of one entity onto another), is equivalent to that between the analog and the digital also.

Recalling the remarks about Mandelbrot's derivation of the discrete from its continuous substratum, which is in fact the derivation which founded phonology, we note that the natural integers are 'carried' by the continuous substratum of at least the real numbers (which are uncountable and upon which depend Zeno's paradoxes of motion) – and perhaps the imaginary numbers too, which set includes all the real numbers as well as the complex numbers (e.g., 5, i, πi, $5+i$, etc.). In relation to 'what falls under it', the concept involves a digital boundary; what falls under it may either be purely analog (e.g., the color 'red') or available to digitalization (a set of homogeneous or of heterogeneous 'entities' derived by abstraction from the relations which constitute them), so long, that is, as we remember that any 'entity' whatsoever consists of an infinity of differences: digitalization is always a matter of SELECTION, PUNCTUATION, or CHOICE.

In this light, I would read the following passage from Frege in the terms of analog continuity and digital discontinuity:

> . . . In the [macroscopic] external world . . ., there are no concepts, no properties of concepts, no numbers. The laws of nature, therefore, are not intrinsically [*eigentlich*] applicable to external things [*Dinge*]; they are not laws of nature. They are, however, applicable to judgments having value in the external world: they are the laws of the laws of nature. They assert not a 'continuous relation' [*Zusammenhang*] or connection between natural phenomena, but something similar [*einen solchen*] between judgments; and among judgments are included the laws of nature (#87).

My point of course is that the 'something similar' is not so similar, since the judgments Frege speaks of are digital.

What the 'entity' 'laws of nature' may be, is of no concern to this interpretation of Frege's logical foundation for the natural integers: it is the relation between the laws of nature and the laws of the laws of nature which is of interest, for the analog differences in nature are of a higher logical type and of a lower level of organization than the digital systems they give rise to. As Lévi-Strauss points out (1964: 58–63), the subtraction of elements from a continuum produces numerical poverty but greater systemic and logical wealth. What allows judgments in Frege's sense are, of course, the mixed analog and digital processes in the brain, which are 'natural'. But since every judgment whatsoever is a selection of possibilities related to the adaptation of some system or other to some environment or other, we have to introduce the notion of analog judgment and digital judgment. This entails making a distinction between analog 'negation' (many-valued, and not involving zero) and digital negation (two-valued, involving zero).

Such a distinction is the same as (and would clarify) that between the diachronic *Aufhebung* of the Hegelian and Marxian 'negation of the negation' and the synchronic *Verneinung* in the Freudian sense of the 'denial of the return of the repressed' (*Standard Edition*, XIX, 239). Both of these processes are distinct from analog refusal, rejection, or disavowal (the Freudian *Verwerfung* and *Verleugnung*). *Aufhebung* and *Verneinung* are processes of a different logical type: the *Aufhebung* of a situation refers to the diachronic overcoming of the contradictions in a referent system and the subsequent emergence of (what is in relation to it) a metasystem; *Verneinung* refers to the statement by some subject or other (who may be a group or a society) that some (actual) state of affairs is NOT the case, and is thus a synchronic metastatement about a statement.

Aufhebung does not include any syntactical use of 'not' (whatever the observer may think about the relationship between the metasystem and the referent system), but it is not equivalent to analog refusal. Refusal in fact is the analog counterpart of digital denial, which is one reason why Freud uses rejection or 'disavowal of reality' to describe 'psychosis', and negation and repression of 'reality' to described 'neurosis'. Whereas the 'psychotic' may entertain two completely contradictory ideas about some state of affairs, the contradiction is not related by 'not'. The 'neurotic' on the other hand, may entertain similar contradictory ideas, but the secondary system negates the primary system presentation, that is, it does not 'bind' it so as to bring it from analog meaning to digital signification, for "repression is a gainsaying (*Versagung*) of the translation" from one system to the other. It is the *Verneinung* of the repressed presentation which provides for the 'suppression and the conservation' (*Aufhebung*) of what is repressed (*Standard Edition*, XIX, 235–6; Hyppolite, 1956, in: Lacan, 1966: 880–2).

Thus I would define analog 'negation' as *Aufhebung* (which suppresses and conserves contradictions) and digital negation as *Verneinung*, while still maintaining the distinction between analog refusal and digital 'no-saying'.

This distinction perhaps allows us to do something more about the curiously difficult concept of negation in general. We have to distinguish the syntactical 'not' of a digital statement from the commonsense idea that negation is equivalent to the absence of something, to nothing, or to absence in general. It should be clear that both 'zero' and 'ϕ' are at least SIGNS in digital or digitalized systems, the sign being defined as whatever represents or re-presents what it is not. The sign is identical to itself and yet not identical to its reference. The signal is defined as being what it is (e.g., a bite, a movement) and both sign and signal are to be distinguished from the signifier, which we reserve for the particular 'mixed' system called 'natural language', which presumably includes all logics. We shall see later whether it is possible to continue to regard 'zero' and 'ϕ' as signs.

The conception of 'non-A' in Boolean or any similar logic, however, can be regarded as founded on the notion of absence. Although the complement of A in set S is B, and B is 'non-A' (therefore B is the sign of 'non-A'), the usual Euler or Venn diagrams of the relation imply that 'non-A' is simply the absence of A (*Figure 1*):

FIGURE 1

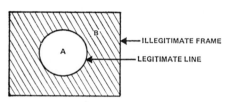

But 'non-A' is an assertion about the existence of A and is opposed not only to A or to other positive statements, but also to all the negative statements it is not (non-B, C, etc.). 'Non-A' is not equivalent to '$-A$', for this would imply that 'non-1' (which could be anything) is equivalent to '-1' (which is a particular).

Now my knowledge of mathematics is rudimentary and I cannot pretend to the logical rigor of a Frege, but in looking at set theory, I am struck by the obvious fact that especially when the sets are representable by some sort of Euler or Venn diagram (which is not true for ϕ, for example), we have an iconic representation of a digital BOUNDARY DISTINCTION. A and B are not in a SYNTACTICAL relationship of negation to each other, for such a relation requires a message between a sender and a receiver in which a negative word occurs. In other words, A and B are in a relationship at a single level, a relationship of EXCLUSION, which is how the relation is used in any yes/no digital system, such as the digital computer. Moreover, they are both excluded from other sets of relations by the frame around then (see p. 187 below).

It seems that saying 'not' about some possibility or concept or state of affairs is a logical operation of a different logical type from that which relates two statements (etc.) by exclusion. 'Not' is in a metalinguistic relationship to what it negates, not in a simple either/or relationship. The use of 'not' in "Don't tell me he's done it again", for instance, has nothing to do with exclusion as such; it is in fact a statement about the sender's attitude, a shifter. The metalinguistic power of 'not' corresponds to Frege's insistence that it is incorrect to speak of positive and negative judgments (by implication in an either/or relationship of identity to each other). All that is required, he points out, is "assertion" and "a negative word" (1952: 130), and these two prerequisites differ in logical type.

We are further led to assume a distinction between identity of signification and identity of meaning, in some sense, for if 2/3 and 4/6 are identical in their signification, they cannot be so in their meaning (this is the argument about the referent signified by 'the morning star' and 'the evening star'). The analog/digital distinction gives us for the first time perhaps an entirely scientific way of distinguishing meaning and signification. We can define meaning in terms of the value system of the ecosystem, that is, in terms of long-range survival. All open systems are goalseeking and adaptive, each with a greater or lesser 'phase-space' of possibilities depending on its level of organization. If only because in French, English, and German, the equivalent terms are related to sensation, direction, desire, intention, and purpose, 'meaning' is the obvious choice for the semantics of survival, the macroscopic domain of adaptation. Meaning can be defined as what real material senders and receivers do with information in order to achieve some goal or other (the goal may, of course, be counter-adaptive). Information organizes the work to be done to this end.

We can restrict 'signification' for the denotative and concept-transferral operations of digital systems, conceived of as composed of signs and or signifiers. The meaning is not simply the use, as Wittgenstein put it, but the use in terms of an end and in relation to a real context. Signification may or may not be involved in a real context, for it can create its own context. Signification (*Bedeutung*) is effectively restricted to names, but to names in the widest sense of systems of names and naming. Meaning thus may or may not involve signification. Meaning is mainly concerned with both–and differences, signification with distinctions, some of which are either/or oppositions. In the terminology of Lacan and of Lévi-Strauss, meaning is of the domain of symbolic exchange, signification belongs to the Imaginary.

Because of the difficulty of defining the line between the analog and the two levels of the digital, especially in play, we should reserve the word 'sign' as a mediator between them. Thus the distinction will allow signals and signs in the analog, and signs and signifiers in the digital. The same distinction applies to that between analog information and digital information. The signification of the Euler diagram as an analog or icon of something is a digital relation of exclusion; its meaning is what it is used for in the analog relation with the receiver of its message. Thus the Euler diagram signifies negation as exclusion; the meaning of the negation it signifies lies elsewhere.

The diagram in *Figure 1* is an icon or analog of a digital distinction; it is therefore a sign. But it also contains a signifier. This signifier is the BOUNDARY between the set of A and the set of non-A. Boundaries between different systems or between systems of different types, as was pointed out above, seem always to involve switching between analog and digital communication. Even if we are not sure in any operational sense of what we mean by 'type', the fact that the Euler diagram involves both a digital and an analog representation of set theory (which is digital) might indicate that we should expect some switching between digital and analog in our discussion of the diagram and what it represents.

The boundary in the diagram is in fact the WAY OF GETTING FROM A to non-A (labeled B). Since in the diagram, A and B can be considered to be different 'organisms' in an environment, one suspects that it might be useful to describe the 'legitimate' line between them as a locus of digital communication between A and B – the locus of the 'non' which makes B part of the set of non-A. This is not in the least farfetched, for the curious thing about this boundary is that it is impossible to decide whether it belongs to the set A or the set non-A. It belongs to neither, it is both neither and nowhere, and it corresponds to nothing in the real world whatsoever. Like 0, like ϕ, it is a digital RULE about relations. In relation to the sets which it divides, it is a metaset, and of course, since it contains no elements, it is the empty set itself. Zero is similarly a boundary or a limit (between the set of positive numbers and the set of negative numbers, for example). But in digital systems, zero is also an empty place, and it depends for its signification on its placing. So too does the line in the diagram, so too does 'not', or its equivalent, in a negative sentence. One notes also in set theory that in order to describe the set S consisting of a point p and a line L (S = [p, L]), the fact that L consists of an infinity of p makes it difficult to represent the union of L and [p] as opposed to S, if p does not belong to L. Any such representation or visualization requires us to draw an artificial boundary around L in order to indicate that it is a whole (element) and not a set, or otherwise S would = L, and p would belong to L.

In other words, boundaries are the condition of distinguishing the 'elements' of a continuum from the continuum itself. 'Not' is such a boundary. Boundaries in fact are the conditions of all communication: the differential boundary of the figure and ground is a primitive digitalization generating a distinction, and the distinction may then become an opposition. Figure and ground form a binary RELATION, one and two form a binary DISTINCTION, A and non-A in analytical logic form a binary OPPOSITION (an identity). 'Not' is a rule about how to make either/or distinctions themselves. The relation between presence and absence, for instance, is that of an analog difference.

We can say therefore that digital distinctions introduce GAPS into continuums (here the gap is filled by the empty set), whereas analog differences, such as presence and absence, FILL continuums. The line between presence and absence is not in fact a line at all. If it were, there would be some way of showing a negative IDENTITY between presence and absence. But there is no such identity in nature as such, whether in homogeneous closed or in heterogeneous open systems, since identity is a pure digital concept. That is to say, it is also a rule about digitalization, like 'not'. With either/or (on/off) and a rule about identity, any digital logic can be constructed.

But there are two kinds of boundaries in *Figure 1*: the boundary between 'A' and 'B', and the boundary between 'A and B' and 'everything else'. It is impossible to draw the first line without SOMEWHERE drawing the second. Even if we think we have successfully divided the whole of reality and unreality into only two sets by drawing a line between A and non-A (and by including within non-A, non-B, etc.), the act of drawing that line defines at least one system or set as belonging to neither A nor non-A: the line itself. And since that line is the locus of our intervention into a universe, it necessarily defines the goalseeking system that drew the line as itself distinct from both A and non-A: it is their 'frame'. This is the sense in which the frame in *Figure 1* can be called logically illegitimate: it is of a different logical type from the line between A and B.

It is the question of boundaries between logical types which generates the limiting paradox of the Russellian theory, as we have seen (pp. 123-4 above), and Russell's antinomy appears to be the absolute first and last in set theory (if not in topology).

Lying behind the oscillations resulting from the question: Is the class of classes not members of themselves a member of itself? is a metalinguistic rule: the notion of an improper 'class not a member of itself'. The metalinguistic function of 'not' is in fact what generates the higher-order paradox, for 'not' is the boundary of the empty set, which like 'the class of classes not members of themselves' is both a member of itself and not a member of itself. And 'improper' turns out to be another, higher-order, substitute for 'not': it defines an Imaginary line which belongs to the

PROCESS of making distinctions, rather than to the distinctions themselves (cf. pp. 219–21 on the splitting of the ecosystem).

If we return to Bateson's analysis of play (1955: 41), we find the following paradoxical definition of the message 'this is play' contained 'in' the nip: "These actions in which we now engage do not denote what those actions FOR WHICH THEY STAND would denote." In other words, the nip denotes the bite, but it does not denote what would be denoted by the bite. This message, Bateson points out, violates the theory of logical types, because the word denote is being used in two degrees of abstraction. But in extending the metacommunicative function of 'this is play' to define the notion of a message which 'frames' another message, Bateson notes that the paradox is unavoidable. In defining a logical class, say, the class of matchboxes, a boundary must be inserted between 'matchboxes' and 'non-matchboxes'. But the items in the 'background set' of 'non-matchboxes' must be of the same level of abstraction as those within the set itself, or the rule of logical typing will be broken. Otherwise it would be possible to include in the class of non-matchboxes the class of non-matchboxes itself (which is a non-matchbox). The paradoxical nature of 'this is play' derives from the fact that it does not discriminate between messages of the same logical type, as a proper 'frame' or 'boundary' should do. It divides items of one logical type from another. In a word, it serves the same function as the limiting paradox of the Russellian theory. For in order to categorize the 'improper non-matchboxes', the theory requires not only that a line be drawn between the 'set' and its 'background' which are of the same logical type, but also that another line be drawn in the background set itself, between items of different logical types (p. 49).

Thus the rule "a class may not be a member of itself" is a paradoxical logical equivalent of the nip.

Since the analog and the digital are always in a similar relationship of figure and ground, or text and context, and since they cannot be of the same logical type, then paradox is inevitable in that distinction also. But this is the fate of all sequences of signs or signifiers: what they say cannot be of the same logical type as what they signify, nor of the same type as that to which they refer.

These arguments lead us to decide that zero, 'not', ϕ, and boundaries are clearly signifiers rather than signs, for they force us to consider them as at the basis of signification. But we cannot consider zero and 'not' to be of the same logical type. Language depends upon punctuation in the widest sense, and especially on the space or the zero phoneme, both of which establish relations between something and something else. The space is a boundary, but not an absence. If the space is equivalent to zero or to ϕ, then we have to say that 'not' is both equivalent to zero and ϕ and also a rule about establishing zero and ϕ. In other words 'not' is both a boundary and a rule (or a 'frame') about the establishment of boundaries. Freud's theory of the relation between ejection and negation, although it does not distinguish between the analog and the digital, is a statement about the emergence of negation in ontogeny. Similarly, the prohibition of incest which we assume to be the hallmark of the passage from nature to culture depends upon the emergence of negation and the defining of boundaries. Only through negation can there be a positive rule of kinship engendering symbolic exchange. We ought not therefore to say with Spinoza simply that every limit is a negation but rather that in language and logic negation is the *sine qua non* of limit.

11. *Some Guiding Principles*

Out of this somewhat tortuous excursus on zero and 'not', we can perhaps extract a number of principles with at least an orienting value. Their validity and their utility are to be established.

1 The question of the analog and the digital is one of relationship, not one of entities.

2 Zero is not an absence, not nothing, not the sign of a thing, not a simple exclusion. If the natural numbers are signs, it is a signifier. It is not an integer, but a meta-integer, a rule about integers and their relationships.

3 The empty set is similarly a rule about sets.

4 The digital has to do with boundaries. In number theory, set theory, and language, 'zero', 'ϕ' and 'not' are the rules for punctuating boundaries. 'Not' is of a higher logical type than zero or ϕ, if only because it is the logical prerequisite for zero or ϕ.

5 Analog refusal, rejection, and disavowal are to be distinguished from syntactic negation.

6 Analog 'negation' (*Aufhebung*) is many valued and does not involve 'not' or zero. Digital negation is two valued and involves 'not' both in the sense of 'zero' and as a rule about zero.

7 Relations of exclusion (digital by definition) establish single-level opposition and identity. Syntactic negation does not necessarily involve more than distinction, and includes levels of relation.

8 Analog differences are the 'smallest possible difference', similar to an

infinitesimal or a quantum. Digital distinctions involve gaps between the discrete elements.

9 Some distinction between digital signification and analog meaning, similar to that between information and meaning, is necessary. Signification controls the creation of signs and signifiers; meaning is concerned with the survival of the whole in which it is involved.

10 Boundaries or frames intrinsically involve paradox. They are always of a different logical type from that which they bound or isolate.

11 Switching from analog to digital is necessary for communication to cross certain types of boundaries. A great deal of communication – perhaps all communication – undoubtedly involves constant switching of this type.

12 The analog/digital distinction, since it involves a boundary, will necessarily generate paradox.

13 The introduction of 'not' into an analog continuum is a necessary (but perhaps not a sufficient) condition for natural language, as is 0 for the integer.

14 A form of digitalization is the *sine qua non* for any limit whatsoever. In human terms, this refers to the emergence of what Freud calls the *Verneinungssymbol* in language (Chapter VI).

15 It is necessary to distinguish between binary relation, binary distinction, and binary opposition.

16 Presence and absence, which fill a continuum, is an example of a binary relation which can be turned into what may be the first linguistic digitalization discovered by the child.

17 Digital thought is analytic and two-valued; analog thought is dialectical and many-valued. (Now see Note 9.)

18 A digital system is of a higher level of organization and therefore of a lower logical type than an analog system. The digital system has greater 'semiotic freedom', but it is ultimately governed by the rules of the analog relationship between systems, subsystems, and supersystems in nature. The analog (continuum) is a set which includes the digital (discontinuum) as a subset.[14]

[14] Cf. von Neumann:

> . . . Whatever language the central nervous system is using, it is characterized by less logical and arithmetical depth than what we are normally used to. . . . Thus logics and mathematics in the central nervous system, when viewed as languages, must structurally be essentially different from [ordinary language]. . . . When we talk mathematics, we may be discussing a SECONDARY LANGUAGE, built on the PRIMARY language truly used by the central nervous system (1958: 81–2).

Von Neumann is presumably referring to his view that the neuron uses a

The concept of the emergence of the socioeconomic discrete element, metacommunication, and negation applies not only to the distinction between animal and human communication and to that between relation and denotation, but also to other communications systems (Chapter IX).[15] I have no doubt that the same distinction is as important for art, literature, and music as it is for economics, psychoanalysis, psychotherapy, anthropology, and human communication theory in general.

---

frequency-modulated system of "counting" (the 'spikes' transmitted in the axon) rather than a "decimal or binary expansion system" (1951: 2087–9). Thus a million signals would be required to express the number of distinctions that can be expressed by a mere 7 decimal digits. Expansion is more economical and efficient, whereas counting is protected against error by a relatively enormous redundancy.

One can perhaps translate 'depth' as level of organization, and 'structurally different', as a relationship of logical types, the higher logical type being more abstract, and therefore more deeply programmed. This is meant in Bateson's sense of the increasing abstraction involved in perceiving, learning, learning how to learn, learning how to learn how to learn . . . habit . . . biological processes. . . . (But see the proviso in section 7 on the relation between logical typing and organization.)

[15] We can perhaps retranslate the statements about 'schizophrenic speech' which describe it as using word-presentations like thing-presentations (images) or words like things (Freud, Goldstein), or as confusing the metaphor with what is meant (Bateson), or as confusing the Symbolic with the Real (Lacan), by saying that the so-called schizophrenic treats the digital as though it were analog. (This perhaps has some bearing on von Neumann's remark about the generalized *in toto* solutions to 'problems' on the part of the brain.) We might even say that the 'schizophrenic' is responding to a pathological environment of digital communication by trying to BE the analog. Cameron (1939: 56), writing from the objectionable viewpoint of the 'expert' on the 'patient', observes that the striking characteristic of 'schizophrenic' patients is their "inability to maintain adequate boundaries", which Goldstein (1939: 33) relates to the figure–ground distinction. All the evidence would indicate that the 'schizophrenic' is most concerned to break the pathological boundaries (oppositions) which are regarded as 'adequate' and 'normal' in our culture.

Appendix I

A Table of Relations

Although it is extremely difficult to avoid reifying the terms, the following table attempts to summarize the various relational distinctions which can be included under the distinction between the analog and the digital. Some items are derived from Ruesch's "Nonverbal Language and Therapy" (1955), but 'language' and 'non-verbal' are not synonymous with 'digital' and 'analog'. Since not all digital communication is linguistic, and since language and the secondary system are both digital and analog, the various

TABLE A

Analog Form	Digital Form
Computation	
Continuous scale	Discrete units (on/off)
Positive, actual quantities	Positive and negative representations of quantities
Quantitative plenitude	Logical complexity
No zero	Dependent on zero
No absence	Dependent on 'gaps' between elements
Always something or something else	All, some, nothing, or less than nothing
Units of computation may be repeatedly divided	Units of computation cannot be divided below the level of the discrete unit
Computation is imprecise and not related to capacity	Precision is a function of capacity
Low signal-to-noise ratio	High signal-to-noise ratio [a]
Concrete, necessary	Abstract, arbitrary
No truth functions	Logical calculus

[a] Cf. von Neumann, 1951.

correlative relationships have been divided into broad categories. The relationships expressed are to be read horizontally in context with each other. The vertical enumerations are not lists of synonyms.

TABLE B

Analog Aspect	Digital Aspect
1. Intraorganismic Communication	
Sequence, rhythm, frequency, spatial patterning	On/off firing of neuron, logical network
Memory trace (pattern)	Decision, recall
Total system	Part of system
2. Interorganismic Communication[b]	
Distinctions established by receiver	Distinctions established by sender
Context of all communication	Text of particular communication
Concerns relations, connections, wholes, systems	Represents limits
Sequence and simultaneity	Combination
Contiguity	Combination
Similarity	Substitution
3. Logical Distinctions	
Concrete	Abstract
Territory	Map
Refusal	Absence, zero
'More or less'	'Either/or'
Difference and similarity	Opposition and identity
No logical typing	Logical typing
Cannot communicate about itself	Communication about communication
Semantic–Pragmatic	Syntactic
Meaning	Signification
Sequence and simultaneity	Space and time coordinates
Continuous	Discontinuous
Full	Full of holes
Whole, relations	Elements, entities
Maps continuums precisely	Can only map boundaries precisely
Presence and absence	Presence or absence
Similarity and contiguity	Code and message, substitution and combination

[b] Not including language.

TABLE B (*continued*)

Analog Aspect	Digital Aspect
'Pre-categorical'	'Categorical'
Can represent successions simultaneously	Indicates simultaneities successively
Observer in the system	Observer assumed to be outside the system
'Subjective' (contextual)	'Objective'
Knowledge of 'relations'	Knowledge of 'facts'
Relativisitic	Absolutist
Ecosystems	Entities
Open system	Closure
Free flow of meaning	Binding of signification
'Untamed thought' (*la pensée sauvage*)	'Scientific' thought; rationalism, empiricism
Connaître	*Savoir*

4. *Human Communication*

Senses	Denotative language
'Emotion'	'Reason'
Evocation of relation	Transmission of abstractions
Presenting	Naming
Rich relational semantics (ambiguous)	Powerful syntax (unambiguous); weak semantics
Position, context, situation	Text, message
Memory	Rememoration
Understandings	Agreements, codicils
Pain is pain, pain is a sign	'Pain' is a signifier
'Natural' body movements	Conventionalized body movements
Sachvorstellung (thing-presentation)	*Wortvorstellung* (word-presentation)
Images, icons	Signifiers
'Natural' symbols	Artificial or conventional symbols
Similarity and contiguity	Metaphor and metonymy
Difference, similarity	Opposition, identity
Interactive	Individual

5. *Language*

Refusal, repudiation, rejection, disavowal	Negation
Referent, goal	Word, means
Relationship	Concepts
Evocation	Information
Connotation (meaning)	Denotation (signification)

TABLE B (*continued*)

Analog Aspect	Digital Aspect
Command or request	Report
Semantics–Pragmatics	Syntactics
Present	Past, present, and future
Shifters	Nouns
Typography, intonation, cadence loudness, frequency	Alphabet, phonemes
Poetry	Prose
Evocation of images	Information about concepts

6. Systems

Analog Aspect	Digital Aspect
Relationships	Entities (or metaphors thereof)
Use value (Real)	Exchange value (Symbolic or Imaginary)
More-or-less	Either/or
Symbolic	Symbolic and Imaginary
Aufhebung	*Verneinung*
Process	Event
Quality	Quantity

TABLE C

General Relationship

(In particular systems)

1. The analog is of a higher logical type than the digital.
2. The digital is of a higher order of organization than the analog.
3. In nature, the digital is the instrument of the analog.
4. In (western) culture, the analog is the instrument of the digital.
5. Both analog and digital communication occur in all open systems.
6. All digitalization generates paradox or oscillation at some level in the system.
7. All control processes require digital communication to set limits on positive feedback.
8. The terms 'analog' and 'digital' describe relationships in context, and not entities or 'objective' categories.

TABLE D

Functional Differences between the Cerebral Hemispheres [c]

Left	Right
Verbal	Pre-verbal
Analytic	Synthetic
Abstract	Concrete
Rational	Emotional
Temporal	Spatial
Digital	Analogic
Objective	Subjective
Active	Passive
Tense	Relaxed
Euphoric	Depressed
Sympathetic	Parasympathetic
Propositional	Appositional

[c] From Bakan, 1971: 67. On the question of the integration of these functions, Bakan suggests that women have better hemispheric integration than men.

Appendix II

Analog and Digital

By Vincent Hollier

INTORGRATED CIRCUIT   HOLLIER

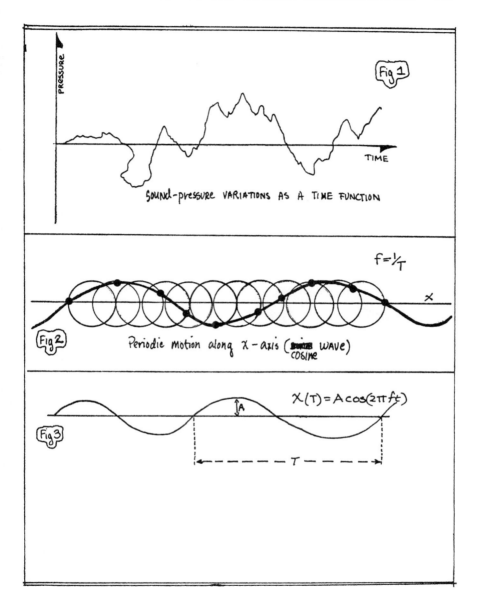

PRESSURE

TIME

Fig 1

Sound-pressure VARIATIONS AS A TIME FUNCTION

$f = 1/T$

x

Fig 2

Periodic motion along x-axis (cosine wave)

$x(T) = A\cos(2\pi ft)$

A

T

Fig 3

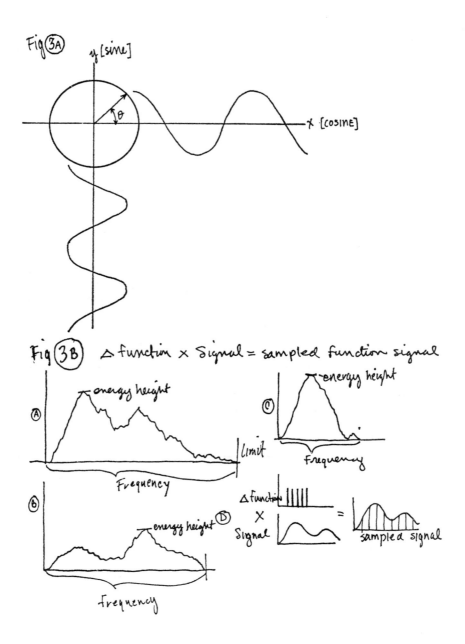

Fig ③A

y [sine]

x [cosine]

θ

Fig ③B   △ function × Signal = sampled function signal

(A) energy height

Frequency | Limit

(C) energy height

Frequency

(B) energy height (D)

Frequency

△ function
×
Signal

=

sampled signal

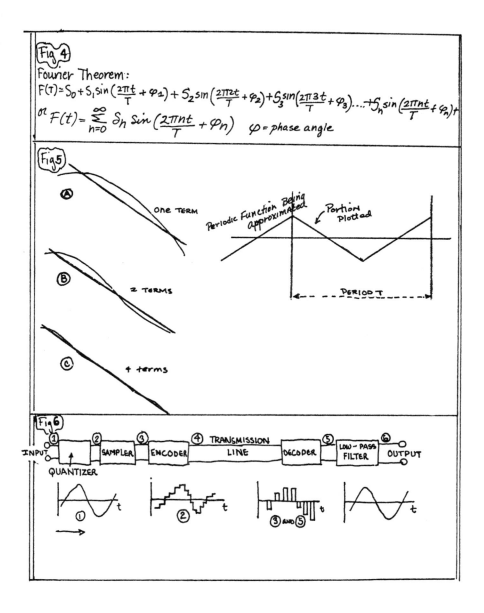

Fig 4

Fourier Theorem:

$$F(T) = S_0 + S_1 \sin\left(\frac{2\pi t}{T} + \varphi_1\right) + S_2 \sin\left(\frac{2\pi 2t}{T} + \varphi_2\right) + S_3 \sin\left(\frac{2\pi 3t}{T} + \varphi_3\right) \ldots + S_n \sin\left(\frac{2\pi n t}{T} + \varphi_n\right) t$$

$$^{or} F(t) = \sum_{h=0}^{\infty} S_h \sin\left(\frac{2\pi n t}{T} + \varphi_n\right) \quad \varphi = \text{phase angle}$$

Fig 5

Ⓐ ONE TERM

Ⓑ 2 TERMS

Ⓒ 4 terms

Periodic Function Being approximated

Portion Plotted

PERIOD T

Fig 6

INPUT ① QUANTIZER ② SAMPLER ③ ENCODER ④ TRANSMISSION LINE DECODER ⑤ LOW-PASS FILTER ⑥ OUTPUT

① ② ③ AND ⑤

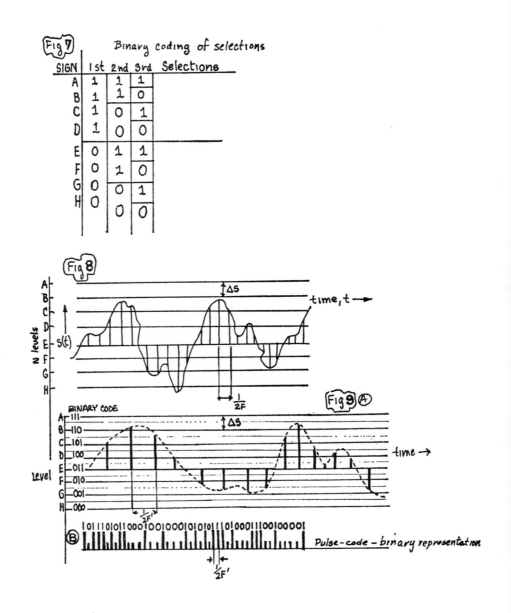

Fig 7   Binary coding of selections

SIGN	1st	2nd	3rd
A	1	1	1
B	1	1	0
C	1	0	1
D	1	0	0
E	0	1	1
F	0	1	0
G	0	0	1
H	0	0	0

Selections

Fig 8

Fig 9 Ⓐ   BINARY CODE

Ⓑ   Pulse-code – binary representation

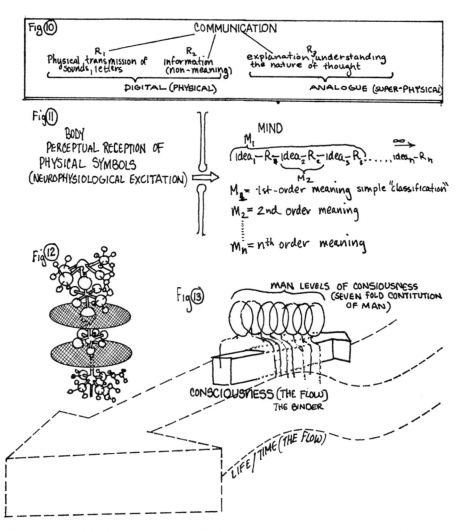

In keeping with the contextual emphasis of these essays, the reader should know that Hollier is black, and that this essay of his was produced independently of anything I had to say on the subject of analog and digital communication.

Chapter VIII

Epistemology and Ecology

THE DIFFERENCE THAT MAKES THE DIFFERENCE[1]

They are a kinde of dancing engines all!
And set, by nature, thus to runne alone
To every sound!
All things within, without 'hem,

Move, but their braine,
and that stands still!
mere monsters,

Here, in a chamber, of most subtill feet!
And make their legs in tune, passing the streetes!
These are the gallant sprits o' the age
The miracles o' the time!
BEN JONSON:
The Staple of News (1625)[2]

1. *Some Tentative Axioms*

That following set of tentative axioms summarizes some of the main distinctions so far employed in these essays. They are further developed in
the chapters which follow.

1 A system is distinguished from its parts by its organization. It is not
an aggregate. We may consequently say that the 'behavior' of the whole

---

[1] This chapter was a direct result of conversations at the Oceanic Institute,
Hawaii, with Gregory Bateson, made possible by a research grant from the
University of California, San Diego. A summarized version of the ideas elaborated here was delivered at the Symposium on Language and Cultural Discontinuities at the State University of New York at Buffalo, April 15, 1970.
[2] Quoted in Wayne, 1971.

is more complex than the 'sum' of the 'behavior' of its parts. However, since the organization of the whole imposes CONSTRAINTS on the 'behavior' of the parts, we must also recognize that the semiotic freedom of each subsystem in itself is greater than its semiotic freedom as a part of the whole, and may in effect be greater than that of the whole (cf. Chapter XII, Section 4).

2 All behavior is communication. Communication, by definition, is an attribute of system and involves a structure. Structure concerns frameworks, channels, and coding; system concerns processes, transmissions, and messages.

3 Every system involving life or mind, or simulating life or mind, is an open system.

4 An open system is such that its relationship to a supersystem (which may be referred to methodologically as its 'environment' or as its 'context') is indispensable to its survival. There is an ongoing exchange of matter–energy and information between them.

5 Every open system is a communication system for which matter–energy and information are functionally distinct. It is goalseeking and adaptive.

6 The primary function of information is the regulation, control, and triggering of energy ('work') in the interests of a goal. Information is defined as negative entropy because it maintains, reproduces, or increases organization ('gradient').

7 A synchronic and diachronic hierarchy of open systems is assumed. What distinguishes them is their level of complexity or their order of organization, and not their degree or extent of complexity.

8 Language includes all the communicational processes and possibilities of less highly organized, primarily digital, communicational systems, as well as specific linguistic properties. Language is not only a means of communication and behavior; it also imposes specific systemic and structural contraints on the ways in which we perceive and act upon the world and each other.

9 Every open system (including the theory elaborated here) exists in a context of selection, survival, and adaptation. Every adaptation has at least a short-range survival value. All such systems are overdetermined, equifinal – e.g., Hughlings Jackson's "final common pathway" (Grinker, ed., 1967: x) – or multifinal.

10 The taxonomy of the hierarchy of goalseeking adaptive systems depends upon the relative semiotic freedom of the 'characteristic response' of each system, type of system, or order of system.

11 Every communications system can be methodologically divided into

'sender' and 'receiver', into 'organism' and 'environment', into 'text' and 'context' (or some set of equivalents). Depending on the original definition of the system, it can also be divided into levels of communication and metacommunication – and for each level, there will be a specific 'receiver' or 'environment' or 'context'.

12 The relation of a system to its anterior states, and the relationship between the various levels of the system, are to be modeled on that between a metalanguage and a referent language.

13 The metasystem can profitably be described as an overdetermined set of propositions in a metalanguage, or as an overdetermined metacommunication, about some overdetermined set of relationships in some referent system or other.

14 Metacommunication, in the strict sense, refers to communication about communication itself. In general it is used here to mean simply a communication about a communication.

15 The privileged model of the communications system is the natural ecosystem.

16 The teleonomy of goalseeking adaptive systems, coupled with selective processes, results in a tendency towards more and more complex levels of organization in evolution and in history. The synchrony of such systems manifests a tendency towards what can be called homeostasis. The goalseeking system borrows free energy from an entropic universe to feed its processes of information and regulation. If the system is homeostatic, it manifests neutral entropy; if it is morphogenic – increasing in order of organization, capable of elaborating new structures – it is negatively entropic (see Chapter XII).

17 Structure is preponderant at the lower levels of organization, system at the more complex levels. The concept of structure concerns the types and the number of relationships or connections between the components (the subsystems) of the system. The concept of system concerns the ways in which these regulations are used and the relations between the relations. This distinction follows in part from the fact that highly complex systems (societies, for example) are capable of changing structure.

18 All communication can be divided formally and/or functionally into analog communication and digital communication.

19 The introduction of closure into the real is an epistemological and methodological act corresponding to the necessity of constructs in explanation and of digitalization in communication. The smallest properly conceivable component of an open system is itself a subsystem (the genes, for example, 'survive' in the environment of the cell and the

organism). If the subsystem is methodologically considered as a whole whose specific systemic properties or whose internal organization is 'put into parentheses' for the purposes of explanation, it is a unit or element. As such, it is an attribute of structure. Thus, depending upon the point of view desired or taken, and provided levels of organization are not confused, any given may be considered from both a systemic and a structural perspective.

2. The Counter-adaptive Results of Adaptive Change

> The things themselves, which only the limited
> brains of men and animals believe fixed and
> stationary, have no real existence at all. They
> are the flashing and sparks of drawn swords,
> the glow of victory in the conflict of opposing
> qualities.
> NIETZSCHE: *Philosophy in the Tragic Age of the Greeks* (1873)

Whether or not the present ecological and social crisis is actually the terminal state of an advanced industrial culture, there is an absolute limit to the possibilities of adaptive change in any ecosystem where adaptive changes in one part of the system set off irreversible and retrogressive changes in its other parts, the environment of the first part. Moreover, all major adaptive changes in any ecosystem tend to trade short-term survival value for long-term counter-adaptive value so long as the adaptation continues to operate within the original 'phase-space' (i.e., a spectrum of multiple and interdependent variables) which allowed the original change. As long as the adaptation is an extreme and not a mean, that is, as long as the phase-space in which it occurred has not been shifted or RENORMALIZED, the adaptive and behavioral flexibility of the system is reduced.

Take for example a hypothetical species whose phase-space of possibilities varies from darkish-brown to red in a reddish-brown environment. Assume that this species is the source of food for another species which can distinguish colors. The variations of color in the first species enable a symbiotic relationship to be maintained between the two: enough of the prey escape the predator both to reproduce themselves AND to prevent the predator species from destroying itself by wiping out its source of sustenance. As in the 'fur cycle' in Canada, both populations will oscillate around a stable size, each constraining the other.

Assume now that the environment of both species starts to become redder and redder. As the environment changes, the normal distribution around brownish-red in the prey becomes a liability; only the few at the red end of their spectrum of possibilities continue to survive. The reduction in their numbers will accelerate in proportion as the number of predators increases, given the conditions of an over-abundant food supply. Both species will be endangered by extinction. Assume, however, that the selection of pre-existing genes which produces reddish members of the prey species begins to occur in sufficient numbers to produce an adaptation to the new environment. The population will now be able to survive, but at the price of a narrow distribution around 'reddish'. Its previous flexibility will be reduced. If the environment continues to change, this distribution will become narrower and narrower. Should the environment eventually become purple, the reduced flexibility of the prey will result in the elimination of both species if neither can renormalize.

We can take the same simple example from another perspective. Instead of assuming changes in the environment of both species, let us assume an INCREASED flexibility in the predator (the environment of the prey). The predator becomes capable of selecting another characteristic besides color in the other species which makes them easier to catch. In the absence of renormalization in this simple ecosystem, the result will be the same: the predators will eliminate the prey and consequently eliminate themselves. In other words, an increased short-range adaptive flexibility in a limited environment tends necessarily to result in a long-range counter-adaptive inflexibility.

The principle of counter-adaptivity is derived from the biology of evolution, but it is equally applicable to psychosocial or socioeconomic systems. The 'security operation' of madness is an adaptation to an intolerable environment – whether that environment be the family context, the value system of a particular culture, or social conditions – and it has at least short-range survival value. It is the beginning of the 'cure'. But if the 'madman' cannot break through at another level, his adaptation may be insignificant as far as his 'environment' is concerned, and psychological death for him – unless he be a Rousseau, a Blake, a Dostoevsky. . . . Worse, however, may be the situation in which his adaptation is essential also to the survival of the 'environment' which made him 'lose his marbles', as they say, in the first place.

The same principle of counter-adaptivity applies to cultural and technological adaptation, but here the effects are qualitatively of a different order from the problems of the 'madman', whose effects upon his environment are minimal. The short-range survival value of the domestication of animals – a typical instance of the short-range extension of a culture's life-span through technology – is in many instances countered by the destruction of the ecosystem in which it occurs, through overgrazing (cf. the effects of modern medicine on the cattle population of the Masai lands in East Africa). Those cultures that survived their own counter-adaptive changes did so in general by switching ecosystems: they moved on and messed around with somebody else's environment.

It seems to be true, as Philip Wylie has suggested, that, because of the irreversible effects of technological innovation on the biosocial ecosystem, the life-span of any culture is in inverse ratio to its per capita "technological index". In distinction from other cultures lasting thousands of years, the advanced industrial culture of modern man seems to be up against the wall after only three hundred.

In the Marxian vocabulary, this particular ecological statement would be known as the 'intensification of the contradictions'.

Rome did not fall because of homosexuality, high living, or marauding 'barbarians'. The Roman Empire fell because its technology could not renormalize when the counter-adaptivity of its original innovations (e.g. colonialism) made itself felt as inflexibility. The Empire became a suitable 'someone else's ecosystem' for the more flexible barbarians to move in on. 'Someone else's ecosystem' is a metaphor of the epistemological error which lies behind the present biosocial crisis. It is an error whose effects may already be irreversibly damaging.

3. *Positive Feedback*

What appears to us as an (counter-adaptive) error was not so for those who introduced it. It was this very epistemological position which was essential to the massive technological advances of the modern industrial system. But its short-range survival value is now countered by its long range counter-adaptive value. Our industrial culture has traditionally depended on an 'ethic of disposability' for which natural resources, other people's ecosystems, 'other' human beings in general, and the disposable beercan have had roughly the same (exchange) value. Having taught that all that it defines as environment is disposable, modern industrial society has only just begun to learn that THE SYSTEM WHICH DISPOSES OF ITS ENVIRONMENT DISPOSES OF ITSELF (cf. Marx's *Grundrisse* [1857–8]: McLellan, 1971: 94–5).

It is common knowledge that the relationship between technological innovation and additional innovation, as well as that between population increase and further increase, generates exponentially increasing one-way processes.[3] Increased population tends to increase the need for and the possibilities of new technology, and increased technology increases the population. The biosocial *hubris* of a value system based on growth and efficiency for their own sakes, on principles of selective affluence, un-inhibited 'progress', the virtue of diversification, and the maximization of profit at all costs, coupled with an almost religious fanaticism about technology, further increases the biosocial deviations of the ecosystem which economic factors are already amplifying. But technology requires human and natural resources. And our global dependence on technology, along with the continuous increase of the technological index of every individual, has brought us to a situation which neither the human nor the natural resources will long stand for.

Each individual makes ever-increasing demands on technology because of the increasing demands technology makes on him. His demands include the psychological gratification and 'escape potential' he seeks in an alienating, objectifying, plastic culture: more horsepower, more mobility, more gadgets, more 'free time', more material status. It is now estimated, for instance, that every single person in the United States depends upon an average of 500 'energy slaves' in order to go about his daily business, each 'slave' expending the energy and producing the waste of an average 'non-technological' human being (*Los Angeles Times*, June 21, 1970).

This increase in the technological index is not deleterious in itself (it could depend upon the recycling of energy and waste, for instance, whereas at present every discarded beercan increases the entropy of our culture). But in the context of an epistemology which refuses renormalization, the technological index becomes an index of decadence. The rapacious building up of quantitative change is leading us inevitably to a qualitative rupture, which may include our own destruction. Whereas in all previous cases of environmental and psychosocial desolation and exploitation, the victims were too localized or too weak to react effectively, mankind may already be facing the kind of massive natural retaliation which could be the genetic result of our turning on to DDT.

In cybernetic thinking, the present relationship of the industrial system and those who control it (state or private capitalism) to the biosocial environment (to me, to you, to nature, to its 'resources') is known as a positive feedback or runaway relationship: the more you have, the more

---

[3] That is, processes generating 'J-curves' on graphs. Such processes can be represented by the formula for compound interest: $y = Ce^{bt}$, where y is the number or amount after time t, e is the base of natural logarithms, and b is a measure of the rate of increase. When b is positive, feedback is positive (Hardin, 1969: 277).

you get. Unlike the primary control system of nature, negative feedback, which seeks out deviation and neutralizes or transforms it, positive feedback increases the deviations between input and output in the communication between the subsystems of the ecosystem. In the short run, this is fine for those who invest their money at compound interest or who draw their profits from underdeveloped countries, but in nature, all runaway systems (such as a forest fire or a supernova) are inexorably controlled, in the long run, by negative feedback at a second level. Second-order negative feedback always takes the form of the emergence of a metasystem (the elaboration of new structures, morphogenesis) or the destruction of the ecosystem involved. In social systems, the first of these responses to positive feedback is known as REVOLUTION. The second is EXTINCTION (cf. Pask, 1962: 238).

Figure 1, which is taken in part from Bateson, seeks to summarize these relationships. It simplifies the complex interrelations between epistemol-

FIGURE 1: *The Relationships of Biosocial Imperialism*

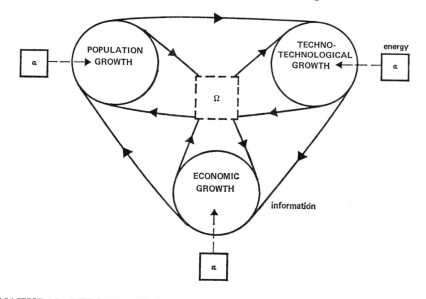

NATURAL RESOURCES (DECREASING) WASTE (INCREASING)

——— INFORMATION LINKAGES (Clockwise = Positive feedback)

α	FREE ENERGY NEGENTROPY FLEXIBILITY

Ω	BOUND ENERGY ENTROPY INFLEXIBILITY

ogy, ideology, economics, and the 'pillage of the Third World', but serves its purpose in demonstrating the form of these relationships.

In the diagram, the term entropy refers to the entropy of the terrestrial biosphere, not to that of the universe.

Simply put, the problem is to know how man-and-womankind can introduce counter-clockwise arrows into the system, without a right-wing revolution which would be dependent on the straightforward elimination of surplus consumers. Note that the conviction that technology will always find an answer is a capital example of the ideological *hubris* which got us into this mess in the first place.

4. *The Paranoia of Symmetry*

Because it seeks to ignore feedback and relationship, the prevailing epistemology is at every level an epistemology which leads inevitably to positive feedback. It is an epistemology of biosocial imperialism. In Bateson's terms, it is an epistemology of lineal causation or 'force' or 'power'. For the general systems theorist it involves the imposition of closed-system thinking on those aspects of reality which are open systems (see below); it denies the relationship between energy and information by splitting symbiotic wholes (ecosystems) into supposedly independent 'things'.

The same epistemological error obtains whatever the ecosystem or the level of ecosystem we are concerned with: biological, psychological, socioeconomic. Deterministic thinking in biology, elitism in genetics and psychometrics, instincts and intrapsychic conflicts in psychology, the free competition of the rational subject in economics, and uncritical attempts to apply the experimental method in the social sciences are particularly obvious examples of the error. In its ideological manifestations (for every ideology is dependent upon a theory of knowledge and vice versa), the same error feeds pollution, racism, alienation, exploitation, oppression, and ALL OTHER FORMS OF PATHOLOGICAL COMMUNICATION.

It is a necessary function of pathological communication to deny its own pathology at some level while admitting and using it at other levels. Thus, since no system can actually ignore feedback relationships, our culture simply converts them into POWER relationships.[4] More precisely, we note

4 As Hardin points out (1969), it is the positive feedback effect of the accumulation of power (control over communication) in economic and social systems which makes the 'competitive exclusion principle' valid for such socioeconomic ecosystems. The notion of 'free' competition is then projected – by 'protective reaction' – onto natural ecosystems, in which, on the contrary, symbiosis or 'coopera-

that any rational argument pinpointing the pathology at any one level will generally be met with a stereotyped set of defense mechanisms: a shift of level (e.g., short-sighted 'pragmatic' considerations in response to long-range economic arguments), a refusal of content through an attack on form (e.g., complaints about the use of proper channels or about 'emotional overreaction'), a refusal to understand ("I don't know what you're talking about"), or a naked challenge ("So what?").

Each defensive response is a further manifestation of the primary epistemological error. The error justifies and encourages an overriding commitment to SYMMETRICAL relationships – such as arms races, corporate mergers, simplistic anti-communism, racism – within which COMPLEMEN-TARY relationships at another level – spheres of influence, exploitation of underdeveloped countries, domestic colonialism, and the like – provide the material for the overall commitment to competitive oppositions.

FIGURE 2

SYMMETRICAL 'MATCHING'   COMPLEMENTARY 'FITTING'

The danger, as I explain in more detail below, does not arise from the nature of human beings or from the nature of symmetry and complementarity as such, but rather from the general tendency of all components of the system to specialize in EITHER symmetry OR complementarity with any given set of other components.

It is all an extraordinary curious business. What happens is that the epistemological error allows our culture to deny the complementary relationships on which it depends, and consequently to justify them as symmetrical. Real relationships of dominance and subservience between UNEQUAL partners are defined as free competition in an open marketplace between free and equal legal, psychological, and socioeconomic subjects. The most obvious example of this pseudo-symmetry lies in our admirable eighteenth-century commitment to 'freedom of speech' (rather than to freedom of communication). Within limits we are all free to say what we think; it is only the channels to the audience that cost money. Similarly, every man has the right to become a conscientious objector – provided he

---

tive competition' is the more general rule. In our economic system, 'cooperative competition' describes the relationship between the industrial giants who monopolize a given area (e.g., automobile manufacturers).

has the education (and the necessary psychological distance from a culture that equates killing with virility) to argue the philosophical and religious premises of his case before the draft board. And on the one hand, we hear (men) talk of 'female chauvinism'; on the other, (whites) talk of 'black racism'.

It is in these ways that the conventional epistemology takes on an ideological paranoia of symmetry (Freud's reductionist and anti-contextual 'narcissism of minor differences' – *Standard Edition*, XVIII, 101), which generates further pathological symmetry. To paraphrase a schizophrenic statement: "If the Russians (Chinese, minorities, hippies, students, etc.) aren't what I think they are, I'll prove it."

5. Cogito ergo sum

> I'm an in divide you all.
> JULIE in *The Divided Self*

For the sake of illustration, let us take Descartes' *Discourse on Method* (1637) as a historical metaphor of this epistemology. A particularly significant passage for our purposes is the following:

> I knew [from the indubitability of "I think, therefore I am"] that I was a substance[5] whose whole essence or nature is only to think, and which, in order to be, has need of no locus and does not depend on any material thing, in such a way that this self or ego, that is to say, the soul by which I am what I am, is entirely distinct from the body . . . and even if the body ceased to exist, my soul would not cease to be all that it is.

Once Descartes had made what is FOR US the crucial epistemological error of founding a philosophy on the *cogito ergo sum* (to say nothing of its psychological and social deficiencies), he had made a COMMENTARY on the TEXT of the relationships of seventeenth-century society – a statement in a metalanguage about the (overdetermined) relationships in the "language of real life" (Marx), the referent language of the existing material relationships. Commentary and the text are mutually interdependent, in the same way that the psychological symptom is a commentary on a text which affects the text and vice versa. Descartes' statement was a CRITICAL commentary on some aspects of a past epistemology (it was a partial metaepistemology), at the same time as, in keeping with Descartes' representative moral conservatism, it was a RATIONALIZATION of the present state of the text. The relationship between commentary and text is a necessary one. There are no accidental relationships.

5 i.e., "*I* is a substance."

In keeping with philosophy's historical function of responding to and elaborating on developments in science, the *Discourse on Method* provided the Galilean revolution with its philosophical paradigm. But, as befits the foundation stone of a new philosophy which sought to overcome the epistemological obstacle of Aristotelian 'final causes' in the physical sciences, the *cogito ergo sum* went much further. It corresponded to the requirements of the existing socioeconomic system that there be an epistemology from which an ethic of personal freedom, individual autonomy, equality, rationality, the universality of *bon sens*, and, above all, an ethic of SEPARABLE AND INDIVIDUAL RESPONSIBILITY could be derived. It was an ethic of symmetry, a doctrine of separate but equal.

The system had begun its counter-adaptive adaptation. It was no accident that Descartes' assertion of the existence of clear and distinct ideas and, correlatively, of CLEAR AND DISTINCT PEOPLE should have paralleled and preceded the introduction of the technics of efficiency, substitutability, and organization in the culture that was soon to dominate the world. The rise of individualism, the invention of perspective, Protestantism, the discovery of alphabetical order for dictionaries, the ordering of practical and abstract knowledge in the *Encyclopédie*, the invention of interchangeable machine parts, the standardization of weights and measures, Linnaeus' ordering of the species, the substitution of legal codes and constitutions for spontaneous common law, and the creation of standardized tasks in the factory system [6] – these and other events were symptoms of the imposition of the 'clear and distinct' on the complex, explicitly oppressive, and hierarchical *communitas* of the Middle Ages. And if Descartes' commentary on the text of an ongoing adaptive change was to strike a blow for the ethic of personal freedom in the Age of Reason, it was also a blow on behalf of an economic system which would lead to the most complex and irrational organization of unfreedom man-and-womankind has ever seen.

Descartes' statement justified the ethics of symmetry by clearly stating the atomistic epistemology upon which we still depend. It is an epistemology related to the forces and energy pushing and pulling bodies about in what was soon to become a Newtonian universe of attraction and repulsion in mechanical equilibrium. Additive, closed-system energy models of all reality – the conception of reality as an AGGREGATE of individual bodies possessing forces, humors, sympathies, affinities, instincts, and the like, [7]

[6] Cf. Ellul's *Technological Society* (1954). The topic of the book is not technology or machines, but *la technique*: the historical development of organization, classification, substitutability, taxonomy.

[7] Cf. Newton, *Principia* (1713):

The motion of the whole is the same thing with the sum of the parts . . . and

in an entropic universe – excluded those minority voices who, like Pascal or Rousseau, to some degree or other protested on behalf of the multiplicative and fractionative communicational relationships of the biosocial open systems which physics necessarily ignored.[8] The 'social physics' which followed, the sociology of the energy relationships of clear and distinct billiard balls,[9] demonstrated the utility and the danger of the Cartesian epistemology. Every *cogito* was free to sell his disposable energy at the best price.

therefore the place of the whole is the same thing with the sum of the places of the parts, and for that reason, it is internal, and in the whole body (Quoted in Laruccia, 1971).

The eighteenth century believed gravity to be a real, innate, physical force. Newton, however, says it is not. But his remarks about the *vis insita* of bodies (i.e., inertia) as not essentially including gravitation are contradicted by his (theological) assumption of a *spiritus subtilissimus* moving and affecting both the inorganic and the organic world. Clearly modeled on electricity, this 'subtle spirit' is the bioenergetic 'force' *par excellence* – i.e., God, the *Primum Mobile* (*Scholium Generale*, 1713, last paragraph).

Cf. also William Gilbert on the magnet (1600):

The magnetic force is animate, or imitates the soul; in many respects it surpasses the human soul while that is united to an organic body (*De Magnete*, Chapter 12).

[8] The following subtle passage was crossed out in the *Pensées* (1670) by Pascal:

Nature has put us so carefully in the middle [*milieu*] that if we change one side of the balance, we also change the other: *Je fesons, zôa trékei*. This makes me think that there are *ressorts* in our head which are so arranged that whatever touches one touches also the contrary (p. 1109).

Pascal has been described as the first dialectical thinker of the modern period, replying both 'yes' and 'no' to all questions (Goldmann, 1955). His use of the colloquialism which places a singular subject with a plural verb (*je fesons*) brings out the reality of the subject as a relation, against the Cartesian conception of the subject as an entity. At the same time, by using the grammatical curiosity in Greek which requires plural neuter subjects to take singular verbs (*zôa trékei*: 'beings is an ongoing process'), Pascal brings out the heterogeneous plurality of 'beings' in relation to their unity of interdependence in a singular 'Being': what touches one touches the other (cf. Montaigne, 1595, III, 2: "On Repentance"). In relation to adaptivity and counter-adaptivity, we find the following: "Everything which perfects itself by progress, also perishes by progress" (p. 1120). Like Feuerbach and Hegel, Pascal also points to the "invisible nature" of informational relationships (p. 1108).

[9] In the *Critique of Pure Reason* (1781) – "The Paralogisms of Pure Reason" – Kant adds a note to explain the possibility of multiple 'identities' of the 'I' over time (in spite of its apparent logical 'identity'). This he does by comparing the 'substance' of the 'I' in each state to an elastic ball impinging upon another ball representing the next state, and thus communicating its "representations together with the consciousness of them" (i.e., its energy) to the other ball.

Following on some aspects of classical ontology and epistemology, of which it is only a variant, the Cartesian 'revolution' made the crucial absolutist and analytical error (for us) of unjustifiably conferring a privileged ontological status on entities ('substance') as opposed to relationships ('attributes', 'accidents').[10] In spite of Aristotle, Hegel, and Marx, the truth that entities do not create relationships so much as RELATIONSHIPS CREATE ENTITIES, was (and still remains) generally obscured. Moreover, the privileged ontological status of entities in the system encouraged the reification of whatever relationships it did recognize. Gravitation, energy, matter, people, and so forth, became THINGS. (cf. Marx on atomism and the general equivalent in exchange [1887, I: 92].)[11]

The second error followed from the first, compounded by Locke[12] and

[10] As Lancelot Law Whyte (1962: 23–5, 59) points out in his remarkable analysis of the conception of non-conscious processes before the specifically Freudian discovery of the unconscious, Descartes sought to "stabilize with final clarity an ancient dualism: the split of subject from object". Whyte regards this as possibly one of the most fundamental blunders made by the human mind (but as I have been at some pains to point out, it cannot be regarded as a blunder for the seventeenth century, whatever it may have subsequently proved to be for us). He goes on: "Until an attempt had been made (with apparent success) to choose AWARENESS as the defining characteristic of an independent mode of being called mind, there was no occasion to invent the idea of UNCONSCIOUS mind as a provisional correction of that choice." The adjective 'unconscious', in the sense of 'not available to consciousness', appears in English in 1712, the noun in German in 1766, but the term *inconscient* does not appear in French until the 1820s.

[11] The same error over substance and attributes and the same emphasis on entities – which are "moved" by the "internal contradictions", which they "contain" as the primary "cause" of their development, their relationship with other "things" being secondary causes – obscures Mao's popular 1937 essay on contradiction (1961–5, I: 311–47). Some of the passages in this essay sound like the orthodox Freudian theory of 'intrapsychic conflict'. I suspect however that the English may make these similarities more apparent than real. But on the face of the text available to us, this essay is an excellent example of the impossibility of dealing adequately with difference (which is what the essay is really about) from Lenin's and Engels's essentially mechanistic conception of dialectics (cf. Jordan, 1967). Contradictions, differences, oppositions, deviations, and paradoxes occur not in entities but in ecosystems, that is to say, in patterns, in organization, in relationships – which are not things. It is true that difference moves the cosmos, but the differences in energy levels which provide the motive power of closed systems tending towards entropy are not the same as the differences between information input and output which control the behavior of open systems tending to neutral or negative entropy.

[12] In a well-known passage, Locke – who believes in "independent, self-determining, unchangeable substances" – compares the understanding to a "closet wholly shut from light, with only some little openings left". These openings let in "ideas of things without" (1690). Perception, for Locke, is of course a one-way process:

the other anti-Cartesians.[13] By imposing analytical logical categories (such as the supposed ontological primacy of the simple over the complex) on the processes of biological, historical, and psychosocial reality, both the Cartesian and the anti-Cartesian epistemology matched the wrong 'organism' or level of the organism to the wrong 'environment' or level of the environment.

As Pascal, the paradoxical thinker who so vehemently opposed Descartes, knew only too well, the epistemological error was to impose an 'either/or' (closed-system) logic on a 'both-and' (open-system) reality. The error has a venerable pedigree, for nowhere is it more clearly demonstrated historically than in the Socratic *elenchus*, which employs the tried and true 'principle of assent' of the encyclopedia salesman (i.e., he begins by asking questions which can only be answered 'yes') against interlocutors forced by their cupidity for knowledge to choose between artificial oppositions.

The socioeconomic reorganization expressed symptomatically in the discourse of science at this period can probably be best described, from a macroscopic perspective, as the DIGITALIZATION of the (fundamentally) analog relationships of the social universe and the social discourse. If we recall the relationship established in Chapter VII between the 'more or less' of analog communication and the 'on/off' or the 'discrete element' of digital communication, the following remarks about the Newtonian discourse by Alexandre Koyré take on a wider signification than perhaps their author intended. The entire article provides most useful support for the thesis of this chapter, especially Koyré's analysis of 'ontological one-

---

the subject contributes nothing to his perceptions; he is an entity which becomes 'imprinted' with 'ideas' (a *tabula rasa*). Against the similar 'copy theory' of perception espoused by Engels and by Lenin, the Marxian psychology is communicational. As Jordan points out, in Marx's words, all such 'one-sided' theories of relation are "obliged to mortify the flesh and become ascetic" (1967: 42).

13 Cf. Leibniz in *The Principles of Nature* and the *Monadology* (1714), where he is writing against the Cartesians:

Our thought of substance is perfectly satisfied in the conception of force and not in that of extension. . . . There is . . . no way of explaining how a monad can be . . . changed in its inner being by any other creature, for . . . the monads have no windows through which anything can enter or depart. The natural changes of the monads proceed from an internal principle. . . . Each monad is a living mirror. . . .

What is interesting about Leibniz, of course, is that in spite of his monadology, his conception of entelechy sought to establish the principle of goalseeking against Cartesian mechanism. As a result, he is one of the first modern thinkers seriously to pose the question of non-conscious mental processes.

dimensionality' on page 7 and his remarks about Newtonian motion as a state on page 10.

> More or less! Somehow this very expression used in connection with Newton strikes me as improper because it is possible that the deepest meaning and aim of Newtonianism, or rather, of the whole scientific revolution of the seventeenth century, of which Newton is the heir and the highest expression, is just to abolish the world of the 'more or less', the world of qualities and sense perception, the world of appreciation of our daily life, and to replace it by the (Archimedean) universe of precision, of exact measures, of strict determination (Koyré, 1968: 4–5).

6. *The Biosocial Unit of Survival*

The Cartesian error appears in many forms, With our present hindsight, it seems almost incredible that Descartes could not have realized that the *cogito ergo sum* was not a "clear and distinct idea" but rather a MESSAGE between a sender and a receiver, and, moreover, a wish-fulfillment, like a dream. Today we would replace it with another slogan: *loquor ergo sumus*.

It is no accident that the Cartesian epistemology entails solipsism. (There are only two kinds of solipsist: those who want to be consciously and those who want to be unconsciously. Solipsism, like what we erroneously call schizophrenia, is a 'security operation'.)[14] Of all the ways in which it is

[14] Since solipsism implies purely logical paradoxes in relation to communication, Descartes could not not take into account the necessity of the communicational circuit in the human ecosystem. In developing the so-called ontological proof of the existence of God in the *Discours* (4th Part), he uses the notion of his own LACK (of perfection) in order to show that a 'receiver' for his own existence is necessary:

> If I were really alone and independent of every other . . ., I would have had in me . . . all the surplus that I know is lacking to me, and thus . . . I would have had all the perfections that I was able to find to be in God.

The inadequate conception of causality in open systems to which Descartes suscribes does not prejudice the 'wish-fulfillment' implicit in this passage. God is thus the mediator of the communications of the individual *cogitos*; he completes the circuit. The eighteenth century, however, by taking over the Cartesian mechanistic materialism and ruling God out of order, did indeed set up a solipsistic individualism and atomism.

Koyré (1958: 276, 274) makes this point from an entirely different perspective:

> The infinite Universe of the new Cosmology, infinite in Duration as well as in Extension, in which eternal matter in accordance with eternal and necessary laws moves endlessly and aimlessly in eternal space, inherited all the ontological attributes of Divinity. Yet only those – ALL THE OTHERS THE DEPARTED GOD

possible to focus on this error, the most important is to describe it as THAT PERCEPTION OF THE BIOSOCIAL UNIVERSE WHICH DESCRIBES THE UNIT OF SURVIVAL AS THE INDIVIDUAL (the individual organism, species, family line, system, and so on). It is the error of the 'survival of the fittest', which is ideologically quite different from the principle of natural selection, for nature selects the survival of the ecosystem, at all its levels, not the survival of the individual (subsystem).

There is no need to elaborate on the often remarked relationship of Darwinism and Social Darwinism to the imperialism of nineteenth-century liberal capitalism.[15] And we are not about to oppose this error with the usual moral arguments about the difference between 'natural' and 'human' selection, nor with the argument that Darwin meant the species and not the individual, nor with the point that Spencer was really thinking about the cooperative relationships of the parts of the organism rather than about the conflict between organisms in a world of restricted possibilities and the 'law of nature red in tooth and claw'.

In their traditional form, these arguments compound the original error by being variations of it. Since such applications of the axioms of the prevailing epistemology are dead wrong, there is no point in tinkering with the axioms; they can only be put back in their place.

The first step is to recognize that THE UNIT OF SURVIVAL IS THE MESSAGE-IN-CIRCUIT IN THE ECOSYSTEM (Bateson), whether the ecosystem in question be methodologically defined at the biological, the sociocultural, the psychological, or at some other level (cf. Emerson, 1956: 148, on sex coloration). Unlike energy, information (messages) can be both created and destroyed,

---

TOOK AWAY WITH HIM. . . . The destruction of the Cosmos [was followed by] its replacement by an indefinite and even infinite universe which is bound together by the identity of its fundamental components and laws, and in which all these components are placed on the SAME LEVEL OF BEING. This, in turn, implies the discarding by scientific thought of all considerations based upon value-concepts, such as perfection, harmony, meaning and aim, and finally the utter devalorization of being, the divorce of the world of value and the world of facts (my emphasis).

Koyré is not quite correct, however. The result was not the divorce of 'value' and 'fact', but rather the REDUCTION of the world of value to the world of fact. (Cf. Goldmann, 1955, on the 'spectator God' of the seventeenth-century Jansenists.)

15 Cf. Darwin in *The Descent of Man* (1871):

At some future period, not very distant as measured by centuries, the civilized races of man will almost certainly exterminate, and replace, the savage races throughout the world.

Or, in the words of the propaganda films of the Moody Bible Institute: "Science Marches On".

primarily because the very possibility of information depends upon a code which is shared by both sender and receiver. (By 'sender' and 'receiver' I mean the heuristic device which enables us to talk about the message in circuit.) The code, in fact, as Bateson points out, is this relationship. Without the reciprocity of the code, the message is received as 'noise'. And when the possibility of information is destroyed by the breakdown of the sender–receiver relationship, the ecosystem perishes.

This is only another way of repeating Schrödinger's maxim that life feeds on negative entropy (information, order, improbability, organization). That is to say, when there is a breakdown of the information flow which maintains organization in living systems and which, carried by energy borrowed from an entropic universe, may also create localized packets of negative entropy, positive entropy (disorganization, randomness) takes back its own.

In order to feed on negentropy, life must have an adequate supply of free energy, that is, it must have "a supply of uncommitted potentiality for change, i.e., flexibility" (Bateson). It is precisely the inflexibility of our present unrenormalized phase-space of potentialities which makes our epistemology counter-adaptive.

Epistemology is a question of where you draw the line, and there are only a restricted number of loci through which to draw it (i.e., everything in this paper has somehow been said before). The line drawn between 'organism' and 'environment' by our conventional model of reality is such a line, and, like all such lines it is a fiction. Unfortunately, we think that it is real.

Psychologically, this conventional epistemological boundary is a refusal or denial of the interpersonal ecosystem; ideologically, it is a (schizoid) justification of the way material relationships are programmed in our culture (biosocial imperialism); epistemologically, it is an arbitrary punctuation of the discourse between sender and receiver, whose supposedly real status in the world is itself defined, by not 'reality', but by the original epistemological error. Some epistemological boundary is necessary (boundaries are the conditions of communication), but it is always arbitrary in the sense of being methodological rather than real.[16] The problem here is

---

[16] All boundaries in this sense involve paradox, for they correspond to the digitalization of an analog continuum, and the distinctions between the various components thus created can never be completely maintained (cf. Chapter VII). Whyte (1962: 40, 42) points to the Gödelian situation involved: "No rational system – logical, mathematical, scientific – can ever be used to define its own boundaries." And further on:

The temptation to treat static ideas as absolute, rather than as partial and provisional, proved irresistible to many Western thinkers; the apparent

that the conventional line serves inappropriate, exploitative ideological ends.

For the sake of this illustration, imagine the message-in-circuit in an ecosystem which is maintaining homeostasis[17] as a spiral in which information – the transformation of difference – flows in one direction. (Leave for the present the complex problem of the relationship between the synchronic and the diachronic aspects of this circuit. This relationship is another aspect of the problem of models – i.e., a question of our consciously chosen point of view. As much as I am suspicious of the geometric metaphor I am using, it is worth noting that, as Robert Nyberg has pointed out to me, projecting a helix on to a plane produces at one transformation a circle – synchrony – at another, a zigzag ladder – diachrony.)

Imagine that there passes through the longitudinal axis of the spiral a plane representing the epistemological line which divides the circuit into two 'sides'. These 'sides' are arbitrarily defined; the barrier between them is imaginary both in the sense of its not being real (the flow of information ignores it) and in the Lacanian sense of the Imaginary. This fiction does define the boundaries of sets of real, material differences in order to allow us to talk about senders and receivers. The problem is that our epistemology reifies the methodological necessity: by reifying the material differences between various sets of components in a symbiotic whole, it turns them into Imaginary oppositions. And any culture that systematically turns difference into what it believes is UNMEDIATED opposition is eventually doomed. (See *Figure 3*, which extends Bateson's original conception.)

The fundamental 'rule of relation' expressed in this diagram is simply this: If you are born on the 'right side of the tracks', you may legitimately exploit or 'dispose of' whatever you define as being on the 'wrong side', whether you know it or not.

We further compound the error of opposition by mixing up the correspondences: we match a biological 'self' to a sociocultural 'other', for example, thus confusing the various LEVELS OF ORGANIZATION within the model. The boundaries of my skinbound biological individuality are quite different from those of my psychic 'self' or my social 'role'. There is not only an environment specific to every system but also to every level of the system; a symbiotic and non-exploitative epistemology will always

---

clarity of such ideas seduces the mind into dismissing change or transformation as a trivial secondary effect of interactions between the 'real' entities. Static concepts proved to be very effective intellectual tranquilizers. . . .

Thus these static oppositions come to represent perfectly the schizoid epistemology of western culture.

[17] See Chapter XII on the difference between homeostasis, homeorhesis, and morphogenesis.

seek to remain aware of these various levels of correspondence at the same time as it remains aware of its own epistemological act – "Nature hath no outline, but Imagination has" (William Blake, 1822).

FIGURE 3
The Imaginary Splitting of the Ecosystem

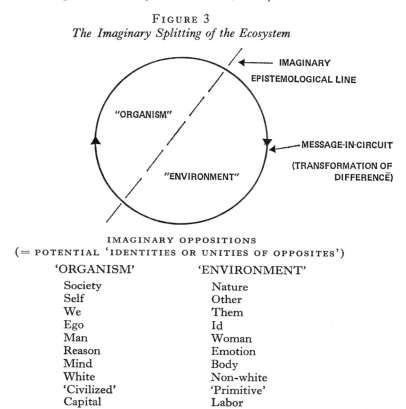

IMAGINARY OPPOSITIONS
(= POTENTIAL 'IDENTITIES OR UNITIES OF OPPOSITES')

'ORGANISM'	'ENVIRONMENT'
Society	Nature
Self	Other
We	Them
Ego	Id
Man	Woman
Reason	Emotion
Mind	Body
White	Non-white
'Civilized'	'Primitive'
Capital	Labor

Language itself (naturally) assists in the confusion, and at a level of categorization more profound than the relativity of conceptual categorization described by the Whorfian hypothesis. At both the phonological and the conceptual level, language (which, like mathematics, is neither superstructure nor base) is constructed on difference (Jakobson's "binary oppositions"). More significant at this point is the actual function of words like 'I', 'me', 'you', 'him' (Postgate's "subjective elements"), which we commonly take to refer to entities when in fact they are simply SHIFTERS. The shifter designates only the locus of the sender of the message; it refers to a relation between sender, receiver, and referent, but it does not of itself supply the context (indicate the code) without which it can have no referent other than itself. Shifters indicate the ATTITUDE of the sender in every sense of the word (most uses of the subjunctive mood, for example, qualify as shifters) – that is, his locus in a context, but not the context itself. 'Me' and 'here' are not entities; they are punctuation marks.

Any act of categorization is a punctuation, and the unit of survival has been wrongly punctuated. The unit of survival is not EITHER this organism (species, etc.) OR that, nor EITHER organism OR environment, nor EITHER this side of the line OR that. IT IS BOTH–AND.

Nor is the unit of survival 'in' entities – 'in' the organism or 'in' the environment – the unit of survival is in their relationship, which is nowhere. It is nowhere because it is information, and information is, first and foremost, difference. When Bateson says that information is the difference that makes a difference, he is referring to that use of distinction, within any given set of variables, which makes the further and continued transformation of difference (e.g., reproduction) possible.[18]

Thus, although the epistemological line has traditionally been drawn in the wrong place – in the place where it creates a (solipsistic) barrier between sender and receiver – its placing corresponds paradoxically with a real, material locus of difference. The error is to turn the distinction between the loci of a symbiotic and non-exploitative relationship into an Imaginary opposition of entities. In our historical example, the error corresponds to Descartes' confusion of the linguistic shifter 'I' with the skinbound biological individual (the organism) which provided the bio-energetic base for the sociocultural subsystem (the man) which emitted it. At this point he chose a difference (between levels of organization and complexity of information flow), matched it with the wrong environment (matched a biological subsystem to a sociocultural environment) and called it IDENTITY. The referent for 'I', which designates the sender, is not however the image of the biological organism, separate and different from his fellow human beings, but rather a LOCUS in the system (perhaps similar to what G. H. Mead would call a role).

And once you have consequently unconsciously correlated 'self' with 'body' (immanence of the self) in order to establish the transcendence or the non-corporeality of 'mind' (which you thought was 'self'), you have a mind–body problem (Bateson, 1971a) to which no satisfactory answers can be given within the epistemology which produced it.[19] The Cartesian

[18] It is information (a spermatozoon, a pin prick) which transforms the bipolar radial symmetry of the frog's egg into the bilateral symmetry of the frog, by defining one meridian as different from all others (Brachet).

[19] The concept of the body as the PROPERTY of the 'self' – complete with fences and boundaries, and, presumably, amenable to real-estate speculation – is deeply imbedded in our culture. In the *Second Treatise on Civil Government* (1690), Locke remarks that "though the earth and all inferior creatures be common to

axioms are perfectly consistent – but they generate Gödelian sentences which we know to be true, but which cannot be 'proved' from those axioms. The axioms generate statements of a logical type different from all other statements within the system, and all attempts to deal with those sentences without transcending the epistemology which produced them result in irresolvable paradoxes. The 'self' becomes one pole of a double-bound oscillation between 'self' and 'other'. In reality, they are together (*Mitsein*), as Heidegger (1927) insisted.[20]

To put it more precisely, the self as SUBJECT (not as entity) is neither transcendent to nor immanent in the subsystem which thinks it. The subject is immanent in the UNIT OF MIND (Bateson), which, isomorphic with the unit of survival, includes the rest of the system in which the appropriate transformations of difference (information) are transmitted. The unit of mind is not either sender or receiver: it is both–and.

There is an environment specific to every organism or subsystem, and

---

all men, yet every man has a property in his own person; this nobody has any right to but himself". The same theme reappears, in an even more alienated form, in the Saint Simonists (*Leçons sur l'industrie et les finances*, 1832):

> Property will not be abolished, but its form will be changed . . . it will for the first time become TRUE PERSONIFICATION . . . it will for the first time acquire its real, individual character (quoted in Marx and Engels, 1845–6: 249).

Some current arguments on behalf of abortion replace the concept of the woman's body as a socioeconomic commodity (as it is represented in advertising, for example) by purely negative or oppositional arguments which refer to it as her own piece of real estate to improve on as she pleases. This is a representation of the principle behind what is described in the Introduction as the 'negative academic', and elsewhere as the 'negative bourgeois'. It is the principle – with a vengeance – of *plus ça change, plus c'est la même chose*. But this cliché is supposed to issue from the mouth of the conservative-cynic. It is not supposed to appear in repressed forms in the political program of the rebel.

[20] In an article whose title is a quotation from Locke – " 'But there is Nothing I Have is Essential to Me' " – Colin Cherry (1967) points out, as others have done, that the word *individuum* in the Middle Ages seems to have meant "indivisible from the community or unit", whereas the Ciceronian use is closer to present-day usage. The Trinity, for example, is "holy and individual". Cherry goes on to quote the 1888 edition of the *New English Dictionary*: ". . . *Self-*, as a living formative word first [appeared] about the middle of the 16th century, probably to a great extent by imitation or reminiscence of Greek compounds in *auto* . . . [whilst] the number of *self*-compound words was greatly augmented by the middle of the 17th century when many new words appeared in theological and philosophical writing, some of which had a restricted currency of about 50 years (e.g., 1645–90), whilst a large proportion . . . have a continued history down to the present time." The noun 'self' dates from 1595, according to the *OED*, with the philosophical sense of 'ego' appearing in 1674. Similarly, the noun *moi* in French dates from the time of Montaigne, *c.* 1588 (Robert).

when either the environment or the organism adapts or changes – i.e., manipulates difference over time – the other must change also. In the terms of viability or survival, their overall relationship is symbiotic; within that relationship, the specific behavior of any two or more subsystems may be complementary or symmetrical, or both.

Either symmetrical relationships – the more of the same, the more of the same – or complementary relationships – the more of the same, the more of the opposite – may lead to runaway. In Bateson's terminology (1936), this progressive differentiation is called schismogenesis, which is beneficial only if controlled.

The possibility of runaway follows from the fact that every piece of information is a difference or a deviation. Every initial message, before feedback, moves the system towards the amplification of deviations. Lack of feedback, misconstrued feedback, or positive feedback can then lead to pathological communication. Unless controlled by deviation-reducing comparisons between input and output that are meaningful at some level or other to all components of the system, both symmetry (e.g., rivalry between father and son) and complementarity (e.g., domination and dependence between mother and child) may lead to the destruction of one component. If the circumstances are sufficiently dangerous, or if there are no other substitute relationships available (as in an arms race or a predator relation), the destruction of the one entails the necessary destruction of the other.

Every transmitted difference is simultaneously a report on a situation and a command to do something about it (McCulloch). When the reports and the commands get mixed up so that deviations between sender and receiver increase, there must eventually occur a situation in which no further 'matching' or 'understanding' – symmetrical imitating or complementary fitting – is possible, and controlled communication ceases. The message-in-circuit had been converted from 'signal' to 'noise' which, for the system, is equivalent to the destruction of the information. In some circles, this phenomenon is known as the generation gap.

Thus neither symmetry nor complementarity are guarantors against destructive schismogenesis. And yet, in nature, either destruction or emergence always rules. What guarantees emergence rather than destruction is not either symmetry or complementarity, then, but both: THE SWITCH FROM ONE MODE TO THE OTHER (Bateson, 1936; cf. also Pask, 1962: 242–3).

The supposed (entity-like) 'inhibitory response mechanism' (epistemologically equivalent to the soporific power resident in opium) which prevents an attacking wolf or dog from rending the exposed jugular of his defeated adversary provides an example, as Bateson has pointed out to me. The vanquished canine switches from symmetry (matching aggression) to complementarity (fitting submission), and it is this substitution of one kind of energy-triggering difference for another which sends the victor off to transfer his symmetrical relationship to the surrounding foliage.

7. *Dialectics and Schismogenesis*

> Quand vous pensez à retrouver
> le temps perdu, vous ne mettez
> rien en danger.
> PAUL NIZAN: *Aden-Arabie*

Of all the representative quotations one might introduce at this point, perhaps the most apposite would be one from the man whose discovery (*inventio*) of the principle of the DIFFERENTIAL ELEMENT in language generated a new paradigm which enabled philology to become a science, a quotation from Saussure's *Cours de linguistique générale* (1916a: 168, 162):

> In language there are only differences. More than that: a difference generally presupposes some sort of positive terms between which it is established, but in language there are only differences without positive terms. . . . [In language] the value of a term can be modified, without its sense or its sounds being affected, simply by the fact that some other neighboring term has undergone a modification.

and:

> Concepts . . . are purely differential. They are not defined positively by their content, but negatively by their relationship with the other terms of the system. Their most exact characteristic is to be what others are not.[21]

[21] Saussure is probably the first linguist to really tackle the epistemological question of punctuation. He establishes a distinction between what can be called the 'relational identity' (exchange value) of one term to another, and their 'material identity' (their orthography, for example). The 'value' of a term depends on its locus in the system, not on anything intrinsic. The errors of previous linguistics and semantics had always been to attribute material identity to signifiers whose relational identity is not the same, e.g., to assume that the 'gentlemen' in "Ladies and Gentlemen" is materially equivalent to the 'same' signifier in, for instance, "an officer and a gentleman" (cf. Ducrot, 1968: 43–7). Such examples would be simply trivial if it were not that the ideological discourse of our culture never fails to repeat this mistake, e.g., the current use of the term 'violence'. Saussure's distinction is equivalent to that between 'attribute' (relation) and 'substance' (entity) in this paper.

Symmetry and complementarity are manifestations in behavior, in ways yet to be fully defined, of the linguistic distinction between metaphor and metonymy, similarity and contiguity, code and message, text and context, substitution and combination, the paradigmatic and the syntagmatic (Jakobson, 1956).

They seem to be related to what Bateson calls selective and progressional integration in decision-making as well as to schismogenesis. Both processes are essential to communication. And just as the choice of symmetry over complementarity (and vice versa) may lead to the destruction of the message-in-circuit, so the choice of the metonymic over the metaphoric pole of language (and vice versa) is a principal characteristic of aphasia, as Jakobson has shown.

The further analysis and comprehension of the relationship between these two differential poles is essential to the continued development of dialectical thought, to say nothing of the destiny of our species. The building-up of contiguous quantitative change in a system, for instance, may be explicable as an analog of the metonymic message processes (combinations) within it, and the dialectical 'quantum jump' from quantity to quality seems to be an analog of a metaphoric change of code (substitution). Opposing messages and codes within the ecosystem may be related symmetrically or complementarily (or both); when the intensification of their deviations ('contradictions') can no longer be controlled by negative feedback, the system will remain viable – be maintained and transformed (*aufheben*) – only if the ensuing exponential schismogenesis leads to the emergence of a metasystem. But goalseeking systems other than people in particular have no ethics other than the ethics of viability; depending on the order of complexity of the system and the semiotic freedom of its 'characteristic response', it will manifest a synchronic tendency towards a steady state (conservation of entropy) and a diachronic tendency towards increasing orders of organization (negative entropy), levels separated from each other by code-switching quantum jumps (cf. Chapter XII). Dialectical reversal (*Aufhebung*) is always the control of schismogenesis in the interests of the system – but how do we equate those interests with our own? Or in other words, how do we learn to control the controls of the system?

The answers to these questions will not come easily. But a materialist, naturalist, anti-reductionist theory of communication and exchange, such as that outlined in this book, a radical and non-mechanistic viewpoint which understands that the unit of survival and the unit of mind are isomorphic, at least points us in the right direction. Cybernetic both–and thinking, combined with an understanding of the hierarchical orders of complexity of organization revealed in systems theory, enables us to deal rationally with the crucial problem of the distinction of logical types (the distinction of codes from messages and from metacodes), upon whose confusion the pathological communication of schizophrenic relationships depends. For any system which comments on itself and confuses meta-language and referent language generates paradox. And paradox, endemic to language and creativity, may be used, in the form of the paradoxical injunction, on behalf of the control of some components of the system by others (Chapter V). IF (and only if) I insist that A is either A or not-A, THEN you are either good or bad, normal or abnormal, sadistic or maso-chistic, American or un-American – and you will oscillate between these impossible contraries as long as you are prevented from metacommunicat-ing about them by the control I exercise over your epistemology.[22]

8. *Better Dead than Red*

Like the (so-called) schizophrenic who cannot answer the double bind of identity, when the analytical epistemology is applied to open systems, IT CONFUSES THE METAPHOR WITH WHAT IS MEANT, the Symbolic with the Real. It denies (*verneinen*) or rejects (*verwerfen*) the symbiotic and reci-procal relationship of sender and receiver by reifying difference, for this epistemology of identity and non-identity can properly account neither for the synchronic transformation of difference (communication) nor for its diachronic transformation (change). Adequate principally in certain formal or static systems and for the energy–entity explanation of physical closed systems, it cannot account for non-lineal or non-causal theories of change, nor for the demonstrable teleonomy of the goalseeking system, which is 'moved' as much by what is not as by what is.

The entities called genes in bioenergetics, for instance, become "ques-tions about difference to which the answers are provided by their neighbor-hood" (Bateson) in cybernetic thinking.

The traditional epistemology is deeply rooted in our culture and in its economics. All remonstrations to the contrary notwithstanding, its adherents manifest the self-alienating and anti-contextual "nostalgia for

---

[22] This oscillation is very evident in Kierkegaard's 'existential' and individualistic opposition to the Hegelian philosophy of the mediation of oppositions, notably in his *Either/Or* (1843). The text is full of double binds, especially as regards S.K.'s inability to follow through with his engagement to the woman he loves: "A man's duty is to marry: Marry, and you will regret it; do not marry, and you will regret it." Later he cries: "Yea, either/or is the key to heaven, both–and is the way to hell." And in the *Journals*: "The idea of philosophy is mediation – Christianity's is the paradox" (1841). He is correct: in Christianity the Father is indeed identical to the Son, for the Creed knows nothing of logical typing.

thingness, for the constancy of stone" which Sartre analyzed in his *Anti-Semite and Jew* (1946): the same rock-like stability which Descartes tells us in the *Discours* he sought in order to establish his philosophy. It is a manifestation of the short-circuited dialectic of narcissism, identity, and identification that Lacan calls the Imaginary, the Manicheism of the 'clear and distinct'.

Even the conservative may understand the essence of the problem, whatever the solutions he considers may be. As Collingwood points out at the end of his *Idea of Nature* (1945):

> I conclude that natural science as a form of thought exists and has always existed in a context of history, and depends on historical thought for its existence. From this I venture to infer that no one can understand natural science unless he understands history: and that no one can answer what nature is unless he knows what history is.

If we ignore Dostoevsky's Russian chauvinism, the situation we are in is particularly well put in his reaction to French culture, as expressed in his *Winter Notes on Summer Impressions* (1863):

> It seems that one cannot create brotherhood, because it creates itself, comes of itself, is found in nature. But in French nature, in Western nature generally, it does not readily appear. Instead you find there a principle of individuality, a principle of isolation, intense self-preservation, of personal gain, self definition in terms of one's own *I*, in placing this *I* in opposition to all nature and all other people, as an autonomous, independent principle completely equal and equally valuable to everything that exists outside it.

The problem is that left, right, and center, we are all riddled with these Imaginary oppositions. They are in our bones, in the corporeality of our own body-images. But these images are not founded on psychological relations, however much they may draw on psychological structures. They are psychological and epistemological communications about the organization of real and material social relationships. In the proper ecosystemic sense of Marx's dictum that "circumstances make men just as much as men make circumstances", we know that the only possible transcendence of these static oppositions lies first and foremost in material, and not in psychological, changes. There can be no escape from digitalized Imaginary communication so long as our social relationships are based on accumulative and Imaginary forms of digital exchange (Chapter IX). There can be no escape from the paranoia of the either/or to the 'more or less' of the both–and relationships of the RATIONAL ecosystem, without the most fundamental changes in values we can conceive of – and perhaps changes even more fundamental than we can actually conceive.

In describing his 'naturalist' or 'anthropological' dialectical conception of history, Marx defined the basic tenets of the program which is necessary if we are to survive our own future. His 'materialism' is of a higher logical type than the traditional oppositions between 'idealism' and 'materialism', for Marx understands that 'information' controls organization, and that it cannot be separated from the matter–energy markers which bear it: Man's consciousness

> is not an original 'pure' consciousness. From the outset, 'spirit' is cursed with the 'burden' of matter, which appears in this case in the form of agitated layers of air, sounds, in short, of language. Language is as old as consciousness, language IS practical consciousness, as it exists for other men, and thus as it first really exists for myself as well. Language, like consciousness, only arises from the real need, the necessity of communication [*Verkehr*] with other men (Marx and Engels, 1845–6: 41–2).

Thus the Marxian conception of history denies all possibility of simple 'spiritual' liberation. This conception of history

> does not explain praxis from the idea but explains the formation of ideas from material praxis, and accordingly comes to the conclusion that all the forms of and products of consciousness can be dissolved, not by intellectual criticism, not by resolution into 'self-consciousness', or by transformation into 'apparitions', 'spectres', 'fancies', etc., but only by the practical overthrow of the actual social relations which gave rise to this idealist humbug; that not criticism but revolution is the driving force of history, as well as of religion, philosophy, and all other types of theory. . . . If the material elements of a total revolution – i.e., on the one hand the available productive forces, and on the other, the formation of a revolutionary mass, which revolts not only against particular conditions . . . but against the whole existing 'production of life' . . . – are not present, then it is quite immaterial . . . whether the IDEA of this revolution has been expressed a hundred times already. . . . (ibid.: 50–1).[23]

For whatever changes we envisage as necessary to halt the one-way accumulation of biosocial surplus value at compound interest, so long as the prevailing epistemology remains an accurate metaphor of "better dead than Red" or "better sick than Bolshevik", there's not much hope.

---

[23] Cf. also pp. 55–6 on pollution and on the necessity of technology for material liberation.

Chapter IX

Nature and Culture

THE EMERGENCE OF SYMBOLIC AND IMAGINARY EXCHANGE

En vérité, comprendre le sens
d'un terme, c'est toujours le
permuter dans tous ses contextes.
LEVI-STRAUSS on Propp's
Morphology of the Folktale

1. *Grammar and Gödel*

The general relationship between Lévi-Straussian anthropology, the Lacanian reading of Freud, and structural linguistics (principally Saussure, Troubetzkoy, Jakobson, implicitly mediated by Russian formalists like Propp), is well known. But the movement in France still called structuralism, for which Lévi-Strauss is principally responsible, has long since ceased to reflect much of a direct link to structural linguistics, which in any case is under heavy attack. In structuralist literary criticism, for instance, with all its somewhat pretentious claims to becoming a science of literature, we find writers either rehabilitating well-established literary positions, or bringing well-known American critical positions into the French corpus, or redoing Vladimir Propp's *Morphology of the Folktale* without paying much attention to Lévi-Strauss's refutation of its formalist, context-independent presuppositions (Lévi-Strauss, 1960a). Fortunately, just as Marx was never a Marxist, Lévi-Strauss has never entirely been a structuralist.

From the work of Chomsky and the reworking of Chomsky by his students (e.g., George Lakoff) it seems probable that structural linguistics has already made most of the significant contributions it will ever make to linguistics proper. And although Chomsky himself seems to commit the same epistemological error as many structuralists, that of trying to separate the subsystems of a coherent whole from each other (separating syntax from semantics, for example), his refutation of the strictly structural position seems to have held good (Chomsky, 1957). Significantly enough, this refutation goes hand in hand with his refutation of the position that natural language can be generated by a finite-state grammar (a Markov process). The theory of grammar as a Markov process is derived from the early development of stochastic theory in information science. Information theory as such, like structural linguistics proper, separates syntax (information) from semantics (meaning) as well as similarly separating language from discourse. The question of the artificial or methodological closure of one part of a coherent system and that of the application of probabilistic analysis to such partial systems is worth dwelling on here.

A stochastic process refers to the lawfulness inherent in any sequence of symbols or events. Those in which the probabilities are fixed and independent of the process itself (such as those involved in considering the letters of an English sentence according to their statistically determined frequency of individual occurrence) are described as zero-memory stochastic sources. Meaningful patterns in the sequence are random and accidental; the system exhibits a high degree of information ('surprise') per symbol and a low or zero redundancy. Those in which the probabilities of the symbols (words, events, letters, etc.) are a function of the symbols previously produced (i.e., a function of context or of the previous states of the system) are called Markov chains.

Both types exhibit redundancy or constraint, terms which are synonymous with pattern and organization in information theory. (The higher redundancy of the Markov process should perhaps be called second-order redundancy, however, since it is supplemental to the redundancy applicable to the frequency of occurrence of its independent symbols. Significantly, second-order redundancy results in a lower information content per symbol and a greater possibility of 'meaning'). The opposite of redundancy is either randomness, where any combination or event is assumed to be unconditioned and equiprobable, or strict determinism, where some combination or event is assumed to have a probability of one. Some Markov processes (e.g., the emission of linguistic messages considered statistically) are further described as 'ergodic': if observed long enough, they will emit sequences 'typical' of the ensemble or repertoire from which they are chosen.

But it is important to realize that although samples of language (*la langue*) can be viewed statistically as a Markov process, the methodological assumptions of such an approach mean that there are no actual senders or receivers involved (whatever ontological status we assign to them in any given context), no referents to be analyzed or acted upon, no context for the sequence of signifiers, no (diachronic) goals for the system outside the manifestation of its own systemic character, no 'work' to be done (MacKay, 1969: 79–93, 95–6). Thus the *langue* of the Markovian analysis is not to be confused with the discourse or the *parole* of the subject, as it seems in fact to be by some contemporary structuralists. The significant point in this context is that whatever the value of the structural method, as method, in linguistics, the methodology of 'structuralism' as such is epistemologically comparable to that of quantitative information theory.

Recent linguistic research, however, seems to show that semantic considerations have repercussions on syntax at deep levels of the utterance (Chomsky also now recognizes this), which makes the isolation of any level of the linguistic system and/or structure methodologically inadequate. Although major aspects of Chomsky's version of transformational grammar are now being revised by both him and his students, he did show that the Markov process is inapplicable to the grammar of natural language. A Markov process (a finite state grammar) will, if it includes recursive loops, produce an infinite number of sentences. But it will either produce ALL English sentences and many non-sentences as well (like the famous monkey and the typewriter), or it will produce ONLY English sentences while not producing an infinite number of other possible English sentences (Chomsky, 1957: 21–5).

In describing the relationship between grammar and language, we can probably say that there is a hierarchy of sets ('languages') and a hierarchy of corresponding algorithms (sets of instructions, grammars). If the grammar and the language are not to be indentical, a valid grammar must enumerate every possible sentence and no non-sentence, and it must also provide a description of the structure and system under consideration. Postal has shown in his "Limitations of Phrase Structure Grammars" (Fodor and Katz, 1964: 137–51) that the equivalent of the algorithm for a higher set, a context-free grammar, is no less inadequate than the Markov process. Natural language is thus at least of a higher logical type than whatever is produced by such a context-free grammar. But there are sets of a yet higher type, such as the set of the theorems of arithmetic or the set of the algorithms under discussion, for which a corresponding algorithm is logically impossible. Thus no material embodiment of the grammar of such a set, no 'machine' – except a human being – can produce those sets. It has not so far been proved that language is not such a set (Fauconnier, 1971). Thus, before we are ready to make any statements about 'structural', 'linguistic', or 'informational' analysis, we must be aware that all analyses, since they depend on boundaries and on closure, are subject to Gödel's proof, or to what I call the digital paradox (Chapters V, VII).

2. *Information, Meaning, and Redundancy*

It is important to distinguish information and meaning. The 'information' of information theory is simply a quantitative measure of improbability, pattern, complexity, or organization. Strictly speaking it is a measure of the degree of (semiotic) freedom, in a given situation, to choose among the available signals, symbols, messages, or patterns to be transmitted (the repertoire), many of which may be entirely devoid of meaning. The smaller the freedom of choice from the given repertoire, the lower the possible information. If all the letters in the English alphabet had an equiprobable frequency of occurrence, the information content of each letter taken singly would be about five 'bits'; on the basis of the probabilities of individual letter frequencies, the content is about four. When the redundancy, patterning, or constraint induced by the grouping of letters, words, and ideas is taken into account, the quantity of information per letter drops to less than two bits.

In the technical sense 'information' is unconcerned with the status of the sender and the receiver. They are no more than heuristic devices, the TERMINALS in a message circuit, and thus involve the arbitrary punctuation of what is in fact a circular process. Whether sender and receiver are actually capable of using language semantically is irrelevant to the measure of information.

Meaning, or more accurately here, signification, can be defined (tautologously) as the significance of the information to the system processing it. The more any given repertoire is analyzed atomistically, and non-contextually, the more information, and the less signification, the repertoire has. Individual letters in linguistic messages carry high information content, for instance, but practically no signification, for signification, like meaning, depends upon context, and the more context there is, the more there is redundancy (low information content) in the use of the repertoire.

As MacKay explains in detail in the passage quoted below, any system emitting, receiving, or processing information uses the information to organize and direct the energy necessary for 'work' to be done by, within, or outside the system (which may be a human being, a machine, a cell, and so on). Thus whereas information is a necessary condition for signification, it is not a sufficient one. The important similarities between information and signification lie in the processes involved: both depend upon coding and decoding, and both depend upon the selection of sequences out of a field of possible sequences. (Cf. Crosson and Sayre, 1967: 3–33, 99–136.)

It is in the sense of power or control over ORGANIZATION that 'information' is legitimately used in the Aristotelian sense of *informare*, for Aristotle distinguishes between form (information) and matter(-energy). The related concept of redundancy is defined by Weaver as "the fraction of the structure of the message which is determined not by the free choice of the sender, but rather by the accepted statistical rules governing the use of the symbols [the repertoire] in question" (1949: 13). Redundancy is therefore a function of syntax.

Technically only in a noiseless channel is it possible to eliminate redundancy in transmission. Otherwise every single error in a given message would change the message into another one. But there is a difference between what we might call the statistical redundancy in the use of the repertoire and the higher-order 'existential' redundancy of human communication. Viewed as an ergodic stochastic process of the Markov type, language is highly constrained by statistical rules which make English from 60 per cent to 80 per cent redundant (depending upon the method of determination used). But the precise redundancy is probably not actually determinable because of the higher-order subjective redundancies involved. To a student of Shakespeare, a message beginning "To be or . . ." involves a repertoire which, however meaningful, is completely redundant (or completely determined, which is the same thing here). There is a difference, which is difficult to characterize precisely, between the *a priori* statistical constraints on a message and the *a posteriori* possibilities of restoring a whole when some of its parts have been lost (which is the usual test for redundancy). Without a high degree of 'existential' redundancy – the constraints of the specific code of communication, codes of behavior, particular lexicons, contexts, intentions, the actual relationship between the sender and the receiver, and so on – there is no signification. Signification must involve shared information; the more sharing, the more redundancy.

I have defined the relationship between QUALITATIVE information (as opposed to Shannon's measurements of the 'amount-of-information') and meaning as essentially PRAGMATIC. The distinction between meaning and signification has been elaborated in Chapter VII. In all communications systems (ecosystems), all information is susceptible to both meaning and signification because it is transmitted by real material senders and receivers, necessarily and essentially linked by the message-in-circuit. Thus one can say that semantics is a subset of pragmatics. Syntactics is simply a measure of the relative semiotic freedom (redundancy) of the

system. We must conclude, therefore, that ALL KNOWLEDGE IS INSTRU-
MENTAL. As Spencer Brown puts it (1969: 1), there can be no distinction
without MOTIVE and the discrimination of differing values.

The preceding definition summarizes that of MacKay, whose 'semantics of the organism' (where 'meaning' covers both meaning and signification, depending on the context) is worth quoting in full (1969: 95–6):

> An organism can be regarded for our purpose as a system with a certain
> repertoire of basic acts (both internal and external) that in various
> combinations and sequences make up its behaviour. In order that its
> behaviour should be adaptive to its environment ["the total world of
> activity of the organism"], the selective process by which basic acts are
> concatenated requires to be ORGANIZED according to the current state of
> the environment in relation to the organism. There are various ways of
> picturing this need. In its most basic terms, we may regard what is
> required as equivalent to a vast constantly changing matrix of CONDI-
> TIONAL PROBABILITIES (the C.P.M.), determining the relative probabili-
> ties of various patterns (and patterns of patterns) of behaviour in all
> possible circumstances. More economically, we can think of it as the
> setting-up of a hierarchic structure of organizing 'sub-routines' to de-
> termine these conditional probabilities, interlocked in such a way as to
> represent implicitly the structure of the environment (the world of
> activity) with which the organism must interact. For many purposes we
> may reduce it to the filling-out of a world-map, ready to be consulted
> according to current needs and goals.
>
> Whatever our thought-model, it is clear that unless the organism
> happens to be organized exactly to match the current state of affairs,
> WORK must be done to bring it up to date: work not only in a physical,
> but in a LOGICAL sense. This 'logical work' consists in the adjusting and
> moulding of the conditional-probability structure of the organizing
> system: the formation, strengthening or dissolution of functional link-
> ages between various basic acts or basic sequences of acts. The total
> configuration of these linkages embodies what we may call the total
> 'state of readiness' of the organism. Some of them will of course have
> purely vegetative functions that do not concern us. What does interest
> us is the total configuration that keeps the organism matched to its field
> of purposive activity, and so implicitly represents (whether correctly or
> not) the features of that field. For brevity, let us call this the ORIENTING
> system, and the corresponding total state of readiness the ORIENTATION
> of the organism.
>
> INFORMATION can now be defined as that which does logical work on the

organism's orientation (whether correctly or not, and whether by adding to, replacing or confirming the functional linkages of the orienting system). Thus we leave open the question whether the information is true or false, fresh, corrective or confirmatory, and so on.

The AMOUNT OF INFORMATION received by an organism can then be measured (in various ways) by measuring if we can (in various ways) the logical (organizing) work that it does for the organism. I have discussed elsewhere some of the different measures that suggest themselves for different purposes, and we shall return briefly to the question later. Meanwhile it is sufficient to note that they are necessarily RELATIVE measures, since they measure the impact of information on the given receiver. 'Amount of information' measures not a 'stuff' but a relation. The MEANING of an indicative item of information to the organism may now be defined as its selective function on the range of the organism's possible states of orientation, or, for short, its ORGANIZING FUNCTION for the organism. It will be noted that this too is a relation. (It must be clearly distinguished from the ORGANIZING WORK DONE on the organism, which is THE RESULT OF THE EXERCISE of this organizing function. Much confusion is caused by attempts to identify meaning with the change produced in the receiver.)

The central question in the semantics of organisms is thus that of goal-seeking. And since goalseeking is not confined to linguistic behavior, but is a property of all open systems – and indeed defines the function of their information processes – we shall have to be very careful about accepting any theory of social systems which is derived solely from properties specific to language alone. A society may depend upon codes and messages, upon metaphor and metonymy, or difference and opposition, but so does DNA, and DNA is not a language.

3. *Structure and Infrastructure: The Question of the Unconscious*

Since all structural, cybernetic, and systemic theories depend on some conception of an 'infrastructure' or 'primary system' or 'primary process', it is necessary to say something about the 'unconscious'. This ambiguous word is often used as a synonym for the primary process, at least in psycho-analysis and in anthropology. Obviously our neural and humoral information processes are unconscious, obviously the code (or rules) from and through which we choose linguistic messages is unconscious, as is most of the 'body language' we use at every moment of our life. Our theory of knowledge is unconscious, the processes of memory retrieval are unconscious, our habits are unconscious, our ideology is unconscious, our economic, psychological, and academic self-interest is unconscious, our choice of survival value is unconscious, our phantasies are unconscious, our relationships are mostly unconsciously (over)determined, and so on.

What this list illustrates is the wholly unscientific way in which the word unconscious, at least in the psychological sense, is generally used. Without going into the details of the redefinitions which are obviously necessary (since I shall generally use the term primary process), it is clear that if the term refers to a supposedly Freudian category, it usually involves a gratuitous confusion between what might be called the *Ur-Unbewusste* (the domain of the primal repression), the dynamic view of the unconscious (for which the unconscious is the repressed), the preconscious (the domain of memory and language), the primary process, and what is simply NON-CONSCIOUS. Hidden within these confusions are all sorts of other confusions, including that which equates consciousness with knowledge (rather than with recognition), that which equates conscious with the spoken word, and that which identifies the unconscious with the latent or with the so-called instincts (the id). We hear of the 'Kantian unconscious' in Lévi-Strauss, for instance, which was not what Freud discovered, but which is clearly what Freud was trying to talk about in positing a level of the unconscious which was never conscious in any sense (the primal repression). Or the Lévi-Straussian conception of the unconscious is suggested to be a 'principle of intelligibility', which it certainly is. But, whether we take it from the point of view that without the Freudian unconscious there could be no intelligibility (no human language) or from the point of view that Lévi-Strauss is talking about principles of organization in systems and that all such principles or rules are necessarily and by definition non-conscious, this is not an explanation but a tautology.

The answer to this problem of the unconscious, the preconscious, and the non-conscious, is, I think, a very simple one, and Lévi-Strauss pointed most clearly to it in 1949 in his "L'Efficacité symbolique" (Lévi-Strauss, 1958). (This is translated as "The Effectiveness of Symbols", a rendering which effectively reduces the dynamic processes of the Symbolic order to the atomistic interpretation of the symbol which has so long obscured the interpretation of Freud. Cf. Wilden, 1968a: 249-51.)

In this article Lévi-Strauss equates the unconscious with what he calls the "symbolic function", a universal set of laws which organizes the personal lexicon available to the individual and "thus makes of [this lexicon] a DISCOURSE". (The English version mistranslates *discours* by 'language'. Note that a discourse has a subject – a relation between a sender and a receiver – whereas a language does not.) In other words, the unconscious is described as a set of rules, and we remember that for Freud the dream, the symptom, the slip of the tongue or pen, and the joke are not the unconscious, but the "royal road" to it. Indeed, the dream is generated not 'in' the unconscious, but by the "regression" of word-presentations THROUGH the unconscious to perception (thing-presentations). In the process, the rules of condensation and displacement distort (*entstellen*) the message (Chapter II).

It is a matter of simple logic to recognize that a rule is of a higher logical type than what it governs. The manifestation of the rule in the phenomenal lexicon of the individual or the social system is thus a commentary on a text; it is a communication about the communication expressed in the rule (a metacommunication) and vice versa, depending on how we choose to define the problem. It is only through an understanding of logical types in communication that we can escape the gross reification of the unconscious by the analytic or bioenergetic epistemology, which mistakenly sets 'unconscious' in opposition to 'consciousness'. Any highly abstract and deeply programmed process is necessarily of a higher logical type than less abstract and more manifest processes. Thus consciousness is of a lower logical type than the unconscious (the symbolic function), and the nonconscious patterns and rules of organization in the brain are of a higher logical type than either the primary process or the secondary process. The natural ecosystem is of an even higher logical type. We can put this another way: the epistemology of a culture or the ideology of a class are necessarily of a higher logical type than their manifestation in any particular 'individual' of that culture or class. Thus the only way in which to understand the processes evident in the collective behavior of those 'individuals' – beyond the level of their Imaginary identification with themselves as skin-bound organisms, of course, they are not individuals in the bourgeois sense – is to seek to formulate the logical typing of the various levels of rules (levels of organization) which created them as 'individuals'. In other words, we must look for the abstract structural frameworks and systemic processes, the codes and constraints, which allow only certain messages to be transmitted in the system. The mistake of all atomistic or organicist anthropology and psychology, and the specious barrier separating dialectical thinkers like Hegel or Marx, and, in some senses, Freud and Lévi-Strauss, from their analytically oriented commentators, is simply that, over and over again, the message is taken as the code. The logical typing of code and message is confused, and the relationship between them is reified

To summarize this point: since the code of the class of 'what is secondary system' is a subset member of the class of 'ruled by primary system', and since both are members of the class 'ruled by the non-conscious', every 'conscious' manifestation, every 'phenomenon', must be dealt with both in terms of its own level of logical typing and in terms of the higher synchronic levels of logical typing which make it possible. The relationship between higher levels of organization and higher levels of logical typing is inverse: the higher the logical type, the lower the level of organization (complexity). Similarly, the lower the level of organization, the more preponderance structure has over system; and the higher the level of organization, the more 'semiotic freedom' in terms of 'characteristic response' the system under consideration may be assumed to have (Chapters VII, XII).

4. *Lévi-Strauss and Systems Theory*

I have never been personally convinced of the methodological adequacy of what might be called the strictly structural approach in either anthropology or psychoanalysis. In fact the current repetition of the word 'structure' all over the place, like a *cheville* in an Alexandrine, begins to sound rather silly. One is led to ask what has happened to the 'system' and why we do not seem to want to deal with the fact that a structure is either a static framework which is predominant at low levels of organization (whereas at all higher levels, system is predominant) or it refers simply to the given code of a system and not to its evolutionary capacities. The term structure is in fact only employed by Lévi-Strauss at the moment that he is going beyond it. The concept of symbolic exchange, for example, which is central to this paper, cannot be properly called simply structural, for it is an attribute of system, a process. The elementary structures of kinship are not so much structure as they are the components of processes of exchange. It is not the structure *per se* that we are interested in, but the code, i.e., the rules which govern the possible selection of messages from the repertoire of 'symbols' available, and the metarules that govern the selection of metacodes.

There are a number of mistaken analogies in the work of Lévi-Strauss, but I do not intend to dwell very much on those problems here. The analogy drawn between language, social systems, and game theory is one of the most significant (one finds it also in the linguist Hjelmslev), for it indicates the same preference for the static and homeostatic rather than for the dynamic and morphogenic that one finds in early structural linguistics and early information theory. The fact that the game theorists state that their theory does not apply to overdetermined open systems is ignored (A. Rapoport, 1959). As pointed out by Dreyfus (1965), a similar epistemological error appears in the overweening claims of the workers in the domain of artificial intelligence, who assume associationist, discrete-step, heuristic qualities to be characteristic of the actual processes of decision in human beings (rather than of their simulation), and subsequently design programs in which the non-heuristic decisions are surreptitiously fitted into the program by the analog complement of the digital machine, the human programmer.

It is perfectly clear that the structuralist movement in France is not 'another opinion', but an aspect of and a contribution to a much wider reorganization of epistemology and methodology in the philosophy of science. Lévi-Strauss said as much in 1945, in his remarks about Troubetzkoy's work in phonology in the 1930s, and the text he quotes does not depend for its basis on anything specific to linguistics:

> First structural linguistics shifts from the study of CONSCIOUS linguistic phenomena to study of their UNCONSCIOUS infrastructure; second, it does not treat TERMS as independent entities, taking instead as its basis of analysis the [synchronic] RELATIONS between terms; third it introduces the concept of SYSTEM; . . . finally, structural linguistics aims at discovering GENERAL LAWS, either by induction "or . . . by logical deduction, which would give them an absolute character". . . . The evolution of a phonemic system at any given moment is directed by the TENDENCY TOWARD A GOAL. . . . This evolution thus has a direction, an internal logic, which historical [diachronic] phonemics is called upon to elucidate (Lévi-Strauss, 1958b: 31, 32).

Taken with the critique of "individualistic and atomistic interpretation" which follows the passages quoted, it is clear that not one of the criteria cited is specific to structural linguistics, nor is any one of them specifically derivable from linguistics as such. The criteria in fact describe the main aspects of the twentieth-century emergence of an epistemological change which is so profound, so widespread, and so important as perhaps to deserve the label 'revolution'.

Lancelot Law Whyte has given us an overview of the culmination of this long process of changing emphasis, in a book which, although it misconstrues entirely the actual novelty of the Freudian discovery, nevertheless provides a most useful epistemological analysis of the changes in the philosophy of science (1962: 177):

> This [new universe] is a universe of contrasts, grouped into complexes of relations, with aspects of order and disorder, including change and tendency. . . .
>
> The stress is on complex systems of changing relations displaying

tendencies towards order and disorder, not on simple unchanging entities. For intellectual convenience, it may be necessary to infer an invisible world of immutables: of gods never directly known, or of one or more classes of persisting atomic particles, to account for the stability of the world of appearances.

Some of these inferred 'atomic particles' may well be the 'invariant laws of relation' of 'structuralism', beyond which systems, cybernetic, and communications theory are now taking us.

It would undoubtedly be interesting to dwell upon the specific contributions of all the various disciplines – from physics, mathematics, and logic, to gestaltism, dialectics, automata theory, information theory, and especially biology – which have been part of this epistemological change. But this is a task of historical analysis for another time and place. All that needs to be said is that the criteria 'unconscious infrastructure', 'relations', 'systems', and 'tendency towards a goal' might have as easily come out of a work on cybernetic theory, communications theory, or general systems theory as out of a revolutionary new approach to phonology. We could trace these criteria to Saussure if we wished, but why not to Freud, to Hegel, to Marx, to Clerk Maxwell, to von Bertalanffy, or to Szilard's solution of the problem of the Maxwell Demon in 1929? Obviously, in such a complex epistemological reorganization as we are experiencing in this century, the new territory staked out by any one discipline, science, or movement cannot be comprehended except in relation to all the others.

The direction taken by the explanatory principles of this radical change in the theory of knowledge can be characterized in a number of different but related ways: from stasis to process, from entity to relationship, from atom to gestalt, from aggregate to whole, from heap to structure, from part to system, from analytics to dialectics, from closed systems to open systems, from causality to constraint, from energy to information, from bioenergetics to communication, from equilibrium theory to negative entropy – in a word, from atom to system and thence to ecosystem.

5. *The Symbolic Function*

> The enigma of the prohibition of
> incest is that it is an answer for
> which there is no question.
> LÉVI-STRAUSS: *Discours*
> *Inaugural*

What follows is not strictly speaking an analysis of the concept of the symbolic function in Lévi-Strauss, but an introduction to its interpretation in the light of Bateson's 'unit of mind' (Bateson, 1970, 1971a), as well as Lacan's conception of the difference between the Symbolic and the Imaginary (Lacan, 1966; Maud Mannoni, 1967), and the ecosystemic notion that the function of analog communication concerns the long-range survival of the whole (Chapters VII, VIII).

The conception of the symbolic function in Lévi-Strauss involves certain major epistemological criteria:

1 It involves a conception of the unconscious as a 'universe of rules' which are empty of content. These rules are assumed to be similar in some way to those which govern language. (Such a viewpoint destroys the notion of an atomistic unconscious and also liberates us from the Jungian archetypes.)

2 It includes a notion of 'system' as a goalseeking unit or ensemble, a conception which parallels that of cybernetics. (Lévi-Strauss has been influenced by cybernetic theory, partly through the Prague School of linguistics.)

3 It also involves a concept of structure which is not a phenomenal given. Structure is the ensemble of laws which govern the behavior of the system. The components thus constrained are to a large degree interchangeable with each other, and do not necessarily derive from the same level of organization as the structure and the system which control or permit their various combinations. Structure and system, in this sense, belong therefore to the domain of INFORMATION, and not to that of the FRAMEWORK of organization, i.e., matter–energy.

4 Lévi-Strauss makes the methodological assumption that what he calls 'symbolic thought' emerged out of the continuum of natural analog relationships, thus constituting a system of communication based on the DISCRETE COMPONENT in the macroscopic domain of communication between human beings.

5 The combinations of the various discrete components are assumed to be of an essentially LOGICAL or LINGUISTIC nature, whether the components are the 'signs' of kinship names or the 'mythemes' of the myth. Lévi-Strauss relates or identifies this process with the phonological laws which turn the 'differential elements', derived from the acoustic continuum, into the so-called 'binary oppositions'.

6 The emphasis is on organization and relationship as such.

7 He further insists on the "total social fact", that is to say, on the context of all communication (cf. in particular his critique of Vladimir Propp in "La Structure et la forme", 1960a).

8 Structure, system, law, organization, and unconscious are intimately

interconnected for him: consciousness does not direct the behavior of the system, nor does consciousness know the structure of the system, unless analysis intervenes.

For Lévi-Strauss, the symbolic function and its expression in the structures of kinship is in some way related to the 'unconscious' structure of the human 'mind' (Simonis, 1968: 169 ff.). It is never entirely clear what he means either by 'unconscious' or by 'mind'. But by using Bateson's conception of the ecosystem as a unit of mind – a set of messages in circuit which maintain the relationship between 'organism' and 'environment' – I think we can cut this Gordian knot. The brain exists as an open system in an essential relationship to the complex 'environment' on which it depends. But in relation to the mind – which is a SOCIAL and not a biological or psychological category – the brain is an entity, whereas the mind is PURE relation. The problem of the relationship between brain and mind is of the same sort as that involved when Lévi-Strauss reduces the woman to a sign (thus confusing female, woman, and sister; confusing energy and information; organism, person, and role; entity and relationship) in the *Elementary Structures of Kinship* (1947), of which more later. But as soon as we conceive of 'mind' as an ecosystemic relationship of communication which involves levels of complexity, we no longer have to worry about where the symbolic function is or ought to be. Since information, minds, subjects, and symbolic functions are relationships, they are nowhere. Nowhere, that is, except in the communication of the message-in-circuit which defines the unit of mind.

There is a reason for Lévi-Strauss's problem with modeling the symbolic function, or the myth, or the kinship system, and for his tendency to locate the source of the model in the brain. For Lévi-Strauss, 'model' seems to mean explicitly only two things: the mechanical model and the statistical model (cf. Simonis, 1968: 172–6). The mechanical and statistical models as such are not in question here, only their application. Both are derived from the closed-system epistemology of classical physics. In physics in general, there is no mediating principle between two types of explanation. One can choose between the precision of ORGANIZED SIMPLICITY (mechanics) and the statistical precision of the study of UNORGANIZED COMPLEXITY (e.g., modern thermodynamics), but classical physics lacks an epistemology and a methodology to deal with ORGANIZED COMPLEXITY. This is the domain of biology, communication, and the human sciences (and possibly that of subatomic physics).

In the study of organized simplicity or of unorganized complexity, the elements (or the statistical aggregation of the elements) are naturally privileged, for this is an atomistic position. But for organized complexity, the structure or the system as such must be primary. The relations in fact constitute the entities. If the world of physics is conceived of as an aggregate of HOMOGENEOUS elements whose sum equals the whole, the world of the more or less open system is to be thought of as a set of combinations which create HETEROGENEOUS elements (Elsasser, 1966). Not only does the question of organization thus become important, therefore, but also that of properly founding the methodological assumption of the homogeneity of the heterogeneous component of (more or less) open systems (the homogeneity which statistics assumes, for example). It is in effect this question which Lévi-Strauss seeks to answer in introducing his conception of system and structure. For, if it is impossible in the study of open systems to guarantee that the observation of the element or of the component isolated from its context (as in mechanics) will yield scientific, repeatable results, then homogeneity must be sought elsewhere: that is to say, in the RELATIONS between components. And in so far as all contextual feedback relationships in open systems defy 'objective' punctuation (Chapter V), one will not waste one's time searching for a positivistic ORIGIN for the system. (As Korzybski's 'structural differential' puts it, we can only know the differences between 'facts', not the 'facts' themselves.)

Thus, although Lévi-Strauss's actual statements about physics (e.g., 1960b: 14), about models, and about the localization of the embodied algorithm often leave much to be desired, his theory itself, like Freud's, is not bound so much by what he thinks he is doing, as by what he does. When he defines the requirements of a structural viewpoint as assuming (1) a system regulated by internal cohesion, (2) the impossibility of understanding this coherence by studying the isolated system, and (3) the necessity of studying transformations which reveal similar properties in systems which are apparently different (ibid.), he is talking about something quite different from a mechanical, statistical, or thermodynamic system as such. Whether or not biological and human systems may be amenable to explanation through some (as yet unknown) form of quantum theory, until such a theory is developed, we are at liberty to pursue the problem of organized complexity in whatever seems to be the most fruitful way. And there is nothing in Lévi-Strauss which compels us to accept his explicit morphostatic prejudices.

The consequence of the relevance or irrelevance of 'origins' is that we must provisionally pursue our researches by accepting the solution offered by the 'myth of the original Event' (cf. Chapter XIII) in the so-called primitive culture. Thus Lévi-Strauss assumes that, like language, kinship, and culture – and at the same moment – the symbolic function is constituted "in one fell swoop". This somewhat cavalier assumption not only saves us a great deal of time we might spend in trying to answer the wrong set of questions, but it is the epistemological and methodological requirement of any systemic theory, as von Bertalanffy (1968: 55) pointed out in 1945: "While we can conceive of a sum [or aggregate] as being composed gradually, a system as a total of parts with its [multiplicative] interrelations has to be conceived of as being composed instantly." This assumption in no way denies or invalidates such speculations on origins as those of Hockett and Ascher (1964), which do not in any case contradict the Lévi-Straussian position. What it does is to allow us to seek out the PRINCIPLES which differentiate nature from culture – rather than remaining caught up in questions of content – and to try to relate them to all the other observable differences between animal communication and exchange and human communication and exchange.

As is well known, Lévi-Strauss bases the distinction between nature and culture on the emergence of the prohibition of incest. I think we can make this an even more general principle, and say that the distinction depends on the emergence of the socioeconomic organization of digital communication and exchange.

6. *Nature and Culture: Anthropology*

The passage from nature to culture as posited by Lévi-Strauss, depends upon two simple principles: (*a*) the introduction of what can be called the 'law of the distinction of difference': the prohibition of incest, and (*b*) the correlative introduction of the discrete, discontinuous, combinatory component into the non-discrete continuum of nature. We have a Bororo myth interpreted by Lévi-Strauss which explains this introduction of the discrete component, the passage of the continuous world of difference into the discontinuous world of distinction and opposition. After a flood, the earth became so full of people that the sun decided to reduce their number. All perished by drowning in a river at his command, except Akaruio Bokodori (who, like Oedipus, limps). Those who were lost in the rapids had wavy hair; those who were lost in the pools had straight hair. Akaruio Bokodori then brought them all back to life, but accepted only those clans whose presents he liked. All the others he killed with arrows. Lévi-Strauss comments:

> It was necessary that men should become less numerous so that neighboring physical types could be clearly discerned. For if the existence of clans and peoples bearing INSIGNIFICANT or NON-SIGNIFYING gifts were

permitted – that is to say, clans whose distinctive originality was as minimal as one could imagine – then there would be a risk that between two given clans or populations there might be interpolated an unlimited number of other clans or peoples which would differ so little from their immediate neighbours that all would end up by being confounded together. Now, in any domain whatsoever, it is only with the introduction of the discrete quantity that a system of significations can be constructed.

(I shall not argue about the word "quantity" here, but read "component".) He goes on to point out that a system made discrete by the subtraction of elements, as in this and other myths, becomes logically richer, even if numerically poorer (1964: 58–63). The point is, of course, that only systems of discrete components are available to COMBINATION and permutation, that is to say, only such systems can properly be said to have anything equivalent to SYNTAX.

The prohibition of incest is to be explained on exactly the same basis. Whatever is assumed to precede the 'magic moment' of the constitution of this primordial law – and with it, language and society – it must presumably resemble what we now find in the animal world. In labeling the natural prerequisite of society an 'ensemble of procreative units',[1] we note that the procreative unit involves exchange processes, communication, and goalseeking. But these macroscopic processes do not involve discrete components beyond the level of the 'skin-bound organism'. These natural 'components' do indeed enter into combinations with each other, but these are combinations of natural differences (e.g., biological sexuality) in which the information (male, female) is not distinct from its organic marker. The relationship between 'organism' and 'environment' – i.e., between the biological 'individual' and that to which he is related, includ-

---

[1] This is often called the nuclear family in anthropology. But this is a notion dependent on an atomistic epistemology which assumes what is to be proved, for it denies what is prerequisite to the emergence of the family as a boundary. It denies the relations within the supersystem of the society which actually generate the family. To make the individual or the individual unit the prerequisite of the system is to constitute the system as an aggregate, or in other words to conceive society on the equivalent of equilibrium models derived from classical physics. The relationships between the 'individuals' of a goalseeking adaptive system are not additive, but multiplicative and fractionative. These relationships are not primarily energy links, but information links. To assume the existence of the 'family' before the existence of the 'society' of which it is a subset, requires an epistemological position derived from, or seeking to justify, a belief in a bioenergetic 'human nature'. One notes that in western culture the nuclear family is indeed the significant unit, since it appears to be the socioeconomic unit of consumption and control.

ing other 'individuals' – has been defined as a relationship of difference (Chapter VIII). The most that can be said of the relation between the sexes or between parents and offspring in the animal world is that their biological 'distinctions' and their temporary competitive 'oppositions' are subsumed under the relation of difference, in such a way that a male is simply a male, a female simply a female, a primate is a primate, and so on.

There is nothing in the macroscopic exchange processes of zoosemiotics which goes beyond the kind of boundaries established by the 'skin', by the 'ecological niche', or by the 'territory'. There are no possibilities of the purely informational or logical combinations of discrete components, dependent on the relationships of logical distinction, opposition, and identity, such as we find in phonology, in kinship systems, in language, and in culture. Although all exchange and communicational processes depend on forms of digital communication, digitalization never represents the primary form or the goal of any natural system. In nature, the analog communication of differences is always of a higher logical type than the digital communication of discrete elements. But this is not precisely the distinction we require here. The distinction between differences in the procreative unit and discrete elements in the family is only true in terms of the RELATIONSHIP between nature and culture, or between animal communication and language, or between use value in nature and exchange value in culture. As long as we remember that distinction and opposition are relational, rather than ontological, categories – except in cultures like our own which confuse the categories of the logical and the ontological (or the 'ontic') – we have no difficulty in dealing with the 'distinctions' and 'oppositions' in the animal world.

It is analog difference which allows the informational relationships between sender and receiver in the natural ecosystem to be constituted, for information is in fact simply transmitted difference. It is the information-in-circuit which ignores the skin-bound 'barriers' between organisms and between 'organism' and 'environment'. Although, as Saussure pointed out, difference is a necessary condition for human language, it is not a sufficient one, nor is difference sufficient to constitute a kinship system. As in the Bororo myth and its interpretation by Lévi-Strauss, a system of signs available to signification depends upon the reduction of the number of elements, the introduction of distinct 'gaps' between them, and the resulting possibility of a very high number of combinations. In other words, the members of the procreative unit have to become LOGICALLY distinct from each other in order for them to become signs (and linguistic signifiers require even more complex levels of distinction, for language is more highly organized – and of a different logical type – than a kinship system).

This is quite apart from the obvious fact that in order to know whom to marry and whom not to marry, you obviously need a nomenclature and a word for 'not'.

Thus the exchange relationships of the family depend upon its constitution as part of a larger whole, the society, and it is usually someone fulfilling the function of the maternal uncle who supplies the necessary CONTACT WITH THE EXTERIOR which provides for the advent of the family in the first place.[2] This contact changes the relationships within the family by introducing, not the differential element (which was already there) but the DISTINCTIVE FEATURE, which is a special sort of bundle of differential elements. And one of the changes within the family, after the event,[3] is that the INDIVIDUAL is retrospectively invented. When female becomes 'sister' or male becomes 'brother', we have in effect a difference which is constituted at a higher level of organization, in other words, a distinction. What is especially significant is that the sign 'sister' or 'brother' not only signifies what it is (a female, a male), but more important, IT SIGNIFIES SOMETHING IT IS NOT (a potential sexual partner or spouse). It would be a mistake in levels of organization to equate this sign with a linguistic signifier (a word always signifies what it is not), or to play the facile game of equating 'not' with absence, but the significance of 'something which stands for something it is and is not' is crucial to the understanding of (how we define) the emergence of culture from nature (and their coexistence).

Above all, the 'sister' or 'brother' who marry someone from another family do not receive a sister or a brother, they receive a man or a woman, a husband or a wife. The sister or brother who are apparently exchanged in the kinship system are never in fact exchanged, for at the moment of exchange they enter a new set of relationships and acquire another designation ('wife', 'partner', 'husband'). (Cf. Lévi-Strauss, 1947: 243.)

This is perfectly logical, for if we are concerned to talk about the FUNCTION of the exchange, it is its symbolic rather than its real function that is important. Procreation can continue in nature without the necessity for the symbolic form of digital exchange. There is no biological reason for the incest prohibition, in fact it is rather the opposite. As Dobzhansky, for

---

[2] As Lévi-Strauss properly points out, the maternal uncle is not an 'invention' or an 'addition' to the 'family', he IS the family. (Cf. Ortigues, 1966: 72, 81–2; or Wilden, 1968a: 303–6.)

[3] Any emergence of a metasystem changes the logical typing of the antecedent subsystems in the referent system. See Chapter XII, Section 9, and Chapter VII, Section 7. Freud's 'theory of deferred action' (*Nachträglichkeit*), and Derrida's *différance* or "post-script" (Chapter XIII), which is derived from Freud's conception, are essential categories here. The emergence of distinctions in levels will change the distinct boundaries WITHIN the system.

one, has pointed out, the evolutionary unit is not the 'individual', but the 'population', i.e., the 'reproductive community'. There is a biological requirement of a certain level of inbreeding (Dobzhansky's bioenergetic 'reproductive isolating mechanisms'), for otherwise a species would disappear in a mass of its own genetic debris. At the other extreme, as Sewall Wright has said, it is necessary for two or three members of any population to go astray and deposit their genes in another 'gene pool' in order to maintain an ideal evolutionary balance. All this operates perfectly in natural ecological niches without the incest prohibition. As Lévi-Strauss says, the prohibition answers a question nobody ever asked. Once constituted in the form in which we know it, however, the prohibition proved, by its survival, to have survival value as simply involving possible genetic advantages. We can posit that the end of oestrus reduced the sexual competitiveness over females and introduced a new level of possible cooperation in proto-hominid groups because of the new order of possibilities of selecting long-lasting male–female relationships. The introduction of forms of incest prohibition – however and whenever its various forms may have appeared, including unstructured forms of exogamy – thus provided for a qualitatively different form of the organization of information-linkages in the group. The 'binding' of matter–energy by information at more and more complex levels proved – after the event – to have a homeostatic value in terms of stability, and necessarily introduced the possibility of ULTRASTABILITY (Chapter XIII). One of the necessary products of the regulation of variation is in fact variation itself.

The incest prohibition which constituted digital communication in its symbolic form, is thus the NON-RATIONAL (i.e., analog) basis of the supposed 'rationality' of culture. The 'symbolic function' must imply that 'something' is exchanged, but it implies a SYMBOLIC something (information) rather than a real something (matter). Symbolic exchange is the elevation of the information processes of nature, by emergence, to another level of organization. It is thus both derived from nature and entirely 'non-natural'. Like the 'nip', it involves a primary communication about communication: but instead of "This is play", we have the equivalent of "This is culture, man". (See Section 7 below, and Section 8 in Chapter VII.)

If the function of Symbolic exchange in culture is the maintenance of relationships at a level different from the maintenance of relationships in the natural ecosystem, then the 'symbolic' object of this exchange cannot actually be expropriated or possessed – no more than the 'difference' exchanged in the ecosystem can be expropriated or accumulated. All that is ever accumulated in nature is energy for future use and information (in memory) for future survival. Under no circumstances is accumulation for the sake of accumulation possible in nature. Similarly, in culture, if the 'sign' or the 'symbolic object' were actually possessed by any member or any family in the system, then the Symbolic exchange would cease, to be replaced by Imaginary exchange, without human relational or survival value. It is not the male or female persons who are exchanged, and we are not concerned with their status here. What is exchanged is the SIGN they RE-present. In our analysis, therefore, we must obey the admonition of Wittgenstein (1945–9: 40) not to confuse the NAME with the BEARER OF A NAME. We must not confuse the sign with the paradoxical 'presence and absence' it represents.

It seems to me that this is altogether a most important distinction and provides further insight into what Lévi-Strauss is talking about. For a sign or a name is information, whereas its bearer is matter–energy. In communication systems it is not entities or energy which are transmitted, but information. The transmission of the information is, however, impossible without the matter–energy markers (like the notches in a key) which bear it (cf. von Neumann, 1958). We can thus rephrase Wittgenstein's admonition in communicational and systemic terms: we should not confuse the information with the matter–energy, the marker, that bears it. Since the whole development of communication theory and general systems theory depends upon the distinction between energy and information, we begin to see some important common elements between the Bororo myth-makers' explanation and cybernetic theory in general. For what distinguishes those who will live and those who will die in Akaruio Bokodori's world is the gifts they bear. THOSE THAT DO NOT CARRY THE REQUISITE KIND OF INFORMATION, THE REQUISITE DISTINCTION, ARE THROWN OUT OF THE SYSTEM. Such is the power of what once was called 'prelogical' thought.

7. Nature and Culture: Zoology

Gregory Bateson's theory of play and fantasy (1955) has already been mentioned in some detail in Chapters VI and VII. The communication about communication 'contained' in the emergence of the nip says something of the order of "This is play". Similarly, the emergence of the 'sister' or 'brother' says something like "This is culture". In the same sense that the nip says 'These actions in which we now engage do not denote what the actions for which they stand denote', the emergence of the kinship name says 'This name no longer denotes what that for which its bearer stands denotes'. The nip and the kinship name denote that some component is no longer what it is, but something identical-but-distinct.

Distinct, that is, not only in LEVEL of logical type, but also from other components of the same logical type.

The prohibition of incest thus sets up the paradoxical metacommunicative rules by which denotation can take place (cf. Chapter VI). Only 'after' the evolution of the communication about the FORM of communication implied in "This is culture", can 'objects' receive denotations. And the *sine qua non* for denotation is a rule about identity, i.e., a word for 'not': "Nature, this is not." The emergence of the digital sign 'sister–brother' both precedes and presupposes the emergence of the 'symbol of negation' itself.

The evolution of the particular form of distinction between energy and information represented by the nip or by 'sister–brother' is precisely what is described in the Bororo myth by the term 'gift'. Unlike a bite, which is simply different from various other behavioral acts of the animal, the nip involves a distinction. One can conceive of a nip as having that kind of boundary around it which distinguishes a sign from other signs. Whereas in the bite, energy and information are one (as in the brake pedal of a car), in the nip the information is distinct from the energy. In other words, the sign (the nip) is distinct from its marker (the mouth) in the same way that the information transmitted by the accelerator pedal of a car is distinct from the matter–energy which bears it. The nip signifies the presence and the absence of the bite, just as 'sister' or 'brother' signifies the presence and the absence of female or male. And whereas the bite is always received in a real sense, like the male or the female, the nip is a primordial symbolic object which CANNOT be received in the real (otherwise it would be a bite). The world of communication of the bite is full of real differences; with the nip, gaps begin to appear, something akin to the zero-phoneme or to the space between one and two. And whatever else the nip may be, it is NO-THING. The nip begins as a real metonymy (a part for the whole, related by contiguity) and becomes a symbolic metaphor (something standing for something else, related by similarity).

8. *Nature and Culture: Economic Exchange Theory*

In the Marxian theory of the constitution of exchange value out of use value, the primary necessity is a 'point of contact' with the exterior:

> Objects themselves are external to man, and consequently alienable by him. In order that this alienation may become reciprocal it is only necessary for men, by a tacit understanding, to treat each other as private owners of those alienable objects, and by implication as independent [discrete] individuals. But such a state of reciprocal independence

has no existence in a primitive society based on property in common. . . . The exchange of commodities, therefore, first begins on the BOUN-DARIES of such communities, at their points of contact with other similar communities. . . . So soon, however, as products once become com-modities in the EXTERNAL relations of a community, they also, by reaction become so in its INTERNAL communal life (1887: 87).[4]

It is not necessary to take Marx to task over his (or Lewis Morgan's) ignorance of the function of exchange within the so-called 'primitive' society, for we can read 'procreative unit' for "primitive society based on property in common", and still pick out the central idea that external contact at a boundary which is constituted by the very act of emergence itself, brings about internal reorganization AFTER THE EVENT and constitutes a system of a higher order of complexity. And for this system to emerge, it is necessary that 'objects' be created out of continuous 'realities', that is to say that objects be alienated from each other and become distinct 'facts' (cf. Kojève, 1947a: 372 ff.).

The distinct, alienable object with exchange value is of course logically equivalent to the discrete component of the Bororo myth, to the 'sister' or the 'brother', and to the nip in animal play, for it is the passage from the analog use values of nature to the digital exchange values of culture that both Lévi-Strauss and the Bororo are describing. Whereas a female or a male have only biological use value, a 'sister' or a 'brother' are invested with symbolic exchange value, and whereas the bite is used, the nip is exchanged.

But what is exchange value? Since it is not directly connected to use value as such, and since any object of exchange may be valued in an en-tirely arbitrary way, it is clear that exchange value has something to do with the symbolic function. AT THIS POINT, from our perspective here, use value corresponds to matter–energy, whereas exchange value corresponds to information. The special characteristic of commodities, however, is that one particular commodity of the original circulation of use value (in which objects are simply different from each other) is thrown out of the system to become the Marxian "general equivalent of exchange": this is gold or silver or shells, or some such similar commodity. There is no such general equivalent in Symbolic exchange, although there is exchange value. The general equivalent is characteristic only of Imaginary exchange. The general characteristic of exchange value is that it is the SIGN OF A RELATION

---

[4] Note the generation of modified subsystems implied here. Freud speaks of the exogamous function of the incest prohibition and of the necessity of external contact very early in his work (Draft N, 1897, *Standard Edition*, I, 257).

(as in language). But in Imaginary exchange, the general equivalent turns all exchange value into the SIGN OF A THING. Marx expresses this by a striking quotation from Revelation (17: 13 and 13: 17):

> These [i.e., the exchangers of commodities] have one mind, and they give their power and authority to the beast . . . that no man should be able to buy and to sell, save he have that mark, even the name of the beast, or the number of his name (1887: 86).

Whatever other processes are involved, the primordial symbolic function of exchange value is self-evident. As in all cases of Symbolic exchange, the value of the 'symbolic object' is that of a symbolic relation. Outside of that relationship, its values are simply real.

The question of money must be historically related to the emergence of alienated labor, for 'money' in the 'cool' society is more nearly a reciprocal gift like other gifts – that is to say a sign of exchange – than it is sign of a commodity. As long as we distinguish Symbolic exchange value – the sign of a relation – from Imaginary exchange value – the sign of a thing – we have no difficulty in distinguishing between digitalization as a necessary FORM for the constitution of exchange value in general (as Marx says, 'individuation' is the product of exchange), and the actual FUNCTION of exchange in different civilizations. Digitalization is necessary, and presupposes no particular function. It allows both for the analog function of Symbolic exchange and for the digital function of Imaginary exchange. We can further distinguish dominant and subordinate functions in various cultures. There is no need to suppose that all 'cool' cultures exemplify only Symbolic exchange, or that Symbolic exchange does not occur, at subordinate levels, in our own predominantly Imaginary culture.

In our culture, money does not represent a relation between people as does the 'symbolic object'. As the valorization of an ENTITY, money under capitalism represents Imaginary relations between things, and the 'things' it represents are the 'clear and distinct' people who are exchanged – as alienated objects – in the system. Money isn't simply 'like' the solipsistic, schizoid entities we call 'individuals' in our culture, it IS those individuals. It is their general equivalent of exchange. In our society, people represent labor time, and labor time – whether energy or organization – is money. This point is obvious, but it nevertheless has to be made: if money can rent people, then money IS people.

We can give a brief historical example of a similar form of emergence, at another level of organization, within the history of our own culture. In his analysis of the alliance against the feudal nobility between the French monarchy and the middle-class 'officers', drawn from the Third Estate, in sixteenth-century France, Goldmann (1955) asks whether the 'offices' constituting the *noblesse de robe* against the *noblesse d'épée* were actually SOLD to the highest bidder or EXCHANGED for services previously rendered. He concludes that the question as such is irrelevant. The sale of 'offices' only becomes a regular economic institution when this institution has developed a POLITICAL SIGNIFICATION. In other words, only when the alliance between the office-holders (jurists, administrators) and the central power is no longer "implicit or natural", can it be called an economic institution, and the Symbolic relation become Imaginary, or the relationship become digitalized at another level.

The same process is repeated in the seventeenth century, when the originally essentially 'homogeneous' class of 'office-holders' splits down the implicit cleavage between the 'jurists and administrators' (the Parlements) and the 'functionaries' or 'commissioners' of the central power, with a resulting opposition between the central power and the Parlements. The absolute monarchy plays a 'politics of equilibrium' through its agents, balancing the aristocracy against the Third Estate. It uses the peasant and other popular revolts as the 'common enemy', the 'outside agitators' to maintain the system in temporary but illusory homeostasis. In the eighteenth century, the positive feedback of this ultrastable system forces a temporary alliance of the upper and middle classes against the central power, taking advantage of the peasantry and the incipient proletariat as its 'agitators', until one ensemble of messages in the system emerges as the new code: the bourgeoisie (see Chapter XII).

Marx pointed to the Imaginary form of the digital relationship of entities in a striking fashion when he compared the relationship between commodities, and between commodities and money, as a mirror-relation of 'body-images' (Marx, 1887: 52): The "BODY FORM" of commodity A becomes the "value form" of commodity B, or, in other words, "the body of commodity B acts as a mirror to the value of commodity A". He adds a footnote which makes explicit the connection with the Hegelian desire for recognition and the Lacanian mirror-stage:

> In a sort of way, it is the same with man as with commodities. Since he comes into the world neither with a looking glass in his hand, nor as a Fichtian philosopher to whom 'I am I' is sufficient, man first sees himself reflected in other men. Peter only establishes his own identity as a man by first comparing himself with Paul as being of the same kind. And thereby Paul, 'in hide and hair', Paul in his Pauline corporality [*Leiblichkeit*], becomes entirely to Peter the phenomenal form [*Erscheinungsform*] of the genus Man.

Marx's 'psychological' footnote is a description of the Imaginary relationship between human beings:[5] the paradoxical relationship of identity (autonomy) and identification (with a model or rival) which generates the paranoid opposition of ego and other in our culture, as opposed to the Symbolic relationship of the 'subject'. The ego is an entity, a commodity in opposition to other commodities, whereas the subject in the sense I use it here is a relation.

One can pursue the constitution and the analysis of the Imaginary throughout literature: Montaigne, Rousseau, Balzac, Stendhal, Flaubert, Dostoevsky, Proust, Svevo. . . . In its sense of specular identification, this Lacanian concept is based upon Freud's theory of narcissism.

9. *Recapitulation: Symbolic Exchange*

> On nous fait du langage des
> premiers hommes des langues de
> géomètres, et nous voyons que ce
> furent des langues de poètes.
> ROUSSEAU: *Essai sur l'origine
> des langues* (1760)

The conception of the Symbolic as that which maintains relationships is very similar to Malinowski's 'phatic communion', as I point out elsewhere. It is also clearly specified at another level in his *Argonauts of the Western Pacific* (1922: 81–104), where Malinowski describes the Kula 'trade' between various islands off the coast of New Guinea. (This book clearly inspired Lacan's conception of the symbol: Wilden, 1968a: 35, 120.) Along the circuit of the Kula, articles of two kinds, necklaces of red shell (*soulava*) and bracelets of white shell (*mwali*) travel in two great circles, in OPPOSITE directions, between tribes differing in language, culture, and even race. Each of these articles meets articles of the other class on its way around, and is constantly being exchanged for them. These exchanges have no objective or subjective economic value. Although the Kula is accompanied by regular trade and barter for use, the symbolic shells involved are not even used for ornamentation, but simply displayed. Many are too big or too small to be worn. Moreover, Kula is specifically distinguished from barter. All exchanges are reciprocal, and no sanctions are involved in the 'debtor–creditor' relationship which occurs when months or a year

---

[5] J.-J. Goux has developed this relationship, but from a phallocentric perspective which does not transcend the bourgeois ideology, in his "Numismatiques I, II" (1968, 1969).

intervene between a Kula gift from one partner and the reciprocal return of another gift from the other partner. All other economic and related activities (e.g., canoe-building) are subordinated to the Kula. The 'valuables' exchanged are not related to each other by any 'general equivalent of exchange' as they would be if they were a form of currency. The articles involved in the many thousands of exchanges between partners (one man will have several or many partners in the Kula, depending on his rank) never stop moving for any length of time: they are constantly changing hands.

Thus the circuit of exchange consists of two vast circles or channels along which the 'bits' of information move, each 'bit' of one type constantly being substituted for a bit of the other type. Thousands of partners are provided with dyadic links through the exchange, but the dyads are a function of the circuit as a whole, not of any individual connection. The whole process is like a sort of undulating web where everything moves but all stands still at the same time. This highly complex network of relations is governed by strict communicational rules as regards the flow of the 'symbolic objects' (bracelets move from left hand to right hand and from North and East to South and West, and never in the other direction), but the 'value' of an object 'owed' is a matter of unarticulated reciprocity and mutual obligation, not of convention.

Particularly significant for the concept of Symbolic exchange employed in these essays is that the 'objects' of exchange in the Kula are UNALIENABLE: they cannot be accumulated, expropriated, or possessed. Whatever enhancement of status may be enjoyed by the 'holder' of a particularly interesting *soulava* or *mwali* – one with a particularly interesting history of previous 'holders', for example – this enhancement bears no relation whatsoever to our conception of status involving the possession of material objects:

> . . . Every man who is in the Kula . . . receives one or several *mwali* . . ., or a *soulava* . . ., and then has to hand it on to one of his partners, from whom he receives the opposite commodity in exchange. Thus no man ever keeps any of the articles for any length of time in his possession. One transaction does not finish the Kula relationship, the rule being "once in the Kula, always in the Kula", and a partnership between two men is a permanent and life-long affair. Again, any given *mwali* or *soulava* may always be found travelling and changing hands, and there is no question of its ever settling down, so that the principle "once in the Kula, always in the Kula", applies also to the valuables themselves (pp. 81–3).

We can ignore Malinowski's repeated projection of western economic and sociological values onto the Kula. Although he states several times that the 'valuable' cannot be possessed, he speculates that the origin of the Kula lies in a "deep desire to possess". Like the gratuitous concept of the 'instinct' in biology, zoology, and psychology, this tautologous conception of the origin of the Kula has more of an ideological than a scientific value. It depends on the preconceived assumptions of western individualism, which seek to make individual factors (the social 'atom') account for all social behavior.

On the one hand, nothing is possessed in the Kula, not even the status involved in displaying an object, for it must soon be handed on. On the other, it is the system of exchange which generates the 'desire' to be involved in it. The Kula 'trade' is in fact another specific example of the use of digital information ('bits') to cross boundaries between different systems (different geographically, linguistically, and probably ethnically) in order to link them together in an ecosystemic relationship, one which uses digital information for analog ends. In keeping with the distinction between information and meaning, the bracelets and the necklaces are useless – that is, meaningless – in themselves; they derive their meaning and use from the context and the goals of the whole. Conversely, they have SIGNIFICATION only in the dyadic relations of each exchange (cf. Chapter VII).

This said, since the concept of Symbolic exchange involves the use of the combination of digital or discrete elements for analog ends, I can think of no more effective way of presenting it than in the analog mode itself. *Figures 1 to 4* are representations of kinship relations by means of kinematic graphs which 'translate' the accompanying tables of transformations. These diagrams are derived from André Weil's formalization of some of the kinship systems described in Lévi-Strauss's *Elementary Structures of Kinship* (1949: 257–65). The demonstrations are slightly different versions of those given by Warusfel (1969: 166–70). In these diagrams, the broken line m defines the marriage relationship: any man of clan X may marry a woman of $m (X)$. The solid line c represents the filiation of the children: every member of $c (X)$ is the child of a woman of clan X.

The poetic simplicity of these diagrams expresses the symbolic communicative function of the exchange relationships which are involved far more effectively than the written word. The fact that the elementary structures which Lévi-Strauss sought to codify in his first full-length work, appear to be far less common than he at first supposed is, of course, irrelevant to the demonstration. The reader will see at once that the circulation of the digital components, while based on distinctions (or 'oppositions' as they are usually called), produces a system dependent on the circulation of information as difference: each diagram thus represents an ecosystemic UNIT OF MIND, the domain of the both–and. The 'symbols' involved correspond to the earliest definition of the term in western culture: *sumbolon*: pact, covenant, communication, LINK.

FIGURE 1 *The Kariera System (four clans: A, B, C, D)*

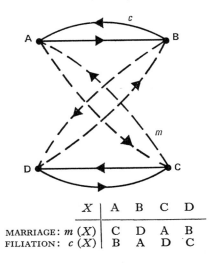

X	A	B	C	D
MARRIAGE: $m(X)$	C	D	A	B
FILIATION: $c(X)$	B	A	D	C

FIGURE 2 *The Tarau System (four clans)*

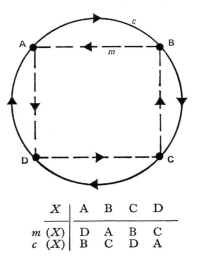

X	A	B	C	D
$m(X)$	D	A	B	C
$c(X)$	B	C	D	A

FIGURE 3 *The Ambrym System (six clans)*

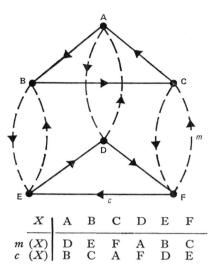

X	A	B	C	D	E	F
$m(X)$	D	E	F	A	B	C
$c(X)$	B	C	A	F	D	E

FIGURE 4 *The Aranda System (eight clans)*

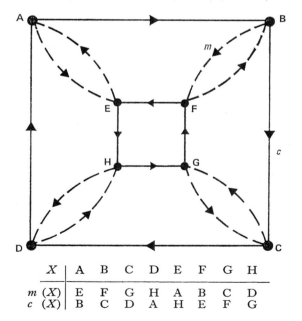

X	A	B	C	D	E	F	G	H
$m(X)$	E	F	G	H	A	B	C	D
$c(X)$	B	C	D	A	H	E	F	G

10. *The Imaginary other in Relation to the Other*

I shall deal in detail with the constitution of the Imaginary order by the 'mirror-stage' in Chapter XVII below. In what follows I am employing the term Symbolic to refer both to the analog exchange of difference and to the digital exchange of distinction. The term Imaginary refers to the mirror relationship described by Marx in the digital exchange of capitalism and to the mirror-stage described by Lacan. Thus the categories I am employing are not precisely the same as those called the Symbolic and the Imaginary in the work of Lacan, for Lacan's Symbolic refers only to 'language' (i.e., to a confusion between 'language' and 'communication': see Chapter XVI), and it is grounded on a logocentric and phallocentric epistemology (Chapters X and XIII).

The Imaginary is the domain of dual relationships, the domain of the either/or. In Lacan, the term derives from the mirror-stage which occurs between the ages of six and eighteen months in child-development (Lacan, 1953a, 1966: 93–100, 178–92; Wilden, 1968a: passim, see Index). This results in a specular identification with the image of another, an *alter ego*, which involves the constitution of the ego as an ALIENATION of the subject. The Imaginary is thus constructed on the double bind inherent in the word IDENTITY: identical to what and to whom, for what and for whom?[6]

The overriding symmetries and oppositional dualities of the Imaginary make it a trap from which the subject could never escape without the introduction of MEDIATION. In a developmental sense, the Imaginary order of the mirror-stage is a necessary stage of (desired) symmetry which is constituted in the overall complementarity of the relationship between mother and child. (This use of symmetry and complementarity derives from Bateson's concept of schismogenesis or differentiation in *Naven* [1936: 171–97]. See Chapter VIII.) Symmetrical relationships are questions of 'matching'; complementary relationships are questions of 'fitting'. The relationship of the part to the whole or the dominant to the subordinate is always complementary. All relationships seem to be either symmetrical or complementary or both (and their definition always involves punctuation); pathology arises if and when there is a specialization in one or the

---

[6] Laing and Esterson (1964: 6) deal with the alienating forms of the 'problem of identity': the 'autonomous ego', the 'free individual', the 'ego as the unity of the person', and so on, in the following way:

> People have identities. But they may also change quite remarkably as they become different others-to-others. It is arbitrary to regard any one of these transformations or ALTERations as basic, and the others as variations.

other, that is to say, an inability to protect against symmetry by switching to complementarity and vice versa. The child's primordial discovery of his distinction from the world is short-circuited by the effects of specularization in the Imaginary. Difference becomes opposition, essential to the concepts of identity, identification, and projection (Chapter VI). Here the child is alienated from himself in a dual relationship of demand with one or other parent, or both. His 'I' is trapped in the demands of his alienated ego, which he seeks to make correspond with the demands of his *alter ego* (his ideal ego). His 'I' is a signifier in somebody else's discourse; he is spoken rather than speaking. Here he can be only what others desire (or in effect demand) him to be. As a 'schizophrenic' patient puts it (Watzlawick, Beavin, and Jackson, 1967: 89), "In other words, I can't be anything but myself, and if people don't like me the way they am – ah, the way I am. . . ."

It is through the symbolic relationship of the oedipus complex – obedient to the social law of what Lacan calls the Symbolic father, the law of the prohibition of incest – that the child is integrated into a dialectical and triangular relationship, where the mediation of desire protects each component from specializing in either symmetry or complementarity with any of the other components. Here his debts and his gifts – theoretically – begin to be safely transferred outside the family. In pathological families, however, the symbolic function of the oedipal relation will be reduced to a set of dual Imaginary relationships.

Lacan's Symbolic order is constructed around the Other as the "name-of-the-father" in our culture. The Other can only be categorized in relation to a corollary, the other (a particular other). If Lacan's use of the term Other is often ambiguous and confusing, it is nevertheless clear that it is designed to be, not an ontic, but an ontological category (to use a Heideggerean distinction). That is to say, it is not of the domain of the existent, but of the domain of Being. To put the same thing in epistemological terms, whereas the other is a FACT, the Other is designated in the theory as a law or PRINCIPLE.[7]

11. *The Problem of Interorganismic Authority*

Lacan's Other represents the patrocentric ideology of our culture. The Other is only theoretically *ne-uter*, for it is not just 'Otherness'. It is the principle of the locus of language and of the signifier, which for Lacan, is naturally the phallus (Chapter X). It is uselessly idealistic to try to say

[7] The Other in Lacan's theory is, however, simply a cultural Other: the Symbolic Father. In other words, it is not in the final analysis ontological, it is ontic.

that Lacan's analysis of our values in these terms is incorrect. The signifier – and the phallus – are indeed the instruments of exploitation in our culture, and the Other is indeed the locus of the violence of the 'law and order' of the system.

For the creative and truly intuitive therapist – a rare bird – the question of the 'cure' never fails to come up against the double bind of trying to 'save' the patient by being forced to 'save' the system which no individual can change. For the 'average' person in our culture – with house, family, car, children, credit-rating, and job, and without the degrees of freedom enjoyed by intellectuals and the more privileged classes – any true 'cure' would amount to an injunction to 'go crazy', as that is defined by the culture, and you can't feed your children that way.

But the Other as a necessary principle in human affairs does not inevitably imply the oppressive characteristics which it actually manifests both in our society and in the Lacanian theory. Waddington (1968: 29–32) has devoted himself to some speculations about the apparent dilemma of 'interorganismic authority'. At first sight his remarks might easily be construed as supporting the particular version of the function of Otherness espoused by Lacan. Waddington has argued in his *Ethical Animal* (1960) that the inexplicable development of language in evolution, as a way of transmitting 'hereditary' information (in culture), "has inextricably connected it with notions of social (usually parental) authority". Or, in Lacan's terminology: "The primary statement or given word decrees, legislates, aphorizes. It is oracular; it confers on the real other[8] the obscure authority of that other" (1966: 808). The Word is inevitably 'command–report' before it can become 'report–command' or report and command. Obviously, the mere fact that language has to be learned from others, engenders this command relationship between the child and 'authority'. This is Lacan's point in describing the Other as the "locus of the Word". Waddington goes on to ask whether "ethics" would ever have been developed if our communications system had remained analog (although he does not use this particular term): "Could symbol transmission have been married to objectification rather than to interorganismic authority?"

> The attainment of 'objectification' – seeing that the world contains certain things with outlines around them . . . – is an achievement which natural selection would certainly have brought about quite independently of any possibility of transmitting information symbolically [i.e., digitally, in language]. . . . If . . . you happen to light on a method of transmitting information . . . in a different sensory mode from that in which you

---

8 The 'real Other' (capital O) in the Lacanian theory, is the mother.

learn the process of objectification [analog perception], then you are likely to finish up with information transmission inextricably mixed up with interorganismic authority . . . [and] ethical values (pp. 31–2).

There is a curious jumble of ideas here, some of which seem surprising coming from the pen of a specialist in animal genetics. In the first place, 'authority' must be distinguished from 'authoritarianism'. The teacher, for example, whose function should be that of a catalyst in a learning (rather than in a teaching) process, must be distinguished from 'the Other' as the representative of the subject-who-is-supposed-to-know (a rare enough situation, it is true). Secondly, there is plenty of evidence of 'authority' in analog zoosemiotics (the weaning of puppies by the mother, for example). And thirdly, Waddington seems to be talking at one moment about ethics and, at another, about morality, which are far from being the same thing.

It seems very obvious that only in a culture with deeply programmed ELITIST metarules does the correlation of 'Other' and 'authority' with particular forms of knowledge, behavior, and status, hold good. I would hope that in the future evolution of humankind, this anti-biological elitist programming can be transcended. For if it is not in fact a transitional stage, it will most surely be the end of all of us. 'Authority' and 'mastery' are only equivalent to 'parent' and 'professor' (or whatever) in a culture which employs Imaginary digitalization to turn dynamic differences into static oppositions.

Otherness is a necessary category of human social systems. But only in the Imaginary does the Other necessarily equal oppression. And only in the Imaginary can you set up a theory of 'counter-opposition' based on anarchist illusions about 'freedom' and 'individualism' – whether in this world of mirrors you describe yourself as left (negative identification with the Other) or as right (positive identification with the Other). The 'purity' of 'absolute' opposition is soiled with the illusions of the existential hero (cf. Chapter XVII); the 'altruism' of liberal tolerance of Imaginary opposition is, if anything, more dangerous, still.[9]

The distinction between morality (the ideology of the present state of the system) and ethics (the ongoing critical theory of systems) is significant. All natural systems are ethical in the sense that they do not allow violence – i.e., exploitative accumulation, accumulation for the sake of itself – but all morality is a locus of exploitation. And so long as the law of

[9] There is a precise elaboration of the sort of values criticized in this chapter and in Chapter VIII, which includes practically every anti-natural and anti-female metaphor I have mentioned, and almost every counter-adaptive, Cartesian, solipsist, elitist, irrational, and Imaginary value one can pack into twenty-odd pages, in Ortega's *The Dehumanization of Art* (1956: 164–87).

incest – the original metaphor of 'No' – is viewed as a MORAL prohibition emanating from the Other, rather than as an ethical injunction to reciprocal exchange, language will indeed remain the agent of violence. Every refusal in the analog and every 'No' in the digital which localize the socially derived aggression of the parent against the child, will necessarily invite the child to internalize it as violence and to re-project it onto others.

12. *The Symbolic and the Veil of Maia*

For Lacan, the Imaginary is related to fetishism, which brings the Marxian perspective on the fetishization of commodities into sharper focus. Lacan refers to the fetishist as clasping the "veil of Maia", and to the castration of the castration complex as a question of what is "beyond that veil" (Wilden, 1968a: 44, 131). Maia is the name of an Italian earth goddess derived from the Greek for "O mother earth". The Greek term also gives rise to the words for midwife in Greek (cf. the Socratic maieutics) and to the appellation 'mamma'. Maya, of course, is the "illusion of entrenched selfhood", and Lacan's conception of the Imaginary is no sense in contradiction with the *Vedanta Sutras* (Thibaut, ed., 1890–6: xxvi) commented by Sankara:

> The unenlightened soul is unable to look through and beyond *Maya* which, like a veil, hides from it its true nature. Instead of recognizing itself to be Brahman, it identifies itself with its adjuncts (*upadhi*), the fictitious offspring of *Maya*, and thus looks for its true Self in the body, the sense organs, and the internal organ (*manas*), i.e., the organ of specific cognition.

The 'enlightened soul' of these ancient texts, for all its apparent mystical apparatus and for all the repressive function of the religious thought in the societies in which these conceptions arose, is a unit of mind. Maya is the Imaginary, in both its essential and its non-essential forms. Ramanuga points out that dreams, as products of Maya, are of a 'wonderful nature' and cannot be brought about by the individual soul alone (p. lxi).

What is essential to Lacan's derivation of the Imaginary order is the confusion of the ego with the body-image, the confusion of the biological 'individual' – the skin-bound organism – with the 'person' or the 'personality'. The dominance of the Imaginary is thus essential to the split between mind and body in western culture (Chapter VIII).

To summarize the relationship which I establish between the Symbolic and the Imaginary orders: The Symbolic is the domain of similarity and difference; the Imaginary that of opposition and identity. The Symbolic is the category of displaced reciprocity and similar relationships; the

Imaginary that of mirror-relationships, specialization in symmetry or pseudo-symmetry, duality, complementarity, and short circuits. Neither Symbolic nor Imaginary can do without the other, and neither can be defined except in terms of and in differentiation from the other. The Symbolic function is collective and the domain of the Law; the Imaginary creates the illusion of subjective autonomy. The Imaginary is the domain of adequacy; the Symbolic the domain of truth. Desire is to the Symbolic as demand is to the Imaginary, as are the subject and the ego respectively. Imaginary debts can never be paid; Symbolic debts can never not be paid. The separation of the organism from the environment is Imaginary; the ecosystem is Symbolic. The *cogito* is an Imaginary 'I'; *loquor* is the next step towards a potential Symbolic 'we'. The being of the Imaginary is either/or; the being of the Symbolic is both–and.

13. C. S. Peirce on Firstness, Secondness, and Thirdness

Peirce's intricate theory of 'semiosis' and communication, seriously misconstrued by Charles Morris's splitting of syntactics, semantics, and pragmatics from each other (cf. Dewey, 1946), is useful in our attempts to establish the levels of logical typing and organization between the Symbolic, the Imaginary, and the Real. On my reading, Peirce's concept of the 'symbol' (the linguistic sign) as having no reference as such to 'objects', does not contradict the essential notion of the intentionality of discourse (its 'referent', its 'goal'). 'Meaning', for Peirce, probably corresponds with 'signification' in these essays (Dewey, 1946: 91, 92). But rather than initiate a critique of Peirce's bioenergetic basis or of his ambiguous category of 'thought', or of his probable confusion of the word 'not' with 'not-I', I shall simply outline his 'levels of being' here.

Writing in opposition to atomistic psychology, Peirce maintained that in so far as thought is cognitive it must be linguistic or symbolical, that is, it must presuppose communication (by means of signs). 'Mental signs', according to him, are inseparable from interpretation by other mental signs; thought is not mosaic or linear, but rather a NETWORK of signs. His lonely phenomenological pragmatism is a typical example of a theory born before its time. Without the benefit of cybernetic and communications theory, his "law of mind", for example, is easily dismissed as idealist anthropomorphism.

Lévi-Strauss has to some extent been influenced by Peirce's semiotics and possibly by his epistemology. Lacan's theory of the signifier corresponds closely to Peirce's 'symbol'. What is of interest here, however, is less the theory of signs as such than the reciprocally related ontology developed by Peirce. Peirce posed the existence of three modes of being, which he called Firstness, Secondness, and Thirdness (Peirce, 1955: 76):

> Firstness is the mode of being which consists in its subject's being positively such as it is regardless of aught else. That can only be a possibility. For as long as things do not act upon one another there is no sense or meaning in saying that they have any being, unless it be that they are such in themselves that they may perhaps come into relation with others.

Secondness is "a mode of being of one thing which consists in how a second object is" (p. 76). This is the domain of "the actual facts". The First is predominant in the ideas of "freshness, life, freedom" – the free being defined as "that which has not another behind it, determining its actions". But, in so far as "the idea of the negation of another enters, the idea of another enters; and such a negative idea must be put in the background, or else we cannot say that the Firstness is predominant" (pp. 78–9).

> We are continually bumping against hard fact. . . . [The] notion of being such as other things make us, is such a prominent part of our life that we conceive other things also to exist in virtue of their reactions against each other. The idea of other, of NOT, becomes a very pivot of thought. To this element I give the name of Secondness (quoted in Dewey, 1946: 90).

The idea of Second is predominant

> in the ideas of causation and of statical force. For cause and effect are two. . . . Constraint is a Secondness. In the flow of time in the mind, the past appears to act directly upon the future, its effect being called memory, while the future only acts upon the past through the medium of thirds (p. 79). The second category . . . is the element of struggle. . . . By struggle I must explain that I mean mutual action between two things regardless of any sort of third or medium, and in particular regardless of any law of action (p. 89).

The bulk of "what is actually done" is Secondness, "or better, Secondness is the predominant character of WHAT HAS BEEN DONE. The immediate present, could we seize it, would have no character but its Firstness" (p. 91). The third mode of being is related to LAW and to PREDICTION:

> This mode of being which CONSISTS, mind my word if you please, . . . in the fact that future facts of Secondness will take on a determinate general character, I call a Thirdness (p. 77).

Thirdness "consists of what we call laws when we contemplate them from the outside only, but which, when we see both sides of the shield, we call thoughts. Thoughts are neither qualities [Firstness] nor facts [Secondness]" (p. 78).

> By the third, I mean the medium or connecting bond between the absolute first and last. The beginning is first, the end second, the middle third. The end is second, the means third. . . . Continuity represents Thirdness almost to perfection. Every process comes under that head. . . . Law as an active force is second, but order and legislation are third. Sympathy, flesh and blood, that by which I feel my neighbor's feelings, is third.

Thirdness is most predominant in "the idea of a sign, or representation. . . . Some of the ideas of prominent Thirdness . . . are generality, infinity, continuity, diffusion, growth, and intelligence" (p. 80). Meaning or intention, in so far as they are related, are an "element of the phenomenon or object of thought" which is the element of Thirdness. "It is that which is what it is by virtue of imparting a quality to reactions in the future" (p. 91). "Every genuine triadic relation involves meaning, as meaning is obviously a triadic relation." Moreover, "a triadic relation is inexpressible by means of dyadic relations alone" (p. 93). The three categories are not sensations; they are interrelated; and if it is possible to "prescind" (i.e., abstract, or cut off) First from Second and Third, or Second from Third, it is not possible to "prescind" Second from First nor Third from Second (p. 97).

> A SIGN ["something which stands to somebody for something in some respect or capacity"], or REPRESENTAMEN, is a First which stands in . . . a genuine triadic relation to a Second, called its OBJECT, as to be capable of determining a Third, called its INTERPRETANT, to assume the same triadic relation to its Object in which it [the sign] stands itself to the same Object. The triadic relation is GENUINE, that is, its three members are bound together by it in a way which does not consist in any complexus of dyadic relations (pp. 99–100).

The similarity of the concept of Thirdness – the locus of meaning, desire, goalseeking, project, mediation, and the highest logical type of law – to the Symbolic and the analog function is very striking. Firstness seems to be related to the Real, and Secondness to the Imaginary, for where Thirdness is the domain of mediated triangular relations, Secondness is ontologically the domain of the apparition of what is other, and psychologically is the domain of reaction, struggle, and duality. As Peirce says, it is in so far as the 'negation' of the other enters Firstness, that

Secondness appears – a conception clearly related to the mirror-stage, to the *Fort! Da!*, to the process of the *Verneinung* in the child, and to the specular opposition of master and slave, ego and *alter ego*, in the Imaginary. I have never met or heard of anyone who understood Peirce's theory of signs, but according to Dewey, the 'interpretant' (another sign) of an 'iconic sign' is an instance of Firstness and the EMOTIONAL; that of an 'indexical sign' is an instance of Secondness and the ENERGETIC; that of the 'linguistic sign' is an instance of Thirdness and of the LOGICAL and the INTELLECTUAL.

Dewey accuses Morris of reducing Peirce's complex triadic theory of meaning, with its integral relation to the world and to other minds, to a binary relation between words and things. We recall that, as Foucault has pointed out (1966: 57–8), the tripartite semiotic theory of the Stoics, for whom the 'sign' included the "signifier, the signified, and the 'conjuncture'" (the *tunchanon*), was reduced to a binary relation between signifier and signified in the seventeenth century. During the Renaissance, however, the relation was ternary, including "the formal domain of marks, the content which they signal, and the similitudes which link the marks to the things designated". "Words and things became separated" in the seventeenth century, which concerned itself with questions of "representation". They continue to remain separated for us, in our concern for "sense and signification" and for the pure taxonomies of "order and classification" (pp. 58, 71) (cf. Chapter VIII). After its binarization by the classical age, says Foucault,

> . . . language, instead of existing as the material writing of things, will no longer find its space except in the general regime of representative signs. . . . Language will no longer be anything more than a particular case of representation (for the classical age) or of signification (for us). The profound kinship of language and the world is undone. The primacy of writing is suspended (pp. 57–8).

14. *Nature and Culture: The Phallus in Exchange*

Lacan's theory of the phallus as a signifier is dealt with in some detail in my critique of phallocentrism in the chapter following this one. To put the matter briefly, if we substitute the sign 'phallus' for the 'sister' or 'brother' exchanged in matrimony and for the 'child' exchanged in the line of filiation (*Figures 1–4* above), we have a representation of the psycho-analytical theory of the exchange of the 'symbolic object'[10] within and

[10] As the next chapter will show, in our culture the phallus serves as an Imaginary object in an Imaginary system.

between generations. The clinical function of the construct 'phallus' in psychoanalysis need not concern us at this point. In psychoanalytical metapsychology it is a 'symbol' of the child, of the breast, and of the faeces, any one of which can enter into the exchange system within or between generations.

The first aspect of the phallus as an apparently symbolic object which is of interest here is that it represents the advent of exchange value in the family itself. It is a cultural object, dependent upon the prohibition of incest and the introduction of distinction, for, like the other symbolic objects mentioned, it is the sign of what it is not (the penis, which has only use value). It cannot be possessed. The second aspect of interest is that, like the nip, the phallus begins in metonymy and ends in metaphor. Melanie Klein describes the penis as a *pars pro toto* (she means phallus). As a representation of the part-object, whatever is a *pars pro toto* at its origin (the breast, faeces, the thumb, and so on) becomes a metaphor in the same way that the originally metonymic nip becomes a metaphor of (a substitute for) the bite once it has been integrated into a higher level of communication (Chapter VII). Once it has become a sign in a system of communication of a different logical type, WHAT WAS ONCE A MESSAGE BECOMES PART OF THE CODE. The phallus – or its 'familial' equivalent – thus emerges – with language, kinship, and society – in the (mythical) passage from nature to culture.

15. *Nature and Culture: Primary Process and Secondary Process*

We have seen that the so-called 'principle of inertia' regulates the free energy of the primary process in Freud's economic viewpoint. This process has been described as an analog continuum of differences. But the reactions of the primary process give rise to a secondary process which discovers certain paths of discharge other than those available to the primary process to be necessary. The primary process and its free energy thus corresponds to the pleasure principle, regulated by inertia, or by the reduction of tension to zero, whereas the secondary process, whose energy is 'bound' (*gebundene*), corresponds to the reality principle, regulated by constancy, or by the maintenance of enough tension (unpleasure) to deal with the exigencies of life (Chapter VI).

The concept of the binding action of the secondary process (*Bindung*) is clearly related to the discrete element and to the discontinuity in the Bororo myth interpreted by Lévi-Strauss. For Freud, the primary process is FULL (*voll*), the secondary process is full of holes (*lückenhaft*). A related viewpoint in the Freudian metapsychology describes the primary process and the secondary process in ICONIC and LINGUISTIC–ICONIC terms, respectively. As early as the work on aphasia, Freud had described the thing-presentation as involving something "which is not closed and almost one which cannot be closed, while the word-presentation is seen to be something closed, even though capable of extension" (Freud, 1891: 214; Wilden, 1968a: 238). What he clearly means by "closed" is that the image is not discrete but that the signifier is. From this vantage point, we can perhaps for the first time make some sense of the curious diagram in Letter 52 (1896), for we realize that it is a representation of levels of a psychic or neuronal process dependent on continuity and discontinuity (*Standard Edition*, I), or in other words, on the distinction between analog and digital communication (*Figure 1*, Chapter VI).

Lévi-Strauss (1950: xlvii–xlviii) poses a somewhat similar analog/digital model of the genesis of the secondary process and of its discontinuous nature, using the expression "symbol" for Freud's "word-presentation":

> . . . Language could only have been born in one fell swoop. Things were not able to set about signifying progressively. . . . At the moment when the entire Universe suddenly became SIGNIFICATIVE, it was not for all that better KNOWN, even if it is true that the appearance of language must have precipitated the rhythm of the development of knowledge. There is therefore a fundamental opposition in the history of the human mind between symbolism, whose nature is to be discontinuous [digital], and knowledge, marked by [analog] continuity. . . .

The result of this difference is

> that the two categories of signifier and signified were constituted simultaneously and jointly, like two complementary units; but that knowledge, that is to say, the intellectual process which permits us to identify in relationship to each other certain aspects of the signifier and certain aspects of the signified – one might even say: that which permits us to choose from the set of the signifier and the set of the signified those parts which present the most satisfactory relationships of mutual agreement between them – only began very slowly. . . .

In other words, in interorganismic communication, the digital emerges as an attempt to 'map' the 'territory' of the analog. Digital knowledge, in the sense of the 'symbolism' of language, concerns the possibility of establishing identities rather than simple iconic similarities (cf. Foucault, 1966: 57–8).

Consequently, Lévi-Strauss can say: "The Universe signified long before we began to know what it was signifying. . . ." Moreover, "the Universe signified, from the very beginning, the totality of what humanity could expect to know about it". The work of equation of the signifier in relation to the signified, he continues, given on the one hand by symbolism (language) and pursued on the other by knowledge, is not fundamentally different in any kind of society, except in so far as the birth of modern science has introduced a difference of degree.

Thus in his attempts to comprehend the universe, man has at his disposition "a surplus of signification". This he divides among things "according to the laws of symbolic thought", in order that "on the whole, the available signifier [signification] and the signified it aims at [meaning] may remain in the relationship of complementarity which is the very condition of the use of symbolic thought" (p. xlix). From these considerations, Lévi-Strauss posits the notion of *mana* as the ZERO-SYMBOL, or the digital gap, in the system of symbols which go to make up any cosmology. It is "a sign marking the necessity of a symbolic content supplementary to that with which the signified is already loaded, but which can take on any value required, provided only that this value still remains part of the available reserve [of "floating signifier"]" (p. xlviii).

One realizes that the concept of *mana* in the 'other civilization' is in effect an informational and not a bioenergetic principle. It is in fact one of the predecessors of what is now called 'information science' (cf. Chapter XI, Section 10).

The relationship between signifier and signified as it is expressed here sounds very much like that between the secondary and the primary process in Freud. Depending on one's interpretation, the notion of a "surplus of signification" may be construed to refer to the free flow of meaning in the Freudian primary process, or it may mean that the logical complexity of the digital aspects of the secondary process allow for a very large number of ways of dividing up the universe "according to the laws of symbolic thought". What is common to both interpretations, and what is common both to the Freudian view and to the Lévi-Straussian conception (no matter how one translates the term 'signified', which seems, however, to mean 'reality' here), is the notion of the binding of an analog continuum by digital discontinuity. A related concept here is Saussure's view of the constant *glissement* or 'sliding' of the signifier in its relation to the signified (Saussure, 1916a: 156–7) – or in the terminology of these essays, the 'sliding' of signification in relation to meaning. (This is also the sliding of 'thought' in relation to 'sound', as in Mandelbrot's theory of the relationship between the phonemes and the acoustic continuum.) In a word, the symbolic function "supplements" the "charge of signification" of the signified, that is to say, through the introduction of the discrete element, it allows analog meaning to come to signification in a context.

A phenomenologist would presumably talk about this passage from nature to culture, or from meaning to signification as these processes are represented here, in the terms of a passage from the 'pre-categorical' to the 'categorical'. But just as many working phenomenologists confuse negation and absence, becoming and communication (cf. Kosok, 1969), they are unable to demonstrate the concrete and material embodiment of these abstractions in the way that the semiotic conception of the analog and the digital is able to do.[11]

16. *Summary: Use Value and Exchange Value*

Analog and digital communication are the unifying concepts which, along with the distinction between energy and information, enable us to make the various isomorphies and relations established here. Analog communication precisely maps Lévi-Strauss's nature, Bateson's animal combat, Saussure's 'sound', Marx's "primitive society with property in common", and the Freudian primary process. The digital, as the domain of the discrete element, precisely maps the notions of distinction, identity, and opposition – all dependent on a form of negation – in culture, in psychoanalysis, in exchange, in language, and in epistemology. It describes the genesis, the form, and sometimes the function of the exchange value of the 'nip', the 'brother–sister', the 'word-presentation', the 'phallus', the 'sign' and the 'signifier'. And it enables us to conceive of the projection of messages from the axis of combination into the axis of the code at a second level, through the process of emergence (Chapter XII).

The distinctions between use value and the two forms of exchange value can be summarized as follows:

1 The exchange and communication processes of the natural eco-system are both analog and digital in form, but invariably analog in function.

---

[11] In spite of Husserl's tendency to speak in terms of an autonomous 'I', the deficiencies of contemporary phenomenology cannot entirely be laid at his door alone. The following passage on his conception of *Einfühlung* (empathy) can be read in two ways: as an expression of a bioenergetic and Imaginary duality and symmetry, lacking any concept of mediation, and as an attempt to talk about the communicational relationships of the unit of mind:

> The first thing constituted in the form of community, and the foundation for all other intersubjectively common things, is the commonness of Nature, along with that of the Other's organism and his psychophysical *I*, as paired with my own psychophysical *I* (1929: 120).

One asks oneself, in Peirce's terms, whether Husserl is talking from the point of view of Secondness or from that of Thirdness.

2 Use value is analog in both form and function and is directly related to matter–energy.

3 Exchange value is digital in form and directly related to information. All cultural systems manifest some form of exchange value related to meaning.

4 Symbolic exchange is digital in form, but analog in function. It thus becomes a use value of a different logical type from (2). It is directly related to both meaning and signification.

5 Imaginary exchange is digital in form and digital in function. In Imaginary exchange, information is reduced to the equivalent of matter–energy. It is the domain of signification in the sense of reification.

6 All exchange value requires digitalization. Symbolic exchange value is the sign of an (ecosystemic) relation; Imaginary exchange value is the sign of a thing (and therefore of relations between things).

Appendix

The Logical Typing of the Symbolic, the Imaginary, and the Real

By Gerald Hall

> The philosopher supposes that the value of his
> philosophy lies in the whole, in the structure;
> but posterity finds its value in the stone which he
> used for building, and which is used many times
> after that for building – better. Thus it finds the
> value in the fact that the structure can be
> destroyed and nevertheless retain its value as
> building material.
> NIETZSCHE

The classification of mental processes into the Symbolic, the Imaginary, and the Real by Lacan has great potential benefit to the extent that we can analyze the nature of their respective contents and explain the relationships between them. These categories are of different logical types, that is, they belong to different levels of abstraction, and are thereby related as sets to subsets.

The most inclusive class of elements is the Real. This class contains everything which is real to the individual, not only in his perceptions of the world but also in his internal thoughts and emotions as they are experienced. It is a subjective and collective reality which may or may not correspond to 'common-sense' reality, i.e., to 'objective' reality. Elements of the Real are distinguished by differences.

The Symbolic and the Imaginary are both subsets of the Real. They are classes of elements which are members of a larger set (the Real). Everything which is Real, but not real (existent), is either Symbolic or

Imaginary. Or, rather, all that is Symbolic or Imaginary is Real, but the Real includes elements which are neither Symbolic nor Imaginary.

The Symbolic, as it has been developed from the work of Lévi-Strauss, is born out of the exchange between subjects. It is the set of elements which are given a meaning which goes beyond the physical nature of the object, gesture, or word exchanged. They are given meaning by distinctive features which define them as units, words, or coins for exchange, and by the context within which the exchange occurs.

Shit and money are Symbolic elements which are important at different stages of people's lives. Their exchange value in defining the relationship between the mother and child, or between the employer and employee, goes beyond the actual use value of such objects of exchange. The father may be Real, but in our culture it is the Symbolic father, the "name-of-the-father" which is given to the child and which defines the relationships between the mother and the child.

The Imaginary is a subset of the Symbolic, just as the Symbolic is a subset of the Real. The elements of the Imaginary are particularly defined as forming pairs of mutually exclusive terms, that is, pairs of binary oppositions. [Cf. *Figure 3* in Chapter VIII.]

The Imaginary is the region of relationship that generates digital reason and logic by creating the principles of identity and negation. But this digital reason is of the lowest logical type of any of these processes. It is the furthest removed and abstracted from reality. Nietzsche was probably the first to understand this. In Part I of *Beyond Good and Evil*, he says:

> The fundamental faith of the metaphysicians is the faith in opposite values. It has not even occurred to the most cautious among them that one might have a doubt right here at the threshold where it was surely most necessary – even if they vowed to themselves, '*de omnibus dubitandum*'.

The emergence of the Imaginary is first expressed in the child's playing with the relation between presence and absence, as in the *Fort! Da!* described by Freud. The development of the Imaginary is also revealed in the child's fascination with his mirror-image, the *stade du miroir* in Lacan. The child's experience is that of looking "through the looking-glass" and seeing himself on the other side where he knows he is not. What 'is' is created in the Imaginary by a relation of opposition with what is not, but what 'is' is projected onto the Real and the Symbolic, while what is not belongs only to the Imaginary. The mirror-image is a condensation of what is and what is not. The condensation of logical types in a single message is the basic characteristic of a joke (Bateson, Haley, Jackson, and Weakland, 1956). The explosive re-evaluation of the logical typing of that message is expressed in laughter; thus the child's laughter when first confronted with a mirror indicates a re-evaluation for which the Imaginary is a prerequisite.

The Imaginary is Real and has effects in the real world. The Imaginary projects 'final causes' toward which the individual is drawn within the overdetermined possibilities of his situation. The processes of play, art, symptom formation, and revolution are all bound up in this process of making the Imaginary Symbolic and Real.

A useful tool in clarifying these concepts and their relationships is the Venn diagram set-notation used in Boolean algebra. The circles define sets, circles within circles are subsets and intersecting circles indicate shared elements. In the individual, the relationship between the Imaginary, the Symbolic, and the Real can be represented as in *Figure 1*.

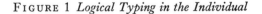

FIGURE 1 *Logical Typing in the Individual*

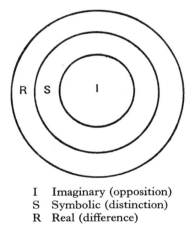

    I   Imaginary (opposition)
    S Symbolic (distinction)
    R Real (difference)

There are messages-in-circuit between individuals on each of these levels, and in normal communication each level supplements the others. The elements of the discourse are the Symbolic and the Imaginary, and conflicting messages on these levels are the basic elements of the double-bind situation, where whichever message a person responds to, he is punished for not responding to the other message. Where the person is locked in this oscillation between levels and punished for appropriate responses on either level, schizophrenia may be the only escape.

Again, the Venn diagrams may be useful, this time for showing inter-personal relationships, as in *Figure 2*.

FIGURE 2

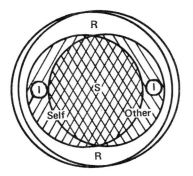

People are separate, atomistic individuals only on the Imaginary level, which is the level of the ego. On the Real and Symbolic levels there is no boundary that can be drawn between them.

The messages between people may be Symbolic and Imaginary, or only Symbolic. Where the content is Imaginary, the message is also Symbolic in the exchange relationship between them. Symbolic meaning refers to the level at which the relationship between the sender and receiver is defined. Where the message is only Symbolic, it may be on the level of gestures and actions without conscious meaning, but which are meaningful nevertheless. The symptom is such a message to an other. The Symbolic is unconscious (and so is the Real for that matter) to the extent that the Imaginary (ego) has not projected onto it.

Messages are also in circuit within the individual between the levels of representation. Imaginary constructs are transformed into Symbolic acts, and Symbolic exchanges are rationalized, mapped into the Imaginary. But in this process, when there is a conflict between the ego and the representation of the Symbolic message, repression takes the side of the ego, and as the gap between the ego and the message perceptions becomes wider, a 'neurosis' develops. We realize that this occurs because the Imaginary is held in higher esteem than the Symbolic, because 'pure' reason is thought to be supreme. But now we know that the Symbolic has the higher logical type, and that in any conflict between these levels, it is the Imaginary that must give way.

Chapter X

Critique of Phallocentrism

DANIEL PAUL SCHREBER ON WOMEN'S LIBERATION

> Being a woman in the true sense – or black or brown or
> working-class or Third World – is not a genetic or
> geographical or economic condition, it is a state of relation, a
> state of political consciousness. Without it you are never
> more than how the others make you.
> ANONYMOUS PAMPHLET: "What the Wizard of Oz Should
> Have Said to Dorothy and her Friends"

> We have the option of regarding a system as composed of
> elements that behave 'as if they couldn't help it' or 'as if they
> decided'.
> GORDON PASK

1. *Therapy and Ideology*

One of the more significant aspects of the various forms of existential
psychoanalysis (Binswanger, Sartre, Rollo May, Ronald Laing) was not
simply the attempt to reduce the overpowering importance of sexual
aetiology, as in orthodox Freudian analysis, but also to reduce the emphasis
on the father-figure represented by the phallus. Since we live in a male-
dominated culture, the relation to the father is undoubtedly of prime
importance. But the continued confusion of the phallus with the penis by
most traditional analysts had engendered a heavy-handed reductionism
which was so unsatisfactory as to result in the baby being thrown out with
the bathwater by younger and more creative therapists.

The changed emphasis – away from the castration complex and towards
being-in-the-world, away from such concepts as the fear of repressed
homosexual wishes and towards interpretations of objectification and

ontological insecurity (e.g., Laing, 1960) – breathed new life into therapy, as did the new emphasis on a conjoint and communicational approach (e.g., Ruesch and Bateson, 1951; Bateson, Jackson, Haley, and Weakland, 1956a; Laing and Esterson, 1964; Watzlawick, Beavin, and Jackson, 1967; Cooper, 1967). But the well-meant flight from the overriding male chauvinism of the Freudian theory (cf. Millett, 1970) did very little to change the continued oppression of women by both male and female therapists. The emphasis on the 'schizophrenogenic' mother – as 'real' as she may be – further contributed to what can only be called the biosocial pathology of the 'opposition' between the sexes in our culture.

Very little attempt has been made, as far as I know, to examine the material social context for the primary sources of this so-called opposition. This is hardly surprising. By calling this psychosocial and economic relationship of mastery and slavery an 'opposition', we (men) typically impute symmetry to what is in fact a relationship of complementarity. (Cf. Mitchell, 1971: 161, on the repressive function of "my wife and I are equals".) The reasons we make this 'error' are not to be found in 'ignorance' or in some 'accidental' confusion of logical typing, which has 'crept into' our definitions. Our refusal to understand – or even to notice – the real context (without which we can understand nothing) has its source in our own vested interest in the *status quo*.

I never met a man – of whatever political or personal persuasion – who did not exemplify in some way this deeply programmed defensiveness. Our vested interest in concealing, by projection, our own inadequacy – not as men, but as human beings – is derived from the objectifying internalization – by transformation[1] – of the same socioeconomic 'performance principle' which creates the alcoholic (Chapter III). But I am not about to say that we objectify ourselves by objectifying women – which is true – without also saying that these two objectifications differ radically in logical typing.

If confusions of logical typing are indeed the source of human creativity, the PROGRAMMATIC confusion of the logical typing of power and responsibility in the primary processes of our society is not simply the source of

---

[1] Formalist, 'structuralist', or 'scientific' theories and methodologies of morphostasis and equilibrium – which are largely useless for the critical analysis of concrete sociobiological reality – are powerful logical tools to use against the ideologies of morphostasis and equilibrium from which they are derived. Thus, Piaget's theory of 'structural transformation' is nowhere more illuminating than when it is applied to the structure of Piaget's own theory (Chapter XI). Similarly, Lacan's Imaginary order is nowhere of greater theoretical and practical use than when it is employed to demonstrate the Imaginary epistemological foundations of Lacanian psychoanalysis (Chapter XVII).

our social psychoses. It is a major instrument of oppression and of the rationalization of exploitation.

Thus, expressions like 'the opposition between man and woman', or 'the opposition between the male and female principles', or 'the battle of the sexes', are most emphatically not the result of faulty definitions. They exemplify the ideological and theoretical rationalization of what our behavior has already defined.

Since the socioeconomic sources of this master–slave relationship between the sexes – in another of their transformations – reappear in the violence inside the bourgeois family, it is not surprising that psychology, psychoanalysis, and psychotherapy – by the studiously artificial closure of their theoretical 'field' – should have in general projected the source of that violence onto the 'schizophrenogenic' mother. (Cf. Ronald Laing on the "self-imposed horizons" of the "clinical interpersonal microcosmos": 1960: 180) The father's complicity in the complex psycho-ontological violence of the parents against the children is often noted (such fathers are 'weak'). But his function as the AGENT, or as the LOCUS, or as the LOCUM TENENS of exploitation in its sexist or male-chauvinist transformation is not. And thus the logical typing of the parents' responsibility (Chapter V) is ignored.

The fundamental principle of our 'civilization' is exploitation. This is an exploitation of nature, of workers, of 'other' races, of underdeveloped countries, of women, of children – and, worst of all, the internalization of this ethic of exploitation to the point that we end up exploiting ourselves (Chapter VIII). Moreover, the internalization of the "ethic of disposability" by the 'experts', by the subjects-who-are-supposed-to-know, has resulted in a situation in which probably the most dangerous place to go for help in time of trouble is the office of a doctor, a clergyman, or a psychotherapist. And now of course we have new versions of gestalt therapy, sensitivity groups, encounter groups, catharsis therapy – some useful, most either decadent or dangerous – but all dependent on denying or disavowing the real socioeconomic context by means of the most naïve assumptions of 'psychological equality', an equality which is supposed somehow to cut across racial, economic, and sexual barriers so that everyone can 'do their own thing'.

From another point of view, the flight from the father to the mother and thence to the family – although it was responsible for the most striking developments in understanding pathological communication (Chapter V) – tended to obscure the enduring insights of Freud, latent within his manifest text. The liberal reaction against the castration theory and the penis–phallus also obscured the symbolic function of the phallus in exchange, which Lacan has so remarkably brought out (Chapters I, IX). The correlative tendency towards a somewhat behaviorist and bioenergetic view of communication left out of account the constraining and structuring function of discourse itself – especially in the way this function operates along class lines (Bernstein, 1958).

Lacan has, of course, reacted by returning us to Freud, via Lévi-Strauss and Roman Jakobson (Chapter I), but his reaction has resulted in a new justification of patrocentrism and phallocentrism in France, which was in any case a culture already so 'rational' as to find that Lacan's theory justified its deepest prejudices. Of course, if psychological theories either restricted themselves to explaining the effects of the dominant ideology of their culture on the psychological 'keyboard' of human beings, without claiming to explain the 'nature' of Man (and Woman), or if they took a truly critical perspective on that ideology, there would be no problem. But, with the exception of Wilhelm Reich, Frantz Fanon, and some of the younger workers in the field, who are seeking to establish a Marxist theory of the personality, therapists have in general done neither.

2. *Lacan's Theory of the Name-of-the-Father*

I hope to show by a critical and communicational analysis of a few representative passages from the text of the most famous 'psychotic' of all, Daniel Paul Schreber, that, as is to be expected, the alienated 'patient' often makes greater contributions to the theory than do his commentators. Just as Freud's theory of psychosis and paranoia depends on Schreber's autobiography (1903), Lacan's theory of the name-of-the-father is dependent on an analysis of the same text (Lacan, 1966: 531–83) – and, it must be added, on the same value system.

In the Lacanian theory, the name-of-the-father REPRESENTS what Lacan calls the Symbolic father. The Symbolic father is not a real or an Imaginary father (*imago*), but corresponds to the mythical Symbolic father of *Totem and Taboo*. The requirements of Freud's theory, says Lacan, led him "to link the apparition of the signifier of the Father, as author of the Law, to death, or rather to the murder of the Father, thus demonstrating that if this murder is the fruitful moment of the debt through which the subject binds himself for life to the Law, the Symbolic father, insofar as he signifies that Law, is actually the dead Father" (p. 556).[2] This primal of all primal scenes is related in Freud to the 'primal repression', for which

---

[2] Besides Lacan's text, see Wilden, 1968a: 270–84, 293–8. Wilden, 1971e contains a version of the present analysis and also corrects some errors in the 1968 English edition.

Lacan substitutes the terms "constituting metaphor" or "paternal metaphor". It is through the failure of this paternal metaphor, according to Lacan, that the psychotic is induced to foreclude or repudiate (*verwerfen*) the name-of-the-father. Since the name-of-the-father has never been successfully repressed, it is rejected, and with it, asserts Lacan, the whole Symbolic order.[3] If the subject employs figures of speech and metaphors in his 'delusions', it is because the signifier and the signified have become coalesced for him. In some respects, says Lacan, his discourse may resemble what linguists call autonomous messages, that is to say, messages about words (i.e., a form of metacommunication) rather than messages employing words. But eventually he will lose all his metalinguistic capacities, or so it will seem from outside.

In the seminar of March–April 1957, summarized by J.-B. Pontalis, Lacan clarifies somewhat his conception of the symbolic function of the father. "Through the oedipus complex", says Lacan, "the child takes on the phallus as a signifier, which supposes a confrontation with the function of the father." Whereas the girl's passage through this stage is relatively simple, the boy's is not. The oedipus complex must permit him to identify himself with his own sex and must allow him to accede to the position of a father, through what Lacan calls the "symbolic debt". He has the organ; the function must come from the Other (the Other beyond the other represented by his father, says Lacan): the Symbolic father.

> . . . The boy enters the oedipus complex by a half-fraternal rivalry with his father. He manifests an aggressivity comparable to that revealed in the specular relation (either *moi* or other). But the father appears in this game as the one who has the master trump and who knows it; in a word, he appears as the Symbolic father.

We must distinguish the Symbolic father from the Imaginary father, "often surprisingly distant from the real father", "to whom is related the whole dialectic of aggressivity and identification". Lacan goes on to say that the Symbolic father "is to be conceived of as 'transcendent', as an irreducible given of the signifier. The Symbolic father – he who is ultimately capable of saying 'I am who I am' – can be only imperfectly incarnate in the real father. He is nowhere . . . ." The real father "takes over from the Symbolic father", which explains why the real father "has a

---

[3] As distinct from my interpretation of symbolic exchange and the Symbolic, the Symbolic order for Lacan is the domain of the signifier (language). It is controlled by the Other. The phallus is for him the signifier of signifiers, the signifier of desire. It is against that position and all similar positions that the present analysis is directed. As I show in Chapter XVI, Section 2, the primal repression has nothing to do with fathers, it has to do with BOUNDARIES.

decisive function in castration, which is always deeply marked by his intervention or thrown off balance by his absence". Lacan continues:

> Castration may derive support from privation, that is to say, from the apprehension in the Real of the absence of the penis in women – but even this supposes a symbolization of the object, since the Real is full, and 'lacks' nothing. Insofar as one finds castration in the genesis of neurosis, it is never real but symbolic, and it is aimed at an Imaginary object (pp. 851–2).

3. *The Phallus as the Instrument of Exploitation*

Lacan's point in reintroducing the phallus into contemporary theory is that traditional psychoanalysis has so concerned itself with the "reduced dialectic" of the subject and his relation to objects, which are conceived of by analysts as either imaginary (hallucinated) or real, that the most essential part of the object relation has been ignored: the notion of the LACK OF OBJECT. Analysts have forgotten that "between the mother and the child, Freud introduced a third term, an Imaginary element, whose signifying role is a major one: the phallus" (Lacan, 1956c: 427). This relationship of three terms, mother, child, and phallus, is changed through the function of the father, which "inserts the lack of object into a new dialectic" and provides for what psychoanalysis calls the 'normalization' of the oedipus complex. It is the lack of object which circulates in symbolic exchange – or, as I would put it, it is the information borne by the sign which is exchanged, as distinct from its matter–energy. But the father involved is not the real father, nor an *imago* of any real father. Thus 'little Hans', through whose phobia Freud first revealed in detail the effects of castration fear in the child, was deprived of either a real or an Imaginary father by the fact that his own father – by whom the analysis and cure were actually conducted – had abdicated his responsibilities in the oedipal triangle in favor of the mother. The Symbolic father in this case, asserts Lacan, was 'the Professor': Freud himself.

Lacan seeks to define the Symbolic, Imaginary, and Real relationships between three subcategories of the lack of object – CASTRATION: "Symbolic lack of an Imaginary object"; FRUSTRATION: "Imaginary lack of a real object", e.g., the disappearance of the breast; and PRIVATION: "real lack of a Symbolic object", i.e., the 'real absence' of the organ in the woman – and the further relationships between the people involved. Thus castration (which is neither real, nor really potential) is part of the child's relationship to the father, that of the "symbolic debt". Frustration is part of the child's relationship to the mother, that of an "Imaginary injury" (*dam imaginaire*), connected with the later symbolization of the relationship of presence and absence through the *Fort! Da!* of *Beyond the Pleasure Principle* (Chapter VI). Privation, however, is real – nothing is lacking (nothing can be lacking in the Real, which is a plenum) – and the subject's relationship is supposedly not so much to a person as to reality itself. Since privation concerns "what ought to be there", the object involved is symbolic.

Why speak of the phallus and not of the penis? asks Lacan.

> . . . Because the phallus is not a question of a form, or of an image, or a phantasy, but rather of a signifier, the signifier of desire. In Greek antiquity the phallus is not represented by an organ but as an insignia; it is the ultimate significative object, which appears when all the veils are lifted. Everything related to it is an object of amputations and interdictions. . . .

He continues:

> The phallus represents the intrusion of vital thrusting or growth as such, as what cannot enter the domain of the signifier without being barred from it, that is to say, covered over by castration. . . . It is at the level of the Other, in the place where castration manifests itself in the Other, it is in the mother – for both girls and boys – that what is called the castration complex is instituted.

Thus it is the desire of the Other which is "marked by the bar" (Lacan, 1958: 252).

The exchange value of the phallus (its function as a sign) comes to it from outside, that is to say, from its function in a system of a higher order of organization which emerges in the new gestalt formed by the emergence of culture. Both the phallus in the family and the 'sister' or 'brother' in a kinship system are signs of an essential absence, or lack. The exchange of the symbolic object[4] is as if it were the exchange of this lack – which is information – rather than the exchange of a thing. Lack is essential to the concept of desire or goalseeking (Chapter XV), and even in the animal world or the world of the cell, the notion of teleonomy implies that the system is controlled not by what is, but by what is not. It is however an error to equate absence or lack directly with negation (Chapters VI, VII).

The phallus and the 'sister' or 'brother' depend on the digital DISTINCTION of a difference, just as the Imaginary, in the development of the child,

---

[4] This term is a residue of a former terminology, and should have been discarded with the other energy-entity metaphors. It is not an object, but a 'bit' of information, or a sign.

is a primary and necessary digitalization of an analog relation of difference. But the 'matrimonial dialogue' of the kinship system has quite a different function from the psychoanalytical MYTH of the exchange of the phallus within and between generations. The first has a Symbolic function, the second an Imaginary one. Unlike the conception of what is usually called the 'binary opposition' in phonology, the term 'distinction' carries no ideological function in itself; it is simply the prerequisite for the constitution of discrete elements out of a continuum. It is only when this particular kind of digital distinction is bent by our epistemology to an overriding Imaginary function which denies or disavows the relationships of the ecosystem from which this difference arises, that it may serve ideological ends inimical to the social, biological, or psychological survival of women and men.

Since symbolic linkages are information linkages (but not necessarily conversely), and not primarily energy linkages, it is through the emergence of the discrete elements of kinship denominations at a higher level of organization than that of the analog exchange of the procreative unit, that 'man' and 'woman' discover their symbolic function, as 'sister' and 'brother', of linking people and generations. But these signs are not the only symbolic 'objects' available. In cultures which make the phallus the measure of all relations between the sexes, the phallus is indeed part of an order of exchange into which the child is born. If the child is identified with the phallus by the mother, he is thus being required to conform to the desire of the Other. According to the theory, the symbolic value of castration – in which the agent is the Symbolic father who incorporates the law – is that of breaking this 'incestuous' circuit, thus opening up 'object choices' outside it. The exchange within the family is thus supposedly free to escape its original duality and enter into a displacement of it at another level of signification. According to the theory, it is through their accession, as subjects, to language (which, for Lacan, governs the Symbolic), that the boy, by repressing castration, and the girl, by rejecting (*verwerfen*) it, emerge from the oedipus complex at another level of organization. At this level, the dual and oppositional rivalry with the parent of the same sex is mediated by the intersubjective and simply DIFFERENTIATED relationship with the parent of the opposite sex. But what is entirely missing from the castration theory, is a critical understanding of the oppression of women it entails.

The problem of castration, which is retrospective for the *infans* and actual for the child, is that it sets up an Imaginary either/or opposition. Castration manifests itself as the question of who HAS the phallus and FOR WHOM does he have it. This is obviously an insoluble opposition, dependent upon an essentially analytic epistemology, for no one has, nor can anyone have, the object of Symbolic exchange. Merely to ask the question reduces the Symbolic to the Imaginary again. This question, which is in fact only one possible metaphor of all the hidden questions that the parents impose on the child (e.g., "Do I have your love?" "Do you have my love?" "Do you dare ask what my love for you really represents?"), in fact conceals an even more alienating possibility, that of asking who IS the phallus and for whom. The only rational answer, for either sex, is that no one is. But it happens that in our culture, for reasons that cannot be considered accidental, the question – which should never have been asked at all – is never properly resolved. With the rather specific organization and manipulation of personal insecurity in western culture, the non-resolution of the question has a controlling power: it is a psychological colonialism of DIVIDE AND RULE.

Whatever the specific reasons for this manipulation of castration may be, the analysis of the process itself is perfectly straightforward. All questions relating to the phallus in our culture depend upon the Imaginary confusion of penis (an entity) with phallus (a relation), a confusion which is necessarily engendered in ontogenesis (the curious expression used to describe the morphogenesis of relationships) by the confusion which the child is induced to make between need and demand. Once the cultural context is taken into account, it is very easy to understand why the girl is supposed to 'reject' castration whereas the boy 'represses' it. In a culture which confuses the psychic or societal individual with the biological organism, the real differences between the sexes can never find their proper level of organization or mediated relationship. That level of the total relationship which is concerned with PERSONS will constantly be confused with a lower level, that of the relationship between ORGANISMS.

As a consequence of this organismic error, it is true (for the system) that the penis is either there or not there, in anatomical terms. The boy can consequently maintain himself in a 'neurotic' relationship to the possibility of its absence by repressing and denying that possibility, whereas the girl, marked by what HER CULTURE REQUIRES her to recognize as a lack, is obviously obliged to take a 'schizophrenic' attitude to castration. Since she can hardly deny what she is taught to call an actual lack (it is not in fact a lack), she cannot repress it, but must reject or disavow it.

What results from the Lacanian analyses of the lack of object and of the primordial relationship to difference, from the fact that the breast is the primary symbolic 'object', and from the distinction he makes between need and desire, is not perhaps precisely what he intended. It is not simply that we must remember to distinguish penis (need) from phallus (demand, desire). The logical consequence of his position is in fact the refutation of his own phallocentrism. The simple notion of the signifier or the sign in Symbolic exchange could free psychoanalytical theory from its cultural function of justifying the subjugation of women. In effect, Lacan's analysis reveals the Imaginary grounds which psychoanalysts of both sexes have used to make of the phallus a privileged theoretical object of THEIR exchanges (whether they use the term or not). Male and female analysts who share the male chauvinism of western culture (to say nothing of other cultures) have contributed powerfully to the maintenance of this aspect of the *status quo*, and nobody of any integrity would want to defend Freud himself on this subject, except to say that he was also a product of his time. The Lacanian theory thus leads us to conclude that the phallus is not in fact a symbolic 'object' of exchange. In relation to the supposed 'lack' in the woman, it is an Imaginary object (entity) beholden to an Imaginary function (opposition).

This is not, unfortunately, the conclusion of most analysts, Lacanian or otherwise. In our culture there is no doubt that the phallus does indeed serve its Imaginary function. As clear as it is that the relation between 'phallus' and 'lack' is cultural and societal, this relation is generally accepted as an ONTOLOGICAL one, even – and perhaps especially – by those who would never use the term 'phallus', or who know nothing of psycho-analysis, or who would reject psychoanalysis as fantasy. The phallus may therefore correctly be said to represent the mediating function of the lack of object in our present psychosocial relationships. There is no doubt a connection between the myth of the 'lack' in the woman and the myth in western thought of the 'full origin' which is criticized so cogently by Derrida (Chapter XIII). (Cf. Laing, 1969: 42–4.)

The question to be answered is why the essentially neutral notion of the lack is used to justify the psychosocial and economic oppression of women. One could perhaps begin to construct an answer along the following lines. In a culture which requires men to be paid for their labor, but requires 'housewives' to labor for 'nothing', the phallus appears as the general equivalent of exchange (just as the commodity gold or its representative is the general equivalent of all other commodities in our economic system). If the alienated labor of the men in the economic system is purchased with money, then the equally alienated labor of the housewife is presumably recompensed in the psychosocial system with some equivalent commodity. Unfortunate as it may be to have to recognize it, this commodity appears in part to be children, long equated with the phallus in psychoanalytical theory. Children are indeed treated in general as accumulated objects of exchange with which to achieve status and by which to mediate one's relationships with others. It has been the anguish of the parents of the so-called 'hippie' generation to discover that many of their children were no longer prepared to accept this role. It has been the anguish of the children to discover that it is almost impossible to escape it, given the alienating and self-alienating values of our society, from which they are far from immune.

What I am trying to say here is that in spite of Lacan's metaphysics of the phallus, the role of the phallus in digital, Imaginary exchange is a product of our socioeconomic system, not a product of human psychology as such. We can therefore surely make use of the notion of the lack of object in symbolic exchange, without necessarily using it to contribute to the alienation and the self-alienation of both women and men (but especially women). The castration fears of men in a culture which equates virility with force, violence, aggression, killing, and the objectification of the 'other' sex, are quite serious enough. But the fears of the master cannot be equated with the effect of those fears on his psychosocial and socioeconomic slaves. It is probably true that the phallus is indeed the general equivalent in most of the psychosocial exchanges in the pathology of our culture. The devastating effect this Imaginary identity has on women, is that the phallus becomes the Imaginary equivalent of the woman herself.

One has only spend a few moments perusing the advertisements in almost any glossy magazine (no need to go as far as *Playboy*) to be entirely convinced that the woman's body and the woman's person are indeed equated, and that she is indeed bought and sold by all kinds of devious means. Advertisers who would never dream of pandering to (outright) racism or (outright) fascism spend many millions pandering to sexism. Literature, philosophy, psychology, and sociology contribute to the spread of these objectifying values by other means (cf. Millett, 1970). The most advanced forms of psychotherapy in England and the United States – dominated by males – show little, if any, consciousness of their implicit justification of the subordinate roles they assign to women. Anthropologists go on and on repeating the expressions the "exchange of women", the "circulation of women", with hardly a flicker of an attempt to understand what they are actually talking about. The contemporary 'love generation' celebrates its 'liberation' by translating what their fathers called 'dolls' and 'birds' into 'chick' – hardly surprising when one considers the actual meaning of the doctrine of 'free love' preached at the beginning of it all by young men to young women: sexual availability one doesn't have to pay for in the terms of the reciprocity and mutual responsibility that such freedom really ought to entail. And just as black militancy is so often overtly or covertly sexist – especially in relation to the black woman (Cleaver, 1968) – Mitchell (1971) and others have pointed to the extraordinary levels of hypocrisy resulting from male chauvinism among men of the so-called New Left. In this context, the mass media then play up the whole question of 'Women's Lib' – to the accompaniment of a sniggering traditionally reserved to 'dirty old men' – in ways guaranteed to get the maximum mileage out of the appropriately related male obsessions with growth, efficiency, performance, and production.

Most women are consciously – and necessarily – unaware of this trafficking in souls, but they – equally necessarily – react very often with a justified unconscious ferocity against whatever representatives of or surrogates for the great white father happen to be around. The exchange of women is thus no anthropological fiction; whatever it may represent in other cultures, it is the most universal manifestation of the reduction of people to things in western culture. It is not for nothing, therefore, that psychoanalytical theory – invented and dominated by males – has always referred to love and hate as a question of the CHOICE OF OBJECT. And since in the real socioeconomic context, men alone are those with the power to punctuate the system in this way, then we must recognize that just as all racism in western societies is (a version of) white racism, all sexism is (defined by) male sexism.

4. *Repressed Homosexuality and Paranoia*

Freud established to his own satisfaction that the 'cause' of 'paranoia' was fear of a "homosexual wish phantasy". Considering the grotesque nature of what passes for love and sexuality in western culture (cf. Marcuse's critique, 1955), and its direct relationship to the cultural schizophrenia in which we live (Chapter VIII), it is entirely possible that such a fear could in fact appear as a kind of 'screen-symptom' re-presenting the basic and constant 'ontological insecurity' of most people in western societies (cf. Laing, 1960). Considering our generalized fear of 'others', and the interrelated fear among men that any manifestation of so-called 'feminine' traits will invite the kind of objectification they themselves project on women, it is very easy to mistake the 'homosexual wish phantasy' for the fundamental social alienation it conceals.

The fact that the run-of-the-mill 'pornographic' movies almost invariably depict lesbianism, but almost never depict male homosexuality, is an indicator of such fears in men. In this case they fear that women in general are 'insatiable' and cannot be satisfied by THEM. Men are not in general afraid of their 'homosexual wish fantasies' as such. They are afraid of other people, and especially of the women to whose reification they have contributed. They are afraid of women because, having consented to their own alienation by the 'performance principle', they now have to perform.

The male myth of 'insatiable' female sexuality is in effect a metaphor of the insatiable demands the socioeconomic system makes on men as human beings. It is not the women that men cannot 'satisfy'; WHAT MEN CANNOT SATISFY ARE THE MACHINES: technique, technology, production, and performance. It appears therefore that the lesbian episodes in the 'pornographic' movie do not serve a primarily titillating function. They are there to perpetrate the myth of female 'insatiability', and to provide comfort against it.

One suspects, therefore, that Freud's homosexual aetiology of paranoia is no more than a rationalization of the irrationality of personal relationships in the culture at large. The Imaginary potential of these fears and oppositions is exploited to the full: they become an internalized means of control which is far more effective than the work of any secret police (cf. Marcuse, 1955, 1964). In a word, there are enough real reasons to be paranoid and schizophrenic in western culture, to make it unnecessary to reduce such manifestations of social alienation to fear of homosexuality or some such equivalent.

The fact that the theory of psychosis in psychoanalysis is closely related to the function of the father in the oedipal triangle, puts Lacan's theory of the paternal metaphor well within the Freudian tradition. And his insistence on its linguistic aspects is also derived from the Freud who said of Schreber's case: ". . . It is a remarkable fact that the familiar principal forms of paranoia can all be represented as contradictions of the single proposition: 'I (a man) LOVE HIM (a man)', and indeed that they exhaust all the possible ways in which such contradictions could be formulated." In delusions of persecution, the verb is contradicted: "I do not LOVE him – I HATE him (because he persecutes me)." In erotomania, the object is contradicted: "I do not love HIM – I love HER (because she loves me)." Alcoholic delusions of jealousy contradict the subject: "It is not I who love the man (women) – SHE (HE) loves him (them)." (Note the double standard of this last example, expressed in the singular 'man' and the plural 'women'.) In megalomania, the whole proposition is contradicted: "I do not love at all – I do not love anyone (I love only myself)" (*Standard Edition*, XII, 62–5).

The relationship established by Freud between fear of 'homosexual' wishes and the aetiology of 'paranoia' has been widely accepted in psychoanalytical theory. In the introduction to their translation of Schreber's *Memoirs* (1903) – commented by Lacan in his "Du traitement possible de la psychose" – Ida Macalpine and Richard Hunter seem to join Lacan in laying the emphasis of their analysis on Schreber's CONFUSION OF SEXUAL IDENTITY. But, as in the whole question of sublimated homosexuality in psychoanalytical theory, it is clear that the 'territory' to which the 'map' labeled 'homosexuality' refers in Freud's interpretation is not at all equivalent to the territory of manifest homosexuality (Bateson, 1955). Freud's theory of overdetermination in any case requires that there be more than one map and more than one territory – and that the map be not a simple indicator, but rather a re-presentation. At another level, as Macalpine and Hunter point out, Freud tends to treat the Schreber case in the terms of his theory of neurosis at the same time as he is trying to maintain a distinction between neurosis and psychosis (Schreber, 1903: 12). (As valuable as such a distinction may be, the attempt to maintain it has a methodological rather than a real value, since any 'patient' is likely to exhibit behavior to which many labels could be applied.) Thus, before we even approach Schreber's text, there are a number of indications that Freud's analysis suffers from purely methodological faults.

5. *Schreber's Desire to be Unmanned*

In order to understand the ideological values of phallocentrism in psycho-analytical theory, we have to examine the relationship between 'castration' and 'unmanning' in Schreber's text. I suggest that Schreber's own analysis of his 'desire to be unmanned', far from being a symptom, is in fact a metacommunication about Lacan's hypothesis of the "paternal metaphor" and in effect goes far beyond Macalpine and Hunter's entirely convincing critique of the "homosexual bias" of Freud's interpretation. In fact, one discovers on reading Schreber's book from a critical perspective, that the chief merit of Freud's interpretation lies not in its faithfulness to the text, but its AESTHETIC simplicity. Like Kepler's stubborn attempts, against all the evidence, to model the planetary orbits on the five 'perfect solids' of Euclidean geometry, Freud's analysis turns out to be an example of the way certain kinds of aesthetic values can misguide the commentator.

Lacan remarks accurately that in their critique Macalpine and Hunter may be confusing the castration of psychoanalytical theory with real castration (1966: 565). But the question of 'unmanning' (*Entmannung*) for Schreber is not a question of castration at all. As Macalpine and Hunter point out in the commentary to their translation, *Entmannung* is always implicitly and most often explicitly a synonym for "being turned into a woman". It is not therefore a negative abandonment of an old state, but rather a positive entry into a new state. The theory of castration will reply, however, that this 'positive' aspect is simply the result of an idealization of women, for which the theory can entirely account. But it is easy to show from the text that the idealization involved does not concern women.

First, however, to Lacan's commentary. On the castration mentioned by Macalpine and Hunter, he remarks: "One realizes that it was not in order to be 'foreclosed' of the penis that the patient dedicated himself to becoming a woman, but rather in order to have to be the phallus" (*pour devoir être le phallus*) (ibid.). (For Lacan's interpretation, "to be or not to be" is in essence the question of "to be or not to be the phallus".) Lacan goes on to point out that Fenichel's "symbolic equation", *Mädchen = Phallus*, has its roots in the processes of the Imaginary, through which, as he says, the desire of the child comes to be identified with the "lack-to-be" or "lack-in-being" (*manque à être*) in the mother, a lack to or into which the mother was introduced by the Symbolic law (of the father), "where this lack is constituted". He goes on to say that it is the same source which accounts for the fact that "in the Real, women – with all due deference to them – serve as objects for the exchanges ordered by the elementary structures of kinship. These exchanges are perpetuated in the Imaginary, whenever the opportunity offers itself, whereas what is transmitted in parallel fashion in the Symbolic order is the phallus" (ibid.). (Cf. the kinship system diagrams in Chapter IX.)

Here Lacan makes the same epistemological error as Lévi-Strauss, an error which is all the more surprising because it was after all Lacan who taught us not to confuse the real object (the penis, the breast) with the symbolic 'object' (the phallus, the part-object). Because both authors regularly confuse energy with information, neither Lacan nor Lévi-Strauss realizes that in the symbolic exchange or 'phatic communion' of the so-called archaic society, it is not the bioenergetic 'entity', the female, nor the psychosocial 'person', the woman, which is the object of symbolic exchange, but the SIGN 'sister' or 'brother'. The sign in symbolic exchange, like the phallus, is what cannot be expropriated, alienated, or possessed. The fact that the WOMAN is indeed an Imaginary object in our culture, as is the PENIS, provides no justification for the error in levels which automatically assigns the same role to the 'SISTER' in the archaic culture. And just as Lévi-Strauss reveals a well-meant guilt about his patrocentric position on the exchange of women in the last pages of *The Elementary Structures of Kinship* (1949) – where he makes an ineffectual sentimental appeal to the "mystery" of the relations between the sexes – Lacan complements this gentlemanly tokenism by his parenthetical "with all due deference".

The critique of phallocentrism does not put the phallus as such in question, but it questions the PLACE assigned to it. A paternalistic position can be justified only by a coherent theory, not by paternalistic apologies like those of Lévi-Strauss and Lacan.[5] Lacan cannot, I would think, have it both ways. If there is indeed a Symbolic, Imaginary, and/or Real difference between 'penis' and 'phallus', then the same distinctions must apply to women and to men. Without even considering what the equation of virgin and phallus means in the application of the theory, the particular equation used contradicts the theory itself. In the case of women, the so-called 'symbolic equation', *Maiden = Phallus*, must in fact represent either an Imaginary equation, *Maiden = Penis*, or a Real equation, *Female = Penis*, or a Symbolic one, *'Sister' = 'Phallus'*. In other words, if one wishes to analyze a relationship between the images of entities in order to account for the reduction of the woman to the image of an entity, the second half of the equation must be an entity for which there is an appropriate image (thus 'Maiden' reduces not to 'Phallus', but to 'Penis'). If, on the other hand, one is talking about real matter–energy, then one should equate one biological use value with another (Female–Male = Penis–Vagina). And if one is talking about a symbolic 'object', then both sides of the equation must be SIGNS ('Sister–Brother' = 'Phallus'). None of these equations can in any case justify, in social or in psychological terms, the reduction of the women's person to her body as an object, a reduction for which the theory is in fact the rationalization. If we drop the ideology of phallo-centrism, we can reformulate the equation in the way the Lacanian theory actually requires us to do: 'Sister–Brother' = 'Part-Object' (the repre-sentative of the breast). The 'sister', the 'brother', and the 'part-object' are neither persons nor things, they are SIGNS.

I have no wish to go any further into the psychoanalytical theory of the 'choice of object', whose alienating terminology is the necessary conse-quence of its instinctual postulates. (Instincts have objects, people have instincts; therefore people have objects, these objects are. . . .) But since we are concerned to demonstrate not only the ideological foundations of much of the current theory, but also its epistemological inadequacies (cf. Chapter XV), it is useful to quote a characteristic example of the mis-leading statements which result from its lack of a communicational perspective. Thus, Winnicott, in his otherwise interesting and useful article on 'transitional objects' (1953: 12), is induced by his inability to

---

[5] All the remarks in this book about the exchange of women are intended to direct attention to the necessity of a critical examination of the idea and the reality, free from rationalization by the dominant ideology. The exploitative male chauvinism of some 'other' cultures is as well known as the lack of it elsewhere is not. Ehrenfels (1964), for example, points to the democratic function of (legitimate) authority in matrilineal groups in India, as distinct from the (ille-gitimate) function of power (with its feudalistic overtones) in most patrilineal systems.

distinguish matter–energy from information to make the following statement about the relationship between mother and child:

> There is no interchange between the mother and the infant. Psychologically the infant takes from a breast that is part of the infant, and the mother gives milk to an infant that is part of herself. In psychology, the idea of interchange is based on an illusion in the psychologist.

The 'illusion' he is referring to is what will become the transitional object (a blanket, a rag doll). Winnicott uses the term 'illusion' to describe a positive transitional phenomenon, but his atomistic basis in instinctual conflict makes it impossible for him to differentiate between an energy–entity relation and the interchange of information. He does not see that this 'object' is what mediates the informational relationship between the mother and the child. Outside its manifestations as a material 'possession' (matter), the transitional object is ALSO a metaphoric sign (information) which has been substituted for another sign, and for which others (e.g., the thumb) may also be substituted.

To return to Schreber: neither Lacan's nor Macalpine and Hunter's interpretations fully fit the text. Moreover, the two interpretations are mirror-images of each other. In keeping with the interpretation of the Imaginary as primarily involving opposition and that of the Symbolic as primarily involving difference, both the phallic interpretation of Lacan (identification with the phallus as progenitor) and the 'unmanning' interpretation of Macalpine and Hunter (identification with the woman as progenitor) are versions of the same man–woman opposition set up by the male-dominated ideology of our culture.

This male domination is common to both sexes. The mother who sought to protect her daughter against the ravages of phallocentrism, as one French mother did (M. Mannoni: personal communication), by telling her that a girl has "three little birds" whereas "a man has only one", not only has a problem with arithmetic. She is doing very well for her daughter in the fantasy world of the birds and the bees, but she is contributing to her daughter's oppression in the real one. Whoever defines the code or the context, has control – as the theory of the double bind so agonizingly shows – and all answers which accept that context abdicate the possibility of redefining it. Phallocentrism is surely most simply defined as that ideology, numismatic or otherwise (Goux, 1968, 1969), which makes the phallus the measure of all things.

It is not enough therefore to replace the phallocentric interpretation of Lacan by the 'question of sex identity' offered by Macalpine and Hunter. Both views depend upon the Imaginary opposition between men and women, and opposition is the correlative of identity. Lacan's interpretation is more subtle, of course. It is easier for him to claim that it is the 'patient' who reads relationships this way, rather than Lacan, whereas Macalpine and Hunter call upon 'archaic' phantasies and myth to buttress their view that Schreber's desire to bear a child is the operative factor in the case. But, when Macalpine and Hunter implicitly replace the so-called 'penis-envy' in women by a form of 'womb-envy' or 'vagina-envy' in men, they build up another set of oppositions, still coded around the ideological opposition of the sexes. The fact that both of these types of envy undoubtedly manifest themselves in our society, is more a statement about the poverty of love relationships in our culture than a statement about psychology.

This is quite apart from the fact that penis-envy is a purely male characteristic. If women manifest it, it is because they have been induced to do so by their cultural upbringing, not as a result of any innate 'inferiority' or 'lack'. It is unfortunate – but inevitable – that most women in our culture have been programmed to interiorize the values of male chauvinism. This process of self-oppression has a parallel elsewhere: even in their very militancy, many Third World people, and many people who suffer from the domestic colonialism within the 'developed' countries, manifest sets of values which turn out to be derived from the exploitative values of whites, or from a simple REVERSAL of those values (Fanon, 1952, 1961). As Marx put it in the *Grundrisse*: "The competition of workers between themselves is only another form of the competition of capital" (McLellan, 1971: 130).

6. *Schreber as a Social Philosopher*

It is only by carefully reading the Schreber case in the terms of the real differences – rather than Imaginary oppositions – between men and women, and with the aid of Macalpine and Hunter's most useful commentary, that one can discover the fundamental factor in it. It is a factor which brings us much closer to Ronald Laing's concern for 'ontological insecurity' than to Lacan's 'castration' and 'foreclusion of the name-of-the-father'.

Schreber manifests a fairly consistent Manicheism in relation to most of the cultural oppositions available to him: male and female, 'higher' and 'lower' gods, self and other, pure and impure souls, soul and body, God and mankind, and so on. But a moment's consideration of the text reveals that whereas, AS A MADMAN, Schreber is oscillating between the poles of various double binds, AS A PSYCHOLOGIST–PHILOSOPHER, he is desperately trying to metacommunicate about them. Schreber is metacommunicating about the Manicheistic ideology of his culture, without being entirely capable of defining that metacommunication. Thus he seems to fall all too easily into what appears to be just one more example of the 'religiosity' of the 'madman'.

The key to Schreber's philosophical commentary lies in his use of the term *Wollust*. It occurs above all in two key phrases: '*Wollust-(weibliche) Nerven*', '(female) nerves of voluptuousness', and in '*Seelenwollust*', 'soul voluptuousness', which is synonymous with 'blessedness of the soul' (*Seligkeit*). The bracketed '(female)' in the first phrase already suggests that Schreber's repeated attempts to catalogue and differentiate 'male' and 'female' attributes (e.g., 1903: S.18, S.164–7) may be of a less significant level of communication than his remarks about the all-encompasing erotogeneity of the Woman he desires to be. As Macalpine and Hunter point out, *Wollust* clearly has the sense of 'lust for life' (*Wollust des Lebens*), rather than a purely or mainly sexual sense, as most commentators have supposed. *Wollust* is as close to Eros, in the Marcusean sense, as it can possibly be. The *Wollust-Nerven* are not therefore so much the 'nerves of lust', but more nearly the 'rays of life'.

We live in a culture which is already dependent on the digitalization of the biosocial and psychological differences between men and women. In our culture, men are primarily viewed as digital. That is to say, they are expected to exemplify the so-called masculine traits: logic, rationality, intellect; manipulative, objective, and instrumental knowledge; being-in-relation-to-objects-in-the-world; and so on. Women, on the other hand, are primarily viewed as analog. They are expected to exemplify the so-called feminine traits: emotion, irrationality, feeling, subjective knowledge, person-oriented knowledge, life-in-relation-to-men, and, above all, BEING-IN-RELATION-TO-RELATION. But in the same way that in the "double dominance theory" of the two cerebral hemispheres (Bakan, 1971; Appendix I to Chapter VII) – which are in any case interfunctional and interconnected – each hemisphere deals with different functions – the left being concerned with processes which are verbal, analytic, abstract, rational, objective, active, and digital; the right, with processes which are pre-verbal, synthetic, concrete, emotive, subjective, passive, and analog – the supposedly 'digital' man is not really in opposition to the supposedly 'analog' woman. There are certainly real physical and biological differences of function between people, and there are undoubtedly hormonal balances which affect men and women differently. But not only are the oppositions I have described purely cultural oppositions which break the essential circuit of difference or unit of mind between man and woman. They are also oppositions based on the IMAGE of man and the IMAGE of woman. Real people can only fit these images by denying or disavowing a part of their analog-and-digital humanity (their 'bisexuality'). In other words, the woman is most emphatically not to be regarded as the 'analog' complement of the 'digital' man: a 'nature' for his 'culture' to continue to exploit.

The cultural opposition between the role of the woman as analog and the man as digital has its correlate in other relations of oppression. As man relates to words and objects, and woman to relations, so exploiter relates to the world of things, and exploited to the world – and words – of the exploiter. These relations are too complex to deal with in any detail in the context of this book. One may simply note that most exploited groups in modern society are excessively male chauvinist themselves, partly because of the level of economic exploitation of their menfolk. Useful in this connection, however, is Bernstein's study of the relation between child and environment in the British working and middle classes (1958). He points out that working-class socialization necessarily evolves a pattern of adaptive response to relationships with words, people, and objects, which is qualitatively different from that of the middle class. The working-class child is induced to be highly sensitive to non-verbal or "immediate" clues and cues in what one would call the digitally simple but analogically complex messages he receives ("Shut up"), whereas the middle-class child is induced to look for similar clues about his relationship with other people in the verbal message itself ("Darling, I do wish you could make a little less noise"). This distinction – which leads to a non-instrumental relationship with words in the working-class child, and an instrumental relationship to words in the middle-class child – must be correlated with the fact that anyone in a social relationship which defines him or her as inferior must necessarily be much more concerned to discover what the relationship is ABOUT than to communicate or receive any particular message within it. He or she will be much more interested in the messages which FRAME the communication, telling them 'where they stand', than in the communication itself, because an inadvertent step outside the frame may have disastrous consequences. (Many Southern lynchings had their source in 'looking up to whites' in the wrong way, for instance.)

The middle-class or white child lives in a much less constrained semiotic environment, where subtle verbal distinctions are encouraged, and where – unlike the situation of the working-class child – they have adaptive (survival) value. Moreover, the middle-class child has been trained in both kinds of communication, whereas the working-class child, in the main, is used to only one mode. Since schooling emphasizes the second (digital) mode, and pays increasingly less attention to the problems of translating from one to the other, the working-class child is rarely, is ever, put into a context in which he can learn the techniques of such translations. From personal experience in the United States and Africa, I would say that the kind of model proposed by Bernstein, once translated into a communicational terminology, is valid for many other relations of oppression. One notes that what he calls the splitting of the continuum of communication and socialization (p. 233) into the qualitatively distinct modes of "mediate/immediate", and "instrumental/non-instrumental" precisely maps the supposed opposition between the 'male principle' and the 'female principle' in our culture. The socialization of women requires them to be acutely aware of their inferiority in relation to men; the socialization of men teaches them to manipulate words and things – as well as other people they have been trained to regard as things.

Although at one level of communication, Schreber is bound by these same cultural oppositions – which he has been trained all his life to recognize (e.g., S.18) – and although he fears for his virility from time to time, he manifests no fear of what he calls 'femininity' at the meta-communicative level. The reason is not far to seek. It is simply that his definition of Femininity goes beyond the oppositions of 'masculinity' and 'femininity' outlined above. For him the Feminine means a total 'lust for life' or eroticism. As he explains in detail, the Female nerves of voluptuous-ness pervade the whole body, whereas the 'male' nerves are simply localized in a GENITAL sense (S.274). 'Female' with a capital F is thus not opposed to 'male' in Schreber's philosophy. The relationship he establishes has to be described in the terms of logical typing. He defines a Female 'totality of being' which is superior to the 'localized genitality' of men. The (actual) 'male' is thus a category which is of a lower logical type then the (desired) 'Female'. The total eroticism or blessedness which Schreber seeks has therefore to be defined as a Symbolic and differential UNION of the Mani-cheistic oppositions of male and female, mind and body, soul and body, which he sees all around him. It is of no small significance, for instance, that one of the primary distinctions in the 'psychotic' *Grundsprache* is a Reichian one: men and women are distinguished by their ARMAMENTS (clothing: *armamentarium*) (S.166). The union of difference posited by Schreber does not repeat the Hegelian error of confusing the (Symbolic) unity of opposites with the (Imaginary) identity of opposites, for his 'unity of oppositions' is a unity of differences which are, in his words, "consonant with the Order of the World".

In this way, Schreber's own interpretation transcends Freud's either/or 'homosexual' bias, Lacan's digitalized 'linguistic' bias, and Macalpine and Hunter's oppositional theory of 'sex identity'. We find that we have to agree with Schreber when he says that he possesses an insight into human thought processes and feelings which any psychologist might envy (S.166).

In spite of all of Schreber's manifest Manicheism – his transvestitism, his love/hatred for his doctor, Flechsig, and so on, at the level of the controlling double bind – he desires above all to live in conditions which he calls "consonant with the Order of the World". Here he speaks at a level which transcends the double binds of his culture. The *Weltordnung* is "the natural bond which holds mankind and God together"; it is an essentially ecological, rather than a psychological, concept. Why is the highest reproach he can find to level against the God who is behaving so peculiarly towards him, the reproach that God "lets himself be f . . . ed" (as he puts it)? The phallocentric theory will respond with an analysis of phantasies of anal penetration and so forth, but in doing so it will be answering at the communicative rather than the metacommunicative level.

The answer of the metatheory is much more simple than any answer explicitly or implicitly contrived to maintain the male dominance of traditional psychoanalytical theory. For Schreber, living in consonance with the Order of the World requires the absorption of his penis into his entrails so that he can become the bride of God and thus repopulate the world, which has undergone a catastrophe. But 'Woman' for him means something quite different from the 'woman' of his time. To be a Woman, for Schreber, does not mean to exchange one set of genitals for another. To be a Woman means to be totally in touch with the source of human life. TO BE THE WOMAN MEANS IN FACT NOTHING LESS THAN TO BE A HUMAN BEING.

Being the Woman is for him the opposite of 'soul murder', and in the text, soul murder always means the EXPLOITATION of one human being by another. Schreber is indeed afraid of being unmanned (turned into a woman) in THIS world, because he fears that this may serve the purposes of soul murder, and such exploitation is contrary to the Order of the World. Thus, for Schreber, 'unmanning' in itself has nothing to do with anything perverse – such as soul murder – which would break what he calls the "natural" link between human beings and between God and humanity.

A glance at a picture of Dr Flechsig provides a clue (frontispiece to the *Memoirs*). He is seated before a huge picture of a single dissected cerebral hemisphere amidst sundry bottles full of preserved 'specimens'. The laboratory is a concrete representation of a psychotic nightmare. If Schreber is afraid more than anything else of being reduced from a 'whole soul', a human being, to the status of an object, the sight of Flechsig studying 'nervous diseases' would be more than enough to set him off.

Schreber explains quite clearly that he is not fundamentally concerned with male–female oppositions, nor with genital sexuality, nor with genital virility, in a revealing passage:

> Since I have wholeheartedly inscribed the cultivation of feminity on my banner . . ., I would like to meet the man who, faced with the choice of either becoming a demented human being in a male habitus or a *Geistreiches Weib*, would not prefer the latter (S.178).

The relation he sets up between the "demented human being in male habitus" and the Woman recalls that made by Eldridge Cleaver, in *Soul on Ice* (1968). Cleaver describes the white man as the "Omnipotent Administrator" who has allowed the black man to be the "Supermasculine Menial", only to discover in retrospect that he has emasculated himself and must therefore emasculate the other.

In our culture, woman is the body, and man is the mind. Schreber seeks to transcend this Imaginary opposition, not by 'changing signs' from positive to negative, but by going beyond the given cultural positives and negatives. The term *Geistreiches Weib* – an 'ingenious' or 'witty' woman, a 'woman full of spirits' – makes this perfectly clear to whoever has eyes to see it. Schreber does not seek to be EITHER a woman ('body') OR a man ('mind'). He seeks to be the unity of their (cultural) difference: to be A WOMAN FULL OF MIND.

But he knows that this process of transformation may be dangerous in the existing social context. This context is the world of the "fleeting improvised men" (*flüchtig hingemachte Männer*, S.4) whose existence proved to Schreber that mankind had vanished and had to be born again through him. He knows that actual transformation into a woman might mean to be treated in the ways a woman is treated in our culture – and in the same way as Schreber himself had no doubt treated women. It might mean to be made into an object for the (psycho-)sexual gratification of men. In a word, it might mean to be treated as a SEXUAL COMMODITY. This Schreber considers to be the epitome of degradation. We can now understand why, for Schreber, the sun (which is feminine in German) is on the one hand the source of all life and the creative principle of God (S.8), and on the other, a whore (S.384). As it appears to Schreber – and no doubt to women – the problem with being even half feminine in our society is that no matter what you do, you may get into situations, where, like God himself, you "let yourself get f . . . ed". Schreber hopes however that all the curious and contradictory behavior of God – who is also an androgyne principle for him – will eventually be corrected and that "inner voluptuousness transfigured and enobled by human imagination [will] offer greater attraction than outer f . . . ing when [that is] contrary to the Order of the World" (S.190).

Schreber's philosophy is an ethical commentary on the organization of aggressivity in nineteenth-century society.[6] It describes a conflict between the way the world is and the way it ought to be. Schreber is above all concerned with the liberation of men and women from oppression and from self-oppression: liberation from the 'is' by means of the 'ought'. The world to come is a world of lust, not for objects, but for life; of voluptuousness, not for the dreary mechanisms of genital sexuality, but for all the dimensions of being human. The condition of voluptuousness he seeks is neither male nor female, but rather a state of BLESSEDNESS, an Order of the World in which "all legitimate interests are in harmony" (S.360).

With that sentence Schreber deserves a place among the great mystics and the great utopian socialist philosophers. His psychological idiosyncrasies remain interesting, but, like those of Montaigne, of Rousseau, of Marx, or those of Freud himself, they are in essence irrelevant to the articulation of his philosophical discourse. If Schreber is schizoid or schizophrenic in his madness, he refuses to be split into the subject of the analog and the subject of the digital in his desire. I have said elsewhere that all great texts are ultimately commentaries on their commentators. Schreber's desperate attempt to liberate the world through his own liberation, against all the odds, is no exception.

[6] In a forthcoming study, Maud Mannoni (personal communication) describes the insane and vicious treatment of the young Schreber by his father, a well-known educational theorist. The father used his son as a guinea-pig to test his views about the value of discipline, deprivation, and frustration in education: the destruction of all originality, creativity, and desire. (See Morton Schatzman, *Soul Murder*. New York: Signet, 1974; and Appendix, Note 30.)

Chapter XI

The Structure as Law and Order

PIAGET'S GENETIC STRUCTURALISM[1]

Madness is the punishment of a disordered and
useless science. If madness is the truth of
knowledge, it is because knowledge is absurd, and
instead of addressing itself to the great book of
experience, loses itself in the dust of books and
in idle debate. Learning becomes madness
through the very excess of false learning.
MICHEL FOUCAULT

1. *The Representative Metaphor*

To write an epistemological critique of the way the term 'structure' has
recently been deified in France requires a representative text. The text I
choose as the axis of this chapter is Piaget's *Structuralism* (1968), which has
just been issued in a useful but rather freewheeling and often defective
American translation by Chaninah Maschler. But to write a critique of
what has become a fad in France and yet is still largely unknown in the
United States would pose a special set of problems, if the critique were
really aimed at 'structuralism' as such. To give the impression that it is
simply 'structuralism' as such which is on trial here, would obscure one of
the objectives of this book, which is to demonstrate the ideological functions and the epistemological inadequacies of the international discourse of
science. Moreover, however difficult it may be to avoid it, I have no wish
to add grist to the mill of those American and British representatives of the

[1] A brief version of this chapter has appeared in *Semiotica*, and a résumé of some
of the central ideas has also appeared in *Psychology Today*. A savagely edited
version appears in a volume on structuralism edited by Ino Rossi (New York:
E. P. Dutton). What follows does not (consciously) depend on Vygotsky's 1932
critique (1963: 9–34), but there are a number of similarities.

scientific discourse who, by the very forms of their opposition to 'structuralism', reveal their own ideological and epistemological identity with it.

I have chosen Piaget's text as the representative pretext for the present critique. His book is taken as a representative metaphor of a way of thought, whose international unity is well demonstrated by the acceptance his work is gaining in the United States. Walter Buckley, for example (1971), has used Piaget's 'constructivism' to try to get at the methodological and epistemological retardation of the American social sciences. I suspect, however, that Buckley's attempt is a step backwards from the potential of the systems perspective he began with. He takes over from Piaget a theory of self-objectification ("the child's development of a sense of the self as an object" in a world of "interpersonal transactions") which is solidly based in the Imaginary, and whose 'transactional' base is, I suspect, a metaphor of commodity exchange in western culture (Chapter IX). As I shall show in detail, Piaget's dependence on a theory of child development involving "actions performed on objects", has its basis in the essentially atomist confusion between energy (entities) and information (relations) that the cybernetic–ecosystemic perspective has so effectively criticized.

Since the traditional epistemology of the life and human sciences is founded on an essentially religious belief in the real existence of such popular fictions as the 'autonomous ego', closed structures, atomistic individuals, and isolable entities (nowhere better expressed than in the Constitution of the United States), it necessarily generates a further fiction, essential to its own survival.

As the product of a goalseeking system which we can label 'the (international) discourse of science' – as the product of a group of (mostly) MEN – a theory occurs only in a specific historical and social context. In that context, then, the theory too, like any adaptive system, must have survival value. It is therefore impossible for a theory not to have a referent or a goal outside itself, since 'pure' truth not only does not exist, it has no survival value whatsoever. The protective fiction engendered by the traditional viewpoint is precisely the denial or the rejection of the INSTRUMENTAL function of all theories in the real and material world of socioeconomic relations. Consequently, the traditional epistemology generates the fiction that a theory can be NEUTRAL. In actual fact, of course, no matter what it is 'about' 'in itself', any theory – or any statement or message whatsoever, as it happens – is also a communication about the context in which it arose and from which it cannot in fact be isolated, except in the imagination of 'science', or through the delusions of the theorist.

Of course, the theory may even be 'true'. But all theories are true, without exception, if they are sufficiently isolated from the context in which they arise or to which they refer. And although the traditional epistemology cannot logically entertain the idea, because it depends upon a one-dimensional criterion of truth as either this or that, the actual way in which theories are accepted or rejected does not depend on examining the 'facts' to which they refer, but on the level of truth about which they communicate. Logic, like mathematics and everything else in the human world, is primarily communication, and the actual behavior of human beings never fails to conform to the requirement of communication, whatever any of us may think or have been programmed to think we are doing.

But the traditional epistemology must refuse the multidimensionality of truth, and it must consequently reject all discussions of this problem outside the domain of what it recognizes as 'science'. The traditional view tends to regard truth as timeless, as non-contextual, and as something to be reached by 'successive approximations', as Cournot or Piaget would put it. But there is no such relation of successive approximation between, say, Newtonian mechanics, relativity, and quantum theory, to give the most obvious example. The traditional view must, however, reject the view that truth is not simply 'either/or', but also 'both–and', just as it must reject the notion that different levels of truth are related to each other in ways that CANNOT BE STATED in analytic logic. If it did not reject these other and dynamic conceptions of truth, the traditional view could not maintain its hegemony in the schools and in our daily lives. It would have to evolve to new levels of organization or communication – it would have to become dialectical as well as analytical – which it obviously could not do and still remain what it is.

Piaget's theory can possibly be rescued from this problematic (cf. Shands, 1970: 274–88). But in the terms of my objective here, I must necessarily concentrate on what Piaget says he is doing, rather than on what he does, in order that a critical theory of what he actually does may become possible. I shall therefore concern myself with the representative metaphors within his text (as a representative metaphor) in order to demonstrate the epistemological foundations of the 'invisible' text immanent to the 'visible' text. Just as Kenneth Burke's "representative anecdote" concerns a nexus of significations which are chosen for the establishment of a theory, the representative metaphor does not communicate to us only about the communication established in the 'theory'. Such metaphors have a life which is all their own. Through their self-articulation in an implicit or invisible discourse, these metaphors may come to captivate the writer to the extent that everything he says may do no more than represent an essentially static ensemble of transformations of an original metaphoric set. The 'labels' he has (unconsciously) chosen for his 'universe of discourse' may in effect exert such fatal fascinations on the writer that, in the end, their self-articulation takes over from him. He no longer speaks his discourse; the discourse is speaking him.[2]

Svevo understood this danger rather well, I think, even if his hero never escaped it. To paraphrase Zeno: "At whatsoever particular spot of the universe of discourse one settles down, one ends by becoming poisoned; it is essential to keep moving" (1923: 287). Or, if we turn to the paraphrase of Montaigne which Pascal incorporated into his discourse on the 'two infinities':

> Nothing stops for us. It is the state most natural to us and yet the most contrary to our inclination. We burn with desire to find a firm foundation [*assiette*],[3] and a last constant base in order to build on it a tower that extends to the infinite. But our whole foundation cracks apart, and the earth opens up to the depths of the abyss (1670: 1109).

In this way we lay our foundations in the statics of the Imaginary. We spend our lives in an Imaginary laboratory, building constructs and entities on an apparently stable base, only to find it a quicksand. Only in the Imaginary can we effectively turn our universe of discourse into this kind of treadmill; in the Symbolic it is impossible not to keep moving.

'Keep moving' is in effect an axiom of metamathematics, as G. Spencer Brown points out (1969: 85, 99):

> . . . The advancement of mathematics consists in the advancement of the consciousness of what we are doing, whereby the covert becomes overt. Mathematics is in this respect psychedelic. . . . There must be mathematical statements (whose truth or untruth is in fact perfectly decidable) which cannot be decided by the methods of reasoning to which we have hitherto restricted ourselves.

Spencer Brown goes on to speak about the "violent pressures" of the scientific discourse. They generate "pride in knowledge" in the place of "recognition of universal ignorance", and thus constitute that discourse as

[2] Cf. Sartre's analysis of the work of Flaubert, notably Part II (1966). Flaubert spent considerable time collecting a dictionary of clichés. He sought to avoid in his writing what he called the *bêtise* of the *idée reçue*. 'Accepted ideas' need no author; like much of the discourse of the social and life sciences, they write themselves.

[3] This is Montaigne's word. As he says: "Si mon âme pouvoit prendre pied, je ne m'essaierois pas, je me resoudrois" (1595a: 782b): "If my being could find its footing, I would not assay myself, make these essays. I would re-solve myself, rejoin myself, dissolve my 'self', re-cover the split in myself." In the bundles of fragments which make up the *Pensées*, the passage from Pascal occurs very close to the *Je fesons, zôa trékei* cited in Chapter VIII.

a kind of psychosis. The quest for truth should be a quest, he says, not for knowledge, but for sanity. Thus, in the utopian socialist universe of Platonic 'reminiscence' represented by some forms of mathematics, the voyager can come to reflect on his journey from axioms to theorems and back again as a *recherche du temps perdu*:

> Coming across [the origin] thus again, in the light of what we had to do to render it acceptable, we see that our journey was, in its preconception, unnecessary, although its formal course, once we had set out upon it, was inevitable (1969: 106).

This is in effect the circuit Piaget completes. In essence, it is the covert epistemological and ideological values concealed 'at the origins' which produce his theory of structure. This is a tautologous journey which goes beyond any necessary tautologies in the 'institution' of science.

2. *Piaget's Review of Structural Theories*

> Instead of criticizing the human
> sciences in terms which their
> practitioner would accept,
> Foucault redefines 'human
> science': this makes his task
> rather too easy.
> PIAGET

Piaget's book is a brilliant and illuminating example of what the Masonic versions of 'structuralism' are not about. It exemplifies a lucid commitment to a carefully elaborated point of view, analytical rigor, and above all, intellectual honesty. There is no trace of the academic racketeering which characterizes many so-called 'structuralists'. Like Lévi-Strauss, Piaget has a position, and he wants everybody to understand what it is. His is the kind of exposition which is so clear and rigorous a statement of a position, that it enables the reader to understand better his own objections to it. It is this very clarity which enables the reader to organize and comprehend those of his reservations about the theory which had previously been incoherent or unrecognized.

To begin with a point of general agreement: Piaget recognizes the value of previous attacks on 'atomism' in the human sciences, at the same time as he points out their various shortcomings. We shall see later, however, in what sense the point in question does not concern 'atomism' or 'positivism' as such. There are many 'non-atomic' thinkers whose conceptions of wholeness, organization, and information, are, to a greater or lesser degree, inadequate for the human sciences. This inadequacy may be the result of a dependence on 'pure' intuition of the 'object' by the 'subject', or on a mechanistic base, or on an organicist one. It may result from a misunderstanding of the role of semiotics and language, or from misconceptions about biology and adaptation, or from a confusion between linguistics and semiotics. It may result from an implicit dependence on bioenergetic causality or from a misunderstanding of goalseeking, or from a purely homeostatic–morphostatic model, or from a misconstruction of context, or from the Buddhistic form of western individualism, or from an ontology and ideology based on class, sex, and racial prejudices (including elitism and paternalism).

Piaget begins by criticizing Chomsky's implication that there must be "innate syntactic laws" to account for generative grammar (pp. 12–13). Since Piaget is concerned to show the relation between "innate structure" and the "construction of structure" (constructivism) in the development of the child, and since Chomsky probably believes that a non-temporal mathematical or logical foundation can be formalized for such grammars (a formal "monoid" structure), the point is well taken. Piaget transcends the curious debate between the Whorfians and the anti-Whorfians over the question of language universals. It is clear in any case that both sides are correct, as the informational analysis of the genetic code surely demonstrates.[4] Piaget goes on to criticize "anti-historical" or "anti-genetic" structuralist theories by further suggesting that a hypothesis of "equilibrium" is perfectly adequate to account for the "stability of transformation rules", without the need for making the rules "innate".

In summarizing the historical development of the structural approach, Piaget remarks that Saussure's ideas about "synchronic equilibrium" were derived from the economic theory of the early twentieth century, just as gestaltism was derived from physics. The Lévi-Straussian models, however, "are a direct adaptation of general algebra". This introduces Piaget's

---

[4] There is an example of an experiment in education in rural Japan, called 'pillow education' (Reps, 1967: 17–19), which we could all learn something from. The children are taught to put all either/or problems – personal, educational, or whatever – to a pillow. The child considers the problem by moving his hands in a relational sequence of four steps around the sides of the pillow. The sides are labeled (in the order of his meditation on the problem): (1) The statement is wrong, (2) The statement is right, (3) The statement is both wrong and right, (4) The statement is neither wrong nor right. The child summarizes his conclusion by cupping his hands in the center of the pillow – which is, as it were, nowhere – and then reverses the sequence, saying "Each of these steps is good". Reps' presentation ends on an unfortunate ideological note, I find, but I cannot think of a more subtle or effective way of teaching a child – in the analog – about the relations in and between logical types.

discussion of group theory, to which I shall return. It is in Chapter III, on physical and biological structures and their relation to group theory, that the epistemological problematic of Piaget's model begins to show through: the confusion between causality and constraint, between 'mechanism' and 'information', between homeostasis and morphogenesis. Piaget is still enough a prisoner of his own past to discuss 'vitalism' and Morgan's 'emergence' theory from his own implicit 'causalist' perspective. He is correct in his critique of von Bertalanffy's tendency to 'organicism' (pp. 46–7), but misses the point that systems theory is not, as such, organicist. In fact, it is here that Piaget's own bioenergetic organicism begins to become evident, especially in his remarks about a supposed "logic of instincts" (p. 51), and in the misconception he has of the work of DNA.

Piaget goes on to analyze the contributions of gestaltism to the theory of structure. Gestalt 'intention' and 'signification' are phenomenological equivalents, he says, of his own 'transformation' and 'self-regulation'. By pointing to gestaltism's basis in physics Piaget effectively questions the concept of 'field' (e.g., Kurt Lewin) in gestalt-oriented theory, and its correlative in the gestaltist discourse: the absence of any genetic theory of the subject:

> Precisely because conceived in this way, the gestalt represents a type of structure that appeals to a certain number of structuralists, whose ideal, whether they acknowledge it or not, consists in looking for structures that may be thought 'pure', because they want them to be without history, and, *a fortiori*, without genesis, structures without functions and unrelated to the subject (p. 55; translation modified).

But, as Piaget points out, the historical significance of gestalt theory was, first, to distinguish additive aggregates from multiplicative wholes and thus to distinguish the gestalt whole from mechanical 'compounding together'. Secondly, by its rule that gestalts tend to take on the 'best' form, the theory provided a psychological equivalent of the physicist's 'principle of least action' (Maupertuis, Max Planck) and the more general principle of equilibrium.

Piaget remarks that it is this principle of "equilibration", and not the law of wholeness, which makes gestaltism a structuralist theory. Piaget's own 'genetic' structuralism is similarly based on a principle of equilibrium. But, according to Piaget, it differs from the gestalt version in that it does not suppose a simple mechanical equilibrium which appears 'out there' in the form. Piaget's theory involves an equilibrated interaction between perceiver and gestalt. "Perceptual acts" therefore change with the effects of memory and maturation (pp. 57–9).

In Chapter V, Piaget deals with linguistic structuralism, beginning with the "systemic" perspective of Saussure. The almost exclusively synchronic emphasis on equilibrium in Saussure, says Piaget, is a result of the "relative independence of laws of equilibrium from laws of development". Although Piaget's lack of a communicational–informational perspective leads him to consider language simply as a "means of expression" (p. 79), or as a means of "description" (p. 38), and thus to entertain closure in all sorts of unexpected places, he does point out – for the wrong reasons – that synchronics and diachronics in linguistics involve a set of relations different from the same processes in other domains.

Piaget then returns to a critique of what he sees as a resurgent Cartesian rationalism in Chomsky's "innatism" (pp. 81–7):

> While the logical positivists, enthusiastically followed by Bloomfield, wanted to reduce mathematics and logics to linguistics and the entire life of the mind to speech, the avant-garde of linguistics derives grammar from logic, and language from a mental life directed [*orientée*] by reason (p, 83, translation modified).

Piaget's point here is to establish (*a*) the genetic principles implicit within Chomsky's 'rationalism', and (*b*) the rights of what Bally called *le langage affectif*: "Why not . . . consider the hypothesis that feeling has a language of its own?" (p. 86).

Piaget's conclusion is that the source of the logical functions required by Chomsky's 'monoid structures' lies in the organization of the 'sensorimotor schemata' which precede language. These he defines as repetition, ordering, and associative connecting (p. 91). But these categories are 'prelogical' categories for him. They have no communicative or semiotic value in his perspective. Consequently, Piaget is forced to introduce another category, which he calls the "symbolic or semiotic function". In his theory, this function "comprises, besides language, all forms of imitation: mimicking, symbolic play, the mental image, and so on":

> Too often it is forgotten that the development of representation and thought (we are not as yet speaking of properly logical structures) is tied to this GENERAL semiotic function and not just to language (p. 93).

Thus, "intelligence precedes language".

Chapter VI of Piaget's book is devoted to the social sciences. Here Piaget makes a most useful distinction between "analytic" and "global" structuralism. All the social sciences involve some form of global structuralism, but only approaches like that of Lévi-Strauss – the analytic uncovering of deep and non-phenomenal structures (which are in essence logico-mathematical) – are said to manifest what Piaget calls 'authentic' structuralism. (This critique takes up at another level the debate between Lévi-Strauss and the British followers of Radcliffe-Brown in anthropology.)

His reference to Kurt Lewin's 'total field topology' (pp. 99–102) brings out the importance of the 'reference to an environment'. But, the definition of 'environment' in the quotation which follows is characteristic of what will prove to be a major inadequacy of Piaget's theory: its antisocial point of view and its rhetorical appeal to the myth of science. Moreover, we discover later in the book that Piaget does not even attempt to conform to his own explicit conception of environment:

> . . . only a psycho-biological account of environment will be sufficiently concrete to enable us to predict or understand the behavior of the human subject (p. 99).

He goes on to point out that Lewin's 'field' topology is not really mathematical. But he says nothing of the 'topology' employed by Lacan, whom he has already mentioned briefly – in the ritualistic way characteristic of many contemporary French writers – on pp. 86–7. According to Piaget, there is "not one known topological theorem that can be given a direct psychodynamic interpretation" (p. 100). This problematic is perhaps connected with the question of invariant relations in topology.[5] In any event, Piaget's approving reference to Lewin's 'force vectors' once again betrays a dependence on energy explanation which grounds the whole of Piaget's own theory.

[5] The following remarks by Sayre and Crosson (1963: 20) presumably apply both to Lacan and to Lewin. In discussing gestalt perception – which is of course a form of communication – they point out:

> . . . The unnoted elements in the perceptual field, in spite of being unnoted, have a functional meaning, i.e., have a function in the constitution of the meaning of the figure or area of focal awareness, and this functional meaning changes when these elements are brought to specification, i.e., explicitly noted. Hence in a real sense the analysis which effects this explanation is introducing new elements rather than merely resolving a complex into its parts. (This is the reason why *Gestalten* resist topological analysis, namely that in such formal analysis the relations of the parts are assumed to be invariant under transformation.)

It seems unlikely that in any self-differentiating system open to an environment, the relations of the subsystems to each other remain invariant.

3. *Piaget's Conception of Structure*

> I am sure the power of vested
> interests is vastly exaggerated
> compared with the gradual
> encroachment of ideas.
> JOHN MAYNARD KEYNES

Piaget's first chapter is devoted to a general outline of his own conception of structure, which he develops and expands in the rest of the book. A structure is (provisionally) defined as "a system of transformations". The structure is "preserved or enriched" by the interplay of its transformations "which never go beyond its frontiers, nor employ elements that are external to it". Structure consequently involves three key ideas: "wholeness, transformation, and self-regulation" (p. 5). A structure is therefore a closed system: it is "a system closed under transformation" (p. 6). It is around Piaget's conception of transformation and closure that any critique of his theory will necessarily be oriented, for it will eventually bring us to put into question his whole conception of what he calls self-regulation.

The criterion of WHOLENESS is based on the necessary distinction between "structures and aggregates" (i.e., between organization and aggregation). It is significant, however, that the example Piaget gives of wholeness is the sequence of the integers – with their properties of forming groups, fields, rings, and so on. In other words, his example is an instance of a structure which is wholly digital. He goes on to distinguish his own conception of wholeness from any kind of structural wholeness which involves no more than a reversal of atomism – e.g., Comte's sociology, Durkheim's "total social fact". In his own theory, which he calls "operational structuralism", the significant reference is not the whole as such, but the RELATIONS within it (p. 9). We shall see later that his term 'operational' goes far beyond its legitimate mathematical sources. Nevertheless, in spite of the demonstrable inadequacy of Piaget's conception of relation – to which I shall return – his point against simplistic totalizing is well taken. It is not either the whole or the part that is primary, but rather "the logical procedures" by which the whole is formed. The whole is therefore "consequent on the system's laws of composition" (cf. Chapter IX).

This, he says, raises the central question in all structural perspectives: Are the composite wholes pure givens? Or are they still "in process" (*en voie de composition*)? In other words, are these structures matters of FORMATION or matters of (eternal) PREFORMATION (p. 9)? Since Piaget considers himself a genetic structuralist, he will necessarily opt explicitly for structures as processes of formation (cf. pp. 114–15, where he argues for a 'genetic' version of Lévi-Strauss's 'symbolic function'). However, it will not be very difficult to show, from Piaget's own premisses, that his 'genetic' structuralism is in fact nothing more than a more subtle version of pre-formational, non-temporal, archetypal structuralism, and "unpolluted" by history.

Piaget's second criterion is that of TRANSFORMATION. The structural laws of composition are not static relations; they are laws which STRUCTURE relations and are structured by them. He suggests that this "bipolar" structuring and structured law of the whole is similar to Augustin Cournot's concept of 'order' in algebra: "A structure's laws of composition are defined 'implicitly', i.e., as governing the transformations of the system which they structure" (p. 10).

The evocation of Cournot's work is no passing reference. The name sets off a whole series of associations with mathematical equilibrium theory in economics (see Newman, ed., 1956: II: 1200–16). Cournot and Jevons were the great precursors of Alfred Marshall and John Maynard Keynes in economics. At the same time as Cournot was developing his theories, Malthus was applying a similar mathematical equilibrium theory to population and Fechner was applying similar principles in psychology. Galton – the founder of the psychometry used by Jensen in the United States and by Eysenck in England – supposed similar 'rational' relations in the application of statistics to the life sciences, and Pareto is well known for his mathematical equilibrium theories – his 'rational mechanics' – in economics and in sociology. Cournot's attempts to explain "duopoly" – the 'rational economic behavior' between partners in equal competition – found their respondent in von Neumann and Morgenstern's rationalist approach to the maximization of utilities in game theory (Newman, ed., 1956, II: 1267–8; Shubik, 1964: 5; cf. Rapaport, 1959). Moreover, Jevons's 'principle of utility' – which is a simple version of Bentham's utilitarian 'pleasure principle' – is essentially identical to the stability theory of Fechner and of Freud, which has been criticized in Chapter VI. Jevons's principle is in effect derived from similar mechanistic conceptions.

The constant reference to equilibrium in Piaget's theory of structure is not simply an association with these names, for he refers explicitly and approvingly to the more well-known exponents of this type of theory later in the book (cf. Section 10 below). He refers also to game theory, as does Lévi-Strauss (Section 11 below). If we keep in mind Elsasser's remarks about the need for a non-binary logic to explain the behavior of open systems (1969, quoted in Chapter VI), we might recall at this point Shubik's cautions about bipolar 'duopolistic', or binary approaches to 'rational behavior'. Shubik points out that there are many features of real 'gaming' situations which game theory has some difficulty in accounting for. They can be summarized as a set of questions: (1) Is precommitment to a strategy actually possible – and does it actually happen? (2) Are there always only two – or a limited number – of major alternatives? (3) Do values stay fixed during the 'game' of negotiations? (4) What is the effect of timing on negotiations? (5) Do individuals think and/or act in strategies? If they do not, ought they to do so? (6) Surely all such negotiations are "part of a larger on-going process and cannot be studied in isolation, but must be investigated in a complete dynamic context?" (Shubik, 1964: 27).[6]

For my purposes here, the significance of Piaget's more than rhetorical appeal to mathematics to support his theory of equilibration, is that all of the theories he mentions are theories which ignore the REAL context of accumulation, socioeconomic status, psychosocial 'socialization', and the accumulative effects of POWER in relations of competition. Such relationships are not in fact 'free' or 'equal' or 'duopolist', for they involve positive feedback weighted on the side of organization (cf. Hardin, 1969). This reference to the context will become even more significant as we pursue Piaget's foundations of a theory of structure.

For the moment, it will suffice to quote a passage from Cournot's pioneering work, the *Theory of Wealth* (1838). His early work on probability reflects an attempt to relate order and chance, continuity and discontinuity, but in an essentially linear way. This is the same method of truth by 'successive approximations' which we have noticed in the alchemy of artificial intelligence (Dreyfus, 1965). The following quotation concerns Cournot's attempt to explain the relation of supply and demand from the interior of the nineteenth-century economic system. He takes a position explicitly disavowing any contextual or historical concerns (Newman, ed.,

---

[6] See also Shubik's remarks subheaded "Noncooperative Equilibrium: Do the Fittest Survive?" (pp. 43–5); and Deutsch, 1963: 51–72. As Deutsch remarks, changes in behavior are exceptions to the rules of game theory. He goes on to quote von Neumann and Morgenstern's insistence on the static nature of equilibria theory like the theory of games: "The essential characteristic of an equilibrium is that it has no tendency to change." But in politics, socioeconomics, and human behavior in general, the 'game' might better be modelled on the croquet game in *Alice in Wonderland* (Deutsch: 57). Here the exploited classes – the hedgehogs, the playing-card soldiers, and the flamingoes – are in a constant state of revolution, with the objective of changing the RULES of the game by taking over the means of production. We are reminded of the abortive "revolution of the colors" in Abbott's *Flatland* (1884) – that curious metastatement about the one-dimensional, digital, and quantified nature of the nineteenth-century 'equilibrium' of class, caste, race, and sex – in which the upper classes are condemned by the 'law of Nature' to perish because of their own 'perfection'.

1956: 1209). His theory is dependent on a Benthamesque principle of utility which equates commodities with labor (ibid.). Thus Cournot sets up in his "social arithmetic" the notion of the relation between supply and demand as a CONTINUOUS function. In his limited perspective, this is undoubtedly the case – even though it does conjure up all the problems of boundaries between steps or states which I have discussed in Chapter VII. But I am more interested in the metaphors of 'gradualism', and 'harmonious change' in his explanation. He finds "sudden revolutions" of any kind, "now very improbable". (This is a few years after Metternich in Europe and the Reform Bill in England, and ten years before the abortive risings of 1848). The metaphor he uses to explain away possible discontinuity or sudden change is physicalist and mechanist (as one would expect) – but it is also almost GEOLOGICAL in scope:

> . . . The principle just enunciated admits of exceptions, because a continuous function may have interruptions of continuity . . .; but just as friction wears down roughness and softens outlines, so the wear of commerce tends to suppress these exceptional cases, at the same time that commercial machinery moderates variations in prices and tends to maintain them between limits which facilitate the application of theory (op. cit.: 1213).

What further facilitates the theory is Cournot's assumption that production involves monopolies. This heuristic device, he says, allows for a more accurate analysis of the effects of competition (p. 1216). Cournot is perfectly correct: The existence – in a supposedly homogeneous (economic) system – of quantitative elements related by 'pure' competition (the 'survival of the fittest') necessarily leads to the generation of the monopolies of power and organization within and between which 'ecosystemic' or 'cooperative' competition is the rule (e.g., the automobile industry).

To return now to Piaget's development of his theory of structure: under the criterion of transformation, we find him tracing the germ of the idea of transformation to Saussure's synchronic conception of dynamic equilibrium (steady state) in language (pp. 10–11). Saussure, says Piaget, used the term 'system' to cover "both laws of synchronic opposition and laws of synchronic equilibration". Piaget's translator provides us with the appropriate references (Saussure, 1916b: 107, 117, 119–22). What we find in Saussure's course notes at this point is an analogy between the GAME of chess – as "the combination of the different chesspieces" – and language – as "a system based entirely on the opposition of its concrete units". In Saussure's words, these 'discrete entities' (which are not immediately perceptible) are "no doubt a trait that distinguishes language from all other semiological institutions". But we know that Saussure's 'oppositions' are, in essence, differential (op. cit.: 117, 120).[7]

There is a more significant point to be made, however, a point brought out most cogently by Edwin Ardener in his Introduction to *Social Anthropology and Language* (1971). Saussure's well-known 'diacritical' theory of signification, based on difference, is closely related to what I have outlined as an analog theory of MEANING in Chapter VII. A 'concept' has meaning by virtue of its difference from all others in the given language. But the more specific statements by Saussure concern the signification of a signifier in a given 'environment' and the change of signification which occurs when the environment is modified. This possibility depends on combination, that is to say, on the DIGITAL possibilities of putting a signifier into new relations by changing its place or by placing other signifiers in differential or oppositional relations with it. This is one reason, as Ardener points out, for the chess analogy, since chess is a game of position. (It is also a relation of competition, of course, which tells us something about the ideological connotations of the term 'oppositions'. See Chapter XIV.)

It is in the terms of the chess analogy that Saussure speaks of the problematic raised in this book in Chapter VII: that of states and boundaries. It will be recalled that I described the boundary between two states or positions (e.g., between 'A' and 'non-A') as "the way of getting from one to the other", the digitalization necessary to cross from one given 'system' or 'state' to another. This digital boundary belongs to NEITHER state or set. In Piaget, however, in everything he has to say about 'frontiers', 'boundaries', and 'bounded structures', we find an entirely different and atomistic relation, which is clearly connected with his Cartesian or Husserlian conception of the 'individual'. For Piaget, these frontiers are not only conceived of as REAL; they are also obviously conceived of as BELONGING TO THE STRUCTURE. (In other words, he does, in his theory, what we all do in our daily practice: we separate figure from ground, and then attribute the boundary between them to the figure.) Thus, whereas for the ecosystemic perspective, the boundary is the locus of communication and interaction, the paradoxical distinction upon which the whole ecosystemic relation depends – and without which we would all be Kantian rubber balls – for the bioenergetic perspective, and for Piaget, it is the barrier to communication. What we see as a Common Market, he sees as a tariff wall, in the terms of a kind of isolationist protectionism.

It follows, therefore, that what is a barrier to communication will also be a barrier to certain kinds of change, and that it is this epistemological

---

[7] See Chapter IX on the emergence of the discrete socioeconomic component, and Chapter XVI on linguistics and semiotics.

attribution of frontiers to a privileged set of entities, called structures, that makes Piaget's conception of the 'genetic' or diachronic relation of one structure to another in child development so dubious. My point here is that Saussure, who is not the equilibrium theorist that Piaget thinks he is (as I shall explain in a moment), had already conceived the problem through the chess analogy and provided an indication of the solution to whoever wishes to find it. He says:

> In chess each move is absolutely distinct from the preceding and subsequent equilibrium. THE CHANGE IF EFFECTED BELONGS TO NEITHER STATE: only states matter (1916a: 126; quoted by Ardener, 1971a: xxxvii, my emphasis).

Thus, each player's moves in chess are the momentary digitalizations which allow the game to pass from analog pattern to pattern. And since the moves do not belong to the patterns, they cannot be explained simply by reference to the patterns (the 'structures'). They can only be explained by reference to the context of meaning in which the game is played, that is to say, by reference to the DESIRE or to the goals of the chess-player. For it is the moves of the player, and not the state of the board, which define the boundary he crosses as he communicates each distinction, each move, as a message to his opponent.

There are two types of 'transformation' in Piaget's view: temporal and non-temporal. This distinction will lead him to discuss later the relationship between structuralism, as such, and his own constructivism. At this point, he introduces his third criterion for a structure: SELF-REGULATION. We discover that this criterion involves a somewhat curious conception of regulation, and one which is directly linked to the concept of equilibrium. Self-regulation entails "self-maintenance and closure" (p. 14). That is to say, the transformations are "inherent" and never lead outside the system. Significantly enough, the example which follows again involves digits. Moreover, the relation of a "bounded substructure" to a larger structure is described by Piaget by the eighteenth- and nineteenth-century political metaphor of CONFEDERATION. In this relationship of parts to wholes, the larger structure does not "annex" the substructure, as he puts it. What happens in this structural doctrine of 'states rights' (*conservation avec stabilité des frontieres*), according to Piaget, is that the laws of the substructure are not impaired by the relation to a larger structure. Rather they are conserved, "and the intervening change is an enrichment" (rather than an impoverishment).

The political metaphors are interesting enough. Piaget has already defined equilibrium solely in the terms of bioenergetic or mechanical inertia or steady state. Now, by this remark implicitly relating alteration and impoverishment (which the translator makes explicit), Piaget goes a step further in articulating the myth of the contemporary scientific discourse. By speaking of interrelations between structures in terms that imply INTERFERENCES and boundary disputes, and by implicitly describing certain kinds of change – specifically interference with internal order – as forms of DEGRADATION, Piaget has effectively defined 'non-programmed' change as a process leading to ENTROPY. To put the matter clearly: In less than fourteen pages, Piaget has outlined a description of structure in precisely the terms of Freud's atomistic energy model. We have, in so many words, both the theory of constancy (mechanical steady state or organic homeostasis) and the theory of inertia (thermodynamic or mechanical equilibrium). My earlier reference to Fechner – via Cournot – was therefore by no means a peripheral one.

Piaget continues to develop his mechanistic model. What he chooses to call self-regulation is defined as the structure's "innermost source of movement" (*moteur intime*). We have some right to suspect that this source of movement may turn out to be either the laws of electromagnetism, or possibly an instinct or two. Or perhaps it is Newton's *spiritus subtilissimus*. Piaget does go on to introduce the key notion of levels of complexity. But once again he is talking about a 'confederation' of levels, presumably with frontiers and passports involved (compare Freud's images of the frontier between the *Pcs.* and the *Ucs.*).

Piaget defines his concept of self-regulation in what he calls "cybernetic" terms. Self-regulation is the equivalent of a "mathematical" OPERATION, which he calls "perfect regulation". What this means, he says, is that in an "operational system", errors are excluded "before they are made", because "every operation has its inverse in the system" (e.g., subtraction is the reverse of addition). In other words, every operation in this type of self-regulating system is REVERSIBLE.

What we cannot fail to see in this definition of cybernetics via mathematics, is an ethical, aesthetic, and ideological hypothesis that perfection and reversibility – in other words, the impossibility of certain kinds of change, or of development, or of evolution – are or should be equivalent to each other. But in the real world of self-organization, the only systems which are reversible in this sense are (*a*) simple closed-loop feedback systems like the thermostat-plus-environment (and even that, given certain environmental changes, can fall into irreversible changes), and (*b*) physical closed systems or machines. The second type are systems of transformation which are reversible in two senses. In the first place, many of them can or could run backwards (e.g., the solar system) – the 'music of the spheres' is, as Wiener says somewhere, a palindrome. Secondly, by a suitable supply of negative entropy, any closed system can IN THEORY be reversed, because it is a determined system in the first place.

Thus we perceive in Piaget's text a metaphor of certain kinds of change as degradation, on the one hand, and a metaphor of perfection as balanced, Newtonian harmony, on the other. Piaget in some sense recognizes the problems raised by this debt of his to the seventeenth century, for he goes on to point out that there is an "immense class" of structures which are self-regulated over TIME, structures whose "regulations" are not "operations" because they are "not entirely reversible". This "immense class" turns out to include everything else in the organic world except mathematics. For if there is a single specific trait characteristic of such temporally oriented feedback systems of self-regulation in an open relation to an environment, it is that they are neither predictable nor reversible.[8]

The peculiar value attached to reversibility in the work of Piaget comes out rather clearly in a colloquium of 1959 (Gandillac, Goldmann, and Piaget, 1965: 37–61), where Piaget explains his rationale for the use of the term *équilibre*. Equilibrium in his sense is to be conceived of as a "mobile or active" state of "stability" in which "external disturbances" of the system or structure are "compensated for by the actions of the subject".

In the following discussion, Abraham Moles tried to simplify matters by pointing out that "active equilibrium" and "compensation" are the same. Using the terminology of mechanistic cybernetics and the example of the dynamic equilibrium of a pendulum, he correctly identified "compensation" as (negative) feedback and the "external disturbances" as "accidents" equivalent to "noise". The activity or work or force of compensation, he pointed out, is proportional to the "structuring force", and the "strength or force" of the structure is precisely its "resistance to noise", which is itself "a measure of the force" (p. 50).

In his reply, Piaget accepted Moles' failure to distinguish energy and information, and went on to explain that he used "equilibrium" with the adjective "active" in order to counter objections that he should really be using the term "stability in an open system" for what he was describing as equilibrium. His reasoning is curious enough to be worth quoting at length:

> When one uses the language of equilibrium, the impression is given that equilibrium is stability in the sense of rest, the end of everything, death, entropy, and so on. On the contrary, mental equilibrium supposes a maximum of activity, but an activity orientated toward compensation.

[8] Cf. Chapter III, and the distinction between homeostasis, homeorhesis, homeogenesis, and morphogenesis in Chapter XII.

I do not use the term 'stability in an open system', he continued, because

first of all, the expression is rather long. But above all I prefer the word 'equilibrium', even if I have to redefine it, because for me it implies compensation. I need the term 'compensation' rather than that of 'stability in an open system', because it is compensation which allows me to explain reversibility (p. 51).

What we can see here is a circular reasoning around a set of implicit values – including that of "intelligence as the summit of life, the most authentic vital phenomenon" (p. 54) – values which, at least in the discussion referred to, no amount of questioning could induce Piaget to recognize as implicit, or as ideological, or even as methodological. We are not surprised to discover at the end of the discussion (pp. 57–61), Piaget's repeated refusals to recognize that simply posing a set of questions to a child – even in the child's "own language" (*sic*), or through a questioner "inexperienced" in Piaget's theory – sets up a particular relation and imposes a set of metarules on the child. At the very least, this relation is ruled by the questioner's dominance, by conscious or unconscious assumptions about 'intelligence' (i.e., performance), by the questioner's desire (or goal), and by the child's desire to satisfy the desire of the questioner (who also re-presents what both he and the child necessarily believe to be 'adult reality'), and so on.

This is not to suggest that the methodological problems of the punctuation of the 'experiment' by the imposition of conscious or unconscious metarules to which the child must conform, are simple ones, or easily resolvable. What has to be pointed out, however, is that so long as discussion of these metarules is interdicted by the theory, the theory may not simply be false, but actually dangerous – notably in the sense that I find Piaget's hidden (and linear) assumptions about logic and intelligence dangerous, and not simply for the children involved, but also for the culture as a whole. It is against the danger of the assumption that one can make 'pure' experiments with open systems (p. 58) – Piaget refuses for example to consider in what sense the questions posed of the child are 'observation' and in what sense they are 'teaching' – that we speak of the principle of punctuation in such systems. Unlike the principle of indeterminacy in physics, which is a tactical question having nothing essential to do with the desires of the observer–participant, the principle of punctuation concerns strategy. It both states that the strategy of the enquirer is 'part' of the system–environment relationship set up by the punctuation (but of a different logical type) and insists that this strategy must be taken into account in the theory itself. But Piaget's theory is necessarily impervious to such considerations because of the assumptions about closure, object-relations, reversibility, linear quotients of intelligence (cf. Jensen, 1969: 10), and structural autonomy on which the theory is built and to which its experimental 'subjects' necessarily conform. In other words, the vaunted 'biological' model of the "equilibrated interaction between organism and environment" that Piaget uses to develop his theory of the genesis of 'intelligence' does not apply, in his view, to the relationship between child and questioner.

Having dealt with the perfect and reversible regulation of mathematical operations outlined above, Piaget goes on to introduce a second type of regularity in his outline of structuralism: rhythm (e.g., biological 'clocks'). "Rhythm, too, is self-regulating, by virtue of SYMMETRIES and REPETITIONS" (p. 16, my emphasis). Having taken as his privileged model the digital and transcendental world of mathematics, Piaget now picks out another form of behavior which suits his preconceptions. By reference to repetition and oscillation – Fechner's "complete stability" – Piaget makes his model even more similar to Freud's bioenergetic model (cf. Chapter VI, Section 4).[9] Lichtenstein – who along with Bernfeld and Feitelberg, was perfectly faithful to Freud in believing that the 'death instinct' was in fact the exemplification of the second law of thermodynamics in the organism – had pointed out in 1935 the contradictions between the concepts of constancy, inertia, and repetition (Jones, 1956–8: III, 292–300). We seem now to be finding a similar set of contradictions, but less immediately obvious, in Piaget.

The point in question, of course, is not the 'facts' Piaget picks – for they are all perfectly valid – but why he picks them, and how he interprets them. What has now to be shown is that in the considered development of his theory of structure, Piaget is indeed perpetuating what we have come to recognize as the Newtonian–Cartesian form of the myth of science.

This myth is the myth of scientism, and like all myths it serves a precise political and organizational function in our culture. With this understanding, we can come back to Piaget's résumé of linguistic structuralism in his Chapter V in order to establish a crucial point about the mythical origins of the myth of equilibrium in contemporary structuralism: its supposed origins in the work of Saussure. In singling out what he will say about Saussure, Piaget takes from the *Cours* those concepts which seem to support his own theory of structure, without dealing in any cogent way with perhaps the most important of the problems raised by Saussure: that of the relation

---

[9] See *Standard Edition*, XVIII, 8. 63, where Freud's reference to "given units of time" implies a rhythmic tendency to repetition. Jones (1956–8: III, 292) wonders to what extent Freud was influenced in this by Fliess's theory of periodicity.

between synchrony ('timeless' patterns) and diachrony (development, history, evolution).

Thus Piaget takes over at face value from Saussure's almost exclusive emphasis on synchronic relations the notion that "laws of equilibrium" are "relatively independent" from "laws of development". Apart from the fact that Saussure's concern for synchrony is the necessary corollary of his successful attempt to turn historical philology into what we now call linguistics, and is consequently an emphasis constrained by the historical context of his discipline, Piaget misconstrues the point entirely. We can put the matter very simply. If synchronic stasis and diachronic process are considered to be independent of each other, it is usually because the theorist in question is unconsciously confusing two different, and essentially incomparable, levels of organization in 'reality'. The 'laws of equilibrium' will in general be found to refer to the processes of mechanics or thermodynamics, based on classical physical theory, with perhaps a bioenergetic conception of organic homeostasis tacked on as an extension (just as there is at the end of Piaget's remarks about Saussure). The 'laws of development', however, can be expected to concern more or less well-understood notions derived directly from biology as the study of organic growth and natural evolution. The first we can expect to be straightforward statements of energy–entity relationships, expressed in the language of physics; the second we can expect to be a similar set of metaphors, but expressed in the language of biology. In neither case do we generally find an explanation of synchrony and diachrony in a scientific discourse which is capable of dealing with their essential – and self-evident – INTERDEPENDENCE: a discourse founded on an informational and ecosystemic epistemology. In the biosphere and the sociosphere, the laws of synchrony and diachrony belong to the theory of open systems (Chapters IX, XII), not to 'physics' or to 'biology' or to 'sociology' or to 'linguistics'.

Of course, some theorists who use the reference to equilibrium are more open about their epistemological difficulties, and are prepared to confess that they use it because they feel that human societies, for example, are too complex for anything but static models (Lewis, ed., 1968: xxiii). Piaget, however, is doing exactly the opposite in that he is elaborating a physicalist equilibrium model *in abstracto* without making anything more than mathematical claims for it, and then quietly attempting to integrate it into his theories about history, evolution, and child development. This becomes clear through Piaget's reference to the probable source of Saussure's apparent position on the relative independence of synchronic and diachronic laws: Pareto's equilibrium sociology and economics. As Buckley has pointed out in his penetrating critique of the equilibrium model in sociology (1967: 8–40), many other theorists – Homans, Parsons, Lewin, for example – have produced or depended on one version or another of Pareto's 'social physics'.

My point is that Piaget's conception of structure depends for its validity entirely on what he quotes as Saussure's position on synchronics, for, without this confusion of levels of complexity, he will be unable to generate his own version of the gestaltist 'good form': what he will call the "perfectly-regulated, autonomously-bounded structure". But, in fact, as Ardener's analysis makes clear (1971a: xxxv–xxxvi), Saussure's course notes are the last place in which to find explicit or implicit support for such a view. Ardener points out that Saussure does speak of separate laws for both the diachronic and the synchronic approach, but that he nevertheless

> achieves an important insight which leads him far beyond Radcliffe-Brown, another believer in laws. . . . He says: 'THE SYNCHRONIC LAW IS GENERAL BUT NOT IMPERATIVE . . . THE SYNCHRONIC LAW REPORTS A STATE OF AFFAIRS.' Synchronic patterns contained no indication of their own stability or lack of it: 'The arrangement that the law defines is precarious, precisely because it is not imperative' [1916a: 131]. Sometimes . . . Saussure loosely uses the term *équilibre* for a synchronic state, but there is here no sideways slip into a view of a self-perpetuating equilibrium of a quasi-organic type, such as has dogged social anthropology into our own days (my emphasis).

The importance of what Ardener brings out here can hardly be overstressed. For Saussure, synchrony and *équilibre* are not in fact imperative states, as structure and equilibrium are for Piaget and for many others who appeal to Saussure as the 'father' of their approach; they are no more than heuristic tools. Their methodological status is not therefore to be confused with their ontological status, nor with their ideological function. There is no reason to suppose, moreover, as some theorists seem to suppose (e.g., Leach), that our 'conceptual models' of, say, social systems, must necessarily be of the equilibrium type, or, for that matter, of its supposed opposite, the equally simplistic 'conflict' type (cf. P. C. Lloyd in Lewis, ed., 1968: 26–7).

4. *A Note on Multifinality*

I shall not dwell on Piaget's explication of the group theory from which his privileged model of structure is derived, except to remark on the gestalt concept of equifinality which he discusses on p. 20. I realize that my own use of this term, and of the term overdetermined, is broader than the concept of equifinality as such, since I discover that I have always viewed it in RETROSPECT. The forgetting of 'Signorelli' is 'overdetermined' in my conception of the process, because it involves unpredictable paths and an unpredictable result (viewed from the result). But, strictly speaking, Piaget's definition, which corresponds to Saussure's in the chess analogy (1916a: 126; Ardener, 1971a: xxxvii) is more accurate: "the end result is independent of the route taken". Equifinality therefore should be retained to mean: "a final state which may be reached from different initial states and/or by different paths." Consequently, we need also an explicit conception of MULTIFINALITY (perhaps similar to the biological concept "equipotential"), which can be defined as a process by which "similar initial conditions, and/or routing by different paths, may lead to dissimilar endstates" (modified from Maruyama, 1963, as quoted in Buckley, 1967: 60).

With this more precise definition of the results of certain types of goal-seeking in an ecosystemic (adaptive) relation to an environment – e.g., the multifinal results of the process of natural evolution itself – we can begin to approach another of the ideological aspects of Piaget's theory. He not only confuses organic development with natural evolution. He also confuses learning – as the 'constructivist' maturation of the individual – with learning in the sense of freeing oneself from the constructions which enslave the individual to his past. Whereas Piaget is perfectly happy with a logico-mathematical theory of equifinality (in the strict sense), a logical or actual process of multifinality is essentially inconceivable for him:

> . . . If termini in group theory did vary with the paths traversed to reach them, space would lose its coherence; what we would have instead would be a perpetual flux, like the river of Heraclitus (p. 20).

I have no idea what is concretely meant by the "coherence of space" here. I assume therefore that it refers to the coherence of mathematical space in group theory. For the river of Heraclitus, however, we have only to refer ourselves to Svevo's Zeno, who knows – but wishes he didn't – that nobody can step into the same ongoing open system twice. Piaget's expression of what is in effect a positive fear of flux or change is already evident in the definition of self-regulation on the same page. Self-regulation is there described as a process of the continual application of three of the "basic principles" of RATIONALISM. These are: the principle of non-contradiction (i.e., the reversibility of transformations), the principle of identity, and the (equifinal) principle that the end result is independent of the route taken.

It cannot be objected that Piaget is talking only about structuralism in mathematics. According to his genetic theory, in the "intellectual development" of the child, the earliest "cognitive operations" – "which grow directly out of HANDLING THINGS" (my emphasis) – involve reversibility under three forms: inversion, reciprocity, and continuity and separation. Thus, he argues, psychogenesis inverts the historical development of geometry but matches the "Bourbakian genealogy" of "parent structures": ALGEBRAIC structures (the group, with reversibility as "inversion" or "negation",[10] ORDER structures (lattices or networks united by the predecessor/ successor relation, in which reversibility takes the form of reciprocity), and TOPOLOGICAL structures (neighborhoods, continuity, and boundaries). In the child, the topological structures are said to "antedate metric and projective structures" (pp. 23–7).

5. *Piaget's Atomistic Rationalism*

The key to the problematic here is Piaget's constant reference to 'intellect', to 'cognition', to the 'handling of things' (*actions sur les objets*): his repeated implicit or explicit references to digital logic or to digital 'entities'. There is no reason to argue with the "parent structures" of the Bourbaki group, nor with the psychogenetic derivation from a topological relationship. Piaget's error derives from elsewhere, from his implicit atomism. Topology is a mathematics of quality and relation. There is no possible way that a 'topological sense' in the child could be derived from 'handling things'. If things are things, then already for the child boundaries 'out there' have been constituted as digitalized limits around 'entities'. Since topology depends on neighborhood and differentiation, the constitution of a possible topological sense in the child is, ontogenetically, long anterior to the institution of any world of 'objects'. Piaget's implicit (and digital) atomism is not therefore derived in any sense from the study of the child. It is derived from the preconceived idea that the first relationship of the child is to objects. Beginning with this energy–entity viewpoint, the rest of the theory simply repeats the same atomism at different levels. It is from this undemonstrated and undemonstrable viewpoint, in particular, that Piaget's theory of causality is derived, whether by causality we mean the theory of the child's discovery of causality, or the causal epistemology in the theory which produces the tautologous explanation of the child's discovery of causality. In effect, Piaget's epistemology of the 'object relation' is produced like a rabbit out of a magician's hat – which is very easy to do if you have put the rabbit into the hat beforehand.

[10] Here Piaget makes the classic error of equating 'minus-one' with 'not-one'. See Chapter VII.

Piaget's epistemology is atomist, intellectualist, rationalist, individualistic. Such foundations generate Imaginary barriers within the ecosystem being studied, and it becomes necessary to invent a special kind of 'action-oriented', 'intentional' construct to get over the obstacles that the epistemology has put in the way. This problematic becomes particularly evident in Piaget's Chapter IV, on psychological structures. Since he assumes that the primary relation is a phenomenological one, a relation between a PERCEIVING or KNOWING or APPREHENDING 'subject' and a set of objects, Piaget is forced to invent a construct called "sensori-motor intelligence". Sensori-motor intelligence is what supposedly allows the subject to construct his own structures "by operations of reflective abstraction". These operations are said not to resemble any activity akin to "perceptual figuration" (gestalts) (p. 60). How a sensori-motor being 'reflects' and 'abstracts' is unexplained. The apparent contradiction which appears here between 'sensori-motor' and 'cognition' is in fact one of the first clues we have to the imaginary construction of Piaget's theory.

In order to arrive at an analysis of Piaget's constructions, we have to follow his argument about theories of the genesis of intelligence. Structures, he says, are either "innate" (preformed, predetermined), or the result of "contingent emergence", or the result of "constructivism". It is significant that the word emergence is modified here by the word "contingent", for Piaget's fear of certain kinds of change is matched by his fear of contingency. He rules out the possibility of innate structures as such. He asserts that contingent emergence is "incompatible" with structure – but then significantly corrects himself to add "in any case, with logico-mathematical structures". What he goes on to describe is, in fact, the emergence of more and more complex structures in the first twelve years of life, but these emergences are called transformations (i.e., forms of self-regulation).

The implicit phenomenological or mechanistic basis of Piaget's 'structural causality' becomes explicit on p. 64. In the early stages of development, the child displays only 'sensori-motor intelligence', which "does not involve representation, and is essentially tied to action and coordinations of action". As a result of his first construct (sensori-motor intelligence), Piaget is now obliged to invent a second: the "semiotic function". This semiotic function "permits the evocation of situations which are not presently perceived", that is to say, it permits a "new dimension": "representation or thought" (French edition, p. 55). The artifice with which this 'function' is conjured up – the rabbit comes out of the hat for a moment, only to disappear quickly back inside – is rather well brought out by the American translation. In response no doubt to the dubious injunction to produce 'readable English', the translator takes considerable liberties with

Piaget's text. At this point, however, the liberty she takes corresponds precisely (and unintentionally) to the necessity of filling up the hole in Piaget's theory:

> As soon as the semiotic function (speech, symbolic, play, images, and such) COMES ON THE SCENE . . . the child . . . uses reflective abstractions (my emphasis).

We ask how? and where from? What process of transformation or self-regulation can account for the mysterious appearance of this so-called 'semiotic function'? Obviously, in a theory dependent on a subject–object causal epistemology, nothing can possibly account for it.

Since Piaget's epistemology is derived from an epistemology of closed systems, there is no way to bring into relation with each other the "closed and autonomous wholes" of his structures, except by providing them with some kind of force or power – something like hollow billiard balls driven by rubber bands, perhaps. Thus, in order to account for the child's 'intentional acts' (anterior to the 'semiotic function'), Piaget must necessarily invent another construct. This we find on p. 48: the instinct. In order to explain that organisms, although 'equilibrated' ("homeostatic"), differ from machines in that they take account of MEANINGS, Piaget introduces the idea of "instinctual structures". We realize that Piaget thinks of the organism itself as a closed and autonomous structure: a monad, but with little holes in it to let things in and out.[11]

In Piaget's theory, the 'organism' is forever separated by an Imaginary and ideological barrier from its 'environment'. Since Piaget sees nothing in the child but an OBJECTIVE ENTITY who pushes and pulls other objects around – and is pushed and pulled by them – and then gets to talk about it, it is impossible for him to fully understand what it means to say that the 'parent topological structure' is constituted BETWEEN the child and his environment (not in his head), and that it is the child's open relationship to the various levels of the environment which accounts for all 'intentional acts' and 'meaning' (Chapters VI, VII). What, for example, is the role of the stimulation of the child's skin as it passes through the birth canal? Push and resistance, the supposed source, according to Piaget, of the child's conception of causality? That this stimulation could also be INFORMATION – that it could be the last set of a nine-month exchange of message sets between mother and child – is inconceivable in Piaget's theory.

Piaget considers the child to be an object in a world of objects, which are

---

[11] Piaget's definition of meaning (1952: 189–95) makes this quite clear. Sensorial images, perceptions, 'indications', 'signs' – and I suspect words also – are OBJECTS for ASSIMILATION.

there simply to be USED (matter–energy) and not also to be LISTENED TO and COMMUNICATED WITH (information). (Quite apart from the relations of the child with other subjects, mediated by these very objects.) He clearly believes in a 'science' of psychology and psychopathology quite separate from the socioeconomic context. Like the early Parsons, for whom 'social deviance' was to be explained by 'individual' psychological factors, and like Lacan, for whom such deviance is simply another manifestation of Hegel's 'law of the heart' (Chapter XVII), Piaget presents us with a theory which does not take into account the objective fact that the child is born into a social system in which it is necessary to sell both one's 'self' and one's labor (one's body) in order to survive. We have therefore to presume that for Piaget the merchandising of oneself as a commodity in our culture is part of the 'natural order of things', and that this is in effect what the theory of self-objectification in "interpersonal transactions" actually means. In a word, one of the tenets of Piaget's theory is that 'self' = 'body' = 'object', and that consequently the child has to learn how to behave like a commodity. Within the context of capitalist ideology, this statement is perfectly true. But, if this is indeed the case, then where in the theory do we discover the logical extension and scientific analysis of this state of affairs? Where do we find it explained why some children have to learn to be BETTER commodities than others – for example, manual laborers, people of color, and (especially) women?

Piaget's 'child' is clearly another monad, replete with the inherent 'human nature' which is attacked by Piaget on p. 106 – but human nature is called "autonomous structure" in Piaget. As with Arthur Jensen's and Ernst Mayr's conception of 'inherent genetic giftedness' (Chapter XIV, Section 6), this notion of autonomy requires a complicated process of projection. Assumptions of consensus and homogeneity – and 'liberal' or 'social-democratic' 'color-blindness' – derived from the social class of the theorist are projected onto the social environment in general, which is consequently viewed in terms of stability and equilibrium. The 'system–environment' relationship of the child is thus conceived in the terms of the equilibrated "bounded structure" of homogeneous elements described (in Piaget) by mathematical group theory. Nowhere in the theory is there any scientific appraisal of this assumption of homogeneity as resulting in fact from the SYNCHRONIC IMPERATIVE of what Marcuse so aptly calls the 'performance principle'.

Moreover, once the theory has projected the liberal assumptions of 'equality' away from the 'individual' and into the contemporary social structure (which is, of course, and in fact, an 'organized complexity' of heterogeneous 'elements' in a context of unequal opportunity), it runs into epistemological difficulties. These difficulties are the result of the pseudo-contextuality of the original definition of the system–environment relationship in which the child or the individual is supposedly constituted. In other words, because the individual is conceived *a priori* as an entity or as a "bounded substructure", the actual open-system relationship of 'individual' and 'environment' – in which boundaries = communication – is implicitly or explicitly conceived of as a relationship between two closed systems, each of which can do without the other until or only for as long as they bump into each other in the street. For this view, boundaries = barriers, and we can use Piaget's unconscious political metaphor of the frontier to explain why. There is never a SINGLE frontier between one nation-state and another, but always TWO. The frontier belonging to France is at the French customs post, and that belonging to Spain is down the street a bit, at the Spanish customs post. The peculiarity of it all is that when you are between one customs post and the other, you are nowhere at all. And, having left one structure of conventions and sanctions in which your passport describes you as such and such a person, without yet having entered another similar structure, you are not only nowhere, you are also nobody. Because of the double frontier (opposition) which replaces the single one (distinction), for a few minutes you are really or potentially stateless, that is, STRUCTURELESS. In actual fact, of course, provided you bear suitable markers, you glide across a single boundary like a bit of information moving from one subsystem in the ecosystem to another.

But the kinds of psychosocial theories we are discussing here ignore the no-man's-land they create between their various structures, because they have no way of dealing with the problem they have generated without destroying their own axioms (cf. Section 12 on Gödel). Consequently, the supposed homogeneity of the 'individual element' which was projected onto the environment is necessarily projected back to the individual, where it all began. In other words, the system–environment relationship posited in the theory is actually an extension of conceptions derived from the study of the individual, as the paradigm of all relationships, to the system as a whole. This perspective is sometimes called 'organicism', but since there are no known organisms on which it could in fact be modeled, this term is itself another denial of the actual state of affairs. It simply provides another label which will allow the 'organicists', the 'historicists', the 'mechanists', and others to continue irrelevant debates about their supposed differences of opinion. For, in reality, they are all in perfect accord on the real source of their models: the political and economic ideology of capital.

We are not therefore surprised that Piaget – since he is incapable of conceiving the primordial semiotic relationship which began with the child's conception – should at other points in the elaboration of his theory, make rhetorical appeals to the myth of artificial intelligence (pp. 69, 114), whose alchemical scientism has been amply demonstrated by Dreyfus (1965). Piaget's imaginary conception of the entity absolutely requires him to say: "To be real, a structure must, in the literal sense, be governed from within" (p. 69). We ask, very simply: IN RELATION TO WHAT? But in fact this internally controlled, closed system is Piaget's "epistemic subject": *cogito ergo sum.*

The whole structuralist movement has relied heavily on an appeal to the relation rather than to the entity. After the phenomenologists' slogan: "To the things themselves", we heard: "Not the things, but the relations between things". However, since the bioenergetic epistemology of classical 'science', for all its evident atomism, is nevertheless (and necessarily) a theory of the relations between things, such an appeal may be no more than an introduction to old wine in new wineskins (or to new wine in old wineskins, if you prefer). What we are really in search of, after all, is not a theory of the relations between things, but a theory far more radical: A THEORY OF THE RELATION BETWEEN RELATIONS.

Piaget's misconception of relation is rather well brought out by his misunderstanding of the work of the genes. Since he thinks of the genes, exactly as he thinks of the child, as entities separate from their environment and related to it by efficient causality, his attempt to explain 'structuralism' in biology reduces itself to another transformation of the atomism he is attacking. He points out that the genes are not "aggregates of individuals", but, as Dobzhansky says, they involve "gene systems". The genes perform "not as soloists, but as members of the orchestra", as Dobzhansky puts it. Piaget's approving reference to this image is highly revealing. An orchestra plays according to a set of coded instructions, but what it produces has nothing essential to do with the nature of, the presence of, or the reaction of the audience. Simple experiments, such as the rotation of the leg nodules in the developing newt – show that changes in a level or a part of the 'environment' result, through the relation of feedback, in changes in the products of the program of the 'system'. When a 180° rotation of the newt's right-front-leg nodule produces, not an upside-down right-front-leg, but a left-front-leg, we realize that the gene system's 'tune' has been altered by the reaction of its audience. As Gregory Bateson puts it (from whom the example comes): "A gene is presumably to be regarded as a question to which the answer is provided by its neighborhood." This example alone makes Piaget's criterion of self-regulation, "which generates elements that still belong only to the structure" (p. 14), entirely dubious in its application.

Similarly, if we take up again the questions raised by Piaget's theory of "instinctual structures", the semantics of the organism are not to be explained by such essentially one-way principles of explanation as 'instincts'. Such terms, derived from the efficient causality of classical physics, are entirely separate from and independent of any environment. They are simply 'causal entities' inherent in one closed system which come into play when that closed system comes into relation with another closed system.

A more promising conception, which speaks directly to the problem of what the term instinct has always covered up – by being the reification of the relationship between teleonomy and constraint – is that meaning is the goal and the result of the way the 'organism' or system uses meaningless information to organize the logical and physical WORK to be done in relation to some environment or other or to some level of the environment (D. M. Mackay). This work may involve matching or fitting or changing the environment (Chapters VIII, IX, XII).

6. *The Confusion between Development and Evolution*

I have said that Piaget is afraid of contingency and certain kinds of change. Random variation in evolution, for example, is impossible in his model. What is perhaps a little surprising, however, is that in criticizing theories of evolution he projects onto the contemporary informational model of evolution – which he does not understand at all – the very adjectives which best describe his own theory. Having developed a reductionist monadology of structures (p. 41) ruled by biomechanistic causality, equilibrium, and inertia, Piaget defines the current evolutionary theory of random variation in the context of natural selection as reductionist, additive, and mechanistic. Piaget seems to think that information-processing involves 'addition' (rather than multiplication). Particularly significant is his equation of random variation and selection in evolution with Descartes' 'animal machines'.

These conceptions are, however, the necessary result of his definition of the organism: "The organism is, in a way, the paradigm structure" (p. 44). As we know, the paradigm structure is not in fact the organism, it is the ECOSYSTEM. In an earlier work (1964: 1), Piaget makes the organism the equivalent of the person, and describes psychic development from birth to adulthood as directly comparable to organic growth. Consequently, because the dynamics of his structure are modeled only on the learning and maturation of the individual organism rather than also on the evolution of the species and the system, no proper concept of natural evolution is possible in his model. In rejecting contemporary evolutionary theory, Piaget does not understand that the theory has to account for morphogenesis, and that the self-regulation of the 'organism' cannot alone account for such violent change.

It cannot account for it because such change is highly improbable and certainly unpredictable. But Piaget depends on a 'flat' or statistical concept of 'causal' probability related to the second law of thermodynamics (p. 43; 1964: 118) and game theory (pp. 104–5). He is aware that the second law describes a probable tendency towards disorganization or randomness, whereas information theory describes an improbable negatively or neutrally entropic tendency towards increasing organization. But he does not employ the theory in an informational sense. Although the random recombinations of strings of DNA (the errors in coding) or the possible errors in transmission by RNA could theoretically be described in the terms of probability, no conceivable theory of probability could predict the possibilities of the survival of the resulting 'mutations'. There is no tendency towards anything except invariant reproduction in DNA, but there is the possibility of error and chance. Since the survival of the error involves a mutually interdependent and equally unpredictable set of variables – the internal and external environment – it is difficult to see how any probability equations could possibly be applied to its potential to survive.

The most satisfactory present account of what may happen in evolution is an informational account. Random variation, probably in the sense of random genetic recombinations, produces novel reorganizations or structures, of which a miniscule number prove to have survival value. These novel structures can be conceived of as the result of the interference of NOISE in the transmission of the genetic information. If selected to survive, then the product of this noise incorporates the noise as information in its own reproduction. There are two ways for a structure or system to maintain its stability in the face of noise. If may either protect itself by massive redundancy, which reduces noise to insignificance and prevents change, or it may maintain itself by changing. The first is a principle of morphostasis; the second a principle of sensitivity to noise, a principle of morphogenesis. It seems clear that the individual organism is an example of the first, and that social systems are an example of the second.

7. Natura non facit saltum

Following his critique of Kurt Lewin's field-theory 'topology', Piaget introduces a discussion of Talcott Parsons's 'structural-functionalism'. He correctly summarizes Parsons's equilibrium model, remarking that it deserves "special attention":

[Parsons's] definition of structure as a stable disposition of the elements of a social system IMPERVIOUS TO EXTERNALLY IMPOSED DISTURBANCES has led him to develop a theory of social equilibrium. . . . As for functions, Parsons conceives them as intervening in the adaptations of the structure to situations which are exterior to it (p. 102, my emphasis).[12]

It was after all Parsons who said, in 1951, just as 'peaceful coexistence' was about to become the explicit keystone of American foreign policy: "Order – peaceful coexistence in conditions of scarcity – is one of the very first of the functional imperatives of social systems" (quoted in Buckley, 1967: 24). Piaget's approving reference here confirms even more strongly the bio-mechanistic epistemological base and the conservative ideological foundations of his theory. As Buckley has pointed out, in equilibrium models of 'consensus', all tensions, problems, deviations, conflicts, and so on are necessarily defined as DEVIANT INTRUSIONS into the system. The fact that Parsons's model also includes a 'law of inertia' more or less equivalent to Freud's 'death instinct' is not to be overlooked. Parsons's 'system' is a mélange of bioenergetics and mechanics. It also includes a concept of structure and function derived from non-informational biology. A little more subtle, perhaps, than the 'veritable organized machine' of Saint-Simon and Claude Bernard (Chapter VI) – but not much.

It is abundantly clear in what sense Piaget is elaborating a theory of structure which represents and confirms the values of the dominant. We are not therefore surprised that his emphasis on consensus, harmony, individualism, and digital intellect – with its necessary corollary: the linear measurement of 'intelligence' against class-, race-, and sex-bound 'success' – should meet with such acceptance in the United States. Piaget's close affinity with Parson's model – elaborated during the McCarthy years and the Cold War – is complemented by his mention of Alfred Marshall's economic "displacements of equilibrium" (p. 104). The epigraph to Marshall's *Principles of Economics* (8th edition, 1920) is Leibniz's comforting dictum: "Nature does not make leaps" (cf. Sweezy, 1970). This ideological denial of quantum jumps in nature is, of course, a characteristic projection onto nature of a desired process of gradualism in socio-economic change. For Marshall, as for Parsons, any sudden change must therefore, by definition, come from outside the system. It must, by definition be NOISE – and therefore, again by definition, it must be VIOLENCE. As Piaget puts it:

The [mathematical] group is . . . an essential instrument of transforma-

[12] I criticize Parsons's 'evolutionism' – identical to Piaget's in essence – in Chapter XII.

tions, but of RATIONAL transformations, which do not modify everything all at once, and which always preserve invariance in some respects (p. 21, my emphasis).

And later:

Scientific structuralism is not a matter of a doctrine or of a philosophy . . . but essentially that of a method, with everything that this term implies of questions of technique [*technicité*], of obligations of intellectual honesty, and of progress by successive approximations (French edition, p. 118).

The seriously defective English translation of this passage – which leads one almost to suspect an unconscious ideological collusion – is, once again, less misleading than it ought to be (note the displacement of the words "intellectual" and "progress"):

Structuralism . . . is technical, involves certain intellectual obligations of honesty, views progress in terms of gradual approximation (p. 137).

A remark by D. M. MacKay is apposite here. MacKay (1969: 112–13) seeks to show how the process of goalseeking, adaptation, and learning in an organism depends on and results in the construction of a simulated mapping of the environment by the organism. In this construction, "aspects of the world which call forth (or have received) no adaptive internal 'matching response' will simply fail to be perceived or conceived of". Consequently, in the absence of sufficient incentive and/or suitable experience or training, there are likely to be "epistemological blind spots" in the structure of the "organizers" evolved in the 'map' as a result of the past experience in the given individual. He compares this limitation to the limitations commonly encountered in mathematics, and specifically to the limitations of Fourier series as descriptions of continuous waveforms, a particularly elegant tool in information science. He points out that although in theory any waveform can be described as the sum of a set of sine waves, "in practice the method becomes infinitely cumbersome for impulse-type functions". His point is that just as the structure of the organism's map may include conceptual blind spots making it inadequate to deal with certain aspects of the world, "the language of frequency-analysis has a 'blind spot' for the concept of 'sudden change'" (cf. Chapter VII). MacKay rather naturally goes on to point out that the "goals pursued in life inevitably condition the terms in which life is perceived and understood". What is required to avoid conceptual blindness says MacKay, is that we "understand our own goal-complexes FROM THE OUTSIDE" (p. 114).

8. *Structuralism and Economics*

There is another dimension to Piaget's mention of Alfred Marshall in support of his theory of "structural equilibration". One of the axioms of Marshall's economics is what is known as Say's Law of Markets. Say's Law holds that a sale is invariably followed by a purchase of equal amount, with the result that the circulation represented by 'commodity–money–commodity' can never be interrupted. Consequently, since supply creates its own demand, no crisis can occur in the system, specifically, the crisis of which general overproduction (positive feedback) is the symptom (Sweezy, 1942: 137). The law supposes a 'natural' tendency to equilibrium under *laissez-faire*, an "automatic self-righting mechanism tending to establish full employment in an unplanned private-enterprise economy" (Robinson, 1948: 105). It is therefore a model of a system in which errors are excluded before they are made.

As Sweezy points out, this theory of a 'natural' self-equilibrating mechanism is Ricardo's also. We note that it is directly related to Ricardo's 'cybernetic' theory of the 'natural' price of labor, which assumes that there exists a 'competitive equality' between 'individual' workers in a 'struggle for existence' governed by Malthusian laws of starvation:

> The natural price of labor is that price which is necessary to enable the labourers, one with another, to subsist and perpetuate their race, without either increase or diminution (1817: quoted by Hardin, 1963: 282).

The point to be made, of course, is that Say's Law was refuted by both Marx and Keynes – and by the economic reality of continuing unemployment before and after the Second World War. Both Marx and Keynes depend on economic factors involving positive feedback which were neglected by classical political economy, such as unemployment and monopoly. Both demonstrated (but in different ways) that economic crises under capitalism are not accidents – that is, 'disturbances' from outside the 'natural equilibrium', as Marshall, the early Parsons, or Piaget would have it – but rather inherent features of the capitalist system of production itself, dependent on factors excluded from the explanatory model of the classical economists.

Apart from the complementary differences between Marx and Keynes over such matters as the Keynesian distinction between "decisions to save" and "decisions to invest", there is an important distinction in the boundaries each ascribes to his model of the capitalist economic system. A cybernetic representation of the Keynesian system (e.g., Tustin, 1952), provides us with an apparently self-regulating model (provided we include within it government control of tariffs, of taxes on capital investment, and of interest rates). These controls over the 'inducement to invest' or the 'expectation of profit' do not however change the occurrence of 'booms' and 'slumps', because the accumulation of capital reduces the profitability of further investment. Increases in unemployment necessarily result from this process of growing wealth and productive capacity, and susceptibility to unemployment is the Keynesian 'weakness' at the heart of capitalism (Robinson, 1948: 111–13).

But government intervention in the economy – new in scope but not in essence – is not in fact a control device in the proper sense of what makes the system stable and self-regulatory, for at most it is a form of DAMPING. In all feedback systems which are stable (e.g., an automatic pilot), damping is essential to prevent the system from going into ever-increasing oscillations around its position of stability. But damping can only come into play if the system is already inherently oscillatory, and a given form of damping can control oscillations only between certain limits within a given CLOSED system of organization. What is not included within the cybernetic model of Keynesian economics, however, is that its 'stability' is dependent on the single factor common to both the 'big-bang' and the 'steady-state' theories of the universe: unlimited expansion (whether or not this includes, as in Hoyle's original theory, the continued creation of 'matter'). Consequently, the system is not closed at the boundaries supposed by Keynes. The "expectation of profit" has no limits defined by any parameter of the system; it is an unlimited input resulting in exponential growth. Such growth cannot be controlled by any manipulation of parameters limited BY the system – such as government intervention affecting the rate of investment in order to damp the oscillation between 'booms' and 'busts' – because 'stability through growth' is precisely what keeps the system operating.

As Tustin remarks, Keynes's understanding of this necessity is the foundation of his theory. According to previous views, the withdrawal of part of the flow of money from the system in the form of savings should make the economy run down and stop, before any re-investment of savings could reverse its trend towards inertia (entropy). However, Keynes showed how a small increase in the flow of money around the circuit of capital goods (buying to invest) is amplified by its effect on the flow of money around the circuit of consumer goods into a much larger change in general economic activity (total incomes). Consequently, what keeps the economic system going is the constant input of demand over and above the supposedly 'equilibrated' supply-and-demand of the system itself: new capital investment dependent on the expectation of profit.

Structuralism partakes of both Marshall and Keynes. Like Marshall, it confuses mechanical equilibrium with stability in open systems; like Keynes, it enlarges its theoretical boundaries enough to take selected new parameters into account, while still closing the theory off from its real relationship to 'metaparameters' like the Keynesian expectation of profit. Unlike Marxian economics, however, Keynesian economics provides nothing but an internal critique of the system, accompanied by suggestions for the treatment of the symptoms. Structuralism, too, while claiming to uncover 'fundamental' structures, remains an analysis of symptoms. Unlike Marx, who is concerned with the whole biosocial context of capitalist economics, Keynes makes no attempt to suggest a cure for the 'disease'. And however novel any suggested treatment may be, it is a long-standing principle in medicine that the only case in which it is legitimate to treat the symptoms, and not the disease, is when the disease is incurable.

9. Bioenergetics and Marxism

Although Piaget is undoubtedly Hegelian, he is probably correct in identifying Althusser's importation of the concept of overdetermination (from Freud, via Lacan) into Marxism, as a causal conception (p. 120). In *Lire Le Capital*, II, Althusser tries to escape efficient causality through a somewhat Heideggerean and not very convincing analysis of the concept of *Darstellung* ('representation', 'performance', 'exhibition') in Marx. Like many of those influenced by Lacan, Althusser conceals his model of causality in the term 'absence':

> . . . Depending on the level at which we place ourselves, it can be said that *Darstellung* is the concept of the presence of the structure in its effects, the concept of the modification of effects by the efficacity of the structure present in its effects – or, on the other hand, that *'Darstellung'* is the concept of the EFFICACITY OF AN ABSENCE (1965b: 170, my emphasis).

By analogy with a theatrical representation, Althusser is saying that it is the whole, which is present but absent at each state or stage of the system, that accounts for 'structural causality'. Absence is, of course, a covert metaphor for teleonomy or goalseeking. But for Althusser, this seems to be an essentially homeostatic conception. Following the Lacanian perspective, and borrowing a term from Rancière, he calls the 'efficacity of an absent cause' "metonymic causality". Given its source in Lacan, this is a straightforward metaphor for desire. Althusser adds that he does not intend to imply that the structure is something exterior to the economic phenomena. The 'absence of the cause' is the "very form of the interiority of the structure, as structure, in its effects". It is a cause immanent to its effects in the Spinozist sense.

The logical contradiction involved in the conception of a cause which is absent, but which is still a cause, arises from that aspect of much of 'structuralist' thinking which is still bound, without realizing it, by energy–entity or closed-system explanation. Cybernetics has provided the methodological constructs necessary to understand the difference between (efficient) causality and teleonomy in open systems. From an ecosystemic perspective, the 'absent cause' is simply the diachronic GOAL or the synchronic REGULATION of the relationship of the subsystem and whatever is defined as its environment. Both goal and regulation involve considerations of constraint, (transmitted) difference, possibility, optimum organization, ideals, and so on, but not the concept of causality as such. Moreover, as Lacan's definition of metonymy as desire already emphasizes, metonymy is not primarily an effect of structure, but an effect of system.

Emmanuel Terray – whose Marxian approach to problems of change in 'other civilizations' is analyzed in Chapter XII – provides a criticism of 'structuralism' which agrees in intent with my critique here: The structuralists

> never conceive the relations between different levels in the terms of efficacy, determination, and reciprocal action.[13] Their object is to discover formal correspondences between structures: homologies, isomorphies, symmetries, inversions. . . . Thus society with its different levels appears as a system of mirrors which reflect a more or less deformed image from one level to another. Such a viewpoint cannot find a place for the event, nor for change (1969: 45).

What is of interest in Terray's critique, however, is that he refuses all 'biological' or 'systemic–adaptive' models, because he believes them to be 'organic' or 'organicist'. Since he lacks any conception of the goalseeking, adaptive, open system, the 'motivation' of the system in his own model necessarily appears in variously disguised forms: as efficient causality, as teleonomy, or as instinct. Thus, whereas he correctly brings out the one-dimensional and Imaginary nature of theories which describe the relationship between the various (non-autonomous) levels or structures in the socioeconomic system by means of a theory of reflection (*Widerspiegelung*) or a theory of homology (e.g., Goldmann), Terray cannot make a systemic critique of 'structuralism'. Consequently he ends up by resorting to

---

[13] Note that these terms conceal and confuse efficient causality, determinism, teleonomy, and feedback.

precisely the very 'organicist' and 'biological–adaptive' metaphor to which he has explicitly denied any theoretical value. Since 'structuralism' cannot account for the event, he says, then

> in relation to structure, change appears as a foreign body, as a sort of poison which the structure must eliminate or die (ibid.).

Terray's phraseology,[14] recalls Zola's 'principle of organic harmony' (derived from Claude Bernard) which is criticized by Lukács. Zola, says Lukács, simply made a "mechanical" identification of the organic life cycle with the social cycle. Thus his novels provide no analysis of relationships; they simply "mirror" late nineteenth-century French capitalism. In Zola's words:

> In society, as in the human body, there is a solidarity linking the various organs with each other in such a way that if one organ putrifies, the rot spreads to the other organs and results in a very complicated disease (quoted in Lukács, 1938: 86).

There seems to be a lot of Zola still with us in the contemporary discourse of science. For the same reasons as Terray, Maurice Godelier's 'structural' discourse on Marx also becomes reduced in its turn to describing change in organicist metaphors. In this case, the organicism appears in an alimentary metaphor which reminds me of nothing so much as of an old monster movie:

> A structure has the property of tolerating and of 'digesting' certain types of events, until such a point and until such a time as it is the event which digests the structure.

On the following pages, Godelier uses the terms *équilibre, mutation, invariance, évolution, paralysie, pratique optimale*, and *inintentionnel* in quick succession.

10. *Games, Probability, Diachronic Linguistics*

Lévi-Strauss uses game-theory metaphors from time to time (e.g., 1947: 574). As I have pointed out, game theory involves INTENTIONAL rationality in the 'pure' competition of equilibrium situations. It is consequently applicable only to the most formalistic kinds of structuralism. Piaget's

---

[14] Godelier (1968) makes the rounds on this question – operations research, teleology, Maupertuis' principle of least effort, the utilitarian pleasure principle, behaviorism, game theory, cybernetics (p. 288) – without ever stabilizing his own system of metaphors: laws, regulation, evolution, logic, combination. Note that the expression "the effects of the structure", as it stands, easily conceals efficient causality.

remarks on closed-loop feedback in the economic theory of 'management' and 'tuning' – following his brief discussion of Marshall – are immediately followed by an implicit reference to the 'free, rational subject' of game theory. Since Piaget believes that human 'intelligence' can actually be simulated in a digital computer, one suspects that he views the 'higher' forms of 'intellect' as only involving 'rational' and binary "mechanisms of decision". It is no doubt this faith which leads him to say that

> once it is realized that game theory is applicable to affects, to perception, and to cognitive development, economic structures become, via game theory, very closely linked to the affective and cognitive regulation of the SUBJECT (p. 104).

Whatever real people in real situations may do, game theory necessarily digitalizes value and utility. I can therefore think of no other explanation for these remarks about affectivity, except to assume an implicit rationalist bias towards binarism in Piaget.

Piaget finds himself largely sympathetic to what he calls the "authentic" structuralism of Lévi-Strauss, and Lévi-Strauss accepts his interpretation with only minor quibbling (1971: 561). It is perhaps in the light of his definition of the "epistemic subject" – as the "cognitive nucleus common to all subjects at the same level" (p. 139) – that we should understand his description of Lévi-Strauss as "the very incarnation of faith in the permanence of human nature [and the unity of reason]" (p. 106. French edition, p. 90. The bracketed phrase is the translator's not Piaget's).

In the second edition of the *Elementary Structures* (1968: xxiv–xxx), Lévi-Strauss employs his earlier dichotomy between statistical models and mechanical models to try to answer his critics. He goes on to introduce the complex problem of the "indeterminate" Crow–Omaha kinship system (which he compares to a "lift-and-force pump fed from an external source", as distinct from an "asymmetrical" system, which is more like "a clock with all its workings enclosed"). Any attempt to represent this kinship system graphically results in impossible problems, because each generation or so requires that a new DIMENSION be added to the diagram. The system is "turbulent", and depends on what the members of the system remember about previous marriages. Such a system – with fifteen clans, let us say, and two types of prohibition – would permit nearly four million different types of marriages. What Lévi-Strauss goes on to do, however, is to compare this huge gamut of possible combinations with those possible in cards, checkers, and chess.

But, since the possible future marriages in the Crow–Omaha system depend on the marriages which have actually taken place in previous generations (the 'memory' of the system), it is impossible to discover an initial state or ORIGIN from which to calculate these probabilities. This is not the case with chess, however. No matter how huge the number of possible moves in chess (probably greater than the estimated number of atoms in the universe), the game can properly be viewed as a Markov process in which the rules are invariable, the initial state is always implicitly given, and the memory process involved is simply the state of the board at each move (and not what the pieces on the board 'remember' about where they have been). Chess is equifinal in the sense that the pathways leading to checkmate or draw are overdetermined. But the Crow–Omaha system does not include only a set of overdetermined pathways. It does not only change state, it also changes rules. The rules of the Crow–Omaha game provide for the emergence, at each given state, of a set of METARULES. In other words, if it is not simply a random system, the Crow–Omaha system is open, multifinal, and homeogenic. In terms of the model elaborated in Chapters XII and XIII, it seems to be a system which creates new information at each state and integrates this information into its memory as TRACE. It cannot therefore reproduce itself; it can only reproduce something other than itself. It seems that it is a system in permanent diachrony, where the metonymic messages in each generation become the metaphors of the next, a game of chess in $n+n$ dimensions.

But the Crow–Omaha system, as such, does not evolve. It simply changes structure or organization without changing its order of structure or organization. Thus, although its complexity results from an unpredictable and open feedback relation in two directions – to its past (memory), and to the actual choices made within it – it does not increase in complexity in a developmental sense ('growth'), nor in an evolutionary sense ('mutation'), nor in a historical sense (the overcoming of paradoxes and oppositions). It is not therefore negatively entropic over time; it simply maintains neutral entropy (organization).

It is this distinction that explains why the linguistic model is incapable of representing evolution or history, and, therefore, why it is inherently conservative. Although the term diachrony in linguistics may well refer to the linear process of the syntagm, it also refers, as it did for Saussure and Troubetzkoy, to the history of a language, or to that of a family of languages, or to phonological change. (Troubetzkoy described the latter in 1930 as a "goal-seeking system". Cf. Mandelbrot's formulation in Chapter VII, or Saussure, 1916b: 121). But no PROCESS of changing complexity in an evolutive or historical sense can be discerned in language change. There is simply a peaceful transition from one set of rules to another set, assisted by noise generated internally and externally. Language complexity bears no relation to social complexity. And if social changes or invasions by other groups accelerate or set off linguistic change, the change from one linguistic code to another remains a pure epiphenomenon with no theoretical value as a MODEL of history. All such change is morphostatic; it is in no real sense whatsoever 'historical' or 'dialectical'.

The question of increasing complexity makes it clear why the 'linguistic–structural' model can be so easily applied to 'cool' systems without writing as such. (In using the term 'cool', I do not of course intend to imply any acceptance of the anti-scientific scientism of Lévi-Strauss's analogy between 'cold' societies and clocks, and between 'hot' societies and steam engines: Charbonnier, ed., 1961.) Such systems tend in general simply to reproduce themselves, or to make non-essential changes in coding, without increasing their ORDER of complexity. Historical evolution occurs, but rarely – and very often as a result of outside events. It is equally clear why the 'linguistic–structural' model applies so readily to myths. Both the myth and the model are essentially timeless. In effect, they prove their timelessness to each other, for the timelessness of Lévi-Straussian structural analysis, like Piaget's 'self-regulation', is mythical time.[15] Moreover, Lévi-Strauss's equation of historical time with anthropological space (1962: 256), and his comparison of Marxism with geology (1955: 61) involve a scale quite different from that of recorded history (cf. Cournot). The same model also necessarily matches the artificial closure of history represented in the psychoanalytical model: homeostasis, equilibrium, repetition, the eternal return, and the *recherche du temps perdu*.[16]

An evolutionary or historical model, on the other hand, not only supposes a negentropic change in complexity, it also supposes a process of GOAL-CHANGING. Similarly, a model of development may involve changes in goals in so far as levels of learning are involved (Chapter V). We can slightly modify Deutsch (1963: 92–3), and list four "orders of goalseeking" in feedback networks:

1 First-order goalseeking: immediate satisfaction: 'adjustment', 'reward'.
2 Second-order goalseeking: self-preservation: the preservation of the possibility of seeking first-order goals by control over (1).

[15] Piaget mentions Waddington's 'chreod' on pp. 49–50 and 89, but seems to have understood nothing of value about its temporal orientation, its implicit informational basis, or its ecosystemic principles. It is of some interest to know that Waddington lived in the room next to Bateson while Bateson was writing his *Naven* (1936) – an unaccountably neglected anthropological study which prefigures much of the cybernetic–systemic perspective.
[16] But not, however, the entropic version of the pleasure principle.

3 Third-order goalseeking: preservation of the group, species, or system by control over (1) and (2), beyond the individual life-span.

4 Fourth-order goalseeking: preservation of the process of goalseeking over and above the preservation of any particular goal or group by control over (1), (2), and (3). This is in effect the preservation of the relations of the ecosystem (Chapter VIII).

These levels of goalseeking differ, of course, in logical type.

11. Lévi-Strauss: One-dimensionality, Autonomy, Closure

The logical laws, which, in the final analysis,
govern the world of the intellect are essentially
invariable in their very nature. They are common
not only to all times and all places, but also to all
particular subjects, with no distinction even
between those we call real and those we call
chimerical. In sum, these laws are obeyed everywhere,
even in dreams.
AUGUSTE COMTE: Epigraph to Lévi-Strauss:
Totemism

On the one hand, Lévi-Strauss apparently believes that his algebraic models are necessarily mechanical. On the other, he invariably takes refuge in an appeal to a statistics derived from the study of homogeneous and unorganized complexity to explain those systems of (heterogeneous) organized complexity which go beyond a certain level of organization. Some authors have even hailed this step backwards – corresponding to Lévi-Strauss's unalloyed scientism – as his "most important contribution to the theory of social structure" (Nutini, quoted in Ardener, 1971b, 233). Kinship names do not however meet the requirement of homogeneity in statistical thermodynamics (probability). They cannot be substituted for each other without a 'change' taking place, whereas in the complete homogeneity of physics, if such a substitution does take place, nothing has happened. Nevertheless, kinship terms are at least of the same logical type. We can probably deduce a rule from this problematic of homogeneity. If the system is so complex as to require a statistical analysis (e.g., the Crow–Omaha), either it is an almost completely random system, or it cannot be modeled by mathematics. It might be possible to SIMULATE it in the organized simplicity of a computer capable of programming the interactions of several thousand or a million particles, but not (I think) if it is an open, structure-changing system.

Lévi-Strauss (1947: xxx) tries to deal with the Crow–Omaha system by suggesting a two-step application of probability. In essence, however, the influence of physics makes him a somewhat one-dimensional thinker. I mean that in spite of his concern for context, his several dimensions or levels of structure (as Terray points out, 1969: 43) are not really inter-related. In *La Pensée sauvage* (1962: 91–2), for instance, he discusses the possibility of demographic changes altering the number or the names of the clans amongst a given tribe, and postulates the solution the 'structure' would give:

> We can see therefore that population changes can explode the structure. But, if the 'structural orientation' resists the shock, it has available to it, each time it is disturbed, several ways of re-establishing an identical system to the previous one, or at least one which is formally of the same type.

He goes on to suggest how the myths and rituals of the system could contribute (as memory) to achieving this re-establishment, because changes at this level would "lag behind" the other changes. The feedback of the system would consequently re-establish its "previous harmony":

> It will orient the disordered ORGAN in the direction of an equilibrium which would at least be a compromise between the system's former state and the DISORDER introduced FROM OUTSIDE (my emphasis).

This is a rather straightforward statement of a cybernetic–organicist equilibrium model, like Piaget's, for which all change is an "environmental intrusion" or an "accident". (I shall return to the question of the 'conflict' or 'tension' necessarily produced within any goalseeking feedback system by its own organization [cf. Deutsch, 1963: 95], in discussing the applic-ability of the terms 'noise' and 'evolution' to societies without writing as such, in Chapters XII and XIII.) In this text of Lévi-Strauss, we have exactly the same kind of internally self-regulated system – whose reference to an environment is taken for granted or posited as secondary – as we have found in Cournot, in Pareto, in Parsons, in mathematical economics, in game theory, and in Piaget (1964: 114–31). The question which lies un-answered here, is therefore the following: Of what possible significance to a multifinal open system like our own, with multiple levels, intersecting structures, and global extension, is such a theory of the behavior of a system or structure which is open to energy, but closed to information? Moreover, in what sense do these elaborate anthropological and psycho-logical theories simply serve the ideological function of maintaining the perennial Cartesianism and Newtonianism of the scientific discourse? For all its emphasis on relations and combinations, and for all its supposed logical structure, this psychoanthropological theory is a myth of harmony, autonomy, imperviousness, repetition, and a comfortable kind of closure. It is a logical form, in the language of the digital computer – Leach also makes this point (1970: 122) – of the 'social physics' of the seventeenth century. For Piaget, it is a universe peopled by Kantian I's, separable, individual, self-regulating, and 'clear and distinct'. For Lévi-Strauss, on the other hand, it is matter in motion, a world of interchangeable atoms spoken by the self-regulating equilibrium of the whole, a "machinery for the suppression of time", like the myth.

Outside the limited domain of certain kinds of analysis – and I have said nothing about Lévi-Strauss's factual and interpretative anthropological inadequacies (cf. Leach, 1970: 101–20), or about the triviality of his analyses of contemporary societies – the only value of the theory may be what it tells us about the position in history of the 'anthropologizing' civilizations of the west. Its preoccupation with autonomy, internal regulation, and closure may be no less than a metaphor of what systemic–cybernetic analysis has shown: that, with increasing population size and increasing internal information transfer and economic exchange, contemporary nation-states demonstrate an accelerating trend to SELF-CLOSURE (J. W. Burton, cited by Deutsch, 1963: x).

12. *Piaget and Gödel*

Since Piaget considers himself a 'genetic' structuralist, he manifests some concern over Lévi-Strauss's philosophical idealism of "permanent structures", and his pure 'synchronics', or "invariant diachronics". Piaget quotes Lévi-Strauss's *Totemism*:

> All social life, however elementary, presupposes an intellectual activity in man of which the formal properties cannot, accordingly, be a reflection of the concrete organization of society (p. 107).

Structures therefore "emanate from the intellect". They are ever the same. These structures are prior to the social order, prior to the mental, and *a fortiori*, they are prior to the 'organic' (ibid.) – which is, for Lévi-Strauss the source of affectivity (1965: 109).

I have already pointed out that Lévi-Strauss's definition of "intellectual activity" involves a confusion of the brain (biological 'entity') with the mind (social relation), and that no relation of reflection can relate different structures or levels of structure. The 'intellectual activity' referred to by Lévi-Strauss is, first, communication, and, secondly, digital communication.

Contrary to Lévi-Strauss's assertion, however, the formal properties of communication are indeed found in the concrete organization of society. Consequently, his hypothesis of the primacy of what he calls 'mind' is untenable. These structures do not 'emanate from the intellect', like a secretion from a gland. They are already implicit in the ecosystemic relation preceding man (in phylogeny) and preceding birth (in ontogeny).

But Piaget does not avail himself of the communicational answer to Lévi-Strauss's false problematic of the 'intellect'. He simply replies that all structures have a genesis (e.g., 1964: 168), and that all genesis is "simply transition from one structure to another". Consequently, Lévi-Strauss's symbolic function is to be viewed as the as yet unfinished product of "continual self-construction". Piaget does, however, speak of "participation" (Lévy-Bruhl) in relation to "analogical thought" (p. 116; Lévi-Strauss, 1962: 348). But Lévi-Strauss incorrectly believes analog thought – the form of "untamed thought" – to be DISCONTINUOUS, whereas "domesticated thought" is characterized by a "concern for continuity": it is "interstitial and unifying". For Lévi-Strauss, this 'continuity' is the very form of analytical reason: analytical reason seeks to "dissolve all differences" (1962: 349).[17] It appears therefore that Piaget's conception of participation is both analytic and digital, for, as he says, it is not to be conceived as "some mystical tie, despising contradiction and identity" (*sic*).

The reason for Lévi-Strauss's curious definition of the analog – whereas he is partly right about the Imaginary quality of analytical thought – lies in the same idealist and rationalist background, founded on philosophies of consciousness and perception, that we find in Piaget. An 'image' or 'analog' for Lévi-Strauss can be only another form of an 'object of thought'. He confuses language and communication by assuming that communication means 'understanding'. The same is true for Piaget. In the following passage, Piaget reveals his intellectualist conception of language by demonstrating his confusion of the 'organism' with the 'subject' (1964: 113):

> Without language . . . operations would remain individual, and they would consequently be unaware of that CONTROL PROCESS which results from interindividual exchange and cooperation (my emphasis).

Considering the emphasis laid on self-regulation in Piaget's work, it is at first difficult to understand why he should think that language is necessary for the regulation of exchange and cooperation between persons. Given the preceding analysis, however, the answer is obvious. Piaget confuses the

---

[17] Lévi-Strauss is confusing the continuity of Symbolic difference in the analog with the Imaginary DESIRE for identity in the digital. Cf. Kierkegaard and Zeno on repetition in Chapter III.

organism and the person. He confuses the skin-bound organismic barrier with the Imaginary line between organism and environment. When he refers to closed, self-regulating structures, he means no less than what he says. These structures are entities, and their processes of communication, exchange, and control are INTERNAL. The structure is, *a priori*, solipsist: it regulates its own self as an object of itself.

Such an autonomy is possible only in machines closed to information (like Ashby's homeostat). As Emerson has pointed out (1956: 148) the individual is never the "ultimate choosing organism" in nature. What is involved in evolution, for example, is invariably the selection of the unit group. No language – only the communication of information – is involved.

For his part, in his *Totemism*, Lévi-Strauss quotes with approval a passage from Henri Bergson in order to exemplify Bergson's intuitive understanding of 'totemic' thought. The passage shows most clearly the confusion between matter–energy and information in Lévi-Strauss. In the passage in question, Bergson describes "a great current of creative energy" – which is "poured into matter' – in order to ORGANIZE the flora and fauna of the world. However, the passage from a Dakota Indian – which Lévi-Strauss quotes alongside Bergson's remarks in order to show their almost "exact" similarity – has quite a different emphasis. If it does indeed concern matter and movement, it also concerns the PRAYERS of the Dakota that everything in the world will find its rightful place. Bergson appeals to the metaphysical and bioenergetic *élan vital* to organize aggregates of matter (the example he uses involves particles of sand). The Dakota, on the other hand, is a materialist with his feet on the ground. In what he describes as a world of birds, beasts, and spirits in motion, he is using information to organize the matter–energy of the world so that he can get on with the business of living in it (1962: 140–1).

Since Lévi-Strauss is concerned with discovering the "permanent" traces of the symbolic function in the kinship organization of 'cool' societies, whereas Piaget is concerned with the ontogenesis of the child, Piaget's theory turns out to be the more dynamic of the two. In spite of his lack of a communicational and ecosystemic perspective, in spite of his bioenergetics of equilibrium, in spite of his misconstruction of language and semiotics, and in spite of his repeated confusion of evolution with development, Piaget nevertheless does offer a way of getting from one structure to another. Genesis involves moving from a "weaker" to a "stronger" structure, which he explains by reference to Gödel's theorem concerning the impossibility of complete formalization in any coherent system (pp. 140–1).

Piaget is consequently led to deny the concept of closure upon which his entire theory is based. Characteristically enough, he sees this as no more contradictory than the fact that the reversibility of his logico-mathematical base-structures makes them "disobey" the second law of thermodynamics (p. 43).[18] Nor does he seem to regard his own denial of closure either as a paradox in his own theory or as a paradox in the domain of 'natural' structures in the real world:

> a logical system, though a closed whole with respect to the theorems it demonstrates, is nevertheless only a relative whole: it remains open at the top with respect to those theorems which it does not demonstrate . . ., and, since the primitive conceptions and axioms have all sorts of implicit elements, the system is open at the bottom as well (p. 30).

My point is that if Piaget could fully translate his intuition about this logico-mathematical structure into the domain of 'natural' structure, he would free himself from the limits he imposes on his theory by his inadequate conception of homeostasis and evolution. Because he insists upon a digital perspective and because he does not see that the child's sensori-motor acts are the communication (in the analog mode) of one open system with another real or imaginary or symbolic 'subject' about the objects he perceives or handles, Piaget makes the same epistemological error of separating the 'organism' from its 'environment' as one finds in all non-communicational approaches to cybernetics, structuralism, or systems theory.

Gödel's Proof is a double bind, and so is the square root of minus one. We are consequently led to remark that Piaget – like all of those outside the poetry of mathematics who use 'mathematics' as a tool to avoid having to think about what they are actually doing – does not understand that most, if not all, of the paradoxes of mathematics are the result of making the discourse of mathematics into a closed system BY EXCLUDING THE MATHEMATICIAN.[19] In the same way, academic linguistics and information science have turned themselves into engineering games by excluding the real senders and receivers of the messages they study. No properly valid metamathematical theory can be constructed which does not include the DESIRE of the mathematician (cf. Spencer Brown, 1969). In a proper metamathematics, the paradox of $\sqrt{-1}$ ceases to be a paradox, and becomes what it has always

---

[18] In a physicalist sense, they do not disobey the second law. The neutral entropy of this sort of thought process, like that of every other open system, requires an input of energy (negative entropy) in order to process the information.

[19] It is the mathematician (not the theory) who sees that the Gödelian sentence is 'true', and inconsistent with the axioms that produced it. But Piaget makes this into a property of the mathematical structure, not of the relation between the mathematician and his mathematics, ignoring once again his own model of the interaction between organism and environment.

been: a 'word' in the discourse of the mathematical subject. That i remains as a sign of higher logical type than perhaps all of the others in a given equation is of small importance. In the first place, it works (mathematics is after all the greatest of the arts of compromise), and in the second, without exactly the same process of vacillation between logical types in the discourse of our daily lives, all HUMAN discourse would simply cease. . . .

13. *The Structure as Law and Order*

> To right a wrong, it is
> necessary to exceed the proper
> limits.
> MAO TSE-TUNG (1927)

It is clear from all that Piaget says about what he calls cybernetics – and he specifically distinguishes his operational self-regulation from "less perfect feedback systems" – that there is a connection between his refusal of random variation in evolution, his disavowals of sudden change, and his conception of feedback. He clearly confuses closed-loop feedback, step-function feedback, and the 'open' feedback of any system which is not only self-differentiating, but also in a reciprocally open, informational relationship to an environment. This would be confusion enough. But there is a more significant error. With his emphasis on control, equilibrium, and regulation, Piaget, like the early Parsons, necessarily assumes that all feedback is NEGATIVE. Consequently, for Piaget – as with 'disturbances' and 'random variations' – the source of any escalating deviations – POSITIVE feedback – must, by definition, be the result of outside interferences with the pre-established harmony of the individual structure. Piaget does not, of course, need a term like positive feedback to explain development or maturation, because he has any number of mixed metaphors to draw from: 'growth', 'instinct', 'force', intentional act', 'assimilation', and so on.

As Walter Buckley has pointed out, the 'order' which Parsons defines as "peaceful coexistence in conditions of scarcity", has very little as such to do with organization. For Parsons, in the final analysis, 'order' means: "institutionalized patterns of normative culture". In a word, it means the ideological and economic values of the *status quo* (Buckley, 1967: 16, 23–31). Parsonian sociology – like Piaget's psychology, like Lévi-Straussian anthropology – consequently makes 'order' a synonym for LAW AND ORDER. Deviations, disturbances, contradictions, conflicts are therefore necessarily and consequently the work of OUTSIDE AGITATORS.

I find the similarity between the structural theories analyzed here and the socioeconomic theory espoused by Mr J. Edgar Hoover, quite striking, not to say alarming.

Piaget's book is lucid, incisive, and (almost) unfailingly courteous to those he takes to task. His work is fruitful even when he is wrong. But, unfortunately, like most psychologists, nearly all academics, sociologists, biologists, and anthropologists, Piaget is a western elitist. He criticizes Lévi-Strauss's attempt to establish the validity of the 'untamed thought' of the 'cool' civilization in relation to our own. He feels that *la pensée sauvage* must somehow be inferior to 'scientific' (read 'civilized') thinking. How it is possible to hold such a view in this age of the possibility of the total annihilation of mankind by global pollution, by overpopulation, by nuclear war, by the depletion of the resources of the planet, or just by suffocating in our own garbage, is beyond me. The only worthwhile criterion I can think of for 'superiority' is a long-range survival value, and the 'other civilizations' have been far superior to our 'advanced' technological culture in that respect.

I find my general evaluation of Piaget's theory borne out by the last chapter in the book: "Structuralism and Philosophy". There is one 'structuralist' in relation to whom Piaget's courtesy and personal objectivity seems to fail. This is Michel Foucault, whose attack on psychological 'science' and whose dismal estimate of the future of man ("an accidental wrinkle in time"), seems to have hit Piaget where it really hurts. There is a sudden change of tone in this chapter, from stringent analysis to almost personal polemic. The central point of Piaget's attack on Foucault is on the notion of CONTINGENCY in evolution and that of SELF-DESTROYING systems in history. Piaget will not, for example, accept the notion of the integration of random noise into the system or the structure as information, which converts some evolutionary accidents into events (cf. 1964: 134–5). But this concept is the only one I know of that can integrate the structural perspective – with its emphasis on synchrony and adaptation within limits – into a truly dialectical view of man-and-womankind emphasizing diachrony and the necessity of a radical mutation of socioeconomic organization if our species is to survive. I would go further, in fact, and say that our species as it represents itself and as it wishes to be has not yet evolved. Indeed, it appears that, as has been recently suggested, the fear of SURVIVAL in a truly humanistic world – and thus the fear of radical change – has become a greater fear in our society than the fear of death itself.

Piaget seems quite honestly afraid to discover the irrationality of what passes for reason in western culture. It is significant that Piaget refers to Waddington's important work in biology without picking up on Waddington's insistence that we cannot survive without a significant change of values. And for Piaget to declare on page 129 that "Foucault has it in for man" – rather than to ask what evidence there is for Foucault to consider seriously that "structuralism spells the end of man" – is a monument to the insulation of the respected researcher from the unadulterated misery in which most men and women spend their lives on this earth. In other words, Piaget, who I am sure is a kind and liberal gentleman, lacks a consciousness of the global biosocial context: the biological environment without which we cannot survive and the global social environment in which, except for the happy few, 'survival' means everything from malnutrition to alienation and death. And here personal values join epistemological values: it is precisely a full and open understanding of the partly controlled and partly random feedback relationship to a CONTEXT which is missing not only from most of the varieties of structuralism that Piaget examines, but most significantly from his own.

Chapter XII

Ecosystem and Metasystem

A MORPHOGENIC MODEL OF EMERGENCE

There is an arrangement in the living being, a kind of
regulated activity. . . . Vital phenomena possess indeed their
rigorously determined physico-chemical conditions, but, at the
same time, they subordinate themselves and succeed one
another in a pattern and according to a law that pre-exists;
they repeat themselves with order, regularity, constancy. . . . It
is as if there existed a pre-established design of each
organism and of each organ such that, though considered
separately, each physiological process is dependent on the
general forces of nature, it reveals a special bond and seems
directed by some invisible guide in the path which it follows
and toward the position which it occupies.
CLAUDE BERNARD: *Leçons sur les phénomènes de la vie
commune aux animaux et aux végétaux* (1878)

1. *Selection and Combination*

Roman Jakobson's analysis of the two poles of language, metaphor and
metonymy, has already been elaborated in Chapter II. In thus using the
Lockean principles of the association of ideas by similarity and by contiguity to distinguish the metaphoric pole – paradigmatic, selective, substitutive, concurrent (similarity) – from the metonymic pole – syntagmatic,
combinatory, contextual, concatenated (contiguity) – Jakobson restricts
his analysis to language alone.

However, metaphor and metonymy are not primarily linguistic processes: they are communicational processes. Selection from the code and
combination in the message must and do occur in any communications
system whatsoever, whether in the genetic code of the DNA molecule, or

in the organism, or in the life processes of bacteria, or in a social system. What distinguishes these processes of selection and combination in different systems is the relative semiotic freedom of the ways in which they are used. Semiotic freedom means freedom within constraints; thus the relative scope of the code and the relative logical possibilities of combination in the message control the information possibilities of the system, and therefore its organization. As I pointed out in Chapter VII, we can methodologically divide the modes of communication found in all such systems into analog and digital communication.

Jakobson does indeed describe metaphor as reference to the code and metonymy as reference to both code and message. But he was writing at a time when the information theory from which these terms are derived was understood as a purely mechanistic and statistical discipline, employed without distinction in physics, at some levels in biology, in engineering, in computer theory, and in the logistics of the Bell Telephone Company. Jakobson has criticized information theory from this perspective.[1] Since that time, however, the continued development of a non-logocentric semiotics (Chapters XIII and XVI) – and therefore of a non-phallocentric linguistics – the development of a communicational and non-bioenergetic biology, that of a non-morphostatic theory of system and structure, and that of a non-mechanistic cybernetics, has invalidated Jakobson's restricted position on information theory (1963: 95).

All communication in systems of communication – ecosystems – involves an axis of selection and an axis of combination. I shall use the terms metaphor and metonymy rather loosely to designate these two axes. This usage is perhaps polemic, for the so-called linguistic model which these terms imply is inadequate to describe the diachronic processes of history and natural evolution, for reasons which will become clear presently. Our present interest in Jakobson's original article concerns the question of THE PROJECTION OF COMBINATION INTO THE AXIS OF SELECTION (1956: 69), for this describes the essence of the dialectical process of *Aufhebung*.

---

[1] His critique is based on a 1952 article by D. M. MacKay, on whose later work I have based my conception of the semantics–pragmatics of communication (Chapter IX). Jakobson, of course, like most information theorists and most linguists (especially structural and generative linguists), is concerned with SYNTACTICS (rules, constraints) and pays only lip-service to semantics and pragmatics (goals). Thus, he deals in general only with signification (digital communication) and not with meaning (analog communication), nor with the problems of the translation from one to the other. It is important to realize that the Shannon–Weaver analysis refers to a CLOSED system of information in which information is conserved or degrades.

2. *System and Metasystem*

From the communicational perspective of these essays we can state that every SYMPTOM (every ideology, every superstructure) is a metaphor. It is a metaphor derived from the metonymic relationships of the system to which it stands in the relation of metalanguage to object language (Carnap). But I shall not employ Carnap's positivistic term 'object language' here, for this term does not simply imply a level of language which is the 'target' of metastatement, but rather an autonomous level of language which talks only about objects, events, and the like. I shall use the term 'referent language' when talking about language, and 'referent communication' when talking about communication. This is a purely methodological distinction, for any statement in a 'referent language' is also a statement in a metalanguage, and vice versa (and the same for communication and metacommunication).

But the use of the term 'referent', in the sense of that to which the metastatement or metacommunication refers, is deliberately double-edged. Every communicative or linguistic statement must and does have a referent. There is no possibility of intransitive communication, for all communication is governed, in the last analysis, by the pragmatics of communication: that is to say, by the goal of the communication. A communications system in this sense is to be methodologically viewed as an open system, which we can continue to define provisionally as a system involving or simulating life or mind. There is no open process which is not teleonomic or goalseeking; there is no signifier for a human being which does not 'mean' (*meinen*) something. Without necessarily signifying a 'thing', every signal, sign, signifier, and symbol is related, in the message, to some 'referent' or other. The signal, the sign, the signifier, and the symbol are information (before they are meaning or signification), and, as D. M. MacKay points out (Chapter IX), the use of information concerns work in or by the system. This work implies that the 'system' or the 'organism' must 'match' itself symmetrically and/or 'fit' itself complementarily to some 'environment' or other, or to some level of the environment as 'other' (or else change the 'environment'), whether this 'other' be Symbolic, Imaginary, or Real. Part of this matching and fitting in human systems includes the metacommunicative commentary on the text of the communication, a process which necessarily involves a metacommunication about the relationship implicated in the communication. Note that the word 'system' here always implies 'ecosystem', or a 'subsystem within an ecosystem'.

3. *Homeostasis, Homeorhesis, Homeogenesis, Morphogenesis*

We can make the following four provisional definitions:

1 SYNCHRONIC PERSPECTIVE: A symptom, an ideology, a superstructure, and every other synchronic level of communication in a system is an overdetermined communication about some (overdetermined) relationship or other at another level. It is a synchronic metacommunication about a referent communication. The steady-state processes involved will be described as HOMEOSTASIS.

2 DIACHRONIC PERSPECTIVE (A): Maturation or learning over time according to the possibilities contained in the 'instructions' or the 'program' of a system (e.g., the genes) involves a continuous temporal metacommunication about antecedent states. This is a process of selection and combination WITHIN the given norms of the system. It may involve quantum jumps in the organization of norms (e.g., language-learning, sexual maturity, the emergence of monopolies in *laissez-faire* economic competition), but it does not involve a change of norms or an essential change of coding. This will be described as HOMEORHESIS, following Waddington's conception of the chreod ('the pathway of desire or necessity'): in other words, the 'developmental trajectory' of the system or subsystem (1968: 12–13).

3 DIACHRONIC PERSPECTIVE (B): Evolution or historical change can be described as the projection of messages in the homeostatic and homeo-rhetic system from the metonymic axis into the metaphoric axis. This process can be described as the metaphoric EMERGENCE of new levels of organization (restructuring, renormalization). It defines an EVENT. Such a discontinuous jump in organization involves some sort of goal-changing. It describes a metaphoric change of code, a second-level metaphor distinct from the code of the antecedent system. As in (2), but at a different level, the emergent system is a metacommunication about the anterior states of the diachronic process. This process of *Aufhebung* is described as the projection of an ensemble of messages derived from the metonymic processes of combination into the metaphoric process of selection at a second level. Thus an originally metonymic message becomes a metaphor in the code. This Event is the result of the combined effect of differences which have been digitalized into oppositions in the proper sense ('contradictions', as opposed to simple binary relations or binary distinctions), of positive feedback ('intensification of the contra-dictions'), and of noise in the ecosystem. 'Noise' refers equally to random disturbances which are products of the behavior of complex systems,

to errors in coding (e.g., random recombinations in DNA whereby a message becomes part of the code), and to outside disturbances (e.g., the effects of radiation on the genes). It will be necessary later to make a distinction between noise WITHIN the system, and 'accidents', which, by definition, are external to it. The metaphoric event will be described as a product of ultrastability (Cadwalladẹr, 1959: 397) or MORPHOGENESIS: the elaboration of new structures through systemic activities.

4 DIACHRONIC PERSPECTIVE (C): There is another form of metaphoric change of code, which does not involve an essential change of structure, or of norms, or of level of organization. For want of another term, this type of change will be called HOMEOGENESIS. The codes involved are homeomorphous or homologous.

Homeostasis, homeorhesis, and homeogenesis are all considered to be examples of MORPHOSTASIS, as distinct from what is defined here as morphogenesis. In morphostasis there is either maintenance of structure, or the elaboration of 'programmed' structures, or the replacement of one structure by a homologous structure. (These definitions may differ somewhat from the accepted use of some of these terms in some disciplines. Cf. Thom, 1968: 152.)

4. *The System as an Ecosystem Subject to Non-Holonomic Constraints*

None of the four types of ongoing process, homeostasis, homeorhesis, homeogenesis, or morphogenesis, can be solely attributed to the behavior of the subsystem itself. They must necessarily involve a relationship to an environment; the system under study is an ecosystem (Chapter VIII; Pattee, 1968b: 219). The question of the necessary environmental relationship is crucial. Many biologists, and sometimes Waddington himself, it appears, tend to take over a cybernetic or information-theory vocabulary and apply it directly to a pre-existing epistemology of lineal causality in biology, which is in fact in contradiction with a cybernetic perspective. Thus 'program' or 'instructions' may become a synonym for 'efficient cause'. But the description of the organism from the perspective of the ecosystem must on the contrary involve a process quite different from efficient causality. The system will demonstrate characteristics similar to the conception of non-holonomic constraints in classical physics (cf. Bateson, 1967). As H. H. Pattee describes this characteristic (1968a: 76):

The very concept of memory in a hereditary system implies the existence of more [semiotic] freedom in the static state description than in the motion of the system, since it must be dynamically constrained so as to propagate only that particular trait which is recorded in the memory storage.

In other words, a description of the possible behavior of the 'organism' 'in itself' is inadequate without a description of the constraints exerted on those possibilities by the 'environment'.[2] Or, in Bateson's terminology, cybernetic explanation is of a different logical type from causal explanation: in this perspective it is not a question of "why such-and-such happened" but a question of what constraints operated so that "the same old thing" or "anything at all" DIDN'T happen.

Like substitution and combination, or metaphor and metonymy, the notion of metacommunication thus covers two correlative and indissoluble processes: the synchronic or paradigmatic aspect of explanation which describes each level of organization in a system as a commentary on the text of another level, and the diachronic or syntagmatic aspect which describes both the developmental pathway and the evolutive passage from one system or level of organization to another.

5. *The Closed and the Open System*

The processes described are subject to the law of entropy. In order to define my use of the term 'entropy', however, it is necessary to distinguish the positive entropy of closed systems from the neutral or negative entropy of open systems. This requires a further elaboration of the methodological distinction between the closed and the open system.

Whatever the DEGREE or the EXTENT of the complexity of a given system or level of system, it is to be methodologically distinguished from other levels, from other systems, and from its anterior states by its ORDER of complexity. This is a conception allied to that of logical types (Russell): the logical typing of the infrastructure is higher than that of the superstructure. The higher the level of logical type, the lower the level of organization (Chapter VII). The extent of a system of communication may be viewed as increasing through the multiplicative and fractionative processes of metaphoric and metonymic combination and substitution; its order of complexity increases by what has already been called a metaphoric process of SECOND-ORDER substitution: a renormalization, restructuring, or essential change of code. Substitution in the first sense is a process; substitution in the second sense is emergence (an Event).

Somewhere between the low order of systemic complexity of the energy

---

[2] Since 'organisms' select 'environments' and vice versa, the terms 'organism' and 'environment' refer to an ecosystemic relationship, not to entities.

relationship involved when two billiard balls strike each other, and the very high order of informational complexity when men, nations, and ideas collide, we pass from the realm of closed systems to that of open systems, from the 'inorganic' to the 'organic'. In a later metaphoric emergence, we also pass from 'nature' to 'culture'.[3]

A closed system can be defined as follows: It is a subsystem which, in reality or by definition, is not in an essential relation of feedback to an environment. Any feedback relationships between variables are strictly internal to the system, or better still, this feedback (as in the relationship between the momentum of a projectile and gravity) has nothing to do with the matching or fitting of the system to the environment, or of the environment to the system. The feedback involved is called 'pseudo-feedback' by some theorists. A self-regulating system, however – such as a thermostat connected to a furnace – involves feedback which serves to maintain a predetermined goal. Feedback means control or command. In the case of the projectile, there is a command aspect (it falls to the ground), but it is a rigid command. Given all necessary information, one can predict exactly the trajectory of the projectile without referring to an environment, for both the projectile and the environment are aspects of the same, essentially closed, system. On the other hand, however, in the case of a guided missile seeking a moving target which is itself trying to avoid being hit, there is a feedback relationship between the missile (system) and the target (environment). The missile may or may not attain its goal, but in any event it is impossible to predict its trajectory. The rules of command are no longer rigid. But such a feedback system does not manifest all of the characteristics of an entirely open system. The usual example given of a cybernetic feedback system is the thermostat. But both the thermostat and the guided missile are CLOSED-LOOP, mechanical feedback systems. They simulate only

---

[3] Kenneth Boulding (1956) maps out a useful 'skeleton' of ascending levels of systemic organization according to their mode of behavior. These he calls FRAMEWORKS (arrangements, structures, maps), CLOCKWORKS (simple predetermined dynamic systems), THERMOSTATS (self-regulating systems, closed-loop cybernetic systems), the CELL (self-maintaining structure, self-reproducing open system), the PLANT (multiplicative ensemble of cells), the ANIMAL ("teleological open system", characterized by an 'image' or 'knowledge structure' which intervenes between stimulus and response), the HUMAN (self-conscious open system), SOCIAL ORGANIZATION (for which the unit or element is not the person, but the role), and TRANSCENDENTAL SYSTEMS (knowledge itself). He points out that the theoretical models of science begin to become very scarce and inadequate at about the third level, that of the thermostat. He concludes that one of the most valuable uses of his schema is to "prevent us from accepting as final a level of theoretical analysis which is below the level of the empirical world which we are investigating".

in part the behavior of the open system, which is neither mechanical nor necessarily subject to closed-loop feedback. Unlike the thermostat and the guided missile, the fully open system may be capable of changing its goals (whether by accident or design), and these changes are REPRODUCIBLE.

The essential characteristic of an open system is its organization. Organization is controlled by information and fueled by energy. Thus, although all processes in the universe obey the second law of thermodynamics, the existence of biological and social organization – i.e., of organized complexity, as opposed to the unorganized complexity of thermodynamics or the organized simplicity of mechanics – can be spoken of as a manifestation of localized packets of neutral or negative entropy, or of order in a universe tending at some unknown rate towards disorder. As Brillouin and others have put it, information is negentropy. Whereas the closed system is explicable in energy terms, the open system is to be described in informational terms. For whereas the probability equations of the second law describe a process of increasing disorganization, the synchronic state of an organism and the diachronic processes of maturation and evolution are examples of systems controlled by information which maintain or increase organization.

Having made this distinction on the grounds of the relationship between negentropy and information, it is necessary to deal with a possible source of confusion in the use of the terms 'open' and 'closed'. A system may be open or closed to energy or to information or to both. For thermodynamic theory, for instance, any system of matter–energy whose entropy cannot be measured is by definition an open system, since the measurement of positive entropy is a function of closure in the sense of equilibrium. The entropy of a flame, for example, cannot be measured because it is not a system in equilibrium (Brillouin, 1949). The dependence of the flame on the ingestion of matter–energy from an environment (e.g., oxygen) makes it an open system in energy terms: without a suitable environment, the flame 'dies'. But this is no different from a steam engine whose environment is the fuel it consumes and without which it comes to a stop.

In order to avoid confusion, we have, first, to distinguish between closed and open energy systems in the theory of physics (as distinct from the reality it studies), for classical physics must close systems in order to study them. Just as contemporary microeconomics has to close the economic system by such devices as the assumption of free competition, classical physics uses such devices as the perfect gas or the massless spring to accomplish similar ends. In this sense, classical physics is the study of closed systems.

Second, in talking about reality, it is necessary to rule out as open systems, by definition, all systems whose relationships concern only the transfer and transformation of matter–energy, and then to introduce a distinction – in systems involving feedback and both information and energy – between systems which are "information tight" or "closed" (to new information) in Ashby's sense (1956: 4) and those which are not.

Closed information systems are consequently defined to include all systems, such as the thermostat, in which 'purpose' or 'goal' is defined by closed-loop negative feedback (e.g., all the systems described by Ashby in his *Introduction to Cybernetics* already quoted). Open information systems are defined to include all systems capable of using or incorporating new information (learning) and/or in which any kind of 'purpose' or 'program' – a kind of 'open', as yet unstructured, feedback relation to an environment – can be conceived of as systematically ANTERIOR to any later construction of closed-loop relationships to certain kinds of information. (The 'imprinting' analyzed by Lorenz would be an example, for instance.) In other words, open information systems are essentially those which are capable of constructing, or are required to construct, within certain constraints, their own relation to an environment, once they have decided it is 'other' than themselves. (As, for example, in what occurs during the development of the cortex after birth in the human child.)

In this way, we dispose of the dubious definitions of open systems which result from the use of a single, simple criterion – such as 'feedback', 'cybernetic behavior', 'goalseeking' or 'purpose' (left undefined) – and we do not have to be concerned with the 'feedback behavior' of pendulums (Ashby, 1956: 54), or with the fact that the circular or goal-directed behavior of closed-loop feedback can be subsumed under the general laws of classical physics as a special case (linear causality being viewed as involving zero feedback). We shall consequently have no argument with the physicist, for instance, who chooses to analyze the radiation of the sun in the terms of quantitative information. As an open system related to a certain kind of environment and communicating with others of his species, he is free within limits, as we are, to define the system he studies in the way most conducive to acceptable results. Margenau points out the kind of definitions involved, and their relationship to the concept of causality:

> By definition, a closed or independent physical system is a causal one, because we call it closed when the laws governing its behavior do not involve the time. But strictly speaking, only closed systems are accessible to physical analysis. Thus it would seem that physics can never inform us of a failure of the causality principle (1934: 445).

Different levels of reality require different levels of explanation. Without being completely able to define the difference, one notes that the biological conception of order or organization (pattern) is not quite the same as the physical conception. In physics, thermodynamic probability is concerned with order, which can be defined as the probability that the microstates of any given aggregate of homogeneous and interchangeable entities will correspond to the macrostate of the collection as a whole. A body whose macrostate corresponded to only one microstate would have the highest internal order or organization, and thus, in terms of the second law, it would be the most improbable. Entropy, the logarithm of thermodynamic probability, is an index of molecular chaos. In physics, order is directly related to FREE energy, disorder to BOUND energy (lack of gradient). In biology, however, as in Freud's 'economic' view of the primary and the secondary processes, the relationship is the inverse. Whereas for the physicist the formation of a crystal amounts to a decrease in free energy (or gradient), and thus, by definition, to an increase in entropy (since the crystal has done 'work'), for the biologist the passage from solution to crystal means an increase in patterning, and therefore an increase in negative entropy (J. Needham, cited in Singh, 1966: 80). In other words, the lack of an energy gradient from which work can be obtained which is represented by 'bound energy' in physics differs from the 'bound energy' of the biologist in that the second refers not to some index of the random distribution of potential, but to THE BINDING OF ENERGY BY INFORMATION.

The open system is open to its environment, without which it cannot survive and on which it depends for those aspects of its time-dependent development which are not controlled by the internal rules and constraints related to self-differentiation. (Note, however, that the 'internal' rules are ecosystemic at another level.) The more complex and the more semiotically free the system is, the more levels of the general environment it will be open to. Many non-organic cybernetic systems, for instance, are open to only one level of the general environment (e.g., the thermostat which is open only to temperature differences), and many organic systems are open only to a restricted environment (e.g., the common tick, sensitive primarily to the presence of certain compounds found in mammalian perspiration). All organisms are open systems. But even the apparently autonomous processes of self-differentiation (internal constraints) require an open-system analysis at the level of subsystems, e.g., the relationship between the genes and their environment within the organism.

Another significant distinction between the closed and the open system is that the first consists of an aggregate of what are assumed to be interchangeable and homogeneous elements, whereas the second consists of an organization of what are known to be heterogeneous and non-interchangeable elements (Elsasser, 1966). In the open system, therefore, homogeneity can only be sought in the relationships of the system. Since information itself is a relation, the study of open systems must involve the dialectics of their informational relationships, whereas the closed system is amenable to additive energy–entity analysis.

In studying a closed system one can follow the classical experimental method of the physical sciences. One can isolate a single variable or change the variables in turn in order to make experiments on the system, without taking its context into account. One would employ the *causa aequat effectum*, which Mittasch (von Bertalanffy, 1968) calls "the causality of conservation" (*Erhaltungskausalität*), to arrive at generalized predictions. In an open system, on the other hand, this same method would yield inexplicable results. Changing the variables of the system would lead to variations in the context (the environment) of the system, which would in turn influence the behavior of the system being studied. If one speaks in this case of causality, it would be a "triggering-causality" (*Anstosskausalität*). In other words, for the open system the input received from the environment will be used to modify the output which the system communicates to it. The environment's reaction will be a function of this output and will consequently communicate a modified input to the system, and so on. Almost everywhere in nature and always in self-regulating mechanisms, feedback is negative. Negative feedback seeks to reduce the deviations within the ecosystem, that is, to reduce the difference between input and output. Negative feedback is therefore a control process tending toward constancy, stability, or steady state. But positive feedback is also found in nature, feedback which tends toward disequilibrium, disproportion, growth, change, and often destruction. As I pointed out in Chapter VIII, the second-order negative feedback which controls such exponential processes is the factor which accounts in part for morphogenesis or emergence.

6. *Complexity and Teleonomy*

The processes of natural evolution seem to involve an APPARENT goal of increasing levels of variety or organization coupled with an increased viability (increased adaptive range) and an increase in the complexity of information transmission (increased semiotic freedom).[4]

Coupled with this general but varying increase in complexity is, first,

---

[4] No linear development is implied, but rather a process of branching, converging, stagnating, and progressing in different orders and in different species. Our friends the bees seem to have a far more complex communications system for indicating distance and location than do dogs, for example.

the increasing separation of energy flow from information flow (e.g., in the evolution of complex nervous systems). Second, relative proximity becomes less and less a requirement for communication between organisms (as in the difference between the chemotactic communication between amoebae and the chromographic communication between sticklebacks). At another level of complexity, beyond that of the signal (e.g., chemical boundaries and trails) [5] – which we can perhaps say is a form of communication mainly dependent on decoding by the receiver – something like the sign emerges.

Although these terms are difficult to define, we can perhaps say that the sign is more dependent on mutual encoding and decoding by sender and receiver than is the signal. It involves levels of communication more complex and less dependent on preprogramming than signals exchanged for the purposes of reproduction, or than 'automatic', non-vocal, 'to whom it may concern' messages about danger. The sign is less an indication about a state of the organism or about what it perceives to be the state of the environment, and more an indication of possibilities, choices, and future intent in specific situations (e.g., play among mammals). The use of vocal means to communicate emerges at another level yet (e.g., gibbon calls), which is still further separated from the requirement of proximity at lower levels of organization.

I suspect that some forms of (symbolic) exchange value appear among birds and mammals which are gregarious; in fact, play is probably the best example of it. But this form of exchange value is still closely tied to biological ends (e.g., learning or practice), and cannot be analyzed as a form of the combination of arbitrarily chosen discrete elements. With the emergence of (symbolic) exchange value and the signifier, we pass from nature to culture (Chapter IX). Here the information linkages become progressively more important, more distant from any 'biological' ends, and for the first time it becomes possible for the system to bind space and time in a qualitatively different way. [6]

Part of the time- and space-binding potential of early mankind necessarily involves DESIGNED tools, and therefore a qualitatively different form of labor from the 'work' done by the animal organism 'on' and 'in' the ecosystem. Tools are undoubtedly the first form of lasting mnemonic trace – or WRITING – to appear in prehistory. (Chapter XIII). Like language, their design and use has to be learned from somebody else; like memory they are something that can be 'recalled' and improved upon.

---

[5] Note that all these examples are examples of a form of writing or trace (see Chapter XIII).

[6] The chemical zoosemiotics described by Sebeok (1967) do bind space and time, but at a qualitatively distinct level of much simpler organization.

The most effective tool invented for any particular job becomes 'grooved' into the network of traces constituting the memory of the system. And a tool which lasts increases the probabilities of its evolving into something new. All early tools are excellent examples of memory systems subject to non-holonomic constraints: there are always more degrees of freedom in their design than in the use they were probably put to. Tools are artefacts, but they are not in essence objects. Since they qualitatively increase a species' possibility of organizing and controlling the matter–energy in the ecosystem, their primary characteristic is that of information. They are forms which inform; they are informed because they remember the past and make possible new types of projection into the future. Tools were perhaps the first properly 'discrete' signs ever employed by what was later to become man-and-womankind.

This process of increasing complexity is not a teleological process. Organisms are goalseeking, or teleonomic, but what they seek is stability, not change; what they reproduce is themselves, not novelties. The increase in levels of complexity in natural evolution seems pretty clearly to be the product of random variation and chance events. All that is required to give it its spuriously teleological character is that the subsystems involved be open, goalseeking, and adaptive, and that they exist in a context of internal and external natural selection. In keeping with the definition of information as the improbable constitution of organization, this process is correctly described as negatively entropic.

Homeorhesis, which concerns development rather than evolution, also involves increases in levels of complexity. In this sense, the maturation of an 'organism' is negatively entropic. Homeostasis, on the other hand, is a neutrally entropic process: organization is simply maintained within certain limits by the importation of negative entropy. Thus the negative entropy in morphostatic systems is controlled by a tendency towards neutral entropy, whereas negative entropy in morphogenesis involves an unpredictable change of organization of a higher order than that involved in the 'program' of an organism.

To put this point another way, the negentropy of homeorhesis is the result of the elaboration of the instructions of the system. It is controlled by such devices as 'inhibitors' and biological 'clocks'. Although it (inexplicably) dies, the mature organism demonstrates that in biological development the end result of homeorhesis is always homeostasis. This is not the case for morphogenesis, where the question lies not in the program but in (unpredictable) changes of program. And until a system has a hereditary transmission system capable of error and modification similar to DNA – e.g., writing and the trace – morphogenesis is impossible. In human terms, learning as a process of maturation is homeorhetic, but learning as a process of political and psychological liberation can be called morphogenic.

7. Entropy and Inflexibility

Although one often finds the term entropy being used in perverse ways (e.g., Lévi-Strauss's equation of "entropic disorder" with "social disorder" in Charbonnier, ed., 1961), the refutation in Chapter VI of the supposed relationship between aggressivity, repetition, and the death drive in Freud in no way prejudices the statistical interpretation of biological death as a form of entropy.

There are two interrelated problems here. As Brillouin pointed out (1949: 149, 151), the second law of thermodynamics says nothing about the rate of irreversible entropy increase in closed systems, nor does it explain the anomaly of metastable systems (systems in "unstable equilibrium"), such as the fuel reserves of the planet, which in general require the catalyst of human intervention to release the energy they store as negative entropy. Living organisms may be similarly described as metastable, with the peculiarity that they use the negentropy of other forms of 'unstable equilibrium' (food, fuel) in order to maintain their own. In this sense, they have a catalytic effect, and catalysts speed up or slow down the rate of entropy in reactions, about which the second law, being unconcerned with the relation between system and environment, has nothing to say. The Freudian Eros may very well be described as an attempt, through the notion of instinct, to talk about this time-dependent process. Nevertheless – and necessarily – the concept of metastability says nothing about the three-score years and ten 'allotted' to human life.

The question of the limits placed on the maintenance of metastability (life) in organisms leads to consideration of the second problem. Biological death can be explained as involving an increase in entropy, but as Brillouin points out, there is no way to define this discontinuous passage from one kind of entropy relationship to another, much less any way of measuring it, and he concludes that the concept of the "entropy content of a living organism" is a meaningless notion (p. 153). But from an informational perspective related to the concepts of instruction, error, and redundancy in the genetic code, we might be able to say that biological death is either programmed into the instructions of the system (as when certain organisms die immediately after completing the task of reproducing their species), or that it is the result of accumulated errors in the transmission of information involved in cell-repair and reproduction (aging). Neither possibility has any relation to the psychoanalytical conception of the death drive, however. The levels of reality involved are different, and biological death is still an 'intrusion' into another level of the system.

Let us assume that aging and natural death in organisms are the result of accumulated random errors in cell-repair and reproduction, with the result that the semiotic freedom of the system is progressively constrained by a form of decreasing flexibility in relation to its own metabolic processes. This notion might seem to go against the extraordinary levels of protection against error through redundancy employed in the control and selective processes of organisms (cf. von Neumann, 1951, on the difference between neural "counting" and the decimal or binary "expansion" of digital computers). Nevertheless, the number of cells being replaced at any given moment in the human body is extremely large, and perhaps large enough to allow for the redundancy of control and selection to be eventually defeated. The accumulation of errors in transmission might therefore be described as the internal accumulation of a USELESS form of variety, called 'noise', a form of variety from which no further variety can be obtained because it cannot be incorporated in the memory trace of the system. In other words, we could speak of a form of 'bound' information or variety analogous to the bound energy of thermodynamics. This kind of bound variety would be a form of random organization, i.e., disorganization, analogous to the increasing statistical randomness in thermodynamic entropy. In aging, some forms of bound variety would occur before others (change of life in women and men, loss of muscle tone and hair pigmentation, and so on).

But obviously this form of entropic wear and tear cannot in any sense be represented as a goal of the living system, as Freud would have it, nor could any organism be conscious of it (or unconscious of it, in the Freudian sense). On the other hand, this organismic process cannot be applied to socioeconomic systems either. The important difference lies in the concept of random error and its relationship to systemic lack of flexibility (Chapter VIII). Whereas it may be possible to say that an organism dies as a result of accumulated accidents, the decline and fall of a socioeconomic system always appears to have been the result of (for it) a necessarily increasing inflexibility in its relation to itself and its environment, an inflexibility which is the necessary result of its 'instructions', and not accidental.

In the case of the Roman empire, for example, it seems clear that the system was organized around the principle of the concentration of wealth and land in the hands of the few in the absence of any technology capable of reversing the continuous decline in productivity which this process of accumulation occasioned in agriculture. This decline was related to the concomitant pauperization of the peasantry and a move to the towns, where welfare payments (bread and circuses) were higher than elsewhere, but insufficiently supported by taxation revenue, in part because of the power of the wealthy to avoid paying taxes (Bernardi, 1965). The difference between the rigidity following on the accumulation of random errors in the organism, on the one hand, and the rigidity resulting from the closing off of an imperialist system dependent on expansion, on the other, is clear. The Roman empire expanded as far as its technology allowed it to do. The lack of any renormalization of its relationships at this point then produced an involution in which external exploitation of human resources (colonialism) necessarily became intensively internalized. For lack of any new mode of economic expansion (mechanization of agriculture, for example), the empire went through a major recession in the third century, recovered through the continued internalization of expansion in the fourth, and definitively collapsed in the fifth. Because this process depended on the exploitation (rather than the use) of its natural and human environment and of itself, there is nothing in the process comparable to 'entropic wear and tear' in the organism. Moreover, the violent oscillations from crisis to crisis in its final years bear no relation to anything we know of about the death of organisms. The catalyst in the system is nothing comparable to 'life', it is the Keynesian "expectation of profit".

From this characteristic of INVOLUTION and subsequent collapse in exploitative socioeconomic systems cut off from evolution by their own rigidity, and cut off from continued expansion for the sake of stability by technological or environmental limitations, we might perhaps deduce a rule: That, in the absence of renormalization, any exploitative socioeconomic system cut off from expansion into what is for it an unlimited environment, for whatever reason, will necessarily end up by exploiting itself. This is a level of exploitation more global than that at which the system has already defined some of its parts as an environment to be exploited (Chapter VIII). One notes, nevertheless, that if such a system were for any reason to close itself off from this second level of exploitation, the same rule of involution and collapse will necessarily apply.

'Competition', 'exploitation', and 'accumulation' – as distinct from 'co-operation', 'use', and 'storing' – thus distinguish our own economic ecosystem (at least) from any kind of natural ecosystem. And, although we can talk about the 'instructions' of a socioeconomic system producing counter-adaptivity (self-closure) as a result of adaptive growth (expansion), we are not thereby sent back to the possible alternative of the 'programmed death' of the organism as a model for this process. The process of increasing rigidity or counter-adaptivity has its analogue in evolution, not in the biological individual, and here too the relation between accident and necessity at one level (evolution) is different from that at another level (human history).

To conclude this section with one last point on entropy, inflexibility, and disorder, it is important to recognize that the counter-adaptive inflexibility of socioeconomic systems in decline is not merely or simply the 'social disorder' which is experienced by their inhabitants at the time. At the moment of its greatest social disorder, the salient informational characteristic of the system would seem to be, not lack of organization or lack of order, but OVER-ORGANIZATION and over-order. It is this very over-organization which threatens its survival, and the social disorder involved is invariably a more or less successful attempt to renormalize the system, in the interests of survival.

8. *Oscillation, Tension, Contradiction*

As distinct from natural evolution, morphogenesis in history involves slightly different processes. The 'instructions' of the system – its economic values, the informational organization of its relations of production according to certain parameters, the matter–energy of its productive 'forces' – are not subject to error or chance in the sense that the errors in coding and transmission by DNA and RNA are the result of random recombinations, 'accidents', or random radiation. Chance – possibly the chance invention of writing (see Chapter XIII) – may indeed set off the 'hot' historical or dialectical process. But once the technology of the system – as expressed in its organization of energy in production – begins to change in a significant quantitative sense the relations of the ecosystem (exploitation of the natural environment, exploitation of some parts of the social ecosystem by others), positive feedback inevitably results, and inevitably leads either to qualitative changes or to destruction (Chapter VIII). The more dependent the system becomes on technology (i.e., on TECHNIQUE, not simply on machines), the more rapid and the more frequent this 'intensification of the contradictions' becomes. And although there are undoubtedly chance events in history which account for particular cases of the triggering of positive feedback, once this exponential process has taken off, it becomes a necessary process, until such a time as second-order negative feedback – just as necessarily – brings the runaway processes to a halt so that the system as a whole may survive by qualitative change (revolution).

Since organization is the source of 'TENSION' in all ecosystems (Chapter VI), it is inevitable that any ongoing system will involve 'contradictions'. Largely homeostatic systems like the 'cool' society, however, are generally capable of keeping this tension in check because they exhibit a low level of the technological exploitation of nature (and therefore of men and women). Thus they will either be controlled by an ecological cybernetics (Rappaport, 1968, 1970) or they will have what is for them an unlimited environment to exploit, and one that does not require technological innovation to deal with (as distinct, for example, from the technology required of the merchant adventurers of the fifteenth and sixteenth centuries). Such societies may emigrate and they may involve feudalistic client/serf relationships (qualitatively different from European slavery), but they never COLONIZE in the sense of mercantilism. Obviously, there is a direct connection between the size of the natural ecosystem in which a social system moves, and the relative severity of the social and economic crises – which promote change – arising within any given society (Davidson, 1970: 38).

All systems controlled by negative feedback are inherently oscillatory – the door buzzer, after all, spends its life in a continual double bind – and in fact the problem is to understand, not why they remain stable, but why they don't oscillate themselves into destruction. The cells, for instance, are such oscillators (Goodwin, 1968). Any inherent tensions resulting from organization will be intensified by any system which is, one might say, 'falling over itself' because of its ability to adapt to adaptation, or which is in some sense 'out of step' with itself, with its fundamental goals, or with the long-range survival value of a symbiotic relationship to its natural environment. It is in those systems where technique, technology, and writing (in the widest sense: Chapter XIII) keep the system in a perpetual state of 'learning to learn', that the oscillations inherent to the system may pass the limits of the control of oscillation by 'damping'. The system then begins to 'hunt' for homeostasis, which is one way of engendering positive feedback (if it does not result in simple 'mechanical' destruction).

9. *The Morphostatic Model*

The self-regulating and the self-differentiating system are homeostatic or homeorhetic from the point of view of process, and morphostatic from the point of view of structure. They maintain a steady state or confine themselves to behavior and development in accordance with structural laws whose violation means the destruction of the system. The distinction between the morphostasis of the individual organism and the morphogenesis of evolution or of highly complex systems like societies, lies in their order of adaptive behavior. The individual organism adapts and develops only within narrow limits – for all growth is positive feedback and must be inhibited – whereas the morphogenic system is capable of adapting by CHANGING STRUCTURE.

Homeostasis, which has no temporal orientation, can be roughly represented as in *Figure 1*.

FIGURE 1 *Homeostasis*

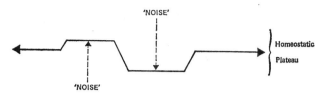

Homeorhesis, which is oriented temporally, can be roughly represented as in *Figure 2*.

FIGURE 2 *Homeorhesis*

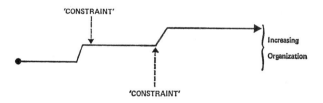

Thus, whereas 'adaptation' in homeostasis is an essential product of 'noise' in the system–environment relationship, 'growth' in homeorhesis is the product of the relationship between the 'internal' program of the system which is following its developmental pathway, and the 'external' constraints on the positive feedback which is engendered by the 'internal' program. The relationship between noise and constraint is essential for the morphogenic perspective (Chapter XIII). For the moment, however, it is useful to try to combine the representation of these morphostatic relationships, as in *Figure 3*.

Any system–environment relationship that goes outside the 'homeostatic plateau' results in the destruction of the system – unless, that is, it can adapt by changing structure in order to survive. Such a morphogenic adaptiveness goes beyond the capabilities of any individual organism. It may of course occur within the life history of a species: the survival of the progeny over the dead bodies of their ancestors. But the only systems which are inherently morphogenic because of their high order of complexity, their semiotic freedom, and the nature of their memory, are social

FIGURE 3 *The Morphostatic Model*

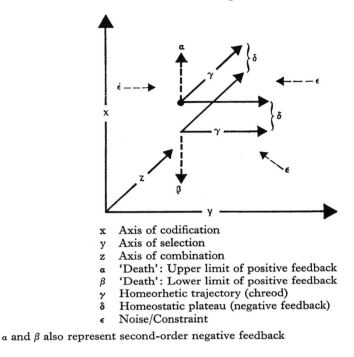

x   Axis of codification
y   Axis of selection
z   Axis of combination
α   'Death': Upper limit of positive feedback
β   'Death': Lower limit of positive feedback
γ   Homeorhetic trajectory (chreod)
δ   Homeostatic plateau (negative feedback)
ε   Noise/Constraint

α and β also represent second-order negative feedback

systems (and their attendant theories, for theories too obey systemic laws).

Figure 3 represents the behavior of all morphostatic systems or theories of morphostatic systems. For example, it represents prey–predator relationships in nature, Adam Smith's 'hidden hand', Malthus's theory of population, Ricardo's theory of the so-called 'natural' price of labor, and the theory of constancy in the Freudian metapsychology.

10. *The Survival of the Fittest*

What it cannot properly represent are the real processes of evolution and history. Recent economic theory, for example, has been influenced by an excessively simple cybernetic model, that of mechanistic closed-loop negative feedback. Part of the error in this economic model derives from its simplistic conception of 'free competition', which is equivalent to the Darwinian model of the 'survival of the fittest'. It is not surprising that this supposedly 'natural' model (in Ricardo's terms) only operates adequately in describing the creation of monopolies in *laissez-faire* capitalism.

The logical contradiction in the implicit assumption of 'pure competition' – which is a projection of ideological values onto nature – is that if the theory were true, there would only be one species or producer left in any given ecological niche, and thus no 'environment' for the species to survive in. This logical error is similar to that of the germ theory of disease, which is similarly dependent on an assumption of non-contextual lineal causality. If the germ theory were adequate, there would be nobody around to think it up. The human organism is quite capable of harboring virulent bacterial strains without succumbing to disease. The emergence of disease involves some TRIGGERING factor (Dubos, 1969) which we can define provisionally as an 'environmental intrusion'. In other words, only an ecosystemic theory can account for organic diseases. This 'environmental intrusion' can be viewed as a message which, IF IT IS RECEIVED AS INFORMATION, triggers the 'pre-existing contradictions' in the ecosystem. It is a form of NOISE.

It is worth giving a specific example here, taken from cybernetics, of the way uncritically accepted ideological assumptions like that of the 'survival of the fittest under free competition' may interfere with rigorous science. W. Ross Ashby, for example, whose contributions to cybernetic theory are justifiably well known, has sought to demonstrate the generalized validity of the notion of competition and natural selection in evolution (1962: 271–2). He represents the "competition between species" as a relation between the numbers in a computer stored with a random collection of the digits 0 to 9. The law of interrelation is that the digits are to be multiplied in pairs, the last digit of the product then replacing the first digit taken from the memory. The "evolution" of this process will show, first, that even figures are favored in the "struggle to survive" (because even times even gives even, odd times odd gives odd, but even times odd gives even); second, that zeros (being uniquely resistant to change by multiplication) will "exterminate their fellow-evens until eventually they inherit this particular earth". The example is said to show that the competition between species is not "essentially biological", but "in fact an expression of a process of far greater generality".

There are, however, only two possible interpretations of the ecosystem Ashby describes. Either the three species (odds, evens, and zeros) are dependent on each other for survival ('food'), or the three species are not dependent on each other at all. If the first is the case, the last few remaining zeros will quickly become extinct after the extermination of the last even number and will inherit nothing but their own destruction (they do not). If the second is the case, then the system is not comparable to a biological ecosystem, and the example is consequently pointless.

Since Ashby well knows that the 'wolf–rabbit cycle' in an ecosystem oscillates around a stable population of both wolves and rabbits in which each population controls the other, the first interpretation cannot be what he intends. But since Ashby is using it to make a point, the example cannot be pointless either. We have therefore to assume that some non-natural principle of extermination is implicit in Ashby's conception of competition. We see at once that it is the nineteenth-century conception of natural ecosystems as systems of exploitative violence and general mayhem: the same conception of 'nature red in tooth and claw' as we find at the beginning of Stanley Kubrick's collection of technological gadgets and metaphysical triviality in *2001: A Space Odyssey*. Ashby's conception of competition in nature is obviously derived from the social relationships of monopoly capitalism, where the environment in which the economic species (corporations) compete is some system OTHER than the relationship between the competitors themselves. In a word, Ashby uses an example to prove the general validity of a proposition which in fact demonstrates its logical absurdity – and, given his theory, he could not assume the general validity of the proposition if it were NOT absurd.

In another example (1956: 69), Ashby uses the same assumption of pure competition to display a different kind of confusion or reduction of logical types. He describes the "self-locking properties" of certain systems viewed as transducers, e.g., a solution of reacting molecules one of whose compounds is insoluble, with the result that it cannot play any further part in the reaction. "The same principle would also apply", he says, "in an economic system if workers in some unpleasant industry became unemployed from time to time, and during their absence discovered that more pleasant forms of employment were available." The implication is that the system would 'self-lock' around 'pleasant' and that the unpleasant industry would suffer from lack of workers. While this is true in the abstract sense of the eighteenth-century view of economics, our current economic system does not operate this way because of the metarules governing the economic possibilities (the highly constrained semiotic freedom) of the worker, even under the conditions of almost full employment (a state which is not assumed in Ashby's example in any case). There is little point in suggesting that Ashby should have read something about Keynes's cybernetic model of crises and unemployment under capitalism, or that he should have understood the function of the reserve army of the unemployed and underemployed (whether in the industrial country in question or in the Third World) in Marx's ecosystemic model of the relations between capital and labor. All that needs to be pointed out is that this example and the previous one are entirely equivalent. Ashby extrapolates on the self-locking characteristics of a set of molecules in a solution and the same characteristics of a set of digits in a computer in order to make statements about levels of organization in nature and in culture to which his model is entirely inappropriate (cf. Introduction). The generalized validity of the model derives rather obviously from ideology, not from reality.

One might object that the second example, in particular, is an illustration, and not a proof. Nevertheless, given the context of Ashby's theory of transducers – which is rigorous, scientific, and extremely useful – we may (or rather must) legitimately ask what rigorous scientific criteria induced him to choose it (cf. Chapter XIV).

11. *The Morphogenic Model*

We have seen from considering the diachronic linguistic model in Chapter XI that the conception of a simple change of code or structure is inadequate to describe the restructuring or renormalization involved in the phenomenon of emergence in morphogenesis.

In order to characterize this process, we can use the methodological distinction between the closed system and the (reproducible) open system to set up the following circular definition: All systems produced by any form of evolution are (1) reproductive (capable of duplication with or without errors), and (2) adaptive (they have memory and are capable of learning at the homeorhetic level and of evolution at the morphogenic level). Such systems are characterized by emergence in two senses: (1) the emergence of new characteristics as the system follows the 'program' of its instructions (e.g., the child's coming to speak, sexual maturity, the 'working-through' of mercantilism), or (2) the evolution of the system to a stage of complexity or organization not forming part of its 'program' (industrial, technological, political revolution).

Modifying the criteria established by Marney and Smith (1964), we can describe the main characteristics of a goalseeking adaptive system as follows:

1 SELF-DIFFERENTIATION, or 'growth'.

2 A CHARACTERISTIC RESPONSE: A response or set of possibilities of response (e.g., 'reaction', 'trial-and-error search', 'learning') which is characteristic of the level of organization of the system and constrained by its relative semiotic freedom. This response is modifiable in systems capable of 'learning how to learn', and will be modified by evolution.

3 SELECTIVITY: The capacity to distinguish between stimuli, to discriminate 'information' from 'noise', to decide between 'figure' and 'ground'.

4 LEARNING: The ability of the more complex systems to modify their

characteristic response. This includes both synchronic and diachronic levels of learning: the more complex the system, the more levels it manifests. At low levels of complexity one finds simple reaction to stimuli on receipt of the selected information: zero learning. At a higher level one encounters COMBINATORIAL structuring: the modification of the timing or extent of the characteristic response by the mediation of some form of MEMORY – more or less complex, as the case may be – or 'knowledge structure' (Boulding's 'image'): first-order learning. At another level, one finds SELECTIVE RESTRUCTURING: a modification of the 'instructions' or 'program', a 'hit' on the structure of the 'image' (Boulding, 1956b), equivalent to third-order learning at the level of highly abstract and deeply programmed 'metarules'. In a human system, this is the level of what I have called second-order metaphor, the essential restructuring of the code.

5 HOMEOSTASIS: Synchronic stability within limits, including self-repair.

6 HOMEORHESIS: First-order developmental stability within limits ('flux equilibrium' in Waddington's terms).

7 REDUNDANCY: The protection of the information processes from random disturbances or noise (implied by 5 and 6). It seems that the more complex the system, the more redundant its code will be. The redundancy of less complex systems seems to lie in their USE of their codes, i.e., in their messages.

8 MEMORY: The *sine qua non* of communication, dependent on the TRACE, and implied by all the other criteria.

9 SIMULATION: The system must be able to map its 'environment' in some way in order to deal with it. Some level of behavior mediated by memory is therefore assumed: mapping, reduction, formation of gestalts, a semiotic system, language.

10 REPRODUCIBILITY: The system must be able to reproduce both past responses and itself.

The criterion of memory is what distinguishes all such systems from mechanical closed loops like Ashby's unfortunately labeled 'homeostat'. Ashby's machine is restricted to random search for stability; it has no memory and it cannot learn. It is in essence a closed system because it is "closed to information and control" and open only to energy (Ashby, 1956: 4). It is in essence its own environment; it seeks the equilibrium of mechanics.[7]

It is difficult to establish any priorities in the enumeration given, except

[7] As valuable as Ashby's work is to mechanistic cybernetics, his happy little machine has been confused by many people with an open system subject to the pleasure principle.

for that of memory. But the list should make clear that the metaphoric–metonymic processes WITHIN the system are governed by the selective possibilities of a set of norms and first-order negative feedback. When the ecosystem is subjected to disturbances that go beyond a certain THRESHOLD, the stability of the ecosystem can no longer be maintained within the context of the norms available to it. At this point the oscillations of the ecosystem can no longer be controlled by the first-order negative feedback which is their source. The ensuing exponential amplification of deviations can be controlled only by second-order negative feedback: the destruction of the system or its emergence as a metasystem.

These disturbances may be the result of learning, of mutation, of the impending dissolution of the environment of the system, of disturbances in the environment, of collision with another system, of the splitting of the system, or of other similar factors. Since all open systems in themselves are primarily conservative of structure, the necessity of a change of structure in order to survive cannot be the result of deterministic laws of evolutionary development. If the open system is determined by anything, it is determined by the goal of STAYING THE SAME. Only when the system enters positive feedback does this determination change. In nature, but not in history, the loss of control described by the term positive feedback is always and essentially the result of error or accident (for the given system). It cannot be triggered by the control processes of the adaptive system itself. There is thus no teleological 'law of emergence' in evolution. But when some accident or other triggers positive feedback, then Malthusian-type laws of the control of exponential growth (the conversion of J-curves into S-curves) do indeed determine the future of the natural ecosystem.

We may expect to see in the emergent metasystem some or all of the following properties:

Increased adaptive range (viability) or increased semiotic freedom.
Increased variety or a new order of organization (complexity).
Structural innovation.
The generation of modified subsystems (after the event).
More sophisticated selectivity.
Changes in the order of adaptivity or learning.
Increased memory storage.
Increased possibilities of simulation.
Increased goal-changing possibilities.
Increased sensitivity to noise.
Increased level of noise between the new system and its environment.

I have tried to represent this process in *Figure 4*, in which homeorhesis (*Figure 3*) is assumed but not represented. The horizontal planes represent first-order codes in which various aggregations, combinations, and selections are possible within the homeostatic limits of negative feedback. The 'time' of these planes is that of homeorhesis. The vertical dimension represents second-order selection (the metaphoric event); the 'time' of this dimension is that of history or evolution. The synchronic–diachronic 'time' of the metasystem as a commentary on the text of the referent system (another level, an antecedent state) is MYTHIC TIME: the time of science.

FIGURE 4   *The Morphogenic Model*
(*modified from Marney and Smith, 1964*)

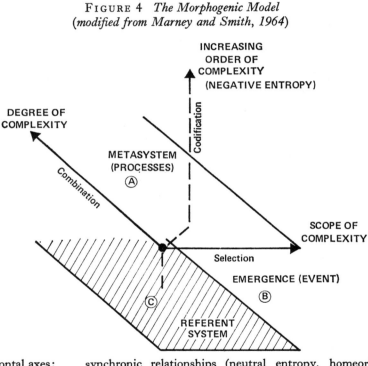

Horizontal axes:	synchronic relationships (neutral entropy, homeorhesis, homeostasis).
Vertical axes:	diachronic relationships (negentropy, morphogenesis).
A (Metasystem):	message PROCESSES (metonymic–metaphoric).
B (Emergence):	metaphoric EVENT (second-order metaphor).
C (Referent system):	(1) System diachronically anterior to emergent metasystem
	(2) System of another level of complexity or organization coexisting synchronically with the metasystem.
	(3) Text upon which the metasystem is the commentary (metacommunication)

How are we to account for the *Aufhebung* of emergence?

In most structural theories and in most cybernetic models, as I have pointed out in detail in Chapter XI, such VIOLENT change is impossible. These models leave out of account the quantum jumps which are evident – after the Event – in history and in evolution. Although evolutionary processes are continuous, the span of time they cover allows us to punctuate the process in discrete steps. The same is true for history, with the added factor that the way we intentionalize and punctuate history changes both the past and the future of (the science of) history. And if 'political consciousness' means anything at all, the reciprocal relationship between material conditions and political action described by the Marxian model suggests that our punctuation of history can have some effect on history itself.

This problematic involves all the practical questions of the context from which we punctuate the process, as well as all the paradoxes of the representation of the analog by the digital. At the theoretical level of trying to understand the essentially morphogenic nature of 'hot' or dialectical societies like our own, the question to be considered is that of the function of writing – as the memory trace – which is the subject of Chapter XIII.

12. *Evolution in the Archaic System*

Having established a theoretical skeleton for distinguishing various types of adaptive system, we can apply it in its outlines to the vexing and fascinating problem of understanding 'instability', 'change', and 'being out of phase' in the so-called 'archaic' system. The following discussion – which provides no simple answers – was inspired by Emmanuel Terray's thought-provoking application of 'structural Marxism' to this anthropological problem, by way of an illuminating commentary on the work of Lewis Morgan (1969: 74–88). I intend to show why Terray's model is inapplicable to the particular question he set himself (the changes in the Kamilaroi kinship system), and how certain unscientific ideological values obscure his analysis. However, it is as a result of his work, as I must point out, that my own understanding of the dimensions of the problem has been greatly extended.

Terray seeks to define the "organization of transition" among the Kamilaroi, by employing Althusser's conception of "dominant" and "subordinate" modes of production (p. 76). From a formal point of view, there is a perfect balance in the Kamilaroi system between the system of classes and the system of clans. But, although, as Terray believes, no logical contradiction is involved in the system – which could theoretically continue in the same form indefinitely – the system generates interference between levels in the sense that it tends to permit the very consanguineous marriages which Morgan believes it is trying to eliminate. Thus, for all its logical harmony, the system is out of step with what Morgan believes to be its goal: the elimination of marriages between consanguineous brothers and sisters. Therefore it is forced to maintain stability by moving to another level of organization (cf. also Godelier, 1966: 832–7).

In *The Elementary Structures of Kinship* (1947: 226–56), Lévi-Strauss makes a detailed analysis of "disharmonic" (stable) and "harmonic" (unstable) systems of kinship. The concrete analysis is too complicated to go into in detail here, but the model involved is highly significant for the three types of diachrony described above. It is not vitiated either by its possibly restricted concrete application (cf. Preface, pp. xviii-xix), nor by Lévi-Strauss's inadequate conception of models (e.g., p. xxiii; 1958: 311–17).

It is this inadequate conception which reduces Lévi-Strauss to defining the difference between 'prescriptive' marriage systems and 'preferential' marriage systems as a difference between "determinist" or "determined" systems and "non-determinist" systems (p. xxiv). The confusion here is not at all trivial. No theory of structure and system in anthropology could remain coherent if it were actually to introduce into its models of social and economic relations a theory of determinism implicitly derived from classical physics and then try to match it with some vague theory of 'non-determinism'. The second principle, whatever it may look like, has nothing to do with 'indeterminacy' in quantum mechanics. Whereas the first principle assumes as its basis a closed physical system, the second describes some sort of (undefined) 'non-determined' system open to change. The distinction depends in fact on that between homeostatic systems which REPRODUCE themselves, and which are dependent on a balance between negative and positive feedback ('contradiction'); and homeorhetic or morphogenic systems which introduce or produce gestalt novelty, as a result of their 'instructions' or because they are inherently paradoxical (cf. Section 13 below). In other words, there is an epistemological confusion of no small importance between an implicit theory of closed (physical) systems and a theory of open systems, which are not closed in the physical sense, but which are SUBJECT TO CLOSURE (in various ways). I have already remarked on this problem in Chapter XI; it accounts for the irresolvable epistemological mismatch between logical explanation and mechanistic explanation in the social sciences at present. Fortunately, the appeal to these models often turns out to be an essentially rhetorical or polemic one. In the more creative authors, such as Lévi-Strauss, and in most of those developing his ideas in a Marxian perspective, the incipient scientism of such appeals, since it IS rhetoric, does not essentially affect what these writers are trying to do or are actually doing. One might compare this problematic with that which results from Freud's explicit bioenergetic determinism – somewhat overdeveloped, it is true – from which he can be rescued by a systemic–communicational analysis, not of what he says he is doing, but of what he does (Chapters II, VI). We have a similar but less serious problematic in the interpretation of Marx (cf. Section 13 below).

Lévi-Strauss's metaphor for the unstable system – which he says is the result of the application of 'heterogeneous' principles at different levels in the kinship rules – is one of STUMBLING. In reference to the Dieri system – which Radcliffe-Brown incorrectly interpreted as a stable system of the Aranda type (cf. *Figures 1–4* in Chapter IX, Section 9) – he points out that it is "only apparently systematic": The Dieri system calls on other principles (its *lignées de fortune*) "in order to impose closure on a cycle which is falling over itself" (*pour boucler un cycle boiteux*) (p. 236). He hypothesizes that the Dieri system comprises an archaic matrilinear and matrilocal system, founded on generalized exchange, which is in the process of adapting itself to the imposition of a neighboring system of restricted exchange (Mara–Anula system) (p. 239).

In systems which include filiation (consanguinity) and residence as markers of the social individual – as distinct from simple or "primitive", systems "harmonically" organized around a dualistic structure of exogamy between moieties – the system will be "in harmony" if the rule of residence matches the rule of filiation, and "in disharmony"[8] (e.g., the Kariera system) if they do not. The harmonic system is not out of step with its rules of filiation; it will consequently tend to keep reproducing a form of exogamic dualism which consists in simply juxtaposing two or more non-conflicting dualist systems, and "nothing will be changed in the degree of integration of the global system" (pp. 247–8). The system cannot therefore evolve, by any internal principle, beyond the stage of moieties.

[8] Terms like 'harmonic' and 'disharmonic', or 'stable and 'unstable', automatically create epistemological problems about the implicit or explicit model in which they have their source. A study of Lévi-Strauss's style and of the metaphors his discourse employs so effectively, would reveal a great deal about the apparent contradiction between his explicit epistemology and his implicit epistemology. The further he moves away from rhetorical appeals to the status he confers on 'hard science', the more explicitly 'metaphorical' or 'poetic' – and the more properly scientific – he becomes.

The example Lévi-Strauss gives of a "primitive" harmonic system (p. 248) is that of a system of patrilocal residence comprising two moieties, A and B, and of two local groups, 1 and 2. Thus if a man from A1 marries a woman from B2, the children are marked 'A1', if B1 marries A2, the children are 'B1', and so on indefinitely.

If the dualistic system of harmonic moieties does change, it cannot do so by any inherent principle of changing the signs borne by the groups (elements, entities) between which there operates direct reciprocal exchange. The system is not of a sufficient logical complexity, says Lévi-Strauss, to "evolve" by this form of substitution and combination. It can, however, evolve by changing the exchange relation itself. It can move from restricted to generalized exchange, by moving from "direct reciprocity" to "indirect reciprocity". This is an "evolution" from the relation expressed by 'A marries (=) B, C = D', to that expressed by 'A = B = C = D (= A)'. Consequently, two general forms of 'evolution' from the 'original' binary relation of the simple 'dualist organization' – which is 'harmonic' because residence and filiation do not interfere with the moieties – are possible. On the other hand the original moieties may become 'disharmonic' by the imposition of a new set of rules upon the original dualism, e.g., 'heterogeneous' rules of residence and filiation. On the other hand, it may evolve in another direction by moving from restricted to generalized exchange.

Lévi-Strauss does not imply that he is discussing anything more than a logical model, which can obviously take many different forms in reality. The general model can be expressed as follows (p. 249, *Figure 44*). There are two possibilities of change: (1) The 'original' dualistic system may move from simple restricted exchange between moieties to generalized exchange (with classes). This represents a common form of "aberrant" system for the anthropologist. It is a movement from a harmonic origin to a first degree of 'splitting' into another form of harmonic system, and eventually to a generalized system of exchange with any number of classes. (2) The original system may, however, retain the principle of restricted exchange-relation, but impose on it a new classification of the signs borne by the various groups and individuals. This is the first splitting into a DISHARMONIC system, which produces a Kariera type of organization (a). (The Kamilaroi system is of this type.) A second splitting of the disharmonic type produces the Aranda type (b). (The Murngin system, which is the significant aberration here – assuming that it did exist – is of neither type as such, because its logical extension involves the splitting of the originally exogamous moieties into two endogamous "sub-societies".) If there is a similarity between the system of generalized exchange (1) and the restricted exchange of the Kariera type (2a), it is because both represent a first-order splitting from the original dualist system. On the other hand, the similarity between generalized exchange (1) and the Aranda system (2b) – which is of a higher order of organization than the Kariera system – lies only in that the NUMBER of elements (names) involved is the same. Thus, in terms of number, the restricted exchange of the Aranda system (2b) is of the same degree of complexity as that of the first-order splitting of the harmonic system which introduces the indirect reciprocity of generalized exchange (1). But the NATURE (the organizing value) of the elements in the Aranda system is not the same as that of the elements of the system of generalized exchange. Only numerically are the two systems of the same logical type. In so far as the Aranda system is the second-order splitting of the DISHARMONIC rule, it differs in logical type from the system of generalized exchange, which is a first-order splitting of the HARMONIC rule. Consequently the organization of the elements in the Aranda system is of a higher order of complexity (and therefore of a lower logical type) than the system of generalized exchange.

To recapitulate: Generalized exchange (1) is similar to the (restricted) Kariera system (2a) because both involve a first-order split from the original harmonic system of moieties. Generalized exchange is similar to the (restricted) Aranda system (2b) because this first-order split in the harmonic system requires the same number of elements as the second-order split in the disharmonic system (p. 250).

The consequence of Lévi-Strauss's analysis is the conclusion that harmonic systems are inherently UNSTABLE, whereas disharmonic systems are inherently stable. I am not sure whether this distinction applies to the 'original' system of dualistic moieties. According to the argument on p. 248, the only inherent tendency of such a system is to go on splitting into more and more versions of its original dualism, without any essential change of organization. It is therefore inherently REPRODUCTIVE in precisely the sense that all open systems tend, as their first principle, to reproduce themselves in a purely morphostatic or homeogenic way. Lévi-Strauss does no more than pose the possibility – rather than the necessity – of the development from the "primitive group integration" of the "original" system of restricted reciprocal exchange, to the higher order of integration (the first-order splitting) represented by the indirect reciprocity of generalized exchange. Similarly, there is no necessity established in the text for the evolution of the original system to the first-order disharmonic restricted exchange of the Kariera type.

In other words, to use the terms employed in Chapter XIII, I can see here no principle which can produce NOISE in the original relation of moieties. The system ought therefore to reproduce itself indefinitely. The binary relation involved is a simple case of homeostatic goalseeking; it includes no principle of overriding positive feedback, no principle of goal-changing. In order to explain its development into other forms, we have therefore either to assume some 'accident' or else to look for the principle of change at some other level in the system. An 'accident' might be, for example, the diffusion of the system, a collision with another system from a different 'ecological niche', or changes in the natural ecosystem requiring some new level of 'integration' to maintain survival. The third of these possibilities seems altogether too weak, because it is based in essence on an evolutionary scale of time which is far too long.[9] The first two, however, seem to be those assumed in many instances by Lévi-Strauss (e.g., the Murngin, the example cited above of the Dieri). It is nevertheless not entirely clear whether, by his assumption of the effects of 'heterogeneous' principles in the same system, he does not in effect mean the introduction of a NEW principle of filiation or residence 'out of thin air'. In other words, it seems that the 'newness' of the principle becomes necessary for logical coherence in the explanation, whereas the origin of the principle remains mysterious.

Obviously the effects of the accidental introduction of noise are a necessary assumption in any developmental–evolutionary theory. But, once we pass out of the domain of adaptive systems controlled entirely by the genetic code and natural selection, and before we reach the level of fully technological systems like our own – which are clearly both homeostatic and morphogenic from internal principles of oscillation and positive feedback (Section 13) – the single principle of noise in the cultural coding of memory and (re)production, seems entirely insufficient for a materialist (i.e., cybernetic–informational) theory of change in the 'archaic' system.

And although the effects of changes in the natural environment can be discerned in the evolution from proto-hominids to man – at an indefinite but extraordinarily lengthy period in which the quantum jump between nature and culture has not yet fulfilled itself – one cannot employ the same principle in the 'evolution' of the 'archaic' society without the danger of confusing levels of organization, of confusing the biological with the socioeconomic and sociocultural.

In spite of Terray's unfortunate confusion between 'closed' and 'closure', (1969: 72), it is this principle of change needed to complement the principle

---

[9] It is this sort of explanation which Engels employs in his ethnocentric and evolutionist *Origin of the Family*, in which all change in 'archaic' organization is reduced, in the final analysis, to a positivist and entirely imaginary "dim impulse towards the prevention of inbreeding", derived from Morgan.

of accidental interference or noise, which he is in fact seeking to define. All of the change-triggering 'inventions' he mentions – which have their source 'outside' the social structure as such (i.e., in the domain of labor) (p. 73) – are indeed noise or accident, which, however, he incorrectly believes to be connected with efficient causality (cf. Chapters XI and XIII). As he points out, it is senseless to assume some 'structure' or 'form of transition', to account for change, such as that supposed by Morgan, for the concept implies a construct derived only from the realm of ideas, and not also from historical reality (p. 75). Terray's escape from this problematic is to assume a form of non-correspondence between the 'juridical' superstructure and the 'economic' infrastructure of the archaic system, derived from Althusser and Balibar (Althusser *et al.*, 1965b: 322). He allies this with Althusser's conception of dominant and subordinate relations between the various coexisting FORMS of production which come to constitute the whole MODE of production of any given system in historical evolution.

As we have seen, Morgan's explanation of the passage from moiety to class to gens among the Kamilaroi people has for its axis the supposition that the logical homeostasis of the system (its 'juridical superstructure') is 'out of step' with its 'infrastructural' goal: the elimination of marriages between consanguineous brothers and sisters. Consequently the 'logical coherence' between the original system of classes and the posterior evolution of a system of gentes (which are "enfolded unchanged" into the previous system – Terray, p. 80) is only apparent. The system actually encourages the very marriages it seeks to eliminate. Morgan's solution is to point out that the system of classes must be eliminated, and he describes the "innovations" actually added to the marriage rules which permit the beginnings of such an elimination (Terray, p. 82). (It is as well to remember Morgan's nineteenth-century upbringing in a Greco-Roman elitist educational tradition, which shows through in his enthusiasm for the Roman gentes.)

However, if we seek in the sort of explanation offered by Terray the solution to the question of the factor other than random noise which might account for the development of organization among the Kamilaroi, we do not find it. Morgan's 'operative factor' is biological; it is Engels's "dim impulse towards the elimination of inbreeding". This is not only a tautology. It supposes precisely what Lévi-Strauss and Marx refuse to suppose: conscious intersubjective intention. It supposes a knowledge of the 'invisible' structures and goals of the system, as well as a knowledge of animal-breeding. We cannot allow the first without destroying the whole theory of systems; we cannot allow the second without some evidence that some such understanding is possible in an 'archaic' system of this type.

We are therefore still faced with three possibilities: (1) The characteristics resulting in change are inherent in the infrastructure of the system itself, which produces forms of variety defined by the system as noise. (2) These characteristics are the result of 'environmental intrusions' or accidents (noise from outside the system). (3) These characteristics are the result of the fact that the logical structure of the system is 'out of step' with some other (undefined) part of the system.

If the first is the case, we are describing a system in homeorhesis, somehow containing at one and the same level its own necessity to produce variations, which may then result in morphogenic evolution. If the second is the case, we are describing a purely homeostatic system with no goals beyond its own reproduction. If the third is the case, however, we have in effect a proper case of dialectical evolution in the Marxian sense, where the tensions inherent between LEVELS of the system (or between different structures in the system) result in morphogenic change. It will be noted that the first is a purely DEVELOPMENTAL theory, which would be applicable to the study of a particular system not subject to innovation and invention in the proper sense of new levels of economic and technical organization. The second is a theory of NATURAL EVOLUTION, for whether noise is actually generated by errors WITHIN the 'genetic code' (or in its transmission), or from outside, this noise is always, by definition an 'environmental intrusion' resulting from accidents. The third is a theory of HISTORICAL EVOLUTION which is applicable to the passage from stage to stage of economic and technical organization within the actual (and minimal) span of recorded history.

By quietly taking on Morgan's assumption of a biological goal in the infrastructure (pp. 63, 81) – which would actually have to be 'visible' to the participants, i.e., learned – Terray seems to opt for a version of the third possibility. He thus destroys his own argument against 'biological adaptation' and his statement that Morgan refused such a model (p. 61) (cf. Chapter XV). Terray, like Morgan, supposes a 'production' of 'better' human 'stock' as a result of reduced inbreeding. He interprets the various overlapping systems of kinship among the Kamilaroi in the terms of the 'dominant' and 'subordinate' forms of production already mentioned (p. 63). One cannot argue against human reproduction as a form of production. But the only place in which to measure a 'better' human being at this level of social development is in the natural ecosystem. 'Better' can only be properly defined in terms of long-range survival, and at this level of development, it is a purely biological value, not a social one.

In fact, one suspects that, as in Morgan, in Engels, and in Marx himself, this 'betterness' is not only a projection onto history of the ideological and elitist status of 'intelligence' as defined by our present society (cf. Chapter XIV), not only the same ethnocentrism about supposedly 'backward' and 'inferior' peoples which is so evident in Marx, not only an entirely unscientific concept which, in the form Terray gives it, is in complete contradiction with the hypotheses of non-phenomenal structures and systems in culture, but a COVERT TELEOLOGY, linear in form and Whig in conception. In the terms of structural analysis itself, there is a non-correspondence between the phenomenal structure of Terray's argument, and the infrastructure of his epistemology. There lies behind his rejection of 'evolutionism' and teleology another form of 'teleological evolutionism'. This failing is directly attributable to Terray's lack of a systemic–cybernetic perspective. As in the case of Piaget, any theory of development or evolution which lacks a conception of informational teleonomy (non-mechanistic cybernetics) will necessarily be forced to invent metaphysical principles to supplement the lack (e.g., Piaget's assumption of the 'constitution' of a "semiotic function", his "semantic instinctual structure").

It may be true, however, that it is Terray's close commentary on Morgan which leads his text astray. In any event, one notes that Lévi-Strauss does not fall into the same trap in his discussion of 'archaic' evolution. He properly avoids the question of supplying a rationale when he has no rationale to give. My main point, therefore, is that without the illegitimate assumption of a (learned) 'biological urge' there is no reason whatsoever why – in the argument offered by Morgan and Terray – the Kamilaroi should not allow the brother–sister marriages which are the logical result of the system. If this result should prove to have deleterious biological effects on their gene pool, the Kamilaroi system would disintegrate before the people in the system could 'find out' about it. We have in this problematic system an excellent example of the thesis of counter-adaptivity sketched out in Chapter VIII. The Kamilaroi have apparently avoided genetic deterioration. (In saying this, however, I confess I am not sure just how serious that deterioration would actually be in the terms of inbreeding itself, nor how often inbreeding in close consanguinity would occur in the system.) But if we do accept the hypothesis of possible genetic deterioration, we can certainly answer the question of why the Kamilaroi avoided it. They avoided it because it did not happen. In a word, they avoided it BECAUSE THEY SURVIVED.

The fact that uncountable other groups may not have avoided this possibility, and that we can never know that they did not, because they perished, reinforces my point about the concealed linear teleology upon which both Morgan and Terray seem to depend. Both of them write history and anthropology from the deeply programmed perspective of the survivor – and all survivors, by definition, are Whigs (Herbert Butterfield).

We can now come back to the original question of how the 'archaic' system changes, from a rather more lucid perspective. We do not assume any covert teleological goals in the development of the Kamilaroi; we assume no more than teleonomy in a multi-dimensional natural and social ecosystem. The question to be asked is, again, that posed in Chapter VIII. The Kamilaroi made an adaptive change which eventually, by its logical consequences, induced a counter-adaptive rigidity in the system. We know that the system was in some restricted sense RENORMALIZED; the question to be considered is whether this limited renormalization was accidental or whether it was necessary (i.e., implicit in the self-regulation of the system itself).

The tautology that adaptive systems which survive, are systems which survive, allows us to assume accident, if we wish (e.g., the influence of another system). We would even suggest that the various changes are the result of progressive errors in coding and transmitting the cultural memory of the kinship system. It might conceivably be possible over some hundreds of years that a number of people 'lost' their signs, or became mispunctuated in some way, and nobody could remember where they belonged in the mnemonic network of the kinship system. But, given the highly speculative nature of this last possibility, we would much prefer to show that the successive changes in the system are the necessary result, either of the self-regulation of the system, or of its being out of step, at the institutional level, with its socioeconomic base.

I do not pretend to be able to solve these questions here. The significance, for me, of the working-through evident in this analysis, is that it provides a way to discover what question we should be asking. Lévi-Strauss furnishes no solution to the question of the 'evolution' from the early moieties, and that part of Terray's analysis which I have criticized, if it were correct, would militate against such an evolution. With two 'original' moieties and matrilineal filiation, the genetic pool of the system could and would maintain its requisite variety within necessary limits on variety. In fact, as regards the moieties, I begin to wonder – not being an anthropologist – whether their supposed antecedence is a workable hypothesis to which some more or less satisfactory interpretation can actually be given, or whether this supposed priority is not just a useful assumption of an original trace of *différance* (Chapter XIII), or perhaps even an example of what Susanne Langer properly called the 'genetic fallacy' (1962: 35–7). (In re-reading Lévi-Strauss's *Totemisme aujourd'hui* [1962b:

69–70], I find him suggesting that this last alternative is the case.) At any rate – provided I have not just totally misunderstood the whole problem – so long as we have only a DESCRIPTION of the development from 'original' moieties to more highly organized forms of kinship, and nothing by way of analysis – except the accident – it is as well to remain suspicious of the status ascribed to the 'origin' of the process. This is especially important if we recall my assumption that changes in level of organization result in changes in the logical typing of the antecedent 'referent system' (Chapter VII).

Since the Kamilaroi are, according to Terray, a Kariera-type system (1969: 77), they form a DISHARMONIC system of the first order (less highly organized than the Aranda system, which is of the second order). A disharmonic system, in Lévi-Strauss's terms, is a stable system (1947: 250). What he clearly means is that a disharmonic system of restricted exchange is capable, in its own terms, of becoming more and more complex because of its multiple levels of logical typing (moieties, sections, subsections, etc.), while still "expressing itself [by] a continuous progression within one and the same series" (ibid.). In the terminology of these essays, the Kariera system – as a result of its own rules of regulation (i.e., its instructions) – is, descriptively speaking, an example of MORPHOSTATIC DIACHRONY. It is essentially a homeorhetic system whose goal is homeostasis. But its regulations are apparently such that, of themselves, they produce novel forms of variety in the system. They generate paradoxes – or Gödelian sentences (rather than contradictions) – which require from time to time the introduction of new levels of logical typing in the organization of the system. But I have no way of demonstrating this. If, without the help of an assumption of the effects of (properly) external noise, the system could be shown to generate its own noise out of its own instructions, and thus be required necessarily to integrate that noise as information in its mnemonic network (cf. Chapter XIII), then we would be able to treat the system as a self-regulating homeorhetic system by means of a purely logical model.

We would not therefore have to hypothesize about biological functions or about the 'production' of people by coexisting dominant–subordinate forms of the mode of production. This hypothesis of Terray's – which is undoubtedly valid for technical–technological systems, and which can be applied over very long periods of natural evolution in which 'accidents' engender technological innovation (e.g., the use of fire) – looks at first to be an ingenious solution to the problem posed by the various 'forms' of production (moieties, classes, clans, etc.) among the Kamilaroi (p. 79). But the underlying BIOLOGICAL principle of increasing 'intelligence' through natural selection (p. 64) can only be applied at the dawn of the human revolution itself, at the level of NATURE, and BEFORE the invention of the discrete element of kinship (Chapter IX). It is a confusion of levels to apply it to CULTURE: to the beginnings of social systems as such, to any system in which a workable form of the prohibition of incest has already appeared. (This presumably emerged in many different forms after the quantum jump in evolution which ended oestrus among proto-hominids, and in connection with postulated climatic or other changes which sent primate or hominid bands out of the forest into the savannahs, where new forms of the [social] organization of energy proved to have survival value.) It is above all an error to apply it to the development of an already constituted social system. I would think that the span of time involved is too short for its effects to be learned by the system. More important, however, is the ethnocentric ideology in which, as it seems to me, Terray's model of 'human production' has its source, possibly derived directly from Marx, as I have said, but certainly characteristic of western culture. What it implies is that 'intelligence' is a LINEAR QUANTITY (cf. my brief critique of Mayr and Jensen in Chapter XIV), which different races and groups can have 'more' or 'less' of. I have never seen any evidence to indicate that what our culture calls intelligence (defined by SOCIAL performance) is in any way superior to that of 'untamed thought', and I would think that Lévi-Strauss has perhaps even demonstrated the opposite. There is no room in Terray's implicit genetic model for different QUALITIES of what we think is intelligent (cf. my remarks on Piaget in Chapter XII). If on the other hand by 'better', Morgan or Terray or Engels mean 'stronger in body', there is not only no evidence for this, but it commits another ethnocentric error, by making the 'primitive' the 'body', and us the 'mind'. And if by 'better' production, Terray means 'more efficient', then the value system which is projected onto the 'archaic' culture is derived from the capitalist relations of production.

Finally, if we look at Terray's model in an epistemological overview, we realize in retrospect that the 'transition' of the 'organization of transition' he analyzes, while explicable in terms of societies developing or evolving at a pace which is relatively high compared to the 'archaic' system, remains unexplained and inexplicable in the 'archaic' system. It remains inexplicable at that level, in my view, because of the relative absence in the Kamilaroi system of the kind of TECHNIQUE which creates a 'hot' or highly multiplicative cultural memory. This question involves the status of the TRACE in the cultural mnemonic network, which is examined in the following chapter.

Since by 'trace' I mean not simply the mnemonic network 'written' ON THE CULTURE by its own activities of self-organization and reproduction, but also the network 'written out' ON THE (natural) ECOSYSTEM by those activities, we can summarize the whole problematic of the preceding discussion in three further remarks:

1 In respect of the distinction established between development, 'natural' evolution, and historical evolution (p. 384 above), some kinship systems which are simply 'developmental' can generate 'historical evolution' when the kinship structure interferes with the political structure. In African history, for example, one of the forms of invention responsible for the repeated splitting of some political systems – with consequent secessions and migrations of parts of the system into other ecosystems replete with new possibilities – is a principle of internally produced 'noise': rivalry within the ruling family over the chieftainship (Davidson, 1968: 37). Such a splitting of lineages and groups as a result of manifest – and, on the surface at least, somewhat chance events – is of course common enough. The possible connection between 'chance' in the manifest structure (e.g., a discontented princeling who sets himself up as king somewhere else) and 'necessity' in the infrastructure leads into the second observation.

2 If there is one point I have consistently tried to make throughout this book, it is that psychology, anthropology, and the social sciences in general, have repeatedly falsified their 'observations' by UNRECOGNIZED epistemological and ideological closures imposed on the system under study. The question of the 'internal' generation of noise 'in' the 'system' concerns precisely the level and extent of punctuation or closure that we impose on the system. Since no open system IS closed, it is always possible that in our definition of a given ecosystem ('system' plus 'environment') we have cut out an essential part of its context. The converse is also possible: that we have included too much (e.g., the influence of the stars – as distinct from the possible influence of astrology as part of the social discourse).

It is not enough therefore to reduce all 'noise' to a simplistic 'principle of contradiction' in the system, as dogmatic or mechanistic Marxism has often tried to do. We have to be able to distinguish types and levels of 'contradiction' ('tension'). In the terms of our own recent history, the beginnings of such a distinction are indeed possible (see 13 below).

3 We must assume levels of chance and levels of necessity in our analysis, just as we assume levels of responsibility, levels of organization, and levels of logical typing. At the level of cosmic history, this word I am writing is a purely random product. At the level of our current socio-economic situation, it is the product of less than random noise generated

between myself as 'system' and the Other as 'environment'. At the level of the argument of this paragraph, the coming word 'necessary' is NECESSARY. The 'random' act of the princeling who secedes does not therefore prejudice a socioeconomic and ecosystemic interpretation of the very same act in the terms of a degree of necessity.

THE RELATIONSHIP BETWEEN CHANCE AND NECESSITY IS THEREFORE DIRECTLY CORRELATIVE TO THE RELATION BETWEEN 'SYSTEM' AND 'ENVIRON-MENT' IN THE ECOSYSTEM WE HAVE DEFINED. As Ashby has said, noise is in no intrinsic way distinguishable from any other kind of variety. In this sense, what we call 'random variation' in natural evolution is not random, but necessary; what is random is only the particular form which the system 'decides' this variation shall take.

13. *Capital and Entropy*

There are in general two kinds of 'tension' or 'contradiction' involved in socioeconomic ecosystems, and they are not of the same logical type. There is on the one hand the 'tension' WITHIN the various levels of the system, a tension which is inherent in any organized (natural) ecosystem, and which negative feedback controls. This inherent tension is in essence the positive feedback of growth and the quest for the goal itself. Every movement towards a goal is necessarily positive feedback, just as every original trans-mitted difference in a system is positive feedback (Chapter VIII). Whether the system is homeostatic (*Figure 1* above) or homeostatic–homeorhetic (*Figure 3* above), it is never actually in a steady state or in an equilibrium, but in oscillation. The paradox of the goal of homeostasis in open systems is that they depend on self-regulation and self-stability and yet their ecosystemic relationship to an environment or to levels of the environment is such that "one of the stable products of self-regulation is variability itself" (Emerson, 1956: 149). In other words, as a group, such systems are in essence ultrastable.

The second type of tension is that engendered BETWEEN the levels of the system or ecosystem. It is not only of a different logical type from the first, but it stems from two (or more) LEVELS of the system (or structures within it), which themselves differ from each other in logical type. Thus if the first type of tension between subsystems of the same logical type can be properly called a form of binary 'opposition', the second type is not opposition, properly so called, but contradiction. It is a relation between levels potentially engendering PARADOX.

The programmatic representation of the ongoing system in this chapter is derived mainly from ecosystemic and logical premises, with some 'sense' of its application to the socioeconomic system. I find in retrospect that, except for the distinction I make between contradiction and paradox, the model begun in Chapter VIII is essentially the same as that drawn from the Marxian texts by Maurice Godelier (1966: 828–64).

Like most contemporary students of Marx and most 'structuralists', however, Godelier fears 'finalism' and 'tensions' in sociology, probably because the words 'sound biological'. Thus he agrees with Lévi-Strauss's critique of Warner concerning the Murngin system, and takes over from Lévi-Strauss the 'scientific' terms 'logical model' and 'mechanism' in consequence (p. 836). But this is to fall out of the frying-pan into the fire. On the one hand, logic and mathematics are themselves goalseeking systems of communication which may well fall into oscillations as a result of paradox and be forced to 'evolve' (Chapter V); on the other, natural and social ecosystems are in no sense mechanical. As with the Althusserian school in general, Godelier believes that 'science' requires 'causality'. He speaks of the same "structural causality" which I have shown in Chapter XI to be one more covert metaphor for goalseeking, and concludes that "no internal finalism regulates either natural evolution or history" (p. 858).

Nevertheless, Godelier's analysis of the two forms of contradiction in Marx is essentially unaffected by the inadequate – and non-Marxian – metaphors which surround it. The first contradiction he defines is that between capital and labor, between the capitalist class and the working class. This contradiction is the SPECIFIC contradiction of the capitalist mode of production. It is "a contradiction which is internal to a structure". It is what distinguishes capitalism from the systems that preceded it; it is there at the very beginning; and it is continually reproduced. In relation to the second, more fundamental 'contradiction' (i.e., paradox), the first is a contradiction between two groups of different logical type, related by exclusion (Chapter VII): those who own capital and those who do not. The profit of the one is the unpaid labor of the other (pp. 845–6).

The second contradiction, however, is "BETWEEN TWO STRUCTURES" (at distinct levels of the system). It is not a contradiction between groups or classes, self-evident to those within the system. It is a 'contradiction' between "the development and socialization of the productive forces and the private property of the means of production", a 'contradiction' between "the structure of the forces of production and the structure of the relations of production" (pp. 846–7).

This is not a contradiction 'original' to capitalism. It is the 'radical' product of the industrial revolution. Two hundred years ago, the machine and the factory system made possible a qualitative leap in the exploitation of the 'productive forces' (cf. Marx on automation: McLellan, 1971: 132–40). According to Marx, this subsequent 'contradiction' is the more fundamental. It involves the relation between the structure of the SUPPLY of natural resources, machines, and workers, on the one hand (matter-energy, free energy, negative entropy), and the ORGANIZATION of the relations between labor and capital, on the other (information). We know from passage after passage in Marx that the first relation of contradiction (between capital and labor) is regulated by negative feedback: the system is homeorhetic–homeostatic (cf. the flow chart in Sweezy, 1942: 91). Whatever the developments in technology, productivity, and efficiency, the relation between those who own the means of production and those who do not, remains essentially the same, with minor variations. The present 'reserve army' of the unemployed, the unemployable, the under-employed, and those who, like the farmworkers of California or the indi-genous populations of the Third World, are the most openly exploited, still fits the Marxian model pretty well. But there is nothing essentially inherent in this SELF-REPRODUCING system which can overcome the contradiction between capital and labor. The negative feedback of the appropriation of surplus value (that part of unpaid labor time which is converted into profit) is maintained by the accumulated power of capital: the system cannot change in any essentials. No amount of purely 'humanistic' protest over 'alienation' or 'exploitation' can have any fundamental effect. Especially as it expands into the Third World, it is always possible for capital to renew the 'buying-off' of some part of the work force (e.g., steel-workers, autoworkers) in order to maintain the principle of 'divide and rule'. This level of the system is homeostatic and reproducible because the negative and positive feedback within it are of the same logical type. It is a stable, oscillatory system.

It is quite another matter with the second 'contradiction', the paradox. In Chapter VIII, I built a model of our runaway biosocial ecosystem on the basis of cybernetic and natural models. In returning to Marx, after the event, we find the same model elaborated in the third volume of *Capital*. The passages I shall quote concern Marx's theory of the necessary "falling rate of profit" which, he believed, was the barrier to continued capitalist development INHERENT in capital itself. This theory has not apparently stood up very well in the purely economic sense (cf. Sweezy, 1942: 100–8).[10]

---

[10] Two remarks suggest themselves. First, the exploitation of the Third World by the 'capitalism of organization' has changed the problem quantitatively, so that the theory has been proved neither false nor true. Secondly, since all labor includes a significant element of 'organizing power' on the part of the worker, the increasing development of technology has meant that the negative entropy

In any case, to employ it in economics as such requires complicated arguments about the form of capital itself, which are of little service to us here, when we have another objective frame of reference to use. Marx describes this second 'contradiction' as the tendency (*Tendenz*) of capital "towards ABSOLUTE development of the productive forces [matter–energy], regardless of the value and surplus value this development contains" and regardless of social conditions [organization] (1887: III: 244, my emphasis). He goes on to apply an implicit Malthusian J-curve[11] to the process: Capital, he says, "has as its goal [*Ziel*] to preserve the value of the existing capital and to promote its self-expansion to the highest limit (i.e., to promote AN EVER MORE RAPID GROWTH of this value" (ibid., my emphasis). In other words, he is describing the inherent tendency in capital to grow for the sake of stability. Capital moves towards "production as a goal in itself". Production is only production for capital and not vice versa. Capital drives towards the "unconditional development" of the productive forces by an unlimited extension of production. Marx believes that this process entails a fall in the rate of profit; thus capitalism will theoretically exhaust itself as a result. Capitalism therefore carries the seeds of a new society within it, in which this fundamental paradox between means of production and relations of production will be overcome.

In our present context, we need not concern ourselves with the economic theory. We have only to apply the model of positive feedback leading to the destruction of the ecosystem through accumulated entropy or rigidity. Although in these passages Marx is primarily talking about the limits of the possible "expropriation and pauperization" of living producers, his reference to the "productive forces" permits us to recall that these "forces" ALSO include the negative entropy of the natural environment:

> The real barrier of capitalist production is capital itself. It is that capital and its self-expansion appear as the STARTING and the CLOSING point, the motive and the goal of production (III, 245, my emphasis).

---

he supplies (to the machine) has become more and more informational, and less and less energetic. In spite of his bioenergetic metaphors, Marx, like Aristotle, is perfectly aware that labor is organization or in-formation, rather than pure energy: "Labor is the living fire that shapes the pattern"; the "metabolism of material" is "regulated by labor", thus producing higher and higher forms of use value (*Grundrisse* [1857–8], McLellan, 1971: 89). The transformation of energy relationships by means of the 'fixed capital' of the earliest machines matches the transformation of informational relationships by the fixed capital of the computer (i.e., by what Marx calls the "automatic system of machinery") (p. 132).

11 In spite of his well-known criticism of Malthus. Note that the following quotation refers, not simply to exponential growth, but to SUPER-EXPONENTIAL growth.

The logic of this pathology is that through unlimited expropriation, capital expropriates itself. Through unlimited imposition of order and organization, it drives the biosphere and the sociosphere to disorder and disorganization. Capital thus becomes equivalent to rigidity, to bound energy, to waste; in human affairs capital is the principle of entropy (cf Marx in: McLellan, 1971: 94–5).

Marx made this ecosystemic perspective clear in 1857–8:

> This contradictory form of capital is itself a transitory one, and produces the real conditions of its own termination. The result is the creation of a basis that consists in the tendency towards universal development of the productive forces – and wealth in general, also the universality of commerce and the world market. The basis offers the possibility of the universal development of individuals, and the real development of individuals from this basis consists in the constant abolition of each limitation once it is conceived of AS a limitation and not as a SACRED BOUNDARY [my emphasis]. The universality of the individual is not thought or imagined, but is the universality of his real and ideal relationships. Man therefore becomes able to understand his own history as a PROCESS and to conceive of nature (involving also practical control over it) AS HIS OWN REAL BODY [my emphasis] . . . (McLellan, 1971: 121).

This second relationship of 'contradiction' is paradoxical in the sense that industrial capitalism is in a global double bind: if it stops producing for the sake of producing, it will destroy itself; if it goes on producing it will destroy us all. Small comfort to anyone as it may be, but this paradox fits the logical model I have been using: The statement 'Production produces itself as the end-product of itself' is in effect a self-reflexive, Gödelian, sentence, as irrational in logic as in life. And whereas I have concentrated here on the limits of negative entropy (energy) available in nature, there are also limits to the form of negative entropy available, as organization, in human beings.

Chapter XIII

Order from Disorder

NOISE, TRACE, AND EVENT IN EVOLUTION
AND IN HISTORY

Relations between logical types
cannot be stated.
BATESON (1956)

1. *The Writing Metaphor in Freud*

In a recent article on the numerous metaphors employed by Freud to
represent the mind, Jacques Derrida (1966) seeks to interpret them in
relation to the partial solution of the problem of memory offered by the
metaphor of the "mystic writing pad": the endlessly erasable children's
plaything in which the original script is always retained in its pristine
newness by the underlying wax, while new 'perceptions' are constantly
inscribed upon it. Dreams and memory for Freud, as we know, are a
succession of comparisons with pictograms, hieroglyphs (*Bilderschriften*),
the palimpsest, the double inscription (*Niederschrift*), *Vorstellungen*, the
rebus, sentences and paragraphs blacked out by the censorship in Russian
newspapers, and so forth. While dealing with many of the more strictly
mechanistic and spatial metaphors employed by Freud (archeology, the
telescope, the microscope, the camera, and so forth), Derrida seeks to
emphasize the metaphor of WRITING in Freud, noting the implication of a
postscript, or supplement, in the concept of *Nachträglichkeit*. One
would add that, for the observer, memory is what is absent from the here
and now and thus what has to be inferred; for the subject, it is the nature
of memory's passage from absence to a particular kind of presence – the
way in which the subject reads the trace – which governs his future
possibilities.

Whatever the relationship between the neurological metaphors and the psychological metaphors with which neurology and psychology seek to formalize the structure and behavior of the mind, it is clear that there are repeating neurological circuits in the brain which can be considered in some respects structurally similar to the memory circuits of computers. And as Derrida points out, this structural similarity is prefigured in the concept of the FACILITATION (*Bahnung: frayage*) of the 'traces of reality' (*die Spuren der Realität*) in the neurological model developed by Freud in the *Project* of 1895. Derrida sees the metaphorical dimensions of the TRACE as that which unites Freud's earliest discussion of memory to the metaphor of writing in the last model he employed, the "mystic writing pad".

The import of Derrida's tentative analysis is indicated well enough by his own preliminary questions: "What is a text? And what must the psychic be for it to be represented by a text?"[1] For Derrida, in so far as the temporality of a text is historical and not linear, that is to say, in so far as a text can be read backwards, comprehended at a glance, written up and down, or from right to left, or permanently modified after it has been written (like a dream), it calls for a method of interpretation allied to the interpretation of the discourse rather than to the interpretation of speech – in other words, an interpretation bound by the laws of the trace and of writing rather than by the laws of phonology. If the distinction sometimes seems rather too nice, it is surely motivated by the necessity of escaping the dilemmas of formalistic binary oppositions as well as by the fact that literature, history, and philosophy are communicational and not simply linguistic forms.

2. *Logocentrism and the Trace*

Derrida's analysis goes far beyond a simple attack on the fetishization of phonology and the so-called binary opposition – more accurately a binary distinction – in the France of the fifties and sixties. Derrida accuses western thought in general of REPRESSING writing in favor of speech. This is what he calls LOGOCENTRISM: the inevitable interpretation of the *logos* in terms of the *phonē*. But he notes that the 'pathways', the 'facilitation' or 'grooving', and the stratified levels of traces or signs in the *Project* of 1895 are 'GRAMMATIC' rather than 'PHONETIC' metaphors. And Freud's inscription

---

[1] Derrida's anti-Lacanian position is partly indicated by his opening words: "If the Freudian breakthrough is historically original, it does not derive its originality from a peaceful coexistence or a theoretical complicity with [a certain type of] linguistics, at least in its congenital phonologism" (p. 11). (Saussure's *Cours* was published in 1916.)

model for memory still remains almost as valid as when he first conceived it.

Derrida's insistence on the trace is significant, for the most recent developments in the study of the genetic code, in the zoosemiotics of animal communication, and in neurophysiology, point to the primacy of the trace rather than to that of the message uttered. Waddington suggests, for instance, that in so far as DNA is a set of instructions, coded in minimally reactive forms in the molecule which bears it, we should regard it as a text. In fact, he says, why not think of DNA as the Bible, of messenger RNA as the preacher, and of the proteins as the congregation ready to perform the good works of the Word of God? (personal communication). Thomas Sebeok (1962, 1967) has examined the chemical signs used by animals and insects (including the celebrated bees) in writing down trails, boundaries, and messages. And from another perspective, while pointing out that almost nothing is known about the neurophysiology of remembering and learning, Karl H. Pribram (1969) has suggested that the interference patterns of the laser HOLOGRAM may prove to be the most fruitful model for memory since Freud's original 'inscription' model.[2]

The primary trace is an ANALOG inscription,[3] and Derrida's comment on

---

[2] The logical consequences of most neurophysiological theories of memory and learning is that memory is impossible (p. 73). In relation to the 'oppositions' involved in logocentrism, see Zopf's attack on the game of 2^{2^n}, where he remarks: "I think part of our confusion . . . comes from equating all thought with logic. . . . I can think of nothing cruder, or stupider, than a Nature which would produce children armed only with logic" (1962: 334, 338).

[3] All writing as such is essentially an analog form. The distinction between the presence of a written sign and the absence of a sign (the 'space') is not an opposition, but something equivalent to the distinction between figure and ground. Opposition is not what is essential to the letters in an alphabetical system, but difference – the ground of distinction – is (cf. Dunn-Rankin, 1978).

Compare Rousseau (1761, Chapter 5):

The first way of writing is not to paint the sounds, but the objects themselves, either directly, as the Mexicans did, or by allegorical figures, as the Egyptians used to do. This state corresponds to the 'passionate' language. . . . The second way is to represent words and propositions by conventional characters, which can only occur . . . amongst an entire people united by common laws. . . . Such is the writing of the Chinese, which is in essence a way of painting sounds and of speaking to the eyes. The third way is to decompose the speaking voice into a certain number of elementary parts, either vocal or articulated, with which one can form all imaginable words and syllables. This way of writing . . . must have been imagined by a commercial people [who needed a set of] characters common to all languages. To do this is not exactly to paint speech, it is to analyze it.

This curious essay includes an attack on Rameau's harmony (metaphor, paradigm) in favor of melody (metonymy, syntagm). According to Rousseau, melody

Freud's conception of levels of signs is apposite: "The trace will become the -gram; and the milieu of facilitation will become a ciphered spacing" (1966: 15). For Derrida the notion of the (memory) trace is intimately connected with the concept of *différence* (as with Bateson) but more especially with its homonym derived from the verb *'différer'*, 'to put off', 'to defer', 'to delay'. *Différance*, with an 'a', is the "after the event" of the post-script (*Nachträglichkeit*), a relation of 'postponement'.

Thus it is possible for Derrida to insist that writing, in the widest sense of the trace, the -gram, or the -graph, is the logical prerequisite for speech. In this he is clearly correct, for speech is dependent on the memory trace: without some form of memory-inscription, no organism can communicate anything whatsoever. This is in fact what distinguishes the 'communication' of energy from communication properly speaking. In information theory, a spectrograph is information as such; for communication theory it is only information because the receiver (the observer) is a communicator with a memory, and not a simple machine. It is from the real and material embodiment of the trace in the organism, says Derrida – the "delayed transmission" of difference (a 'prerecorded' or 'delayed' broadcast in French is *une émission différée*) – that MEANING arises. In my terminology, meaning is analog in function and distinct from signification, which is digital in both form and function. (Meaning, however, cannot occur without some form of signification or digitalization, and signification in the linguistic sense depends for its ground on meaning.) Memory seems to rely upon the sets or networks of analog patterns retained by the 'grooving' of the pathways in and between the organism or the system, and recall could be described as a sort of 'plucking' at these patterns (Bateson, personal communication). It is the 'grooving' of patterns in social systems which accounts for their Lamarckian inheritance of 'technological' and 'organizational' acquired characteristics through culture.

In terms which are remarkably consonant with Bateson's conception of information as "the difference which makes a difference" (which we can now translate as "the difference which leaves a postscript after-the-event"), Derrida attacks the positivistic conception of the "full origin". Speaking in epistemological rather than in historical or chronological terms, Derrida views the "full origin" as the illusory quest for the paradise lost, for the lost object, for u-topia, a quest which seeks to rediscover "being" or "substance" or "subject" or "plenitude" or "presence" at the origin of

---

is the "voice of nature". Thus the tendency towards harmony in western music in the eighteenth century is for him an index of decadence. See also Vico (1725: II, iv; IV, v) on "the origins of hieroglyphs, laws, names, family arms, medals, and money".

life. But "life must be conceived of as trace before being is determined as presence". The "essence of life" (which is no essence, but rather no-thing) is *différance*. This I translate here as 'goalseeking' in the sense that both origins and goals are Imaginary illusions: it is the SEEKING and not the goal which is at the origin of human affairs.

Derrida's somewhat Heideggerean penchant for the etymological and homophonic use of words creates what are probably unnecessary difficulties for the reader, but his analysis is profound:

> . . . The appearance and the functioning of difference suppose an original synthesis which is not preceded by any absolute simplicity. This is the original trace. Without the possibility of retention in the minimal unit of temporal experience, and without a trace which retains the other as other in the same, no difference would do its work and no meaning would appear. Thus it is not a question here of a constituted difference, but rather, before any determination of content, that of THE PURE MOVEMENT WHICH PRODUCES DIFFERENCE. The (pure) trace is *différance*. . . . *Différance* is therefore the formation of form. . . . THE TRACE IS IN FACT THE ABSOLUTE ORIGIN OF MEANING IN GENERAL [but the trace is nowhere]. This amounts to saying . . . that there is no absolute origin of meaning in general. The trace is the *différance* which opens up the world of appearance [*l'apparaître*] and signification (1967a: 91–5, my emphasis).

(I would put this last proposition in a slightly different fashion, however: It is *différance* which opens up appearance TO signification.[4]) Difference, like information, is a relation, and it cannot be localized: *différance* is the IN-FORMATION of form.

Derrida does not distinguish between the analog and the digital, or between energy and information, or between information, meaning, and signification, as I have sought to do. But his philosophical commentary

---

[4] Cf. Husserl's committment to the *phonē* in the domain of signification:

> Every 'intentioned object' [*Gemeint*] as such, every 'intention' [*Meinung*] in the noematic sense (by which I mean the noematic nucleus) is susceptible, no matter what the act may be, of receiving an expression [*Ausdruck*: a 'spoken word'] by means of 'significations' [*Bedeutungen*]. . . . Logical signification is an [act of] expression . . . (1950: 419).

Compare also the theory of digital knowledge in Wittgenstein (1937–44: #133):

> The propositions of logic are the 'laws of thought', 'because they bring the essence of human thinking to expression' or, more correctly, because they bring to expression or show the essence, the technique, of thinking (translation modified).

helps to link together the various conceptions of a symbolic and properly dialectical – 'naturalist' and 'materialist' – epistemology.

3. *Noise in Evolution*

> Noise is in no intrinsic way
> distinguishable from any other
> form of variety.
> W. ROSS ASHBY

The synchronic aspect of Bateson's unit of mind is the trace of the message-in-circuit, a circle of deferred difference. What breaks this circuit in nature, whether at the level of the genetic code or at higher levels, and provides for the transformation of homeorhesis into morphogenesis, is not so much the 'internal contradiction' alone in the classically bioenergetic, materialist sense,[5] but rather random variation or noise. Noise triggers and escalates pre-existing 'oscillatory' or 'contradictory' potentialities.

In natural evolution, noise is by definition an 'environmental intrusion', even when it is generated internally (e.g., random recombinations of DNA). But the noise does not necessarily remain as noise, because of the adaptive capabilities of the naturally morphogenic open system in relation to a changing environment. By the process of *Aufhebung* or emergence, the noise may be incorporated into the system as information. The 'intrusion' is converted into an essential part of the system so as to maintain the relationship between system and environment (survival of the fittest eco-system). Thus, a random event in nature, once it has become incorporated in the TRACE, becomes an Event. The accidental characteristic of the event in nature, its very improbability, is all we have to account for the negentropic bridge between homeostasis, homeorhesis, and invariant reproduction (structure and synchrony), on the one hand, and morphogenic evolution (system and diachrony), on the other. The natural Event is improbable in itself, but its occurrence changes the probabilities of other 'random intrusions'. The inexplicable evolution of bisexuality, for ex-

---

[5] I have criticized the confusion between contradiction and difference in Chapter VIII. The English text of Mao's essay on contradiction confuses the unity of contraries (which I would call difference) with the identity of contraries (which I would call opposition). This seems to be one more residue of the Imaginary reduction of difference which powers Hegelian idealism. Godelier (1968:86) makes a similar point and goes on to cite Marx from the *Grundrisse*:

> There is nothing simpler than for a Hegelian to consider production and consumption as identical. . . . The result I arrive at is NOT that production, distribution, exchange, and consumption are identical, but rather that they are elements of a totality, differentiations in the interior of a unity.

ample, vastly increased the pace of natural evolution. The incorporation of these morphogenic "catastrophes" (René Thom) as information in the genetic coding makes error and variation more probable. The more complex a system is, the more sensitive to error it will be, and the more likely it will be to make errors. One notes that, unlike writing, protected by redundancy in its use of the alphabet, the DNA molecule employs redundancy in that its chains of three-letter 'codons' are written down twice. Redundancy provides one form of protection from noise; this, combined with the minimally reactive chemistry and the 'self-repair' of DNA, protects the articulation of the genetic instructions from errors in 'copying' (duplication of DNA), in 'transcription' (into the alphabet of unstable messenger RNA), or in 'translation' (of the four-letter coding of the instructions into the twenty-letter coding of the proteins, by stable forms of RNA). When an error does occur, it is of course an error in the message. Like the metonymic 'nip' which emerges by contiguity from the message of the 'bite' and becomes a metaphor, the noise or the event begins as a (random) message and then, by emergence, becomes part of the coding of the instructions as Event. In this way, the digital quantum jumps in evolution become reintegrated in the continuum of the analog. In the sense that the growth of the human embryo recapitulates the evolution of man, the accumulated 'catastrophic' messages or Events in that evolution are present for the embryo as parts of the code.

The same sort of process occurs elsewhere. Pask's experiments with the acrasin (chemotactic) communications system of amoebae (1962: 248–9) show that the emission of acrasin controls the timing and placing of the combination of the individuals into a new whole, a slime mold. There is a resultant reorganization of the logical typing of the individual subsystems which create the mold, for they take on specialized functions (Chapters VII and XII). With a sufficient output of acrasin, an Event takes place different from all other events. There is a passage from quantity to quality. This event is a quantum jump in organization which converts each individual amoeba from the status of being a code (at its own level) and a potential message (at the level of the whole) into a message in the code of the slime mold. We can look on this process in retrospect as one in which a series of random contiguous messages in an unstructured system of individual amoebae – unrelated at the level of the code – become combined in such a way that their 'last' set of individual messages 'emerges' as a qualitative leap into a structured whole. This new whole, as a code, is a second-level metaphor generated by the contiguous and originally random messages of the antecedent 'system'. It is a metaphoric Event – after the event – which is retained in the trace represented by the mold.

The random distribution of energy levels of which the second law of thermodynamics speaks is not a series of improbable accidents in the sense that an error in the transmission of the genetic messages of an organism is an accident. The random distribution of energy is rather of the domain of necessity (i.e., of probability), since the second law in both its energetic and its informational aspects is a probability equation. This is only another way of saying that random information (noise) is epistemologically distinct from matter–energy. (In another sense they are the same, for whatever is not information for a communications system can only be matter–energy. It is not a question of their nature, but rather of their FUNCTION and of their effect.) Noise in the sense it is used here is a measure of the actual disturbance of organization, which is why it can become an event; it is not a measure of a TENDENCY towards disorganization, as entropy is.

4. *Noise in History*

Once we leave the level of noise in the genetic code and approach the level of ecosystemic relations in the broad sense, we can redefine noise so as to allow us to define the relationship between noise and event in history. As Ashby puts it (1956: 187): "In biology . . . the 'noise' in one system will be due to some other macroscopic system from which the system under study cannot be completely isolated." All open systems are necessarily related to other open systems and to their own subsystems, as well as to the differing levels of organization 'within' themselves as systems. As I pointed out in Chapter XII, noise in history is not in fact an 'environmental intrusion', although it is necessarily DEFINED as one by those parts within the whole which perceive it as a disturbance. Noise is a necessary product of the tension between the various subsystems or levels of the historical ecosystem. As Buckley (1967: 50–1) points out:

> The typical response of . . . closed systems to an intrusion of environmental events is a loss of organization, or a change in the direction of the dissolution of the system (or possibly a move to a new level of equilibrium). . . . The typical response of open systems . . . is elaboration or change of structure to a higher or more complex level. . . . The environmental interchange is not, or does not long remain, random or unstructured, but rather becomes selective due to the mapping, or coding, or information-processing capabilities . . . inherent in this type of system.

In other words, only a system which believes itself to be a mechanical equilibrium system, or a Newtonian harmony of entities and forces, will be unable to recognize itself as the source of the noise which disturbs it (cf. Chapter XI). Whereas in natural evolution, errors in DNA can be defined as the effects of 'outside agitators' – in the sense that the errors are purely random – this is not the case for the history of a dialectical society like our own. Although there undoubtedly do occur random events in history which can trigger pre-existing tension at certain times rather than at other times – for this is the only way we can account for the actual timing of revolutions, or for the acceleration and deceleration, at different epochs, of historical processes which, on the face of it, seem to involve the same components – the noise in the historical ecosystem is necessarily engendered by its character of being OUT OF STEP with itself. Nevertheless, the RELATION between noise, event, and Event in history remains the same as that between the same factors in natural evolution.

Negentropic evolution in levels of organization – i.e., localized negative entropy drawing its energy from an entropic universe – is a measure of improbability. In the theorization of the dialectical interaction between structure and system, between synchrony and diachrony, it is the failure to recognize or to deal with 'noise' or with the improbable 'event' that accounts in large part for a tendency towards an implicit preference for a 'flat', homeostatic theory among many formalists and structuralists (Chapters IX and XI).

5. *Hegel on* Erinnerung

Evolution and revolution are the results of the creative integration of noise into the system as a memory trace.

The system that evolves RE-MEMBERS (*er-innern*) noise. Derrida's 'original trace' is noise, for life is an improbable accident. We can now translate more freely the celebrated Hegelian metaphor of truth as process (*Bewegung*) (quoted more literally in Wilden, 1968a: 211):

> The true is the Bacchantic *ek-stase* in which no member of the whole, no link in the chain, is not drunken. And because as soon as it differentiates itself, each difference immediately dissolves [itself] – becomes REDUNDANT, as it were – the ecstasy of the whole is as if it were simple and transparent repose. . . . In the totality of process, which we now see as repose, what comes to differentiate itself in the whole, and to give itself a particular being-there, as SOMETHING, is preserved and retained as that which REMEMBERS itself, that for which its being-there is the knowledge [*Wissen*] of itself . . . (Hegel, 1807a: 39; 1807b: I, 40).

In the domain of communication both within and between organisms, or between systems of different types or states, it is the choice or punctuation of one trace, one difference, as different from all others which sets up the boundaries between sender and receiver, between one state of the system and another state, or between one system and another. This punctuation always involves some level of digitalization: the difference chosen to be different is rendered DISTINCT.

For Hegel, it is precisely the extraordinary and surprising digital activity of the understanding (*Verstand*) – the activity of dividing (*scheiden*) – which is, in his bioenergetic language, the 'power' behind 'man as discourse'. Let us leave to one side the privilege accorded to energy and equilibrium (inertia) in the scientific discourse of the eighteenth and nineteenth centuries (to say nothing of our own). Although Hegel's 'organicist' opposition to Newtonian mechanism does not make him that much less Newtonian – any more than Locke's empiricist opposition to Descartes made him much less Cartesian – we can nevertheless see Hegel struggling to distinguish the closed-system mechanism from the open-system man. Although he gets himself trapped in the Imaginary by his view of opposition and identity, he never ceases to try to distinguish the subject-in-becoming from the substance-in-being.

Just as the memory trace is for Derrida the IN-FORMING OF FORM, so the distinction between organism and mechanism, and between man and nature, is for Hegel the explanation of improbability or SURPRISE VALUE, both of which, of course, are technical synonyms for information. To be transmitted, information, as difference, depends on the *Er-innerung*, the retention, of the trace, and it is not for nothing that re-membering is so essential to the *Phenomenology*, nor that the German prefix 'er'- refers both to origins and to goals. After all, for Hegel, as for Aristotle, the beginning is the end, the goal: *der Anfang Zweck ist* (1807a: 22; 1807b: I, 20).

In the following passage, commented at length by Kojève (1947a: 540–2), two distinctions are grafted the one upon the other. The distinction between energy and information (closed and open systems) overlaps that between analog and digital communication (continuity and discontinuity), Of course, Hegel supports the 'digital prejudice' of (at least) western man – we know he prefers the digital (and technologically efficient) alphabet of the west to the emblematic ideograms of the Chinese, for instance. For this reason, and also because the Hegelian "cunning of reason" (*Luft der Vernunft*) and the deification of the Absolute Spirit, for all their totalizing power, seek in the end to reduce Imaginary oppositions to an equally Imaginary identity, we must read him with care:

The circle which remains closed upon itself and which holds its constitutive elements [*Moment*] as a substance would is a non-mediated relationship [i.e., a 'natural', 'given', relationship] which has nothing surprising about it. But the fact that the accidental as such, separated from its boundary – that which is bound and effectively real only in its connection with what is other – the fact that the contingent obtains its own empirical being-there [*Dasein*] and a separated or isolated liberty, is the expression of the prodigious power of the negative [*des Negativen*]. It is the energy of thought, of the pure *I* (1807a: 29; 1807b: I, 29).

We see once again the *Bindung* of the primary (analog) process by the secondary (analog/digital) process (Chapters VI, IX).

Kojève's commentary returns us to our starting-point: to the macroscopic distinction between nature as the analog and culture as the digital, to the trace as *différance*:

> . . . It is in separating and recombining things by and through his discursive thought that man forms his technical projects which, once they are made real through labor, really transform the aspect of the given, natural World by creating in it a cultural World . . . (1947a: 542).

Perhaps Kojève's commentary is too much impregnated with concern for the same existential – and bourgeois – anguish over the death of the individual which we can see in the work of Lacan. But even if for Kojève the being of mankind is "death delayed" (*la mort différée*, p. 550), his Marxism will not allow him to leave this "creativity of man" ("the affirmation of nothingness by the negation of the given") hanging in the metaphysics of idealism or spiritual 'liberation'. Man creates himself through labor. The Concept is signification; it is the information which organizes the work to be done. We can interpret unalienated human labor – the transformation of the given, the production of the artefact – in the terms of the 'work' of the organism or the species (transformation, adaptation, reproduction, evolution) in relation to its environment. Labor or work changes or reproduces the organization of matter–energy. The trace the 'organism' leaves on (or in) the 'environment', and the trace the 'environment' leaves on (or in) the 'organism' is precisely *l'écriture* in Derrida's sense of the -gram. When in evolution 'work' comes to involve the production of exchange values (production proper) rather than simple use values (reproduction), the matter–energy involved is transformed from energy to information (from entity to 'sign' from male to 'brother', from penis to 'phallus'). It is at the (mythical) moment of the creation of the 'symbolic object' (Chapters VI, IX), that 'transitory' or 'unembodied' or 'uninscribed' information – in other words, SPEECH – can come to control the non-natural or non-biological communication and exchange of the system, which will later give rise – by accident – to writing proper.

6. *Redundant Synchrony and Permanent Evolution*

If the trace is the STORAGE of difference so that it can be transmitted later, and if the analog patterns of storage account in some sense for memory (the act of recall involving digital processes), then Derrida's extension of the category of writing throws some light on the function of writing in societies like our own, as opposed to the relative synchrony of 'other' civilizations.

In biological terms, the simpler the organism or the lower the level of organization, the greater the preponderance of structure and reproduction over system and evolution. No individual organism is capable of evolution, although it does of course display adaptation and learning within certain limits. Only the species (the genotype) evolves, and this over the dead bodies of its progenitors. Evolution depends on death, but the past is retained as trace in the genetic pool of the population, which is exterior to the individual organism as such. Evolved characteristics must be retained in the instructions which govern the reproduction of generations; these instructions are the memory bank through which individual potentialities are constrained.

In Chapter XII, I tried to analyze the problematic of 'evolution' in an 'other civilization',[6] without making any assumptions about environmental intrusions. My conclusion was that, so long as no 'invention' takes place, we should be talking about development rather than about evolution. In this chapter, I shall set up a distinction between 'hot' civilizations and 'cool' civilizations on the basis of the presence or the absence of writing, properly so called. This is a methodological distinction, from a macroscopic perspective, and is not intended to imply that 'cool' civilizations are static.

---

[6] In writing this book, I have been constantly concerned about finding a suitable descriptive term for what used to be called the 'primitive' or 'archaic' culture. As Robert Jaulin has said, the expression 'so-called primitive' – which I have constantly used – will not do either. Moreover, by using the word 'culture', one tends to imply an opposition between 'cultures' ('all cultures are equal') and civilizations (we regard only certain 'cultures' as 'civilized'). It is logistically difficult at this point to catch all the previous uses of 'so-called primitive' in my text, but I can at least point to the error here. One cannot substitute 'pre-literate', because (*a*) it sounds like 'illiterate', and (*b*) it contradicts the thesis about writing in this chapter. Nor can one say 'non-technological', because (*a*) it is not a valid description, and (*b*) it contradicts my thesis (from Ellul) about 'technique'. I have therefore used Jaulin's term "other civilization" where appropriate. Elsewhere, I have used the terms 'hot' and 'cool', but not in the Lévi-Straussian sense.

In other words, I am employing a digital distinction between the relative pace of change in the hot and in the cool civilization.

In the cool civilization without writing as such, the past of the society – its memory, its set of instructions, its sacred text – is literally embodied in every domicile, in every person or group marked by a kinship term or by a taboo, in every person or group who exemplifies a ritual or who recalls a myth. Except in so far as the ground plan of the village and/or various cultural objects and implements provide a minimal objective memory for the survival of the organization of the society from generation to generation, the significant distinctions in such a society have to be maintained, reconstructed, represented, and, in essence, RE-INVENTED in the very flesh of each generation. In the Crow–Omaha system, for instance, even the kinship organization is reinvented by what each generation actually remembers about past sets of rules. The distinction between code and message in this type of society must be a minimal distinction; the system is as if it were both language and speech at the same time. Or to put it another way, the text ('DNA') and the messengers ('RNA') are almost the same, the genotype is very nearly the phenotype. Every living member of the system is both a message in the code and a message which maintains the code, a message which retains and remembers a part of the code. Since the tendency of the system is towards invariant reproduction, or towards the logical extension of a set of instructions, the analogy with the information-processing text of DNA in the organism is particularly striking.

It is clear that hot societies, on the other hand, require a different level of explanation. Buckley (1967: 133–6) tries to deal with this question in his discussion of Talcott Parsons's later, more systemic, and less equilibrium-oriented models. But the discussion falls into the ethnocentric fallacy of 'evolutionism' (cf. Terray, 1969: 15–91, who cites Lévi-Strauss, 1952: 13, 15, and Mercier, 1966: 54–5).

After the period of quiescence which followed the neolithic revolution – the invention of pottery, weaving, agriculture, and the domestication of animals – those societies which chose to 'take off' into other forms of evolution must have done so as a result of the fortuitous invention of WRITING and, presumably later, of the ALPHABET. The crafts and techniques of the neolithic revolution are, of course, forms of writing: they inscribe a memory on nature and on objects used by the society. But they offer only restricted COMBINATORIAL possibilities. Although the smelting of copper seems to have been an offshoot of the art of pottery (Lévi-Strauss, 1962: 22) – the use of powdered malachite as a coloring agent – and can thus be seen as a form of combination in the message which later evolved into a metaphor in the code, all the inventions of the neolithic, as well as the later accident of the invention of the wheel in some societies, provide what is only an essentially analog memory with restricted digital possibilities. All these arts are passed on by IMITATION rather than by INSTRUCTION. It is significant that Lewis Morgan,[7] in whose remarkable structural-evolutionist model both Marx and Engels saw prefigured their own historical materialism, fully comprehended the 'technical' invention as the kind of 'noise' whose integration as trace set off new processes of change. But he left entirely out of account the invention of the alphabet, as does Terray (1969: 73). The invention of such a digital form of objective memory is of a different logical type from all the other techniques. It provides vastly increased possibilities of combination and restructuring. The invention of writing as such – however, wherever, and however often it occurred – necessarily accelerates the possibilities of change. One assumes that it must lie at the origin of the hot societies.

A society in which forms of objective memory with greater semiotic freedom, such as writing, have been invented, is necessarily more open to increases of complexity. It has no need to ask its members actually to embody the cultural code and the history of the society to the same extent as the cool society must do, for its code is also inscribed elsewhere. In a hot society, the cultural code is to a far greater extent 'outside' the individual. The extent to which he effectively internalizes and represents it as he becomes 'socialized', has less effect on the status of the code than it would have in the cool society. One might say that the hot society records itself in an essential way, on the world outside – on nature, on stone, on wax, on clay, on paper, on film, on tape, in its railway networks, its streets, its freeways – whereas the cool society is more nearly WRITTEN ON ITSELF. The cool society – which is not 'preliterate' in its ability to read its own memory system – is both itself and the memory of itself. In relation to the highly efficient digital coding of the recall of the trace in the memory patterns of the hot society, the cool society is analog at all levels. It is not an alphabetical system, but an ICONOGRAPHY in which those mnemonic icons which are not objects or patterns of objects (tools, houses, the ground-plan of the village) are in fact people.

It is quite clear, therefore, why cool societies have such complex kinship systems. With the invention of writing as a new form of technique, there is no longer any need for the 'neurons' of the 'mnemonic network' to be

---

[7] *Systems of Consanguinity and Affinity of the Human Family* (1871) and *Ancient Society* (1877). Both the contemporary Marxist school and the structuralist school object to the 'evolutionism' of *Ancient Society* (Terray, 1969).

represented by people who carry and reproduce the organization of the society in their kinship names. And in those societies which do have writing as well as complicated kinship systems (e.g., the Manchu in China), we might expect to find that the form and the function of writing is different from that of the hot society.

The accidental invention of writing as such provides for qualitatively different possibilities of differentiation and therefore of specialization, because its digital characteristics multiply the possibilities of the transmission of information. With its available cultural dictionaries, a society with writing will necessarily be potentially more efficient. After all, the actual invention of the dictionary and the encyclopedia in western civilization, as Jacques Ellul has pointed out (1954), was a technical–technological innovation in the interests of efficiency. And whereas the unit of communication in the cool society is the person, that of the hot society is the 'role' or the 'skill' or the standardized 'replacement part', something which can be digitalized, specialized, alphabeticized, something which can be looked up, filed, localized, and retrieved at will.

Since all communication depends upon redundancy to guard against error, the redundancy of a communications system is a measure of its stability in the sense of resistance to change. Stability is also achieved by sensitivity to change; morphogenesis, evolution, revolution, are all adaptive responses seeking to restore stability at another level. But, for the homeostatic stability of the cool society assumed here, it is clear that redundancy plays a relatively large role in the transmission and retention of the cultural code. The repetitions of myth and ritual, in myth and ritual; the complicated preparations and ritualizations of daily events; the carefully constructed rites of passage: all these contribute to the reduction of the accidental event to the probable, of the novel to the prearranged, and of the (digital) event to (analog) process. Everything is designed to minimize the effect of noise on the cultural code. There are similar effects in hot civilizations, of course, but it is the relative role of TIME, and therefore of the utilization of energy, which distinguishes them. A hot society has a sort of instant memory in its stored information, whereas for a similar amount of information to be 'printed out' in the cool society, it may take a week or a year of feasting, dancing, and so forth by a relatively large number of people. The expenditure of energy required for recall is therefore much greater in the cool society, especially in relation to the total energy available in it.

In the hot society, it is the way that the cultural memory is STORED which depends heavily on redundancy; in the cool society, it is the way the cultural memory is USED which is so heavily redundant. In the terms of the inverse relationship between redundancy and the efficient use of energy, the hot society uses or recalls its highly redundant cultural memory (code) more efficiently than the cool society can recall its highly efficient code by its highly redundant message system.

The more efficient the use of the material and energy necessary to transmit information in the system – essential information, that is, for we are not concerned here with redundancy in the sense of wastage – the less redundant the information transmission will be. The system will be more complex and, in the long term, more fragile. Thus it will be more sensitive to noise, and in order to deal with noise (which increases with complexity), the efficient system must be morphogenic. In other words, instead of maintaining stability by homeostatic resistance to noise, it will seek to maintain stability by ACCEPTING noise, by incorporating it as information, and moving to a new level of organization (evolving). It is in this sense that change becomes an internal or internalized principle of the system, a product of its forms of organization, since the stability of the system is a product of its continuing evolution.

This somewhat speculative analysis is neither 'evolutionist' nor is it representative of the 'archaic fallacy'. It has nothing to do with any bourgeois notion of 'progress', for we know that the cool society is as ancient as the hot society – and, as such, has greater long-range survival value. In the best sense, it is from a purely descriptive point of view that we can say that the cool society guards itself against innovation by seeking to minimize the 'surprise value' (the information) of the event – its digitalizing and dividing function, its either/or quality, its demand for a decision, its function as a boundary between states of the system. In the cool system, the real occurrence of the event is reduced to the domain of the synchronic, to the natural and to the given.[8] This is to say that whereas the cool system is homeostatic and synchronic, its consciousness of itself (its myths) consists of the trace of a single event (its origin), which explains all subsequent events. And whereas the hot system is essentially morphogenic, its own consciousness (its science), particularly since the Galilean revolution, has invariably represented the trace of (Newtonian) equilibrium and harmony.

Both systems have a science to explain away the event. In a system which is surrounded by dangerous events, this science is myth and magic. As Evans-Pritchard has said (quoted in Lévi-Strauss, 1962: 18), witchcraft is a natural philosophy of causality which explains the nefarious event as a combination of sorcery and of natural forces over which man has no

---

[8] Compare Zeno's attempt to reduce diachronic time to repetition in Chapter III.

control. If a granary riddled by termites should fall down and kill a particular person, the termites are recognized as being responsible for its collapse, but witchcraft is responsible for the 'organization' of the collapse in such a way that it killed a particular person, and not somebody else, or nobody at all. And since natural forces are beyond human control, any protection against them even must come through witchcraft, since it alone is the result of human design in a social context. In so-called civilized society, on the other hand, it is the 'natural forces' which we can control, and on whose laws of equilibrium, inertia, and degradation all science is supposed to be constructed. Thus the socioeconomic and psychosocial processes of writing which account for the transition of event into Event in the real lives of human beings in the hot society, are necessarily relegated by the myth of scientism to the status of witchcraft. On the other hand, since witchcraft deals with the theory of the organization and triggering of matter–energy, it is surely the immediate precursor of contemporary information science.

For the cool society, the improbable is the expected and since it is itself the memory trace, the event rarely becomes history. In the evolving system, however, the event is recorded as trace and thus may pass from message to code (metaphor) as Event. The event in the cool system on the other hand, tends to remain at the (metonymic) level of the message. If western science, in Derrida's terms, has always REPRESSED the memory trace, then the 'archaic' myth has always, and necessarily, DISAVOWED the event. This means that each type of civilization, caught in the apparent contradiction between synchrony and diachrony, has responded in a different way to the same problem. The statistical and mechanical pre-dispositions of western science have, until recently, generated an archaic myth of an unchanging metaphoric code (structure, equilibrium, determinism) – for which all change is entropic degradation – to explain away the real significance of the internal or internalized event in a system which is highly susceptible to the Event, and in fact dependent on it. This is a system whose stable status depends not upon the maintenance of a Golden Age, but upon adaptivity in the sense of quantum jumps in evolution (system, self-differentiation, improbability). The Imaginary and romantic illusions of this myth, derived from scientism, are obvious enough.

The ecological and symbiotic concerns of the myth of the cool society, on the other hand, generate a science of the event (the absolute and accidental origin, the 'once upon a time') in the form of a message from the ancestors or the gods, in order to explain the eternal recurrence – and therefore the non-significance – of these 'acts of God'. The myth of origins thus establishes the original event as a metaphor of the behavior of the system and explains the non-internalization of subsequent external events, the lack of the TRACE of the subsequent event, in a homeostatic system highly resistant to noise. For, where every event is a catastrophe, there is no catastrophe.

The ideological function of the Imaginary and bioenergetic epistemology of the scientific discourse in our own civilization, balancing opposition against identity, attraction against repulsion, has nothing surprising about it. It has already been pointed out that noise is a form of violence. But for the dominant ideology and for the scientism of our culture, above all in structuralism and in the human sciences, all violence is necessarily the work of randomly distributed outside agitators, who come to disturb the pre-established harmony of a closed (social) system, which necessarily remembers nothing, and which can therefore learn nothing. . . .

Chapter XIV

The Scientific Discourse as Propaganda

THE BINARY OPPOSITION

TODAY TEXTILES, TOMORROW THE WORLD!
The techniques and strategies derived from sound
psychological research and theory should be equally applicable
to problems that you consider to be socially significant and
personally relevant. Your task is to use an approach like the
textile sales campaign [in Uruguay] as a model for solving a
problem whose content is meaningful to you – whether it be
prejudice, cigarette smoking, birth control, political candidate
preferences, or even trying to change the entire establishment.
ZIMBARDO-EBBESEN (1969): "When it's April in Uruguay,
only Science Sells Curtains"

1. *Epistemological Considerations*

Derrida's critique of logocentrism and phonologism in the previous chapter
provides further grounds for a re-evaluation of the use of the terms 'opposition' and 'binary opposition' in the discourse of science. The use of these
terms is by no means trivial, for they are the kind of words which have a
special controlling power in the discourse, especially at levels which are
unconscious or unrecognized. Most people do not, of course, believe in the
oppressive and violent functions that simple words may serve – quite. apart
from any controls exerted by linguistic structure – unless, of course, they
happen to belong to those very groups or subgroups against whom the
linguistic violence of words is most obviously directed: racial and ethnic
minorities, women, children (on the experience of the 'educated black', see
Fanon, 1952). To "animal categories and verbal abuse" (Leach), we need
therefore to add the categories of things, objects, commodities, and any
number of various forms of paranoid projection used by the dominant to

define the subordinate, whether the subordinate recognize the function of these terms or not (cf. Chapter XVII).

We have seen a new form of the category of opposition in the work of Lacan and Lévi-Strauss. In spite of the fact that in phonology the category of the binary opposition has a purely heuristic – and aesthetic – function; that in the binary system of the digital computer, it has a logistical function related to efficiency and to the behavior of certain kinds of machines; and that the brain does not depend solely on either/or decisions (Chapter VII); the binary opposition comes to be used to explain everything and anything in a way that rather clearly shows its Imaginary determination in the epistemology of western culture.

And in spite of the many critiques of Lévi-Strauss's assumptions, methodology, distortions, and failure to abide by his own rules (cf. Rayfield, 1970a; Scholte, 1968) – many of which nevertheless betray serious misunderstandings at the methodological and epistemological level – his tendency to translate a heuristic device into an ontological statement of some supposed fundamental structure of the human mind, still lies heavy on us. As Bakan suggests (Chapter VII, Appendix I), any apparent binarism of the brain, at least, is a special kind of connected relation, rather than an opposition. In any event, opposition requires that the terms opposed be of the SAME LOGICAL TYPE. The 'duality' of such supposedly opposed terms as nature and culture, energy and information, meaning and signification, analog and digital which have been used throughout these essays, has nothing to do with the binary opposition between equivalent logical types. These 'dualities' are essentially heuristic rather than ontological. But what is much more important is that they do not define opposed terms, they define BOUNDARIES BETWEEN TYPES OF LOGICAL TYPES – a "relation which cannot be stated" as Bateson says. It is the failure to recognize the distinction between the relations of members of a class (structure) on the one hand, and the relations between classes of members (systemic levels and connections), on the other, which vitiates, at the epistemological and methodological level, most of the supposed binary oppositions one finds being used. In other words, although these do indeed perform an ideological function in the scientific discourse – which is 'unscientific' enough – they are not 'scientific' in the very terms of that discourse itself.

2. The International Unity of the Scientific Discourse

The importance of this method of critical analysis cannot be overstated. The relation between binarism, its ally, digitalism, and the Imaginary epistemology are immediately obvious. Thus we can come at the one-dimensional linearity and the non-contextuality of the scientific discourse from another point of view, in order both to exemplify and to ground the multidimensionality and the contextuality of the dialectical epistemology (cf. Introduction).

There is another significant preliminary point to be made. Although I refer to Lévi-Strauss in this chapter, and to Lacan in Chapters X and XVII (in particular) – because of the necessity of close critical analyses of particular texts – and although Chapter XI is based on a critique of French 'structuralism' – because of the necessity of exposing its function as a repressive mythology which projects the violence of the City out of the City – the analysis in this chapter seeks to expose the essential UNITY of the exploitative function of the scientific discourse in western culture at large.

The biographic, social, historical, and ideological context of structural anthropology and its critics has been examined at length in an article by Bob Scholte (1968), in which he brings out the intellectual rivalries, the nationalistic motivations, and the personally directed jealousies – representatives of the instrumentality of the 'circulation of knowledge' at its crassest levels – on which the debate is often articulated. My point is that, whatever the function of structural anthropology may be, the opposition it generates in 'empiricists' is a real example of a binary opposition. In other words, it is a real example of the Imaginary opposition in which the critic who speaks at the same level as what he criticizes refuses to recognize himself in the others he condemns (cf. Introduction). This is particularly true of American and British critics. Their criticism of 'structuralism' is in effect of the same logical type as what they criticize, and in general it depends on exactly the same set of metavalues (i.e., values derived from at least the third or the fourth level of learning). The scientific discourse on both sides of the Atlantic serves the same social function. The apparent critical opposition between them is an illusion; it is an Imaginary construction concealing an identity of simple, and essentially linear, oppositions.

The criticism of Lévi-Strauss is replete with references to his Jewish origins, to the 'Gallic mind', to a supposed French 'rationalism', to 'Cartesianism', to a French 'obsession for order', and so on. There are, of course, significant cultural, historical, and environmental differences between the intellectuals of France, the United States, and England. But, as I have already pointed out in the Introduction, the real – but still potential – contributions to the understanding of mankind made by Lévi-Strauss tend to be neutralized on both sides of the Atlantic or the Channel, if in different ways. Moreover, in spite of the nationalistic chauvinism of the French and their understandable anti-Americanism (given the cultural and economic imperialism of America in Europe), their particular forms of social, class, and racial prejudice are logically, psychologically, and economically identical to the prejudices of those who call themselves, in their characteristic ethnocentrism, Anglo-Saxons – or of those who implicitly or explicitly identify themselves with the cultural values metaphorically represented by the term 'Anglo-Saxon': the 'British tradition' and the 'American way of life'.

Unfortunately for the critic, the scientific discourse is well protected against any real questioning from a metascientific position. The metascientific position is a commentary not only on science, but also on the philosophy of science. One can, of course, choose to remain at the level of general observations, but sooner or later it becomes necessary to choose an example. And the moment that one seeks to show in a particular case the articulation of the social and political values of the existing order under the guise of science, one will have stepped outside the level of criticism permitted by the discourse of science.

The scientific discourse has its automatic defense mechanisms ready. One of the most common is the accusation that the critic is using *ad hominem* arguments. The binarism of this reaction is an example of what I seek to refute, for it says that all arguments are either *ad theorem* or *ad hominem*. This position not only misconstrues the indivisible connection between digital information and analog relation, it also misrepresents the actual values and behavior of the speakers in the scientific discourse itself. For we are not concerned here with particular speakers as men or women. We are concerned with particular speakers as representatives of a CLASS of men and women, with a particular class of characteristics, a set of representative metaphors.

But, as Marx himself so clearly demonstrates by his personal vilifications of his opponents and by his own anti-Semitism, the necessary act of stepping outside the values of your opponent in order to criticize them AS VALUES can very easily be confused by the critic with the personal characteristics of the opponent. It is this level of the *ad hominem* critique which is unacceptable to a critical theory, whatever its value in the symbolic exchange of gossip may be.

If the class of characteristics I refer to should turn out also to be a class of characteristics which are descriptive of schizophrenia and paranoia in the scientific discourse itself, we should not be surprised. Scholte (1968) brings out this possibility rather effectively when he points out that the supposed "rigidity" and "reifications" in French structuralism are in fact characteristic of international and intercultural RATIONALISM, rather than characteristic of any particular theory. He cites Peter Worsley's (chauvinist) quotation of Henry Miller's (chauvinist and objectifying) observation: "The

insane have a terrific obsession for logic and order, as do the French"
(p. 20).

3. *The Scientific Discourse as Propaganda*

The discourse of science is loaded with propaganda. In Ellul's sense (1962)
of the unthinking and uncritical reinforcement of controlling values which
justify existing social conditions, ESPECIALLY BY INTELLECTUALS, the word
propaganda is not too strong a term. It describes the habitual and deeply
programmed projections of current socioeconomic categories and stereo-
types into the scientific discourse. And since I have drawn on Ellul's definition, it is as well to point out that Ellul's book is in fact a fine example of his
own thesis about the function of the intellectual. The book is replete with
an institutionalized and unconscious exploitative ideology, which is objectively racist, paternalist, and colonialist (e.g., pp. 42, 73, 74, 134, 150–1).
Ellul does not actually say 'Some of my best friends are Algerians', but
one expects to hear it every time he mentions the FLN and the Algerian
war of independence.

In treating FLN propaganda as equal and equivalent to French propaganda during the war (p. 79), he makes the usual 'liberal' error of denying
the real context of the struggle, its historical origins, and the real relations
of power and responsibility involved. He conveniently omits mentioning
a half-century of ontological oppression and economic exploitation, the
bombing of defenseless civilians, the repeated murder of hostages, OAS
atrocities, and the systematic use of torture as an instrument of government.

As the script of the film *The Battle of Algiers* took care to point out, any
such real equivalence at any level whatsoever would have been most welcome to the FLN. In the film, an 'objective' journalist asks about FLN
terrorism against the European population, implying, of course, that only
the FLN have been responsible for terrorism, and demonstrating at the
same time his ignorance of its historical antecedents in the institutionalized
terrorism of the French. The FLN had employed women carrying bombs
in their purses to blow up European restaurants and theaters. The captured
FLN leader in the film replied that he would be most happy to exchange
the purses and the home-made bombs for an equivalent number of French
warplanes loaded with napalm.

But Ellul does more than posit an Imaginary symmetry where there is in
fact power, force, and dominance on only one side. He also implicitly
reduces the whole struggle for liberation to a simple war of ideas, and his
unconscious identification of the 'superiority' of certain ideas with the
economic interests of France, is a superb example of the exploitative

characteristics of the 'objectivity' and 'neutrality' of the master. He treats the war, not as a war of liberation against oppression, but exactly as if it were what the French propaganda tried to make it: a question of whether the 'natives' were going to allow the French to continue to 'help' them, all in the name of their future 'betterment' by the 'civilizing influence' of 'we who know better', and who offer our 'continued cooperation' (and so on). Thus the apparent symmetry of his analysis – which is inexcusable enough – conceals a real superiority which remains unacknowledged as propaganda, and which goes beyond anything that could be accepted as unavoidable subjective bias in a critical discourse.

4. *The Enemy Brothers*

> Oppositions are not subject to
> the logic of exclusion, but to that
> of participation, of which
> exclusion is in any case a
> variant.
> HJELMSLEV

We can approach the linear symmetry of the scientific discourse from another perspective. René Girard has often spoken of the relationship of the 'enemy brothers' in the Oedipus trilogy, represented by the physical battle between Eteocles and Polynices in *Antigone,* and by the verbal violence of the debate between Oedipus and Creon, on the one hand, and that between Oedipus and Tiresias, on the other, in *Oedipus Rex.* This is the classic relationship of mediated desire for an object – the Father's inheritance, in this case – which results in the reciprocal objectification of the protagonists by means of a Real or Imaginary struggle for mastery. In this struggle, guilt circulates as a repressed symbolic object between them, until all that can be said is "Whatever you say I am, you're another one". Oedipus' way of transcending the Imaginary in the myth is to accept to be the scapegoat of the City. The myth itself thus fulfills its function of repressing and disavowing the contextual relations of power and responsibility in the City. In exactly the same way, the Judeo-Christian mythology depends on an egalitarian responsibility for violence – the 'original sin' of human 'nature', the 'tragic flaw' in humankind – in order to maintain the 'law and order' of the system.

At the risk of our lives, we cannot afford to believe in this mythology, especially as it comes to be represented in the discourse of science, particularly in the mythology of the binary opposition.

What is Christ in fact but the original martyr to original sin? He is sacrificed to the Other by the Establishment of the Jewish nation. But the Other in question is not God, and the Establishment in question is in no sense representative of the Jewish people. The Other is Imperial Rome, and the Establishment is the compradorist local 'bourgeoisie'. Christ is indeed the original martyr of western culture, but he is not a martyr to 'original sin'. Just as Oedipus is the model of the original outside agitator, Christ is the original martyr to COLONIALISM.

One cannot help seeing the laws of relation in all the various forms of French structuralism as the laws of the relation between the enemy brothers as they are developed by the brothers themselves. But this relation is not confined to structuralism: it appears everywhere in the discourse of science.

The efficacy of the promotion of the binary opposition and its attendant scientism in France is a side-effect of the real contributions Lévi-Strauss has made to anthropology. Whatever relation of empathy one might establish between one's own quest for life and Lévi-Strauss's version of the quest for lost time – and however profoundly one may understand the personal social alienation from which he proceeds – his status as a subject-who-is-supposed-to-know requires that we examine the social function of what he is supposed to know, in order to establish the function of his ignorance of that function.

I do not agree with all of Rayfield's criticisms of Lévi-Strauss (Rayfield, 1970a). But her analysis of his tendency towards binary reductionism and her objections to his ideological insistence on describing the women of the 'other' culture in the terms of the actual status of women as objects and commodities in our supposedly 'civilized' culture, points up the problems of closure and confusion of levels in his work.

However, the tendency towards binarism in Lévi-Strauss is not a personal characteristic. In Lévi-Strauss, the Cartesian rationalism of the international discourse of science appears in the way he conceives the 'dichotomy' between the *I* and the *me*. For Lévi-Strauss, this dichotomy is an effect of the phenomenological paradox of 'self' and 'other'. In spite of his references to the unconscious as a mediator, and in spite of his contributions to the understanding of symbolic exchange, Lévi-Strauss remains beholden to the myth of individualism represented in the alienated ego and the theory of the social contract. This confusion of entity and relationship is rather clearly shown by his misinterpretation of Lacan's mirror-stage (1950: xx and note; Wilden, 1968a: 256). The mirror-stage is of no small import to an anthropologist involved in such a quest for personal lost time in the Other of the 'primitive' culture. The analogy with Proust is no literary metaphor: it describes precisely the Imaginary origins of Lévi-Strauss's quest – which he has had the engaging integrity to tell us about (Lévi-Strauss, 1955). But to confuse Lévi-Strauss's personality with his representative function in the discourse of science is all too simple. When he himself refers to his "adolescent absolutism" (Scholte, 1968: 21), it is the fundamentalism of the discourse of science which is revealed.

5. *Philosophies of Opposition*

> Mythical thought always
> progresses from the awareness of
> oppositions towards their
> resolution.
> LÉVI-STRAUSS

No one would seek to deny the validity of yes/no decisions in logic and in life, but the inveterate use of the term 'opposition' to describe all supposedly logical processes corresponds to the rationalist reversal of the logical typing of the analog and the digital which is described in Chapter VII and taken up again in Chapter XVI. After all, switches and relays do lack a certain sense of *finesse*; they are indeed either 'on' or 'off'. But even in the binary code itself, a sequence of digits like '011011100101010111' cannot LOGICALLY be described as a sequence of oppositions, because we have first to PUNCTUATE the system in order to find out what is supposedly opposed to what (cf. Hollier's graphic essay following Chapter VII). We cannot tell *a priori* which gaps are 'syntactic' and which are 'morphemic' (consider, for example, the 'codon' of DNA). Nor can we logically assume that the mere manifestation of a binary relation between '0' and '1' in such a message has anything more than a purely syntactic, rather than a semantic, value. Unfortunately, the confusion of levels in epistemology and linguistics is such that syntactics are constantly confused with semantics (cf. Chapter XII, note 1).

In Chapter VII, I tried to supply some of the communicational subtleties which are missing from the writings of those who confuse or equate such distinct but interrelated categories as absence, 'not', 'no', zero, minus-one, refusal, the 'negation of the negation', and relations of exclusion. I have sought to establish the principle that there are differences of logical typing between the supposed oppositions or identities in these erroneous equations. In language, at least, affirmation and 'not' are not in a relation of binary opposition, for 'not' involves a metacommunicative level of relationship. The establishment of this principle does not, of course, solve the paradoxes involved, nor do I believe any ultimate solutions to be possible. But I hope thus to encourage the application of a little more creativity, and a little less 'intelligence' to these problems.

If the word 'opposition' had a connotative or analog innocence, the problem I am discussing would not of course arise. I have suggested that, at least in communications and in semiotics, we ought to learn to cool the potential violence of our own rhetoric by asking ourselves whether by 'binary opposition' we do not in fact mean a 'digital decision', a 'binary relation' a 'binary difference', or a 'binary distinction', and so on.

In her two valuable papers on 'Philosophies of Opposition' (1970b), Joan Rayfield culls many examples of the illegitimate use of the term 'opposition' from the 'literature'. She begins by quoting a long passage from C. K. Ogden's *Opposition* (1932) in which every single analog and differential relationship of the human body is simplistically labelled an opposition. She remarks on the 'opposition' in Cassirer between 'I' and 'not-I'. Thus to describe the differential relation of the subject to the rest of the ecosystem without which he cannot survive (biologically) or exist (ontologically) not only makes us wonder whether the word 'opposition' has been correctly applied, but also to ask some pertinent questions about the status of the boundary implied by this use of 'not'. The fact that human beings in their analog goals constantly and consistently confuse logical types is small justification for elevating epistemological errors into the domain of ontology. Such a confusion of the logical with the ontological is in fact the most obvious characteristic of the 'schizophrenic discourse' (cf. Chapter II, Postcript).

What has to be shown, and what can be shown, is that it is the APPLICATION of the binary opposition that is in question, and that it is in its misapplications that it serves the unscientific ideological ends of the particular social discourse which speaks through the discourse of science. In other words, the question of the binary opposition is only a matter of individual values for him who speaks from within the ideology it may come to represent. From the critical and contextual perspective of these essays, it is no longer an ideological question, but a scientific question – in other words an epistemological one. It is a question of confusing 'the metaphor with what is meant', a confusion of levels of discourse.

Edmund Leach has recently attacked the tendency to wholesale use of the binary opposition. His is a perspective which locates the source of this concept in a LEARNED binary code with specific social effects (1968, quoted in Rayfield, 1970b, II: 18). He is well acquainted with Lévi-Strauss's demonstrations that the sacred elements of myth mediate between oppositions, and in his other works, Leach has sought to elaborate the function of ritual as a mediator. He has criticized Lévi-Strauss (1962) for setting up a binary and oppositional classification of the 'sacred' and the 'not sacred', suggesting that the categories of MORE or LESS sacred are equally important: "So also in social classifications it is not sufficient to have a discrimination me/it, we/they; we also need a graduated scale close/far, more like me/less like me" (Leach, 1964: 62).

But although this well-known article on categories deals with the continuous, the discrete, the 'more and less', and gaps between discrete elements, it does not employ the analog/digital distinction. It is of interest to note that the analog relations of 'more' and 'less' described in Leach's article are in fact presented as already digitalized into forms of "discrimination" which are presented as 'oppositions'. There is a reason for the implicit binarism behind Leach's attempt to introduce differential graduations. In 1962 – and I speak from the privileged position of one who has done exactly the same kind of thing (e.g., Wilden, 1970a) – Leach made the following programmatic statement:

> Binary oppositions are intrinsic to the process of human thought. Any description of the world must discriminate categories in the form 'p is what not-p is not'. An object is alive or not alive, and one could not formulate the concept 'alive' except as the converse of its partner 'dead'. So also human beings are male or not male, and persons of the opposite sex are either available as sexual partners or not available. Universally these are the most fundamentally important oppositions in all human experiences (quoted in Rayfield, 1970b: 2).

One wonders what happened to Saussure's distinction of 'what is' and 'what is not' as a differential relationship (Chapter VIII; Saussure, 1916a: 102, 109), or to Wallon's emphasis on the COUPLED opposition in the child (1945: 41), or to Freud's theory of bisexuality, or to symbolic exchange corresponding to requirements which are not based simply on genital sexuality. What Leach does here is first to confuse the relation of exclusion and the function of 'not', and secondly, implicitly to lay all the stress of the (negative) prohibition of incest on BIOLOGICAL differences, when it is surely its positive and CULTURAL function which should be most of interest to an anthropologist. This passage is an excellent example of the coalescence of levels of organization criticized in Chapter VIII. But more significant, it presents the conscious and manifest rationalizations of a man (Leach) or a supposed group of men (the 'primitives') as epistemology or as science.

The quick-step from level to level in this statement from Leach is an example of what Kenneth Burke called the 'essentializing strategy" (1941: 228). As it turns out, we cannot even get from the p to the not-p of the first sentence without having already made an illegitimate shortcut, a jump over a boundary between logical types. Whereas in logic the algebraic metaphor p is indeed of the same logical type as not-p, and can be called an opposition, the same is not true for most of the real metaphors that can be substituted for this equation. A simple example would be 'figure' and 'ground'. The 'figure' is certainly 'not the ground'. But in no useful sense can we say that the figure is 'opposed' to the ground when we know (1) that the figure is simply made distinct from the ground, and (2) that the figure implies a metacommunication about the ground because it introduces a PUNCTUA-TION into the ground, which is not a 'syntactic' part of the ground (or of the figure) itself. It is a punctuation which establishes a LEVEL of logical typing. I have already mentioned the illegitimate punctuation in the theory of logical types itself. The theory requires us to establish a permitted relation of equivalent logical types. The only way this rule can be properly obeyed is by disobeying it at a different level: that of establishing a boundary between types of types, that of setting off the relation of equivalence (as figure) from its background (as ground) (Bateson, 1955; Chapter VII). And this is not simply something providing food for thought – although I obviously wish people would stop forgetting about it. It is a representation of the unavoidable DISCORDANCE between all maps and all territories which, in Lacan's theory, provides for the dynamic constitution of the subject's world through the mirror-stage. Just as we find ourselves tripping over ourselves in our attempt to short-cut levels of logical typing by trying to reduce their multidimensional phase-space to a single linear, dimension, so the child finds himself falling over himself in his attempt to obey the equivalent paradoxical injunctions in the Imaginary (Chapter XVII).

Hegel – who nevertheless confuses 'minus' and 'not' – has already provided us with a preliminary form of the critique of the supposed opposition between p and not-p (1830: 90–3: #116–20):

> If 'A' must be either '+A' or '−A', then the third term is already expressed: 'A' which is NEITHER '+' NOR '−', and which is posited as well as '+A' and '−A'.

> . . . The emptiness of the opposition of so-called contradictory notions is perfectly described in the somewhat grandiose expression of a 'universal law'. This is the law that to EACH thing there refers ONE, and not another, of all the predicates which are thus opposed to it. The consequence is that the mind must therefore be either 'white' or 'not-white', either 'yellow' or 'not-yellow', and so on *ad infinitum*.

According to Hegel, these abstract, either/or relations are the product of the "understanding" (i.e., of illegitimate abstraction from sensuous experience). They are not to be found either in nature or in the mind (reason). (Cf. also Jordan, 1967: 171–5, and Engels, 1885: 27–9.)

Leach unfortunately emphasizes a supposed opposition of entities, where in fact we see no more than differences, distinctions, and relation. (Cf. Ruwet's citations from Hjelmslev and Jakobson, and his remarks on the 'opposition' of terms of different logical types, 1963: 570.) Because this binarism is described as a fundamental process of human thought, we find our deepest social prejudices confirmed in it. We do not discover anything about the complex analog and digital process of the human brain (von Neumann, 1951, 1958), or about the cooperative control processes of the natural ecosystem (Pask, 1962: 242; Shepard and McKinley, eds., 1969), or about the subtle control of difference and opposition in some non-western cultures (e.g., Rappaport, 1968). No matter what Leach intends, what he says is that all human thought, all human relationship, and all human experience are founded, in the last analysis, on opposition – which is precisely what the social ideology of the survival of the fittest also says.

Moreover, it can be no accident that the 'opposition' he most stresses in this passage is that supposed to exist between the biological male and the biological female (cf. Chapter X). In other words, he takes a real biological relation of difference and grafts onto it the social opposition of BODY-IMAGES (Chapter VIII). Consequently, his formulation of the question of the availability of sexual partners coalesces together or short-circuits a zoological question (reproduction), a physical question (matter–energy), a question of communication and exchange (information), a psychological question (the body-image), and a human question (the person). Outside of electrical wiring, all such shortcircuits derive from the Imaginary.

6. A Note on Genetic Difference

Derrida's attack on binary oppositions in what he calls the "congenital phonologism" of our time leads us to consider seriously the function of writing and the trace (Chapter XIII). The word 'opposition' tends to disappear as a result, to be replaced by distinction and difference. But the transformation of labels is not enough.

One can find innumerable instances of the use of the term 'difference' in such a way as to conceal an ideological commitment to social oppositions imposed from the top down. The most obvious example occurs in the current use of the real genetic differences between human beings, but in a linear, quantitative, and one-dimensional fashion which projects the liberal assumption of egalitarianism, away from the real differences between classes and races into an assumed egalitarianism of the environment. Both Ernst

Mayr (1963: 653–62) – somewhat ineptly[1] – and Jensen (1969) – rather subtly – assume variation in people (correctly) and uniformity in the environment (incorrectly). By reducing all QUALITATIVE differences to a quantitative measure of 'performance' in a society tending towards its own destruction, they effectively attempt to reduce real political questions about the quality of life in the United States to a new form of original sin (the inherent quantity of 'giftedness to perform').

The subtlety of Jensen's assumption of uniformity and homogeneity is such that he at first appears to be accounting for environmental differences. But what his work carefully and deliberately ignores is the positive feedback effect of power, economic status, and class in a system of institutionalized racism, where the psychological costs of conformity to its values produce fleeting-improvised people and Uncle Toms of all hues. As P. E. Vernon pointed out (quoted in Bernstein, 1958: 222), the influence of the environment is cumulative (i.e., multiplicative rather than additive). The panoply of scientific rigor masks the real context – physical, social, and economic – of the relationship between 'tester' and 'testee', mediated as it is by unspoken white values. Not only do the psychometric tests themselves reinforce the enforcement of 'disciplined performance' for its own sake, and consequently expel creativity and originality from the domain of 'science', but they also depend for their validity on concealing the reasons for and the results of attempted refusals to perform or conform in many 'accepted' ways by large numbers of people, especially from amongst the minorities and the poor in general. IQ tests, 'achievement' tests, and 'culture-free' tests which test tests or which test people's willingness to take tests are all in essence one-dimensional measures of class-conditioned good manners, complicated by the whole gamut of contextual inputs from the cultural past, present, and future which 'objective' academic psychology necessarily rules out of order by the very design of its 'experiments'. When – if ever – such tests can also measure the multidimensional effects of the burning hatred of the oppressed – a hatred which is inevitably double-bound, often almost entirely unconscious, and usually directed away from the real enemy for reasons of personal security – their hatred for anything that smacks of (white) 'science', (honky) 'objectivity', (liberal) 'education', and every other form of crackerjack; then we may have something of positive value to human beings. Until such a time, however, these and all similar

---

[1] Mayr's complaint (p. 661) that the "genetically gifted" pay high taxes and have to spend too much money to send their children to private schools (and to Harvard?) is not only a grotesque example of the misuse of 'science'. It ignores the fact that, proportionate to income, those near the bottom of the economic 'ladder' pay higher taxes than anyone else. Today genetics, tomorrow the world?

measures of the effectiveness of the performance principle will remain the vehicle of the oppressive values of our society.

But the most significant question of all raised by Jensen's work – a question to which I shall return in detail at another time and place – is that of the SOCIOECONOMIC FUNCTION of Jensen's discourse. Why was this genetic question asked in the first place, and why at this time? Why did the 'genetic question' suddenly become 'scientific' again, and why is it now protected by 'academic freedom' when it was not so protected before?

It is pretty much self-evident that Jensen's question could be asked ONLY at a time when it is immediately obvious to all that the very 'American way of life' which the educational tests measure has all but broken down. The situation has all the marks of the subtle and unspoken revenge of the liberal establishment, which offered 'equality' to all (down South) and (necessarily) failed to deliver the goods, but which still feels like a gift horse which has been kicked in the mouth. By directing the scientific discourse towards the supposedly 'biological' values of genetics and adaptation under 'pure' competition, the question of linear genetic difference does not simply serve to confirm and justify the exploitative and paranoid concerns of the white middle class, who project their own alienation onto the 'others'. It also directs the discourse of science away from any consideration of the POLITICAL questions of quality and multidimensionality (as distinct from the linearity of 'pluralism') in American society.

The fundamental role of Jensen's work as propaganda is to short-circuit any real attempts to direct questions at the ANTI-BIOLOGICAL and ANTI-HUMAN characteristics of our social environment and of our whole conception of intelligence. This is a question which requires more detailed analysis than I can give here, but it is clear that the fundamental error is to confuse biological 'intelligence' – in the sense of increased flexibility, semiotic freedom, and adaptivity in an essentially homogeneous environment – with social 'intelligence' ('mental ability', 'cognitive capacity', and so on). Unlike biological intelligence, social 'intelligence' in our culture is simply a measure of the ability to conform to the rigid and inflexible norms of a heterogeneous social environment, the norms by which we measure 'progress', 'achievement', 'superiority', and 'making it'. Thus Jensen's work, by its very demand for an answer, has the effect of directing scientific inquiry away from any questioning of the very socioeconomic values against which the psychometrics of genetic 'giftedness' are measured. The whole of western culture is so enslaved to the concept of intelligence as a form of economic competition – on the part of both 'intellectuals' and 'anti-intellectuals' at all levels – that questions about whether the average IQ of the population is increasing or decreasing can actually appear to have relevance for human beings. The fact that the 'intelligence' of the 'intellectual' or the 'stockbroker' is probably a measure of self-alienation and counter-adaptivity – like the vaunted verbalism used by men against women – becomes completely obscured.

Jensen and Mayr succeed in imposing a code on their critics in the scientific discourse to which those critics cannot effectively reply without putting science – and the society it represents – in question. Given the socioeconomic constraints on the maintenance of their status as 'men of science', given their own psychosocial vested interests, and given the control of science by those who provide the funds for research, this they can rarely, if ever, afford to do (e.g., Bodmer and Cavalli-Sforza, 1970). Gunnar Myrdal effectively puts his finger on this question – even though in the text from which the following quotation is taken, he regrettably manifests his own bias by continuing to talk about the "Negro problem" and "race riots" in the United States, instead of about the problem of white racism:

> Generally speaking, we can observe that the scientists in any particular institutional and political setting move as a flock, reserving their controversies and particular originalities for matters that do not call in question the fundamental system of biases they share (1967: 53).

Jensen's careful articulation of academic and social values may be bad science – if indeed 'science' has any meaning at all – but in relation to the vested interests of the economic and intellectual elite he represents, his work is damned good politics.[2]

---

[2] According to newspaper reports at the time of going to press, recent work of R. Heber and Howard Garber at the University of Wisconsin has refuted Jensen's position. Newborn black children raised in a special environment of stimulation develop markedly higher IQs than those of a control group raised at home. Significant as such studies may be, they have however the unfortunate effect of reinforcing the very standards – the quantitative measure of performance represented by the IQ – which it should be the task of science to put in question. The creation of an artificially homogeneous environment for these children immediately raises two questions: (1) What are the values represented by the 'strategy of the inquirer' in the creation of that environment? (2) What will be the effect on the children when they discover the real nature of their environment? Will they have sold their birthright for a mess of pottage?

7. *Postscript*

> Ignorance, like knowledge,
> is purposefully directed.
> GUNNAR MYRDAL

A year after writing these lines on Jensen and Mayr, I was presented with a copy of a new Penguin book dedicated to the refutation of Galton, Burt, Jensen, Eysenck, and Shockley (Richardson and Spears, eds., 1972). Of course, Jensen's views will survive in the public consciousness in spite of all refutations, but the commentators in this most useful volume demolish the quackery of psychometrics and demonstrate its political and ideological function pretty effectively.[3]

Nevertheless, I was dismayed to perceive between the lines of many of the articles in this book the same old set of uncritical and elitist assumptions about intelligence and culture that allowed Jensen to put forward his thesis in the first place – as well as anti-American intellectual snobbery (p. 19). Instead of an attempt to understand why racism, in one form or another, seems to be a structural necessity in state and private capitalism, one finds the standard clichés about "getting people to use their brains", "raising intelligence", "chronically poor race relations" (note the assumption of symmetry), "assimilation into the mainstream", the implicit correlation of "creativity" with "productivity", and so on. This is the kind of book that, although it performs the necessary function of making steps in the right direction, ends up by negating its positive value because of the profound – and class-conditioned – ambivalence of many of its contributors towards their subject. It is in effect the kind of 'solution' to a problem that, by its very timidity, on the one hand, and by its implicit acceptance of socially conditioned academic or educational valuations, on the other, ends up by becoming part of the problem itself.

This is particularly evident in the editors' concluding essay. Whereas the

---

[3] Peter Watson deals with the positive feedback effects of discrimination (pp. 56–67); John Hambley explains the difference between biological and social 'genetics' and between causality and constraint, as well as attacking paternalism and the assumption of the homogeneous environment (pp. 114–27); Donald Swift attacks linearity (pp. 147–66). Other contributors provide a most useful historical background, point out the commitment of psychometrics to propaganda in favor of a changeless social order, the oppressive function of most psycho-therapy and "meritocratic" education, the falsity of Jensen's comparison between the IQ of American Indians (in one historical and social context of deprivation and discrimination) and that of American blacks (in a different historical and social environment), the biological effects of the oppressive social order, and so on.

editors do seek – with the best of intentions – to demonstrate the direct correlation between race and class origin (but not sex) and subsequent educational opportunity and social status in western societies – a fact that cannot be too often emphasized – the book nevertheless ends with precisely the ideological rationalization of the 'objectivity' of science that supports the socioeconomic *status quo*. Not only are we offered Piaget as a remedy for Jensen, but we are told that since prescriptions for the solution of social problems "involve questions of evaluation of human worth and the division of goods between individuals", there are "ethical, political and moral judgements which have no place in science, at least as currently conceived". "Socially responsible science" must maintain this distinction, even if there is "doubt" about the possibilities of a "value-free psychology".

As a result of this politic judgment by the editors, and as the result of their abdication of the human responsibility of the scientist – as well as of their refusal (as I predicted) to put the ideological function of the 'neutrality' of science in question – the editors blunder along into their last two sentences. Here they fall headlong into the trap laid for them by Jensen and his 'interventionist' use of social science (which has in fact always been the rallying cry of the liberal 'new dealers' in science):

> Even if psychologists were able to demonstrate the unlikely phenomenon that a socially defined group of people had quite different COGNITIVE capacities from THE REST OF US, this could not on its own provide a reason for treating them in a special way. That decision rests with the whole of society (pp. 194–5, my emphasis).

One asks: What is meant by "cognitive" capacities? Why are people "treated differently" in actual life, and who decides on the treatment? What is "the whole of society"? Does that "whole" include the people who are "treated differently" now, or who may or may not be treated differently in the future? Why does the book end – as it begins (p. 16) – with the "wholly unlikely example" of an "us" and a "them" that feeds into the very prejudices the book is supposedly refuting? But above all: Who is "us"?

The anomaly of it all is that whereas Jensen *et al.* have at least enough of the courage of their convictions to come out clearly in support of a certain socioeconomic order, with the result that the enemy is clearly defined, the sort of flabby Uncle Tomism expressed in the conclusion quoted leaves us with nothing more than another symptomatic statement of the human bankruptcy of the 'social democrat' so vigorously attacked by Sartre (cf. Introduction). As the blacks discovered from their experience with well-intentioned whites during the civil rights movement of the sixties in the United States, with friends like that, you don't need enemies.

Chapter XV

Language and Communication

Not the binary form, but UNITY is the
ultimate residual. . . . Binary analysis is
illuminating, but if erected into an absolute and
universal metaphysics, instead of being used
heuristically, it becomes numerology and fashion,
not science.
WORSLEY (1967)[1]

In current French thinking, a somewhat tendentious opposition is sometimes set up between 'language' and 'communication'. It seems that in
France the extent of the new and fruitful understanding of the function of
speech and language is unfortunately matched by the extent to which
communication is misconstrued in some circles there. The concept of communication is also commonly misunderstood in America, but here the
misunderstanding is not so much between language and communication as
between 'communication' and 'stimulus–response–reinforcement', that is
to say, between the theory of communication and the theory of systems, on
the one hand, and the more traditional energy-oriented 'behaviorism' (in
the classic sense), on the other.

An earnest young student of academic psychology told me the other day,
for example, that light-seeking organisms do not communicate. What she
meant, of course, is that they don't 'talk' to each other, they don't 'understand' each other. I pointed out that the behavior of tropismic organisms is
indeed communication: there is a sender and a receiver, a message, a code,
and a goal. It is rudimentary communication and at a very low level of
organization, of course, but it is communication nevertheless.

[1] Note Worsley's use of Vygotsky's 1932 critique of Piaget in this article.

1. *The Goalseeking System and the Law of Absence*

The behavior of these organisms corresponds, at another level of organization, to Lacan's conception of the discourse as "filling up a lack" – filling up a breach or a break – in the circuit of communication. Without attempting to reduce one level to another, we can point to the distinguishing feature of communication, which is shared by language: that of directiveness, intention, or goal. What probably distinguishes human communication, of which language is an integral part, from all other levels of communication, however – especially in the sense that is far removed or displaced from self-evident or strictly biological survival value – is that the primary goal of human communication appears to be the INVENTION OF GOALS. In other words, the goal of human goalseeking is the process of creating goals; or, in a Lacanian terminology, the primary function of the lack is the articulation of lacks, whether they be effectively Symbolic or effectively Imaginary.

Sartre has said that "it is by the lack that human reality comes into the world" (1943: 392). We must now retranslate this to say that it is the elevation of the lack (the goal) from simple absence, which is analog, to NEGATED PRESENCE, which must be digital, which distinguishes human communication (project, 'symbolizing') from animal communication. In spite of a certain ambiguity amongst animals that play, we can say that lack is at the level of need in animals – the domain of the analog continuum of presence and absence – whereas for the human world it emerges at the level of demand, controlled by desire. It is in this sense that we can also say that the distinction between need and demand, both in ontogeny and in phylogeny, concerns the emergent passage of lack from the level of the message (gratification) to that of the code (desire). Need can be fulfilled, desire cannot. In the human world of discourse, one can choose any number of metaphoric substitutes for the primordial lack or for its supposed fulfillment. The theory of penis-envy is such a metaphor, and clearly reveals its ideological foundations. Any number of messages can be constructed around and with the lack, which is the neutral mediator in the system, and thus pregnant with a symbolic violence (Marin, 1971). But no matter how one may try to exorcise the lack from the message, it cannot be exorcised from the code.

2. *Communication and the Impossible Dialogue*

> In mathematics and logic,
> process and result are
> equivalent.
> WITTGENSTEIN (1937–44: #82)

If we look at the supposed opposition between language and communication at another level, I recall the literary critic who, in response to the statement that "all behavior is communication", replied that the dream is not a communication. The misunderstanding involved concerns the difference between the everyday and the critical or scientific sense of the labels 'language' and 'communication'. This is so much so, in fact, that more often than not those who make an opposition between the terms are usually using one of them to include the other. On the one hand, one hears talk about the 'language' of film and the 'language' of the bees, for example (the first of which belongs to what might be called 'iconosemiotics' and the second, to 'zoosemiotics'). On the other, one hears much about the 'need for more communication', the 'need for dialogue'. In this sense 'communication' is simply being used as a substitute for 'understanding', and the error involved in the assumption that monologues are really possible, is that communication requires an other, a 'species-specific' and tangible or 'real' receiver. The encounter-group therapist blissfully announces: "Ah, now we are communicating", by which he means that certain analog agreements have been reached. The alienated college student complains: "I can't communicate with my father", when, of course, his difficulty is that he can't STOP communicating with his father. He can't stop his repeated demands for love, and in any case, since in a communications system nothing never happens, it is impossible for any living organism not to communicate.

It never ceases to surprise me at what an uncritical and unscientific level the debate about communication is sometimes maintained. Obviously the critical use of the term 'language' ('natural language') should be confined to those systems of communication displaying a set of characteristics which are not met with together in any other system of codes and messages, characteristics such as double articulation, selection and combination of digital components, binary distinctions and oppositions, signifiers in the proper sense, signification as distinct from meaning, tense, and above all, syntactic negation. Neither speech, nor language, nor communication, in the properly critical sense, has anything *per se* to do with understanding in the everyday sense. No communicational or linguistic message is ever 'misunderstood' or 'understood' as such; if it is heard, read, or felt, it is simply received. The implication of complete understanding or true dialogue in the common-sense use of the word communication is an Imaginary illusion of the reduction of difference to identity, and it has nothing to do with the theory of communication. The implication of total understanding between sender and receiver may almost be possible for simple organisms like the planaria, for once a certain threshold of information is received (i.e., once a certain level of noise in the environment is decided to be information), the little worm is in complete accord with the source and has no doubts about his own intentions. (He will oscillate nevertheless.) In any highly complex system, however, the function of levels and thresholds, the function of unavoidable error, and that of unpredictable contextual relations, are such that no message of any complexity can be completely and unambiguously understood at all times and in all places. And when the relationship is that between subjects and signifiers in the human world, no true dialogue is possible. The really important aspect of this last point is that a full dialogue is not possible because such a situation has no survival value. It would amount to an overload of information and thus to death. So much for the romantic, utopian illusions of the *parole pleine*.

3. *Bioenergetic Thinking and Rationalism*

What one first notices about some structuralist (rather than structural) approaches to the problem of language and communication, on the one hand, and the polemical exposition of the Lacanian 'linguistic' position, on the other, is a tendency to misconstrue the real dimensions of the problem, complemented by a precious literary style which buries the problem itself. One can quickly point to a number of general methodological and epistemological inadequacies in the structuralist and Lacanian schools. Some of these defects result from the structuralist or linguistic approach itself and are inherent in any structural theory not complemented by an ecosystemic perspective. But in general these defects are defects because of the imperialism of the theory and the scientism of many of its adherents. By claiming too much, and as a result of a certain parochialism, the structuralist and the Lacanian programmes reveal themselves as inadequate in the following ways:

1 There is a tendency to be mesmerized by language and linguistics (cf. Derrida's critique, Chapter XVI), exaggerated by the tendency of younger writers to deal only with fashionable authorities.
2 There is a general lack of willingness to deal adequately with context

and levels of context, especially as regards the sociobiological context and the material conditions of men and women.

3 The universality of feedback, and the difference between negative and positive feedback, are misunderstood or ignored.

4 The universality of overdetermination and multifinality – as well as that of other apparently linguistic processes – in communications systems is not understood.

5 There is a tendency to write from the interior of a movement which is ideologically and culturally ethnocentric – paternalistic in its references to the 'primitive' – and phallocentric. (There is a lack of global context.)

6 The movement tends to refuse history in any real sense of the term and thus to confuse evolution with development or learning. (There is a lack of a temporal context.)

7 One finds a lack of a dialectical or morphogenic conception of levels of organization in diachrony, a lack which is complemented by a restricted conception of the hierarchy of synchronic levels. (Change is thus reduced to maturation, or to homeogenesis and homeorhesis.)

8 The movement tends to treat most analog communication as if it were digital.

9 The relative logical typing of analog and digital communication is inverted.

10 There is little conception of the complexity of levels of logical typing and levels of coding and communication.

11 As a result of (9) and (10), 'negation' remains a catch-all for absence, zero, minus, 'off', *Auhebung*, *Verneinung*, and sometimes implicitly for *Verwerfung* and *Verleugnung* also. Similarly, 'language' becomes the catch-all for linguistics, communication, and symbolism, as well as for signal, sign, and signifier, or symbol.

12 Partly reflected in the privileged position accorded to the so-called binary opposition, and like a metaphor of all the inadequacies already mentioned, the movement tends to think in mechanical, statistical, probabilistic (in the 'flat' sense), or energy–entity terms. This is partly the result of its emphasis on invariant structural relations. Thus the movement still tends to think in the metaphors of the bioenergetic, closed-system epistemology, rather than in communicational, open-system terms. Some writers, for example, avoid terms like 'cause' and 'instinct', only to replace them with other covert metaphors of lineal causality.

13 These faults result in (and are the result of) a general refusal of noise, of the trace, and of the event.

14 Many writers still depend upon a set of uncritical ideas about information, cybernetics, learning, adaptation, behavior, evolution, goalseeking, and the science of biology.

But the most important question is one which does not seem to be properly posed at all: the question of the relationship between linguistics and semiotics, which I take up again further on. One can focus on this problem as follows: it is self-evident that language has evolved from communication and exchange in nature, and that it cannot be separated entirely from these natural, non-cultural, processes. It is evident also that every emergence of a new level of semiotic freedom must necessarily change the relations of logical typing anterior to such an event. But if this statement can be applied without any difficulty to the question of the child's learning of language (Chapter VI), it becomes thoroughly paradoxical when we talk about evolution, for without language we could not conceive of logical typing. It has to be pointed out, therefore, that it is not the fact of this emergence, but our CONSCIOUSNESS of the evolutionary emergence of language, which changes these relationships. This consciousness (which may in fact be 'unconscious') applies therefore, on the one hand, to reality (to the child), and, on the other, to the theory (to the 'observer').

This point has an important consequence for understanding the relationship between linguistics and semiotics. If the researcher is interested in zoosemiotics, he will tend to maintain the paradoxical frontier between animal and human communication by uncovering the resemblances between the two fields of communication. If his interest is mainly in language, he will maintain the same frontier by uncovering the differences between the two. The first will tend to make general references to the purely human area of what he will call the 'symbol' (i.e., the signifier) and go on to reduce language to communication, leaving aside the 'ambiguity' and the 'structuring function' of language. The second, for his part, will make equally general references to what I have called analog communication, but he will tend to confer on it a linguistic function, leaving out of account the equally structuring – but more clearly sociobiological – function of communication and exchange.

But semiotics in the proper sense is not restricted to an animal as opposed to a human point of view, nor to a cultural as opposed to a natural perspective, nor to a view which is either intraorganismic or interorganismic. Semiotics has as its theoretical task the understanding of all exchanges of signs, whatever may be their nature or their function.

The researcher who is concerned with that aspect of the consciousness of the emergence of language which is represented by the child who learns or exemplifies language, will tend to make language the measure of all things. He will be right. The researcher who is concerned with natural evolution rather than with learning as such will also be right in viewing this consciousness in quite another way. The first will say that language structures (human) communications, the second, that communicational processes structure language. But it is in opposing each other that these two points of view will reveal their commitment to a single bias: the bias of RATIONALISM.

In this sense, rationalism, which derives from the bioenergetic epistemology, forgets that there is a third point of view, that of semiotics, which goes entirely beyond such an opposition. From the semiotic perspective outlined in this book, the essential question of defining the context in which and the level at which one speaks cannot not be addressed. From this perspective, it must surely be understood in what sense the systemic function of communication is primary, on the one hand, and in what sense language structures and organizes that function at the human level, on the other. The feedback relationship between language as structuring and as structured, and between communication as structuring and structured, will become evident – as will the fact that one cannot hope to understand either the one or the other by speaking only from the viewpoint of (either) one or the other. The problematic is an epistemological one, but involves vested interest. It is fundamentally a problem of values. Whatever it may be called, only a critical point of view which tries to escape the bias of rationalism and to reduce its vested interest to a set of values concerned with the long-range survival of real men and women can hope to escape this false dichotomy between language and communication. In the final analysis, this dichotomy is of course only one more version of the Imaginary opposition between 'organism' and 'environment'.

These inadequacies, which are not of course restricted to French thinking or to one area of French thought, are multiplied in some circles by an entirely unjustified ideological mythification of psychoanalytical therapy, whose position in the culture continues to remain essentially supportive of the *status quo*. In other words, the values of psychoanalytical therapy tend to be drawn from the interior of a historically (over)determined culture, and then promoted to a theoretical universality, rather than remaining as values critical of ALL culture.

In Lacan and amongst many of his disciples, these inadequacies give rise to an interesting paradox. In a doctrine which seeks to expose the reifications of the Symbolic by the Imaginary and to demonstrate the controlling power of discourse, it is altogether curious to find the exposition of the theory caught up by the reification of words, on the one hand, and by the controlling power of the forbidden or absent words, on the other. Just as certain names which once were mentioned with some pride by the École freudienne can no longer be mentioned (for fear of deviationism), so certain words, such as 'metalanguage', 'biology', and 'communication', may be invested with entity-like significations, and practically outlawed from the discourse.

The process is the same as that found in almost all originally revolutionary or radical organizations or cliques (political or not). As the group becomes established, the critical faculties of the individual members tend to enter a process of increasing atrophy: the doctrine no longer remains an attack on illusion and resistance, it becomes an illusion and a resistance in itself. There is an increasing tendency to identify positions with words and slogans, and thus to fall into a specular identification with the RHETORIC of the group. One hesitates to USE a certain word or to LOOK LIKE the embodiment of a forbidden or deprecated word, for fear of being 'fingered' by the others. The groups that maintain their original integrity are those which know how to transcend or how to metacommunicate about the facile oppositions they once depended on, and which their own actions necessarily render problematical. Most often, however, the attractiveness and protective pseudo-security of the Imaginary is such that the critical inquiry becomes dogmatism, the radicals of one generation become the reactionaries of the next.

4. Communication and Biology

Since the opposition between language, behavior, and communication is not self-evident, but rather a position taken by certain schools of thought, we should look at a specific example. Thus, O. Mannoni, in his *Freud* – a remarkable distillation of the 'truth' of Freud, an unparalleled work of analysis and synthesis (1971) – makes the following statement in the Afterword to the American translation (p. 178):

> [Winnicott] is the inventor of the concept of the transitional object, which is obviously the exact though silent equivalent of the *da* of the child Freud observed. . . . The transitional object is already part of a symbolism and almost a language, a fact which escapes those who confound language and communication.

If the transitional object is part of a symbolism which is ALMOST, but not quite, a language, then what is that symbolism? Is it energy? or matter? a set of 'objects'? a set of images? Is it real? Is it localizable? The transitional object is none of these things because it can only be part of a system of communication. In the system in which it is being used, this object is not an object, it is the marker of a message. Its function is already differentiated from the lower level of organization represented by its biological source, its matter–energy. It is information in the technical sense, information used by one of the terminals of the message-in-circuit in the interests of the work to be done (here: adaptation in the sense of learning or maturation, not in the sense of evolution). Like all information, it is a non-localizable difference; it is a difference which has been chosen to be different from all other differences. The transitional object is the constitution of information out of NOISE; it will be integrated into the system as TRACE. It is thus invested with a particular meaning, a signification, by the receiver in the system (and by the sender too, but at another level). As a primordial Imaginary digitalization, it is a sign (a symbol in the Saussurean sense of its rudimentary analog connection with its origin) which has been chosen to emerge from the infinite multiplicity of signals transmitted by the other. It is thus ready to emerge at another level, in a more complex context. It is ready to be re-represented, through the equivalent of the child's *Da!*, as a signifier in a discourse. At this higher level, it will no longer be a communication about the relation between presence and absence, but a metacommunication about them, the negation of absence or the negation of presence, as the case may be.

All that Mannoni can mean by the last line of his statement is that some people confuse language and understanding, or language and speech. Thus when he says language, he really means communication, for all communication of any complexity is 'almost' a language, whereas language itself either is language or it is not. What then does 'communication', as the *inter-dit*, mean for Mannoni? It is only in following what he goes on to say about the biologizing tendencies of British psychoanalysis that we can understand what he is trying to criticize. His critique of the British is correct. But since the discovery of the genetic code of DNA – made possible by the more or less accidental and temporary coalescence of the generally separate structural and functional schools in biology – it is no longer possible to attack 'biologizing' without being very careful to define one's terms. What Mannoni is attacking here is not biological thinking, but bioenergetic thinking. Thus, on the one hand, he seeks to differentiate the Symbolic from the Real (critique of bioenergetics); on the other, he seeks to differentiate it from the Imaginary (critique of 'understanding').

He is trying to distinguish the domain of the Symbolic from that of gratification and the instinct. But the Lacanian school is not itself free from the residues of bioenergetic and Newtonian thought. The promotion of 'language' as an escape from 'behavior' turns out in some instances to be a defense of the pulsion, one step removed from the instinct. As in much current thinking in France – to say nothing of the United States – the closed-system concepts of attraction and repulsion, of equilibrium and, in Lacan's words, "the field of forces of desire" (1966: 319), point to the surreptitious energetic model still lying behind many supposedly new ideas.

The bioenergetic perspective reduces information either to matter–energy or to the everyday sense of the term (cf. Lacan, 1966: 299). Such a confusion involves exactly the same epistemological error as confusing Imaginary relations and Symbolic relations. When the epistemology of opposition and identity between entities is not sufficiently distinguished from the epistemology of the relation, the old bioenergetic forces tend to reappear, if under new names. To conceive of desire as project is the essential of the non-mechanistic cybernetic viewpoint, for example, but if behind the definition of desire as metonymy there lurks, the drive, the *pulsion*, or the force, then the perspective remains essentially lineal, energy-bound, and causal. Open systems – goalseeking and goal-changing systems, communications systems – are not ruled by causality except at the level of the closed system which supports them and from which they draw their energy. Their very overdetermination – multifinality, equifinality – rules out causal explanation. It is rather in the sense of POSSIBILITIES or of *potentia* (in the Aristotelian sense) in relation to an environment that they must be explained. Obviously, however, so long as it is assumed implicitly that biological systems are deterministic and that overdetermination ('ambiguity') is confined to language – a point of view which is itself a residue of Newtonian thinking among non-biologists – communication will not be understood.

Let us take the most striking example of the work of teleonomy in biology: that of DNA. DNA is the molecular coding of a set of instructions for the growth of a certain living system of cells. But these instructions do not CAUSE growth any more than the directions of a cakemix cause the mix to become a cake. They do not cause growth, they control its possibilities. In other words, the instructions of DNA CONSTRAIN or limit growth. (All growth is positive feedback – the amplification of deviations – and, without negative feedback control, all growth would be cancerous, leading to destruction.) But it is not only the instructions which constrain growth; so does the environment in which they operate. If DNA were all there were to the 'blueprint' of the cell, then, since all cells in an organism contain the same genetic instructions, no differentiation or division of labor in the cell would ever occur. Differentiation is the product of inhibitors: the constraints of the feedback relationship to the environment in which the messengers carrying the instructions (RNA) find themselves.[2] Thus the articulation of the genetic code – which we know to be in some way double, like language, and punctuated, like writing – depends upon processes of combination-in-context (contiguity) and substitution-by-selection (similarity). Like language, also, it is a combined analog and digital process. Like language, it is not ruled by causality, but by goalseeking and constraint. It is not ruled by what is or what was so much as by what is not, by what may be.

But DNA is not 'almost' a language. It is not a language at all. Unlike language – and this difference is more important than all the resemblances – the genetic code is an 'original' system of writing. It is a redundant system of communication and is protected against noise, but it is the product of such a vast span of time that, linked to natural selection (negative feedback) which prevents random variation from resulting in total chaos, the code reveals itself in retrospect to be sensitive to mutation, open to enduring errors and to changes in level of complexity.

5. *Extension of the Critique*

Whereas Lévi-Strauss and most contemporary French thinkers use language as a catch-all for language, communication, and exchange, the English-speaking person usually separates all these forms of relationship in a positivistic or behavioristic way.

To take a French example first: In discussing whether film (*cinéma*) should be described as *langue* or *langage*, Christian Metz concludes that it is really neither, but rather a "partial" system of communication (1968: 39–93). However, the lack of an adequate methodology of communication and the trace in this article (originally published in 1964), needlessly complicates his attempt to divide and organize the "semic domain" (p. 47, note 5). One could point out that the silent cinema, for example, represents a classic instance of an iconic or analog BIOGRAPH.[3] The biograph employs

[2] According to Whyte (1965), this conception of 'internal selection' – which I arrived at through the purely logical implications of regarding natural systems as cooperative ecosystems of communication consisting of levels and subsystems – is a wholly new idea in evolutionary theory. But Whyte remains beholden to the idea of 'external' (Darwinian) selection as purely competitive: ". . . External selection is comparative, statistical, and competitive; internal selection is intrinsic, singular, and coordinative. . . . Only confusion can arise from treating together the competition of free individuals and the harmonious cooperation of the ordered parts of a unit" (p. 58).

[3] Some of the names applied to the new invention and to the early film companies are: Vitascope, Mutoscope, Biograph, Vitagraph, Pathé Exchange, Kinetograph. Metz almost comes to define the film as primarily analog, textual, communication: "As a rich message whose code is weak, as a rich text with a weak system

a first-level digitalization of the analog in its images, which it then reconstitutes at another level of continuity and discontinuity. It also involves a second-level digitalization in the written captions which mark a special type of boundary between the image-units. The film in general is not only articulated on continuity and discontinuity in the traditional sense; it is also articulated on frames, contexts, communications, and metacommunications. Moreover, the addition of the sound-track does not create a 'talking picture' in any proper sense. The 'pictures' already communicate. The sound-track adds another essentially analog dimension, that of music, and another analog/digital dimension, that of speech. But if any particular movie actually TALKS to us in such a way that we find ourselves LISTENING to it, then it has left the domain of film: it has become a book (Bergman: 1960: 142-6).

Metz's argument is primarily that the film does not conform to Martinet's linguistic criterion of the double articulation. On p. 89, he restates the question posed by Martinet about the trace and the discrete unit, a question which is the axis of Metz's entire problematic. But, because it assumes that the message is anterior to the written code, the question is still the wrong question. It is posed in logocentric terms which effectively preclude any useful answer:

> . . . Can there be a "perfect ideographic system", a "language which is NO LONGER spoken but which is still written", a system in which the "units of content are not separate from the units of expression" – whereas the double articulation divides the discourse into units of expression [phonemes] which have no corresponding content? (my emphasis).

In essence, then, Metz's entire argument is already compromised by the implicit primacy of linguistics in his perspective. Once he has enclosed his discussion in the terms of a distinction between expression and communication, there is no way out. This he does by the argument on p. 79 that the film is not a *langue* because it does not match the characteristics which are (supposedly) specific to the "linguistic fact":

> A particular language is a SYSTEM OF SIGNS destined for INTERCOMMUNICATION. But the film, because it is one of the arts . . . is a one-way communication. It is in fact much more a means of EXPRESSION than it is a means of communication.

[i.e., 'syntax'], the cinematographic image is first and foremost SPEECH." The following sentence completes this 'filmolinguistic' circuit: "Everything in the image is an assertion" (1968: 74). Later, however, he speaks of the 'more or less' of the film (p. 77).

To give a second example: Emmanuel Terray (1969) becomes trapped in the same difficulties in another way. Believing that "social forms" are closed systems, he attacks 'biologizing', 'communication', and the ecosystemic perspective of feedback and adaptation by confusing this perspective with British–American functionalism (e.g., Leach, Parsons). These confusions lead to misleading statements like the following:

> [In this conception] society appears as a cluster of functions which are independent of each other. In such a conception, the coherence of the whole society is lost. In order to restore the lost holism, a mythical image is fabricated of a 'organism-society', which is capable of maintaining its 'equilibrium' as it passes through the vicissitudes of its history, capable of inventing or finding 'responses' to the questions put to it by its environment in order to 'adapt itself' to environmental modifications.

In so far as this is an attack on the separation of 'system' and 'environment' in contemporary sociological and anthropological theory, and especially on the pseudo-organicism of equilibrium theory, Terray is correct. But to tie the words 'environment' and 'adaptation' only to a 'biological' viewpoint is an error derived from the biological DISCOURSE, not from biology as such. In Terray's conception, 'environment' means an entity called the environment, not a relationship of 'environments' and 'levels of environment' as contexts, both within and outside the specific social system one has isolated for study. But the Althusserian conception of dominant and subordinate relations in the socioeconomic system, which Terray uses elsewhere, is in fact a theory in which the relations between the two are levels of feedback relationships between 'organism' and 'environment'. Althusser nevertheless manages to attack 'communication theory' in his work on Lenin.

The third example comes from the one work in French I have happened across that recognizes the mechanistic prejudices of Jacob and Monod and, more important, understands the essentials of the unit of mind, while completely misunderstanding the social and systemic nature of 'mind'. Thus Jeanne Parain-Vial (1969: 43, note 22) remarks correctly that contemporary biological research confirms the "relative character of the autonomy of the organism" and that it marks the end of the "romantic" biology of the *élan vital* and of the Darwinian "struggle for life". But because of her inability to get outside of efficient causality and the current overvaluation of language in France, her correct understanding that this research necessarily confirms the relative character of "the conceptual cutting or splitting into 'organism' and 'environment'" (ibid.) cannot help her to avoid confusing language and communication in her discussion of the genetic code. By reading 'code' as 'cryptography' and by assuming that the genetic code is to be represented either as a mechanism, like a computer, or as a language, she makes the mistake of thinking that terms like 'messenger-RNA' are LINGUISTIC metaphors. Thus she says: "The way the notion of structure is employed in linguistics and in biology, there is a risk of believing that the organism is a language" (p. 47). Parain-Vial is unaware of any mediator between 'thought' and the 'organism'. Consequently she becomes trapped in a false opposition:

But whereas we can know the man who finalized the electronic circuits [in the computer], we have no knowledge of the CAUSE which has imposed an orientation or direction on the chemical laws which living beings obey. This lack of knowledge forbids us to consider the living being as a language (my emphasis).

The point is, of course, that either living beings do not obey chemical laws, but simply depend on them in order to obey higher-level systemic laws, or else those chemical laws are not causalistic, but teleonomic. Although the first possibility is most likely the case, and thus allows for closed-system description at one level of reality and open-system explanation at another, it really makes no difference here. So long as language and communication are confused, so long as logical typing is misunderstood, and so long as language remains the *patron* of semiotics (see Chapter XVI, Section 4), no escape from the irrelevancy of such oppositions is possible.

The last example comes from Edmund Leach. It is an interesting one because Leach is arguing against Lévi-Strauss's erroneous promotion of the language model (1958: 69). Lévi-Strauss's error depends upon a confusion between language and communication, which is similar to the confusion I have pointed to in Metz and Martinet. Leach argues against the error of saying that a language and a kinship system are "identical phenomena". He does so, however, by making an even more elementary blunder. He confuses matter–energy and information, as does Lévi-Strauss, but then goes on to add another element to this confusion:

If I give an object into the possession of someone else, I no longer possess it myself. Possibly I shall gain something else in exchange and possibly I retain some residual claim on the original objects, but that is another matter.

If, however, I speak a message to someone else,

I do NOT deprive myself of anything at all; I merely share information which I originally possessed but my listener did not (1970: 119–20).

As his text indicates, Leach conceives of the symbolic gift only in the terms of the circulation of Imaginary commodities and entities in his own culture. He consequently assumes that all forms of giving – except speech – involve PROPERTY relations of 'propriation' and 'expropriation'. In other words – as in the quotation from the same author criticized in Chapter XIV – Leach assumes that 'distinction' necessarily involves some form of 'opposition' between the exchangers. For Leach, the exchangers are oppositional entities who exchange other entities (objects) in order to mediate their opposition through 'reciprocity'. In his text, reciprocity – "the exchange of distinct, but equivalent resources" – is opposed to mutuality – the "sharing of common resources" (ibid.). According to Leach's argument at this point, the former corresponds to the "exchange of women" and the latter, to "conversation".

What Leach calls a "diametrical" opposition between reciprocity and mutuality is said to be derived from Lévi-Strauss's "Structural Analysis in Linguistics and in Anthropology" (1958). But what Leach has done is to transpose one term of the relation Lévi-Strauss establishes between 'bilateral' and 'unilateral' relationships from one category into the other. In his attempt to generalize the relation of the avunculate, Lévi-Strauss distinguishes (1) the 'bilateral' categories of MUTUALITY ($=$) ("affection, tenderness, and spontaneity") and RECIPROCITY ($\pm$) (the reciprocal exchange of gifts), and (2) the 'unilateral' categories of RIGHTS ($+$) (the creditor) and OBLIGATIONS ($-$) (the debtor). Through his conception of the property of the individual, Leach effectively transposes reciprocity into the unilateral categories of debtor and creditor in his own culture. We can put this critique another way: We can interpret Lévi-Strauss's four categories as an attempt to distinguish between (1) symbolic exchange of use value in the analog ('mutuality'); (2) symbolic communication of exchange value by means of digitalized distinctions ('reciprocity'); and (3) the Imaginary relations of debtor and creditor in relation to objects ('rights' and 'obligations'). Leach simply makes the second and the third categories the same, and then goes on to extend the contradiction by implying, on the one hand, that information is a possession (i.e., an Imaginary object) and, on the other, that it is a "common resource" (i.e., a symbolic link).

Chapter XVI

Linguistics and Semiotics

THE UNCONSCIOUS STRUCTURED LIKE A LANGUAGE

I suspect that we have not yet
gotten rid of God, since we
still have faith in grammar.
NIETZSCHE

1. *Preliminary Critique*

In what sense is Lacan's slogan "the unconscious is structured like a language" a really significant statement?

What is essential to any approach to this problem is to define as far as possible the level of the system in which or about which one is speaking, and it is very obvious to the reader of the *Écrits* that it is the consistent refusal to do this which provides Lacan with his most powerful strategic weapon against criticism. Like the schizophrenic, the discourse of the *Écrits* refuses to label the metaphor, refuses to 'frame' the text, to provide the context without which interpretation is impossible. This careful orchestration of a context which is somehow never there is the mark by which one recognizes a passed master in the art of the double bind, for the double bind depends on the deliberate confusion between referent language and metalanguage, on the refusal to allow contextual definition. The double bind is used in this way by some American therapists as a clinical technique. It is not for nothing, then, that Lacan's Other so closely resembles the impossible God of Sartre's *Being and Nothingness*, nor that the *manque* of which he is the locus turns out to be a sort of displacement of the bourgeois anguish of the existentialists (Chapter XVII). But one can always metacommunicate about a double bind, through counter-violence if need be, if the Other is the locus of either symbolic or real violence. (Cf. Lacan's attempt to reduce this question of the socioeconomic context to a psychological question, via Hegel's "law of the heart", 1966: 172.)

Since Lacan specifically refuses semiotics (Wilden, 1968a: 116), the phrase "the unconscious is structured like a language" either means that the primary process depends upon processes peculiar to language alone – that is to say, language represents a model – or it means that there is some sort of analogy or similarity between language and the primary process.

If we assume that the first is what Lacan intends, what might Lacan's slogan mean, especially in reference to the Freudian texts? We can easily dispose of some aspects of this question by summarizing and adding to the criticisms which have already been made:

1 Since overdetermination is not confined to language or to the Symbolic (unless the Symbolic is interpreted in communicational terms), the linguistic model is useful, but not exhaustive. For Freud, overdetermination is a communicational concept, sometimes akin to redundancy in information theory.

2 Language is distinguished from all other forms of communication by negation and tense. Freud asserts however that the primary process never says 'no' or 'not' and that it involves no 'time'. Nor does it involve logic, according to him, and all analytical logic is founded on syntactic negation. (See also 8, 9, and 12, below.)

3 Freud's description of the thing-presentations of the inscriptions or signs of the primary process is a description of a process which is analog in form. Similarly, his energy model of the primary process is a continuous analog flow of difference. Natural language, however, is digital in form; is articulated on the gap. As a description of a digital process, the linguistic model more closely maps the *Bindung* of the SECONDARY process (which is where Freud does in fact seek to locate language). Once again, the communications model seems more flexible.

4 Since the primary process depends on the TRACE (which never fades), it is not the laws of speech or phonology, but the laws of writing, that we must seek in it. In communication theory, the trace is the condition of both message and code.

5 Language is highly restricted, by its digital form, in the generation of signification out of meaning. Freud's primary process is *voll*; in Lacan's terms it is a plenitude of meaning.

6 The differentiation between matter–energy, signal, sign, and signifier depends on the definition of the particular RELATION one is describing, and necessarily generates paradox. (In American terms, this set of dis-

tinctions would read: metabolism, signal, sign, and symbol. In Saussure's terminology, what I call a sign is in general what he calls a symbol and, in general, what I call a signifier is what he calls a sign.) The Freudian concept of layers of signs which can be trans-lated (or can emerge) from level to level through the process of 'binding', makes the concept of signal/sign as ambiguous as that of the nip in animal play. Some sort of boundary distinction, which implies digitalization, is involved. But so long as we are talking about communication between organisms, the signal/sign is analog in form, rather than digital, because it is not fully discrete and because it is bound to a 'natural' rather than to an 'arbitrary' support. (Its function remains analog: the definition and maintenance of a relation.)

It is through intentionalization (cathexis) that there is translation from the digital/analog secondary process to the analog primary process, and back again (as in the dream). It is the interference of the analog primary 'discourse' with the digital aspects of the secondary discourse which accounts for the *lapsus calami*. The primary process uses associations in the digital discourse related to objects, facts, concepts, and events to talk about relationships. It is for this reason that no dream or symptom can be fully interpreted. Cathexis is thus a form of the digitalization of the analog, just as hypercathexis (attention) is a singling out of one analog difference or set of differences as different from all others (distinction between figure and ground). But the boundary is always ascribed by the subject to the figure, and not to the ground.

7 The laws of 'syntax' of the primary process, which translates words into images in the dream, are not simply the laws of linguistic syntax. The relation between primary process and secondary process is undoubt-edly the locus of the laws of the symbolic function (Lévi-Strauss), but these are the laws of selection/substitution and combination/contexture which are present in all communications systems, not in language alone. Moreover, it is the highly developed syntax of language, and not seman-tics, which allows language to metacommunicate about itself. The pri-mary process is always communicated about by the secondary process (and vice versa); it cannot comment on itself. Thus the word 'syntax', or the implication of a syntax in the primary process, does not refer to syntax in its rather specific linguistic sense, and such a usage tends to encourage a confusion of levels of organization.

8 Presence and absence, as a binary relation in an analog continuum without gaps, are in a relation of difference which may be digitalized as a distinction or as an opposition. 'O' and 'a', however, as with all so-called phonemic oppositions, involve a non-semantic binary distinction with

only a trivial and purely analogous connection with the non-binary SEMANTICITY of presence and absence. It is the PRAGMATICS of the arbitrary 'o' and 'a' as used in Freud's celebrated example which is of interest: the relation between the meaningless information and the work to be done, and the relation between digitalization and the Imaginary (Chapter VI). It is impossible seriously to conceive of an opposition between presence and absence 'in' the unconscious (cf. Lacan, 1966: 594): such an opposition can only arise, as an opposition, in the relationship between primary and secondary systems (which is nowhere). In the linguistic model, there is a well-defined boundary between speech and silence. But there is no such boundary in the communicational model between communication and non-communication, or between presence and absence. No organism can not communicate, and all communication, at every level, is founded, not on absence, but on what is DECIDED is absent (in the analog or in the digital), that is to say, on goalseeking.

Consequently we must conclude that either the analogy between the phonemic opposition, on the one hand, and presence and absence, on the other, is inadequate, or this opposition between presence and absence is not an essential characteristic of language alone (or both). This is not to say that the relationship between presence and absence is not a crucial one. The question must be to examine it outside of our digital prejudices, that is to say, to examine it in relationship to the goalseeking characteristics of the open system. For both man and animal are ruled by the law of absence. (What presence and absence may become in language is not in question here.)

9 The relationship between the primary and secondary process is not one of double articulation. It is rather a relationship of commentary and text in which the 'text' continually quotes itself in the 'commentary'. The relationship of the phoneme to the semanteme, on the other hand, is that of an arbitrary building-block which is essentially unaffected by the semantics–pragmatics of the system it supports. Freud does not posit such a one-way relationship between primary and secondary systems.

10 Apart from its bioenergetic source, the opposition between Eros and Thanatos in Freud's most developed model of the primary process is not derived from observation, nor from simple speculation. It is derived from nineteenth-century Newtonian physics, above all from G. T. Fechner. Thanatos is entropy, a metaphor of the second law. It is not a systemic, cybernetic, or communicational principle – however much it fills in for one – but a principle of thermodynamic or mechanical inertia (equilibrium). Not only is there no similarity whatsoever (within the analytical

model) between this sort of bioenergetic attraction and repulsion, opposition and equilibrium, and the so-called binary opposition of phonemes, but the death instinct – which is in Freud's own terms a tendency towards disorganization – is a gratuitous construct, since 'tension' is a product of organization itself (Eros) (Chapter VI). Tension in relation to another system is not innate at the level of the individual system, for it can be engendered only in relationships between systems.

11 Consequently, the two 'drives' which are supposedly 'represented' in the primary system are in fact singular. Any complex goalseeking network operates in a relation of asymmetry or oscillation in relation to its goals. This asymmetry is a form of entropy: it is a qualitative or quantitative measure of 'missing information'. If the circuit were ever fully completed so that the system was in a state of 'total information', the system would either be in perpetual motion or it would no longer be a system (both of which are the same thing).

If we are to rid the theory of the lineal causality of the drive, we must say that what is represented in the primary process is a lack in the sense of a goal. This lack is engendered, as difference, at the most primordial level of ecosystemic communication with the real other who bears the child. The lack is simply missing information. It is the original breach in the analog unit of mind; when the missing information can be digitalized, through the Imaginary order, it will generate a distinction.

This process involves an emergence from the organismic level of combined analog and digital communication in the ecosystem – for no goals can be sought without digital decisions about thresholds. It is therefore the emergence of a system of communication between the child and his environment by means of distinctions (perception, 'objects out there'), at a higher level of complexity. This emergence also constitutes the primal repression, and with it, the secondary process (see below, Section 2).

With the constitution of the secondary process, the missing information can be brought to the level of opposition and identity, in which the child himself becomes a digital sign in his communication with the world (the mirror-stage). This process of emergence constitutes the second barrier: that between 'organism' and 'environment' (Chapter VIII). It would seem that the internal split and the external split are essentially constituted at the same time.

In the mirror stage, the missing information is the child as a 'self', as a totality (Chapter XVII). What is therefore 're-presented' in the primary process by this passage from organismic difference to perceptual distinction, and thence to bodily identity, is the missing information, now identified with the *alter ego*. The intrasubjective splitting is constituted as a result of an intersubjective (ecosystemic) splitting.

The name of the *alter ego* is Eros. 'O' and 'a' can now come to represent the relation of self and other; the child's goals have been completely digitalized at the first level (Chapter VII). Later he will learn to say 'No'.

12 The 'opposition' between phonemes is purely mechanical, an instrument used in the service of other goals. But the opposition between self and other, in the Imaginary, is semantic–pragmatic. It re-presents the original goal based on difference. The relation sometimes established by Lacan between the *Todestrieb* and Heidegger's *Sein-zum-Tode* is essentially a statement about the Imaginary, not about a 'biological' goal of entropy, not about an 'innate' aggressivity, and not about the 'goal' of existence (authentic or otherwise).

13 Much has been made by a number of commentators of the supposition that Freud (or Lacan) successfully disposed of the notion of instinct and thus somehow liberated psychoanalytical theory. But to replace 'instinct' by *pulsion* or 'drive' or *dérive* (Lacan) is no more than a play on words within the bioenergetic model. This is only a 'detour' which is a necessary result of the emphasis on language rather than on communication, and of the confusion between the two. There is no principle in the language model to account for analog intentionality. Since language begins in the SERVICE of the analog, and has no goal outside its own structural constraints on the closure of the sentence, some bioenergetic construct must necessarily be introduced into the linguistic model from outside, in order to account for human purpose. Language, as the locus of the illusory 'identity' of the 'I' may, under given social conditions, come permanently to alienate human goals. In this Imaginary discourse, one seeks oneself in an identity with words. But this is not some inherent tendency resulting from language as such.

2. *The Unconscious and the Primary Process: The* Urverdrängung

Having made these points, we can now turn to the question of why I have talked about the primary process rather than about the unconscious in criticizing Lacan's slogan. The main reason is simply that of perspective: I am not concerned with psychoanalytical therapy as such, nor do I believe that there is anything particularly 'specific' about psychoanalysis except in so far as it is a historical product of a certain type of socioeconomic system. Thus I speak from outside psychoanalysis, for the concept of a primary process or system applies in both a synchronic and a diachronic sense to all systemic or structural theories. A secondary reason is simply that this is Freud's preferred terminology in the *Project*.

As Gerald Hall has emphasized, there is a particular Freudian point of view on the unconscious to which Lacan's slogan applies more directly. This is the dynamic view, where 'repression proper' is equated with the repressed.

In this view, which is both genetic and structural, the unconscious as such is constituted by the 'primal repression'. This *Urverdrängung* is said to "fix" a primary "ideational representative"[1] by attaching it to a "drive". The drive in this sense is a need which cannot enter the unconscious, but which is re-presented there (as desire). Thereafter, the term 'unconscious' refers only to "repression after-the-event". In Lévi-Strauss's terms, this original repression could presumably be conceived of as constituting the "world of rules" of the symbolic function, for the task of the primal repression is indeed to institute a new set of relations.

According to Freud, repression proper "affects mental derivatives of the repressed representative, or such trains of thought as, originating elsewhere, have come into associative connection [*Beziehung*] with it. On account of this association, these presentations experience the same fate as what was primally repressed." Just as important as the so-called "repulsion" or "after pressure" – which operates "from the direction of the conscious upon what is to be repressed" – is the so-called "attraction" exercised by what was primally repressed. This 'force' attracts "everything with which it can establish a LIAISON" (*Verbindung*) (*Standard Edition*, XIV, 148). However, the thesis of the complementary economic viewpoint in the *Project*, is that the primary process is 'free' and 'unbound'. What can it mean therefore to speak of the "fixation" or the "recording" (*Fixierung*) of the primal repression? What is meant by the *Verbindung* of "conscious" presentations by what was primally repressed?

According to the model in the *Project*, the relationships of linking, binding, or liaison are the reverse of those just stated. The secondary process 'binds' the 'free' energy or 'free' meaning of the primary process. (Later Freud speaks of the ego sending "signals" to "control" the id.) We might translate the term 'binding' here as the imposition of a pattern on the 'energy', thus converting it into a set of markers.

The answer to this apparent contradiction must necessarily lie in how we define the relationships of the various systems. Repression is a process

---

[1] (*Vorstellungs-*)*Repräsentanz*, possibly meaning: "What re-presents or stands-in-for the presentation in the domain of representation". One could presumably also translate it as: "The signifier which re-presents (or holds the place of) the subject for another signifier" (i.e., a shifter in language; see below).

involving presentations at the FRONTIER, or on the boundary, between the system *Ucs.* and the system *Pcs.* (*Cs.*) (*Standard Edition*, XIV, 180). We can expect that positing this boundary will create difficulties over logical typing. Although the primary process is described as 'free' or 'unbound' or 'full', Freud in fact often speaks of UNCONSCIOUS CATHEXES (intentionalizations) or bindings. However, since, as we have seen, his theory is in general an equilibrium viewpoint which conserves energy, and since it involves attractions and repulsions, we can say that what he probably intends by an unconscious cathexis will have a 'translational' equivalent in the other part of the system. In other words, the unconscious cathexis can be said to be the equivalent of an investment of a *Pcs.* presentation in such a way as to block the return of a repressed presentation (*Pcs.* COUNTERCATHEXIS), or that of the withdrawal of *Pcs.* cathexis. In such an essentially electromagnetic viewpoint, unconscious cathexis does not have to be regarded as a separate 'force' in the system, but simply as the opposite of *Pcs.* cathexis. As such, then, 'unconscious cathexis' is identical to 'absence of *Pcs.* cathexis' or to '*Pcs.* countercathexis' – and Freud says as much (XIV, 181). He goes further, in fact. He says that countercathexis is "the sole mechanism of primal repression" (ibid.). We do not therefore have to suppose any process of intentionalization or binding which has its source in the primary system.

The (mythical?) genesis of the primal repression is clearly connected with the genetic viewpoint by which Freud describes the emergence of the secondary process in the *Project*. The bioenergetic displeasure principle which controls the primary process comes to be governed by the reality principle of the secondary process in response to the "exigencies of life" (i.e., the ecosystemic relationship to an environment). Consequently the principle of inertia (reduction of tension to zero, positive entropy) comes to be governed by the principle of constancy (homeostasis, neutral entropy). We can see therefore that this genetic view matches the later 'new topography'. The new topography describes the differentiation of the 'ego' from the 'id' by a process apparently modeled on organic growth, which is possibly to be viewed as the differentiation of the ego, as a gestalt, from the 'ground' of the id.

The new topography fits the processes posited in the *Project* rather accurately, because it clearly maintains the difference in logical typing between the two systems. It is the primal repression which accounts for the differentiation between primary and secondary systems. It accounts in effect for the genesis of the BOUNDARY between them, and therefore for their institution as distinct systems out of some supposed undifferentiated anterior state. Like the difficult concept of censorship, such a boundary must depend on an elementary DIGITALIZATION, and it necessarily involves paradox.

The *Verbindung* (liaison) or *Fixierung* involved in the primal repression now appears, however, as *Entbindung* (releasing) by the secondary system. We may assume as a consequence that the primal repression and its "connections" with "ideational representatives" are "fixed" or "recorded", not by or in the unconscious as such, but by the actual emergence of the secondary system. The primal repression is maintained not by unconscious cathexis, but by *Pcs.* countercathexis. This emergence describes the division of the undifferentiated, anterior, analog ecosystem into an analog primary process and an analog/digital secondary process.[2] But this division can be effected only by the digital aspects of the system. The emergence is similar, at some level, to Bateson's example of the emergence of the sign in play, to Piaget's conception of a reflective form of cognition, and presumably to the child's learning of language. It would seem to provide for a system of discrete elements (first- or second-level digitalization) in the secondary process, perhaps arrived at through the 'subtracting' described by the Bororo myth in Chapter IX, with a consequent reorganization of logical typing. From this perspective, *Pcs.* countercathexis is a form of digital signification corresponding in some sense to analog, *Ucs.*, meaning.

We assume, with Freud and with the ecologists, that it is the analog process which governs the goals of the system as a whole, and that the secondary system is its (digital) instrument. If this is the case, then the freely flowing messages of the primary system must constantly go through a process of translation, in Freud's terms, into messages in the secondary system. THIS TRANSLATION IS CLEARLY THE PREREQUISITE OF REPRESSION. A presentation must at least be recognized by the *Pcs.* before "after-repression", "withdrawal of cathexis", or "countercathexis" can operate. In other words, the presentation must first become SIGNIFICANT for the *Pcs.*, before any attempt can be made to 'designify' or to 'decathect' it.

There are two reasons for this assumption of digitalization in the *Pcs.* before repression. The first is that any cathexis or intentionalization, whether of word- or thing-presentation, presupposes a form of attention, recall, or binding, all of which are necessarily digital. The second reason is that it seems to be more or less established that digitalization is necessary wherever a boundary between systems or states of systems is crossed (Chapter VII).

[2] Since memory depends on analog patterns, and recall on digital 'selections', the secondary system may perhaps be divisible, at some level, into an analog preconscious and a digital/analog consciousness.

We can sum up this question of the dynamic view by saying that we have still not been required to posit any kind of 'unconscious language' or 'structure of language' in the unconscious. The analog status of the *Ucs*. processes involving primal repression and after-repression remains untouched. The passage "through the unconscious to perception" in the dream also continues to fit the model, for the dream images are digitalized in crossing the boundaries between the systems. There seems therefore to be only one coherent explanation of the dynamic relation between the two systems, which also accounts for the economic view, as well as for the iconic–linguistic view. This is an explanation which allows for a digital binding – or process of signification – to be applied to some aspect of the analog primary process as the precondition for any decision to repress that signification. Thus, if we consider the unconscious only in the dynamic sense of after-repression, we can see that it is on secondary-process digitalization, related, but not confined, to language, that repression depends. In the same way, the primal repression is the result of the emergence of the secondary process.

We also discover an unexpected compatibility with the Lacanian theory I am criticizing. The assumption of digitalization makes it impossible in normal circumstances for any unconscious MEANING ever to arise in language (which is the domain of signification). One of Lacan's central assumptions is that unconscious desire is ineffable, incompatible with speech. Since this Lacanian conception of desire is wedded to the metonymic displacement of 'unachieved' or 'unanchored' meaning ('energy') in the primary system, Lacan's 'desire' can be directly correlated with meaning under the rubric of the analog (*Trieb*: inclination; *Meinung*: intention; *sens*: feeling, direction). The aside in Chapter VII to the effect that the 'schizophrenic' may be treating the digital as though it were analog, seems therefore to be correct. This assumption gives us a precise reason for condensations like 'manzanita wood' and for condensations in the dream. Since the analog has been defined as of a higher logical type than the digital, but of a lower order of organization, then any analog meanings – words or images – which can bypass the digital process of signification, will necessarily be LACONIC, to use Freud's term. Lacan's *points de capiton*, his *épinglage*, and his *ancrage* thus all turn out to be metaphors for digital signification.

I have defined the analog as the domain of the overall goals of any 'normal' system. Desire then becomes, like the lack, a 'measure' of missing information. The definition is undoubtedly tautologous – but the reason that desire can never be satisfied is precisely what we always supposed. Such satisfaction would be equivalent to total information, or to death. And Lacan's 'demand' properly fits the digital domain of signification.

The repressed content of after-repression, or the content of some derivative of the primal repression can find its way into the system *Pcs.* (*Cs.*) only if it is sufficiently far removed from its association with the original aim of the repression. As a message originally digitalized and then retranslated into the analog, the return of the repressed may reappear in analog or in digital forms (the hysterical symptom, the dream-text, denegation), but it will always carry the imprint of the secondary process in doing so. It is only in this sense that we can understand Freud's insistence that the 'not' of a denial or denegation is the hallmark of its unconscious origin. Similarly, the psychosomatic symptom, like the dream-image, is often if not always an analog representation of a linguistic and digital message. The problem of recognition therefore lies not in the 'meaning' of the symptom, but in its TRANSLATION and in its TRANSCRIPTION from one mode of communication to the other.

The processes of symptom formation can obviously have nothing to do with attraction or repulsion, however, for the subject is not a magnetic or a gravitational field. They can only be the result of the cybernetic relationship of 'system' and 'environment', in which both condition each other, and in which both are constrained by certain rules regarding the attainment of goals. And under no circumstances is energy repressed as such: it is the information, the *Vorstellung*, which is repressed (Chapter VI).

What of the condensation and displacement within the primary process? Since the transmission of information invariably depends upon differential boundaries and thresholds which are introduced into the system and its relationships by the sender, by the receiver, by both, or by 'reality' (in the sense that one organism or cell, and so on, is 'really' biologically distinct from another), the primary process involves an 'easy flow' of difference, which can be selected from and made to combine. But, since analog and digital communication always occur together in any particular system or level of the system, we would have to assume some (inaccessible) level of digitalization in the primary process if it were not already in a relation with the secondary process.

In order to avoid the most obvious of the possible confusions about the supposed metaphoro-metonymical processes 'in' the unconscious, two distinctions are essential. The first is that in the sense of similarity and contiguity, metaphor (condensation) and metonymy (displacement) are not primarily digital, linguistic, processes but primarily analog processes. Thus they correspond more closely to the LOGIC of the association of 'ideas' – which include signs and icons as well as signifiers – than to anything specifically linguistic. I have assumed both an analog and a digital logic; these categories match those of the "identity of perception" and the "identity of thought" in the text of Freud.

The second distinction has already been pointed out: it is that analog coding and digital coding are fundamentally different in form. Whereas a digital code lies 'outside' the sender and the receiver and depends upon an 'objective' repertoire of discrete elements (distinctions) for the selective and combinatory choices that are made, the analog code is neither 'outside' nor composed of discrete elements. The analog code is nothing more or less than the very relationship between sender and receiver, hence its primacy. It is thus available to digitalization, via the Imaginary, for example, but it is not digital in itself. Consequently, the question of condensation and displacement 'in' the unconscious depends entirely on whether one is speaking of these two processes *grosso modo* as analog or as digital. Depending on the level of analysis, they can be viewed both ways. But it is significant that Freud considered all properly linguistic processes (which for him are both analog and digital) to be part of the system *Pcs. (Cs.)*.

If we do move to another level of analysis, it is clear that the processes of condensation and displacement 'in' the primary process are not 'in' it at all, but rather arise in the relationship between the two systems. The topographical regression through the unconscious to perception, as the dream thoughts become the dream, or the analog statement by a somatic symptom about some previously digitalized analog relationship, are not processes involving rules of selection and combination 'in' the unconscious. They are rather to be viewed as processes of symptom formation controlled by the RULES OF CROSSING BOUNDARIES between systems, for which digitalization is always required. This conception is no less paradoxical than Freud's conception of the censorship, but I find it a good deal easier to understand and to justify.

Only because of this constant interactive translation between the analog and the digital in all complex systems of communication is it possible to use the dynamic view as the basis of the statement that the unconscious is structured like a language. On the one hand, this statement means that the unconscious is structured like a communications system. On the other, it means that since language is the most highly digitalized and the most semiotically free of all such systems, the interference of the unconscious 'discourse' with the conscious or preconscious discourse is structured BY language. It is through language that the primary-system *Sachvorstellungen* are brought to signification, and it is through language that the analog psychosomatic symptom must be digitalized in order to be interpreted and thus overcome.

3. *Freud's Two Languages*

In speaking of a translation between two types of communication, I am obviously not referring to the translator who renders one word by another one. By this term I mean to emphasize the sense of the metaphors of writing, of the hieroglyph or pictographic script (*Bilderschrift*), and of the rebus as applied to the dream by Freud, and thus to re-establish the status of the two 'languages' (*Sprachen*) of which he speaks in the *Traumdeutung*.

In criticizing the error of those interpreters who see in the dream or in the rebus only a pictographic analogy, Freud takes up again the semiotic terminology of the *Project*:

> The dream thoughts and the content of the dream are there for us as two representations or descriptions [*Darstellungen*] of the same content in two unlike languages. Or better, the content of the dream appears as a translation, a transference, a transcription [*Übertrâgung*] of the dream thoughts into another means of expression, whose signs and laws of articulation it is our business to learn by comparing the original with its transposition [*Umsetzung*] into this other mode of expression (*Standard Edition*, IV, 277).

It would be an error, Freud goes on to say, to try to read the signs of the dream according to their value as images (*Bilderwert*). On the contrary, they must be read "according to their semiotic connections, according to their RELATIONSHIPS-AS-SIGNS" (*Zeichenbeziehungen*).

There is no mistaking Freud's conception of the differences between the two types of articulation. In the *New Introductory Lectures* (1933), he goes back on his earlier position that a dream is not a communication. Here he speaks of the dream as a communication (*Mitteilung*) like any other communication in analysis, but with the following characteristic features:

> All the linguistic instruments by which we express the subtler relations of thought – the conjunctions and prepositions, the changes in declension and conjugation – are dropped, because there is no means of representing them. Just as in a primitive language without any grammar, only the raw material of thought is expressed, and abstract terms are taken back to the concrete ones that are at their basis (*Standard Edition*, XXII, 9, 20).

(The inadequate understanding of grammar and linguistics and the inadequate genetic view of language represented in this quotation is of course of no consequence to the point Freud is trying to make.)

4. *Linguistics, Semiotics, Ideology*

In utilizing the Lacanian perspective, we can continue to retain the notion of the phallus as a sign, but as a sign which is converted by the ideological discourse of our culture into a signifier. It is a sign governed by the signifier, and in our culture the signifier (*savoir*) is the agent of exploitation (*pouvoir*) We can still go on to analyze the ways in which language does indeed "structure the relationships between human beings" (Lacan) but without making the unnecessary error of taking language or its structure as the supreme model of those relationships, an error which Lévi-Strauss has been careful to warn against.

To model human behavior, or the phantasy, or social structure, on the phonemic relation of opposition is an interesting metaphor of the digital ideology of our culture. It is through the Imaginary that we are programmed to think in terms of the irreducibility of oppositions, rather than in the terms of the dialectic between difference and opposition in history. In other words, the actual fact of irreducible DIFFERENCE becomes the 'fact' of irreducible OPPOSITION posited by Lacan (Wilden, 1968a: 153), through which is justified the application of the either/or epistemology of the bio-energetic perspective to the both–and realities of the open system.

We can therefore agree with Lacan that, within our present culture, digital language does indeed structure human relationships in the "synchronic register of [what is defined by the culture as] opposition between irreducible elements" in the code (ibid.). But we cannot agree that the psychoanalyzable symptom is "sustained by a structure which is identical to the structure of language" (op. cit.: 116). That structure is not a linguistic structure, but a systemic and communicational one.

In respect of the French linguistic model of relation and communication, I find myself in complete agreement with Jacques Derrida's epistemological critique of it. He has pointed out that 'semiology' in the Saussurean sense and in its usual present sense in France (but not in the United States), has been SUBJECTED to the control of linguistics, without any theoretical justification:

> Although semiology was in effect more general and more comprehensive than linguistics, it continued to be controlled by the privilege accorded to one of its parts. The linguistic sign remained exemplary for semiology. It dominated semiology as the master-sign, as the generative model, as its pattern, and as its 'boss' [*patron*] (1967: 74–5).

Commenting on Barthes's assumption that semiotics is a part of linguistics, Derrida goes on:

This reversal . . . makes clearly explicit the function of a linguistics which has historically been dominated by a LOGOCENTRIC metaphysics, a linguistics for which in fact there is, and [which believes] there ought to be, "no meaning which is not NAMED" [Barthes]. . . . If we wish to describe the fact and the vocation of signification in the closing-off of our epoch, the closure of our civilization – which is on the way to disappearing by its very universalization in the world [*mondialisation*] – Barthes's reversal of the relationship between linguistics and semiotics is indispensable . . . (my emphasis).

I have pointed out that semiotic communication is of a higher logical type (and therefore of a lower order of complexity) than language. Semiotics and linguistics are not therefore in opposition. A proper understanding of this non-oppositional relationship of logical typing also invalidates the supposed opposition between analytical and dialectical reason. One does not therefore have to take sides for or against Lévi-Strauss *vis-à-vis* Sartre in this respect (Lévi-Strauss, 1962a: 324–57). As with the relationship between the bioenergetic epistemology, which is analytical, and the communications epistemology, which is dialectical, the one cannot do without the other. Analytical reason is simply a SUBSET of dialectical reason. The supposed opposition between them is generated by relations between people, and by the way the two perspectives are applied.

Similar false oppositions occur elsewhere. Because of its original misunderstanding of the analog, French semiology began by being trapped in the binary opposition. Roland Barthes's *Éléments de sémiologie* of 1964 provide a good example of the attendant deification of binary forms:

Finally, some authors state that digitalism itself – which is the RIVAL of the analogic – in its PURE form, binarism, is itself a 'reproduction' of certain physiological processes, if it is true that vision and hearing, in short, function by alternative selections (p. 112, my emphasis).

In this text – as befits the colossal one-dimensionality of western civilization – the inverted logical typing of the analog and the digital is not unexpectedly reduced to a binary opposition of symmetry. Similarly, in Lévi-Strauss's early work (1949: 136), the "basic and immediate data of mental and social reality" are said simply to be "duality, alternation, opposition, and symmetry".[3]

---

[3] This epistemological choice is in fact invalidated – in a way characteristic of all of Lévi-Strauss's writings – by the following qualifier: "whether presented in definite forms or in imprecise forms". But I know of no commentator who has realized that this statement concerns – and denies – the distinction between

There is enough of a confusion in France on these questions. If we add to these epistemological and ideological problems those of British and American exponents and opponents, the entire problematic of language, communication, system, and structure really turns into a can of worms. I shall quote just one example, Edmund Leach (1970: 105):

> My disagreement here is basic. Lévi-Strauss has said somewhere that social anthropology is a 'branch of semiology', which would imply that its central concern is with the internal logical structure of the meanings of sets of symbols. But for me the real subject matter of social anthropology always remains the actual social behavior of human beings. . . .

And so on.

5. *The Splitting of the Subject*

Although Lacan's *Écrits* are a veritable epitome of analog communication, Lacan's own theory is a fine example of the logocentric metaphysics. It is in fact only by understanding the inversion of the relationship between linguistics and semiotics, and the attendant problematic of logico-mathematical structuralism, that one can deal critically with the Lacanian texts.

Let us take for another example the Lacanian slogan: "The signifier is what represents the subject for another signifier." This statement is derived from the simple linguistic fact that the subject who speaks (*le sujet de l'énonciation*) is different from the subject of what is said (*le sujet de l'énoncé*). In other words, the *I* that says, 'I' is not the same as the 'I' that re-presents the subject in the message, the shifter which 'takes the subject's place' in the discourse. Lacan apparently interprets this 'displacement' of the subject in relation to his own discourse as a manifestation of an irreducible "splitting of the subject" (*Ichspaltung*). This splitting makes a 'false consciousness' of the multiple representatives of, or spokesmen for, the subject in the social discourse. The notion is similar in some respects to the split between the 'I' and the 'ego' in Lacan's earlier formulations, except that the first bespeaks a 'neurotic' relation, the second, a 'psychotic' one. It is also similar to Ronald Laing's existentially based concept of the false self (1960).

I would be the last to deny the collective psychosis of our culture, but this split is by no means an irremediable adjunct to the 'human condition'.

---

analog and digital communication. Moreover, in 1971, Lévi-Strauss was still talking about the "opposition" between consciousness and the unconscious (*Psychologie*, December 1971; translated in *Psychology Today*, May 1972).

At one level at least it is no more that what Laing calls "necessary de-personalization". But Lacan's "true subject" is not, however, the same as Laing's. It is the INEFFABLE subject of the unconscious (Wilden 1968a: 142, 176–83). It is an unrepresentable 'true self', as it were.

From the perspective of this book, however, this *Ichspaltung* turns out to be no more than a rather complicated way of saying that the analog can never be properly represented in the digital, and that in our culture the digital has taken over almost all the functions of the analog. It says in effect that the EPISTEMIC or SEMIOTIC subject and the LINGUISTIC subject are not the same: that the subject of analog knowledge can never be properly represented by the subject of digital knowledge. What is important to understand about this is that only if one inverts the significance of the semiotic and linguistic subjects can one make such a splitting of the subject into a locus of existential anguish, as Lacan seems to do. The somewhat doomladen tone of many of Lacan's remarks on this question can, in essence, be derived from two contradictory factors in his work: one, his commendable desire to demonstrate the futility and the danger of the notion of the *cogito* once and for all, and, two, his personal commitment to a form of bourgeois elitism and individualism which is in effect that of an UNCONSCIOUS COGITO (ibid. 177–83).

Only in a culture where most communication and practically all exchange is highly digitalized – and in which the average person has been persuaded to believe in the high moral, ethical, and technological values of digitalization for its own sake – is it possible to speak of such a splitting of the subject. This 'psychotic' relation is that engendered by a specific kind of social organization: it is a splitting between two varieties of the logocentric, phallocentric, individual. It is simply the inevitable splitting of the analog from the digital in an Imaginary system of caste, class, race, and sex.

In order clearly to perceive this reincarnation of the bourgeois individual in analytical theory, it is necessary to take a metacommunicative position outside the tendency to one-dimensionality in psychoanalysis and in (western) culture. The not entirely unexpected conclusion which forces itself upon us is that, so long as the logocentric model is retained, explicitly or implicitly, Lacan's position on the status of the subject is no more than a simple reversal of the Cartesianism he attacks.

Having begun in the Imaginary, having attempted a long traverse of the Symbolic, we can now return to our starting-point in the mirror-stage in order to consider how it may be transcended.

Chapter XVII

The Ideology of Opposition and Identity

CRITIQUE OF LACAN'S THEORY OF THE MIRROR-
STAGE IN CHILDHOOD

Classical Political Economy
nearly touches the true
relation of things, without,
however, consciously formulating
it. This it cannot do so long
as it sticks in its bourgeois skin.
MARX: *Capital*, I

1. *Introduction*

On reading Fanon's *Black Skin, White Masks* (1952), one finds a number of
references to Lacan and to the Lacanian school, and especially to the
mirror-stage. J.-J. Goux (1968, 1969) has attempted to use the Imaginary
relationship between ego's and the 'symbolic function' of the phallus, in
Marxist exchange theory (cf. Chapter IX), and Lacan's 1949 article on the
mirror-stage has appeared in a British journal, *The New Left Review* (1968),
as did an article on Lacan by Louis Althusser.

But the theory of the mirror-stage cannot be lightly used in any critical
sociological or economic theory, because it depends on a set of psychoanalytical values which are non-critical and anti-contextual. It is replete
with Hegelianism; it is phallocentric; it is based on the equivalent of a
'human condition' which is then used to support the theory of the 'splitting
of the subject' criticized in Chapter XVI; and it smells of the graveyard:
the existential anguish of individual being-for-death. It is in fact tinged
with the same ideological and personal dangers as those brought out in my
analysis of Freud's theory of paranoia in Chapter X: it is aesthetically
simple; it serves an unstated ideological function; and it invites identification on the part of the 'alienated' intellectual, on the one hand, or on that
of his 'integrated' counterpart, on the other.

It is therefore of some importance to outline the theory and its sources, and to assay its deficiencies so as to indicate how it can be used in a critical theory of communication and exchange without its contributing unknown or unrecognized oppressive factors to the theory. We must of course recognize that, as the psychological source of the Imaginary commodity relationships between human beings under capitalism, the mirror-stage cannot be wished away, it must be dealt with.

2. The Mirror-stage[1]

> Tuer la fortune d'un homme,
> c'est quelquefois pis que de le
> tuer lui-même.
> BALZAC: *Sarrasine*

Between the ages of six and eighteen months, the child who sees himself in a mirror demonstrates a rather particular kind of fascination with his own image. Lacan describes the child's relationship to his double in the mirror as that of an identification. It produces a transformation in the child's relationship to his 'self', which Lacan relates to the psychoanalytical theory of the *imago* (Jung). The child joyfully "takes on" his specular image; for Lacan, this represents the first stage of the emergence of the *I*, preceding that in which the child will objectify his *I* by an identification with a particular other (in the Imaginary) and preceding that in which his learning to speak will provide him the possibility of subjectivity in the linguistic sense. The specular identification is with the ideal ego – one of the avatars of Freud's later conception of the superego.

This primary identification is the root of all others. Thus the ego is constituted in the Imaginary before any significant 'socialization' has occurred. Since the child's motor functions are far from being coordinated at this age, what he sees as his double is the total gestalt of a body which he has not so far experienced as a totality: "This gestalt is pregnant with correspondences which unite the *I* to the statue towards which man projects him-

---

[1] The mirror-stage, first mentioned by Lacan in 1936, is prefigured in an article by Henri Wallon (1931), whose later work was used by Jakobson and Halle in justifying the theory of the binary opposition of phonemes (Wallon, 1945; Jakobson and Halle, 1956: 47; cf. Wilden, 1968a: 154, 159–77).

The first published article dealing with the mirror-stage appeared in 1947 (Lacan, 1966: 178–92). It is mentioned again in 1948, in an article on aggressivity (Lacan, 1966: 110–20). The main article, entitled "The mirror-stage as formative of the function of the *I* as this function is revealed in the psychoanalytical experience", appeared in 1949 (Lacan, 1966: 93–100). A summary later appeared in English (Lacan, 1953a).

self" (p. 95). Lacan goes on to discuss the role of the BODY-IMAGE, as a double or reversed mirror-image, in hallucinations, dreams, and phantasies.

He then introduces zoological evidence to support this conception of the role of the IMAGE OF THE OTHER in maturation.[2] There is a question, he says, of "homeomorphic identification", on the one hand, and of *mimesis* conceived of as "heteromorphic identification", on the other. The latter poses the problem of the "signification of space for the living organism", and *mimesis* cannot, he says, be "ridiculously" reduced to the supposed "master law of adaptation" (p. 96). The "insidious capturing effect" (*captation*) of the specular image on the child is an indication of an "organic insufficiency". It is somehow related to the premature birth of all children, in the sense that considerable neurophysiological developments continue to take place after birth, notably the development of the cortex, which Freud tried to link to the development of the ego. (And which is sometimes referred to as the cortical mirror.) Thus the image in the mirror – or that of another person – presents to the child at this period an anticipated form of maturation which he has not as yet achieved. The image is consequently the locus of a relation of "primordial discord": the child's sense of his body as an uncoordinated aggregate is matched against an image of unity or harmony, whether in the mirror or in other people (p. 96).

This "discordance" between the child as an organism and his *Umwelt* is part of a process of development which Lacan describes as involving periods of the "stagnation of the forms of the ego" (*moi*). These stagnated forms give rise to "the most common structure of human knowledge". This structure is that which constitutes the ego and its objects in such a way that they can be characterized by attributes of "permanence, identity, and substantiality", which effectively make both ego and objects into "entities or 'things'" (cf. Chapter VIII). But these constituted structures are 'out of step', as it were, with the gestalts of the child's actual lived experience, which is governed by "animal desire" (p. 111). In a sense, the

[2] He mentions Jean Lhermitte, *L'Image du corps* (Paris: NRF, 1939); the work of Silberer; the work of Harrison, *Proceedings of the Royal Society*, Series B Vol. 126, No. 845 (February, 1939); and that of Chauvin, *Annales de la Société entomologique de France*, Third Trimester (1941). In studying the processes of larval maturation in *Schistocerca* and *Locusta*, and their development into solitary or gregarious adults, Chauvin showed that the visual perception of another individual of the same or a similar species could result in morphological and behavioral changes. Lacan interprets Chauvin's work in gestalt terms, and quotes Chauvin's conclusion: "There must be a sort of recognition involved here, however rudimentary it may be. And if one says recognition, then surely we are implying that there is some sort of psycho-physiological mechanism involved?" The image thus has a "morphogenic effect" (p. 191) in a "homeomorphic identification" (p. 96).

child is 'falling over himself' in front of his own image. According to Lacan, it is this "fixation of forms" which introduces a certain "rupture" into man's relationship with the world. It is consequently the condition which "indefinitely extends man's world and his power", and it confers on man's objects, "their instrumental polyvalency and their symbolic polyphony", as well as their potential as "armament" (ibid.). All human knowledge therefore begins as formally or structurally equivalent to "paranoid knowledge" (*la connaissance paranoïaque*), since each stage of the development of the ego represents a stage of "objectifying identification", similar to that in paranoia.[3]

The mirror-stage represents a sort of "structural crossroads" in which the "conflictual tension internal to the subject crystallizes" in the form of the ego. It is an erotic relation in which the human individual "fixes on himself an image which alienates him from himself". The mirror-stage provides the "energy" and the "form" in which the "passionate organization" which will be called the ego finds its origin (p. 113). Or, in the Hegelian vocabulary affected by Lacan at this period: "The subject identifies himself in his sentiment-of-Self with the image of the other, and . . . the image of the other comes to captivate and master that sentiment in him" (p. 181).

3. Sartre's Transcendence of the Ego

> Man exists only in so far as he
> is opposed.
> HEGEL

Thus the *stade du miroir* is an ALIENATION of the subject. One assumes that when he wrote these lines, Lacan had read with care Sartre's early phenomenological essay, *The Transcendence of the Ego* (1936–7), or at least that he was very well acquainted with Sartre's *Being and Nothingness* (1943) and his *Anti-Semite and Jew* (1946). Sartre makes a distinction between the *I* and the *me* in the early essay (pp. 43–60): "The *I* is the ego as the unity of actions. The *me* is the ego as the unity of states and of qualities." These

---

[3] Lacan finds support for this theory in the work of Charlotte Bühler, Elsa Köhler, and the Chicago School. He speaks of the originally "undifferentiated" relation between the young child and his counterparts at around eight months of age. The mirror-stage comes to dominate all such relations until about the age of two and a half. Lacan denies any primary relation of *Einfühlung* or empathy. He cites the phenomenon of transitivism as proof. This describes a situation in which one child will attribute his own actions to another, or so identify with the other child as to feel injured when the other child falls down (p. 113).

categories of the *I* and *me* later become the *pour-soi* (nothingness, existence, desire,[4] *projet*) and the *en-soi* (being, essence, self as past, the alienation of the *pour-soi*). In spite of their foundations in a theory of non-intersubjective consciousness,[5] the Sartrean categories have lost little of their relevance as relational metaphors: "The *me* is given as an object [of consciousness]" and remains unknown to us unless we look at it as OTHER (pp. 86–7).[6] "The ego is not the REAL totality of consciousness . . . but the IDEAL unity of all the states and actions" (ibid.), for the ego is "by nature fugitive" (p. 89). Sartre goes on to discuss the "degradations" and "refractions" of the *I* in real life: ". . . The body and BODY-IMAGES can consummate the total degradation of the concrete *I* of reflection [the transcendent or psychically intuited ego] to the level of the '*I*-concept'." The body may consequently serve as the "ILLUSORY FULFILLMENT" of the *I* (my emphasis). One assumes from these passages that Sartre may also have read Wallon's article (1931) on the child.

In a later work Sartre deals with the alienation of the ego in the terms of anti-Semitism. He speaks of the "longing for impenetrability" of certain people. They do not wish to change:

> What frightens them is not the content of truth, of which they have no conception, but the form itself of truth, which is of an indefinite approximation. It is as if their own existence were in continual suspension. But they wish to exist ALL AT ONCE and RIGHT AWAY (Sartre, 1946: 18, 19, my emphasis).

[4] Cf. Chapter III on the Hegelian-Kojèvian theory of desire, and Chapter II, Section 4, on cathexis and intentionality.

[5] For Sartre, as for Husserl, consciousness is a monad (Sartre, 1936–7: 108; Husserl, 1929: 148–51, 157). Husserl's "transcendental intersubjectivity" represents an ideal, rather than a state of affairs that can be grounded in phenomenology. It is in the domain of communication, not in that of consciousness, or of unconsciousness, or of perception, that Laing's "false self", Lacan's *moi*, and the phenomenological and psychoanalytical "(choice of) object" are both constituted and open to transcendence. As distinct from his personal relation to his readers (Sartre, 1964), Sartre's epistemology seems never to have gone beyond the monad: "It is impossible to exist in an environment of men without their becoming objects for me, and for them through me, without my being an object for them, without my subjectivity taking on its objective reality through them as the interiorization of my human objectivity" (1960: 186). The remarks on the gift as reciprocal debt which follow this passage in his text, demonstrate very clearly the relationship between marker and information (Chapter VI) but without any manifest consciousness of this function on Sartre's part.

[6] Both Lacan and Sartre quote Rimbaud's "Je est un autre". Cf. also Heidegger: "Everyone is the other and no one is himself"; "I myself am not the 'who' of Dasein, the they-self [*das Man-selbst*] is its 'Who' " (1927: 165, 312).

4. Being and Madness

Lacan's description of the splitting of the ego from Being (p. 187) matches rather precisely the Sartrean description of alienation. Lacan defines the paradox of man as "the madness by which man believes he is man" (p. 187) (i.e., by which he believes he is the territory of his own map). In this paradox appears the "fundamental illusion" to which man is enslaved – and, far more enslaved to it than to all the "Cartesian passions of the body". This illusion is the PASSION TO BE A MAN, which is "the passion of the soul *par excellence*" or in other words, the passion of NARCISSISM. "Narcissism imposes its structure on all of man's desires, be they the most sublime" (p. 188).

The ego is a locus of formation, information, and deformation. The identification involved is not only "the GLOBAL assimilation of a structure", but also "the VIRTUAL[7] assimilation of the DEVELOPMENT which that structure implies for an undifferentiated state" (i.e., the child) (pp. 88–9). This development is lived like a "temporal dialectic" which "projects the formation of the individual into the plan of history". The mirror-stage is a drama whose "internal force" is a precipitation of "insufficiency into anticipation". For the subject, who is caught in the trap of the "spatial identification" with another, it not only "machines" the fantasy of "the image of the body in bits and pieces" (*corps morcelé*), but also that of the body as a totality, which has an "orthopedic" value. Precipitated from insufficiency to anticipation, the subject then takes on "the armor of an alienating identity", whose rigid structure will thenceforth mark his whole mental development.

Thus Lacan's analysis of this "passionate organization" called the ego, not only extends and elaborates the Sartrean existential analysis of psychosocial alienation, but grounds it in human development and in the Freudian terms of narcissism and identification. But Lacan's analysis also depends on the existential anguish of being-for-death. Lacan describes the genetic passage from the mirror-stage to the actual identification with an *alter ego* or counterpart, as that which dates the beginning of the paranoid alienation which is constituted when the "specular ego" becomes the "social ego". This movement marks that at which "all of human knowledge" (*savoir*) falls under the law of "mediation by the desire of the other" (p. 98). (Cf. Kojève, 1947: Chapter I.) This narcissistic process is linked to the Freudian death instinct, through the supposed opposition between the "sexual instincts" and the "destructive instincts".

In other words there is no social dimension to the foundation of the

[7] The adjective 'virtual' is commonly applied to 'intention' in theology, to 'image' in optics, and to 'displacement' in mechanics.

Imaginary, and it is ruled by death rather than by life. Consequently Lacan's critique of Sartre (pp. 93, 99) does not in fact greatly distinguish his premises from those of existentialism, by which Lacan has been far more influenced than is usually admitted. Everything he says here about the "folly of being man" is in effect a commentary on the well-known passage in the last pages of *Being and Nothingness* (1943: 708):

> Every human reality (human being) is a passion in that he projects the loss of himself in order to found being. He projects his own loss in order to constitute, by the very same act, that in-itself which escapes contingent existence because it is its own ground: the *ens causa sui* which religion calls God. Thus the passion of man is the reverse of the passion of Christ, for man loses himself in order that God may come to life. But the idea of God is contradictory, and we lose ourselves in vain: *L'homme est une passion inutile.*

(The idea 'of God' is in fact paradoxical rather than contradictory, for He is the locus of a double bind.)

5. *Death and Narcissism: The Solipsist and the* Salauds

Lacan elsewhere describes the narcissistic relationship as the first implicit experience of death (Lacan, 1953b). The pure duality of the discordance of the Imaginary engenders a 'tearing apart' (*déchirement*, in the Hegelian sense), or an 'abandonment' (*déréliction*: Heidegger's *Verlassenheit*), as at the origin of the 'human condition'. The anticipation of a future 'coming to realization' is like death, for in order to realize his 'identity', the subject has to take over his own mature functions in the world, on his own account, and escape the Imaginary situation of being the alienated witness of the acts of his own ego. (This is in fact how Freud describes the splitting of the subject in psychosis: *Standard Edition*, XXIV, 201–4.) Death, says Lacan, is the fourth element in the oedipal relationship (which is usually conceived of as three-way). According to Lacan, the real father in our contemporary social system is most often a discordant, deficient, or humiliated father (Claudel), who is incapable of sustaining his Symbolic function as the Other who is the locus of the Law (the prohibition of incest). Consequently, the oedipal relation is more often pathogenic than normalizing in its effects. The family is thus pregnant with narcissism, rivalry, jealousy, and Imaginary identifications or doubles. If one interprets the Imaginary relationship as a Hegelian struggle for recognition (Kojève, 1947), as Lacan does, then one understands that the "struggle for pure prestige" in the Imaginary cannot depend on any kind of real death. It is in effect dependent on an implicit or unconscious pact between the participants: that they shall both survive, for one cannot be recognized alone. The dialectic must depend therefore on IMAGINED death, and this is the form of death that Lacan believes to be the significant mediating factor in all narcissistic relationships (relationships between ego's) and in neurosis.[8] No Hegelian reciprocal recognition is therefore supposed, although the asymptotic goal of reconciliation remains latent in the relationship. Thenceforth the subject's "original, intrapsychic rivalry with himself", discovered in the discord of the mirror-stage, is projected into the "aggressive interpsychic triad" of self, other, and mediating object which is described by the Hegelian theory of desire (p. 113). ('Intrapsychic' is, of course, hardly the correct term to describe the child's relation to his environment, but the preceding essays should make it unnecessary to go into detailed criticisms here.) In keeping with the lack of a socioeconomic dimension in his work, Lacan recalls at this point the metaphysical principles of Love and Strife, and remarks on the supposed "cosmic polarity of the male and female principles". This polarity, he says, is abolished by the "battle of the sexes" in contemporary society (pp. 121–2). (Cf. Chapter X.)

Metaphysical anguish over death, like psychoanalysis in itself, is a middle-class or aristocratic intellectual luxury. One need hardly mention Montaigne or Zeno on the theme of death, or the existential hero, who represents for the twentieth century the Hegelian and schizoid 'unhappy consciousness' – which results from the internalization of the master–slave dialectic by consciousness on its journey towards Absolute Knowledge. (In the sense that the Hegelian *Phenomenology* is a history of literature, Montaigne could presumably represent the sceptic consciousness, Pascal, the unhappy consciousness, and Rousseau, the antecedent of the romantic 'noble soul'.) The existential heroes are still with us. The Roquentin of Sartre's *La Nausée*, Stendhal's 'outsider', Julien Sorel (discovered 'after the event' by existentialist critics), Kafka's 'creature' in *The Burrow*, Dostoevsky's underground man, Beckett's absurd tramps, Camus's Sisyphus – and so on – continue to fulfill their function in the rationalization of socioeconomic alienation, especially as they continue to be represented by all whose moral alienation and impotence encourages them to identify

[8] See also M. Safouan (1968: 267–8). Elsewhere Lacan makes the phallus the fourth term. He is apparently trying to map the oedipal relation onto the four terms of the family of the 'other civilization', which must necessarily include the maternal uncle or his equivalent as the condition of its existence (Lévi-Strauss, 1958: 56–7; Ortigues, 1966: 72–82; Wilden, 1968a: 100, 146–8, 303–6; Lacan, 1966: 348, 362). Lacan does say that all dual relationships are mediated by death or by *le mort* (the 'dummy' or the 'dead man'); death is the Absolute Master (Hegel) (p. 121); the Symbolic Father is the dead father, and so on.

with such 'romantic solipsists': to identify with them, FOR and AGAINST the *salauds* who re-present themselves:

> The ultimate signification of the 'project', according to *Being and Nothingness* (1943), is the desire to be god. God is in any case defined as a projection of the Other. . . . In *Being and Nothingness* the Other who is desired is a tree, a stone, a statue, a tragic mask. In *Nausea* (1938), the despised *salaud* is a tree, a stone, a statue, a grotesque mask (Girard, 1965a: 426, 441).

In this "theology of the Ego", in this " 'Jansenism' of the anti-hero",[9] says Girard, every desire is, in the last analysis, "a desire for the obstacle because it is a desire for the sacred". Roquentin is the OPPOSITE of the heroes of Sartre's youth, "and this opposite is a SAME who is blind to his sameness" (ibid.).

Proust's Marcel is another, perhaps more striking, twentieth century representative of the morbid narcissism of self-alienation:

> The idea of death installed itself definitely in me like an *amour*. . . . But, after I had reflected on death from time to time as if she were a woman that I no longer loved, now the thought of death came to adhere so completely to the deepest level of my brain that I could not pay attention to any particular thing without that thing first traversing the idea of death. . . . The idea of death kept me company as incessantly as the idea of the self [*moi*]. . . . [I realized that] at the time I became like one half-dead . . . , this great mirror of the mind was reflecting a new reality (1913–27: III, 1042–3).

Except for Svevo's hero, who is remarkably Proustian anyway, one could hardly find a better example of Lacan's 'imagined and Imaginary death'.

---

[9] Goldmann (1955) distinguishes four political types of Jansenism in the seventeenth century:

1 The Moderates (Arnauld d'Andilly, Choiseul): Compromise (unwillingly) with the evil and hypocrisy of the world.
2 The Centrists (Antoine Arnauld, Nicole, Pascal before 1657): Fight within proper limits for truth and good in a world where the Jansenist has a place, however reduced.
3 The Non-Tragic Extremists (Jacqueline Pascal): Profess good and truth in a radically evil world, which persecutes and proscribes, but withdraw from it.
4 The Tragic Extremists (Racine's heroes before 1689; Pascal after 1662, Barcos): Say nothing, withdraw.

All condemn the world with no historical hope of change. Only Pascal's *Pensées* (1670) provide any sort of metacommunication about the role of truth in the world.

But whereas a simple, uncritical, human sympathy and empathy might make one receptive to the 'security operations' of these writers, or to their commentators (such as Lacan), an equally simple understanding of the social function of the discourse of science forbids us to fall into the Imaginary trap offered here. We cannot accept an invitation to identify man-and-womankind – and therefore ourselves – with the false consciousness of the academic, psychological, and literary 'false selves' (subjective or objective) of those who earn their livelihood in the production and distribution of the ideal commodities of the dominant ideology (Marx and Engels, 1845–6: 60–1). We see nothing less in this than another resurgence of the anarchistic –individualistic traits represented in the nineteenth century by the young Hegelians – characteristics which are particularly conservative of bourgeois morality, if in displaced and 'denegated' forms.[10]

6. *The Confusion of the Symbolic with the Real: Science and Theology*

> The limits of tyrants are
> prescribed by the endurance of
> those whom they oppress.
> FREDERICK DOUGLASS

In his promotion of the digital oppositions of phonemes and the uncertain status of the digital subject as shifter in his speech, Lacan seems to confuse the Symbolic with its alienation as a form of commodity exchange (Chapter IX). There seems to be a characteristic confusion of the structure of the Symbolic (difference) with its superstructure or content ('irreducible oppositions') (Chapter XVI, Sections 4 and 5). Thus Lacan either actually identifies the Symbolic with its Imaginary representation by the dominant ideology of digital identity and opposition, or else he implies that this is the state of affairs for modern man and woman. And since this ideology is a statement about the relationships in the material life of human beings, we discover that, like the so-called schizophrenic, our culture effectively confuses the Symbolic with the Real:[11]

---

[10] Cf. Marcuse on the concept of repressive desublimation (1962).

[11] Cf. Lacan's commentary on the Freudian *Verneinung*, which he confuses with *Aufhebung* (Lacan, 1966: 369–99):

> In the Symbolic the gaps [i.e., the absence of 'Signorelli'] are as significant (as signifiers) as are the plenums.

In reading Freud today, it looks as if it is

> the gaping of a void [the forgetting of 'Signorelli'] which constitutes the first step in his whole dialectical movement. This perhaps explains the schizo-

For the bourgeois, it is so much the easier to prove on the basis of his language, the identity of the commercial and the individual, or even universal, human relations, since this language itself is a product of the bourgeoisie and therefore in actuality, as in language, the relations of buying and selling have been made the basis of all others (Marx and Engels, 1845–6: 249).

We can put this point another way: Lacan's statement that "there is no dialogue" betrays a particular definition of the Symbolic (language) which is peculiar to our culture. It reveals in fact a quest for communion – and a misunderstanding of communication – in terms all too similar to Sartre's description of the quest for the *ens causa sui*, or to the existential hero's desire for the obstacle. I have already pointed out the theological, rather than human, character of the principle of the Other in Lacan. Both death and being will remain equally theologized so long as the model of the dialogue is language in its digital, analytic, aspects, because it is through these categories that death and being can be reified. Lacan's psychoanalysis is not dialectical; it is epigenetic. As such, it is itself founded on analytical reason and deprived of any way of transcending itself by reference to the material context of death and being: the analog.

In other words, whatever may be said about the signifier as DIFFERENCE in the Lacanian theory, it is always implicitly conceived in the terms of ABSOLUTE difference, i.e., as (Imaginary) opposition, rather than in the terms of simple digital distinction. We do not therefore discover the categories of Symbolic (digital) exchange value in Lacan, but solely those of Imaginary (digital) exchange (called the Symbolic). This is, of course, a metaphor of the actual alienation of exchange value in the Real. Moreover, since – according to the implicit values of the theory – both signifier and subject must be NAMED in order to signify, the category of the Symbolic exchange of (analog) use value is entirely missing from the model.

If meaning is reduced to naming in this way, then all linguistic categories become theological categories. After all, the characteristics of God in our culture are, on the one hand, that he cannot be named, and, on the other, that he is the only being capable of saying "I am who I am". This is how Lacan describes the Other's locus in the Symbolic (Wilden, 1968a: 271). Consequently, the trap opened up for the subject in the Lacanian theory is

---

phrenic's insistence on reiterating this step. But in vain, since for him all the Symbolic is Real (p. 392).

The last sentence refers to the Wolf Man's 'rejection of castration'. The 'rejection' returns to him from 'outside' in the form of a hallucinated injury to his finger and to a tree.

precisely that of the institutionalized LEGALISM of the Judeo-Christian culture itself: The Father is the only Being identical to himself. Is the Son therefore either IDENTICAL to or SIMILAR to the Father? But the Father says: "You must (but you may not) be I, who am what I am." The rationalistic and legalistic categories of reification which underlie the theory thus remain a simple representation of the double bind of the theological discourse itself. This is the inevitable result of defining all dialogue in the terms of language alone, rather than also in terms of the LABOR of relation.

The theological discourse is a metaphor of the scientific discourse: as a system of communication and exchange which seeks to discover the Word of God in Nature, through the digitalization of the Real and through the myth of 'pure' digital knowledge, the scientific discourse alienates itself in the reification of the lost object. The myth of 'objectivity' necessarily generates bad faith, accompanied by a necessary guilt – after all, even those trapped in the discourse of science are nevertheless human beings, whatever their behavioral values may manifestly represent. This filial guilt resulting from one's inadequately representing the Truth of the Word in one's productions, is a manifestation of the researcher's own reification in the COMPETITIVE quest for Truth. Truth is represented by the myth of science as unmotivated and not subject to the relations of rivalry and desire. But so long as Truth continues to represent a vehicle of status rather than the 'quest for life itself', the fleeting improvised men of academia remain trapped in the oedipal relation of the 'enemy brothers' of Sophocles' *Antigone*, destroying each other in a battle of pure prestige for the Father's inheritance. But Antigone's absolutism is, of course, no solution. (In retrospect, the political message of Anouilh's 'modernization' of the play during the German occupation of France has been reduced to one more representation of the existential hero in his – her – solipsistic martyrdom. Martyrdom is a fine symbolic business – if it has political ends.)

Thus, according to the Lacanian theory, because the dominant ideology is one of the reification and the entification of human beings as objects of Imaginary exchange, the dominant category of LINGUISTIC signification – that of the human function which becomes an 'identity', a Name – drives the subject, already reified in the Real, to alienate himself in the Word. But language – through and because of its essence as relation – necessarily refuses all such possibilities of an actual linguistic reification to the subject, who is consequently lost in his pathological attempts to correlate and identify all the possible maps with all the possible territories in human existence. Lacan was quite correct in saying in 1953 that the Symbolic (language) cannot actually be reified, and that reification (or psychosis) confuses the Symbolic with the Real (Wilden, 1968a: 124). But so long as, in a real world of oppressive relations, the question of subjectivity is necessarily posed for the INDIVIDUAL – rather than for the collective – then the subject's quest for identity will remain a quest for a justification of his alienation: a quest for a name in an Imaginary discourse, an empty word.

The category of naming as reification in our culture is not to be confused with the essential category of TAXONOMY in human thought. Classification requires denomination, but the classificatory categories of *la science du concret* in "untamed thought" (Lévi-Strauss, 1962a, 1962b) do not name entities; they name relations. But it is precisely this epistemological confusion which betrays the utopianism of structuralism as a defense against real alienation. In transplanting the categories of a Symbolic discourse (concrete science) into an Imaginary one ('abstract' science, ideology) by a process of reducing the first to the second, the structuralist 'law of relation' reveals its social function: that of concealing the categories of real responsibility and punctuation in socioeconomic communication. In other words, it is through this reductionist confusion of logical typing that logical typing is denied. The punctuation of categories in our society is not a one-dimensional question of linguistic syntax; it is a multidimensional economic question.

So long as one approaches the Lacanian text from an extra-psychoanalytic perspective, there is much of value in that text. I believe that we can separate what is valuable in it from the oppressive ideology which accompanies the text, just as we can separate Freud from his bioenergetic models and from his oppression of his followers, or Marx from his inability to transcend in his personal life the categories of nineteenth-century racism (e.g., Hyman, 1959: 142). But this requires us to remain intransigently critical about those overriding characteristics of the Lacanian perspective which reveal it to be a classical theory of political economy which cannot get out of its bourgeois skin.

Other readers may perhaps find themselves more sympathetic to the Lacanian text as a whole than I find myself to be. If so, however, they should perhaps ask themselves about the form of exploitative violence represented by Lacan's STYLE, to say nothing of its manifest elitism. I have said elsewhere that the *Écrits* represent an ensemble of double binds directed at the reader. But there is nothing 'benevolent' about them. The reader has not simply to follow Lacan's directions to "put himself into the text" in order to understand it (at the analog level). If he is to escape his own ideological self-alienation, and if he is to break the chain of aggressivity which Lacan's text invites him to turn upon those who 'don't know' – as I have repeatedly seen done by those using Lacan's work – then he must be able to transcend that text as the locus of the Other as violence.

No text which retains the characteristic of a mystery religion or of a secret society can ever be trusted. So long as the High Priests are the only ones who can read and write, or who can interpret the sacred texts, or who can read the messages of auguries and dreams, the people at large will be forced to trust in the 'leadership' of those whose values can never be the values of humanity at large.

The supposed expertise in 'reading the secret hearts of human beings' which our society confers on the psychoanalyst makes him a particularly dangerous culture hero. In a culture of the expert like our own, there are few people who, whereas they revere the 'scientist', are not in fact afraid of the analysts – and they, in turn, are afraid of themselves. Their expertise is illusory. One must reply to the constantly unspoken question behind this fear: No, Virginia, he cannot read your secret thoughts the way you once thought your parents did. There is no Santa Claus (cf. Lacan, cited in M. Mannoni, 1970: 195, footnote).

So long as the discourse of science continues to represent the Word of God who is dead but does not know it, and so long as we use that discourse as a protective image which we more or less successfully place between ourselves and our own 'finitude', no transcendence of the values of that discourse is possible. Our own finitude is not, however, our own individual death, as Heidegger or Lacan would put it, but rather the objective necessities of closure at the digital level of a human 'discourse' which is in fact collectively open at each and every level to restructuring.

In a word, we must be able to transcend a discourse in which paradox is insoluble in order to deal with a discourse in which paradox is inescapable, and therefore essential. A rule which is universal and to which there are no imaginable exceptions ceases by that fact to be a rule (Whorf).

7. One Way Out

Unlike Lacan, Marx fully understands the values – if not the processes – of symbolic communication and exchange in the 'cool' culture, and without any trace of a utopian desire for the lost object. For Marx, exchange is the major agent of the evolution of "human individualization" (Marx, 1857–8: 96. Cf. Chapter IX). And, he says, in a particularly eloquent passage, when we peel away the narrow bourgeois form of "production as the aim of man" and the bourgeois form of "wealth as the aim of production" (as distinct from the "ancient conception" of "man as the aim of production"), we can ask a new question:

> What is wealth, if not the universality of needs, capacities, enjoyments, productive powers, etc., of individuals produced in universal exchange?

What is this, in fact, "if not a situation where man does not reproduce himself in any determined form, but produces his totality?" (pp. 84–5).

In the face of repressive material and spiritual alienation, the intellectual may well decide to choose to oscillate between the paradoxical injunctions of the Imaginary – to lose himself in the endless Kierkegaardian circles of repetition, unable to choose either the *either* or the *or*, always in mortal fear of his mastery, constantly seeking recognition, lost in the objectification of his own individualism, 'sick unto death' in his narcissistic anguish. Or he may decide to take the way out offered by the example of Marx, the way of political and personal growth, of morphogenesis, of constant evolution, the way of critical metacommunication. It is probably more likely, however, that he will alienate himself in the impossible lost object of his illusory quest for 'pure knowledge' – for all knowledge comes with dirt under the fingernails – or subsume his alienation in the Dostoevskian underground, in Kafka's courtrooms, or in his Skinner boxes and his pages of equations, in his 'consultations', in his mortgage, and in his 'service to the university'. He may indeed take the path Zeno took, for whom the most important decisions have to do with cigarettes, for whom the lived time of human experience is an unbearable responsibility, and who endlessly repeats his voyeur-sadistic relation to the rest of humanity from whom he has been severed by his own parasitism.

But, on the other hand, he may take the pathway of higher logical type offered by someone like Frantz Fanon, as in his eloquent appeal to Symbolic unity over and above Imaginary identity and schizoid opposition. Since the settler defines the colonized person as an absolute evil, says Fanon, then the *colonisé* can only begin his redefinition (his repunctuation) of the relationship by similarly defining the settler. The relation is, however, a Manichean one only for the colonialist – and for his representation by liberal newsmen in the mother country – for it is the colonizer who is in fact responsible for the violence of the colonized. The necessary reaction against the settler's violence generates the collective labor relationship through which the colonized's communication surpasses in logical typing that of the atomistic and individualistic colonialist. In the struggle for liberation, the colonized comes to transcend the original violence of the colonizer. Thus

> for the colonized person, life can only spring up again out of the rotting corpse of the settler. . . . It so happens that for the colonized people . . . violence, because it constitutes their only work, invests their characters with positive and creative qualities. The practice of violence binds them together as a whole, since each individual forms a violent link in the

great chain, a part of the great organism of violence which has surged forth in reaction to the violence of the colonizer in the beginning. The groups reciprocally recognize each other and the future nation is already indivisible (1961: 93, translation modified).

But how long does it take for the intellectual to learn that he too – if more on a spiritual than on the material plane – is a victim of (internalized) colonial oppression?[12]

8. *Master and Slave in Context*

We know from the study of other cultures that the particular form of the master–slave dialectic posited as 'at the origins' by Lacan is a socioeconomic, rather than a purely psychological process. But we nevertheless have to recognize its actual existence and function. If we want fully to understand the controlling functions of this principle of 'divide and rule' in contemporary society – the real existence of this form of the societal manipulation of learned insecurity – then Lacan's analysis of it in the terms of the Imaginary is essential. However, Lacan has never drawn the logical consequences of his own theory in this respect, as his phallocentrism and his virulent attacks on his own ex-disciples (e.g., Laplanche and Pontalis) amply demonstrate. And the lack of a contextual reference in many of those beholden to the Hegelian–Freudian perspective is rather unfortunately demonstrated in a very bad book by O. Mannoni (1950) on colonization. (Mannoni, now a member of the École freudienne, lived for some time in Madagascar before its independence.) In reading Fanon's remarkably restrained critique of this text, one sees Mannoni seeking to reduce all real socioeconomic and psychosocial relationships to psychological equality and Imaginary identity. (Cf. also my remarks on Ellul's *Propaganda* in Chapter XIV.) Mannoni has since moved to a 'white-liberal' position (1969), but the work continues to exist as an example of the mispunctuation of context or relationship (it 'arrived' in the U.S. in 1964). Fanon's remarks turn out to fit rather precisely my own critique of closure, of one-dimensionality, of the way analytic reason is used in the scientific discourse, and of the imperialism of the 'professional' who illegitimately extends his knowledge of part of the field to the field as a whole (Introduction).

---

[12] This statement is not intended to encourage any romantic illusions about brotherhood between the races in a social system which makes it objectively impossible. And these passages must be read in the context of the following:

> The settler is not simply the man who must be killed. Many members of the mass of colonialists reveal themselves to be much, much nearer to the national struggle than certain sons of the nation (1961: 146).

After making the necessary corrections to Mannoni's absurd statements to the effect that only a psychological approach can properly analyze the colonial situation; that because white laborers in South Africa are as racist as the managers, racism cannot be the result of economics; that colonial exploitation and racism are different from 'other' forms of exploitation and racism; that "European civilization and its best representatives are not responsible for colonial racism"; and that France is one of the least racist of all countries;[13] Fanon summarizes:

> After having sealed the Malagasy into his own customs, after having evolved a UNILATERAL analysis of his view of the world, after having described the Malagasy within a CLOSED CIRCLE, after having noted that the Malagasy has a dependency relation toward his ancestors . . . O. Mannoni, in defiance of all objectivity, applies his conclusions to a BILATERAL totality – deliberately ignoring the fact that since the [French subjugation of the island], the Malagasy has ceased to exist (1952: 94, my emphasis).

If it were not that on any university campus, in the mass media, and in social science, one is regularly faced with similar examples of class- and race-bound vested interest masquerading as science, it would hardly seem necessary to refer to such an obviously racist book. Fanon knows only too well the double bind of the people of color under white oppression: turn white or disappear (p. 100). But Mannoni interprets the Malagasy's behavior as the result of an innate "dependency complex". Replies Fanon: "What Mr Mannoni has forgotten is that the Malagasy alone no longer exists; he has forgotten that the Malagasy exists WITH THE EUROPEAN" (pp. 96–7). Fanon then turns to Mannoni's interpretations of Malagasy

---

[13] It is in fact the extraordinarily subtle manipulation of racism which distinguishes French colonialism from the British form. The overt superiority of the British colonialist was that of a man who would not in general ever accept on personal terms what he called the 'educated native' in a system of colonial schools in which at least literacy was widespread. In contrast, the covert superiority of the highly limited French colonial education system created a 'native bourgeoisie' thoroughly identified with French values. These 'lucky few' were accepted as being 'practically white'. Their poets write in French. Their leaders represented the colony in the French Assembly. Thus they became completely alienated from the 'ignorance' and the 'backwardness' of their own people.

It is the French system which is in general being practiced by American universities today, through their policies of 'compensatory education', although there is still plenty of evidence of the British attitude among the faculty. The white-dominated university is an ever-present cooptative danger to the minorities; it is also at least the repository of technological information – e.g., medicine, health science, communications – which is essential to them.

dreams – nearly all dreams of terror – and insists that they must be restored to their proper TIME and PLACE: and the time is a period in which thousands upon thousands of Malagasy were massacred; the place, an island where Third World troops from other French colonies, imbued with white racist attitudes (there are no others under colonialism and neocolonialism), not only make up the army, but the police torturers as well (pp. 104–6).

"THE RIFLE OF THE SENEGALESE SOLDIER IS NOT A PENIS, BUT A GENUINE RIFLE, MODEL LEBEL 1916."

9. *The Violence of the Reduction of the Cultural to the Ontological*

The Imaginary is the domain of the 'either/or' – and therefore of the double bind (Chapters IV and V). In 1956, in an unpublished seminar (M. Mannoni, 1970: 68, note 1), Lacan spoke of the "ambiguous echo", constantly felt by the subject, of the "relation of exclusion" set up by the master–slave relationship in the Imaginary. The subject will always fear that the 'other' who has conceded an 'ego' to him will take back his mastery. This schizoid relation to the other is a metaphor of the subject's relation to himself. The ego, as a product of Freud's 'reality principle' – or rather, I would say, of Marcuse's far more relevant 'performance principle' (1955) – is said to be necessarily a "function of mastery". Thus the master and the slave are both 'outside' and 'inside': "Every purely Imaginary equilibrium or balance with the other is always marked by a fundamental instability."

I would suggest, however, that Fanon's version of the relation, in which the colonial master 'frees' the slave in order to put him to work, is a more accurate depiction of the real situation of the oppressed in relation to the violence of the system in which the slave – woman, man, child – must perform. Elsewhere Lacan compares the situation of the Imaginary subject to the Hegelian 'noble soul' – who appears elsewhere as Laing's 'disembodied' false self (1960) – but Lacan takes a position which is the opposite of Laing's. Lacan describes every manifestation of the ego as "compounded equally of good intentions and bad faith". The usual "idealistic or revolutionary protest against the chaos of the world" only betrays, "inversely, the very way in which he who has a part to play in it manages to survive". However psychologically true of some people this may be – of the negative bourgeois, for instance (cf. Mitchell, 1971: 27) – the members of Fanon's 'wretched of the earth' might find this recapitulation of Hegel's 'law of the heart' – which reduces all real situations of oppression to paranoid relationships in which "the persecutors are identical with the (once-loved) images of the ego-ideal" (Lacan 1953b: 13) – entirely typical of the way the 'objectivity' of the discourse of science almost invariably turns out to be a renewed attack on the oppressed and a justification of the oppressor.

According to Lacan, the question of the subject's existence is posed for him "in the discourse of the Other" (the unconscious), not only as the simple anxiety (at the level of the ego) that is described by the term 'instability' above, but more profoundly as a question about his status in the "unconscious discourse": "What am I there?" (Lacan, 1966: 549). Lacan replies that the subject is represented in the conscious discourse by a signifier (a shifter), which allows him to "identify himself" in language by "losing himself in it like an object" (Lacan, 1953b: 11; Wilden 1968a: 63). I have already criticized this proposition from an epistemological point of view (Chapter XVI). At the level of the primal repression, however, according to Lacan, the subject is represented by a missing signifier, by a signifier which is LACKING. This definition, which seems to say only that the primary process cannot SAY 'I' – as the domain of the analog, it IS I-in-relation-to-the-others – is, of course, related by Lacan to the Symbolic value of castration as a lack, and to the phallus as what represents that lack in the Symbolic order.

The question "What am I there?" is said by Lacan to concern two primordial questions: sex identity and "contingency in being" (cf. the quotation from Sartre on the contingency of the *pour-soi*, in Section 3 above). These two questions "conjugate their mystery and bind it to the symbols of procreation and death" – which presumably include Eros and Thanatos, at one level, and, at another level, the phallus and the Other (or the dead father) (Lacan, 1966: 549). Since it is language – the locus of the Other – which is responsible for the "synchronic precedence of the signifier over the subject" in his genetic development, then what is required in psychoanalysis, says Lacan, is a 'topological' or 'pre-subjective' logic of the signifier. Significantly enough, that is a logic of differential relations in which all contextual punctuations are possible. Its 'pre-subjectivity' however, is presumably that of what precedes the digital subject. Since that is the analog subject-in-relation, there is some possibility that, used in context, such a topology could be useful to the theory of communication and exchange.

Nevertheless, a moment's thought about the psychosocial violence of our culture might lead us to frame our answers to the demand of the digital subject: "What am I there?" in a radically different way.

We might consider the institutionalized sexism, racism, and corruption of the university, the sciences, and the arts (Ridgeway, 1968; Millett, 1970). We might wonder at the 'soul-murdering' activities of our schools

(Clark, 1965; Herndon, 1968; Kozol, 1969[14]) – which can apparently be differentiated in their approach to their 'socializing function' by the quantitative measure of Rytalin dispensed daily to children possessed of 'MBD'. We could remark on the manipulative functions of the 'American Way of Death' (Jessica Mitford), or of institutionalized guilt, competition, performance, and individualism. One could examine the mechanization and merchandising of sexuality as a commodity in our culture (Brown, 1959). We could consider the wholesale psychological, sexual, and economic violence of male chauvinism or sexism against fifty-one per cent of the population (Millett, 1970; Morgan, ed., 1970). We would not have to mention the violence of psychoeconomic racism, of television, of movies, or of our present colonial wars, both at home and abroad (Graham and Gurr, 1969), if it were not for the fact that the very existence of these manifest forms of violence provides a refuge for us (mostly male) intellectuals against our own daily acts of violence. This is a violence often committed in the name of 'education', 'standards', 'objectivity', 'rationality', 'science', and 'both sides of the question'.[15] The source of this violence presumably lies in the social manipulation of our fear of others (i.e., of ourselves) (Sartre, 1946: 53), especially of students, women, and the 'masses'. It is often triggered by jealousy of the young, but it is more usually the straightforward result of paranoid justifications of our own insecurity, which we project as aggressivity emanating from the others we control. We have said nothing about the violence of psychiatry and 'mental health' (Cooper, 1967: 14–33; Goffman, 1961: 171–320), or about that of the family,[16] or about the destructive and anti-human effects of restricted, non-qualitative, cultural definitions of intelligence, rationality, and retardation.[17] Nor have I mentioned the escalating technological and organizational violence of our culture, or the institutionalized intellectual elitism and paternalism of anthropology, in its persistently ethnocentric relation to the 'others', the 'savages',

[14] And many personal communications from teachers in extension classes.
[15] Cf. Ridgeway, 1968:
    ... While the activities of the professor-entrepreneurs are cast in the form of corporations, their values are those of the university, patronizing and authoritarian. The essence of their propaganda is efficiency, the governing myth of American corporate society. Thus they offer for sale different ways of achieving the same thing: a static, boring consumptive middle class through a constant change of machine parts (pp. 71–2).

    Cf. also pp. 57–68 on the activities of the academic 'gamesters' in domestic and foreign counter-insurgency.
[16] Laing and Esterson, 1964; Bateson, Haley, Jackson, and Weakland, 1956; Watzlawick, Beavin, and Jackson, 1967.
[17] Millett, 1970; M. Mannoni, 1964, 1967; Fanon, 1952, 1961, 1964. Cf. Piaget, 1968; Jensen, 1969; E. Mayr, 1963.

which has been paternalistically refuted by Lévi-Strauss.[18] I doubt whether I have remembered everything that I could have mentioned, but an omission here or there does nothing to change the general picture. However, there is also another form of violence, a covert form which is perhaps the most devastating of all for those subjected to it. This is the PASSIVE VIOLENCE OF THE REFUSAL TO RECOGNIZE COVERT OR REAL VIOLENCE.[19] It may be expressed in deeds; or in positions, stances, attitudes, rules, codes, manners; in inertia, cynicism, 'scientific objectivity', coyness, humor; in refusal, disavowal, negation, or disconfirmation – but also and especially at all levels, in words.[20]

[18] Cf. the remarks on Piaget in Chapter XI. The American publishers of *La Pensée sauvage* (which is the name of a wildflower) in fact destroy Lévi-Strauss's thesis before you can even open the book by entitling it *The Savage Mind*.

[19] Consider the following statement by a "Professor of Educational Sciences", taken from the introductory chapter of a book intended to refute the racist use of the psychometrics of so-called intelligence (Richardson and Spears, eds., 1972: 16) (cf. also Chapter XIV, Section 7):

> Our aim – in research as in teaching – is to discover what constraints limit the growth of an individual's full intellectual powers. Yet even if, for the sake of argument, we were to grant the most extreme possibility – that ALL black children are born less intelligent than ALL white children, a wildly unlikely state of affairs – we are still little the wiser. Dimly, we may feel that something of educational importance is at stake; yet when the proposition is examined in detail, its practical implications trickle away. [It] . . . does not tell us, for example, whether black children and white children should be taught separately or together, it gives no clues as to how each child should be lured into the use of his brains. . . .

What can one say about this complex and grossly insensitive interweaving of alienating values about children, 'intellect', and 'education', and the concomitant use of a "wildly unlikely" example which reveals the identity between the writer and those he is supposedly opposing?

[20] Cf. Fanon, 1952: 138, note 24, on the white as the Real or Imaginary master. On pp. 161–4 Fanon offers a contextual criticism of the mirror-stage, pointing out that only for the (middle-class) white is the particular other an "absolute not-self" in the Imaginary. For the Antillean, ALL perception is Imaginary, in other words, white; and all whites are the Other. Fanon remarks on Lhermitte's conception of the body-image on p. 111: "The elements that I used had been provided for me not by 'residual sensations and perceptions primarily of a tactile, vestibular, kinesthetic, and visual character', but by the other, the white man, who had woven me out of a thousand details, anecdotes, stories." Any woman in our culture could say the same.

Compare also the effects of white exploitation in Africa, as represented by the importation of the mechanistic and objectifying vocabulary of industrialization from English into the indigenous languages: sexual intercourse is described as *ukushanta* (shunting), a light complexion is referred to as a *passport*, a mistress becomes a *spare wheel* or a *piece-work woman*, and so on (Epstein, 1959). This

I therefore choose to answer Lacan's question with Fanon, whose discourse on the violence of the Other puts all the phantasies and aggressions of the discourse of science in their proper place:

> Because it is a systematic negation of the other person and a furious determination to deny the other person all attributes of humanity, colonialism forces the people it dominates to ask themselves the question constantly: "In reality, who am I?" (1961: 240).

This is not a metaphysical question to be answered by a simple recourse to logic, linguistics, psychoanalysis, or communication theory. It is a real and material question – but we may have already run out of time in which to answer it.

10. *Summary of Lacan's Position*

To sum up Lacan's position: the subject is alienated from himself by the perceptual relationship of the Imaginary, founded on the mirror-stage, which generates the ego as an entity modeled on the body-image. The subject then seeks to discover his identity in language (Lacan's Symbolic order), which is articulated on the lack and, it appears, is ultimately reducible in the Lacanian theory to the circulation of the phallus as an Imaginary representation with a Symbolic function. The phallus is a signifier for Lacan, and since for him the signifier is ultimately no more than a bundle of binary oppositions, he is able to play on the supposed opposition of presence and absence between the phallus and the lack (of object) in order to describe the phallus as Imaginary in form (founded on opposition) and Symbolic in function (because it mediates human relationships, because it is a gift, like a word, because it circulates like a 'sign' in the 'matrimonial dialogue'). If the subject seeks to identify himself in language, the Lacanian theory implies that he becomes identified with a signifier (rather than with an entity, as in the Imaginary). This may mean that he is identified as the phallus – as a signifier in someone else's discourse, as a correspondence with the desire of the mother (that he be the phallus). It may mean that he is identified with a name, position, or title; in other words, that he is identified by a reification of words (like Sartre's anti-Semite). Thus, where the subject seeks his own identity in the realm of being, he finds the other; where he seeks identity in language, he finds a

---

article is distinguished by the total absence of consciousness on the part of the 'objective' observer in question, about what he is actually in the process of describing.

lack. According to the theory, he may however, discover his "Symbolic identification" with his repressed, unconscious desire. This is in effect his identification with the desire of the Other, from which all the demands he places on others in the Imaginary are assumed to derive (Safouan, 1968: 267–8).

The Symbolic identification, therefore, by definition, is an identification with the values of the *status quo* – or rather with those of the *status quo ante*.

11. *The Ego's Attempts to Square the Circle*

Lacan has attacked the use of the term 'adaptation' to describe the child's relationship to his environment. And yet, in spite of the essentially static or repetitive character of the Lacanian theory, there is a restricted level at which it can be said to be dialectical, which requires Lacan to use the language of adaptation. The description of the function of the *imago* in the article on the mirror-stage, in fact defines a psychological ecosystem. The function of the *imago* is "to establish a relation of the organism to its reality" or, in other words, "of the *Innenwelt* to the *Umwelt*". And even if this proposition fails to bring out the fact that this relation had already been established, at various other levels, by the communicational processes originating with conception, Lacan does not, in this early text, simply leave the question of relation at this gestaltist level.

To those readers accustomed to the terminology of linguistics or to the phenomenological and existential concept of intersubjectivity, now much less fashionable than it was, the terminology of these essays may sound strange. But terminology is not simply a question of fashion, for the new epistemology which this terminology attempts to articulate fulfills its function in the dialectical movement of the 'lack of object' we call truth by its suppression and conservation (*Aufhebung*) of the theoretical antecedents without which it could not be. The concepts I have used are all as new as the dawn and as old as humankind. Thus, as I now look back on the work of Lacan from a different perspective, it is of no small interest to discover that the same basic gestalt notions of wholeness, relation, goal, organization, and the observer's contribution to the observed which founded general systems theory and structural phonology in the nineteen-thirties, led Lacan to begin his early theoretical development by an implicit definition of the symbiotic sender–receiver relationship of the natural ecosystem. Moreover, he situated the origins of the existential and methodological distinction between the sender and the receiver in the Imaginary, and carefully defined the pathological reification of this essential difference there. He strikes at this reification of the line drawn across the message circuit between (what we define as) 'organism' and (what we define as) 'environment' in a particularly poetic way, drawing on Jacob von Uexküll's imagery:

Ainsi la rupture du cercle de l'*Innenwelt* a l'*Umwelt* engendre-t-elle la quadrature inépuisable des récolements du *moi* (1966: 97).

Récolement refers to a bailiff's inventory, to the reading back of an affidavit or deposition to the depositor, to the old practice in forest law of verifying the terms of the exploitation of a timber sale by a judicial process involving the act of *contra-diction* (a relationship of legal adversaries, technically called *contradicteurs*). Thus this passage might be rendered as follows:

Thus is it that the rupture of the circle joining the *Innenwelt* ('organism') to the *Umwelt* ('environment') engenders those inexhaustible attempts to square the circle which characterize the ego as it verifies its inventory in the Imaginary, as it reviews the possessions it has expropriated, as it checks the symmetries of word and deed, map and territory, as it makes sure that the statements on both sides match each other.

The ego thus makes sure there are no differences, only Imaginary identities and oppositions. And therefore it breaks the ecosystemic relation of the unit of mind.

12. *Phallocentrism in the Body-image*

> Upon this penis-envy follows that hostile
> embitterment displayed by women against men,
> never entirely absent in the relations between
> the sexes, the clearest indications of which are to be
> found in the writings and ambitions of
> 'emancipated' women.
> FREUD: "The Taboo of Virginity"

Later on, however, Lacan put the question of organism and environment in another way: "What relation does the 'libidinal subject' whose relationships to reality are in the form of an OPPOSITION between an *Innenwelt* and an *Umwelt* have to the ego?" (1953a: 11, my emphasis). In this restatement in English of the article of 1949, Lacan goes to some pains to demonstrate a 'social consciousness'. He makes connections between technology, industrialization, and organization, on the one hand, and the "psychological impasse of the ego of contemporary man", on the other, which is demonstrated in the "progressive deterioration in the relationships between men and women". He speaks of the context of psychoanalysis in the history of mankind, and of the possibility of "more human relationships" which are offered by the analytical dialogue. He recognizes the paradox of the analytical situation, which is

> one in which the one who knows admits by his technique that he can free his patient from the shackles of his ignorance only by leaving all the talking to him (p. 13).

But Lacan does not recognize that freedom can never be given, that it can only be TAKEN. And the different use of the term 'opposition' in his preliminary question already begins to reveal the rationalist, linguistic, and digital epistemology upon which all the rest of his work will be based, as one might well expect, given its primarily phenomenologist, existentialist, and logocentric sources. For, latent within this manifest context of concern for "man", we find an original Imaginary opposition at the basis of Lacan's value system. This opposition is revealed in his further discussion of the body-image. He refers to the "imaginary anatomy" on which the body-image is constructed. This anatomy varies with the more or less confused ideas about bodily functions in different cultures. Such phenomena seem to exhibit the autonomous structure of the gestalt, he points out. And then he makes the correlation which will become a prime mover in his system:

> The fact that the penis is dominant in the shaping of the body-image is evidence of [these autonomous gestalt structures]. Though this may shock the SWORN CHAMPIONS OF THE AUTONOMY OF FEMALE SEXUALITY, such dominance is a fact and one moreover which cannot be put down to cultural influences alone (p. 13, my emphasis.)

It is indeed the societal rupture of the circle of difference between man and woman which engenders THE IMAGINARY CHAMPIONS OF THE AUTONOMY OF PHALLOCENTRISM.[21] It is their 'narcissism of minor differences' which results in the 'paranoia of symmetry' by which the oppressor projects his own desire onto those he oppresses. Lacan's world is at first sight simply a Manichean one, but the objectively demonstrable colonialist designs of 'man' on 'woman' in our society mean that no man is for woman simply her other in the mirror. He is also her master and exploiter; he is the Other. Lacan forgets that the woman is not alone, that she is defined by men, and that with the coming of sexism, 'woman' ceased to exist.

Just as the colonialist creates the 'native' – and the liberal creates the 'black intellectual' – by destroying the Antillean, the white creates the 'black' or the 'brown' or the 'red' or the 'yellow' by destroying the human

---

[21] As Melanie sings it: "Freud's mystic world of meaning needn't leave us mystified – It's really very simple – What the psyche tries to hide – A thing's a phallic symbol if it's longer than it's wide. . . ."

being. And just as it is the anti-Semite who creates the 'Jew' by refusing his 'Jewishness', the social democrat makes his contribution to the alienation and objectification of the other's differences, by being 'color blind', by accepting him in the universal – as 'Man' – but never in the particular (Sartre, 1946: 55). So too Man in the flesh creates 'woman' in the body, and he raises her on a pedestal the more effectively to objectify her. He makes 'phallus' = *pouvoir* = *savoir*, and justifies the violence of his verbal, psychological, and economic oppression by conferring ontological status on it. He replies to the woman's anguish, necessarily expressed in her questions about being and identity – and addressed (God forbid!) to HIM – by one form or another of the defensive words of the petrified anti-Semite:

> There is nothing I have to do to merit my superiority and neither can I lose it. It is given once and for all. It is a THING (p. 27).

13. *Concluding Unscientific Postscript*

The theoretical questions around which this book is articulated are those which lie behind – in a real and material sense – every other question about future evolution, ecology, revolution, and the liberation of women and men throughout the world, at every level, from the oppressive values of a decadent civilization.

I know little – yet – of the possible solutions – but the first step is to discover the real nature of the questions. And only when man-and-womankind can truly say: "We and the earth, our mother, are of one mind", will these questions have been answered in the most real and material sense. Then and only then will the human revolution have finally taken place. . . .

Oui, mais il faut parier. Cela n'est pas volontaire, vous êtes embarqué.

Every natural substance (I mean a compound body) is composed of matter and form, as of her principles . . . But the Form hath such singular vertue, that whatsoever effects we see, all of them first proceed from thence; and it hath a divine beginning; and being the chiefest and most excellent part, absolute of herself, she useth the rest as her instruments, for the more speedy and convenient dispatch of her actions: and he which is not addicted nor accustomed to such contemplations, supposeth that the temperature and the matter works all things, whereas indeed they are but as it were instruments whereby the form worketh . . . Therefore whereas there are three efficient and working causes in every compound, we must not suppose any of them to be idle, but all at work, some more and some lesse; but above all other, the form is most active and busie, strengthening the rest; which surely would be to no purpose if the form should fail them, in as much as they are not capable of heavenly influences. And though the form of it self be not able to produce such effects, but the rest must do their parts, yet are they neither confounded together, nor yet become divers things; but they are so knit among themselves, that one stands in need of anothers help . . . Wherefore that force which is called the property of a thing, proceeds not from the temperature, but from the very form it self.

GIAMBATTISTA DELLA PORTA: *Natural Magick* (1558–89, English translation of 1658)

The only Thought which Philosophy brings with it to the contemplation of History, is the simple conception of REASON; that Reason is the Sovereign of the World; that the history of the world, therefore, presents us with a rational process. This conviction and intuition is a hypothesis in the domain of history as such. In that of Philosophy it is no hypothesis. It is there proved by speculative cognition, that Reason . . . is SUBSTANCE, as well as INFINITE POWER; its own INFINITE MATERIAL underlying all the natural and spiritual life which it originates, as also the INFINITE FORM – that which sets this Material in motion. On the one hand, Reason is the SUBSTANCE of the Universe; viz., that by which and in which all reality has its being and subsistence. On the other hand, it is the INFINITE ENERGY of the Universe; since Reason is not so powerless as to be incapable of producing anything but a mere ideal, a mere intention – having its place outside reality, nobody knows where; something separate and abstract, in the heads of certain human beings. It is the INFINITE COMPLEX OF THINGS, their entire Essence and Truth . . . It supplies its own nourishment, and is the object of its own operations . . . The movement of the solar system takes place according to unchangeable laws. These laws are Reason, implicit in the phenomena in question. But neither the sun nor the planets which revolve around it according to these laws, can be said to have any consciousness of them.

G. W. F. HEGEL: *The Philosophy of History: Introduction* (Student Notes: 1832)

Appendix

Additional Notes (1980)

The following notes seek to correct significant types of error in the text, as well as to clarify by means of new definitions certain themes that could not be dealt with in the Introduction. The contrasting passages from della Porta and Hegel used to introduce these notes are intended to re-emphasize the repression of the reality of levels of relation in the scientific discourse, as a result of the capitalist revolution. In particular, these two passages serve to indicate the collapsing of the Form/Matter distinction and its replacement by a viewpoint that no longer distinguishes between information and matter-energy.

1. "In the terminology of communications theory [Lévi-Strauss] is describing the emergence of the digital from the analog in interorganismic communication" (p. 16).

This reference to the emergence of a new form of production and exchange (i.e., society) out of bioecological exchange processes (nature) should not have identified digital communication as such as a novel emergence. Both analog and digital communication occur in all communication systems. What is novel about the emergence of society from nature is the USE to which digital communication is put by kinship organization, in particular. Here named kinship DISTINCTIONS between people, which imply both the evolutionary novelty of human language and that of human society, are employed according to the constraints of coded rules about permissible and/or prescribed socioeconomic relationships. Given the role of kinship in the other societies' organization of the processes of socioeconomic PRODUCTION, and its related role in the organization of individual and collective REPRODUCTION, kinship and the novelty of its emergence are significant markers of the open-system boundary between the natural ecosystem and the socioeconomic ecosystem.

2. "And in our present culture, most of us have agreed to let language and economic relations make those decisions for us" (p. 25).

(1) Apart from the implication of a relative semiotic freedom of choice which we do not have, the major error here is to imply that language as such

(in the Sapir-Whorf sense, or in Korzybski's sense), might be the locus of a particular kind of problem in relation to the Real.

But every language is as adequate to its socioeconomic reality as it needs to be. What may or may not be adequate to a given social and ecological reality, however, are the various DOMINANT DISCOURSES derived in specific times and places from the potentials made available by a given language. It is the conjunction of the constraints of socioeconomic relations with the dominant discourses they permit that makes – or codes – so many decisions for us.

The same problem occurs also on p. 57, where "the controlling function of language" should be: "the constraints of the dominant discourse" (cf. also p. 221). In the *German Ideology*, the same understandable mistake occurs in the discussion of the "language" of the dominant value system, capitalist exchange value (cf. the quotation on p. 472 above).

(2) The mistaken position which confuses language with the dominant discourse(s) that language permits seems to be a residue not simply of the evident realization that language is not a copy of reality, but more significantly of theology. For implicit in this common view of language is the notion that language representation is a 'deterioration' of 'reality' – whereas for humans language is a part of reality – whether this deterioration be assumed to be the result of the loss of the *lingua adamica* (which turned out to be the communication system of DNA-RNA), or the result of the loss of the only 'eternally perfect' and 'self-sufficient' language known to the western tradition: the voice of God said to be inscribed in nature and in human hearts.

3. ". . . Although the system [of communication] is indeed determined in some sense by the repertoire or the code from which the possible elements of the message are drawn . . ." (p. 35).

(1) The term 'determined' here implies the very Newtonianism and determinism it is questioning, and the uneasy phrase 'in some sense' does not help. What the passage is trying to say is that in all communication systems, including language, the codes and repertoires CONSTRAIN the possible messages that sender-receivers mediated by the code can select and combine, emit and receive.

Similarly with the expression 'overdetermination', derived from Freud. What is needed here and elsewhere is the notion of synchronic and diachronic hierarchies of constraint, and the concept of the diachronic convergence of choices made within constraints, conscious and unconscious choices that eventually produce the particular 'overdetermined' message (cf. p. 39; and Notes 8 and 29 below).

(2) On the topic of the determinism invented in the nineteenth century, two forms are now recognizable. When the present system-state is determined by its past states, we have the one-to-one linearity of efficient causality. When the present system-state is determined by its future state, we have the determinism of traditional philosophical teleology. The teleonomy of goalseeking is distinct from both of these determinisms, just as it is distinct from the fantasy of the opposition between determinism and so-called 'free will'.

(3) 'Many-to-one' relations (convergence) represent equifinality; 'one-to-many' relations (divergence), multifinality. Neither of the latter are linear (proportional); nor are they necessarily lineal (single level, unidirectional). 'Cybernetic causality' has been termed 'reciprocal' and 'reticulate' or 'reciprocally determinant'. But the attempt to describe a process in which feedback relations produce effects that come to affect their own sources, which new effects affect the previous effects, and so on, may still end up with a theory of 'reciprocal causality' that is akin to the mechanical action and reaction that enables the reciprocating engines in cars to carry people down the road.

4. ''Redundancy' (pp. 35–7, 231–4, 331, 365–6, 409–12).

The best single definition of 'redundancy' I know of is Hassenstein's in his very useful outline of information-processing in the organism (1971: 75–8). Redundancy is POTENTIAL INFORMATION, i.e., types and levels of variety which are available for use if necessary. Compare Bateson's definition of (future) flexibility in ecosystems, p. 219 above.

Provided we are careful not to confuse the terms 'free' and 'bound' with their usage to label the 'free' and 'bound' energy of thermodynamics – 'bound' energy being that from which no further work can be obtained (cf. p. 136) – redundancy may be said to represent 'free' variety available to the system, in relation to the information (the coded variety) actually being used. In this sense, information may be said to represent 'bound' variety in relation to redundancy. 'Bound' variety here signifies variety from which no novel uses can be obtained; 'free' variety, as one type of noise (uncoded variety) for the given system, signifies an apparent 'disorder' (or non-signifying 'order') for the given system, from which novelty or 'new order' can be obtained if necessary.

Note here that, following the work of Heinz Von Foerster, D. M. Mackay, and Gregory Bateson, organic metabolism and socioeconomic maintenance, including in both cases production and reproduction, may be said to be based on a principle of ORDER FROM ORDER. (Order ingested or taken from the environment or from a subsystem is broken down by various agents, such as enzymes in organisms and basic production processes in society, and then re-ordered as an order usable for the system in question.) Organic evolution and socioeconomic revolution, in contrast, may be said to be based on the principle of ORDER FROM DISORDER. (Disorder external or internal to the system – i.e., noise or variety uncoded or previously uncodable by the system – is converted by the changing system into novel information or new order.)

An organic example of the second principle would be that expressed in the many processes by which the production of disorder by industry – including both the deliberate use of disorder, e.g., biocides, and the 'externalities of production' – and its subsequent injection into the natural and human environment, may over time be taken up as 'new order' by organisms, resulting in mutation, disease, death, or extinction. One instance of this kind of order from disorder is provided by the new varieties of insect species created by the use of pesticides; the drug-resistant bacteria created by the use of modern drugs provides another.

A socioeconomic example of order from disorder in history occurs in the three or four hundred year process of deep-structure change which we now label the 'capitalist revolution'. The increasing disorder represented by the masses of 'landless laborers' created by capitalist enclosures was successfully turned into new order useful to the economic system and protective of its novel social relations. This process of converting 'noise' into 'information' was accomplished in proportion as the predominantly mercantile form of capitalism transformed itself into a new form by means of the invention of the factory system. (See the contemporary account of the later stages of this process by the technocrat, Andrew Ure, in his *Philosophy of Manufactures*, London, 1835.) In this way, the unusable disorder represented by the 'landless laborer' was transformed by the wholesale commoditization of unused creative capacity (labor potential) into the new order of the modern proletariat, i.e., into that of the mass of so-called 'free laborers' constrained by the newly dominant 'labor market' to sell their creativity at the going price.

Finally, it will be noted that 'order' and 'disorder' – like all of the other terms discussed here (amongst many others) – are definable only in relation to each other and in relation to the goals of the system involved. 'Order' and 'disorder' 'as such' or 'in themselves' no more exist than does the 'thing itself' of the phenomenologists or the 'noumenon' of Kant – or the 'structure as such', or the 'history' or the 'structure' 'without a subject', of later writers. To give one obvious example, mutations and new varieties that are useful new order for populations of microbes and insects may well be dangerous forms of disorder for human beings.

See also pp. 400–12, Note 7, and the diagram on p. 209.

5. ". . . The Thelemic injunction of Rabelais" (p. 89n).

'Do whatsoever thou wilt' is the injunction inscribed over the door of Rabelais's imaginary utopia, the Abbaye de Thélême (*Gargantua*, 1534, Book I, Chapter 57). The Abbey is open to "free men", who are "well-born, well-educated, and used to living in honest company".

6. ". . . Because there is no metalevel within the Imaginary (which . . . cannot comment on itself as language and digital communication can), the notion of reflection has the curious result of implicitly denying that there is any relationship between what reflects and what is reflected . . ." (p. 94).

The problem here is that forms of metacommunication are indeed possible in the Imaginary, but will not ordinarily be recognized as involving a different level of communication. What is missing when the Imaginary is the dominant relation, is the CONTEXTUAL PERSPECTIVE, including the perspective of hierarchical relations, which allows us to relate the Imaginary to a reality other than the one it is impersonating.

The relationship of 'reflection' being attacked here is that espoused in a number of common misreadings of the Marxian texts (as well as misreadings of the work of Engels). It is a viewpoint whose use of an Imaginary mirror-relation to characterize the relationship between 'superstructure' and 'base' presumably results from some kind of optical illusion. (The key word in the Marxian texts is not reflection, but 'translation'.) This monocular and monoplanar conception of levels in socioeconomic systems has been aptly characterized by Paul Heyer, who calls it 'the periscope theory of relations'.

7. ". . . Tension is one of the products of organization itself" (p. 143).

The discussion of 'tension' on pp. 143–4, social and otherwise, should be translated into the non-mechanist, non-organicist terminology of META-STABILITY. It is their metastability which distinguishes (organic and social) systems from their various environments. (The same principle will apply to the concrete subsystems and levels of organization 'within' a given organic or social system.) These systems include once-living systems, such as fossil fuels (stored sunlight), whose metastable molecular order can be catalyzed by fire, by organisms, or by human intervention so as to be useful as energy (nine-tenths or more of present usage) or as information (in this case, the molecular organization used in the synthesis of new products, including biocides and plastics). Organic and socioeconomic metastability involves open-system boundaries which may be described in terms of the repeatedly renewed and constantly maintained thermodynamic gradients between 'system' and 'environment'. Such descriptions may be made in energy terms (e.g., 'free' and 'bound' energy, energetic 'order' and 'disorder'), or in informational ones (e.g., 'free' and 'bound' variety – cf. pp. 136 and 365 – informational entropy, 'order' and 'disorder' in the organizational sense). In nourishment, for example, carbohydrates are important principally as sources of energy, and proteins (chains of amino acids) are important principally as information. Both are ordinarily measured in kilocalories, however, by means of combustion in the 'bomb-calorimeter' technique. This process adequately measures available energy; but, as with the use of fossil fuels through combustion, it destroys the information. See also Note 4.

8. ". . . The digital computer involves a code, and any code considered in its totality is an analog of something (a 'map' of some 'territory' or other)" (p. 157).

(1) Here and on original page 158, there is a code-message confusion. A code is (at least) a set of constraints and a set of rules about how messages may be constructed; it is not as such an analog. The confusion appears to stem from a failure to distinguish a code from a cipher. Unlike a code in the proper sense, a cipher is a REPRESENTATION, e.g., the so-called 'morse code' which represents the alphabet, and which is by that circumstance an indirect analog of it. A code in the proper sense does not involve a map-territory relationship, whereas the messages constructed according to the rules and constraints of a given code do indeed involve the representation of a 'territory' by means of a 'map' (cf. also p. 219).

(2) The constraints of a code – which may include rules about the construction of the 'elements' of what in (digital) information theory is called a 'repertoire' – mediate the relative semiotic freedom available to goalseekers in the system for the invention of messages. The code thus mediates the relations of the sender-receivers that employ it. A code – in reality sets of codes and metacodes – is in effect the creative principle that makes messages and relationships possible in the first place, at the same time as its

constraints make an even greater variety of qualitatively distinct messages and relationships impossible or unimaginable in the system AS IT STANDS.

A code is thus of a HIGHER LOGICAL TYPE (and therefore less complex) than its messages and messengers. Deep-structure socioeconomic revolution – as distinct from surface-structure change mediated by the given codes – provides an example of the reordering or restructuring of the dominant socioeconomic codes that make one kind of society qualitatively distinct from others. This kind of restructuring nevertheless takes place within the context of codes and constraints – e.g., inorganic and organic (ecological) constraints; the constraints of social organization as such; the requirements of metabolism, maintenance, and subsistence; the genetic code; and so on – none of which appears to have changed in any significant way since the evolution of society.

In human affairs, the structure of the code-message and the code-messenger relation can in part be represented by a version of the Hegelian and Marxian 'triangle of mediation', as in *Figure 1*. The use of solid and broken lines in this diagram is intended to serve as a reminder that the relation involves a hierarchy of logical types.

FIGURE 1
Code-Message Relations: The Triangle of Mediation

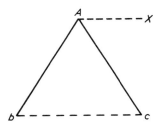

A:	Locus of the code (mediation)
b,c:	Goalseeking sender-receivers mediated by the code
b-c:	Locus of the messages (message channels)
A-b, A-c:	Coding channels
X:	Relationship to an environment

It will be noted that this relationship is also a definition of the minimal requirements of a communication system. And if *b* and *c* are taken to be children, then the diagram may be used to represent the bourgeois family (introducing relations of sex merely requires a permutation of triangles, with the male dominant). Or *A* may be taken to represent the Great White Father in our society. Similarly, *b* and *c* might represent workers whose competition with each other (or indeed, their cooperation with each other) is mediated by the competition of capital with capital, or that of capital with its environments: the competition of A with X and with b and c. (If A represents a monopoly, then its restraint of competition – the cooperation of capital with capital – is mediated by competition at other levels in the system.)

Last, but not all and not least, if b and c are taken to be commodities communicating in what Marx calls "the language of commodities", then A comes to represent the 'general equivalent of exchange' in our society: MONEY in the surface structure, VALUE in the deep structure. (Here the entire relationship of mediation operates at a distinct level, since the code-message relation involves levels within levels.) Readers will recall that although Marx (obviously) does not use the term, money (e.g., gold) is a commodity of a distinct logical type, different from that of ordinary commodities; and that the 'mirror relation' between commodities described in the first volume of *Capital* is grounded in metaphors of a semiotic relationship mediated by an Imaginary discourse (cf. for example, pp. 251–5, 295 above; also pp. 210n, 370–3).

Codes and mediation are evidently properties of all social systems. The reality that mediation in our society involves alienating and exploitative CONTENTS should not be confused, as it often is, with the structure of mediation. If in a given socioeconomic system, the apex, A, represented the locus of cooperation, for example, then all competition in the system would be primarily constrained by the organization of the system itself (rather than by its natural and human environment, as is the case, ultimately, under capitalism).

(3) On the role of the dendrites in the information-processing activities of the nervous system, mentioned on p. 158 of the text, see Shepherd (1978). "The discovery of [these] dendro-dendritic synapses [in 1965], together with our functional model, contradicted the classical doctrine that the nerve cell could only receive signals with its dendrites and cell body and transmit them through its axon, since it suggested that neurons can communicate with each other through their dendrites without the intervention of an axon or a nerve impulse. . . . Recently . . . several examples of neurons have been found that communicate only through graded potentials. . . . It is becoming evident that the nervous system is built up of hierarchies of functional units of increasing scope and complexity" (Shepherd, 1978: 96, 100, 103).

9. "Many-valued . . . dialectical thought" (p. 132); "a dialectical . . . logic of degrees" (p. 158).

The major problem here is the result of the text's failure to distinguish between a 'many-VALUED logic' and a 'many-LEVEL logic' (which will also be many valued). The expression 'logic of degrees' betrays the uneasiness. The many-valued logics as commonly discussed by western philosophers are only many valued in a linear and probabilistic, even quantitative, sense. That is to say, these logics of degrees of 'truth' and 'falsity' do not involve distinctions between qualitatively distinct levels of relationship. In these logics, 'true' and 'false' are arranged along a single either/or dimension: the linear spectrum of the distance between (EITHER) 'probably completely false' OR 'probably completely true'. Thus these logics may well display 'many values', but they cannot display the many levels of the logical typing of levels of value which is characteristic of human socioeconomic organization, e.g., the hierarchical relationship between exchange value and use value, where one or the other may be 'principal' or dominant in relation to the other (cf. also Mao's 1937 essay on contradiction, revised 1952).

This same problem reappears in the discussion of what is called 'analog negation' on pp. 182 and 189. The confusion stems in part from the translation of *Aufhebung* as 'negation' (e.g., p. 96). Negation in the proper sense is a term that should be restricted to linguistic negation. 'Dialectical negation' (*Aufhebung*) is a residue of Hegelian idealism, of the Hegelian dialectic of CONCEPTS – as distinct from the dialectic of realities and the dialectic of class conflict and contradiction in history.

Similarly, the correlation of 'analog' with 'dialectic' should be taken with a grain of salt (e.g., p. 189). The error is derived from recognizing that analytic logic is a digital logic, without also recognizing that it is a subset of dialectical logic, which is both analog and digital. See Note 10; and Wilden and Wilson, 1976.

10. "There is no 'either/or' for the analog computer because everything in it is only 'more or less', that is to say, everything in it is 'both-and' " (p. 162).

(1) Partisans of the position that the digital computer can be programmed to simulate any type of relation should note that, as stated in the text, this simulation is subject to McCulloch and Pitt's 'nerve-net theorem' (1943) which states that such simulations are possible only if they can be described in a finite number of unambiguous words.

(2) On page 162 and elsewhere (e.g., pp. 113, 132, 174), readers will have noticed that a synonymous equivalence is drawn between the 'more-or-less' and the 'both-and' of the analog domain. This is misleading. What is misleading, however, is not that there is no such possible relationship in the

analog mode of communication, but rather that it is a red herring to draw the equivalence in the first place.

This is a tactical error stemming from a strategic problem. The problem is that of the dominance in our society of the 'either/or' of analytic logic. As has been pointed out, this logic IN OUR CONTEXT believes and represents itself to be (purely) digital in its syntax. (If it really were, it would not exist.) Moreover, this logic is also one-dimensional and discontinuous in its communication; also objectifying and objectified; also atomistic, reductionist, and static; also 'oppositional-identical'; also symmetrizing. Indeed, in our context, it is the logic of the classical machine, the logic of the locomotive and the railroad, treating 'truth' and 'falsity' like boxcars in a marshalling yard. It is the diagnostic logic of technocracy and engineering; and in its effective dominance it supports the Imaginary in masquerading as the Real.

As a result, and given the actual socioeconomic context which mediates and structures our relations, the either/or logic permits us to enter into Imaginary identifications with it and into Imaginary oppositions against it. Indeed, so completely may our concerns be mediated by the either/or syntax of this logic that we will happily and incorrectly identify as 'both-and' relations any number of processes that do not happen to display 'either/or' characteristics. In this way, we obey the injunctions about relations implicit in analytic logic, and create a 'both-and' which is an Imaginary OPPOSITE of the already-given 'either/or'.

Thus, since the 'more-or-less' of the analog is NOT an 'either/or', it is all too easy to respond to the Imaginary context by translating such a relationship of 'NOT either/or' into its symmetrized equivalent: 'both-and'.

What has been further by-passed in the passages referred to is the circumstance that 'NOT either/or' could refer to any number of different kinds of relations, whereas 'both-and' in this context refers to a particular relation (cf. pp. 183, 324n; and the quotation from Hegel on p. 423). The kind of implicit logical syntagm involved in this violation of logical typing, which also identifies a general with a particular, is as follows: 'If not "either/or", then (necessarily) "both-and".' But this syntagm displays precisely the symmetrizing rule about relations that makes analytic logic an either/or logic in the first place – we have jumped right out of the frying pan into the fire.

11. ". . . Survival is an analog function" (p. 171).

This phrase should read: "survival is impossible without analog relations."

The form-function distinction used here and on pp. 164–70 is not well worked out. There seem to be two major sources of this problem:

1. The text is attempting to maintain at the same time an analog-digital distinction derived from analyzing language and human communication (where the analog communicates primarily about relationship) and a similar distinction derived from considering the distinctions between animal communication and human communication (including language).
2. The text is then extrapolating on these distinctions in such a way as implicitly or explicitly to make 'nature' = 'analog' and 'culture' = 'digital'. (Hence, for example, the original subheading of Section 8, p. 172: *Play: The Emergence of the Digital.*)

One immediate source of this second problem appears to be the mentalism of the nature/culture OPPOSITION in Lévi-Strauss (cf. pp. 242–3).

FIGURE 2
Logical Typing in Communication

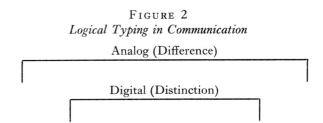

All that is actually needed here in place of the rather tortuous argument is a statement that the ordinary relationship between the COEXISTING digital and analog communication in any given system appears to be the hierarchical relation of logical typing represented in *Figure 2*. This is the perspective derived from considering the use of either/or digital communication (competition) as an instrument of both-and relations (cooperation) amongst the Tsembaga (pp. 159–60). In our society, in contrast, digital communication – as well as competition – is commonly treated as if it were invariably dominant over analog communication – as well as over cooperation – i.e., as if the digital were in the long term of a higher logical type than the analog. In another common mispunctuation of the analog-digital relationship, the hierarchical relationship between these two forms of communication is neutralized by considering the one to be the binary alternative or the opposite of the other (cf. for example, the quotation from Barthes on p. 459).

12. "Because of the difficulty of defining the line between the analog and the two levels of the digital, especially in play, we should reserve the word 'sign' as a mediator between them" (p. 184).

For the five senses, the mediated relationship between the analog aspect of a message and the digital aspect of the same message is commonly an ICON – icons of touch, taste, smell, hearing, and vision, of which the last is the most readily recognized. In this chapter, as elsewhere, a theory of iconic relations is the missing third term – the icon being both analog and digital, often in several dimensions, at several levels.

In this passage – as also on pp. 165, 177, 185, and elsewhere – there is an attempt to translate the communicational distinction between analog and digital communication into the semiotic distinctions between signal, sign, signifier, and symbol. (Mathematical and other such 'symbols' are classified as signs.) The translation suffers from the same problems noted in 11 above. The translation was attempted in this way in order to bring together the dialect of communications theory with that of European linguistics and semiotics. But in the end the translation is not really necessary. Symbols are commonly icons (analog infinities of information framed by their digital borders). Signals, signs, and signifiers may be, and generally are, primarily digital (i.e., discretely bounded), except in so far as in non-verbal communication and in animal communication certain signs or signals may act as icons (e.g., 'displays'). In other cases, the 'fuzzy' framing of the message, as noted on pp. 165 and 169, distinguishes the non-linguistic sign or signal from the verbal-linguistic signifier. But even the signifiers of language, for example, depend at the acoustic level both on relatively clear 'either/or' digital distinctions (e.g., the distinction between 'voiced' and 'voiceless') and on recognizable 'more-or-less' differentiations of continua (e.g., that which distinguishes a phonemic production as 'tense' or 'lax').

13. ". . . This is a task of historical analysis for another time and place" (p. 241).

There exist technological, economic, metaphysical, psychological, linguistic, philosophical, managerial, and literary 'histories of communication' or 'histories of communication technology'. But the communicational history of communication has yet to be written – just as the founding of communications as a critical and social science has yet to be accomplished. Indeed, judging from the 'communications' textbooks now flooding the North American market, even the communicational approach to communication is still relatively unknown (cf. for example, the telling quotation from an unfortunately representative text, *Communication and Behavior* (1975), on p. xxviii).

14. ". . . The mind is PURE relation" (p. 243).

In this attempt to distinguish the mind from the common confusion of levels which identifies it with (the image of) the brain, the text should have pointed out that the mind is a social, and therefore REAL, category of relationship. In contrast, idealist interpretations of 'mind' abstract this relationship from its actual context – and this is as true of Lévi-Strauss's concept of mind and its relation to social structure as it is of Bateson's use of the concept of the 'unit of mind' in a Buddhistic sense. Following on this process of abstraction, it does indeed become possible to dream of 'pure' relations (cf. in this context Zeno's dreams of perfection cited on p. 82).

15. "The Imaginary other in relation to the Other" (pp. 260–1).

The discussion of the Imaginary here fails to include the key words: 'the Imaginary, when dominant'. This relationship of dominance has been particularly emphasized in the revision of the Introduction, whose more appropriate formulations should be read into the deficiencies of the explanation given here in the original text.

A corollary of the failure to distinguish between the dominant and the subordinate in describing Imaginary and Symbolic relationships appears in the inadequately explained use of the term MEDIATION in this passage. Although all socioeconomic relationships are obviously mediated – as has been pointed out – the implication of the passage on p. 260 is that mediation is 'introduced' for the subject at some particular time.

The problem is actually quite a simple one, and its ideological sources correspond very closely to those of other misinterpretations already remarked on. The point is that it is one of the tasks of the Imaginary so to mediate our relations as to deny or to disavow that the mediation of the Imaginary is involved in their constitution. Hence, in the first sentence of the last paragraph on p. 260, the words "without the introduction of mediation" should be replaced. The sentence should read: "The overriding symmetries and the oppositional dualities of the Imaginary when dominant make it a trap from which the subject could never escape without the DISCOVERY OF IMAGINARY MEDIATION. This discovery in its turn provides the possibility of putting Imaginary mediation in its place: under the rubric of the Symbolic and the Real" (cf. also Hall's diagram of interpersonal relations on p. 277 above).

Similarly, the use and interpretation of Lacan's version of the oedipal relation should come under critical scrutiny. As a 'socialization' device proper to the bourgeois family, most if not all references to oedipal relations serve in the end to separate the organization of the family from its socioeconomic context. Moreover, the supposedly 'beneficial' aspects of the child's passage through this socializing relationship on the way to adulthood in our society are restricted almost wholly to males. For women, in contrast, the 'oedipal relation' stands as the Imaginary representation of a lifelong disaster. On this topic, see the revealing analysis of this relation in terms of power by Shulamith Firestone (1970: 47–55). In the world of Freud and Lacan, even the 'other' (little 'o') is a bourgeois male – or a 'person' defined by one.

16. "Thing", "something", "anything", "amongst other things" . . . and so on.

It may seem overly purist to single out for criticism these aspects of the dominant discourse. However, in the context of the atomistic closures of the dominant epistemology and the mechanical objectifications of the dominant ideology – i.e., in the context which, in its relation to the Real, confers on these terms their particular sociohistorical significations – the use of such metaphors to refer to relations that are not things does in effect bring with it a whole series of associated value judgements about reality, judgements which treat reality as if it were simply a collection of things.

That these implicit value judgements are 'unintended' or unconscious does not render them any the less alienated or significant. And we cannot go back in time (nor would we want to) to a sociohistorical context, such as that of the Middle Ages or the Renaissance, where – before the culmination of the capitalist revolution, before the invention of the mechanical philosophy, before the characterization of nature and the human body as machines, before the industrialization of capital – an organic, and in many ways systemic, epistemology prevailed, an epistemology in which 'things' were not considered to be dead objects, but rather to be ANIMATE components of the great chain of being in a Nature pervaded by the information of the Spirit of God (cf. Wilden, 1976a; Lovejoy, 1936; and, on Newton's personal organicism, Dobbs, 1975).

The same contextual critique of course applies to the use of 'mechanism' for 'process', or 'social forces' for 'class conflict', or 'selection pressure' for 'environmental relations', and so on (cf. also Schon, 1963). Indeed, in this respect, much as Flaubert made a collection of clichés and 'received ideas' to be avoided in writing novels (cf. p. 305n), someone should set out to collect and annotate the vast panoply of mechanistic, hydraulic, electrochemical, inertial, equilibrial, gravitational, electromagnetic, thermodynamic, and other physicalist and inorganic metaphors which, in both the social and scientific discourses, we commonly use every day to refer to living nature, to communication, to society, to human beings, to our relationships, and to ourselves.

17. "Piaget's fear of certain kinds of change . . ." (pp. 323, 325).

This moralistic imputation of a form of motivation to the person, Jean Piaget – an imputation derived from the Imaginary and about which his text does not inform the reader – is not only arrogant and condescending, but it also betrays one of the central principles on which I attempt to base this text. This is the principle that what we have before us to learn from, and if necessary to criticize, is never the author but always the TEXT (which may of course include the text of the author's life where necessary). To impute motivations to the author, or to assume that we can know 'what the author really meant' (even when we are dealing with authors who believe they are 'supposed-to-know'), are both examples of what in literary criticism is called the 'intentional fallacy'. Moreover, the imputation of motivation, as distinct from the analysis of contexts and effects, is not only particularly characteristic of modern western society, but it is also a dead end. Psychoanalysts and others have long had a field day over motives but, when all is said and done, all we glean from this approach is that in psychology all motives are equal – which is not true of actions and effects.

What, for example, are my motives in writing these words? You and I could easily come up with a dozen motives or so – but, apart from perhaps satisfying our idle curiosity, in what relevant way would knowledge of those motives illuminate the REASONS for, or the goals of, this necessary apology?

18. "Unequal opportunity" (p. 327).

This phrase is a fine example of an Imaginary trap. Recognizing that 'unequal opportunity' exists in the world does not save one from reinforcing the iniquity of the system one is criticizing – and doing so by one's very use of the expression. What one is reinforcing here is the notion that all would be well if 'opportunity' were 'equalized'. But 'equal opportunity' is an example of a TRANSITIVE expression which – like many, many others in the dominant discourse – is masquerading as an INTRANSITIVE one. Once we complete the incompleteness of this phrase by answering the hidden question, 'opportunity for what?' or 'in relation to what?', we realize at once that we are reaffirming the one great 'right' and the one great 'freedom' that the capitalist revolution promised us: 'equal' opportunity to compete – and in a 'zero-sum game'.

The same kind of question should also be asked about other pseudo-complete received ideas, e.g., 'intelligence', 'subjective', 'progress', 'self-regulation', 'efficiency' (economic, ecological, thermodynamic), and so on. (Also on this topic, see the Introduction, pp. xli–xliv; and the remarks on the liberal attack on racism in genetics, pp. 428–9, 482n.)

19. "Selection . . . and combination . . . occur in any communications system . . ." (p. 351).

Selection and combination involve digital activities. They are to be found in all communications systems because all such systems are both analog and digital. However, it seems evident that whereas one cannot have the analog without the digital in communication, one can certainly find systems of communication so dominated by digitalization that they effectively reduce their analog support and sustenance to the status of information travelling incommunicado.

20. ". . . The word 'system' here always implies 'ecosystem', or a 'subsystem within an ecosystem' " (p. 353).

(1) This clarification comes rather late in the text, but it is in general true of its use of the term 'system', except where the reference is to the systems and subsystems of physics. It is not that physical systems do not have an environment (Kilmister, 1965), or that they do not constitute an environment – indeed they constitute the effectively closed environment of the cosmos as a whole – but rather that their environments are no more essential to their structure or to their activities than are the open-system ecological realities of memory, ecotime and ecospace, and hereditary reproducibility.

In contrast with physical systems as such, living and social systems – as well as systems of ideas – can obviously have no actual or continuing existence, whether in reality or in representation, apart from their essential reference to their environments.

(2) Depending on precisely what is punctuated as 'system', the environments of 'humans' include the ecological and/or socioeconomic environment, as well as the temporal environment of the system's memory, and the environment-to-come through the system's pursuit of its goals. (Note that the major and long-term goal in biological and social systems is stable reproduction, rather than the reproduction of instability which characterizes our present socioeconomic system.) These environments will also include the rememorative environment of the system's actual deep structure – deep structure, in any adaptive system or at any coherent sublevel of the system, being necessarily of a higher logical type than the surface structure.

In considering social systems, we must also include within their context both the inorganic and the organic environments, as well as the environment of their actual history. Included here in some way must also be the mythological or ideological environment permitted and constituted by the material forms in which the social system chooses to store and to recall the memory of its past – the memory, both real and fantasied, linguistic and non-linguistic, of the dominant and subordinate codings of its predecessors, as well as of their 'mutations' in time.

Obviously – and philosophical or metaphysical idealism notwithstanding – ideological systems, epistemological systems, and systems of ideas can have no signification, much less any meaning, except in relation to their various material contexts. The possibilities of this signification are encoded and embodied in the real structure of social systems, as in their functional relations.

(3) We recognize this essential TRANSITIVITY of relations in social systems, as well as their material grounding, in the simple circumstance that all ideologies – whether dominant (as code) or subordinate (as subcodes) – are themselves adaptive, reproductive, and goalseeking systems. Ideological systems may obviously involve the organization of ideas and even the reproduction of unrealities, but they can have no signification if divorced from their functions of rationalizing or 'explaining' the material social and ecological world which gives them existence. At least it is this essential relationship between ideas (information) and reality (other levels of information as well as matter-energy) that we must recognize, unless we share the traditional delusion that "ideas have a life of their own".

(4) Not that ideas did not once seem to have this special form of existence. But this life that they once had was considered real only as long as the cosmos was inhabited by God. Ideas were indeed more real than reality itself so long as the totality of the cosmos was said to constitute the 'Mind' or the 'Body' or both (the 'sensorium') of an amazingly incorporeal and supreme being or beings – was said to constitute attributes of the same God whose body had turned into a gigantic machine by the end of the seventeenth century.

21. "Since organisms select 'environments' and vice versa, the terms 'organism' and 'environment' refer to an ecosystemic relationship, not to entities" (p. 356n).

It is true that within the constraints of the general environment, organisms select *milieus*; and that organic systems (e.g., forests) can modify some aspects of the local environment in their own interests and those of others (e.g., temperature, soil retention, and so on). But it is incorrect to reduce 'organism' and 'environment' to a single-level relationship, as implied in this sentence by 'vice versa' (cf. the Introduction, p. xxxiii). However, if one were analyzing, say, a group-to-group relation of, say, economic equals, then it would be quite legitimate to treat each one, within the levels of the more general environment, as the 'environment' of the other.

On the relation between a social system and its environments, it should be noted that the natural environment is not simply the finite 'resource environment' of soil and minerals and fossil fuels and foods, but also the equally finite 'waste-sink environment' – i.e., the environment which through recycling and other processes uses or neutralizes the disorder injected into it by society. In the case of industrial capitalism, this disorder includes any number of so-called 'externalities of production' through which the environment of nature and the flesh of human beings are presently required to subsidize the production process, for much of this disorder can neither be neutralized nor recycled into useful order by ordinary organic and inorganic processes.

22. ". . . The more dependent the system becomes on technology . . ." (p. 367).

'Technology' and 'technique' here obviously mean 'the social organization of technology', which in its turn must refer to the organization of the social relations of production in the Real. All socioeconomic systems obviously have technology and they are all dependent on it. The error here is a common one: a confusion between 'Technology' as we now experience it, and the capitalist mode of production, with all that its invention of the factory system and the modern consumer entails. As it stands, the noted passage is naïvely 'anti-technological'. This is of course a considerably safer position than being anti-capitalist – which presumably accounts for its continued popularity.

23. "The ensuing exponential amplification of deviations can be controlled only by second-order negative feedback: the destruction of the system or its emergence as a metasystem" (p. 375).

Here, as elsewhere in the text, the two kinds of 'orders' of positive and negative feedback are being visualized in part on the model of the graph represented by *Figure 3*.

Since the graph is an attempt to represent numerous qualitative and quantitative relations in an n-dimensional reality by means of a two-dimensional diagram – with a concomitant loss of information – it should be understood as merely illustrative (Bruce Carruthers). By 'ecospace' is meant all those ecosystem variables which act as constraints on the subsystems in the ecosystem, e.g., types and forms of food supply and energy transforma-

FIGURE 3
Accumulation of Productive Capacity (Capital)

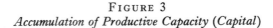

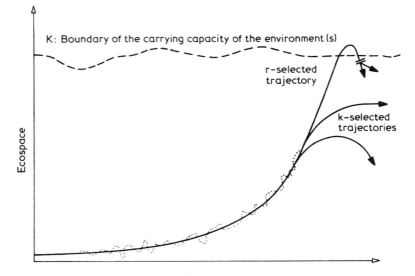

Ecotime

r-selected: Population or system dependent on high reproductive rates to survive.
k-selected: Population or system protected by 'symbolic competition' and other
similar processes from approaching actual carrying capacity (cf.
Wynne-Edwards, 1972, 13–21, 224–8, 389–95, amongst others).

K: Boundary at which the various effects of significant limiting factors
and the production of uncodable disorder come together – catastro-
phically (cf. Zeeman, 1976).

. . . . . . 'First-order' positive-negative feedback oscillations (analog), e.g., the
'business cycle' in the surface structure of 'wages, price, and profit.'

⟶ 'Second-order' positive-negative feedback trajectory, e.g., the exponential growth and/or the increasing accumulation of productive
capacity (capital) in the deep structure of use value, exchange value,
and surplus value.

tions, the topological organization of the system, the patterning of ecological
niches, the resource environment and the 'waste-sink' environment, and
so on. By 'ecotime' is meant that kind of biological and socioeconomic
time in which the reproduction of the past in the present comes to affect the
future of the system. 'Carrying capacity' should be understood as a dynamic
and interdependent factor which is defined both by the resources and the
recycling capacities of the environment, as well as by the capacities of the
various systems within it to make use of these environmental capacities.
Actual carrying capacity can be expanded by innovation and reduced by

'overloading', both qualitatively and quantitatively. (For a summary of research into socioeconomic systems which alter their behavior as they approach some percentage of carrying capacity – some as low as 7 per cent, more generally in the neighborhood of 60 per cent, i.e., systems labeled as 'k-selected' here – see Sahlins, 1972: 41–69.)

The break in the 'r-selected trajectory' in the diagram is intended to indicate that by virtue of passing outside the constraints represented by K, the system in question has passed through a catastrophic and irreversible discontinuity which may represent extinction or morphogenesis – 'catastrophe' in the Thomian sense. (On oscillation and stability, see Wilden and Wilson, 1976.)

24. "Opposition . . . paradox . . . contradiction" (pp. 390–2).

(1) The original text contained an inconsistency in the use of the terms 'opposition' and 'contradiction'. The references to 'opposition' in the original were references to Imaginary oppositions, i.e., to binary and bilateral 'oppositions' – e.g., 'capital' and 'labor' (cf. the revised diagram on p. 221) – which conceal and distort the actual hierarchical relationships they represent.

(2) The key terms in this passage on the two basic contradictions of capitalism have now been corrected. In considering further the communicational and socioeconomic categories of relationship often obscured by the term 'opposition' (cf. pp. 12–14, 414–24, on Lévi-Strauss and others; and the Index entry 'opposition'), one can discern a developmental and dialectical sequence of possibilities, beginning in (analog) DIFFERENCE, moving to digital DISTINCTION (which may or may not involve levels), and thence to the BILATERAL OPPOSITION in which each item is either actually of the same logical type as the other, or is treated as if it were. Such dyadic and symmetrical relationships, some of which are Real, are the products of mediation (i.e., of a relation to a third term); and when this mediation symmetrizes the non-symmetrical or bilateralizes the hierarchical, then the mediation will be seen to be Imaginary.

From (binary) opposition at a single level, the relationships discussed here may move to a CONTRADICTION BETWEEN LEVELS (and between more than two terms). Such hierarchical contradictions may so 'intensify' under certain circumstances as to become translated into double-binding PARADOXES, where opposition runs amuck, it seems, i.e., into paradoxical relations which must be transcended if the socioeconomic system is to survive (cf. Wilden and Wilson, 1976).

(3) On the general topic of opposition, it is worth reiterating that dyadic

oppositions of the same logical type are products of mediated – triadic – relations in which the third term commonly remains unrecognized. This is all the more true when the purported 'opposition' is between terms of distinct logical types (e.g., 'nature' and 'culture', 'consciousness' and 'the unconscious', 'analytics' and 'dialectics', and so on). This occultation of the third term is the relationship partially formulated in the discussion of the mediation of 'God' in the world of Descartes (p. 217n above). Victor Turner (1966 : 71) points up a significant aspect of the problem by citing the following remark from the symbolic logician A. B. Kempe (1890), where we would want only to substitute 'characteristically modern' for Kempe's "characteristically human":

> It is characteristically human to think in terms of dyadic relations: we habitually break up a triadic relation into a pair of dyads. In fact so ingrained is this disposition that some will object that a triadic relation is a pair of dyads. It would be exactly as logical to maintain that all dyadic relations are triads with a null member.

(Compare here C. S. Peirce's category of 'Thirdness', outlined on pp. 265–8 above; and the role of a code as a thirdness outlined in Note 8 above.)

(4) In a topological sense, it is the boundary between (what is called) 'system' and (what is called) 'environment' which is the locus of mediation even for a Leibnizian 'monad' – for the boundary is neither part of the 'system' nor part of the 'environment' (cf. pp. 315–17); and yet without it the monad does not exist. In the same topological sense which thus makes even a monad the product of a triadic relation, a dyad involves at least two distinct locuses of mediation: that which mediates the relation of the dyad to its general environment; and that which mediates the two parts in their relations to each other. When considered as if mediation did not exist – i.e., when considered as they are usually considered – dyads appear as two (digital) atoms with one link between them (the dyadic axis) or in other words as Imaginary 'systems'. In contrast, the triadic relation is explicitly systemic and explicitly hierarchical (as, for example, in the mediation of all relations between others by the Other) – the locus of mediation of one triad becoming a mediated position at the next higher level.

(5) In the socioeconomic and socioecological sense, it will be seen that the original structural contradiction between 'capital' and 'labor', the one that makes capitalism capitalist, is indeed a contradiction in which it is possible to 'take sides'. (In a paradox one is obliged to take both sides at once.) In an infinite environment, there is no reason for this contradiction to change in its essentials. But the second contradiction in Godelier's important re-reading of the texts – in essence the contradiction between the industrial-

ization of capitalism, at one level, and all its resources, including people, at another level – may indeed lead into the paradoxical and ecological conflict between 'land, labor, and capital', and to the ensuing conflict over growth and stability. Hence it is that the 'intensification' of this originally secondary and subordinate contradiction (the socioecological contradiction), may be seen to be contributing to the 'intensification' of the first (the socio-economic contradiction), the principal and structural contradiction between capital and labor, which of course includes, but now also goes beyond, the nineteenth-century realities of the 'class struggle'.

(6) On the question of opposition, contradiction, and hierarchical relations, consider also the following passage from the *Grundrisse*, where the term 'organic' clearly implies 'systemic' – as also in 'the organic composition of capital' – and where Marx does not use either of the terms that a reader of Lenin might expect: the 'identity of opposites' or the 'unity of opposites'.

(In Lenin's notebooks on Hegel, these two terms are not only confused together, but they are used to imply one-dimensionalized and pseudo-dialectical analogies between distinct orders of complexity in reality, e.g., between positive and negative numbers, positive and negative electricity, Newtonian action and reaction, and "the class struggle" – each of which is said to constitute an 'identity of opposites' (1961: 359–60). The one common property they might manifest to someone in Lenin's situation is that each can be regarded as a dyadic 'either/or'.)

Marx is concerned with 'Say's (so-called) Law of Markets', which makes production and consumption equal and opposite, as in mechanics (1857–8: 93–4, 99):

> There is nothing simpler for a Hegelian than to consider production and consumption as identical. And this has been done not only by social belletrists but by prosaic economists themselves, e.g. Say. . . . Storch demonstrated Say's error, namely that . . . a people does not consume its entire product, but that they also create [new] means of production . . . fixed capital, and so on. . . .
>
> The conclusion we reach is not that production, distribution, and exchange are identical, but that they all form members of a totality, distinctions [*Unterschiede*] within a unity. Production dominates not only over itself . . . but also over all the other moments [of the economic process]. . . .
>
> That exchange and consumption cannot be predominant is self-evident. . . . Mutual interaction takes place between the different moments. This is the case for every organic whole.

(7) Such passages have of course to be interpreted without taking over at

the same time the language of 'determinism' which, as a generally available metaphor, forms part of the text from which they are taken. What seems to be particularly significant about the terms used by Marx for relationships within the whole, however, is that the general synchronic relation and the potential diachronic sequence which we can derive from considering analog and digital communication and the double-bind theory is made quite explicit (with the exception of the place of paradox) in one highly significant discussion of use value and exchange value in the *Grundrisse* (1857–8: 147, translation modified):

> The simple fact that the commodity exists doubly, in one aspect as a specific product whose natural form of existence ideally contains (latently contains) its exchange value, and in the other aspect as manifest exchange value (money), in which all connection with the natural form of the product is stripped away again – this double, DIFFERENTIATED [*verschieden*] existence must develop into a DISTINCTION [*Unterschied*], and the distinction must develop into OPPOSITION [*Gegensatz*] and CONTRADICTION [*Widerspruch*].

(8) This one passage alone puts into question the entire category of opposition as used by many exponents of dialectical materialism (along with 'antagonism', 'antithesis', and the like). And in the context of the previously quoted passage on levels of relation, it obviously begs to be interpreted in terms of logical typing. I do not know at present whether there is a basic consistency in Marx's use of these expressions, apart from this notably revealing one, but the quoted passage certainly makes a nicely phrased commentary, before the event, on the position taken on these relations by Troubetzkoy (1939: 33), one of the founders of the category of 'distinctive opposition' – later the 'binary opposition' – whose ideological and epistemological basis and contemporary heritage has occupied the attention of much of this book:

> The idea of difference presupposes the idea of opposition [*Gegensatz*]. Two things can only be differentiated from each other in so far as they are opposed to each other, i.e. in so far as there exists a relation of opposition between them.

Such upside-down and inside-out ways of placing the cart before the horse tell us a great deal about how we should read Hegel's celebrated dictum (taken up by Marcuse: p. 128 above): "Man exists only in so far as he is opposed" – in the Imaginary.

25. ". . . The macroscopic distinction between nature as the analog and culture as the digital . . .' (p. 405).

This 'macroscopic' distinction between nature and culture is one that may indeed be made, and it has a long history in western ideology. But, as was pointed out in Note 11, the distinction ceases very quickly to be useful or even utilizable, once one begins to analyze more closely the actual communication processes in nature at organic levels, where both analog and digital communication are to be found.

It is this realization which accounts for the word 'macroscopic' in this sentence. When one considers the possible sources of this way of describing the nature/culture distinction, the following probabilities emerge: (1) Hegel's reference (p. 405 above) to a 'natural' relationship as supposedly 'immediate' or 'non-mediated'; (2) Hegel's attention to the role in representation of the digital (dividing) aspect of 'understanding' (*Verstand*), as well as his attention to the 'power' of the Negative (which is not simply digital, but also social); (3) Kojève's distinction of culture from nature by means of the (linguistic) categories of concept, negation, and discourse (cf. pp 64–6, 179n, 75n); and (4) Sartre's categorization of 'nature' (the *en-soi*) as 'full', as distinct from the introduction of LACK into nature or 'being' by the human project, the *pour-soi* (cf. p. 66 and p. 431), in *Being and Nothingness* and elsewhere. Moreover, in describing the Real as 'full' (e.g., p. 284), Lacan displays a similar influence, as does the early Barthes in his contention that there is no 'meaning' which is not 'named' (cf. p. 459). The same kind of categorizations are also evident in Lévi-Strauss's conceptions of culture and the signifier (cf. pp. 244–8, for example). Note, moreover, that, as applied to SOCIETY, 'nature' and 'culture' are the ideological equivalents of 'body' and 'mind'.

The key distinction brought into nature by the evolution of society is not the digital 'gap', or the discrete element, or the 'lack' (and so on) as such. It is rather the way in which digital communication is used. Kinship and Symbolic production and exchange are not possible without digital boundaries around the exchange values, for example. But digital communication in a dominant position is also necessary to the exploitative processes of Imaginary (production and) exchange.

26. ". . . The 'other civilizations' " (p. 406 and note).

(1) As Paul Heyer has most pertinently pointed out, the use of the term 'civilization' in this context reinforces the very opposite of what one wants to say. If we use 'class' in the proper sense of the institutionalization of long-

term hierarchical and 'unearned' relations, divorced from the mediation of kinship (as distinct from shifting or generational heterarchies of 'earned status' dominated by kinship relations), then 'civilization', so called, marks the introduction of exploitation by class into human society. 'Civilization' also marks the arrival of manipulated scarcity and institutionalized slaughter. Thus, 'civilization', precisely because it combines savagery with barbarity, is surely the most inappropriate state of affairs to project onto the other societies.

The same kind of critique applies moreover to the use of the term 'myth' – e.g., 'the myth of science' – as a synonym for 'fable' or 'illusion' in the original Introduction to this book. The values expressed by civilized science cannot legitimately be equated with the science spelled out in the values of myth. As a good nineteenth-century 'progressivist', Marx falls into the same trap laid by the dominant discourse in his use of the term 'fetish'.

(2) 'Hot' and 'cool' – this is a poor choice of terms, to say the least. What is meant by 'hot society' here is of course CLASS society, which should be substituted throughout. It should be reiterated also that in his use of the terms 'hot' and 'cold', Lévi-Strauss takes the extraordinary step of equating 'hot societies' with steam locomotives, and 'cold societies' with clocks.

27. "The invention of writing as such . . ." (pp. 408ff).

(1) With some exceptions, writing as we know it is of course the invention – indeed, it is commonly one of the symptoms – of class society. Amongst the many examples of written memory-systems which we would not ordinarily call writing, the stone markers of the Polynesian *marae* are an explicit instance. The stones are arranged in patterns delineating kinship relations over time. Emigrating groups took with them the reference stone that would enable them to reconstruct the written memory, and their locus within it, wherever they settled down.

(2) On the general topic, and especially on the economic basis of what we recognize as writing, see the remarkable research of Denise Schmandt-Besserat (1978). Earlier archaeologists failed to recognize that small, hand-molded (and sometimes inscribed) geometric shapes – made of fired clay and found on numerous sites dating back at least 11,000 years – were actually TOKENS in an economically-based communications system. The result has been a continued and sometimes amusing mispunctuation of these signs, along with classifications which failed to understand any of the significations common to them in the system. In keeping with the predominance of psychological and individualistic interpretations in social

science and history, these patterned signs have been called amulets, toys, and tokens of "personal identification" (a classic case of ideological projection). Perhaps even more typically, the molded cones which appear to stand for the numerals 1, 60, and 600, as well as for traded products such as bread and perfume, have been identified by other archeologists both as schematic female figurines and as phallic symbols (cf. the quotation from Lacan on p. 486 and the footnote).

Schmandt-Besserat has turned the noise of this system – the noise maintained and multiplied by the implicit and explicit codings projected onto it by earlier archeologists – into information. She also puts into question the always suspiciously simplistic 'concrete-to-abstract' pictographic theory of the origin of writing as we know it – as does the *marae* example, representing as it does essential aspects of social organization (cf. also p. 397n). It would appear that this discovery, based on earlier work and on the exhaustive analysis of the many museum collections of these "objects of uncertain purpose", is considerably more significant than the justly celebrated decipherment of Linear B by Chadwick.

(3) Like the relatively recent interpretations of Stonehenge and of the so-called 'medicine wheels' of the plains and foothills of North America as being astronomical computers, Schmandt-Besserat's research forms part of a novel pattern of discovery and rediscovery which in many different fields is providing us with more and more reliable evidence that 'the problem of primitivism' does not lie in the past – where it has been conveniently located by the *hubris* of our dominant ideology – but right here, in the present, in the 'primitivism' of our attempts to understand nature, history, and society, including our own society.

(4) For another indicative recent instance of the recognition of a basic pattern or structure – 'technological' structures common to such diverse realities as the burrows of prairie dogs, the oxygen supply of flying beetles, the stomata of leaves, the ventilation of termite mounds, and the feeding processes of sponges – see "Organisms That Capture Currents" (Vogel, 1978).

(5) A minor, but representative, example of the kind of ideological projection remarked on in (2) above concerns the so-called 'slave-maker' ants, popular with witting and unwitting 'sociobiologists'. Such ants raid others for workers, which are transported back to the nest. How this activity can be confused with slavery is a mystery. Slavery involves a situation in which a dominant group forcibly restricts the relative freedom (the semiotic freedom) of individuals and puts them to work (under capitalism, the relative freedom of the 'free' individual is restricted, not so much by force as by economic and social constraints). In contrast, amongst ants, the

division of labor is oriented by genetics and by feeding, not by any properly social or economic constraints. A worker will work wherever she finds herself, even with a different species, and she will do her work in the same way. Consequently, it is impossible for one group of ants to make 'slaves' of any other group.

28. ". . . The rationalist reversal of the logical typing of the analog and the digital . . ." (p. 420).

What is actually involved here is not of course a 'reversal' of logical typing, but an INVERSION.

29. ". . . These instructions do not cause growth, they control its possibilities. . . . The instructions of DNA CONSTRAIN or limit growth" (p. 439).

(1) In its quest for a terminology that will not explicitly or implicitly stand for ordinary efficient causality or (Newtonian) (atomistic) determinism, the text repeatedly hovers between the concept of 'control' and that of 'constraint'. It would clarify somewhat the relations concerned if 'control' were reserved for the positive cybernetic sense of 'steering' (and in some of its uses, for 'channelling'). 'Constraint' could then be used in the sense of 'limits, at a given level, on the phase space of relative semiotic freedom available to goalseekers within the system'. (A common example in ecology is the role of 'limiting factors' which, by deficiency or excess, make specific activities impossible.)

In this way, proper emphasis would be placed on the 'non-positive' function of constraints, i.e., on the reality that constraints do not define or indicate what goalseeking subsystems must or ought to do, but rather what, within a given hierarchy of constraints, they CANNOT do – e.g., generate the sound 'nga' in the Twi language of the Ashanti out of the phonemic deep structure of English or French.

(2) This use of 'constraint' in a ecosystemic perspective frees social theory from the nineteenth-century spectre of 'determinism' – whether 'economic', 'ecological', or 'environmental' (as the current idealist fashion has it), or otherwise.

Figure 4 represents a useful way of considering major aspects of the synchronic hierarchy of constraints, at distinct levels of complexity, which makes the activities of human beings in society possible. The relations of relative dependency and order of complexity are to be read from top to bottom, each higher order or level constituting the environment of the one below it. (These distinctions in complexity are of course also some of those represented in every individual human being.)

FIGURE 4

Hierarchy of Constraints Between Orders of Complexity

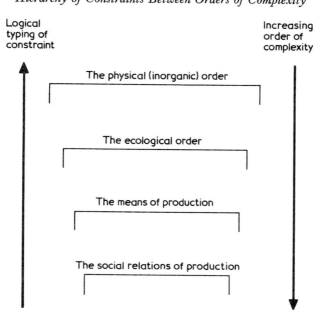

Logical
typing of
constraint

Increasing
order of
complexity

The physical (inorganic) order

The ecological order

The means of production

The social relations of production

Three distinct ORDERS of complexity are represented in the diagram: the physical (the inorganic), the ecological (the organic), and the social. The social order of complexity is divided into its two major levels: the 'means of production' and the 'social relations of production'. These two levels together constitute the possibilities made available to individuals by the various dominant and subordinate MODES of production in various societies. We note of course that each one of these orders and levels is itself made up of hierarchies of constraints.

30. ". . . This recapitulation of Hegel's 'law of the heart' – which reduces all real situations of oppression to paranoid relationships in which 'the persecutors are identical with the once-loved images of the ego-ideal' (Lacan 1953b: 13) . . ." (p. 479).

Readers acquainted with the real source of Daniel Schreber's 'paranoid hallucinations' (Chapter 10) – the mental, logical, and physical abuse to which he was treated in the name of morality and education by his famous father (see Schatzman, 1974) – will fully appreciate the error of Lacan's neutralization of radical dissent. Most of the younger Schreber's descriptions of oppressive and hurtful "miracles" in the *Memoirs of My Nervous Illness* (1903) – particularly the mechanical ones – can be traced back directly to 'educational' and 'moral' restraining devices invented by his father, a famous educator well acquainted with modern forms of brainwashing and conditioning. Moreover, these peculiar devices are fully illustrated and explained, along with extensive directions for a program of manipulation designed to make the child an imaginary slave to the parents' wishes for life, in the father's many books in numerous editions in several languages.

But in spite of the father's fame and Freud's expressed awareness of it, this essential context of the younger Schreber's text – this context of physical force and logical violence – went practically unrecognized for most of this century. As we know, Freud's theory of paranoia was directly based on an interpretation of the younger Schreber's *Memoirs* (he never met Schreber). By the process of making the oppressed responsible for their own oppression – as with the 'human nature' of the 'oedipus complex' – Freud's analysis of this text set the scene for a reading of the dominant ideology, remembering, repeating, and working through, which has been similarly rationalized by most psychological theories and psychotherapies since, whether or not their proponents, male or female, were actually familiar with the work of Freud or with this famous 'case'.

For that aspect of Freud's life and work which is occupied with the psychoanalytical theory and practice of counterinsurgency, the fundamental blunder for which psychoanalysis continues to be responsible in this case is probably surpassed only by Freud's unthinking cruelty to Dora, a young female victim of the nineteenth-century bourgeois family and society – and of the sexism in which psychoanalysis was grounded (*Standard Edition*, VII, 7ff. (1901); cf. Chesler, 1972).

Schreber, Dora, 'Wolf Man', 'Rat Man' [*sic*] – all this violence is of course entirely in keeping with the denial and the disavowal of actual relations of class, race, and sex by means of which most of psychology, along with its offshoots in economics and the 'social' sciences, continues to insist on enforcing the Imaginary instead of interpreting the Real.

31. Miscellaneous Comments

(1) ". . . there simply aren't any gaps or holes in the natural world . . ." (p. 178).

This is another Imaginary lapsus, an ideological paralogism. Amend to read: ". . . there simply aren't any gaps or holes in OUR PERCEPTION OF the natural world. . . ." And in the last sentence of this paragraph read "models" in the Montaignian sense of "patterns", as suggested on the first page of the Introduction.

(2) Note that "Imaginary" and "digital" are not synonymous. Symbolic exchange values, for example, are digital or digitalized (pp. 273, xlvi), but they are not Imaginary – although they may well be reduced to the Imaginary in certain contexts.

(3) "Reversibility", "inversion", "symmetry", "symmetrization", "invariant transformation", "equilibrium", "one-dimensional", "virtual", "repetition", "harmony", "confusion of levels", "confusion of logical types", and so on (cf. for example, pp. 317–20, 310n).

In the final review of this text, I have been struck by what may of course be obvious to others, by how often the argument, in different domains, is based on an epistemological and practical critique of the ideological MISAPPLICATION (or 'misplacing': *Entstellung*) of principles of symmetry, reversibility, and repetition, derived most obviously from the physical sciences, in the explanation of socioeconomic and biological matters. This critique goes hand in hand with the critique of the ideological 'leveling' of the system-environment relation (at least two distinct logical types) and the ideological 'homogenization' of systems and environments, which have for some time now kept in almost perfect step with the real capitalist process of homogenizing the entire planet and its inhabitants: the reduction of the many varieties of diversity in every sphere, while concentrating constraint and control in society in fewer and fewer hands in supposedly 'diversified' corporate relations.

For an elegant and not excessively technical account of the role of symmetries in physical theory, see Freedman and van Nieuwenhuizen's article on supergravity and supersymmetry (1978). This article also provides us with a kind of sketch map of the sources of the many misappropriated echoes from the theory and practice of physics which are still to be found in the work of the English-speaking 'systemists' and 'communicationists', on the one hand, and in that of the French-speaking 'structuralists' and 'semiologists', on the other.

(4) "Renormalization" (e.g., pp. 124, 205–7, 354–6, 366–7, 386).
This is a term which I believe I first heard used in an 'adaptive' sense by Gregory Bateson during the crucial few weeks in Hawaii in 1970, when he somehow managed to make me begin to understand, in spite of my years of training, just what it could mean to say that the survival of the ecosystem

depends on the survival of "both organism and environment", and that (digital) information is a "difference that makes a difference" (a distinction) circulating between them.

In its strict sense, as I discover, 'renormalization' has been applied in physics since the late 1940s as a label for the process of 'making over' a physical theory (Freedman and van Nieuwenhuizen, 1978). It is a way of getting rid of unmanageable noise in the form of the theory being renormalized (e.g., infinite probabilities). One of the relations concerned in renormalization is the status of the system-environment relation between an electron and its own electromagnetic field (its infinite "self-energy"). The noise of such infinities in the theory is either quenched or turned into information (both appear to be the case) by altering the basic parameters of the theory. In one sense, then, the term in its strict sense refers to a restricted and ideal 'dialectic' operating within the basic codes of theory construction in physics; in another, to an instance of re-punctuation (but from 'outside' the theory itself). With these and its other connotations, the term was an unsuitable borrowing. It is used in the text largely as a way of avoiding the tiresome or misleading representations of the concept of *Aufhebung* ('sublating', *dépassement*, 'negation', 'suppressing and conserving', and so on). It is used as a synonym for the dialectical emergence of a real and/or ideal 'metasystem' from a 'reference system' (cf. p. 376).

32. Imaginary Terminology

In the original plan for the revision of this edition, I had intended to indicate the inappropriate use of certain terms, and the inaccuracy of particular sentences in the original, by marking them with square brackets in the text itself. This has not proved feasible. So most of the more significant of the errors I am aware of have now been corrected directly. Most of these involve such mistakes as the following: the use of 'analog' for what should be 'iconic' or 'analog-iconic'; of 'reversal' for 'inversion'; of 'control' for 'constraint'; of 'difference' for 'distinction'; and of 'opposition' for 'contradiction'.

You will undoubtedly have noticed that many of the errors corrected and/or commented on are ideological and epistemological errors of exactly the same type as those the text is criticizing. Given the power of the dominant ideology and its associated epistemology in our society, this is hardly surprising – and there must be others.

It remains to remark on mistakes that have not been corrected, most of which are so profoundly coded into the ordinary rhetoric of the dominant discourse in English that they are particularly difficult to recognize. These appear to fall into two main classes: errors of Imaginary symmetrization, and errors of Imaginary decontextualization.

Into the first group falls the use of 'on the one hand . . . and on the other', when the relationship being discussed is actually hierarchical, and therefore requires the use of the expression 'at one level . . . and at another' (e.g., pp. 93, 127, 163, 174, and elsewhere). Similar to this error is the use of 'vice versa' to refer to distinct levels of relation (e.g., p. 447 and the passage remarked on in Note 21). The commonest offender here, however, is the seemingly innocent use of the expression 'as opposed to'. I doubt that I have caught them all, but this expression is used in a way that symmetrizes levels into Imaginary oppositions on pp. 21, 50, 81, 98, 113, 114, 118, 215, 234, 255, 354, 358, 406, also pp. 67, 128, 183. In each case, this mistake can be corrected by substituting the phrase 'as distinct from'. Like 'difference', 'distinction' involves no covert judgements about levels (cf. Note 24).

Into the second group, decontextualization, falls the use of a type of expression to be found in Marx and in many other writers: 'accumulation for the sake of accumulation' (e.g., pp. 250, 263) and 'growth for the sake of growth' (e.g., p. 208). Like 'art for art's sake' or 'knowledge for its own sake', these expressions make a transitive relation (of goalseeking) appear to be intransitive, a mediated relation appear to be 'self-mediated' (Imaginary), and a contextualized activity appear to be independent of its context. They make a closed-system relationship out of an open-system reality (cf. also 'digitalization for its own sake' on p. 461). Capital is accumulated for the sake of power, for instance; capitalism grows for the sake of (temporary) stability; digitalization exists for the sake of control; and so on.

Similar to this pattern of error is the use of the terms 'subjective' and 'objective' (e.g., pp. 90, 91, 94, 327, 393). As was outlined in the Introduction, in the dominant discourse these two terms form an Imaginary opposition in which each is the mirror-image of the other. 'Objectivity' says in effect, '*This* is the only reliable context', i.e., the objects, the 'facts'. 'Subjectivity' replies that '*This* is the only reliable context', i.e., the subject, the opinions about the 'facts'. Objectivity really exists only in theology, in the timelessness and spacelessness of God; subjectivity certainly exists, but so much of our experience is collective that no one's view of reality is simply subjective. Within the Imaginary, there is no appeal from the dogmatism of these two positions. One subject's subjectivity is no more directly given to another subject's experience than objectivity has an unmediated relation to its objects – and yet each position implies that its view of the world is unquestionable and real.

A final remark: I note that I have often implied that relationships are 'nowhere' (e.g., p. 448). This, too, comes out of the Imaginary subject/ object dichotomy of the dominant epistemology – and it falls into the Imaginary space between the traditional 'two stools' and the traditional 'two sides of the question'. The error arises out of realizing that relationships are neither 'in' the 'subject' nor 'in' the 'object', but without also recognizing that their actual locus 'between' will signify (or appear to be) 'nowhere' only in the atomistic and mechanical world of the Imaginary.

33. Other Corrections

(1) The misreading of Frege (original pp. 180, 186–7) has been corrected. On original p. 124, the words 'and is' were missing from the phrase 'is and is not' in the last sentence, an error that passed unnoted into Wilden and Wilson, 1976: 278, as well as into the Spanish version of *System and Structure* (Madrid: Alianza).

(2) As used in this book, 'the Symbolic' emphasizes the linking function of certain kinds of production and exchange, i.e. their cooperative function. In contrast, Imaginary production and exchange fulfils a competitive function (cf. the diagrams on pp. 688–9 of Wilden, 1976b; also the analysis of Imaginary and Real relations in Wilden, 1980). But information – including signals, signs, signifiers, and symbols – may represent Real relations and Imaginary relations, i.e. may be 'symbolic' of such relations. And just as information at one level may represent, constrain, or communicate about information at other levels, so also may it be 'symbolic' of Symbolic relations (as in the case of the cooperative relations of the *kula* exchange, pp. 254–7 above).

Bibliography

ABBOTT, EDWIN A.
1884   *Flatland* (New York: Barnes and Noble, 1963).

ALTHUSSER, LOUIS, JACQUES RANCIÈRE, AND PIERRE MACHEREY
1965a   *Lire Le Capital* (Paris: Maspero). Volume I.

ALTHUSSER, LOUIS, ÉTIENNE BALIBAR, AND ROGER ESTABLET
1965b   *Lire Le Capital* (Paris: Maspero). Volume II.

ARDENER, EDWIN
1971a   "Introductory Essay", in: Ardener, ed., 1971: ix–cii.
1971b   "The Historicity of Historical Linguistics", in: Ardener, ed., 1971: 209–42.

ARDENER, EDWIN, editor
1971   *Social Anthropology and Language* (A.S.A. Monographs, No. 10) (London: Tavistock).

ASHBY, W. ROSS
1954   "The Application of Cybernetics to Psychiatry", *Journal of Mental Science*, **100**: 114–24. Also in: Smith, ed., 1966: 374–86.
1956   *An Introduction to Cybernetics* (London: Chapman and Hall; New York: John Wiley, 1963).
1960   *Design for a Brain* (London: Science Paperbacks, 1966). Revised version of 1952 edition.
1962   "Principles of the Self-Organizing System", in: Von Foerster and Zopf, eds., 1962: 255–78.

AUGUSTINE, SAINT
1963   *Confessions*, trans. by Rex Warner (New York: New American Library).

BAKAN, PAUL
1971   "The Eyes Have It", *Psychology Today* (April 1971).

BARTHES, ROLAND
1964   "Éléments de Sémiologie", *Communications*, **4**: 91–134.

BATESON, GREGORY
1936   *Naven* (Stanford: Stanford University Press, 1958). Second edition.

1955　　"A Theory of Play and Fantasy", *Psychiatric Research Reports*, **2**: 39–51.

1956　　"The Message 'This is Play'", *Transactions of the Second Conference on Group Processes* (New York: Josiah Macy, Jr. Foundation), 145–242.

1963　　"Exchange of Information about Patterns of Human Behavior", *Information Storage and Neural Control*, ed. by W. S. Fields and W. Abbott (Springfield, Ill.: Charles C. Thomas).

1967　　"Cybernetic Explanation", *The American Behavioral Scientist*, **10**, 8: 29–32.

1969a　"Metalogue: What is an Instinct?", *Approaches to Animal Communication*, ed. by T. A. Sebeok (The Hague: Mouton), 11–30.

1969b　"Double Bind, 1969" (Waimanalo, Hawaii: Oceanic Institute). Draft for the American Psychological Association, August, 1969.

1970　　"Pathologies of Epistemology" (Waimanalo, Hawaii: Oceanic Institute). Contribution No. 64.

1971a　"Towards a Theory of Alcoholism: The Cybernetics of 'Self'", *Psychiatry*, **34**: 1–18.

1971b　"The Message of Reinforcement". Forthcoming in *Festschrift for Elwood Murray*.

1972　　*Steps to an Ecology of Mind* (New York: Ballantine). (Contains articles referred to.)

BATESON, GREGORY, DON D. JACKSON, JAY HALEY, AND JOHN WEAKLAND
1956　　"Toward a Theory of Schizophrenia", *Behavioral Science*, **1**: 251–64.

BERGMAN, INGMAR
1960　　"Film Has Nothing to Do with Literature", *Film*, ed. by R. D. MacCann (New York: Dutton, 1966).

BERNARD, CLAUDE
1865　　*An Introduction to the Study of Experimental Medicine*, trans. by H. C. Greene (New York: Collier, 1961).

BERNARDI, AURELIO
1965　　"The Economic Problems of the Roman Empire at the Time of its Decline", *The Economic Decline of Empires*, ed. by C. M. Cipolla (London: Methuen, 1970), 18–83.

BERNSTEIN, B.
1958　　"Some Sociological Determinants of Perception. An Inquiry into Sub-Cultural Differences", in: Fishman, ed., 1968: 223–39.

BERTALANFFY, LUDWIG VON
1962   "General Systems Theory: A Critical Review", in: Buckley, ed., 1968: 11–30.
1968   *General Systems Theory* (New York: Braziller).

BEURLE, R. L.
1962   "Functional Organization in Random Networks", in: Von Foerster and Zopf, eds., 1962: 291–314.

BINSWANGER, L. VON
1963   *Being-in-the-World*, trans., with an introduction, by J. Needleman (New York: Basic Books).

BLACKHAM, H. J.
1961   *Six Existentialist Thinkers* (London: Routledge and Kegan Paul).

BODMER, WALTER F., AND LUIGI LUCA CAVALLI-SFORZA
1970   "Intelligence and Race", *Scientific American* (October 1970), 19–29.

BOULDING, KENNETH
1956a   "General Systems Theory: The Skeleton of Science", in: Buckley, ed., 1968: 3–10.
1956b   *The Image* (Ann Arbor: University of Michigan Press).

BRENTANO, F. VON
1874   *Psychologie von empirischen Standpunkt* (Berlin).

BRILLOUIN, L.
1949   "Life, Thermodynamics, and Cybernetics", in: Buckley, ed., 1968: 147–56.

BRONOWSKI, J.
1967   "Human and Animal Language", in: Sebeok, ed., 1967, I.

BROWN, NORMAN O.
1959   *Life Against Death* (New York: Vintage Books; London: Routledge).

BRUNER, J. S.
1967   "The Ontogenesis of Symbols", in: Sebeok, ed., 1967, I: 427–46.

BUCKLEY, WALTER
1967   *Sociology and Modern Systems Theory* (Englewood Cliffs, N.J.: Prentice-Hall).
1971   "A Systems Approach to Epistemology" (Santa Barbara: University of California). Unpublished draft.

BUCKLEY, WALTER, editor
1968   *Modern Systems Research for the Behavioral Scientist* (Chicago: Aldine).

BURKE, KENNETH
1941   *The Philosophy of Literary Form* (New York: Vintage, 1957).

CADWALLADER, MERVYN L.
1959   "The Cybernetic Analysis of Change in Complex Social Organizations", *The American Journal of Sociology*, **65**: 154–7. Also in: Smith, ed., 1966: 396–401.

CAMERON, NORMAN
1939   "Experimental Analysis of Schizophrenic Thinking", in: Kasanin, ed., 1939: 50–63.

CHAO, YUEN REN
1959   "How Chinese Logic Operates", *Anthropological Linguistics*, **1**: 1–8.

CHARBONNIER, G., editor
1961   *Conversations with Claude Lévi-Strauss* (London: Cape Editions, 1969).

CHERRY, COLIN
1967   '"There is Nothing I Have is Essential to Me'", in: Sebeok, ed., 1967, I: 462–74.

CHOMSKY, NOAM
1956   "Three Models for the Description of Language", *I.R.E. Transactions on Information Theory*, Vol. IT-2: 113–24. Also in: Smith, ed., 1966: 140–52.
1957   *Syntactic Structures* (= *Janua Linguarum*, series minor, 4) (The Hague: Mouton).

CLARK, KENNETH
1965   *Dark Ghetto* (New York: Harper Torchbooks).

CLEAVER, ELDRIDGE
1968   *Soul on Ice* (New York: McGraw-Hill).

COLLINGWOOD, R. G.
1945   *The Idea of Nature* (New York: Oxford University Press, 1960).

COOPER, DAVID
1967   *Psychiatry and Anti-Psychiatry* (London: Tavistock).

COOPER, DAVID, editor
1968   *The Dialectics of Liberation* (Harmondsworth, Middlesex: Penguin).

CORNFORD, FRANCIS M.
1934   *Plato's Theory of Knowledge* (New York: Bobbs-Merrill, 1957).

CROSSON, FREDERICK J., AND KENNETH M. SAYRE, editors
1967   *Philosophy and Cybernetics* (New York: Clarion, 1968).

DANCE, FRANK E. X.
1967   "Toward a Theory of Human Communication", *Human Communication Theory*, ed. by F. E. X. Dance (New York: Holt, Rinehart and Winston), 288–309.

DAVIDSON, BASIL
1970   *Old Africa Rediscovered* (London: Gollancz).

DELEUZE, GILLES
1968   *Différence et répétition* (Paris: Presses Universitaires).

DERRIDA, JACQUES
1966   "Freud et la scène de l'écriture", *Tel Quel*, No. 26. Reprinted in Derrida, 1967b.
1967a   *De la grammatologie* (Paris: Editions de Minuit).
1967b   *L'Écriture et la différence* (Paris: Le Seuil).

DEUTSCH, KARL W.
1963   *The Nerves of Government* (New York: The Free Press, 1966). Second edition.

DEWEY, JOHN
1946   "Peirce's Theory of Linguistic Signs, Thought and Meaning", *Journal of Philosophy* (February 1946), **63**: 85–95.

DOSTOEVSKY, FYODOR
1960a   *Three Short Novels* (Garden City, N.Y.: Anchor).
1960b   *Notes from Underground and the Grand Inquisitor* (New York: E. P. Dutton).

DREYFUS, HERBERT L.
1965   "Alchemy and Artificial Intelligence" (Santa Monica, California: Rand Corporation). Publication No. P-3244.

DUBOS, RENÉ J.
1969   "Second Thoughts on the Germ Theory", in: Shepard and McKinley, eds, 1969: 223–9.

DUCROT, OSWALD
1968   "Le Structuralisme en linguistique", in: Wahl, ed., 1968: 15–96.

EHRENFELS, U. R.
1964   "The Common Elements in the Philosophy of Matrilineal Societies in India", *Cross-Cultural Understanding*, ed. by F. S. C. Northrop and H. H. Livingston (New York: Harper and Row), 105–24.

EHRMANN, JACQUES, editor
1966   "Structuralism", *Yale French Studies*, Nos. 36–7. Republished as: *Structuralism* (Garden City, N.Y.: Anchor, 1970).

ELLUL, JACQUES
1954   *The Technological Society* (New York: Vintage Books, 1964).
1962   *Propaganda* (New York: Knopf, 1966).

ELSASSER, WALTER M.
1966   *Atom and Organism* (Princeton: Princeton University Press).

EMERSON, ALFRED E.
1956   "Homeostasis and Comparison of Systems", in: Grinker, ed.,
        1967: 147–63.

EMERY, F. E., AND E. L. TRIST
1965   "The Causal Texture of Organizational Environments",
        Systems Thinking, ed. by F. E. Emery (Harmondsworth,
        Middlesex: Penguin, 1969), 241–57.

ENGELS, FREDERICK
1885   *Anti-Dühring* (New York: International Publishers, 1939).

ESCHER, M. C.
1960   *Graphic Work* (New York: Hawthorn).

EPSTEIN, A. L.
1959   "Linguistic Innovation and Culture on the Copperbelt, North-
        ern Rhodesia", in: Fishman, ed., 1968: 320–39.

ESCH, HARALD
1967   "The Evolution of Bee Language", *Scientific American*, **216**:
        96–104.

FANON, FRANTZ
1952   *Black Skin, White Masks*, trans. by C. L. Markmann (New
        York: Grove, 1967; London: MacGibbon and Kee, 1968).
1961   *The Wretched of the Earth*, trans. by C. Farrington (New York:
        Grove, 1968).
1964   *Toward the African Revolution*, trans. by H. Chevalier (New
        York: Monthly Review).

FAUCONNIER, GILLES R.
1971   "Theoretical Implications of Some Global Phenomena in Syn-
        tax" (San Diego: University of California). Unpublished Ph.D.
        dissertation.

FISHMAN, JOSHUA A., editor
1968   *Readings in the Sociology of Language* (The Hague: Mouton).

FLIESS, ROBERT
1950   *The Psycho-Analytic Reader* (London: Hogarth).

FODOR, JERRY A., AND JERROLD J. KATZ, editors
1964   *The Structure of Language* (Englewood Cliffs, N.J.: Prentice-
        Hall).

FOERSTER, HEINZ VON, AND GEORGE W. ZOPF, JR., editors
1962   *Principles of Self-Organization* (New York: Pergamon).

FOUCAULT, MICHEL
1966   *Les Mots et les choses* (Paris: Gallimard). English translation, *The Order of Things* (London: Tavistock; New York, Pantheon, 1970).

FREGE, GOTTLOB
1884   *The Foundations of Arithmetic*, trans. by J. L. Austin (Oxford: Blackwell, 1959).
1952   *Philosophical Writings*, trans. by P. Geach and M. Black (Oxford: Blackwell).

FREUD, SIGMUND
1891   *On Aphasia* (London: Imago, 1953).
1953–   *The Complete Psychological Works of Sigmund Freud*, ed. by James Strachey (London: Hogarth). Twenty-four volumes. Referred to as *Standard Edition*.
1954   *The Origins of Psychoanalysis*, ed. by A. Freud, M. Bonaparte and E. Kris (New York: Basic Books).

GANDILLAC, MAURICE DE, LUCIEN GOLDMANN, AND JEAN PIAGET
1965   *Entretiens sur les notions de genèse et de structure* (The Hague: Mouton) (Conference of July–August 1959).

GIRARD, RENÉ
1964   "Camus' Stranger Retried", *Publications of the Modern Language Association* (1964): 519–33.
1965a   "L'Anti-héros et les salauds", *Mercure de France* (1965): 422–49.
1965b   *Deceit, Desire and the Novel* (Baltimore: Johns Hopkins).

GODELIER, MAURICE
1966   "Système, structure et contradiction dans 'Le Capital'", *Les Temps Modernes*, **246**: 828–64.
1968   *Rationalité et irrationalité en économie* (Paris: Maspero).

GOFFMAN, ERVING
1961   *Asylums* (Garden City, N.Y.: Anchor Books; Harmondsworth, Middlesex: Penguin).

GOLDMANN, LUCIEN
1955   *Le Dieu caché* (Paris: Gallimard).
1959   *Recherches dialectiques* (Paris: Gallimard).

GOLDSTEIN, KURT
1939   "Methodological Approach to the Study of Schizophrenic Thought Disorder", in: Kasanin, ed., 1939: 17–39.

GOODWIN, BRIAN
  1968   "The Division of Cells and the Fusion of Ideas", in: Wadding-
          ton, ed., 1968: 134–9.

GOUX, J.-J.
  1968   "Numismatiques I", *Tel Quel*, 35: 64–89.
  1969   "Numismatiques II", *Tel Quel*, 36: 54–74.

GRAHAM, HUGH DAVIS, AND TED ROBERT GURR, editors
  1969   *Violence in America* (New York: Bantam Books).

GREGORY, R. L.
  1966   *Eye and Brain* (London: Weidenfeld & Nicolson; New York:
          McGraw-Hill).

GRINKER, ROY R., SR., editor
  1967   *Toward a Unified Theory of Human Behavior* (New York:
          Basic Books). Second edition.

HARDIN, GARRETT
  1969   "The Cybernetics of Competition", in: Shepard and
          McKinley, eds., 1969: 275–96.

HEGEL, G. W. F.
  1807a   *Phänomenologie des Geistes*, ed. by J. Hoffmeister (Hamburg:
          Felix Meiner, 1952).
  1807b   *La Phénoménologie de l'esprit*, trans. by Jean Hyppolite (Paris:
          Aubier-Montaigne, 1939–41). Two volumes.
  1830   *Précis de l'Encyclopédie des sciences philosophiques*, trans. by
          J. Gibelin (Paris: Vrin, 1952).
  1845   *Hegel's Philosophy of Mind* (Oxford: Oxford University Press,
          1971).

HEIDEGGER, MARTIN
  1927   *Being and Time*, trans. by J. Macquarrie and E. Robinson
          (London: SCM, 1962).

HERNDON, JAMES
  1968   *The Way It Spozed To Be* (New York: Bantam).

HESSE, HERMANN
  1927   *Steppenwolf* (New York: Holt, Rinehart and Winston, 1957).

HOCKETT, CHARLES F.
  1960   "The Origin of Speech", *Scientific American* (September 1960).
  1963   "The Problem of Universals in Language", *Universals of
          Language*, ed. by J. H. Greenburg (Cambridge: MIT).

HOCKETT, CHARLES F., AND STUART A. ALTMANN
  1968   "A Note on Design Features", in: Sebeok, ed., 1968: 61–
          72.

HOCKETT, CHARLES F., AND ROBERT ASCHER
1964   "The Human Revolution", *Current Anthropology*, **5**, 3: 135–68.

HOFSTADTER, RICHARD
1944   *Social Darwinism in American Thought* (Boston: Beacon, 1968).

HUSSERL, EDMUND
1929   *Cartesian Meditations*, trans. by Dorion Cairns (The Hague: Martinus Nijhoff, 1960).
1950   *Idées directrices pour une phénoménologie*, trans. by Paul Ricoeur (Paris: Gallimard).
1952   "Universal Teleology", transcribed by Marly Biemal (Manuscript E-III-S), *Telos* (Fall, 1969), **4**: 176–80.

HYMAN, STANLEY EDGAR
1959   *The Tangled Bank* (New York: Grosset and Dunlap).

HYPPOLITE, JEAN
1946   *Genèse et structure de la Phénoménologie de l'esprit* (Paris: Aubier-Montaigne). Two volumes.
1957   "Phénoménologie de Hegel et psychanalyse", *La Psychanalyse*, **3**: 17–32.

JAKOBSON, ROMAN
1956   "Two Aspects of Language and Two Types of Aphasic Disturbances", in: Jakobson and Halle, 1956: 54–82.
1963   *Essais de linguistique générale*, trans. by Nicholas Ruwet (Paris: Editions de Minuit).

JAKOBSON, ROMAN, AND MORRIS HALLE
1956   *Fundamentals of Language* (The Hague: Mouton).

JALÉE, PIERRE
1969   *Le Pillage du Tiers Monde* (Paris: Maspero).

JENSEN, ARTHUR R.
1969   "How Much can We Boost IQ and Scholastic Achievement?", *Harvard Educational Review*, **39**: 1–123.

JONES, ERNEST
1913   *Papers on Psychoanalysis* (New York).
1956–8   *The Life and Work of Sigmund Freud* (London: Hogarth). Three volumes.

JORDAN, Z. A.
1967   *The Evolution of Dialectical Materialism* (New York: St Martin's).

JOSEPHSON, ERIC, AND MARY, editors
1962   *Man Alone* (New York: Dell).

KAFKA, FRANZ
1925   *The Trial* (Harmondsworth: Penguin, 1953).
1931   "The Burrow", *Metamorphosis and Other Stories* (Harmondsworth: Penguin, 1964).

KASANIN, J. S., editor
1939   *Language and Thought in Schizophrenia* (New York: W. W. Norton, 1964).

KATZ, BERNHARD
1961   "How Cells Communicate", *Scientific American*, **205**: 209–20.

KIERKEGAARD, S.
1843a   *Repetition*, trans. by W. Lowrie (New York: Harper, 1964).
1843b   *Either/Or*, trans. by D. F. and L. M. Swenson and W. Lowrie (Garden City, N.Y.: Anchor, 1959). Two volumes.

KLIMA, EDWARD S.
1964   "Negation in English", in: Fodor and Katz, eds., 1964: 246–323.

KLINE, MORRIS, editor
1968   *Mathematics in the Modern World* (San Francisco: W. H. Freeman).

KOJÈVE, ALEXANDRE
1947a   *Introduction à la lecture de Hegel*, ed. by Raymond Queneau (Paris: Gallimard).
1947b   *Introduction to the Reading of Hegel*, trans. by J. H. Nichols, Jr. (New York: Basic Books, 1969).

KOSOK, MICHAEL
1969   "A Note on 'Dialectical Logic Today'", *Telos* (Fall, 1969), **4**: 188–91.

KOYRÉ, ALEXANDRE
1958   *From the Closed World to the Infinite Universe* (New York: Harper).
1968   *Newtonian Studies* (Chicago: University of Chicago Press).

KOZOL, JONATHAN
1969   *Death at an Early Age* (New York: Bantam).

LACAN, JACQUES
1949   "The Mirror-Phase", trans. by Jean Roussel, *New Left Review* (1968), **51**: 71–7.
1953a   "Some Reflections on the Ego", *International Journal of Psycho-Analysis*, **34**: 11–17.
1953b   "Le Mythe individuel du névrosé ou 'Poésie et Verité' dans la névrose" (Paris: Centre de la documentation universitaire). Unpublished mimeograph.

1956a   "The Function of Speech and Language in Psychoanalysis", in: Wilden, 1968a: 1–87.

1956b   "The Insistence of the Letter in the Unconscious", trans. by Jan Miel, in: Ehrmann, ed., 1966: 101–37.

1956c   "Seminar of November–December, 1956: La Relation d'objet et les structures freudiennes", *Bulletin de Psychologie* (April 1957), **10**, 7: 426–30.

1957   "Seminar of March–April, 1957: La Relation d'objet et les structures freudiennes", *Bulletin de Psychologie* (June 1957), **10**, 14: 851–4.

1958   "Seminar of April–June, 1958: Les Formations de l'inconscient", *Bulletin de Psychologie* (December 1958), **12**, 4: 250–6.

1960   "Seminar of November 1958–January 1959: Le Désir et son interprétation", *Bulletin de Psychologie* (January 1960), **13**, 5: 263–72.

1966   *Écrits* (Paris: Le Seuil).

LAING, RONALD D.

1960   *The Divided Self* (London: Tavistock; New York: Pantheon).

1961   *The Self and Others* (London: Tavistock).

1969   *Self and Others* (London: Tavistock; New York: Pantheon). Second edition of Laing, 1961.

1970   *Knots* (London: Tavistock; New York: Pantheon).

1971   *The Politics of the Family* (London: Tavistock; New York: Pantheon).

LAING, RONALD D., AND A. ESTERSON

1964   *Sanity, Madness, and the Family* (London: Tavistock).

LAKOFF, GEORGE

1970   "Linguistics and Natural Logic", *Synthèse*. Forthcoming.

LAMB, G. G.

1968   "Engineering Concepts and the Behavioral Sciences", *General Systems Yearbook*, **13**: 165–9.

LANGER, SUSANNE K.

1962   *Philosophical Sketches* (New York: Mentor Books, 1964).

LAPLANCHE, JEAN, AND SERGE LECLAIRE

1961   "L'Inconscient", *Les Temps Modernes*, 183: 81–129.

LAPLANCHE, JEAN, AND J.-B. PONTALIS

1964   "Fantasme originaire, fantasme des origines, origine du fantasme", *Les Temps Modernes*, **19**. English version: "Fantasy and the Origins of Sexuality", *International Journal of Psycho-Analysis* (1968), **49**: 1–18.

1967   *Vocabulaire de la psychanalyse* (Paris: Presses Universitaires).

1972 *The Language of Psycho-Analysis*, trans. by D. Nicholson-Smith (London: Hogarth Press).

LARUCCIA, VICTOR
1971 "The 'More Perfect Structure': What is it? An Analysis of the American Constitution of 1787" (San Diego: University of California). Unpublished draft.

LEACH, EDMUND
1964 "Animal Categories and Verbal Abuse", *New Directions in the Study of Language*, ed. by E. H. Lennenberg (Cambridge: MIT).
1970 *Lévi-Strauss* (London: Fontana; New York: Viking).

LENNENBERG, ERIC H.
1964 "The Capacity for Language Acquisition", in: Fodor and Katz, eds., 1964: 579–603.

LÉVI-STRAUSS, CLAUDE
1949 *Les Structures élémentaires de la parenté* (Paris: Mouton, 1968). Second edition.
1950 "Introduction à l'œuvre de Marcel Mauss", in: Marcel Mauss, *Sociologie et anthropologie* (Paris: Presses Universitaires, 1966).
1952 *Race and History* (New York: UNESCO).
1955 *Tristes Tropiques*, trans. by J. Russell (New York: Atheneum, 1964).
1958a *Anthropologie structurale* (Paris: Plon).
1958b *Structural Anthropology*, trans. by C. Jacobson and B. G. Schoepf (Garden City, N.Y.: Anchor, 1963).
1960 "La Structure et la forme", *Cahiers de l'Institut de science économique appliquée*, **99**: 3–36.
1960b "Discours inaugural au Collège de France," *Aut Aut* (Milan, 1965), **88**: 8–41.
1962a *La Pensée sauvage* (Paris: Plon).
1962b *Le Totémisme aujourd'hui* (Paris: Presses Universitaires).
1964 *Le Cru et le cuit* (Paris: Plon).
1971 *L'Homme nu.* (Paris: Plon).

LEWIS, I. M., editor
1968 *History and Social Anthropology* (A.S.A. Monographs, No. 7) (London: Tavistock).

LUCAS, JOHN
1961 "Minds, Machines and Gödel", in: Sayre and Crosson, eds., 1963: 255–71.

LUKÁCS, GEORG
1920 *Die Theorie des Romans* (Berlin: Luchterhand, 1963).

1938   *Studies in European Realism* (New York: Grosset and Dunlap, 1964).

MACKAY, DONALD M.
1969   *Information, Mechanism and Meaning* (Cambridge: MIT).

MCLELLAN, DAVID
1971   *Marx's Grundrisse* (London: Macmillan).

MALINOWSKI, BRONISLAW
1922   *Argonauts of the Western Pacific* (London: Routledge; New York: E. P. Dutton, 1961).

MANNONI, MAUD
1964   *L'Enfant arriéré et sa mère* (Paris: Le Seuil).
1967   *The Child, his 'Illness', and the Others* (New York: Pantheon; London: Tavistock, 1970).
1970   *Le Psychiatre, son 'fou' et la psychanalyse* (Paris: Le Seuil).

MANNONI, O.
1950   *Prospero and Caliban: The Psychology of Colonization* (New York: Praeger, 1964).
1969   *Clefs pour l'imaginaire ou l'Autre scène* (Paris: Le Seuil).
1971   *Freud* (New York: Pantheon).

MAO TSE-TUNG
1961–5 *Selected Works* (Peking: Foreign Languages Press).

MARCUS, ROBERT L.
1962   "The Nature of Instinct and the Physical Bases of Libido: Part II: The Instinct Machine", *General Systems Yearbook*, **7**: 143–56.

MARCUSE, HERBERT
1955   *Eros and Civilization* (New York: Vintage, 1961).
1964   *One-Dimensional Man* (Boston: Beacon; London: Routledge).
1968   *Negations* (Boston: Beacon).

MARGENAU, HENRY
1934   "Meaning and the Scientific Status of Causality", *Philosophy of Science*, ed. by A. Danto and S. Morgenbesser (New York: Meridian, 1960), 435–49.

MARIN, LOUIS
1971   "The Neutral and the Philosophical Discourse", *Neutrality in Academics*, ed. by Alain Montefiore (London: Routledge and Kegan Paul).

MARNEY, M. C., AND N. M. SMITH
1964   "The Domain of Adaptive Systems: A Rudimentary Taxonomy", *General Systems Yearbook*, **9**: 107–31.

MARUYAMA, MAGOROH

1963   "The Second Cybernetics: Deviation-Amplifying Mutual Causal Processes", in: Buckley, ed., 1968: 304–13.

1969   "Epistemology of Social Science Research: Exploration in Inculture Researchers", *Dialectica*, **23**: 229–80.

MARX, KARL

1844   *Early Writings*, ed. and trans. by T. B. Bottomore (New York: McGraw-Hill, 1963).

1857–8 *Pre-Capitalist Economic Formations*, trans. by J. Cohen, ed. by E. J. Hobsbawn (New York: International Publishers, 1965).

1887   *Capital* (London: Lawrence and Wishart, 1964). Three volumes.

1956   *Selected Writings*, trans. by T. B. Bottomore (New York: McGraw-Hill).

MARX, KARL, AND FREDERICK ENGELS

1845–6 *The German Ideology* (London: Lawrence and Wishart, 1965).

MAYR, ERNST

1963   *Animal Species and Evolution* (Cambridge: Harvard University Press).

MAYR, OTTO

1969   *The Origins of Feedback Control* (Cambridge: MIT).

MERCIER, PAUL

1966   *Histoire de l'anthropologie* (Paris: Presses Universitaires).

METZ, CHRISTIAN

1968   *Essais sur la signification au cinéma* (Paris: Klincksieck).

MILLER, JAMES G.

1965   "Living Systems: Basic Concepts; Structure and Process: Cross-Level Hypotheses", *Behavioral Science*, **10**: 193–237, 337–411.

MILLETT, KATE

1970   *Sexual Politics* (New York: Doubleday).

MILLS, C. WRIGHT

1963   *Power, Politics, and People* (New York: Ballantine).

MITCHELL, JULIET

1971   *Woman's Estate* (Harmondsworth, Middlesex: Penguin).

MONOD, JACQUES

1970   *Le Hasard et la nécessité* (Paris: Le Seuil).

MONTAIGNE, MICHEL DE

1595a   *Essais, Oeuvres complètes*, ed. by A. Thibaudet and M. Rat (Paris: Pléiade, 1962). Revised edition.

1595b   *The Complete Essays of Montaigne*, trans. by Donald Frame (Stanford: Stanford University Press, 1958).

MORGAN, ROBIN, editor
1970   *Sisterhood is Powerful* (New York: Vintage Books).

MYRDAL, GUNNAR
1967   *Objectivity in Social Research* (New York: Pantheon, 1969).

NAGEL, ERNEST, AND JAMES R. NEWMAN
1956   "Gödel's Proof", in: Kline, ed., 1968: 221–30.

NEUMANN, J. VON
1951   "The General and Logical Theory of Automata" in: Newman, ed., 1956, **4**: 2070–98.
1958   *The Computer and the Brain* (New Haven: Yale University Press).

NEWMAN, JAMES R., editor
1956   *The World of Mathematics* (New York: Simon and Shuster).

NORTHROP, F. S. C., AND HELEN H. LIVINGSTON, editors
1962   *Cross-Cultural Understanding* (New York: Harper and Row).

ORTEGA Y GASSET
1956   *The Dehumanization of Art* (Garden City, N.Y.: Anchor).

ORTIGUES, M.C., AND EMILE
1966   *Oedipe africain* (Paris: Plon).

PARAIN-VIAL, JEANNE
1969   *Analyses structurales et idéologies structuralistes* (Toulouse: Edouard Privat).

PASCAL, BLAISE
1670   *Oeuvres complètes*, ed. by J. Chevalier (Paris: Pléiade, 1954).

PASK, GORDON
1962   "A Proposed Evolutionary Model", in: Von Foerster and Zopf, eds., 1962: 229–53.

PATTEE, H. H.
1968a   "The Physical Basis of Coding and Reliability in Biological Evolution", in: Waddington, ed., 1968: 67–93.
1968b   "Comment", in: Waddington, ed., 1968: 219–20.

PEIRCE, CHARLES SANDERS
1955   *Philosophical Writings*, ed. by J. Buchler (New York: Dover).

PENROSE, L. S.
1931   "Freud's Theory of Instinct", *International Journal of Psycho-Analysis*, **12**: 87–97.

PIAGET, JEAN
1952   *The Origins of Intelligence in Children* (New York: W. W. Norton, 1963).
1964   *Six études de psychologie* (Paris: Gonthier).
1968   *Structuralism*, trans. by C. Maschler (New York: Basic Books, 1970. London: Routledge).

PRIBRAM, KARL H.
1962   "The Neuropsychology of Sigmund Freud", *Experimental Foundations of Clinical Psychiatry*, ed. by A. J. Bachrach (New York: Basic Books), 442–68.
1969   "The Neurophysiology of Remembering", *Scientific American* (January 1969), 73–86.

PROUST, MARCEL
1913–27 *A la recherche du temps perdu* (Paris: Pléiade, 1954).

QUINE, WILLARD V.
1962   "Paradox", *Scientific American* (April 1962). Also in Kline, ed., 1968: 200–8.
1964   "The Foundations of Mathematics", *Scientific American* (September 1964). Also in: Kline, ed., 1968: 191–9.

RAPOPORT, ANATOL
1959   "Critiques of Game Theory", in: Buckley, ed., 1968: 474–89.

RAPPAPORT, ROY A.
1968   *Pigs for the Ancestors* (New Haven: Yale University Press).
1970   "Systems and Sanctity" (Ann Arbor: University of Michigan). Unpublished draft.

RAYFIELD, J. R.
1970a   "The Dualism of Lévi-Strauss" (Toronto: York University). Unpublished draft.
1970b   "Philosophies of Opposition: I and II" (Toronto: York University). Unpublished draft.

REPS, PAUL
1967   *Square Sun, Square Moon* (Tokyo: C. E. Tuttle).

RICHARDSON, KEN, AND DAVID SPEARS, editors
1972   *Race, Culture and Intelligence* (Harmondsworth: Penguin).

RIDGEWAY, JAMES
1968   *The Closed Corporation* (New York: Ballantine).

RIFFLET-LEMAIRE, A.
1970   *Jacques Lacan* (Brussels: Dessart).

ROBINSON, JOAN
1948   "Marx and Keynes", *Marx and Modern Economics*, ed. by

D. Horowitz (New York: Monthly Review Press, 1968), 103–16.

ROSOLATO, GUY
1969   *Essais sur le symbolique* (Paris: Gallimard).

ROUSSEAU, J.-J.
1761   *Essai sur l'origine des langues* (Paris: École Normale Supérieure), *Cahiers pour l'analyse*, Supplement to No. 8 (Le Graphe).

ROY, J. E.
1967   *Mechanisms of Memory* (New York: Academic Press).

RUESCH, JURGEN
1955   "Nonverbal Language and Therapy", *Psychiatry*, **18**: 323–30. Also in: Smith, ed., 1966: 209–13.

RUESCH, JURGEN, AND GREGORY BATESON
1951   *Communication: The Social Matrix of Psychiatry* (New York: W. W. Norton).

RUWET, NICOLAS
1963   "Linguistique et sciences de l'homme", *Esprit* (November), 564–78.

SAFOUAN, MOUSTAFA
1968   "De la structure en psychanalyse", in: Wahl, ed., 1968: 239–98.

SARTRE, JEAN-PAUL
1936–7 *The Transcendence of the Ego*, trans. by F. Williams and R. Kirkpatrick (New York: Noonday, 1957).
1938   *Nausea* (New York: New Directions).
1939   "Une idée fondamentale de Husserl", *Situations*, I (Paris: Gallimard, 1947), 31–5.
1943   *L'Etre et le néant* (Paris: Gallimard).
1946   *Anti-Semite and Jew*, trans. by G. J. Becker (New York: Schocken, 1965).
1960   *Critique de la raison dialectique* (Paris: Gallimard).
1964   *Les Mots* (Paris: Gallimard).
1966   "La Conscience de classe chez Flaubert: II", *Les Temps Modernes*, 241: 2113–53.

SAUSSURE, FERDINAND DE
1916a   *Cours de linguistique générale*, ed. by C. Bally and A. Sechehaye (Paris: Payot, 1965).
1916b   *Course in General Linguistics* (New York: McGraw-Hill, 1966).

SAYRE, KENNETH M., AND FREDERICK J. CROSSON, editors
1963   *The Modelling of Mind: Computers and Intelligence* (New York: Clarion, 1968).

SCHOLTE, BOB
1968   "The Ethnology of Anthropological Traditions" (Philadelphia: University of Pennsylvania). Unpublished paper for the Wenner-Gren Foundation, New York.

SCHREBER, DANIEL PAUL
1903   *Memoirs of My Nervous Illness*, trans. and ed., with notes and discussion, by Ida Macalpine and Richard Hunter (London: Wm. Dawson, 1955).

SEBEOK, THOMAS, A.
1962   "Coding in the Evolution of Signalling Behavior", *Behavioral Science*, 7: 430–42.
1963   "Communication in Animals and in Men: Three Reviews", in: Fishman, ed., 1968: 14–37.
1967   "On Chemical Signs", in: Sebeok, ed., 1967, III, 1775–82.
1967   *To Honor Roman Jakobson* (The Hague: Mouton). Three volumes.
1968   *Animal Communication* (Bloomington: Indiana University Press).

SHANDS, HARLEY C.
1970   *Semiotic Approaches to Psychiatry*. (*Approaches to Semiotics*, ed. by T. A. Sebeok, Vol. 2) (The Hague: Mouton).

SHANNON, CLAUDE E., AND WARREN WEAVER
1949   *The Mathematical Theory of Communication* (Urbana: University of Illinois Press).

SHARPE, ELLA F.
1940   "An Examination of Metaphor", in: Fliess, ed., 1950: 273–86.

SHEPARD, PAUL, AND DANIEL MCKINLEY, editors
1969   *The Subversive Science: Essays Toward an Ecology of Man* (Boston: Houghton Mifflin).

SHUBIK, MARTIN
1964   "Game Theory and the Study of Social Behavior", in: Shubik, ed., 1964: 1–77.

SHUBIK, MARTIN, editor
1964   *Game Theory and Related Approaches to Social Behavior* (New York: John Wiley).

SIMONIS, YVAN
1968   *Claude Lévi-Strauss ou la 'passion de l'inceste'* (Paris: Plon).

SIMPSON, GEORGE G.
1949   *The Meaning of Evolution* (New York: Bantam, 1971). Revised edition.

SINGH, JAGIT
1966   *Great Ideas in Information Theory, Language and Cybernetics* (New York: Dover).

SMITH, ALFRED G., editor
1966   *Communication and Culture* (New York: Holt, Rinehart and Winston).

SPENCER BROWN, G.
1969   *Laws of Form* (London: George Allen and Unwin).

SPERBER, DAN
1968   "Le Structuralisme en anthropologie', in: Wahl, ed.: 167–238.

SVEVO, ITALO
1923   *The Confessions of Zeno*, trans. by Beryl de Zoete (New York: Vintage, 1958).

SWEEZY, PAUL M.
1942   *Theory of Capitalist Development* (New York: Monthly Review).
1970   "Toward a Critique of Economics", *Monthly Review*, (January 1970), 1–9.

TERRAY, EMMANUEL
1969   *Le Marxisme devant les sociétés 'primitives'* (Paris: Maspero).

THIBAUT, GEORGE, editor and translator
1890–6 *The Vedanta Sutras of Badarayana, commented by Sankara* (New York: Dover, 1962).

THOM, RENÉ
1968   "Une théorie dynamique de la morphogénèse," in: Waddington, ed., 1968: 152–79.

THOMSON, GEORGE
1940   *Aeschylus and Athens* (London: Lawrence and Wishart, 1966).

TOURAINE, ALAIN
1971   *Systèmes et conflits* (Paris École Pratique des Hautes Ètudes).

TUSTIN, ARNOLD
1952   "Feedback", *Scientific American*, **187**: 48–55.

VICKERS, GEOFFREY
1959   "Is Adaptability Enough?" in: Buckley, ed., 1968: 460–73.

VICO, GIAMBATTISTA
1725   *Scienza Nuova*, trans. by T. Bergin and M. Fisch (Garden City, N.Y.: Anchor, 1961).

VYGOTSKY, L. S.
1962   *Thought and Language* (Cambridge, Mass.: MIT).

WADDINGTON, C. H.
1968   "The Basic Ideas of Biology", in: Waddington, ed., 1968: 1–32.

WADDINGTON, C. H., editor
1968   *Towards a Theoretical Biology* (Chicago: Aldine).

WAHL, FRANÇOIS, editor
1968   *Qu'est-ce que le structuralisme?* (Paris: Le Seuil).

WALLON, HENRI
1931   "Comment se développe, chez l'enfant, la notion du corps propre", *Journal de Psychologie*, 705–48.
1945   *Les Origines de la pensée chez l'enfant* (Paris: Presses Universitaires).

WARUSFEL, ANDRÉ
1969   *Les Mathématiques modernes* (Paris: Le Seuil).

WATZLAWICK, PAUL, JANET BEAVIN, AND DON D. JACKSON
1967   *The Pragmatics of Human Communication* (New York: W. W. Norton).

WAYNE, DON E.
1970   "Ben Jonson: The 'Anti-Acquisitive Attitude' and the Accumulated Discourse" (San Diego: University of California). Unpublished draft.

WEIL, ANDRÉ
1947   "Sur l'étude algébrique de certains types de lois de mariage", in: Lévi-Strauss, 1949: 257–65.

WHORF, BENJAMIN LEE
1956   *Language, Thought, and Reality*, ed. by J. B. Carroll (Cambridge, Mass.: MIT).

WHYTE, LANCELOT LAW
1961   *Essay on Atomism* (Middletown, Conn.: Wesleyan University Press).
1962   *The Unconscious Before Freud* (Garden City, N.Y.: Anchor; London: Tavistock).
1965   *Internal Factors in Evolution* (London: Social Science Paperbacks, 1968).

WIENER, NORBERT
1948   *Cybernetics* (Cambridge, Mass.: MIT).

1950   *The Human Use of Human Beings* (Garden City, N.Y.: Anchor).

WILDEN, ANTHONY

1966   'Freud, Signorelli, and Lacan: The Repression of the Signifier", *American Imago*, **23**: 332–66.

1968a   *The Language of the Self: The Function of Language in Psycho-analysis*, by Jacques Lacan. Translated, with notes and commentary (Baltimore: Johns Hopkins; New York: Delta, 1975).

1968b   "Par divers moyens on arrive à pareille fin: A Reading of Montaigne", *Modern Language Notes*, **83**: 577–97.

1969   "Death, Desire, and Repetition in Svevo's *Zeno*", *Modern Language Notes*, **84**: 98–119.

1970a   "Marcuse and the Freudian Model: Energy, Information, and *Phantasie*", *Salmagundi*, **10–11**: 197–245: Also in: *The Legacy of the German Refugee Intellectuals*, ed. by R. Boyers (New York: Schocken, 1972).

1970b   "Montaigne's *Essays* in the Context of Communication", *Modern Language Notes*, **85**: 454–78.

1971a   "Epistemology and the Biosocial Crisis: The Difference that Makes a Difference", *Coping with Increasing Complexity: Applications of General Semantics and General Systems Theory*, ed. by D. R. Smith and D. E. Washburn (New York: Gordon and Breach, 1974): 249–70.

1971b   "Analog and Digital Communication: On Negation, Signification, and the Emergence of the Discrete Element", *Semiotica* (August, 1972), **6**, 1: 50–82.

1971c   "L'Ecriture et le bruit dans la morphogénèse du système ouvert", *Communications*, **18** (February 1972): 48–71.

WINNICOTT, D. W.

1953   "Transitional Objects and Transitional Phenomena", in: Winnicott, 1971: 1–25.

1971   *Playing and Reality* (London: Tavistock; New York: Basic Books).

WITTGENSTEIN, LUDWIG

1937–44   *Remarks on the Foundations of Mathematics*, trans. by G. E. M. Anscombe (Cambridge: MIT, 1967).

1945–9   *Philosophical Investigations*, trans. by G. E. M. Anscombe (Oxford: Blackwell, 1967).

WORSLEY, PETER
  1967   "Groote Eylandt Totemism", *The Structural Study of Myth and Totemism*, ed. by E. R. Leach (A.S.A. Monographs, No. 5) (London: Tavistock).

ZIMBARDO, PHILIP, AND EBBE B. EBBESON
  1969   *Influencing Attitudes and Changing Behavior* (Menlo Park, Calif.: Addison-Wesley).

ZOPF, GEORGE W., JR.
  1962   "Attitude and Context", in Von Foerster and Zopf, eds., 1962: 325–46.

Additional References and Suggestions for Further Reading (1980)

The following list includes all the new references cited in the revised edition, as well as some suggested readings on related topics. I have indicated by an asterisk those items, other than the classics, that I have found particularly useful.

The *Scientific American* articles cited are readily available as offprints. In a number of them you will notice the classic contradiction of the dominant discourse of western science: its basically materialist approach to physical nature and to physiology, and its generally idealist-Imaginary approach to practically all aspects of history and society. These two perspectives are often combined together in the 'sociobiological' realm: the realm of the confusion of the logical typing of organic nature, at one level, with that of society, at another.

ANGYAL, A.
*1941   *Foundations for a Science of Personality.* Excerpt in: *Systems Thinking*, ed. by F. E. Emery (Harmondsworth: Penguin, 1969: 17–29).

ANON
1923   *Struggle for Existence.* John Player & Son, Branch of the Imperial Tobacco Company of Great Britain and Ireland. Series of 25 cards.

ATLAN, HENRI
*1972   *L'Organisation biologique et la théorie de l'information* (Paris: Hermann).

ATTNEAVE, FRED
*1971   "Multistability in Perception", *Scientific American*, **225** (6): 63–71.

BAR-HILLEL, YENOSHUA
1967   "Theory of Types", in: *The Encyclopedia of Philosophy*, ed. by Paul Edwards (London: Collier-Macmillan, **8**: 168–72).

BARNES, RICHARD
    1936   "Mystery of the Black Poacher", in: Uncle Dick, ed., *The Pip
            & Squeak Annual for 1936* (London: *Daily Mirror*, 25–8).

BAUDRILLARD, JEAN
    1976   *L'Echange symbolique et la mort* (Paris: Gallimard).

BELL, WILLIAM
    1936   "The Way of a White Man: A Thrilling Tale of the Canadian
            Lumberlands", in: Uncle Dick, ed., *The Pip & Squeak Annual
            for 1936* (London: *Daily Mirror*, 200–3).

BERNSTEIN, BASIL
    *1971   *Class, Codes and Control* (London: Routledge and Kegan
            Paul).

BERTON, PIERRE
    *1975   *Hollywood's Canada: The Americanization of our National
            Image* (Toronto: McClelland and Stewart).

BLACKBURN, ROBIN, editor
    1972   *Ideology in Social Science* (London: Fontana).

BLOCH, MAURICE, editor
    1975   *Marxist Analyses and Social Anthropology* (London: Malaby
            Press).

BOWER, T. G. R.
    1976   "Repetitive Processes in Child Development", *Scientific
            American*, **235** (5): 38–47.

BRUSH, STEPHEN
    *1974   "Should the History of Science be Rated X?", *Science*, **18**:
            1164–72.

BRYANT, SUSAN V., AND VERNON FRENCH
    1977   "Biological Regeneration and Pattern Formation", *Scientific
            American*, **237** (1): 66–81.

CADE, TONI, editor
    *1974   *The Black Woman* (New York: Signet).

CAMPBELL, DONALD T.
    *1964   "Distinguishing Differences in Perception from Failures of
            Communication", in: F. S. C. Northrop and Helen H. Living-
            ston, eds, *Cross-Cultural Understanding* (New York: Harper
            and Row: 308–36).

CARRINGTON, JOHN
   1971   "The Talking Drums of Africa", *Scientific American*, **225** (6): 90–4.

CLARKE, BRYAN
   1975   "The Causes of Biological Diversity", *Scientific American*, **233** (2): 50–60.

CHESLER, PHYLLIS
   *1972   *Women and Madness* (New York: Avon).

COE, RICHARD M., AND ANTHONY WILDEN
   1977   "Errore", in: *Enciclopedia Einaudi*, general editor: Ruggiero Romano (Turin: Einaudi, 1977–). Volume V.

COMMONER, BARRY
   1971   *The Closing Circle* (New York: Bantam, 1972).

COOPER, MAX D., AND ALEXANDER R. LAWTON III
   1974   "The Development of the Immune System", *Scientific American*, **231** (5): 58–72.

COOPER, W. E., T. K. EDENS, H. E. KOENIG, AND A. WILDEN
   1973   *Toward an Economics of Environmental Compatibility* (East Lansing: Michigan State University). Mimeographed.

CORBALLIS, MICHAEL C., AND IVAN L. BEALE
   1971   "On Telling Left from Right", *Scientific American*, **224** (3): 96–104.

CUNNINGHAM, BRUCE A.
   1977   "The Structure and Function of Histocompatibility Antigens", *Scientific American*, **237** (4): 96–107.

DALEY, HERMAN, editor
   1973   *Toward a Steady-State Economy* (San Francisco: W. H. Freeman).

DELONG, HOWARD
   1971   "Unsolved Problems in Arithmetic", *Scientific American*, **224** (3): 50–60.

DEREGOWSKI, JAN B.
   1972   "Pictorial Perception and Culture", *Scientific American*, **227** (5): 82–7.

DEUTSCH, DIANA
1975   "Musical Illusions", *Scientific American*, **233** (4): 92–104.

DOBBS, B. J. T.
*1975   *The Foundations of Newton's Alchemy* (Cambridge: Cambridge University Press).

DUNN-RANKIN, PETER
*1978   "The Visual Characteristics of Words", *Scientific American*, **238** (1): 122–30.

EDWARDS, RICHARD C., MICHAEL REICH, AND THOMAS E. WEISSKOPF, editors
*1978   *The Capitalist System: A Radical Analysis of American Society* (Englewood Cliffs, N.J.: Prentice-Hall). Second edition.

EHRENREICH, BARBARA, AND DEIRDRE ENGLISH
*1973a   *Witches, Midwives, and Nurses: A History of Women Healers* (Old Westbury, N.Y.: The Feminist Press). Glass Mountain Pamphlet No. 1.
*1973b   *Complaints and Disorders: The Sexual Politics of Sickness* (Old Westbury, N.Y.: The Feminist Press). Glass Mountain Pamphlet No. 2.

ENZENSBERGER, HANS MAGNUS
1974   "Critique of Political Ecology", *New Left Review*, **84**: 3–31.

EPEL, DAVID
1977   "The Program of Fertilization", *Scientific American*, **237** (5): 128–38.

FEKETE, JOHN
1977   *The Critical Twilight: Explorations in the Ideology of Anglo-American Literary Theory from Eliot to McLuhan* (London: Routledge and Kegan Paul).

FERGUSON, EUGENE S.
1977   "The Mind's Eye: Nonverbal Thought in Technology", *Science*, **197**: 827–36.

FIRESTONE, SHULAMITH
1970   *The Dialectic of Sex* (New York: Bantam, 1972).

FREEDMAN, DANIEL Z., AND PETER VAN NIEUWENHUIZEN
*1978   "Supergravity and the Unification of the Laws of Physics", *Scientific American*, **238** (2): 126–43.

FROMKIN, VICTORIA A.
1973   "Slips of the Tongue", *Scientific American*, **229** (6): 110–17.

GARDNER, MARTIN
1971   "On the orders of infinity. . . .", *Scientific American*, **224** (3): 106–9.

GODELIER, MAURICE
*1972   "Structure and Contradiction in *Capital*" (1966), in: Blackburn, ed., 1972: 334–68.
*1973   *Horizon, trajets marxistes en anthropologie* (Paris: Maspero). Selections in: *Perspectives in Marxist Anthropology*, trans. by R. Brain (Cambridge: Cambridge University Press, 1977).
*1975   "Modes of Production, Kinship and Demographic Structures", in: Bloch, ed., 1975: 3–27.

GREGORY, R. L.
1970   *The Intelligent Eye* (London: Weidenfeld and Nicolson).
1977   *Eye and Brain* (London: Weidenfeld and Nicolson). Third edition.

GRIERER, ALFRED
1974   "Hydra as a Model for the Development of Biological Form", *Scientific American*, **231** (6): 44–54.

GROBSTEIN, CLIFFORD
*1973   "Hierarchical Order and Neogenesis", in: Pattee, ed., 1973: 29–47.

HANNEMAN, GERHARD J., AND WILLIAM J. MCEWEN, editors
1975   *Communication and Behavior* (Menlo Park, Calif.: Addison-Wesley).

HARMON, LEON D.
1973   "The Recognition of Faces", *Scientific American*, **229** (5): 70–82.

HASSENSTEIN, BERNHARD
*1971   *Information and Control in the Living Organism* (London: Chapman and Hall).

HENDERSON, HAZEL
* 1976   "Statement before the Joint Economic Committee, 94th Congress of the United States, November 18, 1976", *Alternatives* (Spring, 1977), **6** (2): 46–7.

HOLLAND, RAY
*1977   *Self and Social Context* (London: Macmillan).

HÖLLDOBLER, BERTHOLD K.
1971   "Communication between Ants and Their Guests", *Scientific American*, **224** (3): 86–93.

HÖLLDOBLER, BERTHOLD K., AND EDWARD O. WILSON
1977   "Weaver Ants", *Scientific American*, **237** (6): 146–54.

IDRIS-SOVEN, AHAMED, ELIZABETH IDRIS-SOVEN, AND MARY K. VAUGHAN, editors
1978   *The World As A Company Town: Multinational Corporations and Social Change* (The Hague: Mouton; World Anthropology Series).

JERNE, NIELS KAJ
1973   "The Immune System", *Scientific American*, **229** (1): 52–60.

JOHANSSON, GUNNAR
1975   "Visual Motion Perception", *Scientific American*, **232** (6): 76–88.

JULESZ, BELA
1975   "Experiments in the Visual Perception of Texture", *Scientific American*, **232** (4): 34–43.

KILMISTER, C. W.
1965   *The Environment in Modern Physics* (London: English Universities Press).

KIMWO, DOREEN
1973   "The Asymmetry of the Human Brain", *Scientific American*, **228** (3): 70–8.

KOSHLAND, D. E., JR.
*1973   "Protein Shape and Biological Control", *Scientific American*, **229** (4): 52–64.

LACAN, JACQUES, AND JEAN HYPPOLITE
1956   "Commentary on the Freudian *Verneinung*", ed. and trans. by A. Wilden (1966). Unpublished.

LEE, RICHARD B., AND IRVEN DEVORE, editors
1968   *Man the Hunter* (Chicago: Aldine).

LEISS, WILLIAM
*1972   *The Domination of Nature* (New York: Braziller).

LENIN, V. I.
  1961   *Philosophical Notebooks: Collected Works,* **18** (Moscow: Progress Publishers).

LEWIS, HARRY R., AND CHRISTOS H. PAPADIMITRIOU
  1978   "The Efficiency of Algorithms", *Scientific American,* **238** (1): 96–109.

LOVEJOY, ARTHUR O.
  1936   *The Great Chain of Being* (New York: Harper Torchbooks, 1960).

MCCULLOCH, WARREN S., AND W. PITTS
  1943   "A Logical Calculus of the Ideas Immanent in Nervous Activity", *Bulletin of Mathematical Biophysics,* **5**: 115–33.

MACPHERSON, C. B.
  *1962   *The Political Theory of Possessive Individualism: Hobbes to Locke* (Oxford: Oxford University Press).

MACKSEY, RICHARD, AND EUGENIO DONATO, editors
  1970   *The Structuralist Controversy* (Baltimore: Johns Hopkins Paperbacks, 1972). Proceedings of conference at Johns Hopkins in 1966.

MAO TSETUNG
  1937   "On Contradiction", in: *Four Essays on Philosophy* (Peking: Foreign Languages Press, 1966: 23–78).

MARGALEF, RAMON
  *1968   *Perspectives in Ecological Theory* (Chicago: University of Chicago Press).

MARGULIS, LYNN
  *1971   "Symbiosis and Evolution", *Scientific American,* **225** (4): 48–59.

MARX, KARL
  1857–8a *Grundrisse der Kritik der politischen Ökonomie* (Frankfurt: Europäische Verlaganstalt, n.d. (1939)).
  1857–8b *Grundrisse,* trans. by Martin Nicolaus (London: Allen Lane, 1973).

NATHANSON, JAMES A., AND PAUL GREENGARD
  1977   " 'Second Messengers' in the Brain", *Scientific American,* **237** (2): 108–19.

MAZIA, DANIEL
*1974   "The Cell Cycle", *Scientific American*, **230** (1): 55–64.

MEADOWS, D. H., D. L. MEADOWS, J. RANDERS, AND W. W. BEHRENS III
1972   *The Limits to Growth* (London: Universe Books).

MÉSZÁROS, ISTVAN, editor
1971   *Aspects of History and Class Consciousness* (London: Merlin).

NEEDHAM, JOSEPH T.
*1956   *Science and Civilisation in China* (Cambridge: Cambridge University Press). Volume 2: 232–345, 533–82.

NICOLAUS, MARTIN
*1972   "The Unknown Marx", in: Blackburn, ed., 1972: 306–33.

ODUM, HOWARD T.
1971   *Power, Environment and Society* (New York: Wiley).

PATTEE, HOWARD H., editor
* 1973   *Hierarchy Theory* (New York: Braziller).

PIERCY, MARGE
1969   "The Grand Coolie Dam", in: *Toward a New America*, ed. by M. Goodman (New York: Knopf, 1970: 57–60).

PIMENTEL, DAVID, *et al.*
*1973   "Food Production and the Energy Crisis", *Science*, **182**: 443–9.

POLLARD, SIDNEY
1968   *The Idea of Progress* (Harmondsworth: Penguin).

POLUNIN, NICHOLAS, editor
1972   *The Environmental Future* (London: Macmillan).

POLYANI, KARL, CONRAD M. ARENSBERG, AND HARRY W. PEARSON, editors
*1957   *Trade and Market in the Early Empires* (Chicago: Gateway, 1974).

POSTMAN, NEIL, AND CHARLES WEINGARTNER
*1971   *Teaching as a Subversive Activity* (New York: Delta; Harmondsworth: Penguin).

RAPPAPORT, ROY A.

*1971a   "Nature, Culture and Ecological Anthropology", in: *Man, Culture and Society*, ed. by Harry L. Shapiro (Oxford: Oxford University Press: 237–67). Only in the second edition.

*1971b   "The Flow of Energy in an Agricultural Society", *Scientific American*, **225** (3): 116–32.

*1974   "Liturgy and Lies", in: *Internationales Jahrbuch für Wissens- und Religionssoziologie* (Berlin: Westdeutscher Verlag) **10** (1976): 75–104.

RATLIFF, FLOYD

1972   "Contour and Contrast", *Scientific American*, **226** (6): 90–101.

RED STAR COLLECTIVE

* 1977   *Canada: Imperialist Power or Economic Colony?* Pamphlet No. 1 (March) (P.O. Box 65723, Station F, Vancouver, B.C.).

REITER, RAYNA R., editor

*1975 *Toward an Anthropology of Women* (New York: Monthly Review Press).

ROSS, JOHN

1976   "The Resources of Binocular Perception", *Scientific American*, **234** (4): 80–6.

ROWAN, MARY KATE

1978   "Our disappearing farmland", *Vancouver Sun*, July 26.

RUBIN, GAYLE

*1975   "The Traffic in Women: Notes on the 'Political Economy' of Sex", in: Reiter, ed., 1975: 157–210.

SAHLINS, MARSHALL

*1972   *Stone Age Economics* (Chicago: Aldine; London: Tavistock, 1974).

SAUNDERS, ROSS, AND PHILIP W. DAVIS

1978   "The Expression of the Cooperative Principle in Bella Coola", in: *Heritage Record* (forthcoming).

SCHATZMAN, MORTON

*1974   *Soul Murder: Persecution in the Family* (New York: Signet).

SCHMANDT-BESSERAT, DENISE

*1978   "The Earliest Precursor of Writing", *Scientific American*, **238** (6): 50–9.

SCHON, DONALD A.
*1963   *Invention and the Evolution of Ideas* (London: Tavistock, 1969).

SCIENTIFIC AMERICAN
1970   *The Biosphere* (San Francisco: W. H. Freeman).
*1971   *Energy and Power* (San Francisco: W. H. Freeman).
1972   *Communication* (San Francisco: W. H. Freeman).

SHEPHERD, GORDON M.
*1978   "Microcircuits in the Nervous System", *Scientific American*, **238** (2): 92–103.

SILK, LEONARD, *et al.*
1974   *Capitalism: The Moving Target* (New York: Praeger).

SLUKZI, CARLOS E., AND DONALD C. RANSOM, editors
*1976   *Double Bind: The Foundation of the Communicational Approach to the Family* (New York: Grune and Stratton).

STAEHELIN, L. ANDREW, AND BARBARA E. HULL
1978   "Junctions between Living Cells", *Scientific American*, **238** (5): 140–52.

TEUBER, MARIANNE L.
*1974   "Sources of Ambiguity in the Prints of Maurits C. Escher", *Scientific American*, **231** (1): 90–104.

TRIBUS, MYRON, AND EDWARD C. MCIRVINE
1971   "Energy and Information", *Scientific American*, **225** (3): 179–88.

TROUBETZKOY, N. S.
1939   *Principes de phonologie* (Paris: Klincksieck, 1970).

TURNER, VICTOR
*1966   "Colour Classification in Ndembu Ritual", in: *Anthropological Approaches to the Study of Religion*, ed. by Michael Banton (London: Tavistock, 1968: 47–84).

UEXKÜLL, JAKOB VON, AND GEORG KRISZAT
1934   *Streifzüge duchr die Umwelten von Tieren und Menschen – Bedeutungslehre* [1940] (Frankfurt: S. Fischer Verlag, 1970). Partially available in French: *Mondes animaux et monde humain* (Paris: Gonthier, 1965).

VAN HEIJENOORT, JOHN
1967   "Logical Paradoxes", *The Encyclopedia of Philosophy*, ed. by Paul Edwards (London: Collier-Macmillan, **5**: 45–51).

VAYDA, ANDREW P., editor
*1969   *Environment and Cultural Behavior* (Garden City, N.Y.: Natural History Press).

VOGEL, STEVEN
1978   "Organisms That Capture Currents", *Scientific American*, **239** (2): 128–39.

VOLOSHINOV, V. N.
1927   *Freudianism: A Marxist Critique*, trans. and ed. by I. R. Titunik and Neal H. Bruss (New York: Academic Press, 1976).
*1929   *Marxism and the Philosophy of Language*, trans. by L. Matejka and I. R. Titunik (New York: Seminar Press, 1973).

VON FOERSTER, HEINZ
*1960   "On Self-Organizing Systems and their Environments", in: *Self-Organising Systems*, ed. by T. C. Yovits and S. Cameron (Oxford: Pergamon: 31–50).

WILDEN, ANTHONY
1972a   "Libido as Language: The Structuralism of Jacques Lacan", *Psychology Today*, **5** (12) (May): 40–2, 85–9.
1972b   "Review of Leiss: *The Domination of Nature*", *Psychology Today* (October): 28, 30, 32.
1972c   "On Lacan: Psychoanalysis, Language, and Communication", *Contemporary Psychoanalysis*, **9** (4) (August 1973): 445–70.
1972d   "Ecology and Ideology", in: Idris-Soven *et al.*, 1978: 73–98.
1973a   "Review of Bateson: *Steps to an Ecology of Mind*", *Psychology Today* (November): 138, 140.
1973b   "Ecosystems and Economic Systems", *Cultures of the Future: Ninth Congress of Anthropological and Ethnological Sciences*, ed. by Magoroh Maruyama and Arthur Harkins (The Hague: Mouton World Anthropology Series, 1978: 101–24).
1974   "Piaget and the Structure as Law and Order", in: *Structure and Transformation: Developmental and Historical Aspects*, ed. by Klaus F. Riegel and George L. Rosenwald (New York: Wiley Interscience, Origins of Behavior Series, 1975: 83–117).
1975   "The Scientific Discourse: Knowledge as a Commodity", *MAYDAY*, **1** (1): 69–77.

1976a   "Changing Frames of Order: Cybernetics and the *Machina Mundi*", *Communication and Control in Society*, ed. by Klaus Krippendorff (New York: Gordon and Breach, forthcoming). Also in: *The Myth of Information*, ed. by Michel Benamou and Kathleen Woodward (Madison: Coda Press, forthcoming).

1976b   "Communicazione", in: *Enciclopedia Einaudi*, general editor: Ruggiero Romano (Turin: Einaudi, 1977–). Volume III.

1977   "Informazione-Rumore", in: *Enciclopedia Einaudi*, general editor: Ruggiero Romano (Turin: Einaudi, 1977–). Volume VI.

1979a   "Culture and Identity: The Canadian Question, *Why?*", *Ciné-Tracts* (Montreal) 2 (2): 1–27.

1979b   *Le Canada Imaginaire*, trans. by Yvan Simonis (Quebec): Presses Coméditex) [Shorter and earlier version of 1980].

1980   *The Imaginary Canadian* (Vancouver: Pulp Press, P.O. Box 3868, Vancouver, Canada V6B 3Z3).

1984a   *The Rules Are No Game: The Strategy of Communication* (London and Boston: Routledge and Kegan Paul).

1984b   *Man and Woman, War and Peace: The Strategist's Companion* (London and Boston: Routledge and Kegan Paul).

WILDEN, ANTHONY, AND TIM WILSON
1976   "The Double Bind: Logic, Magic, and Economics", in: Sluzki and Ransom, eds., 1976: 263 86 [cf. Note 33].

WILLS, GARRY
*1969   *Nixon Agonistes: The Crisis of the Self-Made Man* (New York: Signet, 1971).

WILSON, EDWARD O.
1972   "Animal Communication", *Scientific American*, **227** (3): 53–60.
1975   "Slavery in Ants", *Scientific American*, **232** (6): 32–6.

WYNNE-EDWARDS, V. C.
*1962   *Animal Dispersion in Relation to Social Behaviour* (Edinburgh: Oliver and Boyd, 1972).

ZARETSKY, ELI
*1976   *Capitalism, the Family and Personal Life* (New York: Harper Colophon; Toronto: Fitzhenry and Whiteside).

ZEEMAN, E. C.
*1976   "Catastrophe Theory", *Scientific American*, **234** (4): 65–83.

Indexes

Name Index

In the following, italic figures indicate pages where an author's work is discussed or employed in more detail than elsewhere. Further information on sources will be found in the alphabetical bibliography preceding the indexes.

Subject Index

Name Index (Additions)

Subject Index (Additions)